Family Law and Family Realities

Family Law and Family Realities

Carol Rogerson, Masha Antokolskaia, Joanna Miles,
Patrick Parkinson and Machteld Vonk (Eds.)

eleven
international publishing

Published, sold and distributed by Eleven International Publishing
P.O. Box 85576
2508 CG The Hague
The Netherlands
Tel.: +31 70 33 070 33
Fax: +31 70 33 070 30
email: sales@elevenpub.nl
www.elevenpub.com

Sold and distributed in USA and Canada
Independent Publishers Group
814 N. Franklin Street
Chicago, IL 60610, USA
Order Placement: +1 800 888 4741
Fax: +1 312 337 5985
orders@ipgbook.com
www.ipgbook.com

Eleven International Publishing is an imprint of Boom uitgevers Den Haag.

ISBN 978-94-6236-927-6
ISBN 978-94-6274-420-2 (e-book)

Table of Contents

Family Law and Family Realities: Introduction

Masha Antokolskaia[*]

This book contains a selection of papers presented at the 16th World Conference of the International Society of Family Law (ISFL) that took place from 25 July to 29 July 2017 at the *Vrije Universiteit* of Amsterdam in The Netherlands. The selection has been made on the basis of the merits of the contributions, bearing in mind geographic representation, inclusion of both established and beginning scholars and authors with different views and convictions.

The Conference "Family Law and Family Realities" was dedicated to exploring whether existing national and international family law adequately reflects the rapidly changing realities of modern family life. It is a cliché to say that family realities are changing rapidly in all parts of the world; even since the turn of the millennium substantial changes have taken place in the field of traditional as well as non-traditional family settings. Unmarried cohabitation has increased; new family forms have emerged; same-sex marriage; the high divorce rate, high-conflict divorce and problematic post-divorce parenting have received increased attention; new reproductive techniques, surrogate motherhood and the rights of transgender and intersex persons are high on the agenda; there is growing awareness of domestic abuse and child abuse and many more changes have proven to be an ongoing challenge for contemporary family law. Westernized countries, for instance, are faced with the major demographic challenge of "ageing": due to a decreasing birth rate and longer life expectancy the median age of the population has risen, creating a larger group of elderly people with their own specific demands for empowerment and protection.

In different parts of the world, academic lawyers and practitioners alike are no longer content to regard family law in isolation outside its social context. Concern about the correlation between family law and family realities have triggered a growing interest in empirical research involving both lawyers and social scientists. The aim of this Conference was to bring together experts in family law and social science research who are interested in exploring the correlation between family law "in the books" and family law "in action". This book is one of the results of that endeavour.

The question that the authors of this volume are trying to answer is whether international and national family laws still adequately reflects these changing realities. The international nature of the Conference reflected in the composition of this book enables us to

---

* Masha Antokolskaia, Professor of private and family law at *Vrije Universiteit* of Amsterdam, The Netherlands, the convener of the 16th ISFL World Conference.

examine the issues in different geographical, political, social, cultural and religious settings (e.g. "western"/"non-western", religious/secular, modern/traditional). This book gives a broad overview of how law relates to actual practices and needs of different types of families (e.g. married and unmarried couples with and without children, different- and same-sex, blended, extended, parallel and polyamorous families) and of various types of family members (e.g. adults, children, elderly persons, persons with disabilities and members of sexual minorities).

Dealing with the issue of whether there still is a match between family law and family realities confronts policy makers with many challenges. What to do if there is no match? Is it a problem if the law is lagging behind? It is clear that not every change in family practices is desirable and should be automatically reflected in the law. After all, the law is also an important policy instrument and is used by society for promoting desirable developments and discouraging or even banning undesirable ones. However, determining what changes are desirable and should be promoted and what changes are undesirable and should be discouraged is a demanding normative quest. As many areas of family law are highly ideologically sensitive, the answer to this question largely depends on the political orientation of the policymakers involved.

Along with the old dilemmas, related to the political sensitivity of family law, the contributions in this book also focus on the new ones. These new dilemmas are of a less controversial and more pragmatic nature and arise when the first normative question has been answered. Once policymakers have decided which changes should be promoted by law and which should be rolled back, the following question arises: "How should this legal change be operationalised?" This follow-up question is of course also not entirely new, but, growing use of a multidisciplinary approach has now made it more explicit and pertinent. Before drafting a law or elaborating a new policy present-day legislatures and policymakers tend to first enquire what works and what does not and what are the preconditions for successful legal intervention. This book provides a variety of examples of how both the normative and the pragmatic dilemmas are currently being dealt with in a whole range of family-law settings in various parts of the world.

The book commences with a Part on several overarching themes that will be coming back throughout the other Parts. This Part I presents fine snapshots of the current ideological and political dilemmas in the family law context. It shows that the ideological and political divide, that has split each and every Westernized society into progressive and conservative camps[1] since the Enlightenment, is still in place. Moreover, in some jurisdictions, such as the USA, the divide has becomes even more pronounced in the last decades. Max Rheinstein's metaphor, that ever since the French Revolution France has been split

1 M. Antokolskaia, *Harmonisation of Family Law in Europe: A Historical Perspective. A Tale of Two Millenia*, Antwerp, Intersentia, 2006.

up into "*les deux Frances*" – one progressive and one conservative[2] – is today equally applicable to the USA. This country is now divided into "two separate countries", populated by two different kinds of families[3]: "the blue families" and " red families",[4] with different political views, levels of economic welfare, family values, and family forms. The divide between those families largely coincides with the divide between the two main political parties: the democrats ("blue") and the republicans ("red").[5] Blue families of the college-educated middle class are characterised by late marriages, higher marital rate, more stable marriages, the first-career-then-children attitude, equal parenting, greater reliance on family planning and contraception and low birth rates. The majority of the red families is represented by working class and poor families and is characterised by declining marriages and high divorce rates. There is a link between growing economic inequality in USA society and growing family inequality.[6]

Another overarching theme taken up in the first Part of this book concerns the great trio from the heritage of the Enlightenment: personal autonomy, self-determination and the right to the pursuit of happiness. This subject is addressed in two different contexts: in the context of the abolition of discrimination and in the context of tensions between the right to the pursuit of happiness and personal autonomy, and responsibility for others.

Using the example of Germany, it has been shown that growing acceptance of sexual and gender diversity has led to an increasing degree of autonomy afforded to homosexual as well as transgender and intersex persons in Westernized parts of the world, which has enabled them to enter into marriages or legally registered partnerships and to adopt children.[7] These changes have had and continue to have significant impact on such fundamental notions of family law as marriage and parenthood.[8]

It has also been shown that even apparently indisputable values can have drawbacks once placed into the context of the responsibility of parents for their children. The pursuit of happiness and romanticized ideas of marital happiness can lead to exalted expectations of happiness in marriage. And if "a person is not 'happy' with a spouse, the person may seek a divorce, a new partner, a new location or a new lifestyle."[9] Adults can exercise their rights to autonomy and pursuit of happiness by choosing for less stable relationship forms, single parenthood, divorce and re-partnering, but the children have to bear the economic,

2 M. Rheinstein, *Marriage Stability, Divorce, and the Law*, Chicago, Chicago University Press, 1972, p. 195.

3 L.D. Wardle, 'Trends, Values, and Changes in Families and Family Law in the USA: Towards Realism, Idealism or Confusion?'.

4 N. Cahn & J. Carbone, *Red Families v. Blue Families. Legal Polarisation and the Creation of Culture*, Oxford, Oxford University Press, 2010.

5 Ibid.

6 L.D. Elrod, 'Changing Families and the Need for Policy to Protect Children'.

7 N. Dethloff, 'Personal Autonomy and Legal Recognition of Sexual and Gender Diversity - The German Perspective'.

8 Ibid.

9 Elrod, op cit, n. 6.

social and emotional consequences of these choices. "Easy come, easy go marriage and casual cohabitation and procreation are on a collision course with the economic and social needs of children."[10]

Last, but not least, an overarching theme addressed in this Part is the relationship between the secular state and religion, in particular Christianity, and the Church in the present-day world. Using the Brazilian example, it is argued that the solution to the existing tension between the secular state and the Catholic Church should be sought in mutual respect and greater tolerance on both sides. It is further suggested that, on the one hand, the state should show more respect for the religious freedom of its subjects, including freedom to choose for traditional family forms and traditional family values. On the other hand, the Church should become more tolerant towards non-traditional family forms and family values. It is emphasised that

> it is not a Christian value to deny the happiness of another because of individual choices, or to exclude a person from protection because he is different or belongs to a non-traditional family form, [as] the essence of Christianity is inclusion, not segregation.[11]

The book is further divided into Parts each covering a rather broad theme.

Part II "Relationship Recognition: Responding to Family Diversity" deals with issues concerning the legal recognition of same-sex unions; the lack of legal regulation of cohabitation outside marriage; the role of certification of marriages in African pluralistic legal systems and the legal position of the members of parallel and polyamorous families.

Part III "New models of Parentage" addresses the legislative responses to both new challenges, such as surrogate motherhood, change of gender identity and further advancement of assisted reproductive technologies; and traditional challenges, such as stepparent families and stepparent adoption.

Part IV "Family Relationships and Financial Obligations" concentrates on the issues of child maintenance, including empirical evaluations of child maintenance schemes across different welfare models; the role of spousal maintenance in Bulgaria; the effect given to marital agreements in Portugal; and the gap between the real financial needs that exist after divorce and the relief provided by Italian law.

Part V "Regulating the Parent-Child Relationship When Parents Live Apart" focuses on various issues of post-divorce parenting such as parental responsibility; parenting

10 H.D. Krause, 'Child Support Reassessed: Limits of Private Responsibility and the Public Interest', *Family Law Quarterly*, Vol. 24, No. 1, Spring, 1990, pp. 1-34 at 16, cited by Elrod.

11 I.N. Paranaguá Carvalho Drumond, 'A Dialogue between Freedom of Religion and the Rights of Families'.

agreements regarding parental responsibility; and problems with contact between children and non-resident parents.

Part VI "Protecting Children's Rights and Interests: New Challenges" covers a whole range of child-related matters, including early interventions aimed at protecting vulnerable children; use of the concept of the best interests of the child; children with atypical gender identity; the negative influence of surname policies on the wellbeing of the children with double nationality in Italy; the protection of children on the internet; practice and legislation in the context of domestic abuse against children in China; child-headed households in the African setting; and guardianship for children in a migration context.

The last Part (VII) "Families and Care for Dependants" addresses the issues related to care for the elderly and persons with disabilities. Special mention has to be made of the chapter by Veerle Vanderhulst: "Taking Care of Rain Man: Interaction between Parental Estate Planning and Disability Benefits", which was awarded the ISFL Early Career Researcher Prize 2017.

The editors wish to thank Jenny Boddy, Stevie Martin and Deborah Kim for their assistance with language editing and Aleatha Cox for her administrative support.

Part I

Family Law and Family Realities: Overarching Themes

Personal Autonomy and Legal Recognition of Sexual and Gender Diversity: The German Perspective

Nina Dethloff[*]

I Introduction

The German perspective on personal autonomy and the legal recognition of sexual and gender diversity changed significantly on June 26, 2017. That day, Chancellor Merkel opened the gateway to the passage of the bill introducing same-sex marriage which passed in Parliament only a few days later.[1] This was a historic event in the growing social and legal recognition of sexual and gender diversity which many Western countries have experienced during the last decades. It is due to changing moral attitudes and growing tolerance as well as scientific advances in the areas of psychology and medicine.

As a result, human rights guarantees have often been reinterpreted both on the national as well as supranational level. Prohibitions against discrimination have increasingly been extended to criteria such as sexual orientation as well as gender and sexual identity. Consequently, existing discrimination has been reduced and the right to self-determination of homosexuals and transgender as well as intersex persons has gradually been recognized. In Germany, these changes in the concept of personal autonomy have led to legal reforms in all three areas, concerning homosexuals, transsexuals and intersex persons.

This article will consider those three areas in turn, starting with the self-determination of homosexuals regarding their private and family life where totally unforeseen events have led to significant changes.

* Chair for Private Law, Comparative Law, Private International Law and European Private Law and Director of the Institute for German, European and International Law as well as of the Center for Advanced Study in the Humanities 'Law as Culture', Bonn University.

1 Gesetz zur Einführung des Rechts auf Eheschließung für Personen gleichen Geschlechts of 20 July 2017, BGBl. 2017 I, 2787.

II Sexual Orientation

The legal recognition of same-sex couples and their family lives in Germany is a fairly recent development: It took until the 1990s before criminalization of homosexuals finally ended. Only when the penal code was reformed[2] the way was cleared for same-sex couples to openly live their partnerships and subsequently also to start forming families. The beginning of the 1990s also marks the point in time when first the Nordic countries and then many others created new institutions of registered partnership.

In the year 2001, when the Netherlands as the first country in the world, opened marriage to homosexuals,[3] Germany introduced the *eingetragene Lebenspartnerschaft*, the registered partnership, exclusively for same-sex couples which conferred considerably less rights and duties on the partners than marriage.[4] The legislator deliberately sought to create a status that was different from marriage because marriage, which is guaranteed special protection under the German Constitution,[5] was considered to be exclusively a union between a man and a woman.[6] Since its creation the German registered partnership has gradually become more and more similar to marriage, in particular with regard to the provisions pertaining to children. The stepparent adoption of a same-sex partner's child, for instance, became possible with the major reform of 2005.[7]

However, whereas in many other countries same-sex registered partners were gradually also granted the right to jointly adopt a child,[8] this was not the case in Germany. A non-biological child could only be adopted by one partner alone and initially the other partner was prohibited to even subsequently adopt the child as well. When the Federal Constitutional Court in 2013 struck down this prohibition of the other partner subsequently adopting the child,[9] the legislator was forced to allow this.

However, joint adoption by registered partners was still not permitted. This means they have to adopt one after the other – often with a considerable time lag, leaving the child with only one legal parent for an extended period of time. This is much to the child's detriment because during that period the adoptive parent could die, which would leave the child without a legal parent, or the partners could separate. In the latter case, the child would have to remain with the adoptive parent, even if the child has developed strong ties to the social, but not yet legal, parent, regardless what his or her best interests are.

---

2 Neunundzwanzigstes Strafrechtsänderungsgesetz - §§ 175, 182 StGB (29. StrÄndG) of 31 May 1994, BGBl. 1994 I, 1168.

3 N. Dethloff, 'Ehe für alle', *FamRZ*, 2016, p. 351.

4 N. Dethloff, *Familienrecht*, 32nd ed., C.H. Beck, 2018, § 7 no. 1.

5 See art. 6 I German Basic Law: "Marriage and the family shall enjoy the special protection of the state".

6 BVerfGE 105, 313 (345).

7 Gesetz zur Überarbeitung des Lebenspartnerschaftsrechts of 15 December 2004, BGBl. 2004 I, 3396ff.

8 Dethloff, op cit, n. 4, § 15 no. 84.

9 BVerfGE 133, 59.

This prohibition to jointly adopt remains the major difference between registered partnership and marriage. With the new legislation same-sex couples will now be allowed to marry and jointly adopt. And those who already entered into a registered partnership will have the option to convert their partnership into a marriage thereby also permitting them a joint adoption.

However, the question remains whether all discrimination has ended and homosexuals' right to family life has been fully recognized with the new law. This has to be answered in the negative when considering the (legal) complications of using assisted reproduction for same-sex couples to create a family. Lesbian couples will need to seek a sperm donor while male couples will have to resort to surrogacy. Whereas there are a number of legal uncertainties associated with the former, the latter is prohibited in Germany. Regardless of any legal uncertainties or prohibitions, more and more children are born to and raised by lesbian and gay couples in Germany.

Whereas in case of lesbian couples in a number of legal systems the co-mother may be recognized as a legal mother of the child of her partner upon birth, in Germany she will have to adopt the child by way of a stepparent adoption. This is still the law after marriage has been opened for same-sex couples. It currently only recognizes the husband as the parent of the child and does not allow him to challenge his paternity in case of sperm donation with his consent.[10] The presumption of parentage of the husband according to § 1592 no. 1 BGB will have to be extended to the female spouse.[11] The Federal Supreme Court has recently refused to apply this presumption by analogy to female spouses.[12] Moreover, in cases where the female couple is not married, the partner should be allowed to acknowledge the parentage of a child conceived by sperm donation. Here, parentage law is in need of a reform to adequately reflect the opening of marriage to same-sex couples.[13]

With male couples frequently resorting to surrogacy abroad, upon their return to Germany they will have to seek recognition of their legal status as parents of the child. In 2014, the Federal Supreme Court ruled that a foreign judgment establishing parentage of the intended parents did not violate German public policy if one of them – and not the

10 § 1600 V BGB states: "If the child, with the consent of the man and the mother, was conceived by means of artificial insemination by sperm donation from a third person, the contestation of paternity by the man or the mother is excluded."

11 Arbeitskreis Abstammungsrecht, *Abschlussbericht: Empfehlungen für eine Reform des Abstammungsrechts*, Bundesanzeiger Verlag, 2017, pp. 70ff.

12 BGH 10.10.2018 - XII ZB 231/18.

13 N. Dethloff, *Abstammung und Verantwortung*, De Gruyter, 2017, pp. 8ff; T. Helms, *in Verhandlungen des 71. Deutschen Juristentages Essen 2016*, Gutachten, Vol. I, C.H. Beck, 2016, pp. 33ff.

surrogate mother – is genetically linked to the child and the surrogacy was performed voluntarily by the surrogate mother.[14]

However, in the absence of a foreign judgment establishing legal parentage of the intended parents, the law applicable to parentage will depend upon the habitual residence of the newly born child which frequently leads to the applicability of German law.[15] In that case, in order to acquire the status as legal parents, one partner will have to acknowledge paternity and the other may subsequently adopt the child, if they are married. Here, too, parentage law needs to be reformed in order to ensure that the intended parents will be recognized as legal parents of children born abroad by surrogate mothers. They are the ones who have initiated the child's existence and will generally want to care for it, whereas the surrogate will not.

Ultimately, the prohibition of surrogacy within Germany should be reconsidered in order to be replaced by provisions regulating the conditions for its permissibility as well as for the legal parentage of the intended parents.[16] Recognizing legal co-motherhood of lesbian couples as well as parentage of male partners of children born (abroad) by surrogates would accept a changed concept of parenthood which no longer builds on biology but on the decision to conceive a child and the wish to raise it. Such an approach would be in line with the changing concept of marriage which is increasingly considered to be protected not because of its procreative potential but as a result of the partners taking on legal responsibility for each other.[17]

III Transgender

When considering developments concerning the legal recognition of transgender persons here, too, significant changes have led to an increase in autonomy in Germany as in many other countries.[18] With the Transsexuals Act of 1980,[19] Germany was one of the world's first countries that allowed transsexuals to change their legal gender. Until the 1970s it

---

14 BGH, *NJW* 2015, 479ff.; see for a review Dethloff, JZ 2016, 207ff.; recently confirmed in BGH, *NJW-RR* 2018, 1473.

15 N. Dethloff, 'Surrogacy in German Law', *in* V. Boillet, M. Roca i Escodar & E. de Luze (Eds.), *La Gestation pour Autrui*, Anthemis, 2018, p. 29 at 39; N. Dethloff, 'Leihmutterschaft in rechtsvergleichender Perspektive', *in* Ditzen & Weller (Eds.), *Regulierung der Leihmutterschaft, Aktuelle Entwicklungen und interdisziplinäre Herausforderungen*, Mohr Siebeck, 2018, p. 55 at 64.

16 Dethloff, 'Surrogacy', op cit, n. 15, p. 41.

17 F. Brosius-Gersdorf, *in* H. Von Horst Dreier, *Grundgesetz Kommentar*, 3rd ed., GG, Vol. I, Mohr Siebeck, 2013, art. 6 no. 50, pp. 76ff; A. Sanders, *in* S. Emmenegger & A. Wiedmann (Eds.), *Linien der Rechtsprechung des Bundesverfassungsgerichts*, Vol. 2, De Gruyter, 2011, pp. 368ff.

18 For a comparative overview see J.M. Scherpe (Ed.), *The Legal Status of Transsexual and Transgender* Persons, Intersentia 2015, pp. 101ff.

19 Gesetz über die Änderung der Vornamen und die Feststellung der Geschlechtszugehörigkeit in besonderen Fällen (Transsexuellengesetz – TSG) of 10 September 1980, BGBl. 1980 I, 1654ff.

was generally understood that a person's legal gender could not be changed, that it was immutable. Advances in medicine and psychology as well as the increasing recognition of the right of a transgender person to privacy and a self-determined life in the perceived gender have subsequently led to the introduction of laws that allow for a change of legal gender and name.[20]

Initially, most countries set out quite strict requirements for such a change of legal gender. Apart from medical and psychological expert opinions this often included operations for sex reassignment, the incapacity to reproduce as well as a prior divorce in case of an existing marriage.

Since then, the scope of autonomy for transgender persons in Germany has further been broadened considerably by a number of rulings of the Federal Constitutional Court.[21] With a view to the right to free development of one's personality as well as to physical integrity the Court struck down several of the requirements of the German Transsexuals Act, inter alia the prerequisite to be operated or sterilized in order to change one's legal gender.[22] Also the requirement of the dissolution of an existing marriage was held to be unconstitutional.[23] However, the remaining provisions even now necessitate a lengthy judicial inquiry. Thus, full self-determination in gender identity still remains to be achieved by legal reform in Germany[24] as a free change of legal gender at will is not yet allowed, as is the case in a growing number of countries, like Argentina, Ireland or Malta for example.[25]

The fact that it is now no longer required to get a divorce before petitioning for a change of legal gender has significantly enhanced the autonomy of transgender persons concerning their family life. Moreover, it has also contributed to a change in the concept of marriage: Since the marriage outlasts the change of gender it continues to exist between two persons of the same sex. Therefore, even before the recently passed bill, which has opened marriage for same-sex partners, the existence of marriages between partners of the same sex was

---

20 Cf. Italy: The Sex Reassignment Act no. 164 of 1982; Czech Republic: Act No. 301/2000 Coll., on Register Offices, Name and Surname and Act. No. 133/2000 Coll., on Population Records; England and Wales: Gender Recognition Act 2004.

21 BVerfGE 60, 123; 88, 87; 115, 1; 116, 243.

22 BVerfGE 128, 109.

23 BVerfGE 121, 175.

24 Der bundesweiten Arbeitskreis TSG-Reform, *Forderungspapier zur Reform des Transsexuellenrechts*, 2012; L. Adamietz, K. Bager & S. Elsuni, *Regelungs- und Reformbedarf für transgeschlechtliche Menschen*, Begleitmaterial zur Interministeriellen Arbeitsgruppe Inter- & Transsexualität, Vol. 7, 2016; N. Althoff, G. Schabram & P. Follmar-Otto, *Gutachten Geschlechtervielfalt im Recht: Status quo und Entwicklung von Regelungsmodellen zur Anerkennung und zum Schutz von Geschlechtervielfalt*, Begleitmaterial zur Interministeriellen Arbeitsgruppe Inter- & Transsexualität, Vol. 8, 2017; Gesetzentwurf BÜNDNIS 90/DIE GRÜNEN, Entwurf eines Gesetzes zur Anerkennung der selbst bestimmten Geschlechtsidentität und zur Änderung anderer Gesetze (Selbstbestimmungsgesetz – SelbstBestG), BT-Drs. 18/12179.

25 Argentina: Ley de Identidad de Género, 2012; Ireland: Gender Recognition Act, 2015; Malta: Gender Identity, Gender Expression and Sex Characteristics Act, 2015.

legally recognized in Germany.[26] However, partners could not yet enter into a marriage if they were of the same sex or gender, the marriage was just allowed to continue to exist. Here we can detect another gradual change or erosion in the traditional concept of marriage as a union between man and woman.[27] Since the reform, transgender persons are free to enter into a marriage according to their sexual orientation either with a person of the opposite or the same sex as their newly assigned one.[28]

However, transgender persons are not yet fully acknowledged in their gender identity when it comes to their role as parents. As sterility is no longer a prerequisite for changing the legal gender, a transman can bear a child and a transwoman is still able to procreate. Currently, the transman will be registered as the mother of the child[29] and the transwoman as the father according to their reproductive function.[30]

To register them in accordance with their *current* legal gender as father and mother would acknowledge their actual legal gender and identity. This would also conform to the interests of the child not to disclose the fact that their parent is a transgender person. The child's interest to know its father or mother according to their respective procreative function, i.e. the person who gave sperm or gave birth, which is also constitutionally protected, could be safeguarded by other measures, such as an additional entry in the registry. Ultimately, it would be preferable to just use the term parent instead of mother or father.

IV Intersex

Lastly, the situation of intersex persons will be taken into consideration. A child that can be neither identified as belonging to the male or female sex at birth, was and still often is subjected to operations in order to be able to clearly assign a sex – in a world of legal norms that until lately only knew two categories: female and male.[31] Recently, however, medical practice is becoming more hesitant as it is not uncommon that later on the assigned sex turns out not conform to the development and wishes of the person concerned.

In Germany, new legislation was enacted in 2013 concerning intersex people:[32] If a child's sex is ambiguous, the field where the child's sex would be registered at birth had to

26 Explicitly acknowledged by the Federal Constitutional Court, BVerfGE 121, 175.

27 Dethloff, op cit, n. 3, p. 353.

28 The revised § 1353 I 1 states: "Marriage is entered into for life between two persons of the same or different gender"; see also M. Wellenhofer, *in Münchener Kommentar zum BGB*, 7th ed., C.H. Beck, 2017, vor § 1303 BGB, Rn. 12.

29 BGH, *FamRZ* 2017, 1855.

30 BGH, *NJW* 2018, 471.

31 Intersexualität, Stellungnahme Deutscher Ethikrat (2012), 116ff.

32 Gesetz zur Änderung personenstandsrechtlicher Vorschriften (Personenstandsrechts-Änderungsgesetz - PStRÄndG), BGBl. 2013 I, pp. 1122ff.; detailed in regard to the reform: I.A. Bockstette, 'Das Personenstandsrechts-Änderungsgesetz', *StAZ*, 2013, p. 169.

be left vacant.[33] This legislation aimed at preventing an operation that was not medically indicated in order to assign a legal gender.[34] A later registration as male or female was possible but the registration could also be permanently left open. It was also considered to be possible for an intersex person to strike a previous registration as male or female.[35] Up until recently, the law was construed as not to allow the entry of a third sex or another option such as "inter", "diverse" or "x",[36] as has been allowed in some countries like Australia or New Zealand.[37]

However, the pertinent ruling by the Federal Supreme Court was reviewed by the Federal Constitutional Court and has been found to be unconstitutional.[38] The possibility to leave the registration empty or to strike an existing entry as male or female, does not suffice to fully recognize the right to self-determination regarding gender identity. Denying a person the entry of a positive third option, therefore, not only violates the general right of personality protected by Art. 2 I GG in conjunction with Art. 1 GG as the assignment of gender is of utmost importance for an individual's identity, but also constitutes a discrimination prohibited by Art. 3 III GG. The Federal Constitutional Court has mandated reform of the law by the end of 2018, explicitly stating that the legislator would be free to either grant an intersex person the right to a positive entry in the registry or to abolish the binary system altogether.

In December 2018 the legislator changed § 22 III PStG and gives intersex persons the possibility to enter "diverse" in the register or to leave the entry open.[39] Moreover, all operations on minors aiming at the assignment of gender which are not medically required should be expressly prohibited.[40] The consent of the minor's parents does not suffice in order to protect the self-determination and physical integrity of intersex children.[41]

Since the reform was limited to just this one provision allowing to leave the registration empty or enter "diverse", other questions concerning the legal situation of intersex persons remain unanswered. In particular, there is no regulation on how parenthood is established

33 § 22 III PStG stated: "If the child cannot be assigned to the female or male sex, the civil status must be registered in the birth register without that information." It was changed in December 2018 (BT-Drs. 636/18).

34 The provision was adopted following the recommendation of the Committee of Internal Affairs, that referred to the opinion of the German Ethics Council (fn. 26, 143), BT-Drs. 17/12192, 11.

35 BGH, *NJW* 2016, 2885 (2886); S.L. Gössl, 'Die Anwendung des § 22 III PStG auf intersexuelle Personen', *StAZ*, 2018, p. 40 at 43.

36 BGH, *NJW* 2016, 2885 (2887).

37 As to the use of "X" for "indeterminate/intersex/unspecified" for purposes of passports and directories maintained by federal authorities see: Australian Government Guidelines on the Recognition of Sex and Gender, 2013, no. 19.

38 BVerfG, *FamRZ* 2017, 2046.

39 BT-Drs. 636/18: Gesetz zur Änderung der in das Geburtenregister einzutragenden Angaben.

40 Adamietz et al, op cit, n. 24, p. 160; Althoff et al, op cit, n. 24, p. 93.

41 Dethloff, op cit, n. 4, § 13 no. 63.

as the law of parentage only contains provisions for a father or a mother. For intersex persons the reproductive function should be decisive to establish parenthood.[42]

The other important question concerns how an intersex person may formalize a partnership. Up until recently intersex persons could practically not enter into any formalized partnership because marriage was limited to different-sex partners thus leaving no options for those without a legal sex. With marriage having been opened to both opposite as well as same-sex couples the legislator clearly omitted to regulate for intersex persons.[43] Since the purpose of the law reform was to end all discrimination on the ground of sex it can be argued that the provision should be applied by analogy and intersex persons without an entry in the registry should now be allowed to enter into a marriage. Following the recent reform of the law and the creation of a third option for intersex persons as "diverse" they will now automatically fall within the realm of the provision of § 1353 BGB allowing them to marry a person of another sex, i.e. a man or a woman, or another intersex person registered by the third option and thus of the same sex.

At the same time marriage should explicitly be open to any "two persons" thereby expressly also permitting intersex persons who do not want to enter a third option but prefer to leave the entry open, to marry. In any event, even though the legislator will not (yet) abolish the binary system altogether, as the Constitutional Court proposed as one option, it is evident that with the current and future provisions for intersex persons the binary system that still marks our legal system, especially in family law, is under consideration.

V Conclusion

The rising acceptance of sexual and gender diversity has led to an increasing degree of autonomy afforded to homosexuals as well as transgender and intersex persons in Germany as in many other states. This growing recognition of their right to self-determination and autonomy not only concerns them as individuals but also concerns their right to enter into partnerships and to form families. As has been discussed, these changes therefore also impact the fundamental notions of family law with the existing concepts of marriage and parenthood currently undergoing changes. The recent law reform in Germany can be considered as a major step for homosexuals in all three respects as they are now not only allowed to lead their lives in accordance with their sexual orientation but are granted the right to enter into marriage with their partners as well as to jointly adopt a child.

However, with regard to their options to start a family by assisted reproduction reforms are still required to reflect their constitutionally protected right to procreate as well as to

42 For an analogy to the provisions for maternity and paternity see Dethloff, op cit, n. 4, § 10 no. 7.
43 BT-Drs. 18/6665, 11.

end the persisting discrimination. For trans and intersex persons substantial changes are yet necessary in order to fully respect their autonomy as persons as well as regarding their right to partnership and the legal recognition of their family life.

A Dialogue between Freedom of Religion and the Rights of Families

Isabella Nogueira Paranaguá Carvalho Drumond[*]

I Introduction

Pluralism is one of the essential symbols of postmodernity. When legal professionals describe the family as the fruit of culture, they refer to the fact that, in the modern world, it is no longer possible to accept a single linear idea about family structures. Family pluralism, therefore, is the characteristic of the multiplicity of family species that coexist in the same public space, however without equality of legal legitimacy, which generates social injustices.

Throughout this work, the discussion of the role of religion in the public sphere and its impact in the area of family law is analyzed, as well as the rupture between State and religion in the Middle Ages and in the Modern Age. There is no doubt that the debate on family law and religious freedom transcends its own historicity and inevitably enters the realm of philosophy of law. Secularization is, therefore, an important topic in the conversation on whether or not there is a possibility to regulate the rights of all family nuclei in the contemporary world.

It is precisely for this reason that today the debate about the death of God in a secularized world is important for the demarcation of the effectiveness of family law. Philosophers, theologians, family lawyers and constitutionalists participate in the debate. Going beyond the frontiers of each specialty is important for the search of the inclusion of all families in the Brazilian legal system.

II Laicism (laicist) and Laicity: Defining the Oppositions

The origin of the word "laïcité" (laicism or secularism in Portuguese) is Greek and derives from laikos, which designates the people as a whole. The term was employed within religious

* Lawyer, PhD in Law (emphasis on Family Law and Philosophy of Law) from the Pontifical Catholic University of São Paulo (PUC-SP), Master in Political Science from the Federal University of Piauí (UFPI), Postgraduate in Civil Procedural Law (FMS) by the LFG, President of the Brazilian Family Law Institute, section state of Piauí (IBDFAM-PI), President of the Family Law and Succession Law Commission of the Brazilian Bar Association, section state Piauí (OAB-PI).

language to differentiate between the Levites and priests from other Jews. The etymological origin of the term contrasts the common religious, "laikos", with the religious who teach and confer sacraments, "clerikos". The term evolved into "laicus" and took its current form "laïque" (secular or secular in Portuguese) in the sixteenth century (author translation).[1]

The meaning evolved between the Middle Ages and the nineteenth century, first designating the individual who did not have the status of cleric, and then what is not religious, ultimately giving meaning to the current term "secularism".[2]

The first use of the word secularism dates from 1871, in the newspaper "La Patrie" ("The Patria", in Portuguese). The term appeared in dictionaries in 1873 first in its adjectival form, then in its substantive form which defined it as being "the characteristic of all that is secular, or of a secular person." The adjective secular was defined as "what is neither ecclesiastical nor religious". Ferdinand Buisson justified laicism as the recognition of State and societal autonomy, to the detriment of religion: "the fundamental notion of the secular state, that is, the deep delimitation between the temporal and the spiritual, is the gateway into our conduct so that we can no longer leave." Émile Littré defined the secularism of the State as being its neutrality in religious matters (author translation).[3]

Modernity established the secular state[4] as a means of overcoming medieval thought, attributing to it characteristics of non-confessionality,[5] emphasizing that state actions are different from all existing religions. This secular state with Renaissance roots, therefore,

1 M.-D. Charlier-Dagras, *La laïcité française à l'épreuve de l'intégration européenne. Pluralisme et convergences*, Paris, L'Harmattan, 2002, p. 22. Available at: http://www.youscribe.com/catalogue/livres/ressources-professionnelles/droit-et-juridique/la-laicite-francaise-al-epreuve-de-l-integration-europeenne-1418131 (accessed 21 feb. 2016). ("Lórigine du mot 'laicité' est grecque et remonte au mots *laikos*, designant le peuple dans sa totalite; le terme frut repris par la langue religieuse pour differencier le Levites et les pretes par rapport aux autres juifs. Lórigine etymologique du term oppose le fidéle ordinaire *laikos* au fidéle qui enseigne et s'occupe d'aministrer *clerikos*. L'evolution terminologuique du mot deviendra *laicus*, pour prendre sa forme actuelle 'laique' au XVIème siècle.")

2 "L'evolucion du sens se fera essentiellement entre le Moyen-âge et le XIXème designant sucessivement l'individu qui n'a pas la qualité d'ecclesiastique ou de clerc, puis se qui n'est pas religieux, donnant au terme actuel de laicite son sens definitif." Ibid, p. 22.

3 "La première utilisation du mot laicite date du 1871 dans le journal intitule 'La Patrie'. Le term figurera sous sa form adjective puis substantive dans les dictionaires en 1873 où ele definie comme étant 'le caractere de tout qui est laique, ou d'une personne laique'. Ládjectif laique se definissant comme 'ce qui n'est ni eclesiastique ni religieux. Ferdinant Buisson justifiera la laicite par la reconossaince de l'autonomie de l'Etat e de la societe par rapport a toute religion. Il précisera: "la notion fondamentalle de l'Etat laique, c'est a dire la delimitation profonde entre le temporel et le spirituel est entree dans nos mouers de maniere à ne plur en sortir'. Emile Littré définira la laicite de l'Etat comme etant la neutralite de celui-ci en matiére religieuse." Ibid, p. 22.

4 Term whose semantic sense derives from the Greek word "laikos", meaning "layman, of the town".

5 "Confessionality" is a set of beliefs, principles, symbols and practices that are made explicit in the life of a person or institution. It is the attitude of assuming and confessing as valuable a set of values, principles of conduct and also answers to the questions of life. "Confession" is the acceptance of something as true and worthy, as well as the proclamation or declaration that this "something" is meaningful and worthy of being applied to our experience of life. "Confessionality" will then have the meaning of a lifestyle, based on the values chosen to direct personal, family, professional, social and spiritual practice.

would not be an environment for particular interests, as it aimed to shelter all types of citizens, respecting their diverse religions, beliefs or ideologies.

The Enlightenment[6] had several exponents of man's emancipation from medieval customs that were against any kind of non-traditional belief. That is because, as already mentioned, in the Middle Ages there was no separation between State and Church. During the Enlightenment, freedom of religious belief became a general will, and many citizens promoted a collapse of traditional structures. The cry of freedom disseminated by the Enlightenment continued in the universal declarations of the eighteenth and nineteenth centuries, resulting in the dissolution of the boundaries of sacredness.

A secular state, therefore, is a state without an official religion, and it treats all its citizens equally, regardless of the religious orientation of each one. The principle of secularity presupposes two fundamental characteristics: the neutrality of the State respecting the religious freedom of the individual, as well as the separation of the State from religion, which guarantees a collaborative non-denominational confessionality, through which State and Church can cooperate mutually for the common good, without interfering in the other's sphere. According to Pierre Caye and Dominique Terré:

> Secularity is defined as the neutrality of the State in relation to society and its beliefs. Such neutrality is not limited to the simple organization of peaceful coexistence of the various communities among themselves. It means that the state refuses to reassert its power in any fundamental instance, other than itself. ... In affirming secularity, the state establishes its power over the emptiness and thus affirms its highest sovereignty. [7]

Marco Aurélio Lagreca Casamasso said the following in respect of this issue:

> ... if, on the one hand, secularism presupposes the supremacy of politics over religion - an inequality - on the other, it presupposes, both for the State and for religious denominations, the possibility of a free and Emancipated existence - an equality. Although it is impossible and to reach an absolute harmony between the two presuppositions, one can seek a more balanced relation between both. For this, the secular state must recognize and guarantee, for believers and

6 R. de Almeida Gallego, *The sacred in the public sphere: religion, law and secular state* (Master in Law Dissertation, PUC, SP, 2010), p. 112. Available at www.Domainpublico.gov.br/dowload/teste/arqs/cp141078.pdf (accessed on 14 Feb. 2016).

7 P. Caye & D. Terré, 'Le neutre à l'épreuve de la puissance' *in Archives de Philosophie du droit* (No. 48), Paris, Dalloz, 2005, p. 26.

> religious confession, the widest possible freedom, always within the limits of secularity.[8]

In times of extreme social dynamism, the limits of secularity are questionable, and the model of freedom based on absolute equality is difficult to implement. The idea that if everyone is equal, everyone ought to respect the rights of others to live in different family structures is one of the great focal points of modern legal philosophy and family law. The secular state has a responsibility to guarantee autonomy and freedom for all, including those who live in non-traditional families. Secularism must support both religious freedom and the right of postmodern families. And for this broad equality to prevail, it is important to observe a secular state that is not hierarchically superior to religions, but which is capable of regulating them in such a way that they all coexist peacefully. The secular state that faithfully respects its limits is one that does not accept religious interference and affords individuals the voluntary choice of the family structure that suits them best.

It is important to consider the evolution of the role of religion in the public sphere, which was based on two types of thinking about the secular state: the secular state committed to secularism, and the lay secular state. In this context, secularism represents the subjugation of religion by the scientist, an argument corresponding to the loss of "religious space" in the public sphere. It is, therefore, a doctrine that gives institutions a non-religious character, in order to secure a state totally indifferent to ecclesiastical doctrine thereby banishing it from political-civil discussions.

Secularism sees the Church as a social institution with its own laws, which may not necessarily reflect those that govern the functioning of the political system. This secular conception disregards the power of the Church, forcing a total isolation between it and the State, diminishing the idea of the divine and subjecting it to criticism: a Church discredited and without any participation in society. In this sense, according to Tavares:

> Secularism means a judgment of negative value, by the State, in relation to the positions of faith. Based historically on rationalism and scientism, it is hostile to full religious freedom, to its broad practices. France, and its recent episodes of religious intolerance, can be remembered here as a more obvious example of a State which, far from allowing and consecrating widely the freedom of religion and the non-religious commitment of the State, undertakes, on the contrary, A devaluing stance of religion, whatever it may be. Secularity, as neutrality, means the abovementioned exemption. [9]

8 Gallego, op cit, n. 6, p. 115.

9 A. Ramos Tavares, *Curso de Direito Constitucional* [Course of Constitutional Law], 7th ed., São Paulo, Saraiva, 2009, *passim*.

The idea of a secular state was promulgated to fight Catholic imperialism in Brazil, and its objective was to distance the Church from the public scene and secular issues. It sought to delineate the Republic on the basis of the radical and exclusive power of the State. This rupture between State and Church led the Church to establish its own defences. In order to maintain hegemony over man's spiritual thought, the Church opposed secularism through romanticised narratives such as the worship of the Sacred Heart and the Pope's infallibility, through which he espoused the State's finitude.

In this sense, the secular state, instead of rejecting or attempting to suppress religion, considers it a public fact, though it does not lose sight of the distinction between religious and secular spheres. The secular state bears a clear resemblance to the atheistic state: its concern is with the administration of man's material needs. Religion is a private matter, an anachronism that science and human progress will do away with. In addition, it is characterized by confusion between the public and the state, since it does not respect the autonomy of the social in its religious dimension.[10]

The secular state is the fruit of Western democracies, in which politics operates without external interference. The secular state is the foundation of a society that respects all types of religion, because it does not adhere to any of them, culminating in a logical separation between State and Church, without one hindering the performance of the other.

One of the manifestations of secularism is atheism, in which the religious idea of political action and of the private life of citizens is totally excluded. It refers to a movement initiated during the Renaissance, in which members of society behaved without reference to any religion or other metaphysical being. This materialistic conception of the world conceived of God as a human invention, to be exempted from socio-political discussions and encouraged citizens to seek only humanistic or existential solutions for their problems. The secular state is different from the atheist state; while the former is constitutionally recognised, the other is ignored by law and politics.

From this standpoint, the secular state - based on secularism - appears to balance the atheist state's ineptitude in the face of social impasses and the tyranny of the confessional nature of the Old Regime. Through this balance, secularism seeks to guarantee the autonomy of each individual, including their freedom of conscience. The secular state advocates of diverse beliefs and is, therefore, a state properly neutral to the sacred. It regards all individuals equal, regardless of their religious choice.

Thus, the cardinal principle of secularism concerns not only individual freedom of conscience, but also the attendant obligation of the State to respect this fundamental right which is enshrined in the Constitution of the Republic.

---

10 Á. de Azevedo Gonzaga & A.B. Gonçalves, *Rethinking the right: studies in honor of Prof. Cláudio De Cicco*, São Paulo, Revista das Tribunais, 2010, p. 292.

The primary mark of a secular state is the acceptance of the freedom of belief and the unavoidable existence of religion in people's private lives. In the words of Giorgio Resta and Guido Alpa:

> Secularity is a method that belongs to believers and non-believers: secularism means that the state (precisely lay) is "non-denominational", does not provide for a legal sanction to the ethical-religious norm of a single confession, but at the same time, recognizes not only the freedom of conscience of that religious institution and the fundamental importance of the religious factor for the life of that political community.[11]

Paradoxically, in contemporary plural society, the role of the State as guardian is the greatest obstacle to the effectiveness of secularity. After all, the State often restricts its field of action to public policies and legal order, aspects aimed at the exercise of the common good and the community. Thus, intervention or abstention in these matters, without observing the principle of neutrality, to which the State is bound by virtue of article 19, I of the Constitution of the Federative Republic of Brazil of 1988, leads to conflicts of a religious nature that can affect the family lives of some individuals. To achieve a balance in the State's neutral action towards religious freedom, it is imperative that the State observe two regulatory elements: verification of the public interest and social outcry, and obedience to the principle of tolerance. Thus, within the limits of a democratic public order and granting due respect to the related constitutional principles, the State will enable persons to freely develop their autonomy and personality, especially within the family unit to which they belong.

III Possible Solutions: A Secular state, but not Secular

By developing in line with constant social changes, family law presents itself as both versatile and evolutionary. Civil law, especially in respect of the family, cannot concern itself only with the hypothetical individual. Man is a social animal and free to constitute a family. The law cannot, without justification, enforce a single model of the family. To do otherwise would be to ignore the glaring social reality of family diversity.

However, there is still a conservative influence which forces our legal system not to protect all family structures, citing religious justifications, which is inconsistent with the secular context in which the Constitution was signed. The Church maintains its conservatism through canonical law, treating marriages celebrated in the civil sphere as mere

11 G. Alpha & G. Resta, 'Le persone and la famiglia. Le persone fisiche e i diritti della personalità', (Giuridica), *in Persona e Principio di laicità*, Torin, UTET, 2006, ch. 10, p. 258.

concubinage, and judging civil divorces as invalid. The Church does not recognize the right of the State to annul an ecclesiastical marriage, just as ecclesial law recognizes no family other than that created through marriage.

According to Sampel, this emphasis on the matrimonial institution derives from the fact that canonical law sees in marriage not a mere contract, but a true alliance that seeks, above all, to generate and provide for children. Even if someone obtains a civil divorce decree, any remarriage will be invalid in the eyes of the Church unless an ecclesiastical court has granted a nullity. According to the late Father Pegoraro, professor in São Paulo:

> The Church, in her millennial doctrine, has always declared herself incompetent to dissolve the bond that comes from the sacrament of marriage validly celebrated and consummated, as well as declaring incompetent any other authority. The way she walks is different. It deepens a growing understanding of the requirements and conditions necessary to take up this project of life in a definitive way, expanding the possibility of declaration of nullity of the marriage celebrated. Many marriages, which appear to be valid, are liable to nullity, since their inner reality is not sufficiently constituted.[12]

The exercise of individual freedoms, particularly in respect of one's family structure, is impeded by the lack of a clear delineation between State and Church. On the one hand, the Church does not recognize the right of plural families, while, on the other hand, the State although secular, has not yet completely detached itself from its Catholic roots.

The problem concerning recognition of new family structures is directly linked to the understanding of what is in the so-called "common good", which is influenced by the complex relationship between the secularized state and the Catholic Church and fails to accommodate the freedom of both secular and non-secular families.

It is important to emphasize that it is not a Christian value to deny the happiness of another because of individual choices, or to exclude a person from shelter because he is different or belongs to a non-traditional family unit. The essence of Christianity is inclusion, not segregation. It is clear that the rupture between State and Church - between the Middle Ages and Modernity - did not lead to their complete separation. The State and Church are two important societal institutions, and the rivalry between them must be overcome, so that each can recognize its role with respect to families and religious freedom and the rights of plural families may each be respected.

The Church has a relevant role in society, and the state should not intervene in its sphere. On the other hand, the Church must also respect the non-secular state. The good Christian cannot prevent the legal regulation of new family models, because what should

12 E.L. Sampel, *Introduction to Canon Law*, São Paulo, LTR, 2001, pp. 79-80.

prevail for families is the elevation of affection as a legal value. The Bible states that "where two or more are gathered together in my name, I will be with you" (Matthew, 18:20), which may mean that the best union is not necessarily between a man and a woman. A non-fundamentalist Christian interpretation accommodates several family structures, as long as they are built under the aegis of love.

For Gisele Groeninga,

> affection entered the world of law through what was previously excluded to it: affiliation relations and homo-affective relations. The search for humanization of the subject and the attempts to understand the relationship between feeling, thought and action was directed towards the search for ethical being, which takes into account the individual without losing sight of the collective, always having in mind the concept of dignity of the human person.[13]

For the State there is a desacralization of the concept of family which, because it is secular, must also support non-traditional family structures. This is not to say that the sacred has lost its place in the secular state, but that the postmodern family, being based primarily on the feeling of love, must be respected by observing the principles of autonomy and dignity.

When Jurgen Habermas described "postconventional morality" and Claude Lefort mentioned the dissolution of "reference marks of certainty," they were both referring to the fact that, in contemporary society, it is no longer possible to form a substantive idea of the good to be shared by all. Pluralism, however, has at least two distinct meanings: the diversity of individual conceptions of a decent life, or the multiplicity of social identities.[14]

In contemporary political philosophy, representatives of liberal thought - John Rawls, Ronald Dworkin, and Charles Larmore, among others - adopt the first meaning of pluralism and describe modern democracies as societies in which different individual conceptions of good coexist. The second meaning of pluralism is used by representatives of community thought, such as Charles Taylor and Michael Walzer, to emphasize the multiplicity of social identities and ethnic and religious cultures that are present in contemporary societies. On the other hand, Jurgen Habermas - debating with liberals and community members and representing what we refer to as critical-deliberative thinking - believes that one conceptualisation cannot be favoured over the other. However, despite the different ways in which they describe and understand contemporary, liberal, communitarian, and critical-

13 G.C. Groeninga, 'Law and psychoanalysis: a new epistemological horizon" *in* R. da Cunha Pereira (Ed.), *Affection, ethics, family and the new Civil Code*, Belo Horizonte, Del Rey; IBDFAM, 2004, pp. 259 and 262.

14 G. Cittadino, *Pluralism, Law and Distributive Justice. Elements of Contemporary Constitutional Philosophy*, 3rd ed., Rio de Janeiro, Lumen Juris, 2004, p. 1.

deliberative societies, it is believed that it is possible to formulate and justify an ideal of justice - especially distributive justice - appropriate to modern pluralism.[15]

When liberals associate pluralism with various individual conceptions of a decent life, they are giving priority to fundamental rights over popular sovereignty. For Rawls or Larmore, the State in a liberal democratic society must be neutral in relation to the various individual conceptions of good. It is the "fact" of pluralism - or the existence of reasonable disagreement - that precludes interference by the state in the substantive views of individuals. The prioritisation of fundamental rights is what ensures the neutrality of the state.[16]

Postmodern families have distinct notions of morality. Peaceful coexistence of these families requires dialogue between Church and State, to promote public policies to judge claims in cases of conflict, otherwise the autonomy of free individuals is lost. No matter how we look at this question, we see that backward thinking makes dialogue between religion and the State difficult. Distortions on one side or the other must be avoided and the dispute between the sacred and the common good - which is not necessarily the collective will, for there are minorities - must be eliminated. On this understanding, it is possible to remodel the law to regulate all family structures.

Some people insist that morality is irrelevant to discovering the content of the law, what it serves and its function. However, since Aristotle's treatise, efforts have been made to demonstrate that the fields are connected; that some laws have a moral basis, especially family law.

In such cases, justice[17] and doctrine will change. The capacity of man to choose different values necessitates the discussion of relative truth and the right of freedom. Such discernment is of secular origin, and also finds a basis in the writings of Augustine: man, while an individual, associates himself with others to meet certain ends which are better achieved through collaboration with others. Society is nothing more than the gathering of several family nuclei, led by a ruler and governed by laws that must secure the common good.

The central question of liberalism is, then, how a just and stable society can exist. The ideal of liberalism is, therefore, a morally, religiously and politically pluralistic society. The basic assumption of liberalism is that people are free to pursue their own conceptions of good.

The most important thing is for the State to fulfil its secular role such that family diversity and religious freedom are respected. The Church must be afforded the conditions necessary to carry out its sacred mission in respect of families, while, at the same time, the State must act in accordance with its secular foundation, as outlined above. In fact, the

15 Ibid, pp. 1-2.

16 Ibid, pp. 129-130.

17 As employed here, "justice" refers to the elimination of the subjective and arbitrary, and the establishment of a neutral, impartial jurisdiction. It is the impartial resolution of the conflict, regardless of a judgment of the content of the applicable law, or of the decision itself. Just judgment is impartial, not arbitrary.

Magna Carta has a plethora of provisions aimed at protecting the Church and the family (including, obliquely, marriage) as institutions. It is imperative that the authorities afford citizens the freedom to choose the family arrangement to which they want to belong.

This paper has demonstrated that respect for various family structures is intrinsically linked with the need to respect religious freedom. And this can be achieved by encouraging cooperation between the Church and State, precisely through their separation, in favour of modern, pluralistic society. The Church is an institution that is part of the body politic and plays a very important social role. The dialogue between State and religion requires an understanding that there are different conceptualisations of "the family". The family can remain unchanged from the Christian model, constituted by the loving union between a man and a woman, just as different forms can (and should) be recognised and respected by the state. Such cooperation requires that the Church act reasonably; the Brazilian State is secular, and it is not possible to give effect to religious freedom without giving freedom to the various forms of family.

Changing Families and the Need for Policy to Protect Children

Linda D. Elrod[*]

I Introduction

> *Unfortunately, the American family is confronted with the problem whether it shall continue to exist, and the American people, whether they like it or not, should look the problems of their family life squarely in the face as the greatest of all their social problems.*
> *Charles Ellwood, 1909.*

American society has experienced numerous changes since the quote from 1909.[1] The most significant change for American families has been the decoupling of marriage and parenthood over the past few decades. Although the divorce rate has remained at about the same rate since 1982, fewer people are getting married and more people are cohabiting. More single persons choose to have a child out of wedlock, adopt, or use assisted reproduction. Today, more children live with a single parent or unmarried parents. While for the most part, children in married families fare pretty well, children in single parent and nonmarital households struggle. These children are at greater risk for a variety of problems partly because these families are not as stable and often lack the resources, monetary and social, of married families.[2] Among the reasons are that the parents are younger, have less

---

* Richard S. Righter Distinguished Professor of Law at Washburn University School of Law and Director of the Children and Family Law Center.

1 L. Henry Elrod, 'Epilogue: Of Families, Federalization and a Quest for Policy', *Family Law Quarterly*, Vol. 33, No. 3, 1999, pp. 843-863 (noting two world wars, women's suffrage, a great depression, wars in Korea and Vietnam, the civil rights' movement, incredible advances in medical research, technology, transportation and space exploration). The 21st century started with a contested presidential election, the 9/11 attacks, a war in Iraq, introduction of the iPod, mapping of the human genome, creation of Google, Hurricane Katrina, illegal immigration hitting record highs (2007), awareness of global warming, the recession of 2008, social networking, the election of America's first Black President, and the election of the first thrice married President.

2 S.S. McLanahan & I. Garfinkel, 'Fragile Families: Debates, Facts and Solutions', *in* M. Garrison & E.S. Scott (Eds.), *Marriage at the Crossroads: Law, Policy, and the Brave New World of Twenty-First Century Families*, UK, Cambridge University Press, 2012, p. 142, at 146-147. See also C. Huntington, 'Postmarital Family Law: A Legal Structure for Nonmarital Families', *Stanford Law Review*, Vol. 67, January 2015, pp. 167-240 at 196-202 (summarizing research).

income, less education, and are disproportionately nonwhite.[3] Single parents may have multiple partners. Nonmarried parents are more likely to separate, find new partners, and have additional children, creating "complex" families.[4] These complex families often include stepparents[5] and grandparents.[6] Unfortunately, often the child's relationship with one parent is dependent upon the other parent's relationship with that parent, which in complex families can be a problem.[7] In most states, these nonmarital families lack a legal framework for cohabitants, partners, relatives, and their children when relationships end.[8] Research also shows these diverging patterns of family life are increasingly based on education and class.[9]

The United States has not embraced positive rights for children – the right to food, clothing, shelter, healthcare and education. The Trump administration's call for a return to small government has meant recommendations to cut welfare spending, undermining universal health care, and limiting access to birth control, among other things. The lack of a cohesive family policy that includes public financial support for families generally leaves American families vulnerable, especially nonmarital families, and a growing number in poverty. Some current federal policies, such as the current immigration policies, undercut even intact marital families.[10] Federal and state governments need to develop policies and programs that support the healthy development of children, regardless of family form.

---

3 J. Carbone & N. Cahn, *Red Families v. Blue Families: Legal Polarization and the Creation of Culture*, UK, Oxford University Press, 2011, p. 2 (noting that for African-American women who do not finish high school, 96% of the births take place outside marriage).

4 McLanahan & Garfinkel, op cit, n. 2, pp. 146-147 (finding causal relationship between family structure and child outcomes).

5 H. DiFonzo & R.C. Stern, 'Breaking the Mold and Picking Up the Pieces: Rights of Parenthood and Parentage in Nontraditional Families', *Family Court Review*, Vol. 51, January 2013, pp. 104-113 (indicating stepfamilies are the fastest growing family form but "rights" for stepparents vary widely from state to state).

6 See Pew Research Center, 'Since the Start of the Great Recession, More Children Raised by Grandparents', 9 September 2009 (indicating that one in ten children live with a grandparent, often with one parent). See also J.E. Cross, N. Palmer & C.L. Smith, 'Families Redefined: Kinship Groups That Deserve Benefits', *Mississippi Law Journal*, Vol. 78, Summer, 2009, pp. 791-831.

7 McLanahan & Garfinkel, op cit, n. 2, pp. 152-155. Note that Donald Trump's family is a complex family – he has had five children with three wives.

8 See C.G. Joslin, 'Marital Status Discrimination 2.0', *Boston University Law Review*, Vol. 95, May 2015, pp. 805-831; C.G. Joslin, 'Leaving No (Nonmarital) Child Behind', *Family Law Quarterly*, Vol. 48, No. 3, 2014, pp. 495-513.

9 McLanahan & Garfinkel, op cit, n. 2, pp. 146-47.

10 H.S. Edwards, 'Bye Dad, I Love You: American's Immigration Policy is Splitting Families and Spreading Fear', *Time*, 19 March 2018, pp. 34-40; S. Inskeep, 'To Curb Illegal Immigration, DHS Separating Families at the Border', *National Public Radio*, 27 February 2018 (discussing a 39 year old Congolese woman who was being detained in San Diego while her seven year old child was being held in Chicago).

II Challenges: Resolve the Conflicting Messages

We live in a time of conflicting messages and values. Marriage has been central to family formation and has offered children a relatively stable family environment. The Pew Report indicated that members of the middle class, who once married in high proportions and formed families, are finding it difficult to enter and sustain marriage. They are, however, cohabiting, having children, and forming nonmarital families. These nonmarital families are less stable than marital families, subjecting the children to multiple changes in living arrangements and parent figures. There is an increasing class divide in family stability.[11] Because children hold the keys to the future health of the country, we must find a way to support children in whatever family they find themselves.

A *Society Pays Lip Service to the Importance of Families but Makes Policy Based on the Marital Family and Its Ability to Provide What Children Need*

> *What we have witnessed ... is the unprecedented decline of marriage as the only acceptable arrangement for having sexual relations and raising children.*[12]

Families are the building blocks of society. The family remains the best form of human organization found to date for providing the nurture, love, emotional support, and instruction children need to survive and to become healthy, happy citizens. Family law traditionally has been based upon marriage.[13] In theory, the marital family provides children a stable environment with the financial and social resources of two adults. In 1960, two-thirds of all men and women over 15 were married and 73% of children lived in intact, different sex, married households. No fault divorce, more equal opportunities for women in the workplace and the removal of legal disabilities for children born out of wedlock, coupled with the acceptance of single parenting, has created options other than marriage. As late as 2000, the legal definition of family for most people meant a married man and woman with their biological or adopted children. Marriage status remains an exalted, personal relationship to which government attaches a large number of benefits and obliga-

11 L.C. McClain, 'Is There a Way Forward in the "War Over the Family?"', *Texas Law Review*, Vol. 93, 2015, pp. 705-742.

12 See A.J. Cherlin, *The Marriage-Go-Round: The State of Marriage and the Family in America Today*, New York, Vintage, 2010, p. 27 (indicating that Americans step on and off the carousel of intimate partnership more than those in other countries, *id.* at 20).

13 C.E. Schneider, 'The Channeling Function in Family Law', *Hofstra Law Review*, Vol. 20, Spring 1992, pp. 495-532 (marriage evolved to channel sexual behavior into religiously and socially acceptable norms); M.H. Weiner, *A Parent-Partner Status for American Family Law*, UK, Cambridge University Press, 2015 (law shapes behavior by attaching consequences to human action and defines responsibility).

tions.[14] If a marriage ends in divorce, state laws provide a mechanism to protect children with judicial oversight of the "best interests of the child" in allocating parenting time and child support.

Today's family, however, is no longer based on marriage. In 2013, less than half of all households consisted of married couples. Cohabiting couples rose by 1700% between 1960 and 2011.[15] In 2015, there were more than 8.3 million households with opposite sex unmarried couples; 39% included at least one biological child under age 18 of either partner.[16] Almost forty one percent of children are born out of wedlock.[17] Fifty percent of children born to cohabiting parents will experience parental separation by age nine, compared to twenty percent of married parents. Sixty percent of all couples who have a child together have a child with another person; only 21% of married couples had a child with another.[18] More than 40% of people between the ages of 19-29 have at least one step-sibling.[19] The family no longer is a fixed social unit with fixed membership and roles. Families today are formed and reformed by high levels of divorce and remarriage, increasing number of cohabiting couples, rising numbers of married and unmarried couples who choose to "live apart together" and separated immigrant families.[20] There has been a decline in marriage among the poor for decades, but it is now increasingly noticeable with the middle class.[21] One commentator notes that "it is becoming increasingly difficult to tell where the boundaries of family lie."[22] There is a disconnect between the real world and what politicians think families are. Policies made for the marital family often have unintended, sometimes negative, consequences on the growing number of nonmarital families.

---

14 Obergefell v. Hodges, 135 S. Ct. 2484 (2015); Windsor v. United States, 133 S. Ct. 2675 (2013).

15 The National Marriage Project, *The State of Our Union:, Marriage in America 2012*, December 2012, pp. 76-77, at http://nationalmarriageproject.org/wp-content/uploads/2012/12/SOOU2012.pdf.

16 U.S. Census Bureau, *America's Families and Living Arrangements: 2015: Unmarried Couples*, table UC3. See also W.D. Manning & B. Stykes, *Twenty-five Years of Change in Cohabitation in the United States, 1987-2013*, National Center for Family and Marriage Research, 2015, at https://www.bgsu.edu/content/dam/BGSU/college-of-arts-and-sciences/NCFMR/documents/FP/FP-15-01-twenty-five-yrs-cohab-us.pdf (65% of women aged 19-44 have cohabited and 23% of all children are born into cohabiting households).

17 B.E. Hamilton et al, *National Vital Statistics Report, Births: Final Data for 2014*, 2015, p. 2.

18 L. Tach et al., 'Parenting as a "Package Deal": Relationships, Fertility, and Nonresident Father Involvement Among Unmarried Parents, *Demography*, Vol. 47, No. 1, February 2010, pp. 181–204.

19 J. M. Krogstad, '5 Facts About the Modern American Family', Pew Research Center *Factank: News in the Numbers*, 30 April 2014, at http://www.pewresearch.org/fact-tank/2014/04/30/5-facts-about-the-modern-american-family/ (indicating only 16% of households have a married couple raising their own children)

20 L. A. Rosenbury, 'Friends with Benefits?', *Michigan Law Review*, Vol. 106, November, 2007, pp. 189-242.

21 I. Sawhill, *Generation Unbound Drifting into Sex and Parenthood Without Marriage*, Washington, DC, Brookings Institution Press, 2014.

22 A.J. Cherlin, 'Demographic Trends in the United States: A Review of Research in the 2000s', *Journal of Marriage & Family*, Vol. 72, No. 3, 2010, pp. 403-419.

B Society Still Pays Lip Service to the Importance of Children Growing Up in Families but Does Little to Support Families with Children

Forty years ago Mary Ann Glendon opined that employment relationships were replacing family relationships in importance.[23] Inflation in the latter half of the twentieth century made two income families a necessity. The cost of the basic American middle class package (home, car, food, health insurance and education) skyrocketed. While once a wage earner could support a family of four above the poverty line on minimum wage, that is no longer the case.[24] The minimum wage, when adjusted for inflation, was 19% lower in 1998 than in 1979. It is even lower today. The federal minimum wage has been $7.25 since 2009. If it had kept up with the economy, it would be about nineteen dollars an hour.[25] It is hard for two wage earners to keep up. A single parent today with two children does not earn enough to stay at the poverty line. In 2013, the average household debt totaled over 100% of annual income.[26] Mothers working for pay outside the home increased from 45 to 78 percent between 1965 and 2000.[27] Today about 70.6 mothers with children under 18 worked for pay outside the home, although working mothers are more likely to choose part time work.[28] Even if working full time, women are more likely to earn 80% of what their male

23 M.A. Glendon, *The New Family and the New Property,* London, Butterworth & Co., 1981.

24 See M. Michaels, 'If the U.S. Minimum Wage had Kept Up with the Economy, Many Low-wage Earners Could Earn Double What They Make Now', *Business Insider*, 22 December 2017.

25 See E. Warren, 'The New Economics of the American Family', *American Bankruptcy Institute Law Review*, Vol. 12, Spring, 2004, pp. 1-41 (showing how the 1973 family could live with one wage earner earning $38,700, stay at home wife, two children and have $17,834 left after fixed expenses while a two earner family in 2000 earning $67,800 with day care, second car and health insurance has only $800 left after fixed expenses).

26 S. Dewan, 'An Ambiguous Omen, U.S. Household Debt Begins to Rise Again', *New York Times*, 18 February 2014, p. B2.

27 S.M. Bianchi, 'Family Change and Time Allocation in American Families', *Annals American Academy Political & Social Science*, Vol. 638, No. 1, 2011, pp. 21-44 at 24.

28 K. Parker & W. Wang, 'Modern Parenthood,' Pew Research Center, 2013, at http://www.pewsocialtrends.org/2013/03/14/modern-parenthood-roles-of-moms-and-dads-converge-as-they-balance-work-and-family/ (26% of women compared to 13% of men). Bianchi, ibid, (lamenting that mothers have shed hours of housework but not the hours they devote to childrearing and continue to scale back paid work to meet childrearing demands).

counterparts do.[29] The Trump administration has made the situation worse by revoking many of the protections put in place for women workers.[30]

In the 1970s male unemployment varied little by class or education. By 2010, however, the unemployment rate for college graduates was 4.6%; for noncollege graduates, it was 10.3%. Between 1980 and 2007, male income increased only for college graduates.[31] College-educated individuals marry at an older age and have children in marriage after establishing their careers.[32] The top ten percent of wealth holders are married. Thirty percent of married couples have incomes above the 80th percentile on income distribution.[33]

There has been a severe decline in marriage among the poor, and increasingly the middle-class who have unplanned children early, often outside of marriage. Diminished economic prospects for men without a college degree have impacted their "marriagability." They marry less and have a higher divorce rate. Divorce rates for less educated mothers have also risen.[34] More than half of unmarried couple households had incomes at or below the 40th percentile of income distribution.[35]

Those parents with the lowest incomes are getting poorer and the rich are in fact richer. The CEO who made 41 times the average worker in 1960; 185 times in 1995; made 335 times in 2016.[36] The divergence between rich and poor is the largest since 1926. In 2016, the top one percent of households held 39% of the wealth. A family structure gap is now being added to the widening income gap between rich and poor.[37] Disparities in family structures can be seen across racial groups as 74.5% of white children lived with two married parents in 2014, while only 34.4% of black children and 57.8% of Hispanic.[38] The income

29 U.S. Dep't of Labor, 'Highlights of Women's Earnings in 2013', 2014 (showing women working full time had median weekly earnings of $706 while men had $860). See also A.T. LoSasso et al., 'The $16,819 Pay Gap for Newly Trained Physicians: The Unexplained Trend of Men Earning More Than Women,' *Health Affairs*, Vol. 30, No. 2, February 2011, p. 193 (in 2008 women doctors made almost $17,000 less than their male counterparts). In 2017, the BBC apparently paid John McEnroe ten times more than it paid Martina Navratilova for broadcast coverage of Wimbledon. In Hollywood, Mark Wahlberg was paid 1000 times more than Michelle Williams for reshooting a movie.

30 M.E. O'Hara, 'Trump Pulls Back Obama-Era Protections for Women Workers', *NBC News*, 3 April 2017 (noting the executive order of March 27, 2017 revoking the 2014 Fair Pay and Safe Workplaces Order of the Obama administration).

31 See J. Carbone, 'Unpacking Inequality and Class: Family, Gender and the Reconstruction of Class Barriers', *New England Law Review*, Vol. 45, Spring, 2011, pp. 527-569 at 554.

32 See A.J. Cherlin, 'The Real Reason Rich People Marry', *New York Times*, 6 December 2014, p. SR3.

33 A.L. Alstott, 'Updating the Welfare State: Marriage, The Income Tax, and Social Security in the age of Individualism', *Tax Law Review*, Vol. 66, Summer, 2013, pp. 695-759.

34 See S.P. Martin, 'Trends in Marital Dissolution by Women's Education in the United States,' *Demographic Research*, Vol. 15, December 2006, pp. 537-564 at 552.

35 Alstott, op cit, n. 33.

36 D. Nicks, 'CEOs Make 335 Times the Average of What Workers Earn', *Time.com/Money*, 17 May 2016.

37 J. Carbone & N. Cahn, *Marriage Markets: How Inequality is Remaking the American Family*, UK, Oxford University Press, 2014.

38 See 'Family Structure and Children's Living Arrangements' *in* Federal Interagency Forum on Child and Family Statistics, *American's Children: Key National Indicators of Well-Being 2015*, 205 at p. 2, at

varied by race also. The medium income of white households with children was $80,800; Black $35,900 and Hispanic $41,000.

The frantic pace of life places incredible stress on families. The need for two wage earners, jobs requiring twelve hours a day, and often hour long commutes put pressures on families. Parents are tired when they get home from work. While men have assumed more responsibilities, women still do the majority of the housework and child care.[39] In single parent households, the stress is magnified. Child care is expensive and hard to find. Many children, especially in single parent families, go home to an empty house and are alone from one to four hours. These "latch key" children text, play on the computer, watch television, and sometimes get into trouble with their free time. Lack of parental supervision has been consistently related to delinquency, teenage pregnancies and juvenile crime. Compared to Western Europe, the United States has the worst statistics on problems with families – the highest child poverty rate (20%),[40] the highest divorce rates, highest incidence of drug (now called the opioid epidemic) and substance abuse, adolescent pregnancy, juvenile crime, and adolescent suicide.[41]

At the same time that expenses are increasing, government support for families has declined in terms of tax policies, housing subsidies and cash assistance. The Trump administration's budget proposals for extensive cuts in welfare spending means less support for poor families and programs, like the Supplemental Nutrition Assistance Program (SNAP, also called "food stamps"), that support them. Most of Western Europe have programs that help families such as universal preschool, paid parental leave, and child support assurance. For example, Norway requires parents to take nine weeks compulsory maternity leave at 100% salary, with the option to take 44 weeks at full pay and another year of unpaid leave. In the United States, under the Family and Medical Leave Act, parents can take up to 12 weeks of unpaid, job guaranteed leave for the birth of a child. Only 16% of eligible employees take it because most cannot afford to. Only slightly over 10% of the U.S. workforce has access to paid leave.[42] Most western nations give family allowances for children in single parent or two parent households irrespective of need and subsidize day care,

---

https://www.childstats.gov/pdf/ac2015/ac_15.pdf. See also R.R. Banks, *Is Marriage for White People? How the African-American Marriage Decline Affects Everyone*, New York, Plume, 2012.

39 See C. Tejada, 'Women Still Do More Chores at Home than Men, Study Finds', *Huffington Post*, 27 September 2017, at https://www.huffingtonpost.ca/2017/09/27/women-chores-home_a_23224733/. E. Goodman, 'System Collapsing Because Congress Won't Recognize It', *Topeka Capital Journal*, 17 November 1999, p. 2 ("Until the past 30 years, the 'system' depended on the unseen, unpaid labor of women. It was supported by a family wage and an ideology. Now women are in the workplace and we haven't figured out a replacement.").

40 Children's Defense Fund, *The State of America's Children 2017* (showing poverty rates are much higher for Black and Latino children). The child poverty rate is 7% in France and 3% in Sweden.

41 L. Holmes, 'Suicide Rates for Teen Boys and Girls are Climbing', *Huffington Post*, at https://www.huffingtonpost.com/entry/suicide-rates-teen-girls_us_59848b64e4b0cb15b1be13f4.

42 C.C. Miller, 'The Economic Benefits of Paid Parental Leave', *New York Times*, 30 January 2015, p. BU3.

health care and higher education for children who pass the entrance exam. Most Western European nations give everyone five weeks of vacation a year - at the same time! The United States does less than almost any other industrialized nation for families.

The United Nations Children's Fund found that higher government spending on family and social benefits is associated with lower child poverty rates.[43] There is a strong argument that if developing healthy children is what we want, then government must provide a safety net for all types of families. What type of programs will help families most is the subject of much debate. Some conservatives, concerned about family fragmentation, want to with strengthen marriage and restore a norm of childbearing and parenting within marriage. They argue that child poverty could be reduced by 20% if marriage rates returned to the levels of the 1970s.[44] Others suggest that the answer lies in community supports like better education, better paying jobs and subsidized child care.[45] Another view proposes childbearing by design. Instead of drifting into parenthood, parents should plan for its responsibilities, rather than incur them by default.[46] Yet another scholar argues for a new "parent-partner status," i.e. the existence of the relationship between parent and child should affect the existence of legal obligations between the adults.[47]

C *Conflict Between the Dream and Reality of Marriage in a Disposable Society*

Marriage remains the "ideal" for personal intimate relationships. A 2006 Gallup poll found that 91% of respondents reported that they were either married or intended to be married at some point. Only 4% dismissed marriage as an option.[48] The definition of marriage has

43 'Child Poverty in Perspective: An Overview of Child Well-Being in Rich Countries,' *Innocenti Report Card*, No. 7, 2007.

44 See N.D. Glenn, 'Values, Attitudes and the State of American Marriage' *in* D. Popenoe et al (Eds.), *Promises to Keep: Decline and Renewal of Marriage in America*, U.S.A., Rowman & Littlefield, 1996. The federal government sponsors a National Healthy Marriage Resource Center: see http://www.healthymarriage-info.org/index.aspx.

45 See H. Clinton, *It Takes A Village*, New York, Simon & Schuster, 1996; M. Albertson Fineman, *The Neutered Mother, The Sexual Family, and other Twentieth Century Tragedies*, 1st ed., Abingdon, UK, Routledge, 1st ed., 1995, pp. 226-236 (arguing society should share the responsibility for nurturing children by providing minimum levels of subsidy to support the single mother-child dyad during dependency). See also M. Albertson Fineman, *The Autonomy Myth: A Theory of Dependency*, New York City, The New Press, 2004.

46 Sawhill, op cit, n. 21 (noting that social policies can only go so far and there must be greater personal responsibility on the part of would-be parents).

47 See Weiner, op cit, n. 13 (creating legal obligations to aid; to not abuse; to do relationship work; fair dealing; to give care or pay compensation for disproportionate caregiving). See also N.D. Polikoff, *Beyond (Straight and Gay) Marriage: Valuing All Families Under the Law*, Boston, MA, Beacon Press, 2008, p. 126.

48 J.H. DiFonzo, 'How Marriage Became Optional: Cohabitation, Gender and Emerging Functional Norms', *Rutgers Journal of Law & Public Policy*, Vol. 8, Spring, 2011, pp. 521-566, at 527.

expanded to include the right of same-sex couples to marry.[49] The general norm of marital parenthood, however, seems unlikely to return. Stable, long term marriage is becoming unattainable for some members of our society. Commentators see a link between growing economic inequality and growing family inequality.[50] Marriage, once perceived as an arrangement for economic security and procreation,[51] was one of the few career options open to women even in the 1950s. Happiness in marriage then was not seen as a goal, but as a by-product. Family members were expected to make sacrifices. Today, spouses choose each other and choose to be married. Americans romanticize the institution of marriage and perpetuate the myth of finding the perfect mate for a lifetime. Romance novels make millions of dollars a year, the Hallmark channel's romance shows are among the most viewed, reality shows like the Bachelor and internet companies like Match.com promise to find the perfect mate. The romanticization of marriage leads to rising expectations of happiness in marriage. If a person is not "happy" with a spouse, the person may seek a divorce, a new partner, a new location or a new lifestyle. While most romance movies and novels stop after the courtship, couples often have to navigate marriage and parenthood without a roadmap. "Happily ever after" does not come without hard work and good communication skills, compromise, and compassion.

There is a disconnect between a religious tenet that says "until death do us part" and a legal system which allows unilateral divorce and serial remarriage. There is no longer a cultural consensus of marriage until death. Our society is geared toward throwing away things that are not working rather than repairing them. The disposable mentality too often has resulted in no continued economic responsibility for children or a former spouse (which was a major motivator for the federal child support reforms). While individual freedom allows one to choose to leave an adult relationship, society should not allow parents to abandon their children.

---

49 Obergefell, op cit, n. 14. As late as 2013, Justice Alito in his dissent in Windsor, op cit, n. 14, argued that the Court should not resolve a debate between the two competing views of marriage – the "traditional/conjugal" model of marriage, which links sex, marriage, procreation, and parenting with a "consent-based" model of marriage that focuses on the adults' emotional commitment to one another and does not rest on gender-differentiated roles.

50 PEW Research Center, 'The Decline of Marriage and the Rise of New Families', 18 November 2010, at http://www.pewsocialtrends.org/2010/11/18/the-decline-of-marriage-and-rise-of-new-families/.

51 See L. Teitelbaum, 'Family History and Family Law', *Wisconsin Law Review*, 1985, pp. 1135-1181.

D The Tension Between the Needs (and Rights) of Children and the Rights of the Parents

> *Easy come, easy go marriage and casual cohabitation and procreation are on a collision course with the economic and social needs of children.*[52]

Although children are being created in more unique ways with assisted reproductive technologies, children need much the same as they have always needed – someone to care for them in infancy, to feed and house them, and to give them guidance and emotional and financial support as they grow. Children benefit from having the emotional and financial resources of two parents. In a case upholding a co-parenting agreement between a same-sex couple when the biological mother argued her former partner was not a parent, the Kansas Supreme Court stated:

> ... without the coparenting agreement these children would have only one parent. ... Denying the children an opportunity to have two parents, the same as children of a traditional marriage, impinges upon the children's constitutional rights. Creation of the 1973 Uniform Parentage Act (UPA), was prompted in part by a series of Supreme Court cases that held that the Equal Protection Clause of the Fourteenth Amendment required that all children – both legitimate and illegitimate – be afforded equal treatment under the law.[53]

When parents have children, intentionally or accidentally, they should support them in whatever ways possible. Parenting and rearing children is its own reward. The continuity and stability children need in their relationships and environments can be achieved in many ways, but not without sacrifice. At the heart of every parent-child relationship is the dependence of the child on his or her parents' willingness to financially and psychologically sacrifice some amount of their immediate self-interests for the development and well-being of the child. In other words, parenting often requires putting the needs of the child first. As one author stated: "... kids have suffered from the me-first, winner-take-all individualism of contemporary culture and that many parents, married or not, are having trouble meeting (or even identifying) their obligations to kids."[54]

---

52 H.D. Krause, 'Child Support Reassessed: Limits of Private Responsibility and the Public Interest', *Family Law Quarterly*, Vol. 24, No. 1, Spring, 1990, pp. 1-34 at 16.

53 Frazier v. Goudschaal, 295 P.3d 542, 557-58 (Kan. 2013).

54 S. Coontz, *The Way We Really Are: Coming to Terms with America's Changing Families*, New York, Basic Books, 1997, p. 7. See also S. Coontz, *The Way We Never Were: American Families and the Nostalgia Trap*, New York, Basic Books, 2016 and B. Dafoe Whitehead, *The Divorce Culture*, New York, Vintage Books, 1997 ("Divorce is never merely an individual lifestyle choice without larger consequences for society.").

Recent articles summarize more than a thousand studies of what children need. They show that the most important factors that promote healthy development and adjustment include:

- the quality of the child's relationships with their parents or parent figures;
- the quality of the relationships between the parents and other significant adults (conflict is associated with maladjustment while harmonious relationships between the adults support healthy adjustment); and
- the availability of adequate economic, social and physical resources.[55]

The Adverse Childhood Experience Study (ACES) conducted by Kaiser Permanente and the Center for Disease Control has produced reliable research that documents the types of negative childhood experiences that can harm children and their health throughout their lives. Among the categories are emotional abuse; physical abuse; sexual abuse; emotional neglect; physical neglect; an incarcerated household member; parental separation or divorce; domestic violence where mother or stepmother was treated violently; household dysfunction, such as substance abuse; and household dysfunction, such as mental illness.[56] Children in nonmarital and single parent families are at the most risk of adverse childhood experiences for a variety of reasons, including the reduced care-giving capacity and instability in relationships.[57] Frequent changes of partners has a negative effect on maternal parenting because there is more stress, often fewer resources, and sometimes additional children. Family instability affects fathers because when the relationship with the mother ends, many disengage, depriving children of a needed father figure.[58] The quality of the relationship between parents is an important factor affecting whether nonresidential fathers see their children.[59] Violence is present in many nonmarital homes. If there is violence in the household between the parents or abuse of the children, children are negatively impacted.[60]

---

55 M.E. Lamb, 'Mothers, Fathers, Families, and Circumstances: Factors Affecting Children's Adjustment', *Applied Developmental Science*, Vol. 16, No. 2, 2012, pp. 98-111 at 99.

56 J. Jeske and M.L. Klas, 'Adverse Childhood Experiences: Implications for Family Law Practice and the Family Court System', *Family Law Quarterly*, Vol. 50, No. 1, 2016, pp. 123-137 at 125.

57 Lamb, op cit, n. 55, p. 1; Huntington, op cit, n. 2, p. 199 (noting "Relationship instability influences the parenting behavior of both mothers and fathers in ways that make it harder for children to get the attachment relationships and attention they need for healthy child development"); McLanahan & Garfinkel, op cit, n. 2, p. 153.

58 Huntington, ibid, p. 200.

59 M.J. Carlson et al, 'Coparenting and Nonresident Fathers' Involvement with Young Children After a Nonmarital Birth,' *Demography*, Vol. 45, No. 2, May 2008, pp. 479-80 (by the time children in Fragile Families study were five, 37% of fathers had not seen their child in 2 years).

60 L. Hecht Schafran, 'Domestic Violence, Developing Brains and the Lifespan: New Knowledge from Neuroscience', *The Judges' Journal*, Vol. 53, No. 3, 2014, pp. 32-37 at 33 (exposure to domestic violence can lead to substance abuse, suicide and depressive disorders).

Divorcing and never married parents who engage in high conflict behaviors impose additional stressors on their children. Contested custody cases often focus more on the rights of parents to see and be with their children rather than the best interests of the child.[61] In these cases, children's voices should be heard as part of the total picture that the judge should consider.[62] Article 12 of the U.N. Convention on the Rights of the Child provides a framework for hearing the child's voice, but not giving the child decision-making power. Many other countries have worked on including the child's voice in custody disputes.[63]

One of the most powerful predictors of children's post-divorce adjustment is the level of parental conflict. Children who witness conflict are more likely to have post-divorce issues. The more intense the conflict, the more likely children are to suffer from depression and engage in acting out.[64] While much of the research has been on children of divorce, children in nonmarital families may be exposed to even more conflict because of the multiple and serial parent figures. Family law judges have the primary role in protecting children from the harmful effects of the parental conflict.[65] Even here, there is a class divide between the rich and the poor. Rich divorcing parents increasingly use private ordering, often selecting and paying for private judging or arbitration. Lawyers help them draft parenting plans. Separating nonmarital parents, who are often poor and unrepresented, have to rely on an overcrowded, expensive court system using laws that were drafted for the divorce of married couples. Often these parents rely on court services' personnel to help them.

Almost all states have a preference for joint legal custody that was developed based on the objective of keeping parents involved in the important decisions of the child's life. The push by father's groups for a presumption of joint physical custody of children in all cases

---

61 L.D. Elrod & M.D. Dale, 'Paradigm Shifts and Pendulum Swings in Child Custody: The Interests of the Children in the Balance', *Family Law Quarterly*, Vol. 42, No. 3, 2008, pp. 381-418. See Ford v. Ford, 371 U.S. 187, 193 (1962) ("Unfortunately, experience has shown that the question of custody, so vital to a child's happiness and well-being, frequently cannot be left to the discretion of parents … [especially] where the estrangement … beclouds parental judgment with emotion and prejudice.").

62 L.D. Elrod, 'Client Directed Lawyers for Children: It is the "Right" Thing to Do', *Pace Law Review*, Vol. 27, No. 4, 2007, pp. 899-903.

63 See N. Lowe & M. Murch, 'Children's Participation in the Family Justice System: Translating Principles into Practice', *Child and Family Law Quarterly*, Vol. 13, No. 2, 2001, pp. 137-158; N. Taylor, 'What Do We Know About Involving Children and Young People in Family Law Decision-making? A Research Update', 20 *Australian Journal of Family Law*, 2006, pp. 14-18; P. Parkinson & J. Cashmore, *The Voice of a Child in Family Law Disputes*, U.K., Oxford University Press, 2009.

64 S.R. Rappaport, 'Deconstructing the Impact of Divorce on Children', *Family Law Quarterly*, Vol. 47, No. 3, 2013, pp. 353-377 at 361. See also C. C. Ayoub, R. M. Deutsch & A. Maraganore, 'Emotional Distress in Children of High-Conflict Divorce', *Family and Conciliation Courts Review*, Vol. 37, No. 3, 1999, pp. 297-314.

65 M.D. Dale, 'Don't Forget the Children: Court Protection from Parental Conflict is in the Best Interests of Children', *Family Court Review*, Vol. 52, No. 4, 2014, pp. 648-654 at 652 (court must match family needs to existing resources).

illustrates a parental "rights" perspective rather than a best interest of the child perspective. Angry, hostile parents often demand joint physical custody in situations that make little sense from a child's perspective.[66] As one commentator said:

> [J]oint physical custody is the best and worst arrangement for children. It's the best when parents can cooperate enough to make joint physical custody work for children. It's the worst when joint physical custody leaves children in the middle of a war zone.[67]

Experts agree that joint custody, legal or physical, should NOT be imposed in high conflict situations, especially not when there is domestic violence.[68] Even married parents who have had a history of co-parenting often have difficulty making joint physical custody work well. Many nonmarital families have little history and little trust, especially if they have never lived together. While awarding joint custody is one way to affirm that both parents should remain involved, many of these complex families need help in making shared parenting work. The focus needs to shift from protecting parents' rights to truly promoting the children's interests. Legislators should support dedicated family courts with resources to help parents, both divorcing and nonmarital, resolve conflicts over parenting time.

III Nationalization and Internationalization

Federal laws, Supreme Court decisions, international treaties and norms, as well as uniform law adoptions have resulted in a nationalization and federalization of many areas of family law, traditionally regulated by the states.[69] Since the 1960s, there has been an increasing volume of federal legislation affecting nearly every area of family law from women's right to work; child support; child custody jurisdiction; abortion, childbirth and family planning;

66 See Bishop v. Bishop, 457 So. 2d 264 (La. App. 1984) (reversing a custody arrangement to transfer a two year old weekly between parents in Louisiana and Texas). See also G.W. Hardcastle, 'Joint Custody: A Family Court Judge's Perspective', *Family Law Quarterly*, Vol. 32, No. 1, 1998, pp. 201-219.

67 R.E. Emery, 'Joint Physical Custody', *Psychology Today*, 18 May 2009, at https://www.psychologytoday.com/ca/blog/divorced-children/200905/joint-physical-custody (joint physical custody is a lousy compromise for disputing parents). See also C.M. Buchanan & Jahromi, 'A Psychological Perspective on Shared Custody Arrangements', *Wake Forest Law Review*, Vol. 43, 2008, pp. 419-439 (there should not be a presumption or undue pressure for joint physical custody, especially in high conflict cases).

68 See M. Kline Pruett and H. DiFonzo, 'Closing the Gap: Research, Policy, Practice and Shared Parenting', *Family Court Review*, Vol. 52, No. 2, 2014, pp. 152-174; A. M. Bailey, 'Prioritizing Child Safety as the Prime Best Interest Factor', *Family Law Quarterly*, Vol. 47, No. 1, 2013, pp. 35-64. See also L.D. Elrod, 'Reforming the System to Protect Children in High Conflict Custody Cases', *William Mitchell Law Review*, Vol. 28, No. 2, 2001, pp. 495-551.

69 Ankenbrandt v. Richards, 504 U.S. 689 (1992).

child abuse, foster care and adoption; bankruptcy; health insurance; pensions; family violence; and tax law.[70] Federal legislation has been piecemeal, however, rather than part of any overall family policy. Congress has utilized its spending power to set policy and provide funding under the Commerce Clause and Full Faith and Credit Clause of the Constitution. The area of child support offers an example. As welfare rolls increased because of growing numbers of mothers and children without child support orders, Congress required all states receiving funds for their welfare programs to set up a child support enforcement agency. Congress then enacted laws, civil and criminal, that dictated standards to states.[71] The emphasis was on establishing paternity, establishing, modifying and enforcing child support. While financial support is certainly important, the effort failed to take into account the differences in family formation and the large numbers of unwed fathers who simply did not have the resources to pay support. In addition, many fathers were unable to maintain contact with their children due to lack of parenting time orders. Only recently has the federal government recognized the importance of preserving the relationship between obligor parents and children.[72]

Since 1965, the United States Supreme Court has heard more than 200 cases involving "family" issues, using the Constitution to strike down a number of state statutes regulating families. The Supreme Court has recognized that nontraditional families are deserving of protection,[73] but much of the emphasis has been on the individual and the right of individuals to choose their family form, rather than on protections for nonmarital families.[74] The Court has protected family life and the freedom of personal choice protected by the Due Process Clause of the Fourteenth Amendment.[75] The Supreme Court has upgraded the status of children born out of wedlock[76] and struck down regulations which discriminated

70 L. Elrod, 'The Federalization of Family Law', *Human Rights Magazine,* Vol. 36, No. 3, 2009, pp. 6-9.

71 See L. Henry Elrod, 'The Federalization of Child Support Guidelines', *Journal of the American Academy of Matrimonial Lawyers,* Vol. 6, 1990, pp. 103 -130; L.D. Elrod, 'Child Support Reassessed: Federalization of Enforcement Nears Completion', *University of Illinois Law Review,* Vol. 1997, No. 3, 1997, pp. 695-710; A. Laquer Estin, 'Federalization and Child Support', *Virginia Journal of Social Policy & The Law,* Vol. 5, Spring 1998, pp. 541-601.

72 U.S. Dep't of Health and Human Services Administration for Children and Families, Office of Child Support Enforcement, *Child Support and Parenting Time: Improving Coordination to Benefit Families,* July 2013.

73 Moore v. City of East Cleveland, 431 U.S. 494 (1977).

74 See C. Huntington, 'Nonmarital Families and the Legal System's Institutional Failures', *Family Law Quarterly,* Vol. 50, No. 2, Summer, 2016, pp. 247-259.

75 Griswold v. Connecticut, 381 U.S. 479 (1965); Eisenstadt v. Baird, 405 U.S. 438 (1972); Lawrence v. Texas, 539 U.S. 558 (2003); Roe v. Wade, 410 U.S. 113 (1973); Obergefell, op cit, n. 14; Troxel v. Granville, 50 U.S. 50 (2000).

76 Levy v. Louisiana, 391 U.S. 68 (1968); Gomez v. Perez, 409 U.S. 535 (1973).

on the basis of gender[77] and race.[78] While the Supreme Court has invalidated state laws that impinge on individual rights, it has not recognized positive rights for children, such as rights to the basics of food, shelter and support. It has, however, recognized a child's right to an education.[79]

The Uniform Law Commission has adopted over sixteen uniform family laws intended for state enactment.[80] The two most successful – the Uniform Child Custody Jurisdiction and Enforcement Act (49 states) and the Uniform Interstate Family Support Act (50 states) – have created much more uniformity in child custody and child support jurisdiction. The Uniform Parentage Act (1973), which served as a model for many states, has been interpreted in a gender neutral manner to protect children born to same-sex parents before same-sex marriage was recognized.[81] The 2017 version of the Uniform Parentage Act contains gender neutral language and adds a new definition of a de facto parent. There is, however, no uniform law on rights for unmarried cohabitants.[82]

International norms, especially as they relate to the rights of children, play a larger role in reform efforts. The United States is now a party to three Hague Conventions on family law, all regarding children.[83] A fourth Hague Convention on Protection of Children might be next to be considered.[84] The United States has signed, but has not ratified, the U.N. Convention on the Rights of the Child (CRC)[85] although 195 other nations have. The CRC sees children as rights holders and imposes obligations on states to protect children's

77 Stanley v. Illinois, 405 U.S. 645 (1972) (parental rights for unwed fathers); Orr v. Orr, 440 U.S. 268 (1979) (allowing equal access to alimony); Sessions v. Morales-Santana, 137 S. Ct. 1678 (2017) (finding it unconstitutional to treat children born out of wedlock differently based on whether they are born to a citizen mother or citizen father).

78 Loving v. Virginia, 388 U.S. 1 (1967); Palmore v. Sidoti, 466 U.S. 429 (1984).

79 Brown v. Board of Education of Topeka, 347 U.S. 483 (1954); Plyler v. Doe, 457 U.S. 202 (1982); Endrew v. Douglas County School Dist., 137 S. Ct. 988 (2017).

80 For example: Uniform Marriage and Divorce Act, Uniform Enforcement of Domestic Violence Protection Orders, Uniform Marital Property Act, Uniform Premarital and Marital Agreement Act, Uniform Child Custody Jurisdiction and Enforcement Act, Uniform Child Abduction Prevention Act, Uniform Family Law Arbitration Act, Uniform Interstate Family Support Act, Uniform Nonparent Custody and Visitation Act, Uniform Parentage Act. See uniformlaws.org for listing of all uniform laws.

81 See Frazier v. Goudschaal, 295 P.3d 542 (Kan. 2013) (Biles J. concurring); Chatterjee v. King, 280 P.3d 283 (N.M. 2012).

82 The Joint Editorial Board on Uniform Family Laws has twice sent recommendations to the Executive Committee to consider drafting a uniform cohabitation act because of the widely disparate treatment of cohabiting couples. In July 2018, the Uniform Law Commission appointed a drafting committee.

83 The 1980 Hague Convention on the Civil Aspects of International Child Abduction as of 1988 (in effect in 95 countries); the 1993 Hague Convention on Cooperation with Respect to Intercountry Adoption in 2008; and the 2007 Hague Convention on the International Enforcement of Child Support and Other Forms of Family Maintenance in 2016.

84 The 1996 Hague Convention on Jurisdiction, Applicable Law, Recognition, Enforcement, and Cooperation with Respect of Parental Responsibility and Measures for the Protection of Children.

85 Convention on the Rights of the Child, G.A. Res. 44/25 (Annex), U.N. GAOR, 44th Sess., Supp. No. 49, at 166, U.D. Doc. A/RES/44/49 (1990), reprinted in 30 I.L.M. 1448 (1989).

interests. It recognizes children's rights to continuity of relationships and to protection in the formation and preservation of their identity, including nationality, name and family relations. Additionally, Article 12 of the CRC provides that children have a right to be heard.[86] The United States has not ratified the International Covenant on Economic, Social and Cultural Rights (ICESCR)[87] which would bestow positive rights to education, health care, food, clothing and shelter.

IV CONCLUSION

> ... without prioritizing the physical, emotional and education needs of children, all the efforts to eliminate crime, poverty, and ignorance are only knee jerk band aid solutions which cure none of society's basic ills.[88]

While we can separate marriage from parenthood, we cannot separate the child from the parent. Not only are American governments unwilling to take a holistic approach to helping families with children, many policies actually work against families. The national debate will continue over how to deal with families who do not fit the marital-family model. As families become less "traditional", the courts are more frequently asked to make decisions for these families. We need more support for parents in these families if we are going to help the children. High divorce rates, out-of-wedlock births and cohabitation are likely to continue. Forty years ago Marian Wright Edelman discussed the instability of the family, increasing societal ills and the impoverishment of children[89] and called for a new comprehensive approach. We need to develop an ethic in this country that says that children are important. Just as a parent's responsibility to a child should be seen as irrevocable, so should the responsibilities of the state and national governments. The greatest threat to

86 See U. Kilkelly, 'The Best of Both Worlds for Children's Rights? Interpreting the European Convention on Human Rights in the Light of UN Convention on the Rights of the Child', *Human Rights Quarterly*, Vol. 23, No. 2, 2001, pp. 308-326 at 311 (the right to participate in all proceedings that affect the child's custody along with the principles of nondiscrimination and best interests form the guiding principles of the Convention).

87 International Covenant on Economic, Social and Cultural Rights, G.A. Res. 2200A (XXI) of 16 December 1966, entry into force 3 January 1976. See D. M. Smolin, 'The Corrupting Influence of the United States on a Vulnerable Intercountry Adoption System: A Guide for Stakeholders, The legal relationship legal relationshipHague and Non-Hague Nations, NGOs, and Concerned Parties, Vol. 2013, No. 2, *Utah Law Review*, 2013, pp. 1065 - 1135 at 1079 (suggesting that the United States has not ratified the ICESCR because constitutional law makes individual rights essentially negative rights while the ICESCR imposes "positive" rights).

88 Costa v. Costa, 429 So. 2d 1249 (Fla. Dist. Ct. App. 1983).

89 See M. Wright Edelman, *Families in Peril: An Agenda for Social Change*, revised ed., Cambridge, MA, Harvard University Press, 1989 (first ed. 1987).

America comes from having a generation of children grow up in poverty, undereducated, and underachieving.

Parenthood should create legal obligations between the parents, whether married or unmarried. The continuity and stability that children need cannot be achieved without parental sacrifices. Federal and state governments also have an interest in having children grow up to be well-adjusted, healthy adults. Therefore, we need more responsibility for children by parents, family members, and by state and federal governments.

Trends, Values, and Changes in Families and Family Law in the USA: Towards Realism, Idealism or Confusion?

Lynn D. Wardle *

I Introduction: The Elusive Balance in Family Law

This paper analyzes recent developments in family law in the United States of America from the perspective of the tension in law between recognizing the real and seeking the ideal. It considers the proper and effective roles of family law in reflecting social reality on the one hand, and in promoting social ideals and aspirations on the other. It discusses some recent developments in American family law regulating parent-child relationships as well as spousal relationships.

There usually is a gap of some size – large or small – between the realities of life and the ideals of the law. The ideal in family law is to foster, support and protect healthy, happy, and effective families. The reality, however, sometimes falls short of that ideal. Sadly, American family law sometimes impedes family success and frustrates the well-beings of families and family members.

The diversity of individual experiences, beliefs and social realities seldom are fully reflected in the law. Some disparity is unavoidable because the law must establish a clear, uniform rule applicable to all members of society including those who hold and wish to observe other (minority) standards. Viewpoints concerning family life and family values vary substantially among the members of any society. Thus, normal individual diversity often impedes or frustrates the pursuit of social and legal uniformity, especially in family law.

Lawmakers generally seek to enact laws that reflect the values and experiences of the majority. Inevitably, the views and values of some other members of society – especially minorities and dissenters – are inadequately reflected in – or are omitted from – the law. That is how democracy works – by respecting and implementing the will of the majority.

---

* Bruce C. Hafen Professor of Law, J. Reuben Clark Law School, Brigham Young University, Provo, UT, USA 84602. An earlier version of this paper was presented at the 16th World Congress of the International Society of Family Law, "Family Law and Family Realities", at the Vrije Universiteit of Amsterdam, The Netherlands, 25-29 July 2017. An earlier version of this paper has been posted online.

However, mature democracies also value and seek to protect the rights and interests of minorities.

One way that the rights and interests of minorities are protected in the United States is through the federal structure of government. The Constitution of the United States of America granted certain - limited - governmental authority and power to the national government (especially concerning defense and national economic interests), but it reserved other governmental authority and power to the state governments - including the power and authority to regulate family relations. That means that, within broad constitutional boundaries, each state determines what its own family laws and policies will be, and they may differ - sometimes markedly - from the family laws and policies of the other states. That also means that there is no (or very little) uniform American (i.e. national) family law, but rather there are dozens of different family laws and policies as each state sets its own family laws and policies.

Discrepancies also exist in American family law between ideals and realities, between majority and minority values, and between aspirations and actualities. The law generally seeks to facilitate and to promote the aspirational, the exemplary, and majoritarian ideals in human life, activities, and relationships. However, the law also strives to protect all persons, especially vulnerable minorities, from dangerous and harmful activities, individuals, and majorities. Sometimes efforts to accommodate minorities frustrate legitimate aspirations of the majority. So diversity in American family law is a guaranteed by-product of the structure of the American government and the constitutional division of governmental power and authority between and among the national government and the state governments.[1]

This paper provides some discussion of current marriage laws in the Unites States of America. American marriage laws vary from state to state, sometimes significantly. Different communities pursue different goals, and they strike different balances between the realistic and the idealistic in their family laws. To unfamiliar observers, those differences may appear to indicate confusion. To the well-informed, however, the differences in American family laws are evidence of tolerance, inclusion, diversity and freedom.

Family law regulates two categories of relationships: spousal (and quasi-spousal) relations and parent-child relations. Family law covers three periods of time: the creation of the relationship, the ongoing relationship, and the dissolution and post-dissolution time of the relationships. Most of the issues that are litigated arise in the time of the relationship dissolution and post-dissolution.

1 See *infra* Part III.

II The Gap Between the Real and the Ideal in American Family Law

Several distinguished family law scholars have noted a trend toward harmonization of family law – especially in European nations.[2]

One of the great and persistent jurisprudential questions is whether the law primarily reflects social reality and values, or promotes certain ideals and aspirational standards.[3] It is commonly said that law emerges out of custom, and, hence, law generally can be expected to reflect social norms.[4] Legal rules and sanctions sometimes can reinforce social values and they also can generate and sustain new social norms.[5]

For example, research by Professor Richard D. Schwarz found that:

> the threat of sanction can deter people from violating the law, perhaps in important part by inducing a moralistic attitude toward compliance. This mechanism seems particularly significant when those subject to sanction threat are not trained by, and associated with, an authoritative institution other than the state. The threat of punishment appears, however, to produce some resistance to compliance. Such resistance can be minimized through alternative techniques of securing compliance, such as the utilization of appeals to conscience and to a sense of civic responsibility, motives which can be more powerful than sanction threat in increasing compliance with the law.[6]

---

2 See K. Boele-Woelki et al, *Principles of European Family Law Regarding Property Relations Between Spouses*, Intersentia, 2013, at pp. 345-56 and *passim*; and K. Boele-Woelki (Ed.), *Perspectives for the Unification and Harmonisation of Family Law in Europe*, Intersentia, 2003. In particular, see the following papers from this latter collection: N. Dethloff, 'Arguments for the unification and harmonization of family law in Europe', pp. 37-64; D. Bradley, 'A family law for Europe? Sovereignty, political economy and legitimation', pp. 65-104; and M. Meulders-Klein, 'Towards a European civil code on family law?: Ends and means', pp. 105-117. See further Commission on European Family Law, Conference, University of Oslo, 7-9 June 2007, at the University of Oslo, Norway.

3 See generally the collection of articles from *Brigham Young University Law Review*, 1980: R.D. Schwartz, 'Law, Society, and Moral Order: Introduction to the Symposium', p. 721; L.D. Wardle, 'The Gap Between Law and Moral Order: An Examination of the Legitimacy of the Supreme Court Abortion Decisions', p. 811; F.E. Agrait, 'In Search of a Role for the Legal System', p. 797; and M. Diamond, 'Law, the Problems of Poverty, and the "Myth of Rights," p. 785. See further 'The Relationship of the Formal Legal System to the Less Formal and the Relationship of Both to the Private Sector of Society", *in* L.M. Friedman & S. Macaulay (Eds.), *Law and the Behavioral Sciences*, 2d. ed., Indianapolis, Bobbs-Merrill, 1977, pp. 171-188.

4 See e.g. R. Benabou & J. Tirole, 'Law and Norms', National Bureau of Economic Research, Working Paper No. 17579, November 2011, at http://www.princeton.edu/~rbenabou/papers/NBER%20WP%2017579.pdf (seen 11 August 2017); C. Bicchieri & R. Muldoon, 'Social Norms', *Stanford Encyclopedia of Philosophy*, 1 March 2011, at https://plato.stanford.edu/entries/social-norms/ (seen 11 Aug. 2017); see further A.E. Hoebel, *The Law of Primitive Man*, Cambridge, Harvard University Press, 1954, *passim*.

5 E. Posner, 'Law and Social Norms: The Case of Tax Compliance', *Virginia Law Review*, Vol. 86, 2000, p. 1781, *passim*.

6 R.D. Schwartz & S. Orleans, 'On Legal Sanctions', *University of Chicago Law Review*, Vol. 34, 1967, p. 274 at 300.

However, there often is disparity between the desirable and the actual. For example, most people desire to be successful – in the sense of having adequate material resources, stable marriages and happy families. Social scientists have identified very clearly the 'success sequences' that most often results in financial and family well-being. As W. Bradford Wilcox and Wendy Wang have reported:

> Millennials are much more likely to flourish financially if they follow the "success sequence"— getting at least a high school degree, working full-time, and marrying before having any children, in that order.[7]

Yet in recent years the "success sequence" has not been popular. The rate of childbearing before marriage and before completing basic education has increased or plateaued at historic high levels.[8] That portends significant individual and social problems. For example, Census Bureau researchers report that "women with a nonmarital first birth are both less likely to ever marry and less likely to remain married if they do marry". Childbearing outside of marriage is also linked to higher risks for poverty, lower educational attainment and family instability.[9]

Some commentators have seen significant competition and conflict between formal laws and informal rules and customs. For instance, anthropologist Stanley Diamond argued that instead of "law *and* order" in society, the more common reality is "law *versus* order". He wrote that:

> We live in a law-ridden society; law has cannibalized the institutions which it presumably reinforces or with which it interacts. ... [W]e are encouraged to assume that legal behavior is the measure of moral behavior. ... Efforts to legislate conscience by an external political power are the antithesis of custom: customary behavior comprises precisely those aspects of social behavior which are traditional, moral and religious – in short, conventional and nonlegal. Put another way, custom is social morality. the relation between custom and law is basically one of contradiction, not continuity.[10]

7 W.B. Wilcox & W. Wang, 'The Millennial Success sequence: Marriage, kids, and the "success sequence" among young adults', AEI, 14 June 2017, at http://www.aei.org/publication/millennials-and-the-success-sequence-how-do-education-work-and-marriage-affect-poverty-and-financial-success-among-millennials/ (seen 11 Aug. 2017).

8 C. Wetzstein, 'Census: More first-time mothers give birth out of wedlock', *Washinton Times*, 8 July 2014 ("The number of first-born U.S. babies born into a home with a married mother and father has fallen below 60 percent for the first time, the Census Bureau said Tuesday, while more than one in five first-born children are now born to cohabiting parents.").

9 Ibid.

10 S. Diamond, 'The Rule of Law versus the Order of Custom' *in* S. Diamond, *In Search of the Primitive*, Transaction Publishers, 1981.

So there are institutional as well as cultural reasons for the gap between law and moral order. Law and custom may compete with each other as often as (or more often than) they complement each other.

III Some Diversity in Family Law Reflects Differences Between Communities

In the United States of America, there is not "one" body of family law, but at least fifty-one (arguably fifty-seven) different family law systems, each with its own diverse, substantive family laws.[11] The Constitution of the United States divided governmental power between the national government and the State governments.[12] The national government was given explicit but limited powers (primarily concerning national defense and national economic interests); the remaining governmental powers (including the power to enact family laws) were reserved for the state governments. That constitutional allocation of power (preserving the state authority to regulate domestic relations) reflects the general belief that state law-makers are closer to the people and better able than federal judges and federal legislators to identify and protect the values and policy preferences of the citizens whose lives and domestic relationships will be regulated by those laws.[13] It also is generally believed that state courts and agencies are better able to grasp, interpret and properly apply domestic relations laws than are federal judges and agencies who generally have much less experience and expertise in family law.[14] Thus, most family law is state law, not federal law, and family law often varies (sometimes quite dramatically) from state to state.

However, some issues – including some family law issues - fall with the jurisdiction of both the state governments and the national government. Thus, almost every year the Supreme Court of the United States decides a very small number of cases involving family

11 The United States of America includes fifty-seven different semi-sovereign legal jurisdictions: the United States (federal government), fifty states, the District of Columbia, and five dependent territories (American Samoa, Guam, Northern Mariana Islands, Puerto Rico, and the Virgin Islands). Each American jurisdiction can and does create family law to some extent – all but the United States have jurisdiction to regulate family relations per se, and the United States has jurisdiction over many areas of human behavior that impact upon and influence family life and family laws.

12 See 'The Federalist Papers, No. 14' (Madison) *in* C. Rossiter (Ed.), *The Federalist Papers*, New York, Penguin, 1961: "[T]he general government is not to be charged with the whole power of making and administering laws. Its jurisdiction is limited to certain enumerated objects, which concern all the members of the republic .... The subordinate [state] governments, which can extend their care to all those other objects which can be separately provided for, will retain their due authority and activity."

13 Ibid. See also L.D. Wardle, 'The Proposed Federal Marriage Amendment and the Risks to Federalism in Family Law', *University of St. Thomas Law Journal*, Vol. 2, 2004, pp. 137-198; L.D. Wardle, 'DOMA: Protecting Federalism in Family Law', *The Federal Lawyer*, Vol. 45, No. 2, Feb. 1998, pp. 30-35.

14 See sources cited above, n. 12.

law.[15] For example, out of nearly 7,000 petitions for review that the Supreme Court receives each term it hears approximately seventy (70) cases.[16] In the most recent term of the Supreme Court (the October 2016 Term, which concluded in late June 2017),[17] the Supreme Court rendered opinions in only seventy (70) cases, and only three of those cases dealt with some aspect of family law. They are discussed in Part IV below.

IV IDEOLOGY VS. REALITY

The Supreme Court of the United States decided only three cases in its most recent (October 2016) term that involved issues of family law. Two of those cases concerned federal laws that implicated family relations. In *Howell v. Howell,*[18] the Court unanimously (7+1) ruled that a state court may not order a military veteran to indemnify his divorced spouse for the loss of some of her portion of his (federal) military retirement pay that was awarded to her upon divorce, when his retirement benefit was reduced due to his later election of disability pay which reduced the portion of his retirement pay that the ex-wife received. That case concerned the regulation of federal military benefits which is governed exclusively by federal law, so the state court order that contravened the federal law was invalidated by the Supreme Court.

In *Sessions v. Morales-Santana,*[19] the six-justice majority (per opinion of Justice Ginsburg) held that gender-based differential treatment in the federal law governing acquisition of U.S. citizenship of a child born abroad was unconstitutional. The U.S. law allowed for transmittal of citizenship if the mother had lived in the U.S. for one year before the birth of the child, but required ten years of pre-birth residence for the father. Again, the issue concerned a federal law (regulating citizenship) rather than traditional state-regulated family law.

15 Among the most notable recent Supreme Court family law decisions are: *Adoptive Couple v. Baby Girl,* 133 S.Ct. 1552 (2013) (declining to protect the paternal rights of a Native American biological father who never had custody); *Kerry v. Din,* 135 S.Ct. 2015) (rejecting wife's claim that denial of visa to her Afghan husband violated due process); *Obergefell v. Hodges,* 135 S.Ct. 1039 (2015) (mandating same-sex marriage); *Whole Woman's Health v. Hellerstedt* 579 U.S. ___ (2016) (invalidating Texas abortion regulations), and *Pavan v. Smith,* 582 U.S. ___ (2017) (requiring listing same-sex spouse of mother on birth certificate the same as opposite-sex spouses – discussed herein).

16 E. Slattery, 'Overview of the Supreme Court's October 2016 Term', Heritage Foundation, 20 Sept. 2016, at http://www.heritage.org/courts/report/overview-the-supreme-courts-october-2016-term (seen 28 June 2017).

17 Supreme Court Calendar, October Term 2016, at https://www.supremecourt.gov/oral_arguments/2016Term-CourtCalendar.pdf (seen 7 July 2017).

18 581 U.S. ___, ___ S.Ct. ___ (15 May 2017). Justice Breyer delivered the opinion of the Court.

19 582 U.S. ___, ___ S.Ct. ___ (12 June 2017).

Only one Supreme Court case decided in the 2016 term concerned a state family law. In *Pavan v. Smith*,[20] the Supreme Court *per curiam* (6-3) struck down an Arkansas birth certificate law requiring the name of the mother's male spouse to appear on the child's birth certificate – regardless of his biological relationship to the child – but not allowing a female same-sex spouse of the mother to be named on the birth certificate. One might well wonder whether the biological facts of human reproduction might justify the gendered birth certificate difference, but the majority of the Court focused narrowly on marital status and gender equality, and invalidated the differential treatment of male and female spouses with no discussion of the dual-gender reality of human reproduction. The Court concluded that mere biological differences relevant to human reproduction do not justify a difference in the legal treatment of male and female partners of birth mothers for the purpose of identifying parentage on birth certificates. The majority held that the federal government's suggested rationales for the gender difference did not survive heightened scrutiny. Critics might ask whether the Court gave ideology priority over biology, and whether the majority's preference for a politically correct relationship or ideal trumped respect for the reality of dual-gender human reproduction. But the holding in *Pavan* was clear (as clear as it was intellectually debatable).

That Supreme Court decision in the *Pavan* case illustrates one of the tensions that is the subject of this paper. There is persistent tension between law's need to acknowledge and reflect social reality and the law's aspiration to promote certain ideals, values or principles. Perhaps the absolutism of the gender-equality goals of the *Pavan* majority weakens the justification for the result they reached. However, the subject is not one of great interest so the implications of the decision and of its interesting rationale may not be of great moment.

In one sense, the Court's recent *Pavan* ruling seems unremarkable under its ruling just two years ago in *Obergefell v. Hodges*.[21] In *Obergefell* the Court invalidated state laws barring same-sex couples from marrying; *Obergefell* mandated that all states and government agencies must allow and recognize same-sex marriages. Traditionally marriage has created a legal presumption of parentage for the spouse of the birth mother, even if the spouse physically could not be the parent (i.e. the spouse was absent at the time of conception).[22]

---

20 582 U.S. ___, ___ S.Ct. ___ (26 June 2017).

21 *Obergefell v. Hodges*, 135 S.Ct. 1039 (2015).

22 "The law has created the presumption that a child born to a married woman is legitimate, and has made it one of the strongest of presumptions. At one point … the presumption was conclusive if the husband was not impotent and was within the fours seas, that is, was in England." H.H. Clark, Jr., *The Law of Domestic Relations in the United States*, 2nd ed., 1987, § 4.4 at 191. See also 'Legitimacy (family law)', in Wikipedia, at https://en.wikipedia.org/wiki/Legitimacy_(family_law) (seen 12 July 2017): "In English common law, Justice Edward Coke in 1626 promulgated the "Four Seas Rule" (*extra quatuor maria*) asserting that, absent impossibility of the father being fertile, there was a presumption of paternity that a married woman's child was her husband's child. That presumption could be questioned, though courts generally sided with the presumption, thus expanding the range of the presumption to a 'Seven Seas Rule'."

So by mandating the legalization of same-sex marriage, the Court cleared the path (to marriage) by which a same-sex partner could not only establish a full, legal marital relationships with a partner, but which would provide the basis for a parentage claim to children born to his or her same-sex spouse during the marriage.

In another sense, however, *Pavan* was a significant and controversial expansion of the same-sex marriage ruling in *Obergefell.*[23] It would have been easy for the Court to distinguish the adult vertical relationship of parent/partner-child in *Pavan* from the horizontal, adult co-equal relationship of marriage involved in *Obergefell.* However, the majority of the Court in *Pavan* apparently wanted to extend the *Obergefell* principle of the equality of same-sex and opposite-sex relationships beyond the marriage context and into the parentage context. Of course, in reality adult-adult relationships and adult-child relationships are not the same and by simply equating them legally the Court seemed to ignore some very important state and social interests in the best interests of children. Critics might suggest that children's welfare was subordinated by the *Pavan* majority to the interests and preferences of same-sex adult partners who want to have a same-sex partner of the mother listed as the parent of a child born to a same-sex spouse. However, even if that criticism were valid, it would not change the outcome or holding of the Court in *Pavan.*

These tensions are not new. For example, in his masterful article "The Seduction of Lydia Bennet: Toward a General Theory of Society, Marriage and the Family", Professor Scott FitzGibbon discussed the "system of rules and principles" that regulated "family, friendship, and social rank" in England in Jane Austen's day.[24] He noted that: "Most societies operate in major part through the medium of obligation."[25] When obligations are violated, "[s]ocieties often afford faculties for setting things straight."[26] In *Pride and Prejudice,* Austen has Elizabeth say of Lydia's unfortunate marriage to Mr. Wickham: "[H]ow little of permanent happiness could belong to a couple who were only brought together because their passions were stronger than their virtue."[27] Perhaps the same might be said of many cohabiting non-marital and same-sex couples in America today. The prospect that the results for the nation will be similar to the results of Lydia's and Wickham's marriage are concerning.

Marriage matters tremendously for society – especially for children and for those who will depend upon their support in the future. For example, college graduates generally

---

23 Justice Gorsuch, writing in dissent in *Pavan*, op cit, n. 20, declared (at 2): "[I]t seems far from clear what here warrants the strong medicine of summary reversal. Indeed, it is not even clear what the Court expects to happen on remand that hasn't happened already. The Court does not offer any remedial suggestion, and none leaps to mind."

24 S. FitzGibbon, 'The Seduction of Lydia Bennet: Toward a General Theory of Society, Marriage and the Family', *Ave Maria Law Review*, Vol. 4, 2006, p. 581, at 583, citing Jane Austen, *Pride and Prejudice* (1818).

25 Ibid, at p. 586.

26 Ibid, at p. 588. See further ibid ("Lydia and Wickham set things straight by getting married.").

27 *Pride and Prejudice,* op cit, n. 24.

earn much more, and have more successful lives and families than those who do not graduate from college.[28] And the evidence is irrefutable that children raised by married parents have much greater likelihood of both college graduation and of their own successful marriages. The Pew Research Center summarizes some of the research as follows:

> Among parents who live with a child under the age of 18, [eighty-nine percent] 89% of college graduates are married, compared with 64% of parents with less than a high school diploma and 70% of those with just a high school diploma.[29]

So the benefits of marriage are not enjoyed equally by all Americans:

> When it comes to matrimony, the United States is *two separate countries.* There's college-graduate America, where getting and staying married is still the norm. Then there's the rest of America, where marriage rates are retreating and divorce is rampant.[30]

As Robert Pollak has explained: "College graduates – men and women – are using marriage as a 'commitment device' to jointly invest a lot in children."[31] Likewise, Brookings Institute scholar Richard Reeves argues that today, American college graduates "are reinventing marriage as a child-rearing machine for a post-feminist society and a knowledge economy."[32]

The benefits of marriage and marital childrearing are found among both the college-educated and the non-college-educated:

---

28 'College graduates earn 84% more than high school grads, study says', *L.A. Times*, 5 Aug. 2011, at http://latimesblogs.latimes.com/money_co/2011/08/college-gradutates-pay.html (seen 15 Aug. 2017) ("On average, a doctoral degree-holder will earn $3.3 million over a lifetime, compared to $2.3 million for a college graduate and $1.3 million for those with a high school diploma."); 'The Rising Cost of Not Going to College', Pew Research Center, 11 Feb. 2014, at http://www.pewsocialtrends.org/2014/02/11/the-rising-cost-of-not-going-to-college/ (seen 15 Aug. 2017) ("college graduates ages 25 to 32 who are working full time earn more annually – about $17,500 more – than employed young adults holding only a high school diploma."); see also 'College graduates earn 56 PERCENT more than high school grads, claims new study', *Daily Mail*, 12 Jan. 2017), at http://www.dailymail.co.uk/news/article-4113486/Pay-gap-college-grads-record.html (seen 15 Aug. 2017).

29 G. Livingston, 'The links between education, marriage and parenting', Pew Research Center, *FactTank*, 27 Nov. 2013, at http://www.pewresearch.org/fact-tank/2013/11/27/the-links-between-education-marriage-and-parenting/ (seen 11 July 2017).

30 J. Weissman, 'Marriage Stages a Comeback (but Mostly Just for College Grads)', *The Atlantic*, 7 Feb. 2014, at https://www.theatlantic.com/business/archive/2014/02/marriage-stages-a-comeback-but-mostly-just-for-college-grads/283682/ (seen 13 July 2017) (emphasis added).

31 A. Kim, 'Why Is Marriage Thriving Among (and Only Among) the Affluent?', *Washington Monthly*, March/April/May 2016, at http://washingtonmonthly.com/magazine/maraprmay-2016/why-is-marriage-thriving-among-and-only-among-the-affluent/ (seen 13 July 2017). See also S. Lundberg & R.A. Pollak, 'The Evolving Role of Marriage: 1950-2010', *The Future of Children*, Vol. 25, No. 2, 2015, p. 29.

32 Kim, ibid.

> Approximately 30% of moms with less than a college degree who live with their kids are living without a spouse or partner, as compared with 7% of comparable dads. In comparison, [just] 13% of college-educated moms who live with their kids are living without a spouse or partner, as are 3% of comparable dads.[33]

Yet, sadly, in America and many other affluent Western nations,

> [m]arriage has been on the decline for decades, particularly *for those with less education*. At the same time, the share of *non-marital births* for the less educated has risen dramatically, and the *likelihood of divorce* remains significantly higher among those lacking a college degree than among those who have one.[34]

However, sadly,

> [s]ince 1950, marriage behavior in the United States has changed dramatically, though most men and women still marry at some point in their lives, they now do so later and are more likely to divorce. Cohabitation has become commonplace as either a precursor or an alternative to marriage, and a growing fraction of births take place outside marriage. We've seen a retreat from marriage within all racial and ethnic groups and across the socioeconomic spectrum. But the decoupling of marriage and parenthood has been much less prevalent among college graduates.[35]

A simplistic interpretation of the data might suggest that those who are smart enough (and/or disciplined-enough) to attend college are also smart enough to marry. But it is likely that the dynamics are more complicated than that.

This is very important because marriage matters for kids – and for those who will depend upon them (and their taxes/support) in the future. In other words, marriage matters for all in society. Distinguished professor Sara McLanahan has concluded: "Children of single-parent families suffer measurable harm."[36] She summarized some of the evidence:

> Children who grow up with only one of their biological parents (nearly always the mother) are disadvantaged across a broad array of outcomes. … [T]hey are twice as likely to drop out of high school, 2.5 times as likely to become teen

33 Livingston, op cit, n. 29.
34 Ibid.
35 Lundberg & Pollak, op cit, n. 31.
36 S. McLanahan, 'The Consequences of Single Motherhood', *The American Prospect*, Summer 1994, available at http://prospect.org/article/consequences-single-motherhood (seen 28 June 2017).

> mothers, and 1.4 times as likely to be idle – out of school and out of work – as children who grow up with both parents. Children in one-parent families also have lower grade point averages, lower college aspirations, and poorer attendance records. As adults, they have higher rates of divorce. These patterns persist even after adjusting for differences in race, parents' education, number of siblings, and residential location.[37]

A Pew Research report notes that:

> Researchers at the National Center for Health Statistics estimate that 78% of college-educated women who married for the first time between 2006 and 2010 could expect their marriages to last at least 20 years. But among women who have a high school education or less, the share is only 40%.[38]

There also are significant differences in the longevity of American marriages between different racial and ethnic groups, as the following graph shows.[39]

37 Ibid.

38 W. Wang, 'The link between a college education and a lasting marriage', Pew Research Center, *FactTack*, 4 Dec. 2015, at http://www.pewresearch.org/fact-tank/2015/12/04/education-and-marriage/ (seen 11 July 2017) ("While the research does not address reasons these marriages last longer, we do know college-educated adults marry later in life and are more financially secure than less-educated adults.").

39 Pew Research Center, 'The Link Between A College Education and A Lasting Marriage. Sharp differences on longevity of marriages by race, ethnicity', *FactTack*, 3 Dec. 2015, at http://www.pewresearch.org/fact-tank/2015/12/04/education-and-marriage/ft_15-12-03-race-marriage/ (seen 11 Aug. 2017).

Sharp differences on longevity of marriages by race, ethnicity

Probability that a first marriage will survive among women (%)

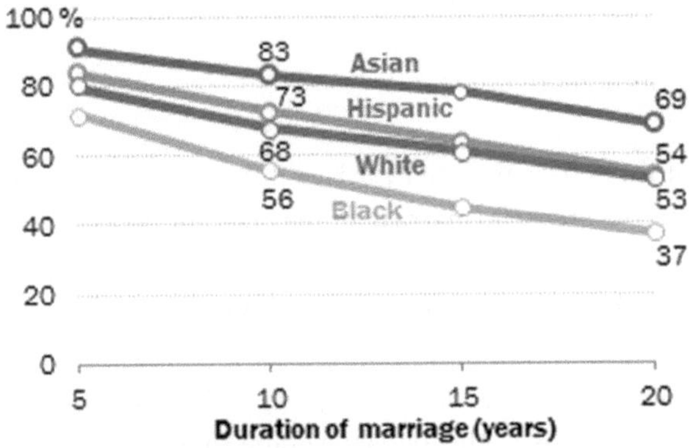

Note: Probabilities are derived from 2006-2010 National Survey of Family Growth (NSFG) data, among women ages 15 to 44 who have ever been married. Whites, blacks and Asians include only single-race non-Hispanics. Hispanics are of any race.

Source: National Center for Health Statistics, NSFG.

PEW RESEARCH CENTER

What about these racial-ethnic differences might explain the huge differences in marriage longevity between the races? I suggest that the cultural differences regarding respect for, commitment to, and practice of marriage are the core reasons for such marriage longevity differences among these American ethnic groups. People from cultures that value marriage more tend to have longer, healthier, and happier marriages – and richer, more fulfilling lives than do people from cultures that value marriage less.

Yet, in America and many other affluent Western nations,

> [m]arriage has been on the decline for decades, particularly *for those with less education*. At the same time, the share of *non-marital births* for the less educated has risen dramatically, and the *likelihood of divorce* remains significantly higher among those lacking a college degree than among those who have one.[40]

40 Livingston, op cit, n. 29.

Marriage and marital families provide a safe and beneficial form of diversity between families. The decline and disintegration of marriage foreshadow serious troubles that will come upon all individuals and families in all of the societies where it occurs. So we have a serious problem to address.

V How to Revive a Marriage Culture

We live in an imperfect world filled with imperfect people in imperfect communities, with imperfect marriages. However, even imperfect people have ideals and aspirations. With patience for the imperfections we all have and see, we must elevate our aspirations. The law must establish and confirm society's core normative goals and values. For the welfare of families – including adults as well as their children and grandchildren – the law must reaffirm, reestablish and convey clearly in laws and public policies the tremendous importance and great value of marriage.

The law must protect and facilitate fulfillment of the marriage aspiration – the desire of a man and a woman to unite in fidelity in a loving, intentional, life-long union to care for and support each other and their children. Yet how to do that seems to be a mystery.

The Universal Declaration of Human Rights famously declares that: "The family is the natural and fundamental group unit of society."[41] Clearly, it is recognized universally that families are enormously important for the well-being of individuals and of societies. The evidence is indisputable that families founded on marriage are the most secure, most happy, and the most successful. Marriage matters greatly for families; and for that reason marriage matters greatly for all nations, peoples and societies. Yet that simple truth seems to get lost from time to time.

It seems to have been forgotten in contemporary American society. As commentator Anne Kim has noted: "Today ... marriage in America seems to be dying."[42] In 2010, according to the Pew Research Center, only about half of all Americans over age eighteen were married, compared to nearly three out of four in 1960. Americans today are marrying later, if at all, and the share of Americans who [have] never married has climbed to record highs. As one result, the share of children growing up with single moms is also skyrocketing; in 2013, 41 percent of all births were to unmarried women.[43]

---

41 UN General Assembly, Universal Declaration of Human Rights, 10 December 1948, G.A. Res. 217A, article 16; see also International Covenant on Economic, Social and Cultural Rights, 16 December 1966, G.A. Res. 2200 ("The widest possible protection and assistance should be accorded the family, which is the natural and fundamental group unit of society, particularly for its establishment and while it is responsible for the care and education of dependent children.").

42 Kim, op cit, n. 31.

43 Ibid.

The percentage of Americans aged 18-45+ who were married declined between 1960 and 2010 for each age cohort, dropping nine percent (for those ages 45+) to dropping 38% (for those ages 25-34).[44] But for the most advantaged Americans, there has been relatively less decline in marriage:

> [T]he share of young college-graduate white women who were married in 2010 was a little over 70 percent—*almost exactly the same as it was in 1950.* College-educated white women are, moreover, half as likely as other women to be divorced, … and they are also refusing single motherhood. Fewer than 9 percent of women with a bachelor's degree or more had an unwed birth in 2011—a level barely higher than what it was for all women in 1950.[45]

The decline in marriage in America continues and is accelerating. According to U.S. Census data, in the year 2000 fifty-five percent (55%) of American young adults ages 25-34 were married. Just nine years later that percentage had dropped to 44.9 percent married.[46] Between 1965 and 2010, the rate of marriage for persons ages 25-34 fell for those will only high school or less education from about 85% to about 45%, and for those with a Bachelor's degree or more from nearly 80% to just over 50%.[47] University of Virginia Professor Bradford Wilcox, director of the National Marriage Project, reports that between 1975 and 2013 the poverty rates for female householders with no spouse present were about six times higher than for married-couple families.[48] Yet, "the share of American adults who have never been married is at an historic high."[49]

The decline in marriage and in support for marriage in America matters for all Americans. But the heaviest burdens and highest costs of those declines will afflict our children:

> [K]ids raised in married-parent households are much less likely to grow up in poverty, more likely to do better in school, and more likely to move up the economic ladder even if they start out poor. "There's no argument about what's best for kids," says the economic and social policy expert Ron Haskins, of the

44 Ibid at Fig. 1, Share of Americans Currently Married, 1960 and 2010.

45 Kim, op cit, n. 31 (emphasis added).

46 M. Mather & D. Lavery, 'In U.S. Proportion Married at Lowest Recorded Levels', Population Reference Bureau, at http://www.prb.org/Publications/Articles/2010/usmarriagedecline.aspx (seen 14 July 2017).

47 Ibid.

48 W.B. Wilcox, *Married Parents: One Way to Reduce Child Poverty,* Institute for Family Studies, 21 June 2017, at https://ifstudies.org/blog/married-parents-one-way-to-reduce-child-poverty (seen 28 June 2017).

49 W. Wang & K. Parker, 'Record Share of Americans Have Never Married', Pew Research Center, 24 Sept. 2014, at http://www.pewsocialtrends.org/2014/09/24/record-share-of-americans-have-never-married/ (seen 11 Aug. 2017).

> Brookings Institution. "It's to be reared in a stable household by married parents."[50]

Yet if recent trends away from marriage in America and other Western nations continue, children, families and our societies will continue to decline and suffer. On the other hand, if marriage is restored and a culture favoring marriage is rejuvenated, children, families and society are likely to flourish and prosper in our once-favored nations.

Baroness Ruth Deech of the British House of Lords (formerly a distinguished family law professor and Principal at St. Anne's College, Oxford) summarized the importance of marriage well when she declared that: "The best thing for children, as the statistics show, is to live with two married parents."[51] Marriage "[n]ot only is ... the safest environment for children, it provides a link to history, to previous generations and generations yet to come."[52] Baroness Deech was also was correct when she declared: "It is marriage that makes all the difference."[53]

The defining question of our time is whether we will revitalize the culture of marriage in our societies. What we do (or do not do) now to revive the culture of marriage will profoundly impact (help or harm) our posterity for generations to come.

Marriage is the key. Marriage makes all the difference! It matters not only (though most powerfully) for children and their caregivers, but ultimately it matters for all members of all societies whose future welfare depends upon those children and their caregivers.

We must work to rebuild and revitalize the culture of marriage in our communities, nations and societies. That will not be easy. But it is a task fitting for our generation to undertake. It is not merely an abstract ideal but is a realistic goal within our reach. If we can make any progress toward reviving marriage that ultimately will benefit not only our own posterity, but it will benefit all of our cultures, all of our societies, and all humanity.

---

50 Kim, op cit, n. 31 (emphasis added).

51 R. Deech, 'Couples don't need the law to tell them how to live together', *The Guardian*, 21 Nov. 2009, at https://www.theguardian.com/commentisfree/2009/nov/22/ruth-deech-marriage-cohabitation-children (seen 15 Aug. 2017).

52 R. Deech, 'Cohabitation and the Law', Transcript, Gresham College, 17 November 2009 (seen 1 May 2017), at p. 7 ("Research tells us that cohabitants have different perceptions of the union: the man normally does not assume commitment until he has made a clear decision about their future together, whereas the woman will see it in the fact of her moving in with him."). See also P. Fagan, *The Child Abuse Crisis: The Disintegration of Marriage, Family, and the American Community,* The Heritage Foundation, 15 May 1997, at http://www.heritage.org/marriage-and-family/report/the-child-abuse-crisis-the-disintegration-marriage-family-and-the (seen 15 Aug. 2017) ("The safest family environment for a child is a home in which the biological parents are married.").

53 Baroness Deech, Marriage-Debate, House of Lords debates, 10 February 2011, available at file:///C:/wardle/Publications/Articles&Chs/1103%20Baham%20Conseq%20Fam%20Disintegra/RES%20Deech%20Speech%2010%20Feb%202011%20%20House%20of%20Lords%20debates%20%28TheyWorkForYou.com%29.htm (seen 14 March 2011). See further J. Elgot, 'We must prioritise saving marriage, says Deech', *The JC*, February 10, 2011, available at http://www.thejc.com/news/uk-news/44964/we-must-prioritise-saving-marriage-says-deech (seen 4 May 2015).

Part II
Relationship Recognition: Responding to Family Diversity

Does the Italian Civil Partnerships and Cohabitants Act n. 76/2016 Answer Current Societal Needs?

Denise Amram[*]

I Introduction

In May 2016, Act n. 76/2016 introduced into Italian law two new family models: civil partnerships for same-sex couples and cohabitation both for same-sex and heterosexual couples. Through analysis of the most recent case law, this paper highlights the critical issues related to the practical application of the new Act.

The aim of this paper is to describe the main features with respect to the two new family models introduced by Act n. 76/2016. In particular, analysing the rights and duties which regulate a civil partnership in case of a rupture of the relationship, the paper will show that differences with respect to marriage are not so significant, despite the exclusion of any recognition of filiation rights. This is so because, in response to this legislative gap, Italian courts have interpreted the principle of *favor filiationis* established abroad in order to extend (case-by-case) parental responsibilities to the social parent (i.e. the partner of the biological parent of a child born through medical assisted reproduction techniques abroad).

As far as the new cohabitation model is concerned, the paper will analyse the legislative intent to transpose the principles stated by the case-law for de facto couples in the last thirty years. However, it will show that, also for cohabitants, the new Act avoided the opportunity to establish a different basis for social parenthood with respect to adoption.

In light of this analysis, the paper will conclude that the Italian reform of family law did not completely deal with the new challenges that current society raises.

---

* PhD in Law, SSSUP 2012, postdoctoral researcher in Comparative Law at Scuola Superiore Sant'Anna (Pisa), adjunct lecturer in European and Comparative Family Law (SSSUP, 2015-2016).

II Rights and Duties under a Civil Partnership

According to the new Italian Act n. 76/2016,[1] civil partners have almost the same rights as married couples in terms of access to justice, welfare and the healthcare system.

A civil partnership is a "specific social formation in accordance with articles 2 and 3 of the Constitution" between two adult persons of the same sex. They can constitute a civil partnership before the Municipality.

It has been introduced to fill the legislative gap that led the European Court of Human Rights to condemn Italy in its judgment of July 21, 2015 in which the Court found a violation of the right to respect for private and family life under the article 8 of the ECHR Convention.[2]

Article 1, paragraphs 11 and 12 of Act n. 76/2016 list the personal consequences deriving from the establishment of a civil union, specifying – as article 143 of the Italian Civil Code does for married couples – that the principle of equality regulates the personal and patrimonial relationships of the couple.

The core of the civil partnership entails the mutual obligations of moral and material assistance, cohabitation, and contribution to common needs. With regard to marital obligations, the current understanding of the "way of family life" requires a common residence.

The cohabitation of spouses constituted one of the milestones of the Italian patriarchal family structure and it was set before the duty of fidelity both in the Italian Civil Code of 1865 and in the current one of 1942. The obligation of assistance was included in the concept that the wife should follow her husband in the decision with respect to residence.[3] The reform of family law in 1975, although not modifying its formulation, renewed the order of the reciprocal duties of spouses in article 143 of the Civil Code, by moving cohabitation to the end of the list.[4]

---

1 M. Gorgoni, 'Le convivenze "di fatto" meritevoli di tutela e gli effetti legali, tra imperdonabili ritardi e persistenti perplessità', *in* M. Gorgoni (Ed.),*Unioni civili e convivenze di fatto L. 20 maggio 2016, n. 76*, Santarcangelo di Romagna, 2016; L. Lenti, 'Convivenze di fatto. Gli effetti: diritti e doveri', *Famiglia e diritto*, 2016, p. 934ff; M. Trimarchi, 'Unioni civili e convivenze', *Famiglia e diritto*, 2016, p. 862; M. Blasi et al, *La nuova regolamentazione delle unioni civili e delle convivenze. Legge 20 maggio 2016, n. 76*, Torino, 2016; G. Buffone, M. Gattuso & M.M. Winkler, *Unione civile e convivenza*, Giuffré, 2017.

2 *Oliari et. al. v. Italia*, ECHR, 21 july 2015, (18766/11 and 36030/11) *Nuova giur. civ. comm.*, 2015, p. 2, comments by L. Lenti at p. 575; *Fam. dir.*, 2015, comments by P. Bruno at p. 1069. From a comparative perspective, see A. Sperti, *Constitutional Courts, Gay Rights and Sexual Orientation Equality*, Vol. 14, Hart Publishing, Oxford, 2017, pp. XXIV-220.

3 V. Roppo, 'Coniugi I: Rapporti personali e patrimoniali tra coniugi', *Enc. giur. Treccani*, VIII, Roma, 1988, p. 3.

4 F. Santoro Passarelli, 'Articolo 143', *in* G. Cian, G. Oppo & A. Trabucchi, *Comm. dr. it. fam.*, II, Padova, 1992, p. 156; P. Zatti, 'Dei diritti e dei doveri che nascono dal matrimonio', *in Tratt. Rescigno*, 3, 2a ed., Torino, 1996, p. 66.

In contemporary society, the increasing mobility of people has led to a rise in the number of married couples who take up separate residences, reflecting the fact that spouses not only have individual interests that necessitate the establishment of separate domiciles (under article 45 of the Italian Civil Code)[5], but also different habitual residences. The same considerations suggest that the obligation of cohabitation is also of little relevance to civil partners.

The duty of fidelity and the duty of cooperation apply only to married couples, not civil partners. With reference to the first duty, some authors have welcomed the initiative, taking the view that fidelity is related to the stability of the couple, which is a significant requirement only in terms of parent-child relationships. According to this opinion, Act n. 76/2016 could also be considered as suggesting that the duty of fidelity should be ousted from the meaning of the personal relationship within marriage.[6]

The exclusion of the duty of fidelity from civil partnerships however marks a failure to take into account the greater complexity of the role it assumes in the couple relationship. The meaning of the duty of fidelity, nowadays, goes beyond the concept of sexual exclusivity between spouses, in ways which cannot always be deduced from a systematic interpretation of other spousal duties.[7]

The omission of obligation of cooperation would not seem to affect the relationship between civil partners, since the same duty can be extracted from the complex relationship of mutual duties that the moral and material assistance obligation, expressly stated by Act n. 76/2016, requires of the partners.

The moral and material assistance obligation, expressed both in active and passive behaviours, aims at facilitating the family life of the partners, as well as spouses. In fact, it was believed that the obligation of moral and material assistance constituted an expression of all the other elements of the relationship – "unity, solidarity, equality, respect for the individual personality" – allowing the couple to live a correct family relationship.

Despite these differences from marriage, the civil partnership is subject to the same conditions of nullity as marriage, as well as to the same property relations model (community of property regime unless different agreement) and inheritance law.

From a procedural viewpoint, the Divorce Act n. 898/1970 is directly applicable to civil partners, including collaborative law procedures, while the separation procedure is not. In fact, married couples may claim for separation because their common life has become unsustainable, asking the court to state a suspension of the marriage and – after a year (or

---

5 M. Costanza, 'Domicilio, residenza e dimora (dir. civ.)', *Enc. Giur. Treccani*, XII, Roma, 1989.

6 See G. Autorino, 'Le unioni civili in Europa', *Nuova giur. civ. comm.*, 2016, p. 1667; F. Viglione, *in* G. Cian & A. Trabucchi, *Commentario*, Cedam, 2016, *sub* 'Note introd. Libro I, Titolo VI: Sez. II', p. 169; P. Logroscino, 'Il diritto fondamentale delle coppie same sex all'unione civile', *in* M. Gorgoni (Ed.), op cit, n. 1, p. 37, spec. 67; see also A. Ambrosi, 'Unione civile e costituzione', *Nuova giur. Civ. comm.*, 2016, p. 1676.

7 E. Quadri, '"Unioni civili tra persone dello stesso sesso" e "convivenze": il non facile ruolo che la nuova legge affida all'interprete', *Corr. Giur.*, 2016, p. 893.

six months in cases where the couple has no children) – they may claim for divorce, the effect of which is – instead – to dissolve the marriage, considering the impossibility to recompose the family unit. Civil partners are not entitled to suspend their partnership, but only to directly ask for its dissolution.

As far as all that has not been regulated by Act n. 76/2016, article 1 § 20 makes a general reference to civil partners possessing all rights afforded married couples, except for rights under Act n. 184/1983 on adoptions.

III The Lack of Recognition of Step-Child Adoption and the Case-Law Approach

As far as the personal relationship between civil partners is concerned, the differences in respect to marriage have less relevant consequences.

However, equality is not expressly granted in terms of parental rights: access to adoption and medical assisted reproduction techniques are still forbidden to same-sex couples. The concept of parenting beyond blood ties has evolved to confer parental responsibilities – and the attendant legal consequences – on the social parent. This is possible under the Adoption Act n. 184/1983 only in certain conditions, which still do not include either single parents or civil partners.

Despite such a legal framework, which does not completely respond to the societal need to afford a parental role to the persons (*recte* "family members" according to EU law)[8] who take daily care of the so called "rainbow children", the case law of the Italian High Court and lower courts reflects a new trend aimed at extending parental responsibilities (rights and duties) to parents who do not share a blood-tie with their child(ren).

For instance, the courts have interpreted the principle of the best interest of the child to give legal recognition to the enduring de facto situation.

The Italian High Court has stated that a broad interpretation of article 44(d) in cases of special adoption when the child cannot be considered "abandoned" complies with constitutional principles and supranational law. From this perspective, step-child adoption

8 On the extended concept of "family member" see M. Verschraegen, 'Family Members, the Rights to Family Life and Family Reunification', *in* P. Lodrup & E. Modvar (Eds.), *Family Life and Human Rights: Papers presented at the 11th ISFL World Conference*, Oslo, Glydendal Akedemisk, 2004, p. 919; E. Bribosia, I. Rorive & L. Van den Eynde, 'Same-Sex Marriage: Building an Argument before the European Court of Human Rights in Light of the US Experience', *Berkeley J. Int'l Law*, Vol. 32, 2014, p. 1; G. Comandé, 'The Fifth European Union Freedom: Aggregating Citizenship … around Private Law, in "The Constitutionalization of European Private Law', *in* H. Micklitz (Ed.), *Constitutionalization of European Private Law*, Oxford University Press, 2014, p. 1 at 61-101 and K. Carr, *Deconstructing and Reconstructing Family Law through the European Legal Order* (PhD thesis on file at the EUI, Florence, Italy, 2014).

by the homosexual partner of the biological parent can be recognized if it is considered in the best interest of the child.[9]

In addition, in those cases where the parent-child link has already been recognized abroad, in light of private international law, courts have applied the principle of *favor filiationis* combined with that of the free movement of people. According to these principles, it is not in the child's best interests to have their familial status affected by a more restrictive statutory law in the country of destination.

In particular, the High Court has stated that in order to assess the compatibility of the foreign birth certificate with public order and to recognize its effects in Italy, the court must verify whether the foreign act is compatible with the fundamental rights protected under the Constitution, and the EU Charter of Fundamental Rights, as well as the European Convention on Human Rights. Indeed, this evaluation does not concern the question of whether the foreign certificate was drafted in accordance with Italian statutory law.[10]

In this respect, the Italian High Court has recently ordered the transcription of an English birth certificate where two mothers were identified as parents. The Court explained that the birth certificate was drafted and registered abroad according to the UK legislation which establishes the presumption of parental responsibility for the spouse of the biological mother, regardless of whether they are a heterosexual or homosexual couple.[11]

In light of these principles, the most recent case-law of the lower courts has started to fill the Italian legislative gap by legally recognizing filiation links between the homosexual partner of the child's biological father, determining a full extension of the parental responsibilities in cases of surrogacy agreements legally effected abroad.

The Court of Leghorn accepted the request to modify the birth certificate in accordance with what the foreign (US – State of California) certificate stated. Thus, while the Register Office of Leghorn initially registered only the biological parent in the birth certificate, now it has been ordered to include the non-biological (male) one as well.[12] It has been remarked, in fact, that the child – who is both an American and Italian citizen – has the right to maintain his own familial and social identity legally achieved under the foreign law.

Similarly, the Court of Appeal of Trento accepted the request to recognize in Italy the efficacy of a foreign (Canadian) judgment which had established the parental responsibility of the non-biological (male) parent of a child born through surrogacy under the article 67 of the Private International Law Act n. 218/1995.[13]

9 Cass. 22 June 2016, n. 12962, in *Giur. It.*, 2016, p. 2573.

10 Cass. 30 September 2016, n. 19599, in *Corr. Giur.*, 2017, p. 181.

11 Cass. 15 June 2017, n. 14878, in *Nuova giur. Civ. Comm.*, I, 2017,p. 1718

12 Court of Leghorn, 3 January 2018. See also Court of Pisa, 26 July 2018 and 18 September 2018.

13 Court of Appeal of Trento, 23 February 2017, *Nuova giur. civ. comm.*, I, 2017, p. 994.

This formal recognition has also occurred in a few cases by the transcription of a foreign adoption and the birth certificate directly at the Register Office of the Municipality.[14]

The Constitutional Court has recently confirmed that surrogacy is in breach of Italian Law, but it also stated that it is important to verify case-by-case the best interests of the child when it has been legally performed under a foreign law.[15]

A homogeneous regulation/interpretation is needed to guarantee the same protection to all children in Italy.

IV Rights and Duties under the New Cohabitation Model

As far as the rights of cohabitants are concerned, the above-mentioned reform introduced rights and duties for couples who have declared themselves as cohabitants in the municipality of their domicile.[16] It regulates several legal tools which were already extended to de facto families by case law in the last 30 years (e.g. bereavement damages compensation).

It also extends some rights traditionally reserved for married couples, like maintenance in case of termination of the relationship. This seems to limit the contractual autonomy of the partners, instead of answering the social need to provide regulation of personal and economic aspects of unmarried relationships.

Article 1 § 36 of Act 76/2016 refers to "two adult persons permanently united by emotional bonds of couple and mutual moral and material assistance, not bound by relationships of kinship, affinity or adoption, by marriage or by a civil union", and attributes to them rights and duties. It is important to remark that the free status condition excludes a significant number of stepfamilies where the members of the couple are only separated and not also divorced from the previous marriage.

The role of the declaration at the municipality is an open issue. Is it necessary just to prove[17] the existence of the cohabitation or to establish it?[18] The second approach could make easier the identification of couples belonging to the "cohabitation" model. However, it could create some issues of compatibility with the above-mentioned previous case-law, which extended some fundamental rights to de facto couples based upon proof that the relationship between the couple was stable (such as in case of bereavement damages compensation).

---

14 This is the case of the Municipality of Milan, http://ricerca.repubblica.it/repubblica/archivio/repubblica/2018/01/25/prima-registrazione-allanagrafe-di-due-bambini-con-due-padriMilano03.html.

15 Constitutional Court, 22 November 2017, n. 272, in www.cortecostituzionale.it.

16 F.P. Luiso, 'La convivenza di fatto dopo la L. 2016/76', *Judicium*.it.

17 Court of Milan, 31 May 2017.

18 L. Miglietta, 'Convivenze di fatto: gli spiacevoli effetti collaterali', *Guida al Diritto*, 2016, n. 25, p. 8; G. Finocchiaro, 'Sottoposti a norme due maggiorenni con un legame stabile', *Guida al Diritto*, 2016, n. 25, p. 59.

Scholars consider that for those couples who do not declare themselves as "cohabitants" all the fundamental rights that the case-law recognized are still applicable, but these "informal relationships" cannot benefit from the new tools introduced by Act n. 76/2016, such as, in case of breakdown in the cohabitation, the right of maintenance if the former cohabitant needs alimony. According to article 1 § 65, the new maintenance obligation should be proportional to the duration of the cohabitation and the criteria for alimony between relatives in article 438 of the Italian Civil Code should be applied.[19]

Another new legal protection instrument introduced for cohabitants arises in cases in which a cohabitant, owner of the "couple domicile", dies. In such cases, the surviving cohabitant may stay in the house for a period of between 2-5 years, depending on the duration of the cohabitation. Despite the fact that cohabitants have no inheritance rights, unless there is a will, Act n. 76/2016 thus introduced a tool of solidarity for the cohabitant who does not own the house in which the couple were domiciled, limiting potential claims by the heirs for a specified period.[20]

As far as parental rights are concerned, differences between children born inside and out-of-the-wedlock were repealed in 2012-2013, with the so-called reform on filiation. The Italian system deleted all the adjectives which described children like adoptive, legitimate (i.e. born inside the wedlock), and natural (born out of the wedlock). However, as stated earlier, social parenting is recognized only in cases of adoption, and adoption by single parents and homosexual couples has been expressly excluded.[21]

V Future Perspectives in Light of Other EU systems

The Italian system has tried to answer the societal needs emerging from the development of new family models by introducing civil partnerships and cohabitation. However, the adopted approach reflects a preference for the "traditional family model" that article 29 of the Constitution describes as the "natural society based on marriage."[22]

Despite the rights and duties that Act n. 76/2016 has established for the relationships between adults, the lack of recognition of parental rights and responsibilities within non-traditional families is still an open issue that the law is asked to solve case-by-case.

The principle of the best interests of the child is the compass usually applied to navigate this legislative gap. However, it should not become an "open" formula left to the discre-

19 F.S. Mattucci, 'Gli alimenti in favore del convivente di fatto', *Fam. dir.*, 2017, p. 705.

20 L. Balestra, 'Le unioni civili e le convivenze di fatto: la legge unioni civili, convivenze di fatto e "modello" matrimoniale: prime riflessioni', *Giur. It.*, 2016, p. 1771.

21 See D. Amram, 'Pursuing the Best Interest of the Children in Non-Traditional Families. A Comparative Overview", *European Journal of Law Reform*, Vol. 17, No. 2, 2015, p. 247.

22 See F.D. Busnelli, 'Il diritto della famiglia di fronte al problema della difficile integrazione delle fonti', *Riv. Dir. Civ.*, 2016, p. 447.

tionary power of the courts. A statutory law becomes more urgent every day in order to avoid discrimination between children.

From this perspective, the Italian system seems to have enacted just a first step towards a complete family law reform able to satisfy the equality needs emerging from the current social context. Other European systems, such as those in Malta, Ireland, Germany, France and the UK, have already moved on from the "compromise solution" of the civil partnership towards a gender-neutral marriage approach.

The latter, in many cases, allows access to adoption for same-sex couples and facilitates the establishment of a legal presumption of parental responsibilities between the spouse of the biological parent and the child born through medically assisted reproduction techniques.

The Certification of Marriages in African Pluralistic Legal Systems with Special Reference to Customary Marriages in South Africa and Zambia

A Case for Parallel and Decentralised Certification Systems

Chuma Himonga[*]

I Introduction

This paper discusses the registration of marriages in African legal systems with special reference to South Africa and Zambia.[1] The focus of the paper is the registration of customary marriages in African legal systems with respect to the "grounded" reality imperative. This imperative is the need to provide more reliable means of enhancing family members' access to family resources within a legal pluralistic context.

---

* Professor Emeritus, University of Cape Town; Chair of the DST/NRF Chair in Customary Law at the University of Cape Town from 2010 to 2017.

1 The paper is largely based on recent socio-legal empirical studies of customary marriages in South Africa and Zambia conducted under two separate projects. The first project investigated the operation of the Recognition of Customary Marriages Act of 1998 (Act 120 of South Africa) and the rules of intestate succession emanating from the Constitutional Court of South Africa in *Bhe v Magistrate Khayelitsha.* This study has been published as a book: C. Himonga & E. Moore *Reform of Customary Marriage, Divorce and Succession Living Customary Law and Social Realities*, Juta & Co. (Pty) Ltd, 2015. The methodology adopted for this study is discussed in the book. A report of the study was also published under the same title (https://juta.co.za/uploads/SAR/mobile/index.html. This study was funded by the South African Research Chairs Initiative of the Department of Science and Technology, managed by the National Research Foundation (Grant No 64825). However, any opinions, findings and conclusions or recommendations expressed in this paper are those of the authors, and the National Research Foundation does not accept any liability in this respect. The second project was an investigation of the formation and patterns of customary marriage in Zambia. The findings of the study, together with the methodology used for the study are reported in C. Himonga, *Research Report on Formation and Patterns of Customary Marriage in Zambia: A Socio-legal Study* (to be published by Juta). This study was funded partly by the South African Research Chairs Initiative of the Department of Science and Technology, managed by the National Research Foundation of South Africa (Grant No 64825) (the disclaimer above also applies here) and the SSHRC, Canada, through the University of Ottawa. Variations of this paper were presented at the following conferences as well: LSA/CLS (UCT) Conference on Dynamism, Liminality, and Reality? Policy, Research and the Law in an Afropolitan Era, 9-11 December 2016 and the 2017 *Celebratory 20th Annual Family Law Conference, Cape Town* 8-9 March 2017, Cape Town. I acknowledge the contribution to this paper of discussions at these conferences.

The certification of marriages in many African legal systems is the gateway to family resources, whether in the form of personal legal status or proprietary consequences of the marriage, during the marriage or after its dissolution. Access to these family resources depends on the existence of the marriage, which is most reliably proved by the certificate of the marriage. Therefore, how the state regulates the certification of marriages is critical to family members' entitlements and rights arising from marriage. Particularly important in this respect in African contexts is how the state takes account of different marriage forms concluded within multiple normative orders of civil law,[2] customary law and religious law and the oral nature of some of these legal orders, such as living customary law.[3] This paper draws from recent studies of customary marriages in South Africa and Zambia[4] to analyse the grounded realities of certification of marriage systems, their impact on people's access to family resources and the need to change the model of certification of customary marriages in order to address the identified challenges.

These studies on which the paper is based reveal grounded realities with a combination of: (a) the absence or inadequacy of state interventions for certification of marriages, (b) the co-existence of uncoordinated formal and informal systems of certification and (c) the narrow concept of certification of marriages restricted to state certification. These factors compromise the prospect of access to family resources by deserving family members. The paper argues that a model of parallel and decentralised certification of marriage systems would address the factors concerned while acknowledging and recognising the "grounded" reality of the co-existence of state and non-state systems of marriage certification in an African context. Put differently, the paper argues for the need to develop parallel and decentralised certification systems that respond to the fact of legal pluralism, the "grounded" realities of the operation of state and non-state certification systems.

The argument of the paper is advanced in seven sections. Following this introduction, the paper briefly discusses the importance of the certification of marriages. This is followed by the third section on the official methods of certification of marriages in South Africa

2 This term is used to designate the systems of law also referred to as received law of European origin introduced to Africa by foreign countries in the context of colonialism.

3 Customary law is conceptualised as official or living customary law. The former generally refers to the customary law that is recognised and enforced by state agencies and is often reduced to writing through codification, legislation and case law. Living customary law refers to the customs and practices that the communities that are subject to customary law in a given territory generate and invest with binding authority to regulate their lives. However, overlaps arise between these concepts in some states, such as South Africa, as a result of the recognition of living customary law by the state and generally due to other factors, such as the unevenness of processes of social, economic and political changes within which the norms of living customary law evolve and are formed.

4 Apart from being sites of recent empirical socio-legal research (see n. 1), these two countries present two other features of interest. The first is that they both have multiple forms of marriage which parties intending to marry can choose from. Secondly, they represent contrasting systems of certification of marriages - one with a mandatory requirement for the registration of customary marriages and the other with an optional registration system.

and Zambia. The fourth section is a discussion of the operation of the certification systems under the concept of strong legal pluralism. This section shows, firstly, how the unofficial systems ignore the official systems, and, secondly, the confusion among both state and non-state actors connected to the interaction of the two certification processes, confusion that, arguably, compromises family members' access to family rights and resources in the state forums where these rights and resources are adjudicated.

The fifth section examines the implication of current certification systems for access to family resources. It draws from the preceding section to show how the state of the marriage certification system and its operation affect the protection of family members' rights and access to family resources, such as matrimonial property upon the dissolution of the marriage. The sixth section draws from all the sections of the paper to consolidate the argument for a model of certification of customary marriages that responds to the need for mandatory certification of marriages and grounded realities of the co-existence of state and non-state systems of marriage certification in African legal systems. This section sets out the essential elements of such a model, the details of which are to be left to each country according to its peculiar conditions. The seventh section is the conclusion.

II The Importance of Certification of Marriages

The importance of certification of marriages may be viewed from two perspectives – the international and regional human rights perspective, on the one hand, and the national perspective, on the other hand.

Several human rights instruments are notable for imposing obligations for registration of marriages on states. The Convention on Consent to Marriage, Minimum Age for Marriage and Registration of Marriages provides that all marriages must be registered in an appropriate official register by the competent authority.[5] The Convention on the Elimination of All Forms of Discrimination Against Women and the African Charter on the Rights and Welfare of the Child both provide for compulsory registration of marriages in an official registry.[6] The Protocol to the African Charter on Human and People's Rights on the Rights of Women in Africa (The Women's Protocol) not only creates an obligation for official registration of every marriage but it also makes such registration a condition for the validity of the marriage. Article 6 (d) states: "Every marriage shall be recorded in writing and registered in accordance with national laws, in order to be legally recognized."

All these instruments require the registration of all marriages, including customary marriages. The certification processes envisaged include recording or certification of marriages in writing. However, the requirement for registration in writing only, may be

5 Art. 3 of the Convention.
6 Art. 16(2) of the Convention and art. 21(2) of the Charter.

criticised as undesirable and unsuited for African contexts, which recognize oral systems of law and traditions regulating the formation of customary marriages. The Women's Protocol is ambivalent in this respect in that it refers to recording and registration "in accordance with national laws." Arguably, the provision in question implicitly recognises and anticipates the oral nature of customary law systems in Africa. Thus, no African state should be charged with violation of human rights regarding certification of customary marriages because it does not require written certification of marriages provided that the unwritten certification procedure is effective enough to signify and prove the existence of the marriage. The counter argument is that because the Women's Protocol makes registration a condition for the legal recognition of the marriage, it anticipates written registration systems that are more certain than unwritten ones. This interpretation should, in any case, be rejected as it does not take account of African realities in which state-sponsored written systems of certification are impractical and do not work adequately.[7] For similar reasons, the stance of the Women's Protocol that invalidates marriages for lack of registration should be rejected.[8]

The importance of the certification of marriage from a national perspective relates to the determination of the existence of the marriage for purposes of access to family rights and resources. The certification of marriages in Africa (as in many other parts of the world) is one of the most reliable methods of proving the existence of a marriage upon which depends the access of different kinds of resources by family members in a marriage setting. Thus, marriage certification acts as a gateway to important family resources a legal system affords the members of a family. The most important of these are the incidents of personal legal status and proprietary consequences of the marriage during the marriage and after its dissolution.

While the non-registration of a marriage may not in itself be fatal to the validity of the marriage,[9] the registration of a marriage makes it easy to prove the existence of a valid marriage as the certificate of registration is considered to be prima facie evidence of this fact.[10] This means that the fierce contestations over resources that often follow the dissolution of marriage by death or divorce may have different outcomes depending on whether the parties to the marriage obtained a piece of paper with a government stamp certifying the registration of marriage.

---

7 For example, see Himonga & Moore, op cit, n.1, in which the authors discuss the inadequate application of the South African law governing the registration of customary marriages.

8 For a contrary view, see F. Banda, *Women, Law and Human Rights: An African Perspective* Portland Oregon, Hart Publishing, 2005.

9 See, for example, s. 4 of the RCMA.

10 See, for example, *Baadjies v Matubela* 2002 (3) SA 427 (W).

III Systems of Certification of Marriages in South Africa and Zambia

The certification systems in the countries under study are characterised by a narrow concept of state certification of marriages that takes no cognisance of other certification of marriage systems operating outside of the state law. The current certification in the two countries takes the form of official registration corresponding to the duality of forms of marriages under civil law and customary law.[11] Under this concept only state institutions can certify marriages.[12]

In South Africa, mandatory state certification of marriages applies to both customary and civil marriages under their respective constituent legislative frameworks. The certification of civil marriages is undertaken in terms of the Marriage Act[13] while the certification of customary marriages is conducted in terms of the Recognition of Customary Marriages Act (RCMA).[14] This Act provides for registration of all customary marriages even though non-registration does not affect the validity of the marriage.[15] The Department of Home Affairs (DHA) is an important point of intersection between processes of certification of customary and civil marriages.

Although civil and customary marriages are registered under different statutes, they are both registered by the DHA, and therefore certified by the same authority. The same officials that register civil marriages also register customary marriages. The DHA issues marriage certificates for both customary law and civil law marriages.[16] The certificate of

11 While the South African Constitution envisages the legislative recognition of religious forms of marriage, such as Muslim and Hindu marriages, for example, none of these forms of marriage have as yet received this recognition in the same way as customary marriages have been recognised by legislation. Customary marriages are recognised and regulated by the Recognition of Customary Marriages Act 120 of 1998, which came into operation on 15 November 2000. Zambian law is completely silent on the recognition of any religious system of marriage outside the legal framework of the civil marriage.

12 Interestingly, the human rights law outlined above does not seem to prescribe narrow concepts of certification of marriages centralized in state institutions such as those adopted by South Africa and Zambia.

13 Marriage Act of 1961.

14 See n. 11 above.

15 See s. 4 (8) of RCMA. The Recognition of Customary Marriages Act Regulation (GN R1101, GG 21700 of 1 November 2000) provides for further details on the certification process. The peculiar effect s. 4(8) has had on the regulation of customary marriages in practice, such as, for example, that non-registration is equated to the invalidity of the marriage or to non-recognition of the marriage, has been noted by several studies: See M. De Souza, 'When Non-Registration Becomes Non-Recognition: Examining the Law and Practice of Customary Marriage Registration in South Africa' *Act Juridica*, 2013, pp. 239-272; L. Mwambene & H. Kruse, 'Form over Function? The Practical Application of the Recognition of Customary Marriage Act in South Africa' *Acta Juridica*, 2013, pp. 292-317; R.N. Ozoemena 'Legislation as a Critical Tool in Addressing Social Change in South Africa: Lessons from Mayelane v Ngwenyama', *PER/PLJ*, Vol. 18, No. 4, 2015, pp. 968-992 at 987-988.

16 The customary marriage certificate is Form C of Regulation 2(5) (a) of Regulation of the Recognition of Customary Marriages Regulations (Government Notice No. R. 1101 of 1 November 2000 (Government Gazette No. 21700) as amended by Government Notice No. R. 359 of 14 March 2003 (Government Gazette No. 25023)), entitled "Customary Marriage Certificate".

registration is *prima facie* evidence of the existence of the registered marriage.[17] This intersection of customary and civil marriage certification in the DHA is important to the operation of the system of certification of marriages in practice as it is at the heart of the confusion that arises among state and non-state actors considered in the next section.

The certification of both customary and civil marriages in South Africa may take place via purely civil processes, involving state official, or via religious authorities who are designated as marriage officers by the state, or via designated traditional leaders.[18] The designation of traditional leaders as registration officers was intended to decentralise the system of certification to rural areas. However, very few traditional leaders have been designated for this purpose,[19] with the result that registration remains centralised in the DHA. Traditional authorities are also involved in the official certification of customary marriages at another level: the forms that the parties are required to complete at the DHA in order to register the marriage must be accompanied with a declaration by the traditional leader.[20] In addition to this procedure for registering marriages, the court may issue a certification of registration of a customary marriage (or if necessary, have the existing certificate cancelled or amended) upon application by an interested party.[21]

It is important to emphasize that, in South African law, in order for churches or traditional authorities to officially certify marriages they must be designated as official registering officer for this purpose by the Minister of Home Affairs or an "officer acting under the Minister's written authorization".[22] This marks the centralisation of the certification system in the State.

Unlike South Africa, Zambia does not provide for the mandatory certification of customary marriages. Mandatory registration only applies to civil marriages.[23] The registration of customary marriages is, therefore, voluntary. Couples who choose to register customary law marriages may do so at the Local Court in urban areas[24] or at Rural District Councils in rural areas. In either case, the parties are issued with a marriage certificate upon the

17 See n. 10 above.

18 A traditional leader is defined as "any person who in terms of customary law or any other law holds a position in a traditional ruling hierarchy" (sections of the RCMA). Traditional leaders operate in rural areas of the country.

19 See Himonga & Moore, op cit, n. 1, p. 118.

20 For a detailed discussion of the South African registration system and how it operates in practice, including how it deviates from the RCMA provisions, see Himonga & Moore, op cit, n. 1, pp. 102-128.

21 See s. 4 (7) of the Act.

22 See, for example, s. 1 of the RCMA. A registering officer according to this section is defined as "any person appointed as registering officer for purposes of this Act by the Minister or an officer acting under the Minister's written authorization".

23 For a detailed discussion of the registration of these marriages and related matters in Zambia see C. Himonga, *Family and Succession Law, International Encyclopedia of Laws*, Supplement 81, the Netherlands, Kluwer Law International, 2016, paras. 91, 110-112.

24 Section 8(2) of the Local Courts Act.

payment of a small fee.[25] No informal certification of customary marriages is recognised. Thus, the limited certification of customary marriages is centralised in the State.

Despite the fact that both South Africa and Zambia do not recognise informal or non-state systems of certification of marriages, these processes do exist, and they represent an expanded form of signifcation of the existence of a customary marriage in practice. Thus, for the purposes of this paper, state and non-state sytems of certification interact and intertwine with each other in practice,[26] and produce consequences that are sometimes detrimental to family members' access to resources within the context of legal pluralism. In the next section I highlight[27] the nature and effect of legal pluralism on certifcation of marriages before I examine the effect of the interaction of formal and infomal forms of marriage certification on family members' access to family rights and resources.

IV The Nature and Effect of Legal Pluralism on the Certification of Marriages

Legal pluralism literature acknowledges two notions of legal pluralism. These are weak and strong or deep legal pluralism. Defined simply, weak legal pluralism is the co-existence of different legal system within one polity but all of which draw authority or legitimacy from state recognition. Strong legal pluralism, on the other hand, accepts the co-existence of state law with other (non-state) legal orders. Thus, the state law (recognised under weak legal pluralism) co-exists with others that owe their existence to entities located in what Sally Falk Moore refers to as semi-autonomous social fields, which have power to generate rules and enforce them on their adherents.[28] As explained by Griffiths deep legal pluralism is:

> The presence in a social field of more than one "legal order" .... a situation ... in which law and legal institutions are not all subsumable within one "system" but have their sources in the self-regulatory activities of all the multifarious

25 See further, Himonga, op cit, n. 23, para. 109.

26 C. Himonga provides a detailed discussion of the interactions and intersections of customary law, civil and religion in the formation of marriage in Zambia. See C. Himonga 'Legal Pluralism and the Adjudication of Matrimonial Disputes in Zambian Courts: Justice Denied in the Intersections?' *in* F. Diallo & A. S. Anamzoya, *Legal Pluralism in African Courts: Actors, Institutions and Governance*, Brill, (forthcoming). See also F. Diallo & C. Himonga 'Interactional Pluralism in Southern Africa: Legal Hybridisation in the Judicial Arena', *in* G. Otis (Ed.), *L'intéraction des systèmes Juridiques Autochtones et Non Autochtones/The Interaction of Indigenous and Non-Indigenous Legal Systems*, Presses de l'Université Laval, (forthcoming).

27 For a detailed discussion of the impact of legal pluralism on customary marriages in Southern Africa see Diallo & Himonga, ibid.

28 S.F. Moore 'Law and Social Change: the Semi-Autonomous Social Field as an Appropriate Subject of Study', *Law & Society Review*, Vol. 7, No. 4, 1973, pp. 719-746.

> social fields present, activities which may support, complement, ignore or frustrate one another, so that the "law" which is actually effective on the "ground floor" of society is the result of enormously complex and usually in practice unpredictable patterns of competition, interaction, negotiation, isolationism, and the like.[29]

By its nature strong legal pluralism represents layered kinds of regulation. The discussion in this section shows how this kind of legal pluralism affects the system of state certification of marriages in the two countries. It shows that certification in reality takes place, as it were, in many rooms represented by state and non-state certification systems, and that people move between these systems. However, these movements or interactions sometimes lead to confusion among both state and non-state actors as to the kind of marriage the parties have "registered".

Two levels of strong legal pluralism in certification of marriages are of interest. The first level of strong legal pluralism concerns the involvement of religious bodies in certification of marriages. In both South Africa and Zambia, while official certification of marriages is restricted to designated or licensed churches (and ministers of religion), churches (and their officials) that are not designated also certify marriages under their own systems, such as recording the marriage in a book or issuing a marriage certificate designed by the church. In South Africa we found cases in which spouses used both designated and undesignated churches to celebrate what they called "white weddings."[30] Interestingly, some of those who used undesignated churches were aware that they did not comply with the state process of registration. Regina and Frank[31] were in this category. Although they both knew that their marriage was not being registered under the state system, having informed their traditional leader, they went ahead with the "white wedding" in the undesignated church. Regina stated:

> We invited family and friends; we also went to the church to say our vows and later had a big feast…yes we just signed in the book. I was very happy and excited to be wearing the white dress. It was the happiest day of my life, my husband waited for 21 years before we got married.

In Zambia, some couples who are married under customary law also seek the blessing of their churches on the marriage. In some cases, even where the couple contracts a civil marriage via the licensed church, the church still gives its marriage certificate on top of

29 J. Griffiths 'What is Legal Pluralism?,' *Journal of Legal Pluralism*, Vol. 24, 1986, pp. 1-50 at 39.

30 See Himonga & Moore, 2015, pp. 116ff.

31 These are not the real names of the parties to the marriage under consideration.

the state marriage certificate, with no explanation to the parties of the difference between the two "certification processes." Because of its stance on the centralisation of the marriage certification system in the state, the law does not recognise the blessing of the marriage as certification and confines that process to a mere marriage blessing.[32]

It should also be noted that some churches in Zambia also play a role in the certification of civil marriages. This leads some parties who wish to convert their customary marriage to a civil marriage[33] to think that they can simply go to the church to have their marriage converted without following the full procedure they would otherwise need to follow to convert the marriage to a civil marriage. This procedure involves a complex official process requiring, among others, the issue of relevant notices at the District Council offices and the licensing of the church and the minister of religion in which the marriage is being converted.[34]

In Zambia, as in South Africa, civil marriages may be certified via state authorities or religious officials that are licensed to solemnise civil marriages, but not all churches are licensed for this purpose. As will be shown in the next section, in practice, the certification of civil marriages by licensed churches is the point at which intersections occur between customary marriages and civil marriages and between formal and informal certifcation processes. It is also at this intersection that confusion arises among state and non-state actors with regard to the certification of marriages.[35]

The effect of the "certification process" under consideration is that where a church which offers marriage blessings is also licensed to celebrate civil marriages, such a church essentially issues two types of marriage certificates among its congregants – the state - generated certificate (for state church marriages) or the church self-generated marriage certificate (for informal and, sometimes, formal church marriages).

The second level of strong legal pluralism in marriage certification involves traditional leaders from different ethnic groups whose customary practices of marriage and marriage signification are not uniform.[36] In South Africa, we found that traditional leaders who were not designated as marriage registration officials play the same roles with regard to the registration of marriages as the few who claimed to have been designated.[37] Some of the traditional leaders had even developed their own forms of certification as a way of implementing the state certification system under the RCMA, or in order to help people to establish the existence of marriages, especially in the context of the customary law of

32 *Chaila v Chaila* 1982/HE/101.

33 The Marriage Act that regulates civil marriages entitles couples who are married under customary law to convert their marriage to a civil marriage. See Himonga, op cit, n. 23, para. 103.

34 For a detailed discussion of the relevant procedure, see Himonga, op cit, n. 23, paras. 110-111.

35 See Diallo & Himonga, op cit, n. 26.

36 See n. 18 above for the definition of traditional leader.

37 See L. Mbatha, *The Content and Implementation of the Recognition of Customary Marriages Act no 120 of 1998: A Social and Legal Analysis* (LLM thesis on file at Witwatersrand University).

succession.[38] An example of these certification forms is where the parties to the marriage and their families drive the *lobolo*[39] cattle or take the *lobolo* cash payments to the chief's homestead to have them counted and recorded as proof of the marriage that has been entered into. One participant described this certification system:

> Those cattle, the *magadi* have to go to [the chiefs house] be registered at the [chiefs place]. We do that so that even if you do not sign anything it will be registered at the Chiefs and there will be witnesses from the man's family and the woman's family. If its actual cattle, they are driven to the Chief so that they can see them and register them, even their colours and everything about them. If its money, they want it as is and it's taken to the Chiefs and counted there. And then there is a letter that they give you to say that *magadi* has been paid and indeed you are married.... Yes, it's like a certificate because it has numbers and registration number and at the bottom the chief signs ... Yes, they have a registration book and then they give you the certificate....[40]

This statement presents a clear method of signification of the existence of the marriage which local people consider to represent certification of marriage even though it is outside the framework of the South African state certification system. Another example of informal certification of marriage in South Africa is the practice of the two families of the parties to the marriage exchanging *lobolo* letters confirming the payment of *lobolo* as evidence of the conclusion of marriage.[41]

The co-existence and interaction of state and non-state certification of marriages in both South Africa and Zambia noted in this section raises two problems. The first problem is that even though the state ignores the existence of non-state certification systems, people use them and in doing this they ignore or bypass the official system designed for certification of marriages. Thus, in practice the certification systems of the state are largely mere paper systems with little relevance to the people for whom they are designed. Moreover, the states' narrow concept of marriage certification causes the state to ignore processes of certification at the local level that might otherwise fulfil the same purpose and goals as official certification processes.

The second problem of the co-existence and interaction of state and non-state certification of marriages is that the interactions between the state and non-state processes are

38 See Himonga & Moore, op cit, n. 1, p. 119-120.

39 Section 1 of the RCMA defines *lobolo* as "the property in cash or in kind, whether known as *lobolo, bogadi, bohali, xuma, lumalo, thaka, ikhazi, magadi, emabheka* or by any other name, which a prospective husband or the head of his family undertakes to give to the head of the prospective wife's family in consideration of a customary marriage".

40 Himonga & Moore, op cit, n. 1, p. 120.

41 Ibid.

largely uncoordinated.[42] This results in confusion for parties to the marriage seeking to register a marriage as to what system to register the marriage under. This statement by one research participant in Zambia amplifies the problem:

> Sometimes people [...] come here [the local court] and get a certificate, go to church and then go to the civic centre [where the Town Council is located and where the certification of certain forms of marriages takes place]. It's a way of securing their marriages and – maybe it's a bit of ignorance on really what they want – because they could go for one.

The confusion among actors involved in certification of marriages processes also arises from the centralisation of the certification of marriages in one state institution. For example our research in South Africa found that officials at the Department of Home affairs register customary marriages as civil marriages, to the shock of parties who later find out that they registered a civil marriage instead of a customary marriage they had intended to register.[43] Furthermore, state actors get confused about how the complex certification system works as evident from the judgment of a magistrate in Zambia who thought that all customary marriages require to be registered:

> One may prove marriage with the production [of] a marriage certificate. Even if a marriage is under customary law, the local court gives spouses a marriage certificate to confirm such marriages. The appellant has not produced the said documents and therefore he has not convinced me that the respondent is married to another man [...] the application is dismissed [lightly edited].[44]

As a result of this confusion, the court denied the petitioner the right they sought from the court. The next section provides further evidence of the implications of the state certification system on the rights of the parties to family resources.

42 Himonga & Moore, op cit, n. 1, p. 121.
43 Himonga & Moore, op cit, n. 1, pp. 112-113.
44 It may well be that in addition to confusion, some officials require the certificate because it is easier to administer. Thus they do not have to try and ascertain the existence of a marriage, deal with fraud, etc. It seems that the certificate avoids the officials being entangled with these issues. Whatever the reason for demanding a certificate where the law does not require it, doing so causes confusion in law and in society.

V THE IMPLICATIONS OF THE CERTIFICATION OF MARRIAGE PROCESSES FOR ACCESS TO FAMILY RESOURCES

The operation of marriage certification systems in the context of strong legal pluralism has important implications for the protection of family members' access to matrimonial rights and resources. We found several cases in Zambia relating to these issues as the following two examples show.

The first case is that of the magistrate above who was confused about the requiement for registration of both civil and customary marraiges, the court denied the petitioner the claim for damages for adultery they sought from the court because, in its view, the marriage was not registered.

In the second case,[45] in 2005, the respondent (the wife) in this case brought an action in the local court, which has unlimited jurisdiction to hear matrimonial causes in customary marriages.[46] The wife's petition was for divorce due to 'matrimonial disputes.' She also alleged that the appellant had deserted the matrimonial home. The local court dissolved the marriage and, in addition, awarded her the sum of K 3 million compensation[47] payable in monthly instalments of K70 000. The husband appealed this decision to the Subordinate Court on the ground, among others, that the amount of compensation ordered was too high. The subordinate court upheld the decision of the local court upon which the husband appealed to the High Court in 2008.

The grounds of appeal to the High Court were, inter alia, that: the magistrate misdirected himself in law and fact when he failed to appreciate the existence of the marriage certificate obtained from the Pentecostal Holiness Church by the parties to the marriage; and both the subordinate court and the local court did not have jurisdiction to dissolve the marriage celebrated under the Marriage Act, as evidenced by the marriage certificate obtained from the Pentecostal Holiness Church.

The parties appeared before the High Court in person (i.e. they were not represented by lawyers). The main argument of the appellant was that the marriage in question was solemnised by the Pentecostal Holiness Church and, therefore, a marriage under civil law which the courts below had no jurisdiction to dissolve. The High Court noted that the copy of the certificate was on record and stated: "the copy attests to the fact that the marriage between the appellant and respondent was solemnised by the Pentecostal Holiness Church on 11th December, 1982."[48]

45 *M v M*. The name of this case is abbreviated as it was not reported.

46 See Rule 4(a) (ii) of the Local Courts Rules in the Local Courts Act Cap 29 of the Laws of Zambia.

47 The local courts have for many years ordered spouses, especially husbands, to compensate each other in material terms upon the dissolution of the marriages. These payments apparently take the place of orders of spousal maintenance: see Himonga, op cit, n. 23, para. 163.

48 At p. 419.

In its judgment the High Court stated that the appeal turned on the narrow question of whether the courts below – the local court and subordinate court – had jurisdiction to hear the dispute. It held, *inter alia*, that: the marriage in question was a civil marriage which could only be dissolved by the High Court. Accordingly, the judge quashed the decision by the lower courts to dissolve the marriage, and the award to the respondent of K 3 million.

The judge in the High Court seems to have arrived at his decision that the marriage was not a customary but civil (or state-church) marriage on the ground that the certificate produced by the appellant attested "to the fact that the marriage between the appellant and respondent was solemnised by the Pentecostal Holiness Church on 11th December, 1982". The record does not show evidence of the Court enquiring into whether the parties had entered into a customary marriage or a civil marriage. The church certificate relied upon could as well have been the certificate issued to the parties to a customary marriage upon the blessing of the marriage by the church. In this case, the High Court would have confused the informal certification process of customary marriages by the churches with the state certification of civil marriages via churches. The confusion in turn resulted in the wife in a customary marriage being denied the right to the compensation or matrimonial property awarded by the lower courts, which the High Court quashed.

The confusion in the certification of marriages arising from the co-existence on the ground of both formal and informal processes of marriage certification, and the consequent denial by the state of justice and family resources to family members whose marriages are otherwise valid, evidently establishes the case for a parallel and decentralised model of certification of customary marriages in Africa with a view to simplification and elimination of confusion, to which I now turn.

VI The Parallel and Decentralised Certification Model

The discussion in the preceding sections of this paper has shown the importance of certification of marriages from both international and national perspectives that underscore the need for mandatory registration of customary marriages. Therefore, countries like Zambia that do not require mandatory registration of customary marriages should be motivated to establish legal mechanisms for mandatory registration of customary marriages just as they provide for registration of civil marriages.

The preceding sections of the paper have also shown that despite the narrow concept of state certification of marriages that South Africa and Zambia maintain at a formal level, there is a prevalence of strong legal pluralism represented by uncoordinated formal and informal systems of certification of marriage. These systems are so closely intertwined with each other that both state and non-state actors are sometimes confused by them in their practical operation. This confusion results in some family members being denied access to their family rights and resources wrongfully.

Arguably, there is a need to dismantle the narrow model of certification of marriages that concentrates the process of certification in the state exclusively. This model of certification should be replaced by a model that encompasses mandatory registration of customary marriages (and any other marriages recognised by the state) while responding to the prevailing strong pluralism in the certification of marriages. In other words, there is a need for mandatory parallel and decentralised certification of marriage systems. Our studies of the operation of certification of marriage systems in the pluralistic legal systems of South Africa and Zambia reveal many problems and challenges for both state and non-state actors.

These challenges may require multifaceted interventions to improve the certification systems. However, our research in both countries under study in this paper suggests that the major intervention needed should, firstly, take account of the grounded reality in which people who use the certification systems live their married lives and, secondly, aim at the management of the pluralistic certification processes in a manner that minimises the confusion among state and non-actors. In my view, the current state models of certification of marriages tend to simply mimic western-style certification systems that are based on a monolithic view of law centred in state authority and sources and characterised by formalism, centralisation and narrow state-based conceptualisations.

The model I propose for the certification of marriage calls for a parallel and decentralised certification system. The model should be introduced by a legislative framework and include the following core and essential features:

- Mandatory certification of customary marriages, but without the effect of nullification of the marriage for non-registration.
- Simplified certification processes that can be operated by ordinary (appropriately trained) citizens.
- Inclusivity of formal and informal processes of certification within the context of strong legal pluralism that characterise African legal systems.
- A high level of coordination of certification processes to avoid multiple certification of the same marriage.
- Sensitivity to the protection of vulnerable family members, such as women and children.
- Embedment of the value of solidarity, which underpins African marriages as reflected by the role the extended family plays in the formation of legal customary marriages, in the certification processes.[49]

---

49 A major finding of a recent study of legal pluralism and customary marriages in Southern Africa by F. Diallo & C. Himonga under the auspices of the research partnership *The State and Indigenous Legal Cultures: Law in Search of Legitimacy*, under the leadership of Professor Ghsilain Otis at the University of Ottawa, has shown that the value of solidarity underlies both customary and civil marriages of black Africans in Zambia

- Separate and decentralised registration processes for civil and customary marriages with clear signage in all languages spoken in the area at each facility.
- Certification of marriages at any stage of the marriage's existence while ensuring that vested rights of third parties are secured.
- Protection of the right of individuals to take any dispute about certification to a court especially established, capacitated and equipped to deal with this kind of dispute summarily and expeditiously.
- Inclusion of mechanisms for determining, from the parties at the time of registration of the marriage, the type of marriage they intend to register, accompanied with a system of referral of marriage couples by one registering authority to another registering authority in appropriate cases.

The exact manner of incorporation of these features of the model into individual countries' certification systems will depend on the social conditions and special characteristics of the legal system of each country.

VII Conclusion

The paper has attempted to show the importance of certification of customary marriages, and to demonstrate that despite the narrow conception of marriage certification adopted by the state, restricting certification to state-recognised authorities, in practice, within the context of strong legal pluralism, marriages are informally certified by multiple authorities and agencies. Not only are the formal and informal forums uncoordinated, they are also intertwined. The result is a complex certification system on the ground level of society, characterised by confusion among both state and non-state actors about the different forms of marriage and the substantive rights attaching to them. In the process of this confusion and state actions, family members' rights and access to family resources are compromised, if not lost.

In order to mitigate the challenges connected with the current marriage certification systems identified in this paper and to respond to the grounded reality of certification of marriages, the paper recommends a parallel and decentralised model of marriage certification with specific core features. Each country is to work the features of this model into its own social conditions and specific nature of the legal system.

---

and South Africa. Four research reports of these studies on Zambia and South Africa have been written by Diallo & Himonga, but they are not yet published.

The Evolution of European Court of Human Rights Case Law on the Right to Family Life through its Milestone Judgments on Same-Sex Couples (2010-2018)

*Dafni Lima**

I Introduction

In recent years, family law in Europe has undergone major changes on several fronts.[1] From increased legal recognition of same-sex couples to more elaborate approaches to parenthood, western jurisdictions across the globe have seen a wave of inclusive developments and sophisticated reconceptions of family law notions. Against this setting, forums that closely follow, identify and propel forward family law trends emerge as crucial convergence points for examining the ongoing changes in family law – and for assessing the direction towards which it might move in the near future.

The European Court of Human Rights (ECtHR) is one of the most significant such forums, bringing together a wide spectrum of jurisdictions in the European area and legal orders at its periphery, like Russia and Turkey. The ECtHR is thus perfectly positioned, amidst a range of jurisdictions with significant differences in how they approach key matters in family law,[2] to assess the emerging trends and consensus on crucial matters.

* Research Student (PhD candidate). The author can be reached at dafni.lima@cantab.net.

1 See especially 'Part IV. Current Family Law: Sweeping Modernisation – Breakthrough of Uniformity or Self-reproducing Diversity?' *in* M. Antokolskaia, *Harmonisation of Family Law in Europe: A Historical Perspective – A Tale of Two Millennia*, Intersentia, 2006; H. Krause, 'Comparative family law: Past traditions battle future trends – and vice versa', *in* M. Reimann & R. Zimmermann (Eds.), *The Oxford Handbook of Comparative Law*, Oxford University Press, 2006; C. McGlynn, *Families and the European Union*, Cambridge University Press, 2006; M. Antokolskaia, *Convergence and Divergence of Family Law in Europe*, Intersentia, 2007; K. Boele-Woelki & T. Sverdrup (Eds.), *European Challenges in Contemporary Family Law*, Intersentia, 2008; K. Boele-Woelki, N. Dethloff & W. Gephart (Eds.), *Family Law and Culture in Europe*, Intersentia, 2014; J.M. Scherpe (Ed.), *European Family Law – Volume II: The Changing Concept of 'Family' and Challenges for Domestic Family Law* and *Volume III: Family Law in a European Perspective*, Edward Elgar Publishing, 2016; K. Boele-Woelki & A. Fuchs (Eds.), *Same-Sex Relationships and Beyond*, 3rd ed., Intersentia, 2017; J.M. Scherpe & A. Hayward (Eds.), *The Future of Registered Partnerships*, Intersentia, 2017.

2 For more about the Court's case law in family law see A. Büchler, 'The Right to Respect for Private and Family Life: The Case Law of the European Court of Human Rights on Parenthood and Family Forms', *in* H. Keller & A. Büchler (Eds.), *Family Forms and Parenthood: Theory and Practice of Article 8 in Europe*,

Bringing together such diverging traditions is no easy feat[3] and precisely because of the politically and socially sensitive nature of family law (and human rights law in general), the Court has a long tradition of exercising its adjudicating competence carefully – sometimes too carefully, some of its critics (or rather, some of the fiercest proponents of the ECtHR project) would argue. Yet the fact that the ECtHR treads lightly is also a crucial aspect of why it is the ideal forum to look for tendencies that have gained firm ground in national legislations and in public opinion.

Furthermore, the European Convention on Human Rights (ECHR) does not provide for rights the content of which is set in stone and should be interpreted in a consistently restrictive way over time;[4] instead, as the ECtHR has reiterated time and again, the ECHR is a "living instrument"[5] and as such the content of the rights enshrined under it shall be adapted to accommodate evolving standards both in legislation and in social realities among Member-States. This quite unique and constantly evolving perspective places the Court in a very interesting position, one that combines its mandate to move forward slowly out of respect for its Member-States and their legislative choices, with the equally strong mandate to keep on moving forward and continue to enrich the content of the Convention rights by incorporating relevant developments.

Thus, each time the Court is called upon to adjudicate, it needs to strike a delicate balance among differing views between the various European countries, yet also accurately reflect where things stand in any matter within its scope. In that sense, the Court is perfectly positioned to assess tendencies and consensus among Member-States as well as provide an indication of further developments both in law and in relevant public opinion. In the field of family law specifically, the Court has in the past decade taken note and subsequently reflected in its judgments an overwhelming move towards legal recognition of same-sex couples.[6] Thus, examining the Court's case-law on the matter will hopefully provide a

---

Intersentia, 2016; D. Coester-Waltjen, 'The impact of the European Convention on Human Rights and the European Court of Human Rights on European family law', *in* J.M. Scherpe (Ed.), *European Family Law – Volume I: The Impact of Institutions and Organisations on European Family Law*, Edward Elgar Publishing, 2016, pp. 49-94.

3 For more on the Court's methodological approach to the right to family life under Article 8, see H. Keller, 'Article 8 in the System of the Convention', *in* Keller & Büchler (Eds.), ibid.

4 See also E. Brems & J. Gerards, 'Introduction' *in* E. Brems & J. Gerards (Eds.), *Shaping Rights in the ECHR*, Cambridge University Press, 2014, pp. 1-14.

5 See *E.B. v. France* [GC], no. 43546/02, § 92, 22 January 2008, and *Christine Goodwin v. United Kingdom*, no. 28957/95, 11 July 2002, §§ 74-75). See also M. Burbergs, 'How the right to respect for private and family life, home and correspondence became the nursery in which new rights are born – Article 8 ECHR' *in* Brems & Gerards (Eds.), ibid, pp. 319ff.

6 See also J.M. Scherpe, 'The Legal Recognition of Same-Sex Couples in Europe and the Role of the European Court of Human Rights', *The Equal Rights Review*, Vol. 10, 2013, pp. 83-96; L. Hodson, 'A Marriage by Any Other Name? *Schalk and Kopf v Austria*', *Human Rights Law Review*, Vol. 11, No. 1, 1 March 2011, pp. 170–179; N. Bamforth, 'Families but Not (Yet) Marriages? Same-Sex Partners and the Developing European Convention "Margin of Appreciation"', *Child and Family Law Quarterly*, Vol. 23, No. 1, 2011, pp. 128-143; C.M. Cerna, 'Introductory Note to Schalk and Kopf v. Austria', *International Legal Materials*, Vol. 49, No.

comprehensive overview of the rapidness of this development: in just five years, from the 2010 *Schalk and Kopf v. Austria* judgment to the 2015 *Oliari and Others v. Italy* judgment, the Court has shown a tremendous shift in its approach on the right of same-sex couples to have their unions legally recognised under Article 8 of the Convention.

Might this shift in fact be indicative of a further-reaching enrichment of our understanding of how we form "families"? To answer this question, this paper seeks to analyse the ECtHR's landmark jurisprudence on the right of same-sex couples to legal recognition of their unions in order to also examine the Court's understanding of the notion of 'family life' and how it has evolved over the years to accommodate changes in how individuals form committed relationships. In effect, this paper will seek to demonstrate that the Court has through its recent case law broadened its understanding of what it means to 'live together' as a couple and as a family to reflect relevant practice across a wide spectrum of European countries – a development extending beyond same-sex couples and pertaining to different-sex couples as well.[7]

II Broadening the Meaning of the Right to Family Life: ECtHR Landmark Judgments on Legal Recognition of Same-Sex Couples (2010-2015)

Family law and regulating family life has traditionally revolved around the fundamental notion of an different-sex couple, married, and bearing children within wedlock.[8] The gradual move towards a broader and more inclusive understanding of "family" was first reflected in the last two elements: children born out-of-wedlock were granted rights, while processes for legal recognition of parenthood by unmarried parents were introduced.[9]

---

5 (2010), pp. 1302-1305; P. Pustorino, 'Same-Sex Couples Before the ECtHR: The Right to Marriage', in: D. Gallo, L. Paladini & P. Pustorino (Eds.), *Same-Sex Couples before National, Supranational and International Jurisdictions*, Springer, 2014, pp. 399-408; D. Lima, 'Registered Partnerships in Greece and Cyprus', *in* Scherpe & Hayward (Eds.), op cit, n. 1; G. Zago, 'A Victory for Italian Same-Sex Couples, A Victory for European Homosexuals? A Commentary on Oliari v Italy', *Articolo 29*, 21 August 2015, available at SSRN: https://ssrn.com/abstract=2689060; A. Hayward, 'Same-Sex Registered Partnerships – A Right to be Recognised?', *Cambridge Law Journal*, Vol. 75, No. 1, March 2016, pp. 27-30.

7 In the future this might extend to other gender expressions as well – besides the currently dominant male-female binary – as these become increasingly recognised in law.

8 Scherpe, op cit, n. 6, p. 83.

9 See e.g. Schalk and Kopf v. Austria, no. 30141/04, 22.11.2010, § 91: "The Court reiterates its established case-law in respect of different-sex couples, namely that the notion of 'family' under this provision is not confined to marriage-based relationships and may encompass other de facto 'family' ties where the parties are living together out of wedlock. A child born out of such a relationship is ipso jure part of that "family" unit from the moment and by the very fact of his birth (see Elsholz v. Germany [GC], no. 25735/94, § 43, ECHR 2000-VIII; Keegan v. Ireland, 26 May 1994, § 44, Series A no. 290; and Johnston and Others v. Ireland, 18 December 1986, § 56, Series A no. 112)."

Similarly, the right to divorce was firmly established, especially as marriage gradually became disentangled from religious connotations and more openly associated with rights, obligations and benefits vis-à-vis the state, while de facto relationships and cohabitation became increasingly recognised in a wide range of European countries.[10]

Against this setting, same-sex couples have consistently pressed for and have gradually gained legal recognition for their unions – in various forms and varying degrees across the European area. In Europe, Nordic countries led the way, with Sweden providing same-sex de facto/cohabiting couples with legal recognition similar to different-sex couples in 1987; just two years later, in 1989, Denmark introduced same-sex registered partnerships. The Netherlands took over in 2001, when it became the first country to open up marriage to same-sex couples, with Belgium (2003) and Spain (2005) following closely.[11] In this context, the ECtHR has been called upon to adjudicate matters pertaining to legal recognition of same-sex couples, resulting in three milestone judgments in the last decade, which will be considered in this paper.

A Schalk and Kopf v. Austria (2010)

A major shift in the Court's approach to the issue of same-sex couples came with its *Schalk and Kopf* judgment in 2010. Mr. Schalk and Mr. Kopf, a same-sex couple and both Austrian nationals, lodged an application with the Court in August 2004, alleging that the Austrian state discriminated against them, as they did not have the option to marry or have their relationship otherwise legally recognised. In particular, the applicants invoked a violation of Article 12 (right to marry) and Article 8 (right to private and family life) in conjunction with Article 14 (prohibition of discrimination).

Prior to resorting to the ECtHR, the couple had in 2002 requested the Austrian authorities to allow them to get married, a request that was rejected as same-sex marriage was not provided for under Austrian law. They then took the matter up with the Vienna Regional Governor and with the Constitutional Court, but in both cases their appeal was rejected, and the authorities reiterated that marriage was reserved for different-sex couples. As a last resort, the applicants turned to the ECtHR. By the time the Court came to adjudicate on the matter, in February and June 2010, the second part of their complaint (absence of any type of legal recognition) had been rendered irrelevant, since as of January 2010 Austria had introduced the Registered Partnership Act (*Eingetragene Partnerschaft-Gesetz*) which regulated – and was limited to – same-sex couples.[12] As such, the Court primarily

10 See for a more thorough account K. Boele-Woelki, C. Mol & E. van Gelder (Eds.), *European Family Law in Action: Volume V - Informal Relationships*, Intersentia, 2015.

11 Scherpe, op cit, n. 6, pp. 83-84.

12 *Schalk and Kopf*, §§ 16-17.

focused on whether the applicants had the right to marry under the Convention, while it also examined whether Austria should have introduced registered partnerships earlier than it did. The Court did not find that Member-States had a general positive obligation to introduce registered partnerships and as such found no violation of Article 8 in conjunction with Article 14.[13]

With regard to Article 12, it should be noted that this was the first time that the Strasbourg Court was called upon to decide on a potential right of same-sex couples to marry.[14] Interestingly, one of the arguments put forward by the applicants in their arguments for opening up marriage to same-sex couples was precisely that the concept of marriage has evolved beyond its traditional association with bearing and raising children. In particular, they argued that

> in today's society civil marriage was a union of two persons which encompassed all aspects of their lives, while the procreation and education of children was no longer a decisive element. As the institution of marriage had undergone considerable changes there was no longer any reason to refuse same-sex couples access to marriage.[15]

The Court had already sided with this broader understanding of marriage, as it had found in its previous *Christine Goodwin* judgment that the "inability to conceive or parent a child cannot be regarded as per se removing the right to marry".[16] Although the Court firmly stated that this previous finding did not allow any direct conclusions with regard to the right of same-sex couples to marriage, it is evident that the dissociation of marriage and procreation was formulated broadly and could thus be transported into the *Schalk and Kopf* reasoning, lending legitimacy to the applicants' argument about the evolution of the concept of marriage. This transposition of a general finding in the case of a transgender party's right to marry to a case involving a same-sex couple is precisely a demonstration of how findings in the framework of legal recognition of same-sex couples could be transported to cases concerning e.g. different-sex couples.

In its judgment, the Court conceded precisely that "the institution of marriage has undergone major social changes since the adoption of the Convention", yet concerning specifically the right to marry, it noted the absence of European consensus regarding same-sex marriage;[17] thus the Court did not side with the applicants and did not find a violation of Article 12, as it held that as things stood there was no obligation for Member-States to

13 Ibid, §§ 109-110.
14 Ibid, § 50.
15 Ibid, § 44.
16 Ibid, § 56, with reference to *Christine Goodwin*, § 98.
17 Ibid, § 58.

grant same-sex couples the right to marry.[18] Tellingly, the Court observed that "marriage has deep-rooted social and cultural connotations which may differ largely from one society to another" and reiterated that "it must not rush to substitute its own judgment in place of that of the national authorities, who are best placed to assess and respond to the needs of society".[19] This last part would be radically qualified in its subsequent *Oliari* judgment just five years later.

Although the applicants lost the case, arguably the most important parts of the Court's judgment are not to be found in the actual rejection of their requests, but in the Court's shift regarding its overall approach to same-sex couples.[20] Notably, the Court found that same-sex couples do fall within the ambit of Article 12, stating that it

> would no longer consider that the right to marry enshrined in Article 12 must in all circumstances be limited to marriage between two persons of the opposite sex. Consequently, it cannot be said that Article 12 is inapplicable to the applicants' complaint.[21]

In its more recent *Orlandi v. Italy* judgment, the Court reiterated that

> while it is true that some Contracting States have extended marriage to same-sex partners, Article 12 cannot be construed as imposing an obligation on the Contracting States to grant access to marriage to same-sex couples.[22]

In *Schalk and Kopf*, the Court also departed from its previous approach which confined its examination of same-sex couples to the notion of "private life" and took the opportunity to clearly state that these also fall under the notion of "family life". In particular, the Court noted "a rapid evolution of social attitudes towards same-sex couples" as a "considerable number of member States have afforded legal recognition to same-sex couples" and "[c]ertain provisions of European Union law also reflect a growing tendency to include same-sex couples in the notion of 'family'"[23] and it went on to famously state that

> in view of this evolution, the Court considers it artificial to maintain the view that, in contrast to a different-sex couple, a same-sex couple cannot enjoy "family life" for the purposes of Article 8. Consequently, the relationship of the

18 Ibid, §§ 63-64.
19 Ibid, § 62.
20 Scherpe, op cit, n. 6, p. 91.
21 *Schalk and Kopf*, § 61.
22 *Orlandi and Others v. Italy*, nos. 26431/12, 26742/12, 44057/12 and 60088/12, § 145, 14.3.2018.
23 *Schalk and Kopf*, § 93.

> applicants, a cohabiting same-sex couple living in a stable de facto partnership, falls within the notion of "family life", just as the relationship of a different-sex couple in the same situation would.[24]

With this radical move in its approach the Court decisively pushed forward both in the level of protection that should be granted to same-sex couples and in the degree of scrutiny that it should impose upon the individual States' well-established "margin of appreciation".[25] Yet further than that, it also enriched the concept of "family life" under the Convention, deeming that a "cohabiting (same-sex) couple living in a stable de facto partnership" should be understood as a family. In its subsequent *Vallianatos* judgment, the Court proceeded even further in adapting its understanding of the notion of family life, by including non-cohabiting couples.

B *Vallianatos and Others v. Greece (2013)*

In its 2013 *Vallianatos and Others v. Greece* the Court had the opportunity to revisit the matter of legal recognition of same-sex couples by examining two applications lodged in 2009 by four Greek same-sex couples that complained of a violation of Article 8 in conjunction with Article 14. In particular, they complained that Greece, in its rather original approach to introduce registered partnerships only for different-sex couples by virtue of law 3719/2008, while marriage was also reserved only for different-sex couples – thus becoming the first European country to provide both options to different-sex couples and none to same-sex couples – infringed on their right to private and family life and discriminated against same-sex couples.[26] The Court agreed with the applicants and found that a violation of Article 8 in conjunction with Article 14 had taken place; in a nutshell, while it noted that opening up marriage remains within the wide margin of appreciation of states, introducing another form of formalising committed relationships and reserving this for different-sex couples did amount to a discrimination that the Greek Government failed to justify.

Among the most striking conclusions of the Court was its focus on the social status and acceptance that legal recognition would confer on same-sex couples, besides rights and obligations. In particular, the applicants complained that

---

24 *Schalk and Kopf*, § 94.

25 Scherpe, op cit, n. 6, p. 91. See also *Schalk and Kopf*, § 77: "It followed from the Court's Karner judgment (cited above, § 40) that the protection of the traditional family was a weighty and legitimate reason, but it had to be shown that a given difference was also necessary to achieve that aim. In the applicants' assertion, nothing showed that the exclusion of same-sex couples from marriage was necessary to protect the traditional family."

26 For a more elaborate account of the case and its significance for Greek law, see Lima, op cit, n. 6.

> instead of taking positive steps to overcome prejudice against gays and lesbians in Greek society, the respondent State had reinforced that prejudice by enacting Law no. 3719/2008 without including same-sex couples. ... [T]he Law in question cast a negative moral judgment on homosexuality as it reflected an unjustifiable reserve, not to say hostility, towards same-sex couples. Having decided to move away from marriage as the sole formal basis of family life, the legislature had shown a clear disregard for same-sex couples by excluding them from the scope of Law no. 3719/2008.[27]

The Greek Government counter-argued that same-sex couples could have the same rights and obligations as those they would have under a registered partnership under law 3719/2008 by simply entering into a contract that would provide for them.[28] Yet the Court noted that registered partnerships "as an officially recognised alternative to marriage" would carry an "intrinsic value" for the applicants, "irrespective of the legal effects, however narrow or extensive, that they would produce".[29] It observed that same-sex couples "sharing their lives" have the same needs when it comes to "mutual support and assistance" as different-sex couples do and highlighted that entering into a registered partnership would grant same-sex couples "the only opportunity available to them under Greek law of formalising their relationship by conferring on it a legal status recognised by the State" and therefore regulate issues concerning property and inheritance "not as private individuals entering into contracts under the ordinary law but on the basis of the legal rules governing civil unions, thus having their relationship officially recognised by the State".[30] Finally, the Court further stressed that

> same-sex couples would have a particular interest in entering into a civil union since it would afford them, unlike different-sex couples, the sole basis in Greek law on which to have their relationship legally recognised.[31]

In adopting this line of reasoning focused on the "intrinsic value" and the uniqueness of having a relationship officially recognised and regulated by the state, the Court ventured out of the confines of a narrow definition of the right to private and family life and took into account factors like the promotion of social acceptance, visibility and status, besides mere rights and obligations. Even if this remains particularly relevant in the context of same-sex unions, the same line of reasoning could be pursued in other cases, too.

---

27 *Vallianatos and Others v. Greece*, nos. 29381/09 and 32684/09, 7.11.2013, § 60.
28 Ibid, § 80.
29 Ibid, § 81.
30 Ibid, § 81.
31 Ibid, § 90.

It is interesting to note at this point, that in its more recent *Ratzenböck and Seydl v. Austria* judgment,[32] the Court examined the application of a different-sex couple who complained that the Austrian law on registered partnerships – mentioned above in the context of *Schalk and Kopf* – violated their rights under Article 8, since it was only open to same-sex couples. The Court found that while both same-sex and different-sex couples were in need of legal recognition and protection of their relationships, since the applicants had access to the similar institution of marriage and as such had access to a form of legal recognition, there was no violation under Article 8. By contrast, same-sex couples in both *Schalk and Kopf* and *Vallianatos* had no other means of protecting their relationship, so the Court found that the applicants in *Ratzenböck and Seydl* were not in a comparable situation to a same-sex couple.

In their dissenting opinion in *Ratzenböck and Seydl*, judges Tsotsoria and Grozev argued instead that the situation between different-sex couples and same-sex couples was comparable and analogous and as such any difference in their treatment should be justified, but the Austrian Government had failed to offer any such strong justification hence a violation of Article 8 had taken place. They further argued that the majority's reasoning was incompatible with the Court's approach to the right of same-sex couples to marry – in the context of which it has found that the situation between same-sex and different-sex couples is analogous yet the exclusion of same-sex couples from marriage is justified – and would lead the Court down a road of a "separate but equal" approach that could prove dangerous.

Returning to the *Vallianatos* judgment, perhaps its most important aspect for the scope of this paper is the fact that the Court enriched its understanding of what it means to live together as a couple and form a "committed relationship" by accepting that couples who do not cohabit fall under these notions. In particular, the Court noted that one of the couples that lodged an application were in a relationship but "for professional and social reasons" did not live together.[33] The Court further took into account that one of them paid for the other's social security contributions, as demonstrated by their bank statements, which it took as evidence of their mutual support and commitment vis-à-vis one another.[34]

While the Greek Government urged the Court to make a distinction between the couples sharing a home and the ones who did not and examine only the former under the notion of "family life" and the latter under the notion of "private life",[35] the Court refused to do so. In fact, it noted that it could

32 *Ratzenböck and Seydl v. Austria*, no. 28475/12, 26.10.2017.

33 *Vallianatos and Others v. Greece*, § 8.

34 Ibid, § 8.

35 Ibid, § 65.

> see no basis for drawing the distinction requested by the Government … between those applicants who live together and those who – for professional and social reasons – do not …, since in the instant case the fact of not cohabiting does not deprive the couples concerned of the stability which brings them within the scope of family life within the meaning of Article 8.[36]

In this sense, the Court accepted a broader meaning of a stable and committed relationship – one that it would further elaborate in its subsequent *Oliari* judgment.

C *Oliari and Others v. Italy (2015)*

In 2015, just five years after *Schalk and Kopf*, came the most notable ECtHR judgment regarding legal recognition of same-sex couples to date, as it found that Member-States have an obligation to provide same-sex unions with some form of legal recognition. This time it was three Italian same-sex couples that lodged applications with the Court in 2011 and quite similarly to Mr. Schalk and Mr. Kopf complained that the Italian state did not afford them any legal status and invoked Articles 12 and 8 in conjunction with Article 14. Again, similarly to the *Schalk and Kopf* case, the first couple (Mr. Oliari and Mr. A.) asked the local authorities for a marriage permit, a request which was denied. They appealed with local and regional courts and the Constitutional Court, to no avail – the judicial authorities instead found that marriage under current Italian law was reserved to different-sex couples. However, the Constitutional Court did suggest that same-sex couples should be granted some form of legal recognition but stressed that this fell within the competence of the legislature and not of the Italian judiciary.

The applicants themselves complained that "the recognition in law of one's family life and status was crucial for the existence and well-being of an individual and for his or her dignity", stressing that they were left to suffer "a state of uncertainty" and be "at the mercy of judicial discretion".[37] They also submitted "empirical evidence" to the Court which demonstrated that countries which did not recognize same-sex unions had lower social acceptance rates regarding homosexuality.[38] Lastly, they noted that wedding ceremonies "brought social legitimacy and acceptance, and particularly in the case of homosexuals", as they denoted that same-sex couples "also have the right to live freely and to live their relationships on an equal basis, both in private and in public" and that total lack of legal recognition "brought about in them a sense of belonging to an inferior class of persons"

36 Ibid, § 73.

37 *Oliari and Others v. Italy*, nos. 18766/11 and 36030/11, 21.10.2015, § 107.

38 Ibid, § 113.

despite the fact that same-sex and different-sex couples had the same needs in terms of emotional support.[39]

It is interesting to note that the Court highlighted facts such as the undertaking of further studies by one partner thanks to the financial support of the other, designating one another as guardians in the event of incapacitation, opening a joint bank account, and formally registering their cohabitation, as indicators of the stability and commitment of the couples' relationships. It further reaffirmed that same-sex and different-sex couples are equally capable of entering into stable, committed relationships and that they share a need for legal recognition; in particular, the Court reiterated that it had "already acknowledged that same-sex couples are in need of legal recognition and protection of their relationship".[40]

Furthermore, it struck down the recurring argument that same-sex couples could regulate their relationship on a contractual basis by noting that "the aim of such contracts is not that of the recognition and protection of the couple", as is demonstrated by the fact that "they are open to anyone cohabiting, irrespective of whether they are a couple in a committed stable relationship".[41]

In one of the most interesting aspects of its judgment, the Court recalled its position in *Vallianatos* and reaffirmed that cohabitation is not a requirement for a stable relationship; instead, it elaborated that

> in the globalised world of today various couples, married or in a registered partnership, experience periods during which they conduct their relationship at long distance, needing to maintain residence in different countries, for professional or other reasons

and concluded that "that fact in itself has no bearing on the existence of a stable committed relationship and the need for it to be protected".[42]

Furthermore, the Court noted that instability and inconsistency in terms of the current protection under Italian law, which relied too much on judicial and administrative discretion (as the country does not have a strict rule of judicial precedent) undermined the Government's argument that current protection was sufficient; it also highlighted in a more general fashion that "coherence of administrative and legal practices within the domestic system must be regarded as an important factor in the assessment carried out under Article 8".[43]

---

39 Ibid, § 116.
40 Ibid, § 165.
41 Ibid, § 169.
42 Ibid, § 169.
43 Ibid, § 172.

In terms of its generally cautious approach with regard to overstepping the margin of appreciation of states, the Court observed a "conflict" between the social reality that the applicants experienced by living openly as same-sex couples and the law's failure to catch up with that reality and grant them legal protection; instead, it noted that introducing legal recognition would not impose any particular burden on the Italian state but would, quite to the contrary, serve an "important social need" when it comes to the large number of homosexual and bisexual individuals living in Italy.[44]

It also stressed that the case at hand did not concern secondary, supplementary rights, where a wider margin of appreciation might be entertained due to sensitive nature of the issue, but core rights such as the very recognition of a legal status for same-sex couples and fundamental protection, which the Court found to be "facets of an individual's existence and identity to which the relevant margin should apply".[45]

After noting a general global tendency towards legal recognition of same-sex unions,[46] the Court departed from its usual overcautious approach and observed that

> while the Government is usually better placed to assess community interests, in the present case the Italian legislature seems not to have attached particular importance to the indications set out by the national community, including the general Italian population and the highest judicial authorities in Italy[47]

and noted that the Italian Constitutional Court "notably and repeatedly" called for legal recognition of same-sex unions by the legislature.[48] The Court further took note of public opinion polls which suggested popular support of same-sex couples and of their need for legal protection.[49]

In conclusion, the Court found that there existed a positive obligation under Article 8 to grant legal recognition to same-sex couples, and found that "the Italian Government have overstepped their margin of appreciation and failed to fulfil their positive obligation to ensure that the applicants have available a specific legal framework providing for the recognition and protection of their same-sex unions".[50] Lastly, the Court stressed that to conclude otherwise would mean that the Court would show unwillingness "to take note of the changing conditions in Italy and be reluctant to apply the Convention in a way which is practical and effective".[51]

---

44 Ibid, § 173.
45 Ibid, § 177.
46 Ibid, § 178.
47 Ibid, § 179.
48 Ibid, § 180.
49 Ibid, § 181.
50 Ibid, § 185.
51 Ibid, § 186.

III Conclusions

Through these milestone judgments, the Court has noted that in a period of just five years that passed between *Schalk and Kopf* until the *Oliari* judgment, a rapid and overwhelming development concerning legal recognition of same-sex couples had already taken place. Recognising this evolution, the Court has considerably enriched its understanding of a same-sex couple's right to family life under the Convention. In *Schalk and Kopf* (2010), it found that it could not be inferred from Article 8 that Austria had a positive obligation to introduce registered partnerships earlier than it did. In *Vallianatos* (2013), it found that while states were still enjoying a particularly broad margin of appreciation on the socially and politically sensitive issue of same-sex marriage, when they introduced another form of legal recognition of couples besides marriage then they had the obligation to open it up to same-sex couples – unless specific and weighty reasoning was provided for their exclusion. In *Oliari* (2015), noting the now widespread legal recognition of same-sex couples in the European area, it found that Italy had a positive obligation to provide some form of legal recognition to same-sex couples – irrespective of whether the country had moved away from the monopoly of marriage in regulating different-sex committed relationships.

More recently, in its 2016 *Chapin and Charpentier v. France* judgment[52] the Court confirmed its earlier position in *Schalk and Kopf* that no right to same-sex marriage currently exists under the Convention.[53] By the time that the application lodged by Mr. Chapin and Mr. Charpentier in 2007, concerning the decision of a French court to annul the marriage they concluded in 2004 in Bègles, was adjudicated before the Court, France had already opened up marriage to same-sex couples.

The Court however did not pass up on the opportunity to affirm that even though changing social views have profoundly affected the concept of marriage, no positive obligation existed yet for states to introduce the right to marry for same-sex couples and that the question of doing so or not remained a matter for national laws. The Court further reiterated that it should not rush to substitute its own assessment in the place of that of national authorities, which are better placed to appreciate the situation, as it had also stated in *Schalk and Kopf*.[54] The same findings were repeated in its *Orlandi* judgment, where the Court, however, found that a violation of Article 8 had occurred when the Italian state failed to offer any form of legal protection to same-sex couples that were married abroad.[55]

Beyond the right of same-sex couples to have their unions legally recognised, the three judgments discussed above also pushed forward the Court's understanding of the notion of "family life" under Article 8 in a more general and far-reaching fashion, such as that

52 *Chapin and Charpentier v. France*, no. 40183/07, 9.6.2016, available only in French.
53 Ibid, § 36.
54 Ibid, § 36.
55 *Orlandi and Others v. Italy*, §§ 210-211.

the now enriched concept might be applied in future judgments not necessarily pertaining to same-sex couples. With *Schalk and Kopf* the Court took a decisive step towards broadening the concept of family in order to include "alternative" committed relationships other than the traditional different-sex couple. By encompassing same-sex couples, the Court demonstrated its readiness and willingness to adapt the notion of "family" in order to reflect social reality, hinting that, in the future, other "non-conventional" types of unions might be considered as families – for example, unions of more than two persons or of non-binary individuals. In *Vallianatos* and *Oliari* it further noted and integrated the social reality of committed, stable couples "living apart together", in long-distance relationships, across borders or sharing a home only for parts of their time together. The Court thus took note of the effect of globalisation on how people nowadays form relationships, especially in the EU area where borders are more easily and conveniently crossed, thanks to the fundamental freedom of movement of EU citizens – and their formal partners.

This increasingly porous nature of borders in the EU area might be precisely one of the springboards of further and more uniform legal recognition of same-sex couples. In his 11 January 2018 Opinion, the Advocate General to the Court of Justice of the European Union advised the CJEU that same-sex spouses recognised in one member-state should be recognised as such across EU member-states with regard to the freedom of movement, even in member-states that have not yet opened up marriage to same-sex couples. The Opinion was given in the context of Case C-673/16 "Relu Adrian Coman and Others v Inspectoratul General pentru Imigrări and Others", concerning the right of the same-sex spouse of a Romanian citizen to be granted the right to live and work in Romania, where foreign spouses of Romanian citizens are generally granted such a right but where same-sex marriage is not recognised.[56]

In its subsequent Judgment of 5 June 2018, the Grand Chamber of the CJEU followed that Opinion and decided that in the case of same-sex couples, member-states are precluded from denying a third-country national a derived right of residence on the basis that their law does not recognise same-sex marriage.[57] It also noted that the term "spouse" used under the relevant EU legislation is gender-neutral[58] and that when member-states exercise their legislative competence they must comply with EU law.[59]

Statistics show that the family landscape and with it the issues that family law is called upon to regulate keep changing in the EU area. According to Eurostat, from 1965 to 2013 crude marriage rates went down by almost 50%, while in 2014 42% of children were born

56 Court of Justice of the European Union, Press Release No 02/18 – Luxembourg, 11 January 2018, available at: https://curia.europa.eu/jcms/jcms/p1_697974/fr/.

57 Court of Justice of the European Union [GC], Judgment, Case C-673/16, 5.6.2018, § 58.

58 Ibid, § 34.

59 Ibid, §§ 37-38.

outside of marriage.[60] At the same time, divorce rates keep rising – triggered also by the gradual legalisation and social acceptance of divorce – and in 2011 there was roughly one divorce for every two marriages.[61] The decline of marriage is also reflected in the rise of alternative forms of living together: in 2011, almost 1 in 10 people aged over 20 lived in a "consensual union" (that is, sharing a household in a committed relationship without being married or in a registered partnership) and the percentage reached 15% among young people aged 20 to 29.[62]

We have come a long way from the traditional paradigm of the married different-sex couple raising children mentioned at the start of this paper. New ways of forming relationships, of living together, of raising children, and of legally recognising these ties are constantly unfolding in most European states. Whether we choose to call these new forms of living together "families" or not is as much a political and ideological question as it is a legal one. In this sense, reaching out to include new social realities into the legal definition of "family life" demonstrates an open-minded approach on part of the ECtHR that could transcend the specifics of the individual cases discussed above and pave the way for future, more inclusive judgments in family law.

60 EUROSTAT, Marriage and divorce statistics, online at: http://ec.europa.eu/eurostat/statistics-explained/index.php/Marriage_and_divorce_statistics.

61 EUROSTAT, Marriage and birth statistics - new ways of living together in the EU, available at: http://ec.europa.eu/eurostat/statistics-explained/index.php/Marriage_and_birth_statistics_-_new_ways_of_living_together_in_the_EU"

62 Ibid.

Cohabitation Laws: Where Do We Go from Here?

*Zanele Nyoni**

I Introduction

Over the past decade, figures from the Office of National Statistics show that across the UK cohabiting couples have more than doubled in number, making it the fastest growing family form.[1] The context of cohabitation is becoming increasingly diverse; with socio-economic factors, religion and ethnic background all playing an important role in the decision of whether or not to marry.[2] In comparison to their married counterparts, cohabiting couples have little financial protection when the relationship ends or upon the death of a partner. It is not that cohabitants do not have any legal rights; instead the law has not yet developed a comprehensive approach to cohabiting couples. In some contexts, they are treated as if they were married, in others they are accorded lesser rights, and in others they have no rights at all, or at least none that are specific to their status as cohabitants. As a result, cohabiting couples have to resort to piecemeal legislation and a legal framework which often produces undesirable outcomes. Instances of inequity and hardship are widespread, and the results have been described as confusing, complex, usually inferior and hardly ever automatic.[3]

Proposals for reform have intensified in recent years, but as yet no action has been taken. This article does not presuppose what policy would be ideal for cohabitants, but instead examines the criticisms of the existing law and considers a possible way forward.

---

* Solicitor, Lecturer in Law, Lancashire Law School, University of Central Lancashire.

1 In 2017 cohabiting couple families reached 3.3 million; see Office of National Statistics, *Families and Household in the UK (2017)*. By contrast, there were 12.9 million married or civil partner couple families and this remains the most common type of family.

2 For example, see J. Eekelaar & M. Maclean, 'Marriage and the Moral Bases of Personal Relationships' *Journal of Law and Society*, Vol. 31, 2004, pp. 510-538.; E. van Acker, *Marriage and Values in Public Policy: Conflicts in the UK, the US and Australia*, 1st ed., New York, Routledge, 2017, pp. 26-34.

3 A. Barlow, S. Duncan, G. James & A. Park, *Cohabitation, Marriage and the Law: Social Change and Legal Reform in the 21st Century*, 1st ed., Hart Publishing, 2005, p. 2.

II Proposed Reforms

In 2007, following consultation, the Law Commission recommended the introduction of a new scheme of financial relief on separation based on contributions made to the relationship by the parties (rather than on the respective needs of the parties as in divorce).[4] The key features of the recommended scheme were that cohabiting couples who had satisfied certain eligibility requirements should be able to apply for financial relief on separation unless they had specifically opted out of the scheme.[5] The applicant would also have to show that the respondent retained a benefit, or that the applicant had a continuing disadvantage, as a result of contributions made to the relationship.[6] The level of financial relief would be determined by the court having regard to a list of discretionary factors that include the welfare of any relevant children, the financial needs, obligations and resources of both parties, and their conduct.

In 2008, the government announced that no action would be taken to implement the scheme in England and Wales until research on the cost and effectiveness of similar principles introduced in Scotland could be studied.[7]

By 2011, the coalition government announced that the findings of the research into Scottish legislation did not provide a sufficient basis for a change in the law, and as a result it did not intend to take forward the Law Commission's recommendations for reform of cohabitation law.[8] The scheme was not intended to provide cohabiting couples with the same rights as married couples and it was not intended that cohabiting couples would be obligated to meet each other's future needs.

Since the Law Commission's recommendations, there have been a number of bills introduced by private members advocating the implementation of these proposals.[9] Previous bills have, so far, failed to generate government support (amongst many reasons) on the basis that it would create a quasi-legal matrimonial structure based on an arbitrary length of time of cohabitation, and that it would be more beneficial for society to encourage marriage rather than cohabitation. The government has argued that rights and responsi-

4 Law Commission, *Cohabitation: the financial consequences of relationship breakdown*, Law Com. No. 307, 2007.

5 Law Commission, ibid, para. 3.24 provides that couples who have had children together or who have lived together for a minimum period would be eligible. The Law Commission recommended that the minimum period for couples without children should be set within a range of two to five years.

6 Law Commission, ibid, para. 1.19.

7 Written Ministerial Statement to Parliament, Hansard HC, col 123WS, 6 March 2008. For information on the operation of the scheme in Scotland, see the briefing paper issued by F. Wasoff, J. Miles & E. Mordaunt, 'No longer living together: how does Scots cohabitation law work in practice?', *University of Cambridge Faculty of Law Research Paper*, No. 11/02, 1 October 2010.

8 Written Ministerial Statement to Parliament, Hansard HL, col WS19, 6 September 2011.

9 The first reading of the Cohabitation Rights Bill 2017 took place in July 2017, However the general debate on all aspects of the Bill is yet to be scheduled.

bilities that come with being a spouse should not be imposed on a couple that has chosen not to marry.[10]

III Current Law: Jointly Owned Property

In order to understand the current position, an examination of the law applicable to cohabitants is necessary to understand what aspects of the law should be corrected through reform. In England and Wales, the court has the power to redistribute the assets of a divorcing couple by virtue of the Matrimonial Causes Act 1973.[11] This enables the court to make a wide range of property orders regardless of the legal ownership of the property. The aim of the court in redistributing the assets is to ensure fairness between the parties[12] by considering the financial needs of the parties, whether there should be compensation for economic disadvantage caused by the way the parties conducted their marriage, and the equal sharing principle which is derived from the basic concept of equality permeating a marriage.[13]

In stark contrast, there are no statutory rights protecting cohabitants on the breakdown of the relationship. Instead, cohabitants must rely on complex property and trust law to establish an interest in the home[14]. The court can only declare ownership of assets and has no power to redistribute property, therefore much will depend on whether the legal title is held solely or in joint names. If the property is held in the parties' joint names, there will be a presumption that the beneficial interest will be held jointly. However, this position is rebuttable if a joint owner can show that it was not the intention to hold the beneficial interest in equal proportions. If the parties have never discussed ownership of the property the court can draw inferences from the parties' conduct.

10 Hansard HL Debate 12 December 2014, cols 2069-2085.

11 When dividing the assets of the parties, a wide range of matters are taken into account, such as the housing and financial needs of the parties; their ages and the duration of the marriage; future earning capacity; their standard of living; and any disability of either party.

12 See *White v White* [2000] UKHL 54 at paras. 24-25 (paraphrased) in seeking to achieve a fair outcome there is no discrimination between a husband who earned the money and the wife who looked after the home and the children and as such, fairness requires that their respective roles should not prejudice or advantage either party. Before reaching a firm conclusion and making an order as to the division of assets, a judge should check his tentative views against the "yardstick of equality of division". Equality should be departed from only if there are good reasons for doing so.

13 *Miller v Miller; McFarlane v McFarlane* [2006] UKHL 24 paras. 8-17.

14 Under s. 14 Trusts of Land and Appointment of Trustees Act 1996, claims can be made for an order declaring the nature and extent of person's interest in property and/or for an order for sale of the property. In determining an application, the court must have regard to the matters contained in s. 15 of the Act.

IV Current Law: Soley Owned Property

Where the legal title to property vests in one party, and there is no formal declaration of trust, the presumption is that "equity follows the law"[15] and the legal owner is entitled to the beneficial interest. If the other party has made a direct contribution to the purchase price,[16] this gives rise to the presumption of a resulting trust and the contributor acquires a beneficial interest. Nevertheless, this presumption is rebuttable if it can be shown that there was no intention for the contributor to acquire an equitable interest.[17] The problems in this area arise in situations where the parties are not joint legal owners and they cannot agree on their respective shares. In such cases the court must determine whether the legal owner holds the property on trust for another party who will have an equitable interest by virtue of a constructive trust.

Since *Lloyds Bank v Rosset,*[18] the courts have dealt with such constructive trust claims through a strict two stage process. First, the finding of a common intention between the parties to share the beneficial interest (a detrimental reliance on that common intention), and second, the quantification of that share.[19] In *Rosset,* Lord Bridge stated that a common intention was "based on evidence of express discussions between the parties, however imperfectly remembered and however imprecise their terms may have been."[20] Where there is no evidence to support a finding of an agreement or arrangement to share, inference can be drawn from the conduct of the parties. Lord Bridge further added that

> direct contributions to the purchase price by the partner who is not the legal owner, whether initially or by payment of mortgage instalments, will readily justify the inference necessary to the creation of a constructive trust ... [I]t is at least extremely doubtful whether anything else will do.[21]

This suggests a restrictive approach to considering financial contributions and poses an obstacle that is too high.[22] This approach has been heavily criticised as it relies on evidence of either an express or implied common intention to share the ownership of the property

15 *Stack v Dowden* [2007] UKHL 17.
16 *Gissing v Gissing* [1971] AC 886 (indirect financial contributions such as paying the household bills will not give rise to a resulting trust).
17 *Re Sharpe (A bankrupt)* [1980] 1 WLR 219 (a direct contribution to the purchase price by way of a gift or loan will rebut the presumption).
18 [1991] 1 AC 107.
19 *Lloyds Bank v Rosset* [1991] 1 AC 107.
20 Ibid at 132.
21 Ibid at 133.
22 *Stack v Dowden,* op cit, n. 15.

and in many cases it is difficult to discern not only what each party might have intended, but also to identify commonly held intentions, assuming that they ever existed.[23]

In *James v Thomas,*[24] the parties had cohabited for 15 years in a property acquired in the sole name of Mr Thomas. When the relationship ended the claimant sought a beneficial share of the home and relied on evidence that during discussion regarding improvement to the property, Mr Thomas had replied that "this will benefit us both". The court found no evidence of an express common intention to share the beneficial title, instead Mr Thomas' remarks were construed as statements regarding the shared use and enjoyment of the property. It is in the context of these uncertainties that it is clear that there needs to be a review of the current law on ownership of property by cohabitants.[25]

Where it is not possible to find evidence of an express agreement to share, it will be necessary to infer an agreement by considering other factors. Unlike the restrictive approach in *Rosset,* in recent cases the courts have been willing to consider the "whole course of conduct in relation to the property"[26] and that the law has moved on since the strict approach on common intention in *Rosset.* In order for the court to ascertain what the parties intended, "many more factors than financial contributions may be relevant to divining the parties' true intentions".[27] These include the purpose for which the home was acquired; the nature of the parties 'relationship and the parties' individual characters and personalities. Inferring common intention is not an easy feat as it depends on the judge's analysis of the facts, which may render outcomes unpredictable, and quite possibly in contrast to the parties actual intentions.[28]

Furthermore, there are limitations as to the types of conduct the courts will consider as sufficient to demonstrate an intention to share the beneficial ownership. Some decisions seem to accept that indirect financial contributions such as making a payment of the bills and therefore, enabling the owner to afford the mortgage, constitutes sufficient conduct.[29]

---

23 R. Probert, 'Equality in the Family Home?', *Feminist Legal Studies,* Vol. 15, No. 3, 2007, pp. 341-353.
24 [2007] EWCA Civ 1212, [2008] 1 FLR 1598.
25 J. Bray, 'Cohabitation: The long slow road to reform', *Family Law,* Vol. 46, No. 12, 2016, pp. 1428-1437.
26 *Stack v Dowden,* op cit, n. 15.
27 Ibid; see para. 69 for a full list of factors.
28 J. Mee, 'Jones v Kernott: Inferring and Imputing in Essex', *Conveyancer and Property Lawyer,* Vol. 2, 2012, pp. 167-180.
29 *Lefoe v Lefoe* [2001] 2 FLR 970; *Gissing,* op cit, n. 16, per Lord Diplock: "The court is not entitled to infer a common intention to this effect from the mere fact that she provided chattels for joint use in the new matrimonial home; and there is nothing else in the conduct of the parties at the time of the purchase or thereafter which supports such an inference. There is no suggestion that the wife's efforts or her earnings made it possible for the husband to raise the initial loan or the mortgage or that her relieving her husband from the expense of buying clothing for herself and for their son was undertaken in order to enable him the better to meet the mortgage instalments or to repay the loan."

Conversely, inferring intention from conduct is difficult and case law seems to suggest that the focus remains on an express agreement made between the parties or capital contributions.

V Lessons from North of the Border?

Under the Family Law (Scotland) Act 2006 (hereinafter 'the 2006 Act'), cohabitants, whether same sex or opposite sex, have limited rights to make claims against each other when the relationship ends or upon the death of one of the cohabitants. These provisions stem from the recommendations of the Scottish Law Commission that the law should strike a balance between protecting the autonomy of those who do not wish to marry and not undermining the institution of marriage.[30] The Scottish government acknowledged that there have been major changes in the way families are built and every family is important no matter how it was formed.[31] Essentially, it was important to safeguard the best interests of children; promote and support stable families; and update the law to reflect the reality of family life in Scotland. Under section 28 the claimant may be entitled to some financial provision where a cohabitant has suffered an economic disadvantage due to the separation, or a party has derived an economic advantage from the other party's contributions. Ultimately, the remedies available under the 2006 Act are both practicable and fair. They do not impose upon cohabiting couples the responsibilities of marriage but redress the gains and losses flowing from their relationship.[32]

The contrast between the treatment of cohabitants in Scotland and those in England and Wales is demonstrated in *Whigham v Owen.*[33] The parties had cohabited for 27 years and Ms Wingham sought a capital sum of one half of the parties' net assets. She argued that virtually all of the parties' wealth had been acquired during their cohabitation. Nevertheless, Mr Owen argued that Ms Wingham had not established any contributions that resulted in an economic advantage to her, nor any economic disadvantage suffered. In other words, Ms Wingham was no worse off at the end of the relationship than she was at the beginning. In considering the legal basis of the claim, the court considered that the overriding principle was one of fairness and not a precise economic calculation.[34] The court held that there was no necessity for Ms Wingham to show that there was a causal

30 Scottish Law Commission, *Report on Family Law,* Scot. Law Com. No. 135, 1992, para. 16.1.

31 Scottish Executive, *Family Matters: Improving Family Law in Scotland, April 2004,* http://www.gov.scot/Publications/2004/04/19220/35697 (accessed 29 January 2017).

32 *Gow v Grant (Scotland)* [2012] UKSC 29.

33 [2013] CSOH 29.

34 See *Gow v Grant (Scotland)* [2012] UKSC 29. Lord Hope noted that it would be wrong to work on the basis that the legislation was entitled only to correct any clear and quantifiable economic imbalance and discouraged such a narrow approach.

link between her contributions and Mr Owen's wealth at the breakdown of the relationship. The significance of the decision is that it marks a further step in the development of the application of section 28 of the 2006 Act.

Whilst the Act has had a positive impact for Scottish cohabitants and their children, the legislation has its limits. Section 28(2) of the 2006 Act gives the court a wide discretion to determine the outcome of a claim, but the Act does not provide any guidance as to how the court should exercise this discretion. According to the Scottish Executive, it was right and proper that the courts could consider any and all relevant factors in order to reach appropriate judgments.[35] This undoubtedly means that there may be inconsistencies and uncertainty as to the factors the court will take into account in the exercise of its discretion.

The application of the legislation is not an exact science and unlike the proposed English law reforms which includes a minimum cohabitation period of two years, the lack of a cohabitation requirement under the 2006 Act means that those in very short relationships could be eligible for statutory protection, should the court exercise its wide discretion.[36] The court also faces challenges in quantifying non-financial contributions, which can include looking after any relevant child or the home in which the parties cohabited.[37] Again, the 2006 Act does not provide any guidance or criteria and therefore those that the legislation was intended to protect may be at a disadvantage because their claim is difficult to quantify with any accuracy.[38]

VI FUTURE DIRECTIONS?

So far, the debate over the reform of the laws relating to cohabiting couples tends to focus on the shortcomings of the law of trusts and the need for a legislative framework. While legislative reform is an option, the merit of pursuing that option should be reviewed in light of the range of other responses that would be worthy of exploration.

A Better Public Legal Education (PLE)

The concern that the law does not adequately protect cohabitants has been the catalyst for empirical research studies over the past 15 years. A study carried out by The National

35 Scottish Executive, op cit, n. 31.

36 T. Guthrie & H. Hiram, 'Property and Cohabitation: Understanding the Family Law (Scotland) Act 2006', *Edinburgh Law Review*, Vol. 11, Issue 2, 2007, pp. 208-229.

37 Sectopm 28(9) Family Law (Scotland) Act 2006.

38 F. McCarthy, 'Cohabitation: Lessons from North of the Border', *Child and Family Law Quarterly*, Vol. 23, No. 3, 2011, pp. 277-301.

Centre for Social Research[39] of former cohabitants found that cohabitants were less likely to reach a settlement based on the parties respective needs, that homes owned by one party were always retained by the owner and jointly owned homes were either retained by one partner or sold. The arrangements that cohabitants made did not reflect their full legal entitlement, and the legal remedies that were available were rarely used. The study also found that cohabitants needed to be educated about the legal implications of their relationship. In light of the level of ignorance uncovered by the studies, the government launched the web-based Living Together campaign, which aimed to make people aware of the legal vulnerability of cohabitants as compared with their married counterparts and to give cohabitants practical advice and options to redress their legal position if they wish to do so.

A study into the effectiveness of the campaign[40] found that the majority of the participants found the website useful and informative about their legal position. But despite this positive impact, few cohabitants had taken any measures to improve their legal position. For example, one of the main reasons for not improving their position was the perceived lack of suitable actions for cohabitants to take.

Also, the discussion of financial affairs in the event of the relationship breaking down was considered difficult. A recent YouGov survey[41] of 1000 cohabiting couples revealed that 41% of cohabiting couples purchased their home as joint tenants and 40% purchased the property without any involvement from the other. Across the age groups surveyed, 54% of younger couples bought as joint tenants compared with 38% in the 55 plus age group. There will of course be a range of factors influencing home ownership (which the survey does not address), however at the very least, the survey serves to highlight that the majority of properties are jointly owned but also that the problem of sole legal owner has not all but disappeared.[42]

While public education may serve to provide cohabitants with a greater awareness and understanding of their rights, there are some obstacles to effective public education. These include isolated initiatives which lack the continuity and sharing of knowledge essential for the spread of learning and short term funding of public legal education projects. In July 2017, the Attorney General's Office launched a new panel to drive forward legal education initiatives and to promote the importance of "teaching people about their legal

---

39 R. Tennant, J. Taylor & J. Lewis, 'Separating from cohabitation: making arrangements for finances and parenting', *Department of Constitutional Affairs*, Research Series 7/06, 2006.

40 A. Barlow, C. Burgoyne & J. Smithson, 'The Living Together Campaign – An investigation of its impact on legally aware cohabitants', *Ministry of Justice*, Research Series 5/07, 2007.

41 Mills & Reeves, 'Our new survey reveals that the myth of the common law marriage leaves cohabiting couples vulnerable', 5 April 2017, https://www.mills-reeve.com/our-new-survey-reveals-that-the-myth-of-the-common-law-marriage-leaves-cohabiting-couples-vulnerable-04-05-2017/ (accessed 1 September 2017).

42 R. Auchmuty, 'The limits of marriage protection in property allocation when a relationship ends', *Child and Family Law Quarterly*, Vol. 28, No. 4, 2016, pp. 303-324.

rights and responsibilities",[43] it is unclear whether this includes matters relating to cohabitation.

B *Cohabitation Agreements*

A cohabitation agreement generally deals with three key areas in relation to how the parties will own and share assets. First, establishing the financial arrangement while living together; second, who owns what at the time of the agreement, and third, how property, assets and finances are to be divided should the couple separate.[44] Despite the increase in cohabiting couples in England and Wales, agreements regulating financial arrangements during the subsistence of the relationship and upon separation are underused. Much of this is partly due to a lack of awareness of their existence. According to the YouGov survey,[45] 76 per cent of participants had never heard of cohabitation agreements and only 10 per cent had an agreement in place.[46] This echoes the findings of the study into the impact of the Living Together Campaign. The study found that in theory cohabitants felt agreements were a good idea, but many were reluctant to enter into one due to the negative connotation and because they did not want to contemplate their relationship ending.[47] The study also found that the fact cohabitation agreements might not be legally binding was a reason why some did not enter into such arrangements.

Until fairly recently, the question of whether or not a cohabitation agreement is enforceable under English law had remained unanswered by the courts. At one point, such agreements were considered to be void on the ground of public policy (that they encouraged sexual immorality),[48] nevertheless, in *Sutton v Mishcon de Reya and Gawor and Co*[49] the court confirmed that a cohabitation agreement that regulated the property and financial arrangements of a cohabiting couple was valid. It should be noted that even where an agreement is found to be valid, it could be unenforceable if it fails to comply with the general law of contract principles which governs these agreements. The court is more likely to find that there is an intention to enter into an agreement if it clearly governs the financial affairs of a cohabiting couple.[50] Furthermore, if the terms are reasonable and each party

---

43 https://www.gov.uk/government/news/new-panel-launched-to-drive-legal-education (accessed 6 January 2017).

44 http://www.advicenow.org.uk/guides/how-make-living-together-agreement#guideAccordians (accessed 19 June 2017).

45 Mills & Reeves, op cit, n. 41.

46 Ibid.

47 Barlow et al, op cit, n. 41.

48 *Fender v St John-Mildmay* [1938] AC 1. Lord Wright said the law will not enforce an immoral promise, such as a promise between a man and a woman to live together without being married, or to pay a sum of money or to give some other consideration in return for an immoral association.

49 [2004] 1 FLR 837.

50 Law Commission, op cit, n. 4.

has had separate independent legal advice, the agreements are likely to be legally enforceable, therefore this might encourage a few more couples to enter into such agreements.[51]

VII Conclusion

When it comes to providing protection to cohabiting couples, England and Wales is some way behind Scotland and many other jurisdictions around the world. It is evident that there is a degree of confusion as well as a lack of clarity as to the rights afforded to those who cohabit. Property lawyers on the other hand have a different view on whether cohabitation is a problem with some considering the concept of family relationships as the problem to the purity and logic of the law of property.[52] Perhaps the answer is not legislative reform, but to better educate cohabitants about the existing law.

The most significant factor that impedes the achievement of reforms is the absence of government support for legislative reform. This argument resolves around the view that governments are reluctant to be seen as supporting a relationship type other than marriage. They have been of the opinion that if legislative reforms were made, cohabitation "would be as expensive and legalistic as divorce" and essentially if cohabitants are dissatisfied with the insecurity that cohabitation may bring then they should opt to marry instead.[53] The Law Commission's recommendations have also been faced with scepticism in that while they are "doing much to address perceived injustices, these proposals are obviously not compatible with a long-term national policy aimed at improving family stability by encouraging marriage and discouraging markedly more unstable cohabitation."[54]

As it stands, cohabiting couples will have to make do with the existing property and trusts law provisions and contractual natured agreements that can be entered into. But the push to be fully recognised and protected as a family type under the existing law, like married couples, remains to be achieved.

51 R. Probert, 'Cohabitation: current legal solutions', *Current Legal Problems*, Vol. 62, No. 1, 2009, pp. 316-345 at 332.

52 Ibid, p. 332.

53 Hansard HL Debate 12 December 2014, cols 2069-2085.

54 The Centre for Social Justice, *'Breakthrough Britain the Family Law Review'*, An Interim Report, November 2008.

Legal Protection of Parallel and Polyamorous Families: A Long Way to Go

*Hannetie Kiyono Koyama Sato**

I Background to Brazilian Family Law

In order to analyze modern day legal and social conceptions of family the deep influence of Brazil's colonial period must be recognized. In the 16th century, men traveling to Brazil would leave their families back in Portugal. Once they arrived, they would form a parallel family with another woman with whom they would have children. As a result, many couples in Brazil were in a common law marriage. Unfortunately, these families were neither recognized by law nor society. On the contrary, the laws at the time rejected these family structures.

The institution of marriage was not directly regulated in Brazil during the Imperial period following the country's independence in 1822. It was only in 1891, when the first Republican Constitution was approved, that civil marriage was introduced in Brazil by article 71 of the Constitution. Up until then, the only type of marriage available was religious marriage, which was between one man and one woman.

In 1916, the Brazilian Civil Code was approved, which regulated civil relationships between or amongst individuals. Under this law the legitimate family was strongly protected, while relationships outside of marriage were strongly disapproved. There was a clear dissociation between norms and factual reality at this point in time: many relationships in Brazil were not legally recognized by the state.

Even legal discourse about divorce in Brazil progressed slowly during the Republican period, probably because of the Roman Catholic Church's influence on Brazilian society. Divorce was only introduced in Brazil in 1977, when the Divorce Act was enacted. Up until then, the only rule recognised by the law in respect of dissolution of marriage was "till death do us part", which, in fact, led to a growing number of "parallel unions" before the Divorce Act's introduction. At this point, it is worth noting that a parallel relationship is not to be confused with an official union. Rather, a parallel relationship refers to a second relationship formed after the marriage has ended.

Following this period of legal evolution in Brazil, partners in a parallel relationship only had a limited right to "compensation for domestic services". According to Professor

* Family Law Lawyer at Peixoto & Cury Advogados.

Maria Berenice Dias this provision put second partners in a humiliating position, since they were not entitled to the protection and provision of the general family law: love was paid as if it were the provision of working services.[1] During this period, specific legal landmark in relation to relationship recognition was reached. However, it is worth mentioning that the Brazilian Courts adopted positions which implied the recognition of certain obligations relating to second relationships.

Obviously, the Brazilian legal system at this time did not reflect the social reality. However, this dissociation was mostly solved by the enactment of Brazil's 1988 Constitution, widely known in Brazilian legal culture as the "Citizen's Constitution" because of its recognition of fundamental rights. After the constitution was enacted, in accordance with article 266 of the Constitution, the Brazilian state began to extend protection to de facto or actual families, recognizing civil unions or domestic partnerships (established as "união estável", roughly translated as stable union) as a valid institution protected by law.

Brazil's legal framework in relation to family structures was also progressed by the new Constitution. The Constitution recognized the importance of the institution of family in protecting the fundamental rights of children and teenagers, leading to the Children and Teenagers Protection Act, the 2002 Brazilian Civil Code and the New Adoption Act. Furthermore, the legal evolution brought about by the 1988 Constitution reached new heights when the Supreme Federal Court's interpretation of the Brazilian Civil Code gave it a broader scope. The Court stated that, according to the Constitution, a family entity exists regardless of the spouse's gender.

Nevertheless, as expected, over time the concept of family brought in by the 1988 Constitution has failed to include new forms of de facto families. Despite the lack of specific legal provisions for these families, they have started to enjoy protection through ordinary legislation and even court decisions which have, little by little, begun to cover such family "structures".

II New Family Structures and the Contemporary Constitutional Framework

The early 20th Century's parallel family has evolved to become today's "plurality of families". The diversification of families was not immediately supported by legal scholars but, with the passage of time, it became a principle that was established and protected under Brazil's 1988 Constitution.

1 M.B. Dias, *Manual de Direito das Famílias*, São Paulo, Revista dos Tribunais, 2010.

According to Zygmunt Bauman,[2] the contemporary family based on the affection shared by its members is liquid and transitory, since relationships are also fluid and short-lived in modern society. This state of affairs makes it possible for one person to be in several relationships at once. Where multiple relationships exist, one relationship is not more important or relevant than the others. Even if there is this underlying idea of impermanence, a family entity may not be so fluid as to include a "one-night stand". Some degree of stability is needed.

Even today, the subject of parallel families and polyamory has a large impact and causes heated arguments. If these families exist, failing to legally recognize them will result in an uncountable number of 'families' being denied protection.[3] In other words, disagreement about whether these families should be formed does not prevent them from existing. If this "second union" is not recognized and the relationship ends, withholding protection from the "second partner" not only results in the unjust enrichment of the other, but also violates the human dignity of the second partner.

However, before giving a detailed account of the two types of family structures considered in this piece – "parallel" and "polyamorous" families – it is important to define and differentiate them. Parallel families are those in which one family member is simultaneously in a relationship with two or more other family members. Polyamory or polyamorous families are defined by the relationship between more than two non-monogamous individuals.

When describing polygamous families, the most common thought is of Eastern societies based around a religion, such as Islam, which permits a man to take as many wives and he pleases. However, in Western societies, multi-member families came to prominence in the nineties, in connection with social movements towards gender equality and sexual freedom.

It is important to emphasize that a major feature of a polyamorous family is that all participating partners are fully aware of the existence of the remaining partners involved. This is the case, regardless of whether the family is a trio or has more persons involved. As a rule of thumb, all partners are of legal age and agree upon having a relationship involving three or more people.

When talking about these families, one must be careful not to use language which conflates parallel families with multi-member families or polyamorous families. Although both family structures involve more than two partners, in polyamorous families every

2 Z. Bauman, *Amor Líquido*, Rio de Janeiro, Zahar, 2004.

3 D. dos Santos Cardoso, *Amando Várias - individualização, redes, ética e poliamor*, (Dissertação de Mestrado em Ciências da Comunicação, Lisboa, Faculdade de Ciências Sociais e Humanas, Universidade Nova de Lisboa, 2010).

member is involved with one another, while in parallel families, there are two family nuclei, but one member is part of the two families.[4]

In Brazilian discussions about parallel families, most scholars divide these families into two groups, dependent on whether "good faith" is present. "Good faith", in this context, means the parties' knowledge about the existence of the other relationship(s).[5] When "good faith" is used in relation to parallel families, it refers to knowledge that a member of that "family" had already formed a previous family. It is worth mentioning at this stage that Brazil's legislation establishes equality of treatment between families that are in a civil union or marriage. According to the Brazilian legal framework, the presence or absence of knowledge of a second partner can be categorized as "pure concubinage"' and "impure concubinage". Pure concubinage is where the second partner acted in good faith and did not know about the existing relationship. Impure concubinage refers to the situation where the second partner was aware of the first relationship and therefore is acting in bad faith in regard to the other relationship.

Most legal scholars and judges are of the view that, where the facts are such that a second partner was unaware and had no means of being aware that their partner already had a family before starting the relationship, the said good faith partner should not be negatively affected. Therefore, the "pure concubinage" is understood as a "putative civil union".[6] There are two perspective on this position. One perspective is that, where the second partner was not aware of the existence of his or her partner's former union, the second partner should not be left unprotected if the second union ends by death or one of the parties' decision. The other perspective is that mere ignorance about the existence of the partner's prior family is insufficient to legitimate a second union. An additional requirement must also be met, which is that the new partner had *no means* of knowing about the former relationship and that all investigatory means were used to check whether their partner had a former family before the new one was formed.

At this point, a question arises: should the quality of good faith be applied only to the second partner? Where, at the end of the first relationship, the first partner has discovered the second relationship, would it be fair for them to lose legal protection because of that knowledge? If the first partner failed to react to the discovery, would tacit agreement to the new relationship be found? Additionally, what if the first partner is aware of the second relationship and agrees to the maintenance of the "parallel family"?

Under the current law, the first partner, as a result of his/her status of "first partner" - regardless of knowledge about the other relationship - will always be entitled to legal pro-

4 C. Klesse, 'Polyamory and Its "Others": Contesting the Terms of Non-Monogamy', *Sexualities*, Vol. 9, No. 5, 2006, pp. 565-583.

5 E.B. de Oliveira, 'Do Concubinato à União Estável,' *Revista do Instituto dos Advogados de São Paulo*, 1988, pp. 665-79.

6 F. Tartuce, *Direito Civil - Direito de Família*, Rio de Janeiro, Método, 2015.

tection; timing of the union is important and not good faith. However, the current law is discriminatory as it treats two equal parties differently. It is pointless to argue that the first and the second partners are differently situated as they both have the same capacity to investigate whether their partner has another family. Discrimination would be prevented if parallel unions were exceptionally recognized as families in the absence of good faith by either the first or second partners.

The above reasoning is also applicable to polyamorous families – families which are based around a union between more than two individuals. For example, a three or four-way relationship. Nevertheless, both family structures – parallel families and polyamorous families – should be entitled to legal protection.

Recently, discussions about recognition of new family structures have attracted more attention. An argument that is persistently made against recognition it is that these families do not form part of Brazilian culture. However, this argument neglects the speed with which principles and even society itself have been changing. Until quite recently, if an individual disclosed their homosexuality they would become an outcast. Nevertheless, young people today do not care about sexual orientation and gender and even understand these matters as transitory or fluid[7]. For example, the same person could be interested in persons of the same or opposite sex during different periods of their life. It is within this context of a liquid society, where love is "liquid" – to use concepts established by Zigmunt Bauman – [8] that we must examine social relations, particularly the formation of families.

People who do not support "new" family structures, generally argue that parallel families and polyamory are not typical of Brazilian culture. However, this argument is strongly opposed by social science scholars, especially anthropologists such as Professor Mirian Goldenberg who has authored many books which study and analyze the body, family, marriage and infidelity.[9] Furthermore, if parallel families did not exist in Brazil, there would not be the numbers of petitions for dividing death pension filed at our courts.

On 15 June 2015, the Regional Appellate Uniformization Court (TRU) of the 4th Region Federal Small Court (JEFs) granted a claim for uniformization, concluding that in cases where marital and extra-marital relationships coexisted, both the "wife" and the "partner" should receive the death pension.

Those who do not support new family structures argue that they are not entitled to direct legal protection because Brazil's Constitution only protects monogamous families. On the one hand, this interpretation could be deemed correct about what the Constitution provides. On the other hand, the existence of family structures cannot be ignored simply because of the principle of monogamy.

---

7 I.M. Chiamulera, 'As Uniões Livres', *Revista Jurídica*, 1992, pp. 71-98.

8 Bauman, op cit, n. 2.

9 M. Goldenberg, *A Outra - A amante do homem casado*, Rio de Janeiro, Best Bolso, 2009.

It is also true that human dignity is among the republican principles established under Article 1, Section III of the Constitution.[10] Accordingly, human dignity grounds fundamental civil rights such as the right to expression of sexual orientation. Dignity therefore encompasses a strong sense of self-assertion and personal appreciation. The principle of human dignity also implies that all persons have the right to seek happiness. As the Brazilian Constitution guarantees that all persons must be treated with dignity and dignity implies a right to seek happiness, the individual beliefs of a person must be respected.

In addition to the principle of human dignity, there is also the guarantee that privacy and intimacy will be protected through the principle of "inviolability of private life". This guarantee is vital for human development and the satisfaction of all human needs. It may be enjoyed "individually or in small groups". Furthermore, there is also the eudemonism principle,[11] which protects individuals and their characteristics, on the basis of production of happiness and, again, human dignity. Overall, the state should not be interfering with relationships by prohibiting persons of legal age from creating the family structure they desire.

III A Paradigm Case and Reflections for the Future

The chosen paradigm case is that of Joana da Paixão Luz, who sought acknowledgement of her civil union with the deceased, Valdemar do Amor Divino, and the consequent *pro rata* division of his death pension with his wife. Despite being married, Valdemar had a domestic partnership style relationship with Joana. While living with both women he had nine children by Joana. Neither woman knew about the other's existence.

The first-instance Court based its decision on the article in the Constitution that holds that the family is the foundation of society. It thereby recognized that the union between Joana Paixão Luz and Valdemar do Amor Divino, that is the union between the second partner and the deceased, was not only a family relationship but also a civil union. After thoroughly analyzing the case, the appeal Court granted the wife's appeal. A civil union between Joana Paixão Luz and Valdemar do Amor Divino was rejected on the facts of the case and the wife was awarded the full pension.

In light of current changes to customs in modern society, recognition and regulation of the family status of parallel and polygamous families is expected with anticipation. Regardless of whether one holds a more traditional position or a progressive outlook on

10 P.L. Netto Lôbo, 'Família e Dignidade Humana,' *in* R. da Cunha Pereira, *V Congresso Brasileiro de Direito de Família*, IBDFam, 2005, pp. 795-801.

11 G.M. Fernandes Novaes Hironaka, 'A família brasileira contemporânea e o ensino do Direito de Família nos cursos jurídicos', *Revista da Faculdade de Direito da Universidade de São Paulo*, Vol. 109, 2014, available at http://www.revistas.usp.br/rfdusp/article/view/89267 (accessed 20 June 2016).

these changes, there is a trend towards granting persons in simultaneous relationships some of the rights afforded to traditional family entities. After all, these are actual families. In this sense, it seems inevitable that the state will perform its role as protector and regulator, providing persons in parallel or polyamorous relationships with minimum rights in accordance with the human dignity of those persons. By doing so, the State would be fulfilling its constitutional promises, for guaranteeing the happiness of these "new" families requires more than merely complying with principle. Instead it is a reference that all families, regardless of their structure, are real families that are entitled to all the rights guaranteed to traditional families.

Cross-Border Recognition of Same-Sex Formalized Unions in the Baltic States and the Challenge of Intersectionalizing Private International Law

Laima Vaigė[*]

I Intersectionality and Private International Law

Those interested in private international law[1] and the theory of intersectionality[2] may notice that both have similar aesthetical metaphors. For instance, intersectionality focuses on "persons at intersections"[3] who are the most vulnerable to different forms of discrimination, and private international law is the law of intersections of different legal systems.[4] Moreover, in private international law, crystallization of a relationship[5] is necessary for recognition of decisions taken abroad, whereas in intersectional studies, a metaphor of multifaceted crystal[6] is used to describe personal identity. Finally, intersectionality has a map-like logic,[7] for which it is sometimes criticized as overly technical and complex.

* Doctoral candidate (Uppsala University), PhD in law (Mykolas Romeris University).

1 Private international law is understood as the discipline encompassing private relationships across the state borders and solving the problems related to determination of jurisdiction, applicable law and cross-border recognition and enforcement of judgments.

2 Intersectionality is a theory that different personal identity markers, such as race, gender, sexuality, class are interwoven and cannot be seen as completely separate, because together they create a lived experience of a certain individual.

3 K. Crenshow, 'Demarginalizing the Intersection of Race and Sex: A Black Feminist Critique of Antidiscrimination Doctrine, Feminist Theory and Antiracist Politics', *University of Chicago Legal Forum*, Vol. 1, No. 8, 1989, pp. 139-167.

4 H. Van Loon, *The Global Horizon of Private international law*, The Hague Academy of International law, Brill Nijhoff, 2016, pp. 25-27.

5 J. Basedow, *The Law of Open Societies: Private Ordering and Public Regulations in the Conflict of Laws*, The Hague Academy of International Law, Brill, 2015, p. 13.

6 C. Dale & L. Sims, 'Faceted Identities: Extending Intersectionality', 2009, retrieved 20 November 2017, from https://www.academia.edu/195897/Faceted_Identities_Extending_Intersectionality.

7 K. Crenshaw, 'Mapping the Margins: Intersectionality, Identity Politics, and Violence against Women of Color', *in* M.A. Fineman & R. Mykitiuk (Eds.), *The Public Nature of Private Violence*, New York, Routledge, 1994, pp. 93-118.

Just like intersectionality, private international law is both complex and map-like. Connecting factors[8] in this field might be seen as creating a neutral system of coordinates and resembling geography. However, it would be an illusion to claim that private international law – or intersectionality, for that matter – is only neutral. Both the method of private international law and intersectional analysis need to be contextualized, and cannot be separated from cultural and political considerations. Neutrality (equal standing of all persons and all legal systems) is only one of the aspirations of private international law but not necessarily its reality. Neutrality has many exceptions and is seriously questioned in the area of recognition of family statuses, where the national family values are often protected at the risk of creating limping family statuses, i.e. marriages or registered partnerships that are recognized as valid in one country but considered inexistent in another.

How important are these aesthetic similarities in theorizing about private international law and intersectionality? I would argue that these aesthetical concepts are not just decorations but serve to "structure experience, shape perception and mediate our relationships with others by constituting reality."[9] The aesthetic characteristics of law make it cognizable as a legal text. Hence, the aesthetic concepts in this given context help to understand the meaning of the problems involved, and deserve a scientific inquiry.

In this paper, I aim to apply intersectional analysis (i.e. to intersectionalize) to Estonian, Lithuanian and Latvian law on cross-border recognition of same-sex formalized unions lawfully created abroad. First, I reflect on the concept of intersectionality and introduce the European standards in this area. Two landmark decisions were recently adopted by the Grand Chamber of the European Court of Justice (ECJ) and the European Court of Human Rights (the ECtHR), which restrict the application of national public policy. Next, I briefly overview the private international law in the Baltic states (Latvia, Lithuania and Estonia) in this area, including the relevant case law, where possible. All the three Baltic states are the European Union (EU) member states, and contracting parties to the European Convention of Human Rights (the ECHR), which have an effect on national public policies. I discuss which couples are more likely to be refused recognition and become invisible. Finally, I reflect on the general idea whether intersectionality could be a helpful concept to include more diverse experiences and identities into the analysis of private international law on the recognition of family status.

8 The most characteristic legal norms to this area of law are created to address the problem of applicable law in case the legal relation is connected to more than one legal system. The choice-of-law norms hence rely on certain connecting factors, such as habitual residence of the persons involved, to establish the applicable law.

9 J.J.A. Shaw, 'Aesthetics of Law and Literary License: An Anatomy of the Legal Imagination', *Liverpool Law Review*, Vol. 38, 2017, pp. 83–104, at 84.

II Intersectional Analysis and Its Uses

"Intersectionalizing" in the title refers to the use of intersectional analysis to focus on multiple and intersectional forms of discrimination of certain persons at intersections. Some groups of persons are more likely to be discriminated, i.e. become victims of injury, precisely because these persons belong to a number of minority groups and that creates a unique experience. The use of the allegedly neutral private international law makes their experiences invisible.

There are different ways in which the intersectionalizing of private international law could work. For instance, it could be used to put forward arguments for legislation – i.e. a common EU solution on recognition of civil status, or an enhanced cooperation instrument (involving at least nine cooperating member states). Intersectionality could be used to provide arguments in a context of judiciary analysis: focusing on the case practice of the ECJ, the ECtHR, or the national courts. Intersectionality could be used as a theoretic analytic tool on cross-border recognition of family status.[10] Moreover, intersectional analysis could be used in putting arguments for claims for political recognition of the family status acquired abroad.[11]

The recognition claims need not necessarily be only one-sided, for instance, favouring a universal blanket recognition of family status. The solution could instead involve a wide discretion for courts to decide in each individual case, whether the status should be recognized in the particular context. Keeping the vision of private international law in mind, neither blanket-recognition of family status, nor blanket non-recognition is plausible, because the contents of the *ordre public* (public policy) exception differ from case to case. In many cases, public policy questions should not even arise in the first place. Only if the result of the application of foreign law is completely inconsistent with the targeted state's public policy, constituted in its essential principles of its law, the family status may not be recognized on this narrowly construed basis. The said public policy of the state also has an *attenuated effect*[12] due to the lack of proximity to the recognizing state, and development of the state's obligations under international law, EU law and the ECHR.

---

10 S. Mustasaari, *Rethinking recognition: transnational families and belonging in law*, Helsinki, University of Helsinki, 2017.

11 I. Isailovic, 'Political Recognition and Transnational law, Gender equality and cultural diversification in French courts', *in* H. Muir Watt & D.P. Fernandez Arroyo (Eds.), *Private International Law and Global governance,* Oxford, Oxford University press, 2014, pp. 318-342.

12 The attenuated effect of *ordre public* may allow the recognition of civil status under foreign law that would have been otherwise disregarded to protect the interests of the *lex fori's* public policy.

III The European Standards in the Area

One may claim that the current ECtHR practice obliges member states to recognize same-sex marriages legally contracted abroad in one form or another. *Family life* of same-sex partners is protected under the Convention,[13] and non-recognition of family status cannot serve as a legitimate basis for refusal to issue residence permits to same-sex partners.[14] In 2017, the ECtHR also concluded that refusal to include same-sex marriages concluded abroad in the civil registry in Italy violates Article 8 (right to family life) of the ECHR.[15] The case concerned eleven Italian citizens and one Canadian, who had lawfully entered into same-sex marriages in Canada, USA and the Netherlands and attempted to register their marriages in the Italian civil registry. The Court reiterated that "States are still free … to restrict access to marriage to different-sex couples."[16] According to the Court's reasoning, contracting states have a wide margin of appreciation to decide whether they will register same-sex marriages contracted abroad as marriages or downgrade them to partnerships,[17] because the practice is inconsistent and a common consensus is lacking. To summarize, states need to protect the family life of same-sex couples,[18] to issue residence permits to same-sex partners, and to include the marriages lawfully contracted abroad into their civil registry in some form.

On 5 June 2018, the ECJ affirmed that the concept of the spouse should be understood autonomously under the Free Movement Directive,[19] and may include same-sex formalized marriages[20] moving across the borders. The case concerned a same-sex marriage between a Romanian American and American men, who were married in Belgium. A residence permit was sought in Romania, which had an explicit rule on non-recognition of same-sex marriages lawfully contracted abroad. Most importantly, the ECJ underlined:

> an obligation to recognise such marriages for the sole purpose of granting a derived right of residence to a third-country national does not undermine the

13 *Schalk and Kopf v. Austria*, 24 June 2010, No. 30141/04, at p. 61; *P.B. and J.S.* v. *Austria*, app. no. 18984/02, ECtHR 22 July 2010, at para. 30.

14 *Pajić v Croatia*, 23 February 2016, app. no. 68453/13. *Taddeucci and McCall v. Italy*, 30 June 2016, app. no. 51362/09.

15 *Orlandi and others v. Italy*, app. nos. 2643/12; 26742/12; 44057/12 and 60088/12, ECHR 14 December 2017.

16 Ibid, at para. 192.

17 Ibid, at para. 205.

18 States have a positive obligation to ensure the legal protection of *core needs* or *core rights* of the couple, however vague the said expression may be. See *Oliari and others v. Italy*, 21 July 2015, app. nos. 18766/11 and 36030/11, para. 172, 174.

19 Directive 2004/38/EC of the European Parliament and of the Council of 29 April 2004 on the right of citizens of the Union and their family members to move and reside freely within the territory of the Member States. OJ L 158, 30.4.2004, pp. 77–123.

20 Judgment of the Court (Grand Chamber) of 5 June 2018 in *Case C-673/16*, Relu *Adrian Coman and Others v. Inspectoratul General pentru Imigrări and Ministerul Afacerilor Interne*, ECLI:EU:C:2018:385.

> national identity or pose a threat to the public policy of the Member State concerned.[21]

The Court considered that Article 21 (free movement) of the Treaty of the Functioning of the European Union may serve as a basis for the derived right of the EU citizen's spouse, a third country national, to family reunification. At the same time, the language of the Court was cautious and limited solely to the discussed situation. It concerned free movement of the EU citizens, who had been married with third country nationals and had genuine residence in the state of marriage, which was different from their nationality.[22] The reception of the said case in the Baltic states will be discussed further; it was broader than one could expect.

Regarding the secondary EU law, it must be noted that EU Regulations in the area of private international law do not provide directly applying rules on cross-border recognition of status but use rather evasive techniques. For instance, Article 22 of the Regulation on jurisdiction, applicable law, recognition and enforcement of decisions and cooperation in matters relating to maintenance obligations (the Maintenance Regulation)[23] states that:

> The recognition and enforcement of a decision on maintenance under this Regulation shall not in any way imply the recognition of the family relationship, parentage, marriage or affinity underlying the maintenance obligation which gave rise to the decision.

Despite this, the Regulation in general ensures the free movement of decisions on maintenance, thus the legal relation may have the intended effects that move freely across the EU borders. It is only one specific area and only one effect but it applies throughout the EU, and it is important. Other EU Regulations in this area also use similar evasive techniques, e.g. explicitly provide that they do not apply to recognition of effects of marriage or partnership but ensure acceptance of a status document[24] or court decision that relates to effect of that status. Thus, rules in the EU Regulations could be seen as requiring at least *quasi-recognition* of the same-sex formalized union in a particular area. It must be recalled that Regulations cannot be used in discriminative manner, and in principle, recognition of a same-sex marriage for a certain purpose (e.g. in the case of succession) could hardly be

21 Ibid, at para. 46.

22 Ibid, at para. 53.

23 Council Regulation (EC) No 4/2009 of 18 December 2008 on jurisdiction, applicable law, recognition and enforcement of decisions and cooperation in matters relating to maintenance obligations. OJ L 7, 10.1.2009, pp. 1-79.

24 Regulation (EU) 2016/1191 of the European Parliament and of the Council of 6 July 2016 on promoting the free movement of citizens by simplifying the requirements for presenting certain public documents in the European Union, OJ L 200, 26.7.2016, pp. 1–136.

argued to undermine the national identity or public policy of a member state, in consideration of *Coman* case.

Unfortunately, intersectionality as such is not part of the European standards. There have been reports[25] and suggestions to institutionalize intersectionality,[26] but so far this has not happened at the EU level. It has been offered to include intersectionality into the ECJ or the ECtHR's reasoning, including the more recent case on same-sex formalized unions.[27] In *Parris* case,[28] the ECJ did not find that an elderly gay man was discriminated because he was ineligible to surviving benefit to the civil partner in Ireland. Neither discrimination on the basis of age, nor discrimination on the basis sexual orientation could be proven, but persons might had been discriminated precisely because they were at the intersections of age and sexual orientation. Discourses that simplify questions of national identity, such as "the tolerant West and the homophobic East"[29] sometimes makes us forget that same-sex families also live in Eastern Europe. Some of them are elderly, some of them (mostly women) raise children together, and some have disabilities themselves, or raise children with disabilities.

IV The Baltic Rules on Marriages Contracted Abroad

The three Baltic states and some other states in Eastern Europe keep their family law centered around marriage between the man and the woman. As an exception, Estonia pioneered a move towards greater tolerance of same-sex relationships in 2014 with the adoption of registered partnership law. In private international law, the impossibility to conclude a same-sex or polygamous marriage under the local family law does not mean that all such foreign marriages must disappear into thin air. Private international law should be seen as much more than a buffer-law for the protection of national values and ideologies. Rather the opposite, it should serve as the law that provides greater room for diversity and allowing tailor-made exceptions. One may have a presumption that all same-sex unions formalized abroad will not be recognized in the Baltic states but that is not true.

25 For example, H. Bielefeldt, *Tackling Multiple Discrimination, Practices, policies and laws*, Luxembourg, Office for Official Publications of the European Communities, 2007.

26 A. Krizsan, H. Skjeie & J. Squires (Eds.), *Institutionalizing Intersectionality: The Changing Nature of European Equality Regimes*, Basingstoke, Palgrave Macmillan, 2012.

27 M. Möschel, 'If and when age and sexual orientation discrimination intersect: Parris', *Common Market Law Review*, Vol. 54, 2017, pp. 1835-1852.

28 Judgment of the Court (First Chamber) of 24 November 2016 in *Case C-443/15, David L. Parris v. Trinity College Dublin and Others*, ECLI:EU:C:2016:897.

29 K. Kahlina, 'Local histories, European LGBT designs: sexual citizenship, nationalism and 'Europeanisation' in post-Yugoslav Croatia and Serbia', *Women's Studies International Forum*, Vol. 49, 2015, pp. 73-83.

A Estonia

Estonia is the only state in the Baltics that provides for registered partnerships for both same-sex and different-sex couples.[30] However, implementing acts have not been adopted to this date due to a lack of political will and therefore the effects of such partnerships are not clear. Notably, the same-sex of the spouses is a ground for treating the marriage as incapable of producing any effects under local family law.[31] Due to the lack of subsequent implementing acts[32] of the law on registered partnerships, partnerships can be registered but they cannot be included in the civil registry. Choice-of-law rules on recognition of registered partnerships are missing because of the said political delay of legislating. Therefore, same-sex registered partnerships concluded abroad also cannot be included into the civil registry at the moment.

On 10 April 2018, the Supreme Court's Constitutional division rejected a request from the Tallinn's administrative court for constitutional review.[33] The request asked the Court to analyse whether the delay in adopting laws on implementation of the Registered partnership law was an infringement of the Estonian Constitution. The Court first clarified that the Registered Partnership law is valid even without an adoption of additional laws. This is a valuable clarification, because the status of the said law was not absolutely clear. Second, the Court did not consider the review substantiated because the application was insufficiently grounded. The Supreme Court wanted to see very concrete violations of specific rights of the persons involved by the lack of adopting the implementing acts. It was true that the same-sex couple at the centre of the review could not enter their relationship into civil registry, did not have any social guarantees, could not use the right to parental leave, survivor's pension, death grant, to submit a joint income tax return, as well as to be registered as joint parents in the civil registry.

Nevertheless, most of these grievances had not (yet) happened to the applicants. The Supreme Court ruled that everyday life difficulties could be overcome by interpretation under the Constitution and did not necessarily need involvement of the legislator.[34] The subsequent practice of courts is not consistent and it is difficult to make any conclusions. For instance, in some cases lesbians could adopt the children of their partners, and in other instances they did not receive the court permission.[35]

30 Registered partnerships act of the Republic of Estonia, passed by Riigikogu (Parliament) on 9 October 2014, translation published 27 November 2014.
31 Family law act of the Republic of Estonia, art. 10, passed by Riigikogu on 18 November 2009, translation published 19 June 2017.
32 Drafts of these laws were prepared but they were never adopted by the Parliament. Alternatively, attempts to abolish the Registered partnership law was also discussed and rejected.
33 Riigikohus põhiseaduslikkuse järelevalve kollegium, 10 april 2018, No. 5-17-42.
34 Ibid, at pp. 31-40.
35 The said cases are marked as confidential and are not available in Estonian database of court cases.

The Estonian Private International Law Act was passed in 2002, and has been amended a number of times since. Part 7 concerns family law and contains Chapter 1 that deals with marriage. Notably, the law does not have provisions on registered partnerships. Article 55 (2) is of the most significance. It provides:

> a marriage contracted in a foreign state is deemed to be valid in Estonia if it is contracted pursuant to the procedure for contraction of marriage provided by the law of the state where the marriage is contracted and the material prerequisites of the marriage are in compliance with the laws of the states of residence of both spouses.[36]

The article contains both the choice-of-law rule on formal and material validity of marriages contracted abroad. The formal validity (as to the form) is established in accordance with *lex loci celebrationis*, the law of registration of marriage. Material validity (as to the substance) is determined under *lex loci habitationis,* the law of residence of spouses. These rules reflect the general tendency in the act to refer to residence as the connecting factor: this also applies to the law governing prerequisites for the contraction of a marriage (article 56) and the law with regards to the general consequences of marriage (article 57).

Article 55(2) refers to "laws of the states" in plural, hence if the spouses do not share a common residence, the material prerequisites are determined separately in accordance with *each* spouse's place of residence. In 2018, the Supreme Court adopted a negative decision regarding a same-sex marriage that was contracted in the USA between an Estonian national and an American national.[37] The Estonian national was in the USA on a tourist visa at the time of conclusion of the marriage and the residence of the Estonian spouse was (arguably) still Estonia. Hence Estonian law was seen as applicable from the point of view of Estonian private international law. At the same time, the American same-sex spouse has been granted a temporary residence permit, pending the final decision. The temporary decision is in line with the ECtHR practice, according to which states are expected to provide residence permits to family members, regardless of the civil status.

The ECJ's decision in the *Coman* case, discussed above, came afterwards. It might be expected that the Estonian case practice will change in the future to accommodate this decision. However, member states are so far under an obligation to recognize same-sex marriages validly contracted in other member states, and not in third-party states, such as the USA. Since 2018, a constitutional case[38] is pending at the Supreme Court concerning

36 Private international act of the Republic of Estonia, passed by Riigikogu (Parliament) on 27 March 2002, official translation, version retrieved late 2017.

37 Supreme court (Riigikohus), 27 June 2017, case no. 3-3-1-19-17, ECLI:EE:RK:2017:3.3.1.19.17.12242.

38 Ringkonnakohus considered it to be unconstitutional, decision of 17 September 2018. See https://www.kohus.ee/et/ajakirjanikule/uudised/ringkonnakohus-elamisloa-mitteandmine-samasoolisele-registreeritud.

the rules which do not provide for the possibility to issue a residence permit based on registered partnership lawfully contracted abroad. In this pending case, the circuit court considered that same-sex couples, who had registered their partnerships abroad, should also be able to receive residence permits.

Article 7 of the Estonian Private international law which includes an *ordre public* clause, also needs to be considered in this context. It provides that:

> foreign law shall not apply if the result of such application would be in obvious conflict with the essential principles of Estonian law (public order). In such an event Estonian law applies.

This rule is relevant only if the law applicable is foreign law, not Estonian law as in the case above. Essential principles of Estonian law relate to values protected by the norms of penal law, norms that relate to national security, as well as the main principles related to justice and morality under the Estonian Constitution.[39] Non-discrimination on the basis of sexual orientation is a part of the Estonian law and same-sex relationships are not considered to infringe the Estonian morality. According to case practice of Tallinn's circuit court (Ringkonnakohus), the fundamental principles and public policy of Estonian law do not in principle include the prohibition of the recognition of same-sex marriage in any country.[40] Due to this reasoning, a same-sex marriage contracted in Sweden by two Swedish nationals could be included into the Estonian registry.

The fact that same-sex marriages were not allowed under Estonian law did not make Swedish law, which allows such marriages, contrary to Estonian public policy. It must be stressed that the concept of public policy is to be applied in extremely rare cases, when the result of application of such law would be completely unacceptable, for instance, a human right would be infringed or the object of the transaction is immoral or the contract as such is prohibited under criminal law. Simply the differences of laws are not offending national public policy. If the laws that are different would be seen as automatically against the national public policy, then choice of law and private international law itself actually loses its purpose.

The commentaries to the Estonian Constitution explained that traditional marriage is to receive a special status and protection in the Estonian society.[41] However, this constitutional protection of marriage only applies to marriages entered in Estonia and not to marriages lawfully contracted abroad.[42] Same-sex marriages contracted in Sweden or

39 Tallinna Halduskohus (Tallinn Administrative court), 7 March 2016, case no. 3-15-2355, para. 2.

40 Tallinn circuit court (Ringkonnakohus), 24 November 2016, case no. 3-15-2355.

41 *Eesti Vabariigi põhiseadus. Kommenteeritud väljaanne*, (*Commentaries to the Estonian Constitution*), Tallinn, 2012, p. 355, para. 24.1.

42 This coincides with the opinion of AG Wathelet in *Case C-673/16, Coman*, op cit, n. 20, at para. 39.

Denmark, for instance, have been contracted lawfully and in accordance to the constitutional protection of gender-neutral marriage. According to Tallinn's circuit court (Ringkonnakohus),[43] the Estonian legislator made a choice to introduce registered partnership instead of marriage for same-sex couples, but this legislative choice does not mean that all other legislative choices, e.g. marriage rather than partnership, are automatically in conflict with Estonian public policy. In other words, the *ordre public* seems to have changed since the adoption of the registered partnership law. As a result of this case, same-sex marriages that are lawfully contracted abroad are included in the Estonian civil registry as marriages.

This reasoning seems to be very pragmatic. It does not underline the symbolic value of traditional marriage but simply considers it as *one of the legislative choices* among the many possible. The court also relied on an article written by Estonian researchers and used their arguments.[44] This is an innovative approach, because the use of academic articles on case practice is not at all common in the Baltic states and even other countries. It is also uncommon for countries to recognize same-sex marriages as marriages, when they do not have such marriages in their local law. Estonia is in fact the only state in the EU to do this.[45] Most states recognize same-sex formalized unions, *adapting* them to the institute that exists within the said state. The reason why it did not happen in Estonia is that court practice filled in the legislative gap. Because the implementing laws on partnership are still lacking, the downgrading to registered partnership could not happen, and the marriages had to be registered in the only form available, i.e. as marriages.

Inclusion into the civil registry has legal effects in Estonia and can be used against the third parties and among the state authorities. However, it must also be underlined that inclusion of a same-sex marriage into the Estonian civil registry does not necessarily mean that this marriage will always have all effects as marriage in the Estonian legal system. It still is not completely clear whether same-sex marriages would be seen as marriages in Estonia to the full extent and, for instance, would allow division of the matrimonial property.[46] Depending on different scenarios, it is for the national courts to clarify this matter further.

43 Op cit, n. 40, at para. 10.

44 K. Jaadla & M. Torga, 'Välisriigis sõlmitud samasooliste abielu ja kooselu tunnustamine Eestis', *Juridica*, No. 8, 2013, pp. 598-607.

45 See para. 113 of the *Orlandi* case, op cit, n. 15.

46 Notably, Estonia does not participate in the EU Regulations on Matrimonial property (2016/1103) nor property consequences of registered partnerships (2016/1104) and neither do other Baltic States. The refusal to participate is directly related to same-sex formalized unions.

B Lithuania

Lithuania has been one of the countries that aimed at introducing a restrictive interpretation of the concept "family."[47] The first attempts resulted in much outrage due to labelling some families as either "incomplete" (e.g. family after divorce) or by failing to label some families as family at all (e.g. single parents). In 2011, the Constitutional Court found such attempts to be unconstitutional[48] and explained that family life is a broader concept than only that based on marriage. At that time, no further explanation was provided whether same-sex couples could have a common family life but it was clear that it is not the form that creates a family, i.e. the registration of marriage or partnership, but the content of the relationship.

In 2017, the Law on Strengthening of the Family[49] was adopted, which provides in the preamble that *complementarity* of man and woman is the basis for the family, which is seen as the initial and natural community and the best basis for the development and education of the child. The consequences of the inclusion of such a traditionalist and seemingly religiously inspired[50] idea of the family within the Lithuanian legal system are not entirely clear. The said law provides for establishment of an institutional framework for "family strengthening," which is described in very vague terms and aims to ensure historical survival of the nation. It seems that the Law aims to promote the *idea* of the traditional family in the Lithuanian society, which is based on complementarity of the man and the woman, as well as motherhood and fatherhood.

Lithuania included registered partnership (only to heterosexual couples)[51] in the Civil Code adopted nearly 20 years ago[52] but the section of the Civil Code that provides for such partnership has never came into force due to the lack of implementing acts. Entering into a registered partnership in Lithuania is not possible, nor is the inclusion into the registry of the partnership contracted abroad. This must be distinguished from the situation described in Estonia, where the Partnership act came into force even without the imple-

47 G. Sagatys, 'The Concept of Family in the Lithuanian Law', *Jurisprudence*, Vol. 1, No. 119, 2010, pp. 181-196, at 192. The author notes that the most conservative family policy model in the history of Lithuania since independence was adopted in 2008, when the new Framework on national family policy was introduced. The said framework – adopted by a parliamentary resolution rather than law – was later recognized as unconstitutional.

48 Constitutional Court of the Republic of Lithuania, Case No. 21/2008, 28 September 2011.

49 Law on strengthening of the family of the Republic of Lithuania, 19 October 2017, No. XIII-700, enters into force on 1 March 2018.

50 Differently from Latvia and Estonia, Lithuania is influenced by the Roman Catholic tradition. The majority of the population is Catholic and the Church is politically very active, both directly and through non-governmental organizations. The idea of complementarity of men and women is provided in the Catholic theology, for instance, the Apostolic letter of the Supreme Pontiff John Paul II Mulieris dignitatem, 1988.

51 Notably, the ECtHR later admitted – by the Grand Chamber decision – that such registered partnership that is limited only to different-sex couples would be discriminatory under the Convention. *Vallianatos v. Greece*, 7 November 2013, app. nos. 29381/09 & 32684/09.

52 Chapter XV of Book Three (Family Law) of the Civil Code of the Republic of Lithuania, adopted by the Lithuanian Parliament on 18 July 2000, No. VIII-1864, official translation.

menting acts. Although incomplete, the Estonian registered partnership could function. In Lithuania, the entry to force was made dependent on the special subsequent legislation, which was never adopted. The Lithuanian registered partnership appeared to be a stillborn.

Lithuania does not have a codified law on private international law, like Estonia, but its Civil Code of 2001 contains a section on Private international law. The key provisions seem to suggest that both nationality and domicile[53] matter. Article 1.25 (4) of the Civil Code provides the *rule of recognition* of marriages validly concluded abroad, with the exception of evasion of mandatory norms of Lithuania.[54] Article 1.25 (1) provides a general rule that Lithuanian law applies to material conditions of marriage and matrimonial capacity. Article 1.25 (3) provides that matrimonial capacity and other conditions to contract marriage in respect of foreign nationals who do not live in Lithuania can be determined under the law of common domicile, if the marriage is recognized in at least one country of the spouses. Finally, article 1.11 (1) provides for a general safeguard against the application of foreign law that contradicts the *ordre public* entrenched in the Lithuanian Constitution and other laws. It must also be noted that the Lithuanian civil registry rules do not allow inclusion of same-sex marriages lawfully contracted abroad into the national registry.[55] In practice, these civil registry rules are applied without proper consideration of private international law, differently from Estonia.

These rules could be interpreted in two different ways. First, it could be claimed that article 1.25 (1) and (3) does not apply at the time of recognition,[56] and only article 1.25 (4), i.e. the rule of recognition of marriages should apply. If so, cases of clear evasion of mandatory norms, i.e. a total lack of connection with the state of marriage at the time of its conclusion, would render some same-sex marriages unrecognizable. Second, it could be interpreted that article 1.25 (1) and (3) are applicable systematically, and if so, same-sex marriages of Lithuanian nationals could be unrecognizable, because there is an exception for material conditions of marriage only with respect to foreign nationals, and

53 Note that the Lithuanian term "nuolatinė gyvenamoji vieta" has been translated as both "domicile" and "habitual residence" in different EU secondary law acts and by different researchers, even though the Civil Code's translation and textbooks consistently use "domicile". It should be further considered whether the said term is adequate.

54 Civil Code of the Republic of Lithuania, adopted by the Lithuanian Parliament on 18 July 2000, No. VIII-1864, art. 1.25(4) states: "A marriage validly performed abroad shall be recognized in the Republic of Lithuania, except in cases when both spouses domiciled in the Republic of Lithuania performed the marriage abroad with the purpose of evading grounds for nullity of their marriage under Lithuanian law."

55 Rules on registry of civil status documents, adopted on 28 December 2016 by the order of the Lithuanian minister of Justice, No. 1R-334.

56 For instance, it has been claimed that only art. 1.25(4) applies in case of cross-border recognition. In this context, V. Mikelėnas has explained that although polygamous marriage contradicts mandatory provision (art. 3.16 of the Civil Code), it can be recognized in Lithuania: V. Mikelėnas, *Tarptautinės privatinės teisės įvadas*, Vilnius, Justitia, 2001, at p. 215.

mandatory norms prohibit same-sex marriages.[57] Considering that EU law allows certain discrimination of own nationals, the scenarios that involve Lithuanian nationality would have weaker prospects of recognition.

In 2019, the Constitutional Court explained that the concept of the family in the Lithuanian Constitution is gender neutral.[58] In other words, a same-sex couple can also have family life. Notably, the Court also concluded that that a same-sex marriage lawfully contracted abroad should be recognized for the purposes of immigration, i.e. a third country national spouse should receive a residence permit. The case concerned a Lithuanian and Belarus nationals, two men, who were married in Denmark. The Constitutional Court's decision did not mention private international law rules at all. The Court relied on the *Coman* case and briefly mentioned local rules on entering into marriage. There was no discussion whether the couple had a "genuine residence" in Denmark or just went there to be married. According to the facts presented to the Migration department and administrative courts, they did not live in Denmark. It would mean that the couple who both were resident in Lithuania attempted to evade the mandatory rules by going to Denmark. Nevertheless, the Constitutional Court relied on the fact that marriage had been entered lawfully in the state of registration. The Court also focused on the concept of human dignity in the Constitution and the right of the Lithuanian citizen to free movement under the Constitution, including his/her right to return to Lithuania. This is a landmark case but it still is not clear whether same-sex marriages recognized for purposes of migration, will have any further effects in Lithuania.

C *Latvia*

Latvia amended its Constitution to provide that marriage is "a union between a man and a woman"[59] in order to entrench the special role of heterosexual marriage. The country does not have a registered partnership. In 2017, it was evaluated by the European Region of the International Lesbian, Gay, Bisexual, Trans and Intersex Association as the worst place for an LGBT person in the European Union.[60] Attempts have been made to adopt a cohabitation law and some strategical litigation for the right to marry in Latvia has taken place, but none of these attempts were successful.

57 V. Mikelėnas stated in 2009 that a same-sex marriage of *Lithuanian nationals* would not be recognized in Lithuania due to mandatory prohibition of same sex marriage (art. 3.12): ibid, at p. 148. He has not developed this idea further, but presumably it related to the applicability of art. 1.25 to nationals.

58 Constitutional Court of the Republic of Lithuania, Case No. 16/2016, 11 January 2019, No. KT3-N1/2019.

59 Constitution of the Republic of Latvia, art. 110. Adopted by the Constitutional Assembly of Latvia on 15 February 1922, amendment of 2005.

60 ILGA-Europe (the European Region of the International Lesbian, Gay, Bisexual, Trans and Intersex Association), annual ranking, retrieved 23 January 2017, https://rainbow-europe.org/country-ranking#eu.

It is fascinating how different the regulation of private international law is between the discussed Baltic states. Latvia does not have a codified Private international law act either. The relevant norms are included in its Civil Law[61] of 1937. Article 11 of the Civil Law provides that Latvian law applies to both material and formal requirements for entering into marriage in Latvia. The same article specifies that in case a Latvian national enters into a marriage abroad, his "right to marry" is to be determined under Latvian law. From the point of view of Latvian law, the law of the foreign state applies only to the formal validity of the marriage. Therefore, under these explicit norms, it would be difficult to claim recognition of same-sex marriages that involve both Latvian nationals. From the point of view of Latvian rules, wherever Latvian nationals live, as long as they have the Latvian nationality, the Latvian provisions on marriage impediments are considered to be applicable to their marriages. Such a strong rule on nationality could be criticized as outdated in the country which to this date has about 12 percent of "non-citizen"[62] population.

Article 35 of the Latvian Civil Law provides a prohibition of marriage between persons of the same sex. The law does not mention partnerships, which do not exist in the Latvian legal system. According to article 4 of the Civil Law, if the direct meaning or teleological explanation of the norms is not available, analogy applies. The Law on the registration of civil status documents[63] provides that when a Latvian and a non-Latvian national marry in the territory of a foreign state, the marriage "shall be valid in the Republic of Latvia" provided that Latvian material family law requirements, including the prohibition of same-sex marriage, have been observed. This seems to suggest that same-sex marriages of mixed nationalities or foreign nationalities would not be seen as "valid", at least for the purposes of registration of civil status contracted abroad.

In the absence of a comprehensive legal regulation, court practice could fill the existing gaps. However, there are few cases on cross border recognition of same-sex formalized unions' family status in general, and even where they exist, they may not be accessible for practical reasons. The author came across only one case of cross-border non-recognition of a same-sex marriage. The marriage was concluded between two women, a Latvian national and non-EU national. The case concerned inclusion of a marriage lawfully contracted in Portugal into the national civil registry, and issuance of a residence permit to the wife and the couple's children. In the context of this case, the Constitutional Court

61 The Civil Law was initially adopted on 28 January 1937 by the Latvian Saeima (Parliament), re-adopted in 1992 and amended numerous times, published in 'Valdības Vēstnesis', 41, 20.02.1937, text consolidated and translated by Valsts valodas centrs (State Language Centre), 2015.

62 In 1990, about a half of the population was not ethnic Latvians and most of them did not receive citizenship, a different situation from Lithuania, for instance, where automatic citizenship was granted to all minorities. The Central Statistical Bureau of Latvia, Latvia 2017, Statistics in Brief. Riga. See http://www.csb.gov.lv/sites/default/files/nr_04_latvia_statistics_in_brief_2017_17_00_en.pdf.

63 Law on Registration of Civil Status Documents of the Republic of Latvia, adopted by Saeima (Parliament) 29 November 2012, no. 2012/197.1, translation by Valsts valodas centrs (State Language Centre), 2014.

rejected a request to evaluate article 35 of the Civil Law and related provisions under the Law on registration of civil status documents in the light of the Latvian Constitution and the European Convention on Human Rights.[64] The Court did not consider the application to be well-substantiated regarding the possible unconstitutionality of the legal norms in question.

It must be noted that the decision came before the case of *Orlandi,* which clarified that non-inclusion into the civil registry of a same-sex marriage contracted abroad can be seen as a violation of the right to family life. The Constitutional court did not analyse the question of residence permits either. The wife and the couples' children did in fact receive a residence permit, without receiving any explanation or written decision. After the *Coman* case, even a conservative interpretation would not allow refusing a residence permit in a similar case. However, this does not mean that marriage has effects that extend beyond immigration law in Latvia. There is also very little room for argument on cross-border recognition of registered partnerships in Latvia, in any context.

V Intersectionalizing the Law on Cross-Border Recognition

Private international law is by its definition the law of intersections. Although it is seen as a part of civil national law for cases with foreign element, it stems from public international law[65] and has close connections to it. The categories of *private international law* and *public international law* intersect when we deal with cross-border recognition of status. In cases where a civil status is finally recognized, despite the local rules prohibiting celebration of same-sex marriages within the country, it is done with the help of public international law. The *Orlandi* and *Coman* cases, as well as the case in the Lithuanian Constitutional Court, clearly show this. It was fundamental human rights and freedoms, such as the right to protection of family life and the freedom of movement of the EU citizen, which required the recognition of civil status. It can be claimed that the method of private international law has been revolutionised by the impact of human rights on cross-border recognition of status. Of course, this is not something entirely new, if we look at the history of private international law. The theory of vested rights suggested that individual rights that had been acquired and "vested" abroad need to be recognized without prejudice to private international law. This theory originates from international public law. As the Permanent Court of International Justice proclaimed, vested rights represent "a principle which, as

64 Constitutional Court of Latvia, ruling of 2 February 2017, case no. 4/2017.

65 For instance, see H. van Loon, *The Global Horizon of Private International Law,* The Hague Academy of International Law, Inaugural Lecture of Private International Law session, Recueil des cours, Vol. 380, Brill, 2016, at p. 108.

the Court has already had occasion to observe, forms part of generally accepted international law."[66]

In the example of K. Crenshow – who coined the term "intersectionality" – when a person is at a traffic intersection, that person is more likely to suffer injury. When same-sex partners cross state borders and lose their rights, duties and the legal connection to each other or their children, these rights are not simply "lost" but they are taken away with the power granted by the national law. Immediately one might object: is the family status really "taken away" or simply unseen (considered inexistent) in that particular country? From the private international law perspective, it would not be considered as having been taken away but as being simply inexistent in that particular state. From the point of view of the persons involved, it is taken away by force of law rather than lost on the way.

It is true that any individual moving across borders always risks being submitted to legal regimes that are disadvantageous for that person. However, when disadvantageous outcome is related solely and primarily to the person's sexual orientation, it is more than just unfortunate or incidental. From the classical private international law perspective, this unseen legal relationship – which is considered as perfectly valid in the country of celebration of marriage and many other countries – is called a "limping" relationship. The word itself signifies bodily harm, a disability, or an injury. Same-sex couples may face very concrete harms, such as the loss of connection with a family member, a family home, and the very status that legalised their love and belonging. This process is not entirely neutral. A legal relation of individuals, despite its lawfulness in the state where it had been concluded, is sacrificed for the protection of national values of the state of non-recognition, which privilege traditional gender roles.

In theory, the *ordre public* analysis under private international law should not be used primarily to protect the local ideology and national ideas on marriage. Private international law analysis should be neutral as much as possible. The analysis should not focus on differences of the laws (e.g. Swedish law differs from Latvian) but instead, on the comparison of the results of application and non-application of the particular rule of foreign law. Would the public policy be harmed, if a same-sex family can reunite? Would it be acceptable to include the same-sex marriage into civil registry, considering that the registry is supposed to reflect the legal reality of marriages contracted abroad? Concrete contents of an *ordre public* clause should only become visible in specific cases and not be presumed in advance in a wide, blanket manner.

Furthermore, considering that there are many different effects of marriage or partnership, the concept of "recognition" should be used with caution and thoughtfulness. Although

66 Permanent Court of International Justice, *Certain German interests in Polish Upper Silesia*, 25 May 1926, PCIJ Series A, No. 7, 42. Also see *Sapphire International Petroleum Ltd. v. National Iranian Oil Company*, 35 I.L.R. 136, Mar. 15, 1963, p. 184, where acquired rights are said to be "undoubtedly one of the general principles of law recognized by international tribunals".

in many countries, information in civil registries is presumed to be accurate before proven otherwise, it is only the court that may take the final decision on material validity of a specific marriage or partnership, again in a concrete case and with specific results. On the other hand, if the court has already adopted a decision that a same-sex marriage should be registered as marriage, identical questions may no longer require new court proceedings. Court praxis can then be relied upon by the other state authorities, such as migration offices or civil registries.

From the private international law perspective,[67] the injury of intersections is most likely to affect same-sex spouses, who are nationals and/or residents of the Baltic states, in particular when they retain close *proximity* to the state where they seek recognition. Intersectionality shows that persons are indirectly forced to choose between the two categories, that of their sexuality or that of their nationality/the place of residence/domicile. Choosing sexuality and hence, personal integrity in a legal sense, means detaching oneself from the state and possible emigration. The ideology of the Baltic states attaches more value to national belonging but from the individual perspective, neither nationality nor residence are more valuable than the person's authentic identity and his/her family ties. In social reality, people tend to be Estonian, Latvian or Lithuanian nationals/residents *and* homosexual. Where nationalism is involved, however, the identity of humans is considered as less important or valuable than the national identity of states.

National identity of Lithuania and Latvia in particular has been tied to heterosexuality and traditional gender roles, including the privileged position of marriage between a man and a woman. Homosexuality has been seen as part of "the decadent West"[68] and traditional ideals as in need of protection against moral colonization. For instance, the Latvian Constitution was changed to entrench that only a man and a woman can enter into marriage. In Lithuania, the principle of complementarity of the man and a woman, and the principle of complementarity of motherhood and fatherhood were introduced in the legislation in 2017.

Nevertheless, protection of same-sex families is also increasing in the Baltic states. Estonia has adopted a registered partnership law and has also ensured inclusion of same-sex marriages contracted abroad as marriages. The courts in Lithuania and Estonia have recognized that family is a gender-neutral concept. These are landmark developments, which build on the development of the European case law. At the same time, they show the readiness of highest instance courts to protect democracy, even if that means going against the opinion of majority. Paraphrasing the ruling of the Constitutional Court of Lithuania, a democratic state protects human dignity and the Lithuanian Constitution

67 I.e. the way it stands in the legal rules and in academic commentaries, but not necessarily in practice.

68 R.C.M. Mole, 'Nationalism and Homophobia in Central and Eastern Europe' *in* K. Slootmaeckers et al (Eds.), *The EU Enlargement and Gay Politics*, London, Palgrave Macmillan, 2016, at p. 100

must be seen as an anti-majoritarian act. Therefore, majority opinion or stereotypes cannot be the basis for discrimination of same-sex couples under the consideration of public policy.[69]

If we look at the reasoning in decisions of the Estonian and Lithuanian courts, which adopted positive decisions, their methodology was rather different. In the Estonian decision, primarily private international law method was applied and the approach was very pragmatic. All arguments on discrimination were rejected in the Estonian case, although the final result was that the same-sex marriage had to be transcribed as marriage in the Estonian civil registry. In the Lithuanian decision, private international law is not analysed at all. Human dignity and equality under the law are central concepts. The Constitutional court of Lithuania also did not explicitly find discrimination but instead provided interpretation that law should apply without discrimination, i.e. regardless of the gender of spouses in the future. This was also done by the Estonian Supreme Court, which even encouraged national state authorities to be creative, in a way, to solve everyday life difficulties of same-sex couples. Same-sex couples as a result can register their lawfully contracted marriages in the Estonian civil registry, obtain residence permits, adopt each other's children and register lawfully obtained parental status. Therefore, although national identity is an authoritative structure, it can expand with time and allow the protection on minority identity categories. In the future, with increasing legal consciousness, it may even include intersectional identities.

In case the same-sex spouses or partners are women, it is also quite common for couples to have children, including in Eastern Europe. The consequences of non-recognition can be additionally harsh for these families with children. The intersections may involve age, as in the *Parris* case mentioned above. It may even involve the category of class, because many emigrants are not rich but instead, are forced to undertake precarious jobs and face the risks of human trafficking for purposes of sex, exploited labour and crime. Litigating for the protection of personal dignity is thus not for everyone, and vulnerability of homosexual couples (especially from rural areas and without any foreign language skills) is high in these situations.

Intersectional analysis would allow for a more individualist approach to cross-border recognition and would encourage adequate consideration of vulnerability of groups that find themselves at intersections. Intersectionality may serve as a useful tool in courts for those individuals, who cannot show that they were discriminated on the basis of only one category, e.g. sexual orientation alone, but they are nevertheless facing injury precisely because they are, for instance, an elderly lesbian couple, who live as Latvian non-citizens. Once the distributive effect of the "injury" for vulnerable groups is realised, the courts could re-think whether justice might be served without such different results. Sometimes

69 Ruling of 11 January 2019 of the Constitutional Court of Lithuania, at 31.3.

the arguments of discrimination do not even need to be used directly but they nevertheless stay between the lines.

Finally, the purpose of intersectionality here in this paper is rather limited, i.e. primarily to highlight some aspects of the problem. If private international law has an effect of intersectionalizing, and I claim that it does, then intersectional analysis seems a worthy tool to illustrate that.

VI Concluding Remarks

The aim of this paper was twofold – first, to introduce the Baltic (Lithuania, Latvia and Estonia) countries' private international law on cross-border recognition of family status, including its recent developments, and second, to suggest an intersectionalized approach to the law on cross-border recognition of family status. As briefly discussed, the Baltic states use different connecting factors to material/substantial validity of marriages contracted abroad: nationality, domicile, residence. The courts in Estonia and Lithuania also used rather different methodologies to recognize the status of same-sex marriages in the contexts of immigration and inclusion into civil registry. Lithuanian and Estonian concepts of the "family" in substantive family law have also gradually been interpreted as gender-neutral. Evolving European standards, and in particular the cases of *Orlandi and others v Italy* (ECtHR, 2017) and *Coman* (ECJ, 2018), clearly had an impact on these decisions.

At the same time, the European courts so far have refrained from applying intersectionality in their reasoning, and neither did national courts notice any intersectional discrimination in cases before them. There are some difficulties in using intersectional analysis in this particular geopolitical area, i.e. the Baltic states. Nevertheless, I argue that an intersectional analysis would allow for a more individualist approach to cross-border recognition and would help to provide adequate consideration of vulnerability of certain groups that find themselves at intersections. Intersectionality may be useful to encourage methodological plurality and to show that the problem cannot be simplified to just one-dimensional analysis. Personal identities of human beings, national identities of the EU member states, and even the identity of private international law, are all multidimensional.

When the Bough Breaks

A Postmodern Approach to Redefining Family Law to Protect Children's Rights in Marriage Equality, Same-Sex Adoption and Religious Freedom Legislation

Crystal Welch[*] *and Melissa Joy Reger*[**]

I Introduction

While traditional ideas of heteronormative families crystallized around the notion that the institution of marriage is circumscribed by the concept of one-man, one-woman unions, this traditional family structure is now experiencing a major paradigmatic shift in favor of more liberal notions of marriage and family. Recent marriage and adoption legislation promoting sexual freedom and marriage equality buttresses the idea that heteronormativity is no longer the status quo for the postmodern family. However, usually ignored in the postmodern family discourse is one of the most significant unresolved issues: the legal protection of children who are affected by same-sex marriage and adoption.

Lesbian, Gay, Bi-sexual, Transgender, and Intersex (LGBTI) describe a person's sexual orientation.[1] *Lesbian* refers to women who love women. While lesbian may be gender specific, all people who prefer people from the same-sex are referred to as gay.[2] Bi-sexual persons prefer both men and women, not dependent on sexual anatomy.[3] Transgender refers to an internal gender identity, not sexual preference. Intersex refers to a person presenting with the physical anatomy of both male and female genders.[4] Some references include a "Q" for questioning, more common amongst youth, which refers to the period in which people realize they may be part of the LGBT community.[5] In an effort to attempt sensitivity, GLAAD Media Reference offers a guide for sensitive reference terms for writing which foster inclusivity.[6] LGBTI, seeming most inclusive of all of the groups, will remain the reference throughout the paper for the purposes of this writing.

---

* Professor at Mississippi College School of Law Family and Children's Law Center.

** M.E.D.L. and J.D., Mississippi College School of Law Alumni.

1 'Supporting your LGBTQ Youth: A Guide for Foster Parents', https://www.childwelfare.gov/pubPDFs/LGBTQyouth.pdf#page=1&view=Creating a Welcoming Home for Youth.

2 Ibid.

3 Ibid.

4 'What is Intersex?', Intersex Society of North America, http://www.isna.org/faq/what_is_intersex.

5 'Supporting your LGBTQ Youth', op cit, n. 1.

6 GLAAD Media Reference Guide - Terms to Avoid, http://www.glaad.org/reference/offensive.

In its *Obergefell* decision,[7] the Supreme Court of the Unites States dramatically challenged the traditional context of family with the controversial overhaul of conventional marriage. But many questions concerning children's rights in the context of same-sex marriage have largely been left unanswered. Specifically, *Obergefell*, declared the battle for marriage equality concluded, giving LGBTI and same-sex parents absolute family rights in all aspects, but did so seemingly without any consideration at all for the children affected by the decision. Legislation often addresses the rights of parents; little progress has been made in children's rights to ensure protection for the most vulnerable factor in the equation.

Intentionally, this paper draws awareness to the *Obergefell* decision lacking comprehensive children's rights advocacy. As children are the most vulnerable humans in the process of adoption, a most severe injustice would be to go without mentioning their constitutional rights as such should be held paramount to the rights granted to adults. As the adults possess the power and capital to bring claims against the courts, most suits entail the struggles of the adults and the rights which must accompany their requests. But at the heart of the matter in adoption cases lies an innocent child, powerless to the system controlling his/her relationships and wellbeing. The paper in no way means to assert that the rights granted by the Court are inadequate, as no advocacy for additional or differing legislation will be found. In fact, children's rights often overlap with parental rights in adoption proceedings. The main goal is to remind attorneys, parents, and other readers of decisions that must prioritize the child's best interest in all adoption proceedings as it is inhumane to disavow the rights of the child in such proceedings with permanent legal consequences.

Section I of this article addresses the state of children's rights in the United States before *Obergefell*. Section II examines the *Obergefell* decision and analyzes the results of that opinion in the context of children's rights. Section III offers a new way to "rock the cradle" by shifting the focus of concern from the rights of parents to the rights of children and offers suggestions. Finally, section IV addresses international efforts in LGBTI family rights including children's rights.

II Rocking the Cradle: Children's Rights, an Afterthought of LGBTI Families and Adoptions?

To best understand exactly how the *Obergefell* ruling ultimately broke the bough on children's rights, one must look all the way back to the original conception of equality and constitutional rights, both penumbral and enumerated, and understand whether the fight against adult discrimination in the family dynamic should also include the children affected. But how? What is "equality" where children are considered? What are "children's rights"?

7 *Obergefell v. Hodges*, 135 S. Ct. 2584, 2600 (U.S. 2015).

How do new family equality rights address and protect children's rights within this new family dynamic? How is the United States working to protect the rights of children in LGBTI adoptions? What is being done on an international scale to protect children's rights in LGBTI adoptions? These questions invite discussion addressing the key issues surrounding children's rights and the new legislation and invite consideration of protections already adopted in other countries.

A *Penumbral Rights in the Constitution: Explaining the* Obergefell *Decision to Grant LGBTI Marriage and Family Rights*

"Equality" means all individuals in the same circumstances should be treated in the same manner.[8] On its face, equality seems to be an easy right with which to comply. Many are taught the Golden Rule growing up, treat others as you would have them treat you.[9] But, in fact, equality, the right to be treated like everyone else in the same situation, continues to invoke the fight of the century. Declaring a categorical win in the fight for equality in LGBTI marriage and family rights failed to comprehensively address a major stakeholder in the fight, the children who are products of these same-sex unions. Family and marriage rights are not explicitly enumerated in the Constitution. Enumerated rights articulated by the Constitution are few. Enumerated rights are rights specifically defined within the Constitution. [10] Penumbral rights, such as privacy rights, are not explicitly stated in the constitution, but are equally protected by language in the Constitution. Black's Law Dictionary defines a penumbra as "a surrounding area or periphery of uncertain extent," and further explains the penumbral rights as "constitutional guarantees ... implied" in the Bill of Rights language in our Constitution.[11] Although privacy rights are not articulated specifically in the constitution, the Supreme Court has held the fourth amendment contains language such as "secure in their persons, houses," implicating rights to privacy in certain places.[12] Although some penumbral rights may be easier to carve out of the language than others, the distinction does not mean those rights should not be respected. Penumbral rights, such as privacy and parental rights, oftentimes spark debate, but understanding these types of rights helps to explain how the Supreme Court debated the *Obergefell* decision.

8 J.F. Gonzalez-Bertomeu & R. Gargarella (Eds.), *The Latin American Casebook: Courts, Constitutions, and Rights*, Routledge, 2016.
9 *Mark* 7:12 (King James Version).
10 'Enumerate', *Black's Law Dictionary*, 4th Pocket Ed., 1996.
11 'Penumbra', *Black's Law Dictionary*, ibid.
12 USCS Const. Amend. 4.

B *Children's Rights: Precious Cargo in the Cradle*

The idea that there is still a fight over equality and discrimination in any category in this century may seem preposterous. But, the fight for equality is not even a back-burner topic in today's courts as many would expect. Discrimination is alive and well, evolving daily. And amid this fight for equality, often the biggest losers are children. Although the United States recognizes "age" as a class deserving of equality rights, very little has been done to ensure children's rights are considered.[13] When discussing family rights, children's rights have been included as an after-thought at best. Policies should start with protections for the most vulnerable, not the most privileged.

Many policies, laws, rules, and statutes grant rights to children in all types of families. Rights such as social security, child support, and custodial agreements all are protected by federal and state statutes. These rights become even more important when considered in adoptions, especially when children depend on the state, as the rights of their natural parents have been terminated. Federal provisions have provided protection for the care of children, such as the Family Medical Leave Act[14] which grants time off for parents when children are ill, including adopted children, and the Omnibus Budget Reconciliation Act of 1993, Title IV, Subtitle D-Group Health Plans, Section 4301, which grants "a provision that guarantees adopted children the same access to health insurance as birth children."[15] Such rights granted to children must be considered in adoptions in order to ensure the well-being of the child.

Before *Obergefell*, LGBTI couples were generally not considered suitable parents for adoption in several states. Only single persons, or heterosexual married couples were considered fit to adopt children. Traditionally, heterosexual married couples were thought to protect inheritable rights of children, provide a clean home in a safe neighborhood with both a father and mother to rear the child to adulthood, and possibly provide the financial benefits of a dual income household.[16] These rights have critical consequences.

For instance, in 2009, April DeBoer and Jane Rowse fostered three boys, each individually since lesbian couples were not allowed to adopt as a same-sex couple in Michigan.[17] If an emergency were to arise, schools and hospitals may treat the three children as if they had only one parent.[18] Were tragedy to befall either DeBoer or Rowse, the other would have no legal rights over the children she was not allowed to adopt.[19] The couple filed a lawsuit in a Michigan federal district court challenging the constitutionality of the discrim-

13 42 USCS § 6101.
14 Family and Medical Leave Act of 1993, 1993 Enacted H.R. 1, 103 Enacted H.R. 1, 107 Stat. 6.
15 103 P.L. 66, 107 Stat. 312, 1993 Enacted H.R. 2264, 103 Enacted H.R. 2264.
16 *Obergefell*, op cit, n. 7.
17 Ibid.
18 Ibid.
19 Ibid.

inatory adoption ban. The couple later amended their claim to challenge the same-sex *marriage* ban, the crux of the national legal debate. The district court overturned the ban; however, the decision was subsequently reversed by the United States Court of Appeals which upheld Michigan's same-sex marriage ban. DeBoer and Rowse then appealed the decision to the United States Supreme Court, where their case was consolidated with the *Obergefell* case. The two women argued that LGBTI families could offer guarantees to rights for children with a favorable holding in *Obergefell.*[20]

III When the Wind Blows, the Cradle Will Rock: *Obergefell*

In the 2015 case, *Obergefell v. Hodges*, the United States Supreme Court decided that the Equal Protection and Due Process clauses of the Fourteenth Amendment to the United States Constitution guarantees the fundamental right of marriage to same-sex couples.[21] In that case, several same-sex couples sued their state agencies in an effort to strike their state's constitutional ban on gay marriage in the following states: Michigan, Kentucky, Ohio, and Tennessee.[22] Each state defined marriage as a union between one man and one woman.[23] The plaintiffs were successful in trial court, however, the appellate court reversed the decision and decided that the states' constitutional ban on gay marriage was valid, and did not violate the Equal Protection or Due Process clauses of the Fourteenth Amendment.[24]

Subsequently, in a 5-4 decision, the United State Supreme Court grappled with the constitutional crisis and addressed two essential questions: (1) Does a state have a legal obligation to license a marriage for a same-sex couple based on the Fourteenth Amendment; and (2) Does the Fourteenth Amendment legally obligate a state to give full recognition of the marital union of a same-sex couple that was lawfully licensed in a different state? The Supreme Court held that the state is legally obligated to license a marriage between two persons of the same sex and the state is also required to recognize the marital union of a same-sex couple which was lawfully licensed and performed in a different state.[25]

Although the *Obergefell* decision established a right to marriage and family, it gives little affect to children's rights other than an understanding of the "closeness of their own family."[26] LGBTI citizens now have the right to adopt children under the family rights granted in *Obergefell.*[27] The Court did consider the "permanency" and "stability" of a

20 Ibid.
21 Ibid.
22 Ibid.
23 Ibid.
24 Ibid.
25 Ibid.
26 Ibid.
27 Ibid.

married family adopting children no matter the sexual orientation to be positive for children living in LGBTI families.[28] Noticeably missing was discussion on rights of children adopted from a heterosexual family into an LGBTI family or vice-versa, or of an LGBTI youth adopted into a heterosexual home. Will their opinions be considered when placed in a home with families with different sexual orientation? Will children's rights be second to the family decisions incorporated into the LGBTI rights granted by *Obergefell*? Is the United States doing enough to ensure children's rights come first in decisions such as adoption? It would be an injustice to these children not to consider their rights.

"Love wins" is the slogan which emphasizes the LGBTI equal rights movement. *Obergefell* defined marriage equality rights and became known as the 'win' for 'love' in the marriage equality movement for LGBTI persons.[29] *Obergefell* addressed family rights specifically as a "unified whole: "[T]he right to 'marry, establish a home and bring up children' [as] a central part of the liberty protected by the Due Process Clause."[30] So, "love wins." But, within the categorical "win" children's rights were universally disregarded. The ruling has rocked the cradle for children's rights in some of the very families the ruling set out to protect.

Obergefell did not establish a broad right against sexual orientation discrimination in all contexts, only under the right to marry and substantive due process under the Fourteenth Amendment to the United States Constitution.[31] While the case categorically created marriage and family rights for LGBTI, the case did not generate rights to LGBTI as a classification applicable to all constitutional rights such as employment and other discrimination under Title II and Title VII.[32] Without recognition as a class, LGBTI persons are forced to have to fight for those rights heterosexual citizens already have.

Obergefell opponents claimed LGBTI family cultures embrace and celebrate immoral behavioral choices.[33] This unbroken tradition argument did not hold up in the context of LGBTI families. The argument being a mere pretext for visceral dislike did not show harm against other people, including children, in any way.[34] Being treated as second-class citizens does hurt the LGBTI people being subjected to the discrimination, by way of "demean[ing] the lives of LGBTI persons."[35] Just as farcical as the opinion given in *Dred Scott* stating "[Negros] ... had no rights which the white man was bound to respect", so seems the irrational parallel to hate encountered by LGBTI people by their opponents.[36] Previously

28 Ibid.
29 Ibid at 2600.
30 Ibid at 2604.
31 *Dew v. Edmunds*, 2015 U.S. Dist. LEXIS 138708, *28-30 (D. Idaho Oct. 8, 2015).
32 Ibid.
33 Ibid at 2596.
34 Ibid at 2621.
35 Ibid.
36 *Scott v. Sandford*, 60 U.S. 393, 407 (U.S. 1857).

unchallenged assumptions were directly addressed by the Court. Once a tradition in society to make laws against sodomy and LGBTI rights, recent laws have shown significant changes over the years in addressing the LGBTI community in a less traditional sense, often granting rights in different categories, and the Court recognized change in the tradition.[37]

IV Preventing the Fall: Shifting the Focus from Parent to Child

The United States should be a front runner for children's rights advocacy instead of rocking the cradle with categorical decisions while waiting to see if the bough breaks, harming those most affected, children. So how do we stop the bough from breaking while respecting the rights granted to parents in LGBTI marriage and families including adoptions? First, states must evaluate current marriage equality statutes identify when the laws are not keeping up with the trends. Second, legal uncertainty threatens children's rights and should be evaluated to ensure children's rights are considered. Intergenerational conflicts should be addressed to ensure that shifts in family dynamics are adapted. Finally, judicial discretion in adoptions should be held sacred to ensure children's rights are considered first in adoptions without the risk of litigation looming over that decision.

A *Marriage Equality: Shifting Winds Bring Change*

Obergefell redefined marriage, but courts can wreak havoc when rulings supersede societal change at a race pace. The Court heard the case when there arose a split in the circuits, Michigan, Ohio, Kentucky, and Tennessee represented in the case as respondent states.[38] Hawaii and Massachusetts began the split with early decisions in favor of same-sex marriage.[39] Just as in *Brown*, "deliberate speed" often means take your time.[40] Judicial remedies for time, as with *Obergefell*, created options for those where the Court could not force the states to change their laws, but could establish constitutional rights for a group of citizens, essentially pushing the fast forward button on the tape player for the states with laws specifically prohibiting LGBTI family matters.

But where rights may be violated by action and omission, normally remedies are designed to be implemented immediately. The changes in LGBTI rights have been sluggish. *Obergefell* offered a sweeping reshaping of those rights of LGBTI people in marriage including family. Some rights, by necessity, are restricted, but there is a bundle of rights which should remain unchanged. Children's rights should be in that list. *Obergefell* failed

37 *Obergefell*, op cit, n. 7.
38 Ibid at 2618.
39 Ibid at 2622.
40 *Brown v. Board of Education*, 347 U.S. 483 (1954).

to adequately consider children's rights, because the only rights on the table in the litigation were those of the LGBTI adults claiming family and marriage rights. Unfortunately, *Obergefell* rocked the cradle, and failed to address the very people those family creations would directly affect, offering very few words, but a big push rocking the cradle of state's rights.

As the family dynamic shifts, it is easy to see where the law is not keeping up with the trends. It is even more evident when the Supreme Court issues a holding that overturns statutes in over half the states in the United States, leaving legislators scrambling to put political differences aside to pass legislation for the states to follow. And that is my main goal here, to encourage legislators, attorneys, and other readers to set aside their political talking points and prioritize the rights of children who have parents who are in same-sex couples. Whether the lawmakers are in favor of the holding, the burden remains to protect the interests of children. What happens when a child builds a relationship with their parent's LGBTI partner who is living in the household and takes the child to school each day? When that child is sick, can that partner take the child to the doctor? Should that partner suddenly die, does the child have any inheritable rights from living with them as a "parent figure" and fostering those relationships? No. So it is important to set aside political views vis-à-vis same-sex adoption in the attempt to secure the same rights for children who are products of such relationships.

Intergenerational conflict is another detrimental factor worth analysis in the fight to encourage states to continue to update their marriage and adoption laws to keep up with trends in the postmodern family. A courtroom steeped in tradition may possibly feel the winds of change more briskly than a millennial judge who approaches domestic relations law with a more postmodern view as opposed to traditional puritanical interpretations of the law.

Although the Supreme Court granted rights to LGBTI persons wishing to adopt in its *Obergefell decision*, Mississippi was still the only state to explicitly ban same-sex adoption.[41] In 2015, four same-sex couples filed a lawsuit challenging Mississippi's ban on same-sex adoption as unconstitutional in the *Campaign for Southern Equality* case. The state statute, Miss. Code Ann. § 93-17-3(5), forbids adoption "by couples of the same gender." However, in March 2016, the court in Mississippi issued an injunction enjoining enforcement of the same-sex adoption ban. The court maintained that the *Obergefell* decision "foreclosed litigation over laws interfering with the right to marry and rights and responsibilities intertwined with marriage."[42] The court concluded that the logic in Obergefell protects the rights of gay persons to marry, as well as all marital rights entangled in that right to marry, including the right to adopt. Thus, the court decided that the state statute is therefore

41 Miss. Code Ann. 93-17-3.

42 Miss. Code Ann. 93-17-5.

unconstitutional as it violates the Equal Protection Clause. However, the statute banning same sex adoption remains in the adoption chapter of Mississippi domestic relations law despite the trend demanding marriage equality. The state faces the legal conundrum in which rights have been granted by the Supreme Court, but state statute fails to reflect the constitutional rights carved out in *Obergefell.*[43]

In a similar case, appellate roulette rocked the cradle for an LGBTI couple in Alabama this past year.[44] In *V.L. v. E.L.*, the parent E.L. had three children through reproductive technology during an extended partnership (1995-2011) with her same-sex partner, V.L., during which the couple rented a home in Georgia and petitioned the Georgia family court to allow V.L. to adopt the children without relinquishing her own parental rights.[45] The Georgia court granted the adoption and both partners raised the children together. However, in 2011, the couple ended their relationship, and E.L. denied V.L. visitation rights with the children.[46] V.L. petitioned the Alabama Family Court to recognize the Georgia adoption and grant visitation rights and won.[47] E.L. appealed arguing Georgia did not have jurisdiction to enter the original judgment based on a third-party adoption statute that did not allow a second party to adopt without the first party having all rights terminated, but the court rejected that argument.[48]

The Alabama Supreme Court reversed, saying without proper jurisdiction, the Court did not have to give full faith and credit to the Georgia judgment.[49] Certiorari was granted by the Supreme Court who reversed and remanded claiming the statute argued was not the jurisdictional statute granting the court in Georgia rights to hear the case, and the jurisdiction was proper under the Georgia statute allowing the court jurisdiction to hear adoptions.[50] Therefore, V.L. was allowed to have visitation rights just as a heterosexual noncustodial parent would. Although the case was not LGBTI-specific at the appellate level, it is a current example of the ongoing legal battles LGBTI families face to retain marital and privacy rights to their children.

43 Ibid.
44 *V.L. v. E.L.*, 136 S. Ct. 1017 (U.S. Mar. 7, 2016).
45 Ibid at 1019.
46 Ibid.
47 Ibid.
48 Ibid at 1020.
49 Ibid.
50 Ibid at 1022.

B *Judicial Discretion: Facing the Winds*

Children's relationships with their family play a large role in their development.[51] In Mississippi, Chancellors have judicial discretion to address many of the psychological needs of children going through foster care and adoption proceedings for placements that may be of controversial change for children, such as new religions, siblings' issues, etc.[52] Mississippi has gone further by its holding in *Brunt:*

> the granting of authority to the court in adoption proceedings to make investigations limited to matters concerning whether the child is a proper subject for adoption, the petitioners are suitable parents for the child, the adoption is in the best interest of the child, and any other facts or circumstances which might be material to the proposed adoption, is not unreasonable, and such procedures do not constitute a denial of due process of law.[53]

In one of my recent cases, a Caucasian client and her Caucasian husband, adopted an African American child in Mississippi. The judge recommended that the parents attend training on how to fix the child's hair as the texture and dryness would require a technique with which the new family was unfamiliar. In like manner, some judges may consider that a child's transition from a heterosexual family to a LGBTI family may bring about psychological changes that could possibly affect the child's development. "In adoption proceedings, the welfare of the child [should be] the primary consideration."[54] However, the *Obergefell* decision may place a judge at risk of litigation should the sexuality of a member of the family be considered, even under the current law allowing for discretion.[55] *Obergefell* did not address the affect to investigations within an adoption proceeding. Currently, a Chancellor has discretion to conduct investigations, often through a court-appointed Guardian ad Litem, to protect the best interests of children.[56] One could potentially argue that the new LGBTI family rights remove the safeguard for family law judges to address issues related to sexuality if the parent's or the child's sexuality becomes an issue for the child, which could necessitate either therapy or alternative placement, without fearing the risk of possible litigation questioning the constitutionality of the judge's discretion. However, it is important to note that differences in sexual orientation may not be an issue for most children's well-being even if the family dynamic is a new concept for the child under

51 J. Dwyer, 'A Taxonomy of Children's Existing Rights in State Decision Making About Their Relationships', *Wm. & Mary Bill Rts. J.*, Vol. 11, 2003, p. 845 at 846.
52 Miss. Code Ann. 93-17-11.
53 *Brunt v. Watkins*, 233 Miss. 307, 101 So. 2d 852 (1958).
54 Eggleston v. Landrum, 210 Miss. 645, 50 So. 2d 364 (1951).
55 Miss. Code 93-17-11.
56 Ibid.

Obergefell. Sexual orientation should not be viewed as a condition that may affect a child's upbringing. A parent should be judged by their ability to provide for and care for a child. However, if a case arises where either a parent's or the child's sexual orientation becomes an issue as far as the child's physical, psychological or emotional welfare is concerned, a judge should have the right to address the issue in child custody and adoption matters without fearing possible backlash.

Many states address sexual orientation by evaluating the effect of the parental relationship on the child's overall wellbeing. Most cases have been unable to find detrimental effect of sexual orientation on the children's welfare. In *Black v. Black*, the Washington court held conduct and conversation of a LGBTI parent could not be limited unless it was found to show specific and severe harm to the children, which the court failed to find.[57] In Tennessee, "parents' sexual orientations can be a factor that the trial court should consider in making a custody decision, but … [only when there is] negative effect on a child's welfare."[58]

In *Murray v. Murray*, however, a Tennessee Court held the mother's sexual orientation with multiple partners along with her drug use constituted a material change in circumstances warranting loss of custodial rights.[59] None of the above cases spelled out a specific test for child welfare considerations for sexual orientation of a parent and the effect of that relationship on the child, nor does it specify which children's rights must be affected before an adverse effect can be claimed.

Luckily, the ruling in *Obergefell* did identify some rights for LGBTI parents which affect children currently living with same-sex parents. In Smith, two lesbian women decided to adopt from Kazakhstan.[60] Due to laws against same-sex adoption, only Smith adopted the child, but both Smith and Gordon contributed financially to the adoption proceedings and to the family.[61] They lived together as a family for years.[62] When the two separated, Gordon sought custodial rights of the adopted child.[63] The Supreme Court of Delaware concluded she had no parental rights to the child.[64] After *Obergefell*, parental rights for LGBTI couples adopting in the United States will be simplified in many ways so that the children can continue to enjoy the same rights of visitation and access to both parents as do children who are the products of heterosexual couples.

57 2016 Wash. App. LEXIS 411, 16 (Wash. Ct. App. Mar. 8, 2016).
58 *C.W.H. v. L.A.S.*, 2016 Tenn. App. LEXIS 808, *25 (Tenn. Ct. App. Oct. 31, 2016).
59 2010 Tenn. App. LEXIS 608 (Tenn. Ct. App. Sept. 28, 2010).
60 *Smith v. Gordon*, 968 A.2d 1 (Del. 2009).
61 Ibid at 3.
62 Ibid.
63 Ibid at 4.
64 Ibid.

V Cradles Rock Abroad: Intercountry LGBTI Anti-Discrimination Adoptions Face Same Winds

In my attempt to analyze the protections granted in Obergefell in the context of intercountry adoption, I noticed that many cases discussed The Hague Treaty and the more recent shift to the United Nations Convention for Rights of Children. An international adoption allows parents domiciled in one nation to travel to a foreign country to adopt a child there under the laws of the child's nation, but only establishes guardianship under United States immigration laws for visas for the child.[65] The process of completing the adoption in the parent's native country is called intercountry adoption.[66] To reference the adoptions discussed in the paper as already complete in both the home country and the parent's country, the paper will be discussing intercountry adoptions. To best understand the trends in intercountry adoption decisions, as well as international LGBTI decisions, one must first know which treaty the country has ratified and what each set of laws entails.

The Hague Convention on the Protection of Children and Co-operation in Respect of Inter-Country Adoption (Hague Adoption Convention), signed into law in the United States in 1994 and came into full force in 2008, is described by the Department of State as "an international agreement to establish safeguards to ensure that intercountry adoptions take place in the best interests of the child." Specific to adoptions, the law aides in defining children's rights, but also guides the drafting of relevant new legislation across the nation. Hague does not prioritize in-country placement over out-of-country placement. It prioritizes connecting children with the family they need and deserve, despite nationality.

The United States professed its interest in protecting children's rights in adoptions by signing The Hague Treaty in 1964, but arguably the last fifty years have brought to light many additional areas of concern in the fight for children's rights, including the new LGBTI family rights granted in *Obergefell*.[67] While The Hague Treaty established comprehensive international children's rights laws affecting intercountry adoptions in the United States, it does not offer enough protection for children's rights. The United Nation's Convention for Rights of Children (UNCRC) provides for a more up-to-date, comprehensive list of rights for children, but has not been ratified by the United States because the convention arguably competes with intercountry adoption laws the United States wishes to uphold. The United States, by not signing the UNCRC, does not wish to send a message against comprehensive children's rights protections, however, at the same time not wanting to

65 'International adoption", Black's Law Dictionary, op cit, n. 10.

66 'Intercountry adoption', U.S. Dept of State, at https://travel.state.gov/content/adoptionsabroad/en/adoption-process/what-is-intercountry-adoption.html.

67 'Understanding the Hague Convention', U.S. Dept. of State, at https://travel.state.gov/content/adoptions-abroad/en/hague-convention/understanding-the-hague-convention.html.

render intercountry adoptions almost impossible for United States citizens wishing to adopt internationally.

The United Nations Convention for the Rights of Children (UNCRC) broadly:

> ensures the rights to each child within their jurisdiction without discrimination of any kind, irrespective of the child's or his or her parent's or legal guardian's race, color, sex, language, religion, political or other opinion, national, ethnic or social origin, property, disability, birth or other status.[68]

On the surface, the UNCRC seems to provide the most up-to-date, comprehensive list of protection of rights of children, but requires the child first be "cared for in a suitable manner in the child's country of origin," language difficult to prove if arguing against the opposing country they are not providing 'suitable care' in order to adopt.[69] The United States signed the UNCRC in 1995, but failed to present the legislation to the Senate for ratification, a major reason being conflicting intercountry adoption law. Ratification of the UNCRC to ensure rights for all children could be considered, but currently faces understandable opposition from intercountry and intercountry adoption proponents in the United States.

The Multiethnic Placement Act (MEPA), as amended by Congress in 1996, eliminating discrimination based on ethnicity in intercountry adoptions directly conflicts with CRC language considering children only be placed with families of their same ethnicity and origin, going so far as to recommend eliminating intercountry adoptions.[70] The UNCRC places emphasis on the interests of child remaining with the country of origin, giving those countries a greater interest in retaining offspring produced, no matter how unwanted or neglected, in their own countries. By ratifying the UNCRC, the United States would effectively render MEPA useless and stagnate intercountry adoption by forcing the U.S. to consider home origin and ethnicity in all intercountry adoptions. By eliminating nurturing, competent, caring homes on intercountry landscapes based solely on an ethnicity argument, the UNCRC takes the side of the country and parent origin over the rights of children in need and awaiting intercountry adoption. So, although the UNCRC may protect children's rights in many areas, until the contention with intercountry adoption is satisfied, the U.S. must continue to follow The Hague Treaty with "due diligence."[71]

How are other countries granting children's rights while also upholding rights to LGBTI people? Columbia, Costa Rica, and Chile have established rights for LGBTI persons, but only Chile instituted a check for children's rights into the test for family protections. Other

---

68 http://www.ohchr.org/EN/ProfessionalInterest/Pages/CRC.aspx.
69 CRC, art. 21.
70 P.L. 104-188, s. 1808(a)(3).
71 Understanding the Hague Convention, op cit, n. 57.

countries are far behind, relying on the UNCRC language, providing institutional care in most areas over the choice of adoption, with over 160 countries having signed the UNCRC.[72]

The Constitutional Court of Colombia established the need for positive and focused action to be taken by authorities to adopt measures and provisions that secure benefits for individuals unable to secure them alone that would allow the individual to lead a dignified life.[73] (Typically marginalized, poorly organized people lack available political or judicial structures that protect class rights.[74]) This same court has since upheld rulings concerning rights for LGBTI groups to free development of personality.[75] Social discrimination cannot be based on behavior.[76] Student rights to free development of personality and education have been granted.[77] In Decision C-481/98, the court found:

> no evidence that these people are more prone to sexual abuse than the rest of the population, and [the teachers' presence] in the classroom affects the free development of the students' personalities ... [and] established ... an intimate part of an individual's identity and has special constitutional protection.[78]

In 2006, Costa Rican Magistrate Vargas Benavides addressed the issue of family rights for LGBTI:

> legal systems must evolve and respond to urgent needs and realities, adapting themselves to the most elementary principles that protect the human being as such.... [The] Constitution and intercountry instruments on human rights does not allow to exclude the LGBTI minority of the institution of marriage.[79]

By humanizing the right to sexual orientation, Costa Rica eased access to courts for a previously marginalized group.

Karen Atala v. Chile, a Supreme Court decision in Chile, granted a father rights to his children because the mother began having a LGBTI relationship with another woman.[80] The Inter-American Court of Human Rights, set aside the ruling when reports were considered proving the children had suffered no harm.[81] The court concluded that the parents'

72 United Nations Human Rights Office of the High Commissioner, Convention on the Rights of the Child, http://www.ohchr.org/EN/ProfessionalInterest/Pages/CRC.aspx.
73 Gonzalez-Bertomeu & Gargarella (Ed.), op cit, n. 8.
74 Ibid at 2.
75 Ibid.
76 Ibid.
77 Ibid at 10.
78 Ibid at 68-69.
79 Ibid at 66.
80 Ibid at 13.
81 Ibid.

LGBTI relationship did not affect child welfare while also recognizing sexual orientation as protected under the UNCRC.[82] The court opposed the idea that LGBTI parents were bad for the children's development.[83] This same court "recognized the legitimacy of the principle of the best interests of the child" by clarifying the child's best interests cannot be used to justify sexual orientation discrimination, but instead saying the court cannot take the social condition into consideration as an element.[84] The decision means children's rights will be considered in family court matters such as custody and adoption, but without consideration for the sexual orientation of the parents.[85]

Cuba holds an alarming position on children's rights, adoption, and intercountry adoption. Although Cuba, meaning to embrace children's rights issues by adopting The Hague Treaty, has done little to improve intercountry adoption rights and children's rights in the country.[86] The country forbids intercountry adoptions, and rarely approves in-country family adoptions.[87] Instead, children sent to orphanages often grow up to commit crimes and are moved from one institution into the Cuban prison system.[88] The Bureau of Consular Affairs for Intercountry Adoptions of the U.S. Department of State reports United States citizens married to Cuban nationals wishing to adopt are allowed to adopt but are met with tough restrictions through United States laws including 101(b)(1)(E) of the Immigration and Nationality Act, and then Cuban laws requiring them to live with the child for two years before "being eligible for U.S. immigrant visas on the basis of the adoption until the U.S. citizen adoptive parents accrue two years of legal custody and joint residence with the child outside the United States, among other requirements."[89]

Similarly, a study in Brazil revealed foster-care statistics that raise questions regarding children's rights. Most children in Brazil are institutionalized under the foster-care system.[90] 37,861 children and adolescents in foster care were part of the study, of whom 36,929 were in institutional care services and 932 in private family home care services.[91]

As intercountry efforts to include children's rights as part of adoption decisions increase with the language of the UNCRC infiltrating in adoption decisions, countries must continue to ensure that the interest remains in the rights of the child. Rights for LGBTI families internationally substantiated through the UNCRC language proves a promising step for

---

82 Ibid.
83 Ibid.
84 Ibid at 73.
85 Ibid.
86 'Cuba', U.S. Dept. of State, at https://travel.state.gov/content/adoptionsabroad/en/country-information/learn-about-a-country/cuba.html.
87 Ibid.
88 Ibid.
89 Ibid.
90 S. Goncalves de Assis, L. Wernersbach Pinto & J. Quintes Avanci 'Nationwide Study on Children and Adolescents in Foster CareIn Brazil', *Paediatrics Today*, Vol. 10, No. 2, (2014), pp. 135-146.
91 Ibid.

both the rights of the adults and the children in these families. However, language stifling intercountry adoption, and increasingly institutionalizing children convolutes the intention of the UNCRC Act in the fight for children's rights and should be evaluated on an international political scale.

VI Conclusion

Intentionally, this paper maintains that the Obergefell decision lacks the spirit of children's rights advocacy. As children are the most vulnerable humans in the process of adoption, a most severe injustice would be to go without mentioning their constitutional rights as such should be held paramount to the rights granted to the adults who are legally responsible for rearing them to adulthood. Much of the court opinion is obsessed with the rights of the adults seeking to adopt. However, the polestar consideration in adoption and child custody cases is the best interest of the child. The paper in no way suggests that the rights granted by the Court in Obergefell are insignificant. In fact, in many aspects children's rights overlap with parental rights in adoption proceedings. The purpose is to encourage legislators, attorneys, and other readers that we must set aside our political affiliations no matter whether we agree or disagree with same-sex marriage and adoption, and first and foremost prioritize the child's best interest in all adoption proceedings as it is inhumane to disavow the rights of the child in such proceedings regarding the permanent rights of a child and their access to benefits such as inheritance, social security, and all other benefits received from the parent-child relationship. Children who are products of same-sex couples deserve the same rights and benefits that children of heterosexual couples deserve. The hope is to continue to rock the cradle in ways that promote children's rights without breaking the bough in which those rights hang in such delicate balance.

Part III
New Models of Parenthood

Argentina's Absence of Regulation of Surrogate Motherhood: A Case of Judicial Activism and Unforeseeable Consequences

Mercedes Ales[*]

I Introduction: Proposals to Regulate Surrogate Motherhood in Argentina

In recent years Argentina has experienced a major transformation in substantive law as a result of a new Civil and Commercial Code (the "Code") that came into force on August 1, 2015.[1] This transformation has had a deep impact in the field of family law and has reshaped most rules relating to parent-child relationships, including parentage and legal parenthood.[2] Given the short period of time the Code has been in effect, the full implications of its new rules are still being explored and clarified by the courts.

Although the new Code was largely based on the draft bill sent to Congress by the Executive Branch in 2012, there were some fundamental changes in matters concerning family law. One such change was the suppression of the proposed legal framework involving surrogacy agreements contained in article 562 of the draft bill, which was to apply when a couple sought to obtain parentage over a child whose birth mother was a third party. When discussed in Congress, this section was eliminated on the ground that the matters involved required a deeper analysis and more thorough research. In other words, Congress seemed to suggest that Argentine society was not yet at a stage where it was ready to discuss surrogacy.

* Professor of Family Law, Faculty of Law, Universidad del Salvador and Professor of Family Law and Succession Law, Faculty of Law, University CEMA, Argentina.

1 The full text of the Code, as updated, is available at: http://servicios.infoleg.gob.ar/infolegInternet/verNorma.do?id=235975. The Code was enacted by means of Law 26.994.

2 For purposes of clarity, "parentage" will be used to indicate a parent-child relationship based on biology and "legal parenthood" will indicate the attribution of legal status to someone in relation to a child. Some of the main changes introduced by the Code include: the recognition of parenthood by means of assisted reproduction techniques as equal to natural and adoptive parenthood; rules determining paternal and maternal parenthood in same-sex couples and also in cases involving use of donor gametes; and a legal definition of "procreational will". The applicable dispositions dealing with assisted reproduction techniques and parenthood can be found in Title V, Chapter 2 ("General Rules Pertaining to Parenthood by Means of Human Assisted Reproductive Techniques"), arts. 560 through 564.

As a result, the rules for determining maternity remain mostly unchanged: the Roman principle of *mater semper certa est* is to be applied when determining biological parentage upon birth. Motherhood can also be intentional in the case of lesbian couples, so long as the birth mother's spouse or partner expresses her autonomous desire to be held as mother to her partner's child.[3] Adoption rules remain unchanged and contemplate adoptive maternity for women regardless of their marital status, including the case of adoption of a partner's or spouse's child. The adoption regime prohibits the direct transfer of parental rights or custody of a child by the biological parents.[4]

II The Current Legal Vacuum

The suppressed article 562 of the draft bill established a set of rules for creating an enforceable surrogacy agreement, including the need to obtain prior judicial authorization by a competent court. Failure to comply with these rules would render the agreement unenforceable and, as a consequence, parenthood would be settled according to the general rules of parentage – namely, the *mater semper certa est* principle.

In order to obtain a judicial authorization, the parties were required to demonstrate: (i) that the child's best interests were the paramount consideration; (ii) that the surrogate was entering into the agreement of her own free will, in a good state of health, without any genetic link to the child to be conceived and without receiving any monetary compensation; and (iii) that the intended parents had no possibility of carrying out a pregnancy and at least one of them was genetically linked to the child to be conceived. A limit of two surrogacy agreements per woman was imposed and fertility clinics were prohibited from implanting any embryo in a surrogate while judicial authorization was pending. Surrogates were also required to have at least one biological child of their own.

Although article 562 of the draft bill was suppressed, the Code contains no explicit prohibition on surrogacy. Even though the rules for determining motherhood through birth remain unchanged, there are no specific provisions in Argentine law to clearly indicate the outcome if a surrogacy agreement were entered into. Would such an agreement be deemed null? What consequences would the agreement have for the parties involved, especially for the child? And what conditions, if any, would be imposed in order for a surrogacy agreement to be held valid and enforceable? Surrogacy involves a broad range of issues from parenthood to contractual enforcement and liability, and even tort. Never-

3 Art. 562 of the Code states that the woman who gives birth to a child will be the legal mother. It also establishes the legal parenthood of the birth mother's partner who had previously expressed his or her consent to be hedl as parent of the child. Art. 565 states the means by which birth can be proved. Art. 599 details those persons who can be held as adoptive parents of a child.

4 Art. 611 sanctions the nullity of any direct transfer of custodial rights or de facto guardianships over a child,

theless, to date neither the legislator nor the judiciary in Argentina have addressed the full extent of such issues.

Despite this legal vacuum, surrogacy is currently offered as an alternative for couples and individuals by several fertility clinics in Argentina. Although no official statistics are available, these clinics claim to have assisted in a large number of cases. Some of them offer international surrogacy arrangements with other Latin American countries (e.g. Mexico) and the United States. The main issue in these cases, assuming that no conflict arises between the parties, is the impossibility under Argentine law of registering the child's parentage according to the desires of the adults involved.

III A Case of Judicial Activism

Despite the decision reached in Congress, since the enactment of the Code about two dozen cases have arisen in which de facto surrogacy arrangements have been considered by the courts, with the majority of cases being decided through 2017 and 2018.[5] These cases have been decided by first instance judges, in both local and national courts. One unpublished decision was decided on appeal and is now pending before the Argentine Supreme Court on extraordinary appeal.

None of the cases have dealt with the validity or enforceability of the surrogacy arrangement entered into. Thus no judge has addressed the issue of the requirements for rendering such an agreement enforceable or, alternatively, the circumstances in which a party may be compelled to abide by the terms of the agreement. Each case sought a legal solution to the parental status of a child born – or about to be born – to whom the existing rules of parentage accorded a status that did not match the agreement between, and manifest desires of, the intended parents and the surrogates. All but three of the cases[6] involved parentage registration of a child already born – or about to be born – where the birth mother was requesting that she be released of her parentage status in favor of the intended parents.[7]

In all cases the intended parents were couples who were Argentine residents and only one involved a Peruvian immigrant acting as surrogate.[8] None of the cases presented a

5 At the time of the initial writing of this paper in July 2017 sixteen surrogacy cases had been presented to the courts. The paper focusses on those cases.

6 "XXX s/ maternidad por sustitución", Tribunal Colegiado de Familia nro. 7 de Rosario, sentencia del 2 de diciembre de 2014 and "Dato Reservado, Expte. Nro. 10178-14", Juzgado de Familia N. 9, Bariloche, sentencia del 29 de diciembre de 2015. "Dato Reservador", juzgado de Familia de Viedma, sentencia del 6de julio de 2017. These three cases involved prior judicial authorization of a surrogacy agreement.

7 The first case seeking prior judicial authorization was filed before the Civil and Commercial Code was enacted and at a time when there was no legal framework for cases of parentage by assisted reproductive technologies.

8 "B.M.A. c/ F.C.C.R. s/ ordinario", Juzgado de Familia de Gualeguay, sentencia del 19 de noviembre de 2013.

conflict between parties (regarding parentage or any other issue). All groups of plaintiffs[9] declared first, that the surrogate had acted out of her own free will and with altruistic purposes and second, that the surrogate did not intend to act as a mother to the child.

Each case allegedly involved an altruistic surrogacy in which the surrogate claimed that she was a relative of the intended parents[10] or a very close friend and that the only money received was to cover medical expenses. Nevertheless, one judge hinted at the possible validity of payments to the surrogate in excess of medical expenses, on the basis that her "services" could not be deemed any less important than those of the lawyers and doctors involved.[11,12]

Regarding the intended parents, both same-sex and heterosexual couples were involved, although the vast majority were heterosexual. None of the intended parents were single – all were couples. Except for those surrogacy agreements entered into by same-sex couples, all but one case (in which there was resort to egg donation) involved genetic material from the intended mother.[13] In no case did the surrogate donate her own eggs.

In each of the cases, the judges granted the plaintiffs' requests, relying mainly on the idea that the lack of an express ban on surrogacy meant an implicit legal permission from Congress. Most judges also referred to the principle of "procreational will" as a necessary element of the constitutional right to procreate.[14]

Procreational will is referred to in article 562 of the Code[15] which deals with determining parentage in the situation where a couple have used donated gametes, intending to be the parents of the child born as a result of the assisted conception. Article 562 provides that legal parentage will be assigned to the birth mother and her partner based on "the will of

9 In all cases the birth mother and the intended parents joined together as plaintiffs.

10 "S.P., B. B. c. S. P., R. F. s/ materia a categorizar", Juzgado De Familia N° 2 de Moreno, sentencia del 4 de julio de 2016 y "H.M. y Otro s/medidas precautorias (art. 233 CPCC)", Juzgado de Familia 7, Lomas de Zamora, sentencia del 30 de diciembre de 2015.

11 "O.A.V., G.A.C. Y F.J.J. por medida autosatisfactiva", Primer Juzgado de Familia, Primera Circunscripción Judicial, Provincia de Mendoza, Argentina, EXPTE.N°714/15/1F, sentencia del 29 de julio de 2015.

12 After completion of this paper more cases dealing with surrogacy were resolved before the Argentine courts. One worth noting is "A., M. T. y Otro s/ solicita homologación", Expte. SAC N° 7057134, Juzgado de Familia de 1a Nominación de Córdoba, Sentencia del 6 de agosto de 2018. The plaintiff was a single woman past her biological fertility age, seeking authorization to enter into an altruistic surrogacy arrangement with a friend. The child was to be conceived using anonymous sperm and eggs, and any resulting embryos were to be transferred to the surrogate. In this way, the child would be born to a single parent with whom she would bear no genetic connection at all. The judge granted authorization on the basis of "procreational will" and expressly refused to consider the child's welfare or the best interest principle in the decision.

13 "B., B. M. y otro c/G., Y.A. s/Impugnación de la Filiación", Juzgado nacional en lo Civil n° 8, Expte. 70522/2014, sentencia del 20 de septiembre de 2016.

14 "C., F. A. y otro c. R. S., M. L. s/impugnación de maternidad", Juzgado Nacional de 1A Instancia en lo Civil n. 102, sentencia del 18 de mayo de 2015.

15 It should be noted that this reference to art. 562 is to the current Code. It is important not to confuse the current art. 562 with art. 562 of the draft bill, discussed above, which dealt with surrogacy. Article 562 of the draft bill was eliminated during the parliamentary discussion of the Code. The current art. 562 of the Code deals with the legal definition of "procreational will" and makes no reference whatsoever to surrogacy.

the birth mother and her partner [male or female] manifested by prior, informed and free consent". However, in the surrogacy cases being studied, different (and much broader) conceptions of "procreational will" have been relied upon.[16] These understandings range from considering procreational will as the desire to be a parent with constitutionally protected rights[17] to expelling the rule of biological truth and deconstructing maternity with a triumph of intention over biology or genetics.[18] In many of the cases the reasoning has been supported by a broad interpretation of the Inter-American Court of Human Rights decision in *Artavia Murillo vs. Costa Rica.*[19] This case dealt with Costa Rica's ban on resort to *in vitro* fertilization and not directly with surrogacy.

These broad understandings of procreational rights have served as a basis for establishing parentage in favor of the intended mother who has supplied her eggs,[20] the intended mother when donated eggs were used,[21] and the biological father's husband.[22] In some cases the judges reasoned that intended parentage should take precedence over any biological factor and should prevail over genetic elements in the construction of a child's – or any person's – identity.[23] Several cases went one step further and declared the rule of *mater semper certa*

16 On the academic front, two opinions may be distinguished. One supports the freedom of any party to enter into a surrogacy agreement based on the constitutional right to reproduction and on procreational will as the determining principle in all cases of reproduction involving third parties regardless of any biological or genetical consideration. Another group of authors points out that an agreement that implicates a woman's reproductive capacity and the handing over of a child would be an invalid contract on the grounds of (i) conflicting with the dignity of women and children involved; (ii) implying an illicit object; (iii) serving as a fraud to adoption laws and the express prohibition in Argentine legislation of handing over parental rights and custody of a child without resort to the judicial proceedings. In the cases being discussed, the courts have invariably sustained their decisions with the repeated quoting of opinions held by: Andrés Gil Dominguez; Eleonora Lamm; María Victoria Famá; Marisa Herrera; Aída Kemelmajer and Adriana Krasnow, who without exception support the first position described.

17 "S. P., B. B. c. S. P., R. F. s/ materia a categorizar", Juzgado De Familia N° 2 de Moreno, sentencia del 4 de julio de 2016.

18 "B., B.M y otro c/ G., Y.A. s/Impugnación de la Filiación", Juzgado Nacional en lo Civil n8, Expte. 70522/2014, sentencia del 20 de septiembre de 2016.

19 "Artavia Murillo y otros (Fertilización in vitro) vs. Costa Rica", sentencia del 28 de noviembre de 2012, Petición 12.361, Caso n° 257.

20 "S. P., B. B. c. S. P., R. F. s/ materia a categorizar", Juzgado De Familia N° 2 de Moreno, sentencia del 4 de julio de 2016 y "H.M. y Otro s/medidas precautorias (art. 233 CPCC)", Juzgado de Familia 7, Lomas de Zamora, sentencia del 30 de diciembre de 2015; "O.A.V., G.A.C. Y F.J.J. por medida autosatisfactiva", Primer Juzgado de Familia, Primera Circunscripción Judicial, Provincia de Mendoza, Argentina, EXPTE.N°714/15/1F, sentencia del 29 de julio de 2015; Juzgado de Familia N. 9, Bariloche, sentencia del 29 de diciembre de 2015. "Dato Reservador", juzgado de Familia de Viedma, sentencia del 6de julio de 2017.

21 "B., B.M. y otro c/G., Y.A. s/Impugnación de la Filiación", Juzgado nacional en lo Civil n° 8, Expte. 70522/2014, sentencia del 20 de septiembre de 2016.

22 "XXX s/ maternidad por sustitución", Tribunal Colegiado de Familia nro. 7 de Rosario, sentencia del 2 de diciembre de 2014.

23 "N.N. O s/ inscripción de nacimiento", Juzgado Nacional de 1a Instancia en lo Civil nro. 83, sentencia del 25 de junio de 2015.

est found in article 565 of the Code to be blatantly unconstitutional. [24] One judge considered article 565 to be contrary both to the Argentine Constitution and international human rights treaties, namely the American Convention on Human Rights.[25] A second unpublished case followed a similar line of reasoning.[26]

In one case the parties converted their request to challenge maternity of the surrogate into an application by the husband of the intended and genetic father to adopt the child and become a co-parent, with the parental rights of the biological mother being severed. This request was granted by the Civil Court of Appeals, although the Court expressly refusal to consider the constitutionality of article 565[27].

IV Currently Unresolved Issues

Thus far, the cases resolved by Argentine first instance judges have not given clear guidelines regarding surrogacy agreements and their consequences. The result is a lack of regulation that leaves several grey areas with potential risks for all parties. Also, no criteria exist regarding potential parentage issues in the event that the adult parties either simultaneously claim parentage over the child (positive conflict) or refuse to accept it (negative conflict).

In the legislative arena, three bills have been presented proposing different rules for surrogacy. To date, Congressional committees have begun their preliminary analysis of two of these draft bills. The draft bills share some commonalities: positive permission to enter into surrogacy agreements; guidelines as to who may become a surrogate; and rules for the determination of parentage according to the desires of the adults involved as manifested at the onset of pregnancy or before, with no provision for the surrogate to change her mind. They differ, most notably, as to the requirement of prior judicial authorization.

None of the bills addresses any issue arising after judicial authorization is granted; thus there is no provision for regulation of the on-going relationship between the parties. None

24 Under the Argentine legal system, a declaration of unconstitutionality can only refer to the case and parties considered and does not carry in itself an *erga omnes* effect.

25 "H.M. y Otro S/medidas precautorias (art. 232 CPCC) (419)", Juzgado de Familia n° 7, Lomas de Zamora, sentencia del 30 de diciembre de 2015.

26 As in every matter concerning minors, judicial proceedings are to be kept secret and cannot be accessed by third parties unless expressly permitted by the intervening court – and with the names of those involved removed. The only reference that can be made is that the case was decided by the Juzgado Civil n. 4 on 30th June 2016.

27 Sala H, caso "Simonelli Teitelbaum, Ayra y otro s/inscripción de nacimiento" (Expte. N° 31.689/16), sentencia del 24 de octubre de 2016.

provide guidelines for the determination of the rights and duties of the parties during and after pregnancy, nor for resolution of potential conflicts of parentage.[28]

If an express legal permission for surrogacy agreements were to be incorporated in Argentine Law, Congress would be faced with an array of issues:

(1) the extent of judicial involvement in the agreement and whether a court should grant prior authorization or only act *ex post* in the event a conflict arises;
(2) the rules for determining parenthood and the resolution of possible positive and negative conflicts that may arise between parties;
(3) contractual rights and duties, as well as liabilities, of all parties involved in a surrogacy agreement (e.g., compensation, right to terminate or continue pregnancy in the event of disagreement; surrogate's right to custody); and
(4) finally, what is possibly the core of any piece of legislation that touches upon children's rights, legal measures aimed at preventing any agreement that may border on child trafficking.[29]

V Social and Economic Reality of Argentina

Family law should reflect the realities and needs of the population to which it will be applied. It is therefore worth focusing on some aspects of the current social and economic reality of Argentina. Any potential regulation of agreements that touch upon women's reproductive rights and the establishment or transfer of parentage over children should thoroughly assess existing vulnerabilities.

Although the GDP per capita in Argentina was last recorded as 10,398.09 US dollars in 2017,[30] the latest statistics indicate that 32% of the population live in poverty and that 6.9% fall into the category of insufficient minimum means of living (implying the impossibility of procuring food every day).[31] About 9% of the total active population are currently unemployed, with women in the majority, and half of the active population have difficulties in the employment area.[32] Approximately 33% of people work in the unregistered and informal economy and, again, women are twice as likely to be affected by these conditions. There is a 27.2% income gap between men and women, increasing to 47% in the case of

28 For example cases where the surrogate chooses to keep the child or where the intended parents reject the child.

29 Among a complex variety of aspects to be considered in this field are: the requirements that at least one of the intended parents be genetically linked to the child, nationality and/or residence of the adult parties, and possibly a time for the surrogate to reconfirm her decision to give up parental rights as well as safekeeping of documents in order to ensure the child's right to identity.

30 https://tradingeconomics.com/argentina/gdp-per-capita.

31 https://elpais.com/internacional/2017/03/09/argentina/1489075264_055333.html.

32 http://www.infobae.com/economia/2017/02/11/la-mitad-de-la-poblacion-activa-tiene-problemas-de-empleo/.

unskilled workers.[33] According to one survey, an average female employee must work two years more than her male counterpart to earn enough to obtain a mortgage for a first home[34].

These factors make it necessary to address requisites of residence, nationality and profit involved in surrogacy, in order to fight risks of abuse of women and the underlying potential for child trafficking.

VI CONCLUSIONS

Through a review of recent judicial decisions and intended legislative reforms, this paper has sought to reflect upon the current situation of surrogate motherhood in Argentina and the urgent need for Congress to legislate upon the matter. To date, the absence of a prohibition on surrogacy agreements in the Civil and Commercial Code has been regarded by a small number of courts as a tacit permission for such agreements. The resulting court decisions have left an array of issues unanswered.

Two bills are currently under preliminary study by Congress and one remains unaddressed. However even though they do regulate the requirements for adults entering into valid agreements, these bills leave a great many questions unanswered. Even if they were to be passed, a high level of uncertainty would remain and courts would be forced to create rules for each potential conflict that arises.

Any piece of legislation enacted regarding this matter must: (i) give a thorough account of all of the issues involved and the rules adopted to deal with these issues; (ii) contemplate the child's best interest as a paramount consideration; and, (iii) consider the adult parties' human rights and the socio-economic reality in Argentina in order to adequately protect and balance the rights and interests of all involved.

33 http://jornadaonline.com/economia/175296-argentina-brecha-salarial-entre-hombres-y-mujeres-es-de-272.

34 Official statistics on gender, gender gap and gender violence available at: https://www.argentina.gob.ar/sites/default/files/3boletinestadisticasdegenero.pdf.

The Japanese Gender Identity Disorder Act: Possible Amendment and Its Implications for Family Law

Mai Ishijima[*]

I Introduction

In Japan, the enactment of the Act on Special Cases in Handling Gender Status for Persons with Gender Identity Disorder (GID Act) made possible the change of one's legal gender in family registers. However, the change is still restricted to those who have been diagnosed with "gender identity disorder" and have undergone the prescribed surgeries[1]. The Act does not reflect the fact that physical intervention does not necessarily ameliorate gender nonconformity and that there are some persons for whom it is appropriate to change their legal gender without undergoing physical interventions. Since the GID Act took effect in 2004, its requirements have been perceived as an indicator of the authenticity of one's gender dysphoria; thus the Act has worked as a normative model which advocates conformity with its requirements. Sterilization and changing the appearance of external genitalia should not be performed if a person is simply prompted by the desire to change their legal gender, nor should acquiring the status of a diseased person be required. The fact that the Act's requirements may have spurred surgeries and sterilisation that were intrinsically unnecessary for the improvement of the life circumstances of those affected should be considered a serious problem.

---

* Ph.D. Guest researcher at Johannes Gutenberg University Mainz, Faculty of Law, Management and Economics, Germany. This work was supported by a JSPS Grant-in-Aid for Research Activity Start-up (Grant No. 15H06681).

1 The physical requirements for changing one's legal gender (namely physical sterilization and modification of the physical appearance of external genitalia) were determined to be constitutional in a recent Supreme Court case (decision of the Supreme Court, Second Petty Bench, 23 January 2019, Case No. (Ku) 269 of 2018). The applicant in the case had requested a change of legal gender without undergoing the necessary surgery, claiming that the requirements for irreversible physical intervention were unconstitutional as they violated the right to self-determination protected under Article 13 of the Constitution and failed to ensure equal treatment as guaranteed in Article 14 paragraph 1. It should be noted that because the GID Act stipulates being diagnosed with a gender identity disorder as a requirement for changing one's legal gender, this paper will often acknowledge that a sense of gender dysphoria is a precondition to determining availability of the legal procedure. However, this should not be taken as an endorsement of the idea that pathological gender dysphoria is an intrinsically necessary requirement for accessing the legal procedure to change one's registered gender.

This paper aims to contribute toward the depathologisation of the GID Act by elucidating the problems potentially arising from it and realigning the Act's future direction. After recommending the elimination of the sterilization requirement and physical modification requirement (hereinafter combined as "the physical requirements") from the GID Act, the paper will examine the problems that may ensue from this change. The specific focus will be on possible solutions to the problem of how to determine legal parent-child relationships if the physical requirements for a legal change of gender are removed and there is a discrepancy between legal gender and reproductive capacitysolutions that will not require significant amendment of the current legal criteria.

II The Current GID Act

A *Background of Diagnostic/Physical Requirements*

According to article 2 of the GID Act, in addition to having gender misalignment, a person seeking a change of legal gender under the Act must obtain a gender identity disorder diagnosis from two or more physicians. Further, article 3(1) requires such persons to: (1) be at least twenty years of age, (2) be unmarried, (3) have no minor children, (4) have no reproductive glands or reproductive glands that have permanently lost their function, and (5) have a body with parts that closely resemble the genital appearance of the other gender. Furthermore, article 3(2) requires a specific medical certificate issued by a physician.[2] Hence, the request for a change of legal gender under the GID Act is substantially restricted to a group of persons characterised by the age of majority, the social attributes of being childless and single, the loss of reproductive capacity, and external genitalia that have a prescribed appearance.

People have dealt in various ways with the gender nonconformity arising from the conflict between their assigned gender and their self-perceived gender, including the rejection of any bodily intervention. The medical profession recognizes that there is no "one size fits all" optimal solution.[3] Although their diverse methods of dealing with the nonconformity were also taken into account when the GID Act was legislated,[4] the Act

2 The specific physical interventions to be shown in the certificate are specified by the Ministry of Health, Labour and Welfare; see Ministry of Health, Labour and Welfare, *Guidelines for Physician's Medical Certificate Prescribed in Article 3, Paragraph 2 of the Act on Special Cases in Handling Gender Status for Persons with Gender Identity Disorder*, 2004, at http://www.mhlw.go.jp/general/seido/syakai/sei32/dl/youryou.pdf.

3 Japanese Society of Psychiatry and Neurology, *Guidelines for the Diagnosis and Treatment of Gender Identity Disorder*, 4th ed. (revised), 2018, available at https://www.jspn.or.jp/uploads/uploads/files/activity/gid_guideline_no4_20180120.pdf.

4 A. Kamikawa, *Courage to Change – My Story as Someone with 'Gender Identity Disorder'*, Tokyo, Iwanami Shoten, 2007, p. 106.

nevertheless imposed physical requirements. The reason may be found in the relationship between the legislation and medical therapies at the time. The legislation was hastily enacted against a backdrop of widely publicised media reports about the sex reassignment surgery ("SRS") performed at Saitama Medical University.[5] The GID Act was intentionally and strategically characterised as being a measure to bring relief to persons with the "disease" of "gender identity disorder". The term "gender identity disorder" was first mentioned in the Diet during its 143rd session,[6] which was held just one month before the surgery was performed. This mention of the term arose from the criminal issues concerning SRS, which may have emanated from the 1969 ruling of the Tokyo District Court[7] that debated whether certain "sex change surgeries" contravened article 28 of the old Eugenics Protection Act.[8] In this ruling, the court laid down the conditions necessary for SRS to be an appropriate medical procedure. Prior to the surgery performed at Saitama Medical University, these conditions were formalised in the guideline established for the diagnosis and treatment of gender identity disorder ("the guideline").[9] On several occasions from this point until the passage of the GID Act, the guideline served as the criterion against which to examine the legality of medical treatments for gender identity disorder.[10]

Although the guideline constituted the medical protocol for appropriate treatments, it must be noted that "medical treatments" for gender identity disorder were still in the process of being developed at the time. In contrast with so-called radical treatments that root out the cause of a disease, alleviation therapies such as SRS do not, technically speaking, eradicate the cause of a disease, but are rather intended to mitigate a patient's suffering. However, for alleviation therapies to be considered proper "medical treatment",

---

5 Although the SRS at Saitama Medical University in 1998 is widely known, this was not the first SRS to take place in Japan; prior SRSs were well reported by Junko Mitsuhashi: see J. Mitsuhashi, 'Returning the "GID Myth" Back to History', GID Society, 19th Research Convention, 19 March 2017, Sapporo.

6 22 September 1998. K. Takeda, 'On the Law Covering Gender Identity Disorder and Sex Status: A Political Perspective', *GEMC (Gender Equality and Multicultural Conviviality in the Age of Globalization) Journal*, Vol. 1, 2008, pp. 94-105, at 101.

7 The so-called "Blueboy Incident" Tokyo District Court judgment, 15 February 1969, *Hanrei-Jihou*, No. 551 (1969), pp. 29-36) and Tokyo High Court judgment, 11 November 1970. This ruling commented that SRS could be deemed an appropriate medical treatment when certain conditions were fulfilled. However, this case set back the development of medical treatment for gender dysphoria in Japan as the defendant was strictly sentenced for violations of both the Eugenics Protection Act and the Narcotics Control Act. See I. Doi, 'What is Gender Identity Disorder?' *in* R. Alexander et al, *Sexual Minorities- Homosexual, Gender Identity Disorder, Intersex and Human Diversity, As Told in Their Own Word*, 3rd ed., Tokyo, Akashi Shoten, 2012, pp. 92-109, at 95.

8 Art. 28 provided that no person may perform operations or X-ray irradiation aimed at removing the ability to reproduce for any reasons other than those provided in the Act.

9 The first edition was published in 1997 by the Special Committee on Gender Identity Disorder, Japanese Society of Psychiatry and Neurology. The current edition is the revised fourth edition.

10 M. Ishii, 'For discussion of a case where after undergoing sex change surgery as treatment for so-called gender identity disorder, the application for family register correction under article 113 of the Family Register Act was denied', *Hanrei Taimuzu*, Vol. 1065, 2011, pp. 168-169, at 168.

it was necessary that they be rationalized as based on eradicating the cause of the disease, and as such distinguished from other expedient use of medical technologies, such as cosmetic surgeries. Thus, when the guideline implementing the standard of appropriate medical treatment of gender dysphoria indicated by the court was being developed, it was necessary to specify the disease causing it. Despite the medical profession's awareness that the burdens on persons experiencing gender dysphoria derive from a social structure that assigns gender roles, gender dysphoria was segregated from the issue of gender roles in society, and gender identity issues were treated in a biological framework.[11] Furthermore, the first (1997) and second (2002) editions of the guideline, which were consulted during the drafting of the GID Act, did not incorporate the current "à la carte" therapy scheme, but adopted the "step-by-step" approach that moved from psychotherapy to sex-hormone treatments[12] and then to SRS as the culmination of therapy. The GID Act is premised on the model of a patient who suffers from a congenital disease causing gender dysphoria, completes surgery, and becomes fully immersed in the "other sex". Targeting this typical model patient, the GID Act adopts a treatment model that leads to surgery.

Given its emphasis on surgery, the GID Act was required to deal with the issue of how to handle the legal gender of the post-operational persons. During the period when it was being enacted, the focus of gender policy merely shifted from a one-sided women's protection model to a gender-free model.[13] According to Takeda, the bill was approved because it was seen as a measure to handle a condition characterised as a "disorder"; gender dysphoria was not seen as an issue of gender or minority, but rather as a deviation from the "normal" male/female dichotomy. The change of legal gender under the GID Act still requires the specification of a male/female gender, so the process is only available to persons who will fit into the framework of sexual dichotomy. The synergistic medical and legislative collaboration that led to the enactment of the GID Act thus produced a legislative scheme that shuts out persons who shun surgery. The Act only accommodates those who transition from a "diseased condition" to the "other sex", and accepts requests for change of legal gender only from those who have completed the physical transformation and intend to immerse themselves totally in the other sex. In so doing, the GID Act incorporates a

11 At that time, it was postulated that gender identity takes shape starting from the prenatal period in tandem with a systematic biological scheme. S. Takahashi, 'Gender Identity Disorder and the Body - Analysing the Guidelines, the Gender Identity Disorder Act, and Transsexualism' *in* T. Yamamoto & K. Kitamura (Eds.), *Research Center for Ars Vivendi Report Vol. 3 - On Dysphoria - Medical Trials x Gender Identity Disorder/Body x Society*, Kyoto, Research Center for Ars Vivendi, Ritsumeikan University, 2008, pp. 133-155.

12 Administration of estrogen to MtFs and androgen to FtMs induces discontinuance or diminution of previous reproductive capacity. Committee on Gender Identity Disorder, Japanese Society of Psychiatry and Neurology, op cit, n. 3, p. 1262.

13 For a detailed account of political developments during the enactment period, see Takeda, op cit, n. 6.

framework based on the conventional male/female dichotomy and is aimed at bringing a person with gender identity disorder back into the fold.[14]

B The GID Act as a Normative Model

As described above, the GID Act presupposes a person who has undergone surgery and the fourth requirement set out in article 3(1) is that the individual must not retain the reproductive capacity of their previous gender. Moreover, to avoid social confusion, the fifth requirement regarding the external appearance of genitalia was instituted.[15] The requirement with respect to the absence of reproductive capacity may be ascribed to a desire to avoid confusion regarding the legal parent-child relationship. However, the physical requirements of the GID Act have been criticized for creating the risk of unnecessary surgery. While the GID Act paved one pathway for handling gender dysphoria, those who do not reach "the finish line" – persons who do not complete SRS and then subsequently change their legal gender through the GID Act – are relegated to the sidelines.[16] Among the persons affected are those who reject surgery and are consequently discriminated against as being "insincere" and not experiencing "genuinely serious suffering" from their condition. In contrast, there are those who seek to prove the authenticity of their condition through adherence to the GID Act's normative model.

According to a recent report by psychiatrists, the post-surgical period for completing the diagnostic certificate relating to the change of legal gender is becoming shorter, suggesting that the physical requirements are motivating persons to undergo surgeries to fulfill the requirements under the GID Act.[17] Yoshino[18] has noted that the requirements of the GID Act have come to be commonly regarded as the criteria for determining the existence of a "true" gender identity disorder, and have engendered an "elite" class of persons who have complied with all the requirements and immersed themselves in the

---

14 Takeda, op cit, n. 6; Doi, op cit, n. 7.

15 C. Nono (compilation supervisor), *[Commentaries] The Gender Identity Disorder Act*, Tokyo, Nihon Kajo Shuppan, 2004, pp. 93-94. Further, in its ruling dated 17 May 2005 (*Kagetsu*, Vol. 57, No. 10, p. 99), the Tokyo High Court acknowledged these justifications.

16 I. Sugiura, 'Possibilities of Linking Criticism of the "Guidelines" and "Gender Identity Disorder Law" to the "Social Model of the Disorder": Towards a Study of the Burden Distribution on Society, Medical Treatment, and the Individual – Review of H. Ishida (Ed.), Gender Identity Disorder: Gender, Medical Treatment, and the Gender Identity Disorder Act', *Queer Studies*, Vol. 2, 2009, pp. 150-159, at 151-152.

17 H. Oda et al, 'A Study on the Gender Identity Disorder Act and Receiving Medical Treatment', GID Society, 19th Research Convention, 19 March 2017, Sapporo.

18 Y. Yoshino, 'A Matter that the "Diverse Body" Casts on the Gender Identity Disorder Act', *Core Ethics*, Vol. 4, 2008, pp. 383-393.

"opposite sex".[19] Meanwhile, Tsuruta[20] has drawn attention to the emergence of a "*Nanchatte* (Pseudo) FtM" discourse. The phrase is used by those who seek distinction from the "Pseudo FtM" by earnestly undergoing physical interventions (mostly hormone therapy), in order to indicate their "seriousness".

The pervasive belief that submitting oneself to physical intervention is a better option has become a serious problem, as one can lose the opportunity to self-determine one's own gender identity and physical disposition, particularly in the case of youth vulnerable to isolation.[21] In the first place, the feasibility of the surgical intervention required by the GID Act does not depend solely on the person's consent, as their physical condition may preclude surgery.[22] The imposition of a prescribed surgery restricts the possibility of legal gender change for those who cannot undergo the required physical modifications. While the requirements can foist surgery on a person who originally had no desire for such intervention,[23] they also restrict the choice of surgical options, thus narrowing the range of a person's self-determination regarding their physical disposition. The Act has also been criticized for reducing an individual's gender to a strictly biological construct, thereby evading the fundamental debate on the essence of gender itself.[24]

Although the GID Act does allow a person experiencing gender misalignment to obtain their proper legal gender marker (thereby preventing immense suffering due to the discordance between one's originally assigned gender and one's self-perceived gender) if they

19 Yoshino, ibid, has reported that in order to obtain a physician's diagnosis and the benefits accompanying it ("formal" coming out in school or in the workplace, etc.), there is "excessive appeal to fitting into gender stereotypes so as to be 'accepted' by the people involved". Medical staff tend to consider male/female assimilation as beneficial and take such an appeal positively. In this scheme of reciprocal influences between medical staff and patients, the GID Act reinforces the conventional gender model. (This does not negate the fact that there are those who intrinsically wish to assimilate themselves completely into the "opposite sex".)

20 S. Tsuruta, 'What did the dissemination of knowledge after the "Kinpachi" broadcasts bring about? A Theory of Utilizing the FtM Category' *in* H. Ishida et al, *Gender Identity Disorder: Gender, Medical Treatment, and the Gender Identity Disorder Act*, Tokyo, Ochanomizushobo, 2008, pp. 161-182.

21 Especially for young persons lacking in socio-economic self-sufficiency and practical experiences, who tend to find their sexual role models outside, impatience to fulfil the GID Act's requirements could result serious harm. Cases already exist involving such actions as personal purchase and use of sex hormones and surgeries performed at inexpensive private clinics (Y. Imamura & D. Miyayama, 'Post-mastectomy death at a private GID clinic', *Asahi Shimbun*, 8 February 2013, evening edition). There are not a few instances in which irreversible bodily harm occurred without sufficient supervision of a person having expert knowledge.

22 For example, allergy to anaesthetics, severe liver damage, etc. Other factors restricting the choice of surgical option include considerations of whether the person can obtain a receptive environment by others, and of sufficient leave time from work, etc. The guideline specifies conditions for transitioning to physical treatment. Committee on Gender Identity Disorder, Japanese Society of Psychiatry and Neurology, op cit, n. 3, pp. 1259-1260, 1266. Also, Yoshino, op cit, n. 18, p. 385.

23 Yoshino, op cit, n. 18, pp. 383-393.

24 N. Kokubun, 'Gender Identity Disorder and the Constitution', *Bulletin of the Faculty of Letters, Aichi Prefectural University (School of Japanese Studies)*, No. 52, 2004, pp. 1-17, at 14. Shimazaki (2004) has also pointed out that gender identity disorder has not been adequately grasped as a human rights issue; see Takeda, op cit, n. 6.

are willing to undergo the loss of reproductive capacity and physical integrity, these physical requirements create a 'choose one or the other' situation. It is now known that surgical interventions are not indispensable to alleviating gender dysphoria and, given the normative effects of the GID Act, there is a compelling argument that the physical requirements should be removed. However, this must be subject to the proviso that we examine the interests safeguarded by the physical requirements and the effects on other legislation if they are rescinded. Although the physical requirements have been regarded as harmful from the perspective of sociology and human rights,[25] exhaustive and detailed domestic legal studies of the elimination of these physical requirements are still scarce in Japan. The following section explores the problems that may arise from the abolition of the physical requirements and the measures that would be required to alleviate those problems, focusing particularly on the establishment of legal parent-child relationships.

III Legal Issues Accompanying the Abolition of Physical Requirements

A *Family Law Issues*

In Japan, the person who gives birth is considered to be the mother.[26] The person who is in a marital relationship with the mother, or who recognizes the child, is considered to be the father.[27] Currently, as the sterilization requirement renders it impossible to produce offspring after the change of legal gender, it seems that confusion regarding the legal parent-

---

25 As for international developments, a United Nations Human Rights Council report raises the loss of reproductive capacity as an issue related to torture and cruel and unusual punishment; see United Nations, Human Rights Council, Report of the Special Rapporteur on torture and other cruel, inhuman or degrading treatment or punishment, Juan E. Méndez, A/HRC/22/53 (1 February 2013) at para. 78, available at http://undocs.org/A/HRC/22/53. Furthermore, a number of international agencies, operating under the auspices of the World Health Organization (WHO), have issued a joint declaration on 'Eliminating forced, coercive and otherwise involuntary sterilization' available at http://www.who.int/reproductivehealth/publications/gender_rights/eliminating-forced-sterilization/en/. There are also quite a few Japanese articles concerning the issue of the physical requirements in the field of sociology and human rights. See for example Yoshino, op cit, n. 18.

26 Although there is no provision in the Japanese Civil Code that regulates the establishment of legal motherhood, judicial precedents have established a definite practice that the person who gave birth to the child becomes the mother of the child (e.g. 27 April 1962, Supreme Court judgement, *Minshu*, Vol. 16, No. 7, p. 1247). In only a few cases, such as when gestation and delivery are difficult to prove, as in the case of abandoned or lost children, is motherhood established by recognition. T. Takahashi, F. Tokotani & M. Tanamura, *Civil Code 7: Families and Succession*, 5th ed., Tokyo, Yuhikaku, 2017, pp. 149-150.

27 The marital presumption and recognition are dealt with under arts. 772 and 779 of the Civil Code respectively. Under Japanese law, paternity is presumed by marital status at the estimated time of gestation. Para. 2 of art. 772 stipulates that a child born after 200 days from the formation of marriage or within 300 days of the dissolution/rescission of marriage is to be presumed to have been conceived during the marriage. Under art. 779, a father or a mother can recognize a child when a legal father/mother has not been assigned to the child.

child relationships is avoided by preventing a legal male from giving birth, and a legal female from impregnating another woman. However, the following circumstances can still arise under the current Act. Take the case of a person who has changed her legal gender from male to female (hereinafter "MtF"[28]), having terminated her marriage to comply with the requirement of being unmarried. If her ex-spouse gives birth within 300 days after the change, a parent-child relationship should be established, as the MtF should be presumed as the begetter (Figure 1).

Figure 1

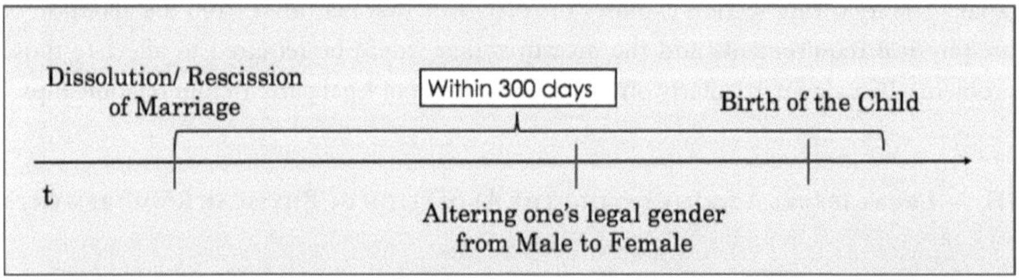

Take another case in which no marital relationship exists. The GID Act does not clarify what parent-child relationships can be established if a MtF tries to recognize a child after her change of legal gender (Figure 2). As the parental relationship is retroactively validated by the recognition, it is also not clear if the change of legal gender will be invalidated due to non-compliance with the third requirement of having no minor children.[29] Moreover, with the possibility of preserving gametes due to medical advances, the goal of preventing confusion in the legal parent-child relationships is not fully achieved by the sterilization requirement.

28 In this paper the abbreviation MtF refers to a person who seeks a change of legal gender from male to female. FtM (abbreviation of "female to male") refers to a person who seeks a change of legal gender from female to male.

29 M. Tanamura, 'Current Legal Status and Issues Surrounding Gender Identity Disorder', *Jurist*, No. 1364, 2008, pp. 2-8, at 6-7. If recognising a child would nullify a person's change of legal gender, that person might avoid recognition. From the child's perspective, this ambiguity in the establishment of parent-child relationships should be regarded as a problem.

Figure 2

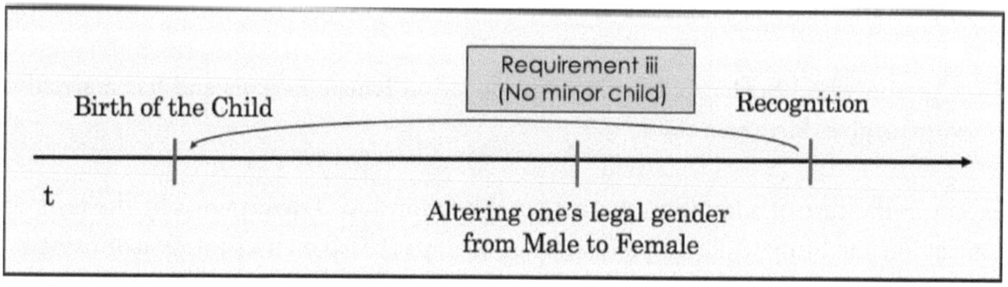

Since the sterilization requirement does not currently achieve the legislative purpose, it is worthwhile to consider removing it. In what follows I attempt to explore in concrete detail the issue of how legal parent-child relationships involving persons who have changed their legal gender would be established if the physical requirements were to be removed. In this process, the following two questions arise: 1) what should be the criteria for establishing the parent-child relationship; and 2) which parenthood – fatherhood or motherhood – should be established. Under the current legal criteria for establishing parent-child relationships the emergence of the following types of parent-child relationships can be hypothesised:

(A) A person who has changed his legal gender from female *to male* (FtM) subsequently marries a woman, and this spouse gives birth to a child;[30]

(B) A person who has changed his legal gender from female *to male* (FtM) then recognizes a child;

(C) A person who has changed his legal gender from female *to male* (FtM) subsequently gives birth to a child;

(D) The ex-wife of a person who has changed her legal gender from male *to female* (MtF) gives birth to a child during the presumption period;[31] and

(E) A person who has changed her legal gender from male *to female* (MtF) recognizes a child.

Although FtM/MtF nomenclature excludes persons who identify themselves as neither male/female, this paper only considers male and female, as its aim is to take advantage of current legislation which is, apart from a few regulations, primarily based on the male/female framework. In order to focus solely on the elimination of the physical requirement of sterilization, the hypothetical scenarios set out above all assume that the requirement of being single at the time of the change of the legal gender is maintained. In

30 In this scenario the spouse could conceive a child either by using donated sperm or having sexual relations with a third party.

31 Within 300 days of the day of the dissolution or rescission of marriage.

addition, I will also introduce a variant on scenario (C), which I will designate as scenario (C') which assumes that FtM has a spouse:[32]

(C') A person who has changed his legal gender from female *to male* and has married a woman, gives birth to a child.

Except in the case of adoptions, the maternal relationship is determined by the facts of conception and birth, while the paternal relationship is based on presumption or recognition.[33] Motherhood is evident, but since it is not always perfectly clear who the father is, fatherhood is determined, in the case of presumption, on the basis of the underlying marital relationship.[34] In this respect, reproductive capacity of the parent is premised in the law only to the extent of the traditional legal maxim "*mater semper certa est, pater semper incertus est*".

For the establishment of a parent-child relationship, the existence of a biological relationship between parent and child is not essential. Civil Code provisions such as the presumption of paternity (article 772), loss of the right to rebut the presumption after a husband's acknowledgment (article 776), the consent of an adult child to be recognized (article 782), and the consent of the mother when recognising a foetus and the consent of an adult lineal descendant when recognising a dead child (article 783), provide examples of the inconsistencies between legal parental relationships and those based on biological connection.[35] Court rulings in recent years have shown that the significance of the presumption system lies in preventing the disclosure of secrets in the spousal relationship, as well as stabilizing the father-child relationship at an early stage,[36] without necessarily clarifying the existence of biological relationship.

By allowing the husband's non-exercise of the right to deny paternity, the presumption system recognizes the intervention of the husband's will in determining the existence of a parental relationship. The presumption system strongly affirms the father-child relationship it establishes by restricting both the right to deny paternity[37] and the period for filing

32 Since same-sex marriages are not yet legally recognized in Japan, in the case of (C'), the spouse of FtM would have to be female.

33 See op cit, n. 27.

34 Ibid.

35 M. Ishii, 'A Re-examination of Parental Relationship Laws – Through Recent Supreme Court Judgments', *Horitsu Ronso*, Vol. 81, Nos. 2 & 3, 2009, pp. 31-51, at 45.

36 Supreme Court judgment, 10 December 2013, *Minshu*, Vol. 67, No. 9, p. 1847 (case where a FtM person sued the family register administrator who refused to register him as the father of the child to which his wife gave birth); and also Supreme Court judgment, 17 July 2014, *Saiji* No. 1608, p. 6 and Supreme Court judgment, 17 July 2014, *Minshu*, Vol. 68, No. 6, p. 547 (in both cases, the wife tried to rebut the presumption of the father-child relationships based on the DNA test she conducted).

37 This can only be done by a court procedure initiated by the husband (arts. 774 and 775 of the Civil Code).

the suit in order to safeguard the child's legal status.[38] Moreover, while a parent-child relationship on the basis of recognition can be denied due to the absence of a biological connection,[39] a paternal relationship established on the basis of the father's will is sustained as long as no other party has initiated an action to nullify the recognition.[40] Furthermore, under Japanese law the person giving birth is deemed to be the mother, even in cases of gestational surrogacy arrangements where the surrogate is not genetically related to the child, since an immediate and clear standard for determining mother-child relationships is required.[41]

Applying the current criteria for establishing maternal and paternal relationships, let us now determine the parental relationships in the hypothetical scenarios set out above, beginning with scenarios (A) and (B). After the change of legal gender, as there are no regulations specifying that FtMs be treated differently from other legal men in the context of establishing paternal relationships, the FtM in scenarios (A) and (B) will be treated no differently from other males.[42] Under current legislation, this person will have a *paternal* relationship with the child. In scenario (A) the wife of a person whose legal gender has changed from female to male may conceive a child, for example by means of AID (artificial insemination by donor). When the child is registered, the FtM will be the father of the child, based on the marital presumption (Figure 3).[43] In scenario (B), when an FtM recognizes a child, a *paternal* relationship is formed, as in the case of any other male recognising a child (Figure 4). Thus in these two scenarios, despite the clear absence of a biological connection, the framework of presumption and recognition validates the relationship.

38 S. Nonomiya, 'Marriage and Presumption for Persons whose Legal Gender Has Changed', *Ritsumeikan Law Journal*, No. 345-346, 2012, pp. 576-610, at 585–587.

39 Supreme Court judgment, 14 January 2014, *Minshu*, Vol. 68, No. 1, p. 1; Supreme Court judgment, 28 March 2014, *Shumin*, No. 246, p. 117; Supreme Court judgment, 14 April 1978, *Kagetsu*, Vol. 30, No. 10, p. 26.

40 Nonomiya, op cit, n. 38. The difference between denials of recognition and the marital presumption is primarily focused on respecting legal marriage. However, the rationality of using biological connection as the criterion only in the case of recognition should be questioned if the stability of the paternal relationship is to be fostered.

41 Supreme Court judgment, 23 March 2007, *Minshu*, Vol. 61, No. 12, p. 619.

42 GID Act, art. 4.

43 Supreme Court judgment, 10 December 2013, *Minshu*, Vol. 67, No. 9, p. 1847.

Figure 3

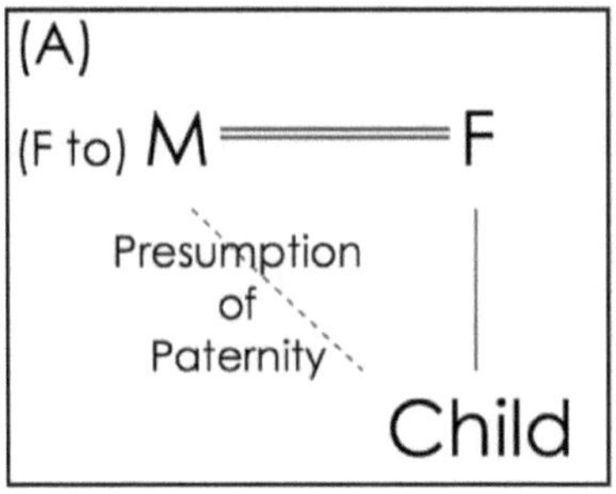

Figure 4

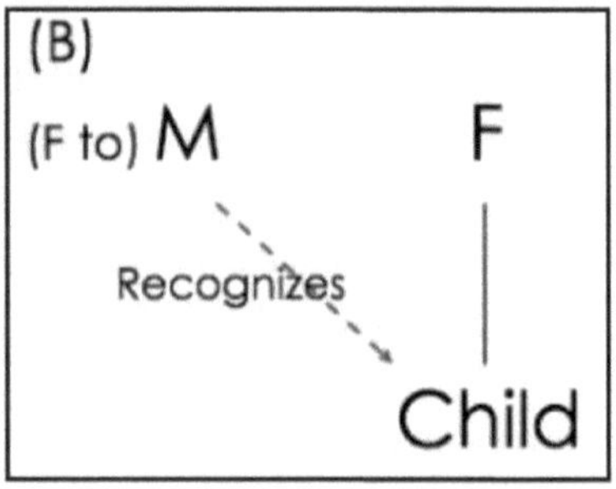

Scenarios (C), (C'), (D), and (E) involve circumstances where the person whose legal gender has changed utilizes their own reproductive functions. In determining the parental relationship in scenarios (C) and (C'), the principle of deeming the person who gives birth to be a parent should be retained, since it assures that the child will have at least one legal parent (Figures 5 and 6).

Figure 5

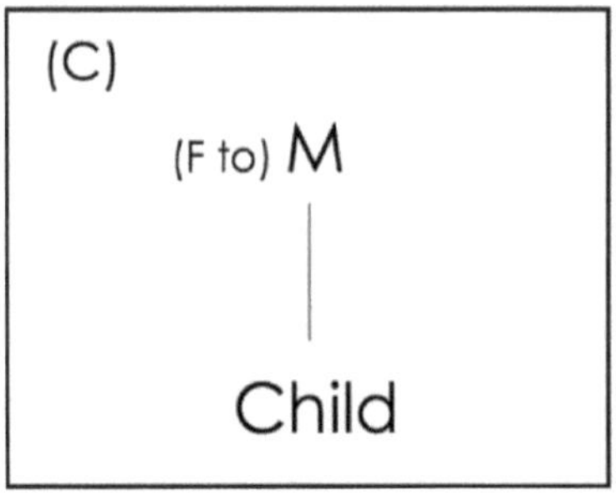

Figure 6

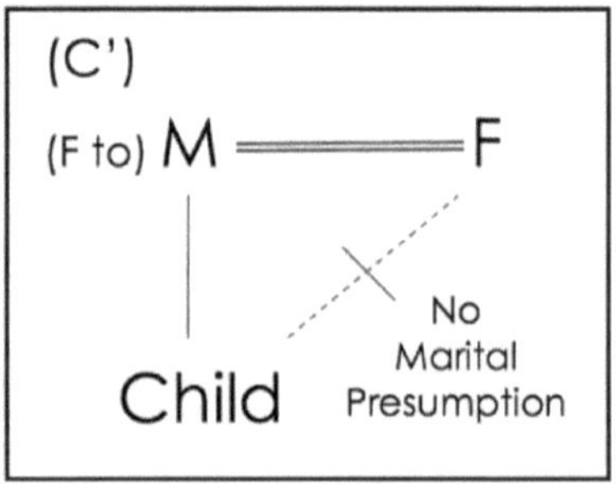

Although there is no difference in the parental rights and obligations ensuing from the registration of a person as either mother or father, a few differences remain in the framework confirming/denying the existence of parent-child relationships. Hence, in scenarios (C) and (C'), the relationship between the FtM and the child would currently be deemed a *maternal* relationship. However, the following issues must be considered:

1. In scenario (C'), how should the relationship between the spouse of the FtM and the child be defined?
2. In scenario (C), if the FtM has a female partner, should it be possible for the partner to establish a parent-child relationship with the child, even if the child already has a mother?
3. Again, in scenario (C), if the FtM has a male partner, this partner can probably recognize the child and be the father, even though the FtM (male/mother) and the male partner

(male/father) cannot marry each other. (This could be problematic for the child involved as a considerable advantage is still given to marital relationships in Japan.)

In applying current criteria to establish parent-child relationships in a gender-neutral manner, it is not unthinkable that the relationship between the spouse and the child in scenario (C') could be considered a father-child relationship. However, establishing a father-child relationship between the female spouse and the child would contradict precedent[44] which suggests that the marital presumption applies only to a male person. In addition, it could be controversial to extend the discordance between father/mother status and male/female status to a spouse who did not request a change of legal gender themselves.

Considering the potential scenario in (2), although article 779 of the Civil Code allows motherhood by recognition, the female partner would not be able to recognize the child, since there is already one legal mother established by childbirth. Thus, in scenarios (C) and (C'), if the female partner or spouse of the FtM wants to establish a parent-child relationship other than by adoption, it would be necessary to permit the child to have two mothers.[45] For such legislation, the co-motherhood scheme, such as the Dutch *duomoeder* system, would be a valuable reference.[46]

Similarly, in scenario (E), the MtF could not have a maternal relationship with the child, since the mother has previously been determined by childbirth. However, it would

44 Ibid. The Court stated that "a person whose gender has been legally changed to male under article 3, paragraph 1 of the Gender Identity Disorder Act ... *since this person is deemed to be male* ... the child is presumed to be the child of the husband."

45 Under Japanese law, it is possible for a child to have two mothers through "regular" adoption, as the original mother-child relationships are not interrupted by regular adoption (unlike "special adoption" which cuts off the original parent-child relationships). There are no procedures in Japan to relinquish one's motherhood status to another person as in, for example, the case of surrogate childbirths.

46 Since the dramatic revision of family law in 2014, Dutch law allows maternity to be established not only by the fact of giving birth, but also by presumption based on relationship with the birth mother and by recognition, thus allowing a child to have two mothers (see M.W. Schrama *in* M.V. Antokolskaia, *Familierecht-Een introductie*, Den Haag, Boom Jurische uitgevers, 2015). About half a year later, the laws governing change of legal gender were also revised in the Netherlands, and the physical requirements, which were similar to the Japanese ones, were abolished. However, a few problems remained; as the presumption of parental status for a female partner of the birth mother requires anonymity of the sperm donor, an MtF person can obtain maternal status by presumption only when the child most likely does not have a biological link with her. When she uses her own sperm, the presumption clause cannot be applied (see M. van den Brink & J. Tigchelaar, 'The equality of the (non) trans-parent: women who father children' *in* M. van den Brink, S. Burri & J. Goldschmidt (Eds.), *Equality and human rights: nothing but trouble?*, Utrecht, SIM/Universiteit Utrecht, 2015, pp. 247-260, at 255). In addition, although the criteria for establishing parental relationships have been made gender-neutral, establishing parental relationships is highly dependent on whether childbirth can occur among the partners. The current Dutch family law has created a substantial difference between male same-sex couples and female same-sex couples since, because of their different physical capabilities, there is a distinct difference in the ease with which they can establish parental relationships. (For more details see M. Ishijima, 'Brief Introduction and Study on Family Relationships Regulations and Civil Registration in Dutch Law: with a Focus on Gender Alternation Clauses (Dutch Civil Code, Book 1, Article 28-28c)', *Comparative Law*, Vol. 50, No. 2, 2016, pp. 235-251.)

be unreasonable to prevent the child from acquiring another parent. Hence, a *paternal* relationship between the MtF and the child should be recognized (Figure 7). If the child is the result of a pregnancy with the MtF's sperm, a parental relationship could be established by the MtF's recognition, unless the MtF was playing the role of a sperm donor.[47] This also leaves room for the child to claim recognition against the MtF.[48] A parental relationship could also be established by recognition between a MtF and a child with whom she does not share a biological link, since the establishment of a parental relationship does not require consanguinity. However, it is undesirable to allow a female person to arbitrarily establish a "paternal" relationship because the person was male prior to the change of legal gender. This would create two sub-categories under "female": "natural-born female" and "female by change of legal gender". It is not appropriate to allow all legal women to establish a "paternal" relationship by recognition at this time, as the discussion over whether a child can have two mothers is not sufficiently developed. For now, it would be appropriate to allow a MtF to recognize a child in restricted cases – restricted from the viewpoint of securing a framework in which a child can generally be guaranteed to have two parents.[49]

Figure 7

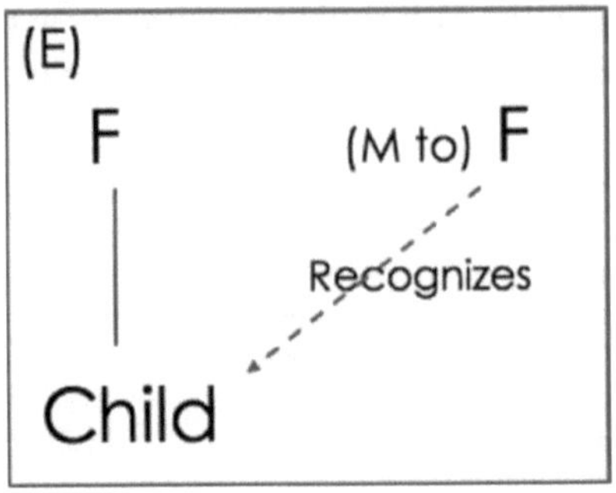

In scenario (D), attention should be paid to the fact that under Japanese law the presumption of paternity is based on the estimated time of the gestation, not the time of delivery. If the child is born within 300 days after the dissolution or rescission of the marriage, the child's conception would be presumed to have occurred when the MtF was the hus-

47 In the case of providing sperm as a donor, there may be already a person who has consented to AID (artificial insemination by donor) and intended to become a father.

48 If the relationship to be established between a MtF and a child is a "paternal relationship", it is conceivable that some MtFs might hesitate to recognize the child. Therefore, it is essential for the child to be able to claim recognition even after the MtF has legally become a female.

49 The same is true in the case of a FtM who gives birth and has a female partner. However, if a MtF and her female partner have a child between them, they cannot marry each other as they are both legally female - even though one can become the father and the other can become the mother. This is an issue with respect to marriage equality that needs to be addressed.

band/legal male of the child's mother. In addition, the presumption only validates paternal relationships.[50] Thus, the parental relationship which the MtF establishes with the child in this case should be deemed a *paternal* relationship, even if the person is a female at the time of the child's birth (Figure 8).

Figure 8

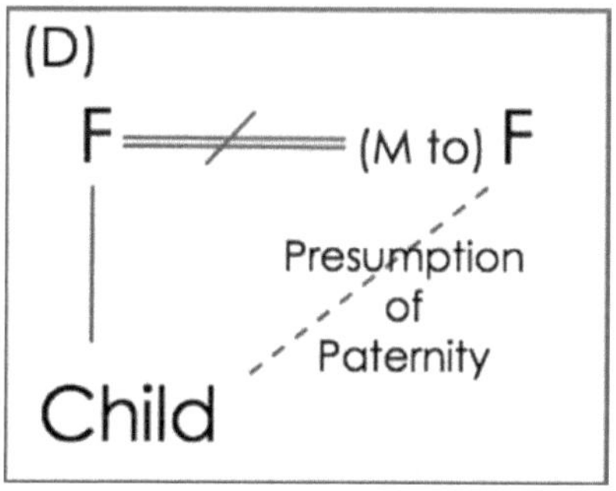

In scenarios (C), (C'), (D) and (E) above, even if a FtM is registered as a male, a "maternal relationship" would be established, and even if a MtF is registered as a female, a "paternal relationship" would be established. This is not an eccentric solution, as the discordance of male/female registration and father/mother registration already exists, since the third requirement of the GID Act, which initially required "having no children", now allows the change of one's legal gender once the child reaches adulthood. However, it should be noted that in the scenarios above, a MtF cannot form a maternal relationship. This disequilibrium between a MtF and a FtM is problematic and could be solved by instituting a scheme of co-motherhood.

B Gender Embedded in Other Legislation

As gender is a vital element in many laws, an exploration of the implications of changing the GID Act must be conducted not only in family law, but also in other legal fields such as those relating, for example, to labour, social insurance, treatment at various institutions and facilities, civil registries, taxation, medical treatment, criminal law, victim identification, and gender equality. In all these areas one can find legal provisions that contain gender-

50 As art. 772 simply provides that the child is presumed to be a child of the husband, it could be said it does not determine whether a paternal or maternal relationship would be established by the presumption. However, other laws presuppose that only the "paternal" relationship can be established by the presumption (for example, art. 773 specifies "when the *father* of the child cannot be determined according to the previous article ..." [emphasis added]). Thus it must be concluded that, under the current legislation, only the paternal relationship can be established by the presumption.

related terms.[51] The elimination of the physical requirements for a change of legal gender – in particular the abolition of the sterilization requirement – will raise issues with respect to other laws that are premised on reproductive capabilities specific to males or females.

The employer's responsibilities in maternal health management are an example. The obligation to protect the worker during pregnancy and childbirth may be applicable to a person who is legally male based on the fact of pregnancy, as such protection is provided not only for the pregnant person but also for the unborn child. However, when the employer perceives the worker as male and the worker is not actually pregnant, it may be considerably more difficult to accuse the employer of failing to protect the worker's fertility or childbearing opportunity, since the worker's fertility is scarcely foreseeable for the employer.[52] Furthermore, compelling the worker to disclose his fertility when his pregnancy has not been ascertained is also inappropriate. On the other hand, in gender equality legislation, when problems related to childbearing are regarded as exclusively female, the employment conditions and considerations applied to a male worker who retains his childbearing function cannot be examined unless the worker reveals his fertility. Moreover, when the registered gender is used as the standard for medical care or the receipt of health information, the risk groups will be determined based on the registered gender (or even on a person's appearance, e.g. at a pharmacy), and spontaneous disclosure of fertility cannot be expected.

The problems which arise from the discordance between one's registered gender and fertility may be distilled into the following two questions: (1) should information on reproductive capacity be collated; and (2) if so, how this should be accomplished. Further questions arise if the registered gender at birth is used for discerning reproductive capacity:[53] (3) how should personal data from the period prior to changes of legal gender should be managed; and (4) under what conditions and to what extent should disclosure be permitted.

As for the treatment of males and females at various facilities, it makes sense to balance the interests of persons in being treated according to their self-perceived gender with the interests of the persons interacting with them in that environment. Enabling the discern-

51 The author conducted a cross-sectional search of gender related terms on the e-Gov Law Search System offered by the Ministry of Internal Affairs and Communications. For more studies on each specific provision see M. Ishijima, 'A Legal Cross-disciplinary Research on Problems that may Arise upon Discrepancy of One's Fertility and Registered Gender - Possible Method to Amend the Japanese Gender Identity Disorder Act', Parts (1) & (2), *Waseda Law Review*, Vol. 93, No. 4, 2018, pp. 87-131 & Vol. 94, No. 1, 2018, pp. 103-143.

52 For example, the regulations for radiation protection provide separate standards for the maximum allowable radiation load for "men, and females who do not have the capacity or intention of being pregnant (declaration required)" and for "other persons".

53 If determinations of reproductive capacity are based on its presence or absence, the question arises of whether everyone should be required to disclose their status, even if a legal gender change is not involved. Since reproductive capacity is highly personal information, it has to be inferred to a certain degree from previously existing information.

ment of gender from physical appearance would protect the interests of the latter group. According to Nemoto, as such discernment depends on the social order, a certain degree of reliability of social order and a basic ability to distinguish a person's gender from outside is required. Thus, the external appearance requirement has been characterised as balancing the interests of the person with society's needs.[54] However, in reality, the fifth requirement of physical modification under the current GID Act applies only to the external genitalia. The situations in which the discernment of a person's gender will be based on the appearance of external genitalia are extremely limited. To ensure a certain predictability of gender, the GID Act only needs to require the consistent continuance of a lifestyle reflecting the gender after the legal change.[55]

IV Conclusion

In light of the normative function of the GID Act in establishing the criteria for "authentic" cases of gender dysphoria, the physical requirements that promote sterilization and physical intervention require immediate revision. As a massive revision of the parent-child relationship system is not realistic at this time, this paper has examined how parent-child relationships could be determined under current family legislation once the physical requirements have been abolished. In future legislation, adoption of a system of co-motherhood may prove an effective means of resolving problems related to obtaining motherhood by MtFs and the spouses/partners of FtMs.[56]

Future developments in family legislation should also include adoption of measures to grant fatherhood to the FtM who gives birth, and motherhood to the MtF who impregnates another person. Procedures to subsequently change paternal/maternal registrations could be introduced, while providing mechanisms to trace how the parent contributed to the child's birth so as to leave a means of later confirming the (non)existence of legal parent-child relationships. At the time of its enactment, the GID Act was promoted as a remedy for those who have a disease; however, it is now preferable to premise it on the concept of "sexual self-determination."[57] Further research should be conducted to

54 T. Nemoto, 'A Study of Laws and Social Systems in Relation to Gender Identity Disorder', *University of Tokyo Law Review*, Vol. 6, 2011, pp. 106-126, at 115-117. He also argues that the current requirement of the GID Act does not contribute much to protection of such a social order, thus this requirement could be replaced with one which protects the social demand more efficiently, such as the requirement of consistent continuance of a lifestyle.

55 However, it should be noted that this "continuance of a lifestyle" only refers to the change of legal gender between male and female, restricting social acceptance of the person as only either male or female. This requirement should be revised when the gender dichotomy reflected in current legislation is abolished.

56 Until then, these problems need to be dealt with within the regular-adoption framework.

57 This concept can be seen in several Western jurisdictions. See, for example, the gender identity cases of the European Court of Human Rights reviewed in European Court of Human Rights, 'Factsheet - Gender

examine the affinity of the self-determination based model with Japanese anti-discrimination regulations, as some of them may be premised on a certain nonselectability of the protected characteristics.

If the physical requirements for a legal change of gender are abolished, the childlessness requirement becomes meaningless.[58] Once irreversible physical modifications are segregated from the procedure for changing one's legal gender, lowering the age limit becomes a possibility. Further, the requirement for a pathological diagnosis also needs to be re-examined. Today, the focus of medical treatment for "gender identity disorder" is not the misalignment of one's experienced gender and the assigned gender itself, but the dysphoria and dysfunction rooted in the discordance. The number of persons requiring a change of legal gender is not necessarily the same as the number of persons diagnosed with this condition and requiring medical treatment. In order to change one's legal gender, it is not necessary to reach a pathologic state and be diagnosed as a person who has a disorder.

The avoidance of unnecessary surgical interventions is rightfully a pressing concern. The issue of the propriety/necessity of a legal gender change should be separated from the issue of the appropriateness of physical modifications/loss of reproductive potential. Reviewing the law requiring sterilization and physical intervention should be deemed critical. Given the normative effect of the Act, new and proper requirements must be promptly adopted.[59]

Identity Issues', (October 2018), available at http://www.echr.coe.int/documents/fs_gender_identity_eng.pdf). Another example is the judgment of the German Federal Constitutional Court of 11 January 2011 (BVerfG, Beschluss des Ersten Senats vom 11 January 2011, 1 BvR 3295/07 - Rn. (1-82)). The German case is remarkable as the physical requirements were essentially nullified by rights-based arguments before amendment of the legislation.

58 Athough it is said that this requirement was instituted to prevent parents from changing their legal gender "for the sake of the child's welfare" (Tokyo High Court judgment, 17 May 2005. *Kagetsu*, Vol. 57, No. 10, p. 99), it does not prohibit a parent from shifting their external appearance and gender in their day-to-day life. If the childlessness requirement prevents legal gender transitions of the parent, the inability to change their gender status may cause the parent psychological suffering, and that may negatively affect the child's mental state and economic conditions.

59 For a more detailed study see M. Ishijima, 'A Practical Study on Elimination of the Physical Requirements in the Japanese Gender Identity Disorder Act', *Waseda Law Review*, Vol. 93, No. 1, 2017, pp. 79-85.

The "Law in Context" for (Stepchild) Adoption in Same-Sex Couples: The Italian Models

*Alessandra Pera**

I Stepchild Adoption in the Statutes

This essay focuses on a recent development in Italian family law with respect to stepchild adoption in cases involving same-sex couples. Resorting to arguments of both the continuity of the affective relationship and the best interests of the child, courts have been willing to permit adoptions in these cases under article 44 of L. 184/1983 ("Adoption Act"), which provides for "adoption in particular cases" ("APC"). This article provides a special (not exceptional) tool, that, at the time it was drafted, was not contemplated for stepchild adoption by a parent's same-sex partner, but could be adapted for such situations. This has remained the case even after the legislative choice not to grant stepchild adoption to the partners of *unioni civili* (L. 76/2016, "Civil Partnership Act").

The starting point for analysis of this recent trend must be the Adoption Act, moving on to the reform of filiation (2012) and the law on the continuity of the affective relationship (2015), and finally to the Civil Partnership Act (2016).

The APC was introduced to protect the child's right to have a family even in those situations that could not end with ordinary and full adoption, but in which the adoptive path still represented the most appropriate solution. The rationale is, as in case of the ordinary adoption, to protect the paramount best interest of the child to be raised within a family, thus ensuring stability and healthy development. However, APC differs from full adoption in its objective and subjective requirements.[1] According to article 44 of the Adoption Act, the APC does not presuppose the abandonment of the child, does not necessarily require

* Associate Professor of Comparative Law, Department of Political Science and International Relations, University of Palermo, Italy.

1 In order to adopt under art. 6 of the Adoption Act (ordinary and full adoption), it is necessary that the *Tribunale per i Minorenni* (Juvenile Court) issue a declaration on the state of abandonment of the child and a decree on the suitability of the adopting parents. In particular, the eligible parents have to be married for three years or, if they are just married, they have lived together as a couple for three years before the marriage; they cannot have been separated or divorced in the previous three years; they must be 18 years older than the child, but not older than 45. The declaration of adoption is preceded by a period of pre-adoptive custody, after which the Juvenile Court can issue the definitive adoption decree. The child then loses any relationship and link with the biological parents, loses their surname and takes the adoptive family's one. Legally, the child becomes the child of the (new) adoptive family.

the severing of the relationship with the natural family (if existing), and in some cases permits adoption by a single individual or an unmarried couple. Under article 44 the APC can be applied for when:

(a) the child is an orphan and the adopting parent(s) has a stable and lasting relationship with the child, regardless of whether that relationship stems from previous family custody (*affidamento familiare*) (para. 1(a));
(b) the child is the daughter or the son of the adopting parent's spouse (para. 1(b));
(c) the child is affected by a serious illness and is an orphan (para. 1(c)); or
(d) pre-adoptive custody (*affidamento pre-adottivo*) is impossible (para. 1(d)).[2]

The APC, like all adoptions, is based on the mutual consent of both the adopting parent and the adoptive child and subsequent control by the court (articles 56[3]-57[4]). Under the original model of APC, the adopted child became the child of the adopting parent, but extended kinship relationships were not affected. However, as a result of the reform of filiation in 2012 this has changed and now, according to article 74 of the Civil Code[5] as unanimously interpreted by scholars and courts, the adopted child establishes relationships with the adoptive parent's relatives. The adopted child also acquires the adoptive parent's surname, which is added to the previous surname.

The APC was conceived as a subsidiary tool to ordinary adoption, with less strict personal requirements on adopting parents with regard to factors such as age, status, and presence of other children in the adoptive family. The rationale was to give answers to many situations where children and weak individuals (also non-minors) would need care, maintenance, education and love, but where full adoption would not be suitable because of the restrictive subjective and objective requisites requested under article 6.[6] One situation clearly contemplated was stepparent adoption by a married couple.

---

2 As briefly explained in n. 1, pre-adoptive custody is a preliminary step in the path to full adoption during which the Juvenile Court, social services and all the other institutions involved in the case monitor the suitability of the potential adoptive parents to determine if they fulfil the requirements prescribed by the law for adoption and if, in the particular case, such solution is in the best interests of the child.

3 Under art. 56 the judge competent to rule on the adoption is the *Tribunale per i Minorenni* of the district where the child is located. Art. 56 also provides that "The consent of the adopter and the adoptee, who is fourteen years old, and the hearing of the legal representative of the adoptee must be personally manifested to the president of the court or to a judge delegated ad hoc".

4 Art. 57 requires the court to verify whether the circumstances in art. 44 apply and whether the adoption is in the child's best interests.

5 After the reform by L. 219/2012 on the unique status of filiation, art. 74 of the Civil Code states: "Relationship is the bond between the people who descend from the same ancestor, whether in the case where the filiation took place within the marriage, whether in the event that it was outside of it or in the event that the child is adopted. The relationship of kinship does not arise in the cases of adoption of older persons, referred to in articles 291 et seq." For scholars' opinion on the recent reform of status of filiation see P. Morozzo della Rocca, 'Il nuovo status di figlio e le adozioni in casi particolari', *Famiglia e diritto*, 2013, pp. 898ff.

6 Described op cit, n. 1.

Due to its flexibility, the APC has been adapted to answer to needs different from those the legislator had in mind in 1983. For instance, it has been used:

- to turn temporary custody into adoption, when the situation of temporary abandonment has become definitive and the "custodial family" seems worthy of protection just as the family of origin;[7] and
- to deal with situations of "partial abandonment", as a form of adoption that does not cause the definitive interruption of the relationship with the natural family.

More recently, it has been applied to situations far removed from the traditional ones, including situations where social or de facto parents have played a crucial role in the growth and education of the child. Such situations include:

- children born through surrogacy, recognized by the father and then adopted by his wife;[8]
- the Islamic Kafalah,[9] which is close to adoption but is not identical, and does not necessarily break the relation between the child and the family of origin;
- the enforcement in Italy of an order of adoption by a single parent, issued abroad;[10] and
- the recognition of relations arising from "reconstructed families" (when the natural parent is dead and the new partner or spouse of the surviving parent applies for the adoption of the family child)[11] or from same-sex couples (de facto, civil unions or married abroad).

These recent judicial developments have been anchored by a legislative framework of reference which has evolved in three different stages: the first represented by L. 219/2012 and d. Lgs. 154/2013 on the unique status of filiation;[12] the second is L. 173/2015, which,

7 Trib. Min. Genova, 14 October 1995, in *Famiglia e diritto*, 1996, p. 346, commented on by P. Morozzo della Rocca; Trib. Min. Roma, 22 June 1987, in *Diritto di famiglia e delle persone*, 1998, p. 947; Trib. Min. Roma, 18 March 1985, in *Diritto di famiglia e delle persone*, 1985, p. 620.

8 Corte di Appello Salerno, 15 November 1991, in *Nuova giurisprudenza civile commentata*, I, 1994, p. 177, with a comment by R. Bitetti; Trib. Min. Roma, 31 March 1992, in *Diritto di famiglia e delle persone*, 1993, p. 188.

9 Trib. Min. Trento, 10 September 2002, in *Nuova giurisprudenza civile commentata*, 2003, p. 149, with a comment by J. Long; *contra* Trib. Min. Brescia, 12 March 2010, in *Rivista di diritto internazionale privato e processuale*, 2010, p. 770; Cass. Civ., 2 February 2015, n. 1843, in *Nuova giurisprudenza civile commentata*, I, 2015, p. 707, with a comment by M. Di Masi; T. Tomeo, 'La kafalah, in *Comparazione e diritto civile*, May 2013, available at http://www.comparazionedirittocivile.it/prova/files/ncr_tomeo_kafala.pdf.

10 Cass. civ., 14 February 2011, n. 3572, in *Foro italiano*, I, c. 728, with a comment by C. De Marzo.

11 Trib. Min. Milano, 28 March 2007, in *Famiglia e minori*, 2007, p. 83; App. Firenze, 4 October 2012, in *Minori e giustizia*, 2013, p. 366.

12 For a complete and interesting analysis see G. Ferrando, 'Stato unico di figlio e varietà dei modelli familiari', *Famiglia e diritto*, 2015, pp. 952ff, who highlights the plurality of affective relationships in which the child's personality develops, regardless of the form of family, but simply because of filiation and parenthood themselves.

modifying the rules on adoption, has expressly codified the child's right to the continuity of the affective relationships; and the third step was L. 76/2016, the Civil Partnership Act, on same-sex civil partnerships (*unioni civili*) and de facto relationships (both same-sex and opposite sex).

The first two statutes explicitly recognized the unification of the child's status and the catalogue of her/his rights, regardless of the nature of the relationship between the parents, expressly introducing into the Civil Code the right to moral assistance, to be loved and to grow up in a family, and to have high-quality and stable relationships with relatives.[13] What seems crucial in the recent reforms on filiation and on continuity of affective relationships is the intention to protect the interest the child has in living in stable, affective relationships, and to afford legal status to the concrete form and way in which such relationships have been built across the years. This has allowed foster parents to adopt. Moreover, through a systematic and extensive interpretation of the continuity of affective relationships' doctrine, courts have recognised the juridical relevance of many social parental bonds, declaring the APC of a minor by the social parent, the person who has acted and has been perceived as such (inside the family and in front of third parties) for a stable and long period of time.[14]

Before the Civil Partnerships Act entered into force, many court decisions on adoption by the partner (even in same-sex couples)[15] were aimed at protecting values such as affection, assistance and care of the child provided by the adopting parent who had behaved in the couple and in the family as a parent, even if biologically they were not. In those cases the judges, as will be discussed more fully below, preferred the solution that protected the best interests of the child, consenting to the request for an APC under para. 1(d) of article 44 of the Adoption Act based on the impossibility of pre-adoptive custody because of the absence in such cases of the prerequisite of the abandonment of the child.

13 See arts. 315 and 315-bis.

14 For an in-depth explanation of the continuity of affective relationships act and its *ratio* see the decision of the *Cassazione* discussed below, in n. 15, at para. 2.

15 Cass. civ., 22 June 2016, n. 12962, in *Diritto di famiglia e delle persone*, II, 4, 2016, p. 1014. And, similarly, Trib. Min. Roma, 30 July 2014, n. 299, in *Nuova giurisprudenza civile commentata*, I, 2015, pp. 109ff, with a note by J. Long; for a contrary point of view see the comments by R. Carrano & M. Ponzani, 'L'adozione del minore da parte del convivente omosessuale tra interesse del minore e riconoscimento giuridico di famiglie omogenitoriali', *Diritto di Famiglia*, 2014, pp. 1550ff. The decision has been confirmed by Corte di Appello Roma, Sez. Min., 23 December 2015, n. 2015, in *Diritto di famiglia e delle persone*, II, 3, 2016, p. 806, with a comment by S. Menichetti. On the cross-adoption by each member of a same-sex couple of the other's child(ren), see Corte di Appello Napoli, 30 March 2016, in http://www.dirittoegiustizia.it/, which has recognised legal effects in Italy of the respective French court decision on adoption. Against these solutions and with a restrictive interpretative attitude see Trib. Min. Piemonte e Valle d'Aosta, 11 September 2015, n. 258 & n. 259, in *Nuova giurisprudenza civile commentata*, I, 2016, pp. 205ff, commented on by A. Nocco, 'L'adozione del figlio di convivente dello stesso sesso: due sentenze contro una lettura "eversiva" dell'Article 44, let. (d), L. n. 184/1983'.

The Civil Partnership Act provided for formal recognition of same-sex unions and affords same-sex partners a status similar to that of marriage. The *unione civile*, even though formally conceived as a separate institution from marriage, shares many of its essential features: the constitutive moment (the act); the interpersonal rights and obligations (the relationship); and the relevance of the relationship for third parties and the community. The main difference from marriage is with regard to children. Paragraph 20 of article 1 of the Act[16] establishes the applicability of all the provisions "relating to marriage" or that contain "the words 'spouse', 'wife and husband' or similar expression, recurring everywhere in the laws, in the acts having the force of law, regulations and administrative measures or collective agreements" to *unioni civili*, but expressly excludes the provisions of the 1983 Adoption Act.[17] Paragraph 20 thus precludes couples of *unioni civili* from being eligible for full adoption (under article 6 of the Adoption Act), which remains reserved to spouses.

As far as APCs are concerned, para. 1(b) of article 44 of the Adoption Act provides for the adoption of the child of the other "spouse". It is thus clear that, according to the wording of para. 20 of the Civil Partnership Act, this provision does not apply to *unioni civili*. However, this exclusion does not cover para. 1(d) of article 44. While 1(b) contains specific rules for adoption by a "spouse", 1(d) instead contains a general framework for cases of "impossibility of pre-adoptive custody" (*affidamento pre-adottivo*).

Subsequent parliamentary debate has focused not on the Adoption Act and the use of the APC in cases involving same-sex parents, but instead on the behaviour of the parents.[18] Calls have been made to strengthen the penalty for having recourse to surrogate motherhood abroad,[19] especially in the case of male same-sex couples, and to limit and/or avoid recourse to artificial insemination in female same-sex couples. The proposed model suggests that the right of children to a legal relationship with their parents should be limited by the supposed need to punish and/or prevent behaviour on the part of parents that is deemed "deviant" or criminal. As will be discussed below, this approach does not reflect the attitude of the Constitutional Court.

16 The Act is made up of just one article, subdivided into many paragraphs.

17 As will be discussed further below, earlier drafts of the Act permitted stepparent adoption by civil union couples, but this was rejected in the parliamentary debates.

18 The proposal (n. 3816) was from On. Binetti, 'modifiche all'articolo 12 della legge 19 febbraio 2004 n. 40 concernenti l'aggravamento delle pene per il reato di surrogazione di maternità e la sua perseguibilità all'estero'. The draft is available at http://www.camera.it/leg17/410?idSeduta=0622&tipo=documenti_seduta.

19 The penalty is provided by art. 12, c. 6, L. 40/2004 on artificial insemination and reproductive techniques, which states that "anyone who, in any form, realizes, organizes or promotes the commerce of gametes or embryos or surrogacy is punished with imprisonment from three months to two years and with a fine of 600,000 to one million euros".

II COURT RULINGS

This analysis of the emerging trend in court rulings on stepchild adoption in same-sex couples will focus on leading decisions of the Italian Constitutional Court and the *Corte di Cassazione.*[20] The starting point will be an important decision of the Constitutional Court in 2016, a case in which the Court was asked to rule on the recognition in Italy of a judgement of a Spanish court allowing a stepchild adoption by the female partner of the child's mother.[21] On the constitutional issue before the Court, it found that articles 34-36 of the Adoption Act were compatible with the Constitution. (These articles provide for giving legal effect and recognition in the Italian legal system to foreign adoptions.) For the purposes of this analysis, the decision is significant for the systematic approach adopted by the Court in clearly delineating the differences between full adoption and special adoption: only the first presupposes a permanent state of abandonment, while the latter seeks to implement the child's right to have a family in cases where, although the requirements for the full adoption are not satisfied, it is necessary or appropriate to adopt, giving a legal status to de facto family relationships.

The Court described article 44 as "a kind of residual clause" for "special cases that do not fit in the discipline of ordinary and full adoption, when the conditions mentioned in the first paragraph of article 7 are not occurring."[22] More specifically, para. 1(d) of article 44 "provides a further solution for cases that do not fit into those more specifically referred to in subparagraphs (a) and (b)". The Court recognized that unlike full adoption, adoption under article 44:

> does not cut the ties of the child with her/his family of origin, but it offers her/him the opportunity to remain part of the new family that welcomed her/him, *formalizing the affective relationship established with specific individuals who are actually taking care of her/him.* [emphasis added, translation by author]

---

20 The highest court of appeal in Italy, which has the role of ensuring the correct interpretation and application of the law, revising mistakes with respect to the law's interpretation but not those with respect to the evaluation of facts.

21 Corte Cost., 7 April 2016, n. 76, commented on by E. Billotti, 'Riconoscimento in Italia di un provvedimento di stepchild adoption: la Corte Costituzionale ritiene inammissibile la questione di legittimità costituzionale degli art. 35 e 36 della legge 184/1983', *Diritto civile contemporaneo*, 2016, available at http://dirittocivile-contemporaneo.com/2016/04/riconoscimento-in-italia-di-un-provvedimento-straniero-di-stepchild-adoption-la-corte-costituzionale-ritiene-inammissibile-la-questione-di-legittimita-costituzionale-degli-artt-35-e-36-d/.

22 Art. 7 requires a declaration by the *Tribunale per i Minorenni* of the adoptability of the child based on a finding of parental abandonment.

The Constitutional Court noted that the European Court of Human Rights (ECHR) has interpreted the right to "family life", protected by article 8 of the European Convention on Human Rights, to include de facto family relationships in adoption cases, where the existing emotional relationship within a family deserves consideration and protection, regardless of whether it is a recognised relationship under domestic law.[23] The Court reasoned that formal recognition of such de facto relationships reflects the interests of the child and provides a certain legal framework through which specific responsibilities and obligations towards the child and third parties can be assumed. Formal recognition secures both the child's legal status and their rights, for example, in the event of the biological parent's death, or the rupture of common life, and it safeguards the child's relations with third parties, such as educational or health institutions. It is aimed at ensuring the stability and continuity of existing affective relationships, in the same way as family custody provided for by L. 173/2015 (law on affective continuity).[24]

According to the Constitutional Court, once the interests of the child and the adoptive eligibility of the parent have been verified, adoption must be granted not only to the spouse of a parent, but also to the parent's partner. The adoption in such a case would be based upon the impossibility of pre-adoptive custody under para. 1(d) of article 44 and the absence of the conditions required for full adoption under article 7 of the Adoption Act.

In support of its interpretation of para. 1(d) the Constitutional Court referred to a 2013 decision of *Corte di Cassazione*'s[25] (not binding for the Constitutional Court, but with persuasive effects) which had criticised the refusal to permit a stepchild adoption by a same-sex partner in the following terms:

> at the base – of a denial - there are not scientific certainty or data of experience, but the mere prejudice that is detrimental to the balanced development of the child the fact of living in a family centred on a homosexual couple. [translation by author]

In reasoning endorsed by the Constitutional Court, the *Cassazione* had stated that it was not permissible to "assume as obvious and assessed something that instead has to be demonstrated", i.e. "the harmfulness of that family environment for the child". In this same decision the *Cassazione* concluded that adoption under article 44 can involve both

---

23 *Moretti and Benedetti v. Italy*, ECHR, 27 April 2010 (R. n. 16318/2007); *Paradiso and Campanelli v. Italy*, ECHR, 27 January 2017 (R. n. 25358/2012); *Zhou v. Italy*, ECHR, 21 January 2014 (R. n. 33773/2011); *S.H. v. Italy*, ECHR, 13 October 2015 (R. n. 52577/2014), all available at www.udhoc.eu.

24 L. 173/2015 specifically recognised the existence of family relationships that can develop in situations of "temporary family custody" and granted the foster family the right to be preferred to other eligible persons if the child became adoptable. However, more generally, the doctrine of affective continuity can be and has been extended to other situations where legal recognition of social parenthood has been requested.

25 Cass. Civ., 11 January 2013, n. 601, in *Giurisprudenza italiana*, 2013, p. 1038 commented on by M. Winkler.

single individuals and unmarried couples, including same-sex couples, and that the investigation into the interests of the child "cannot be based ... on the sexual orientation of the applicant and the consequent nature of the relationship established by her/him with her/his partner." [translation by author]

More recently, in a 2016 decision that was issued one month after the entering into force of the Civil Partnership Act and which involved a case of stepchild adoption by the female partner of the mother, the *Cassazione*[26] clarified that there are

> two patterns of adoption, the legitimizing (full), founded on the abandonment of the child and the non-legitimizing (simple), based on different requirements with regard both to the factual situation in which the child lives and to the relation with the adopting applicant. [translation by author]

In this regard, the Court pointed out that the *Tribunale per i Minorenni* is required to determine if there is compliance with the requirements of the regulatory framework, and in doing so it "must make a specific assessment of the 'emotional suitability' of the adoptive parent". Such "evaluation can only be done on the basis of a pre-existing relationship between the adopting parent and the child" [author translation] and this is obviously incompatible with a situation of abandonment (prerequisite for full adoption).

Two recent decisions by *Tribunale per i Minorenni di Milano*, likely influenced in part by the recent legislative choice to preclude stepchild adoption in same-sex civil partnerships, stand in contrast with this interpretation of article 44.[27] The first decision was in a case of a request for an APC by the mother's male partner in a de facto relationship and the second was in a case of cross-adoption by two co-mothers. Both decisions employed a strict literal interpretation of article 44 which did not take sufficient account of the legislative evolution of the APC or, more generally, the evolution of family law, particularly in the light of rulings by the Constitutional Court and European case law. Moreover they were founded on two misleading premises.

The first is that APC is allowed only in cases of abandonment, interpreted by the court as a "serious lack of parental figures", which obviously does not occur in the case of a child who has grown up with and been educated by a parent and the parent's partner. There is no abandonment, even in the literal or technical meaning of the words, as there is no lack of moral or material assistance (either permanent or temporary) by the parent or the relatives, who are obliged by law to grant it. However, as confirmed by the Constitutional

26 Cass. Civ., 22 June 2016, n. 12962.

27 Trib. Min. Milano, 17 October 2016, n. 261, which denied the cross-adoption of the respective children in a female same-sex couple; Trib. Min. Milano, 20 October 2016, n. 268, which refused the adoption by the male partner of the mother of the child (not in a same-sex couple). Both decisions are available and commented on at www.Ilfamiliarista.it, 22 November 2016.

Court and the *Cassazione*, the APC does not presuppose the status of abandonment of the child.

As for the second false premise, the court considered the APC unavailable in both cases because the exclusive model for the ACP is the "traditional family founded on marriage". However this interpretation is not supported by the legislative framework. As has been outlined above, the family originating from marriage is not the paradigmatic model in the APC. Above all, para. 3 of article 44 provides that in cases falling under subparagraphs (a), (c), and (d) of para. 1 adoption is permitted even by a single parent. Only if the adopter is married, and not separated, is the consent of the spouse required. In contrast to full adoption, for the APC of a minor child, the statute refers to adoption by a married couple as one of the possible options, but not the only one.

Furthermore, the *Tribunale per i Minorenni di Milano* seems to have forgotten its mission to protect affective relationships by granting them formal recognition. Instead it approached the applications as if the decisions concerned the issue of the equal treatment of a family founded on marriage with one founded on a para-matrimonial partnership rather than the issue of the best interests of the child, regardless of the marital status of the adopter and the child's parent. The reform of filiation has clearly made the child's equal opportunity the paramount consideration, in the sense that every child has to be granted the same rights within the family, regardless of its origin or form, as the family is the primary place where the child's personality develops.

In its 2016 decision,[28] the *Corte di Cassazione* has underlined that whenever the circumstances for pre-adoptive custody are absent and the child is already living in a de facto family relationship with the adopter, the judge is required to determine whether that relationship can be considered to be in the best interests of the child. Such scrutiny can lead to a negative conclusion regarding best interests, even if the adopter is the partner of the parent, when the partner's relationship with the child is not stable, established or reciprocated, or is for any other reason not worthy of protection and formal recognition. The "juridification" of the de facto relationship and the decision to grant the APC should be made by the judge, considering the best interests of the child as an "insuperable limit and interpretative key of the institution"[29] according to the Adoption Act, article 3 UN Convention on the Rights of the Child[30] and article 24 of the EU Charter on Human Rights.[31]

---

28 Op cit, n. 26.

29 Trib. Min. Roma, 30 July 2014, n. 299, in *Diritto di famiglia e delle persone*, II, 4, 2015, p. 1335, with a comment by G. Miotto.

30 Entered in to force in Italy by means of L. 176/1991, available at http://www.camera.it/_bicamerali/infanzia/leggi/l176.htm. Art. 3, para. (1) establishes the primacy of the best interests of the child principle.

31 Art. 24, para. 2 provides: "In all actions relating to children, whether taken by public authorities or private institutions, the child's best interests must be a primary consideration."

III Social Change and Policy Choices in the Context of Same-Sex Couples Forum Shopping for Artificial Insemination and Surrogacy

The strict interpretation of article 44 offered by some courts and the statutory omission of stepchild adoption in the *unioni civili* deny members of a same-sex couple (de facto or *unione civile*) the right to parenthood. If the Italian legal system promoted parenthood as a life project of the couple, eligible forms would include: full adoption of an abandoned minor; artificial insemination (female couples); and surrogacy (male couples). However, none of these options are now contemplated by statute. The request for full adoption, under article 6, para. 1 of the Adoption Act must come from a married couple. Access to artificial insemination, governed by article 5, L. 40/2004, is reserved to opposite-sex couples, married or cohabiting. Surrogacy is banned and criminally prosecuted by the same L. 40.

These elements must be read together, as they point out a crucial controversy: the way in which parenthood is conceived is connected to the way politicians, who are members of the legislature, interpret how their base (civil society) feels about the relationship between marriage and the *unioni civili* and about the idea of parenthood for same-sex couples. In the drafting phase, stepchild adoption was included in the reform on *unioni civili*, but during the parliamentary debate it was set aside, otherwise the *unioni civili* "would never have seen the light".

Recently in 2017, even after the entering into force of the Civil Partnership Act, some *Tribunali per i Minorenni* (Trento, Torino and others) have recognized the APC for female same-sex couples where the child is the product of artificial insemination, is genetically related to one of the women, and the other female partner undertook the pregnancy, so that the latter is the natural mother and the first is biologically linked to the child. The real controversy arises in the case of male same-sex couples. In those couples, the interests involved are not rights, because L. 40/2004 prohibits recourse to surrogacy, so that the parents' joint life project is illegal from the outset. Despite the prohibition, surrogacy is quite widespread, as demonstrated by the increasing number of cases brought before the Italian civil and criminal courts. Couples travel abroad to more permissive jurisdictions in order to overcome the prohibition and to fulfil their desire to become parents.

The prohibition of surrogacy has different rationales. The legal system wants to protect children and prevent them from being treated as goods that can be bought and sold.[32] There is also the need to ensure a degree of certainty of motherhood which, in the case of

---

32 On the different - and sometimes contrasting – interests of the child and the parents see V.S. Browne-Barbour, 'Bartering for Babies: are preconception agreements in the best interest of children?' *Whittier Law Review*, Vol. 26, 2004, p. 429; J.B. Reich & D. Swink, 'Outsourcing human reproduction: embryos and surrogacy services in the cyber-procreation era', *Journal of Health Care Law & Policy*, Vol. 14, 2011, p. 241.

surrogacy, can be split having regard to the various mother figures.[33] This is alleged to have negative consequences for the psychological and social development of the child. Looking at the position of the surrogate mother, the state wants to avoid the economic or social exploitation of women,[34] especially when the choice to act as a surrogate mother is determined by the amount of compensation offered by the commissioning couple, such that it is not a free decision, but rather one based only on economic reasons.[35]

Italian law does recognise paternity if there is a genetic link with the commissioning father. This is easily verifiable through a DNA test, allowing the commissioning father to formally recognise the child and be registered as the father in the birth certificate. The determination of maternity is more complex as, under article 269, para. 2 of the Civil Code, the "mother" is the woman who gives birth to the child. At present, the Italian legal framework is unable to respond to social change and to deal with the question of who should care for and bring up the child after birth.

There are many controversial issues surrounding surrogacy upon which there is no general consensus in public opinion in Italy nor amongst European countries or other western jurisdictions. Does the right to procreate, which may even be recognized as constitutionally protected - as in Italy - extend to using a surrogate mother? Is it reasonable to conclusively presume as a matter of law, without looking at the particular circumstances of the case, that a woman is unable to decide freely to become a surrogate mother? Is it possible to consider surrogacy as a lawful means of procreation, comparable to blood donation? The answers to these controversies are tied to the concept of parenthood, which is of course culturally specific. In Italy the concept of parenthood is founded, on the one side, on notions of procreative choice (articles 2 and 32 of the Italian Constitution) and, on the other side, on notions of procreative responsibility (article 30, para. 1 of the Italian Constitution).

Adoption has not only a domestic dimension, but also a private international law dimension, as demonstrated by two recent decisions of the *Tribunale per i Minorenni di*

---

33 See J. Wallbank, 'Too many Mothers? Surrogacy, Kinship and the Welfare of the Child', *Medical Law Review*, Vol. 10, 2002, p. 271; C. Achmad, 'Protecting the Locus of Vulnerability: Preliminary Ideas for Guidance on Protecting the Rights of the Child in International Commercial Surrogacy', *in* T. Liefaard & J. Sloth-Nielsen (Eds.), *The United Nations Convention on the Rights of the Child: Taking Stock after 25 Years and Looking Ahead*, Leiden, Brill, 2016, p. 513.

34 For further discussion of these rationales, see C. Shalev, *Birth power. The Case for Surrogacy*, New Haven and London, Yale University Press, 1989; M. Coleman, 'Gestation, Intent, and the Seed: Defining Motherhood in the Era of Assisted Human Reproduction', *Cardozo Law Review*, Vol. 17, 1996, p. 497; R. Schuz, 'The Right to Parenthood: Surrogacy and Frozen Embryos', *in* A. Bainham, (Ed.), *The International Survey of Family Law*, 1996, The Hague, Kluwer/Int. Society of Family Law, 1998, p. 237; M. H. Baughman, 'In Search of Common Ground: One Pragmatist Perspective on the Debate over Contract Surrogacy', *Columbia Journal of Gender and Law*, Vol. 10, 2001, p. 263.

35 In the Italian literature see I. Kriari & A. Valongo, 'International issues regarding surrogacy', *Italian Law Journal*, Vol. 2, 2016, pp. 331ff.

Firenze[36] which enforced in Italy foreign decisions on adoption involving male same-sex couples.[37] It is important to emphasize that the rulings in these cases concerned both the recognition of an adoption certificate issued abroad, when the adopting couple was in a same-sex relationship, and the subsequent transcription of the adoption in the civil status register, which was essential for the children to obtain legal status and Italian citizenship.[38]

One case involved two men who were Italian citizens but had lived for a lengthy period of time in the U.K. They had become registered partners under the U.K. Civil Partnership Act (2004) and, as permitted by that Act, had adopted two children. The rights of registered partners to adopt were afforded both to U.K. citizens and foreign couples as there were no restrictions relating to citizenship or the domicile of the applicants. Another case concerned a family of two Italian-American men who, in 2014, had adopted a girl in compliance with the applicable foreign law, which provided for an authorized agency to evaluate the family of birth, the adoptive parents, and the conditions within the adoptive home, before and after the placement with the adoptive family.

In the Italian legal system, article 36, para. 4 of the Adoption Act allows for the recognition of an adoption by Italian citizens resident abroad if the adoption was in compliance with the principles of the Hague Convention on Protection of Children and Co-operation in Respect of Intercountry Adoption.[39] In particular, article 24 of the Convention states that "the recognition of an adoption may be refused in a Contracting State only if the adoption is manifestly contrary to its public policy, taking into account the best interests of the child". Thus, the only impediment to the recognition of the foreign adoption is public policy, interpreted according to international norms.

Many court rulings in Italy,[40] including rulings of appeal courts, have considered same-sex parenthood to *not* be contrary to public policy. In a very significant 2016 decision involving recognition of same-sex parenthood, the *Corte di Cassazione*[41] established the boundaries of the public policy exception in cases involving child status having regard to four key principles: (a) respect for human fundamental rights; (b) legislative discretion;

36 Trib. Firenze, 7 March 2017, available at http://www.articolo29.it/wp-content/uploads/2017/03/Trib-min-fi-1.pdf.

37 See M. Winkler, 'Riconoscimento di sentenza di adozione straniera e nozione "perimetrata" di ordine pubblico internazionale: le due decisioni del Tribunale per i Minorenni di Firenze', 23 March 2017, available at http://www.diritticomparati.it/riconoscimento-di-sentenza-di-adozione-straniera-e-nozione-perimetrata-di-ordine-pubblico-internazionale-le-due-decisioni-del-tribunale-per-i-minorenni-di-firenze/.

38 See art. 34 of the Adoption Act.

39 The convention was concluded on the 29th May 1993. The text is available at https://www.hcch.net/en/instruments/conventions/full-text/?cid=69.

40 See Corte di Appello Napoli, ord. 30 March 2016, which gave legal effect in Italy to the French crossed *adoption plénière*; see also Corte di Appello Milano, ord. 16 October 2015, which upheld the Spanish step-child adoption of same sex partner's daughter.

41 Cass. Civ., 30 September 2016, n. 19599, available at http://dirittocivilecontemporaneo.com/wp-content/uploads/2016/10/Cass.-30-settembre-2016-n.-19599.pdf. This was a case involving the recognition and transcription of a Spanish birth certificate that listed two women as mothers.

(c) the interests of the child; and (d) patent incompatibility with legal order.[42] The two recent decisions of the *Tribunale per i Minorenni di Firenze* which enforced foreign decisions on adoption involving male same-sex couples made reference to these principles.

On the first principle, the *Tribunale per i Minorenni di Firenze* considered that an adoption that violates fundamental rights protected by the European Convention on Human Rights and the EU Charter on Human Rights would be contrary to the public international order.

As for legislative discretion, the *Corte di Cassazione* had ruled that the public policy exception can only be used to protect the constitutional dimension of public policy. The public policy argument thus had to be based upon a constitutional provision (implicit or explicit) and that, in the absence of such provisions, statuses acquired abroad through surrogacy and medically assisted reproductive techniques could not be limited by reference to the public policy exception.

The *Tribunale per i Minorenni di Firenze* determined that the same reasoning could be applied to adoption, particularly given that it was not in the interests of children to have their parental relationships limited by a "limping" legal status. Non-recognition of a parental status legally acquired abroad would affect the child's rights to personal identity (origins, citizenship), to the free movement of people, to be free from discrimination based on their parents' sexual orientation, and to affective continuity, including recognition of the link with both parents, and other relatives.

On the issue of whether the adoptions were patently incompatible with legal order, the *Tribunale per i Minorenni di Firenze* ruled that the court should concentrate on the facts of the individual case. Thus, it considered sufficient the numerous documents offered by the applicants with respect to the children's condition which provided evidence of a "life happily conducted in a stable family", of positive relationships with the parents, relatives and friends, and of a social environment in which the children practised sports, went to top schools and expressed their personal attitudes with adults and other children. After these acknowledgements, the court stated, in one of the decisions, that "there is a real and genuine family (…) there is a plain relationship between children and parents and as such it has to be treated and protected." In both cases the court upheld the full adoption, with the consequence that the families lawfully built abroad were fully recognised by the Italian legal system.

---

42 All these parameters must be evaluated through a constitutionally oriented hermeneutic work, as suggested also by Corte Cost., ord. 1 July 1983, n. 214, available at www.giurcost.org/decisioni/1983/0214s-83.html.

IV Concluding Remarks

Analysis of the emerging trend in judicial decisions with regard to stepchild adoption in same-sex families reveals that there is a key distinction between the right of a same-sex couple to parenthood, which is not recognized by statutory regulation, and the minor's right, effectively enforced by judges, to a juridical status corresponding to the factual situation lived within a same-sex family founded on affection, moral and material assistance, and care of the child. The fact that the law does not expressly regulate the child's adoption by the same-sex partner of the parent has led courts to resolve these cases so as to ensure the right of children to legal certainty and stability of their relationships with those who exercise the parental function.

At the same time, considering the legal system in its entirety, while courts are required to promote the importance of the nature and stability of the bonds created between the individuals involved, they must do so without neglecting their public function, which includes evaluating the "ways" through which these ties have been established, especially if they are illegal. In this regard, a minority of the judges of the European Court of Human Rights have argued, in their dissenting opinions,[43] that no one can sue for a right based on an illegal action. In particular, according to these opinions, the law cannot offer protection to people who have acted in clear violation of legal rules and fundamental principles by conceiving a child via a technique which is forbidden in their country of origin, and then transferring the child from one country to another.

The extreme consequence of such reasoning is that any intervention of the state authorities in the family or private life of the individuals involved is legitimate since the intervention is not directed at denying their wish to become parents, but at stopping and eventually punishing the means by which they seek to obtain such result. This restrictive position considers the child to be a victim of human trafficking as the commissioning of their birth and their acquisition by the "eligible parents" has been in violation of national and international provisions.[44] This position also condemns surrogacy, especially when paid, as an inhumane practice, which violates the dignity of both the woman and the child.

The opposing approach stresses the importance of the family life lived, even if for a short period, by the couple and the child. According to this line of reasoning, courts must give paramount consideration to the impact that separation would have on the welfare of the child. This approach implies that the bonds between the minor and the family must be preserved and protected (with some exceptions if the family is patently inadequate), and that this choice ensures the child's safe and healthy development. It appears that the

43 *Paradiso and Campanelli*, op cit, n. 25, opinion by De Gaetano, Pinto De Albuquerque, Wojtyczec and Dedov, para. 3.

44 Such as the Hague Convention on Intercountry Adoption, op cit, n. 39.

Corte di Cassazione has endorsed this approach. In a 2016 decision the *Cassazione* consented to the recognition and transcription of a foreign birth certificate indicating that the parents in a female same-sex couple had each contributed to the generation of the child: one through the use of her egg and the other by carrying and giving birth to the child.[45]

Post-modern legal theories emphasize a change of perspective in the relationship between legal categories and social facts, underlining the strong trend towards the "factuality of the law."[46] The facts assume a central function and can result in alteration of the law as the legal system tries to read such facts in light of the interests and values involved.

In Italy, the existence of children inside same-sex families has necessitated new forms of protection for minors. Answers have been provided by the judiciary and not by the legislator, with results that are quite similar to those that would have been secured if the possibility of stepchild adoption had not been removed by Parliament from the final text of the Civil Partnerships Act. Of course, the effects are not identical, but are in fact of even greater relevance, because in the cases examined the granting of the APC has not been linked to the constitution of a *unione civile*, but instead has been recognized as a tool to protect the personality and the development of the child. It is also important to stress some secondary effects: protecting the paramount interests of the child has meant, indirectly, promoting new forms of families and rights to parenthood, and has given certainty to familial relationships and reinforced their stability for the partners or spouses in same-sex couples. These secondary effects are not of minor importance.

However, in Italy, which is a civil law system not based on case law and binding precedent, entrusting the courts with the role of creating legal rules, in the absence of a legislative framework, has led to inconsistencies and contrasting decisions. As long as ethical issues are involved, political choices are needed and value choices have to be taken by Parliament. It is unsurprising, then, that during his speech held during the inauguration of the judicial year (2017) the First President of the *Corte di Cassazione* asked the legislature to provide rules on stepchild adoption.

With respect to future reforms, the option of enlarging the sphere of eligible parents could be considered, even for full adoption, by abandoning the prerequisite of the married couple and opening adoption to unmarried couples living together in a stable relationship, and even to single persons. Such widening must not exclude same-sex cohabitants, *unioni civili* couples or single persons because of their sexual orientation or gender, otherwise the legislation would be in violation of the principles of equality and non-discrimination contained in article 3 of the Constitution. In this regard it should be noted that in 1994,

45 Op cit, n. 41. This is the decision, discussed above, in which the court laid out the boundaries of the public policy exception under international law in cases involving recognition of child status.

46 The reference is to P. Grossi, 'Sulla odierna fattualità del diritto', *Giustizia civile*, 1, 2014, pp. 10ff. The translation of the expression "fattualità del diritto" is literal in order to remain (hopefully) faithful to the intention, as expressed in Italian, of this extraordinary author.

the Constitutional Court - in a case on the constitutional legitimacy of the exclusion of single individuals from those eligible to adopt - argued in *obiter dictum* that there were no constitutional obstacles to the legislature, at a future date, finding it "appropriate to expand the scope of eligibility for adoption of a child by a single adoptive parent".[47] Such an option would be consistent with the European Convention on the Adoption of Children,[48] which obliges contracting states to provide for adoption by a single person and by homosexual couples.[49]

47 Corte Cost., 16 May 1994, n. 183, available at www.giurcost.org/decisioni/1994/0183-94.html.

48 The Convention has been revised on the 7 May 2008. The text is available at https://rm.coe.int/1680084823.

49 See Article 7, which states:

1. The law shall permit a child to be adopted:
   (a) by two persons of different sex
      (i) who are married to each other, or
      (ii) where such an institution exists, have entered into a registered partnership together;
   (b) by one person.
2. States are free to extend the scope of this Convention to same sex couples who are married to each other or who have entered into a registered partnership together. They are also free to extend the scope of this Convention to different sex couples and same sex couples who are living together in a stable relationship.

Stepfamilies and the Law in Japan

Maia Roots[*]

I Introduction

The number of second and third marriages is on the increase in Japan, and with it the number of stepfamilies where at least one party brings children from a previous relationship into the new marriage. However, despite this increase in numbers, stepfamilies remain a largely hidden family form in Japanese society[1] and their unique realities and special needs are as yet largely unacknowledged. This is also true for law. There is a definite tendency visible in Japanese law to forcefully approximate stepfamilies to the "traditional" two-parent (one mother and one father) first-marriage nuclear family. This is most plainly evident first, in a clear tendency of the law to push the stepparent to adopt, as is apparent from the extremely weak legal position of a stepparent unless they adopt their stepchild, and the fact that the legislator has facilitated adoption of a stepchild by their stepparent; and second, a strong tendency to exclude the non-residential parent, both when that parent is seeking contact with the child, and when (s)he attempts to regain parental authority for the child. In light of the actual situation and needs of stepfamilies, as highlighted by research done in Japan in recent years in the field of family sociology, the current state of the law is unsatisfactory.

This paper provides an overview and critique of the current state of legislation and case law concerning stepfamilies, concentrating in particular on (1) the legal position of a stepparent in relation to their stepchild, including the regulation of stepchild adoption, and (2) the legal position of the non-residential parent.[2] Following the overview of the current state of the law, I provide a very brief overview of relevant sociological findings. Finally, I propose some amendment of the existing statutory law, and point out the need for a change in the way the best interests of the child are interpreted by the Japanese courts when handling cases concerning children living in stepfamilies.

---

* Associate Professor of Law, School of Law, Tohoku University, Japan. This work was supported by JSPS KAKENHI Grant Number JP16K17017 and Tohoku University Center for Gender Equality Promotion (TUMUG) Support Project (Project to Promote Gender Equality and Female Researchers).

1 S. Nozawa, 'Remarriage and stepfamilies', *in* S. Quah (Ed.), *The Routledge Handbook of Families in Asia*, Oxon, Routledge, 2015, p. 345 at 346.

2 Although the legal regulation of support and maintenance, family names and other aspects of family life and family law are undoubtedly also relevant to this topic, due to space constraints they are not the focus of this paper.

II The Legal Position of a Stepparent

A *The Legal Position of a Stepparent Who Does Not Adopt*

According to Japanese law, a stepparent has virtually no rights or obligations in relation to their stepchild unless they adopt the child. Without undergoing adoption, a stepparent and stepchild are related by affinity in the first degree.[3] This means that the stepparent and stepchild have a rather abstract mutual obligation to "help each other" as "relatives who live together"[4] and only if "special circumstances" exist, can the family court impose a duty of support between a stepchild and stepparent.[5] Although the stepparent will, in most cases, exercise de facto care for a stepchild in the same way as the residential biological parent, there is no legal basis for the exercise of such parental or parent-like care in Japanese law.

Furthermore, if the relationship between the residential biological parent and the stepparent who has not adopted their stepchild breaks down and the couple separate and/or divorce, the stepparent is unlikely to be granted contact with the child. In the only published case concerning an application for contact from a stepmother (no adoption) who had been raising the child since babyhood, the court simply stated, without providing further explanations or reasons, that contact was not necessary from the point of view of the welfare of the child. Prior to 2011, when article 766 of the Civil Code was amended, there was no express limitation on who might apply for contact with a child. With the 2011 reform, the words "mother or father" were inserted into article 766, which could be read to limit the persons who can apply for contact to the parents of a child.[6]

B *Stepchild Adoption*

At present, adoption is the only means of establishing a legal parent-child relationship – with all its attendant legal effects, such as parental authority, obligation to support, and rights concerning inheritance – between the child and stepparent.

1 General Rules for Adoption in Japanese Law

There are two types of adoption under Japanese law: the so-called "regular adoption" (simply referred to as "adoption" in the Civil Code) and special adoption. Regular adoption

3 Art. 725 III of the Civil Code (Law No. 89, 1896). Hereafter the articles referred to are articles of the Civil Code, unless otherwise stated.
4 Art. 730.
5 Art. 877 II.
6 Adjudication of Tokyo Family Court, 15 Nov. 1974 (*Kasai Geppou* 27-10-55).

has a long history in Japan and has been used for a variety of reasons which do not necessarily relate directly to the best interests of a minor, for instance to enable a person to take over the family business. In contrast, special adoption was introduced in 1987 as a new type of adoption that would further the welfare of the minor being adopted, by providing a child who had no parents with a loving home and family.[7]

The two types of adoption differ considerably with respect to their formal conditions and legal consequences. Whereas regular adoption will become effective when the parties agree and submit a notification of adoption to the appropriate authorities,[8] in the case of special adoption a court ruling is necessary. Only a child younger than six years of age can be adopted via special adoption,[9] whereas there is no age limit for regular adoption. The law has also set stricter requirements in the case of special adoption including the age of the adopting parents, consent to adoption, and a period of care of the child by the persons seeking to adopt.[10] Furthermore, the Civil Code stipulates that a court can only make a ruling of special adoption if both biological parents are incapable or unfit to care for the child or there are any other special circumstances, and it is found that special adoption is especially necessary in the interests of the child.[11] Whereas it is extremely difficult to dissolve a special adoption,[12] regular adoption can be dissolved by simply submitting a notice of dissolution of adoption, as long as the parties agree.[13]

The stricter regulation of special adoption is justified, in part, by the more serious and final consequences of special adoption, particularly the extinguishing of the legal parent-child relationship between the child and its biological parents (and other relatives of the parents).[14] In the case of regular adoption, the child will retain a legal parent-child relationship with the biological parents, with the attendant rights and obligations concerning, among other things, maintenance, and inheritance rights, while parental authority will be exercised by the adoptive parents.[15]

2 Stepchild Adoption

In the case of adoption of a stepchild, both types of adoption are, in principle, possible. This is clear from the wording of the Civil Code, which includes specific stipulations concerning the adoption of a spouse's child.[16] In the case of special adoption, the legal parent-

7 K. Hosokawa, *Kaisei Youshihou no Kaisetsu*, Housoukai, 1993, pp. 33ff.
8 If the child is younger than 15 years of age, the child's representative may give their consent to the adoption of the child on behalf of the child (art. 797 I).
9 Art. 817-5.
10 Arts. 817-4, 817-6, and 817-8.
11 Art. 817-7.
12 See art. 817-10.
13 Art. 811 I and art. 739 applied mutatis mutandis (art. 812).
14 Art. 817-9.
15 Art. 818 II.
16 Such as proviso to art. 795, art. 817-3 II, proviso to art. 817-9.

child relationship between the child and the non-residential biological parent (and that parent's relatives) is dissolved. This is not the case with regular adoption, where the child retains a legal parent-child relationship with the non-residential parent, and therefore has three legal "parents" following the adoption.

Japanese case law and scholarly opinion tend to deem special adoption by a stepparent inappropriate in most cases. Therefore, most adoptions by stepparents are regular adoptions.

2.1 *Regular Adoption of a Stepchild*

Stepchild adoptions via regular adoption are not uncommon in Japan.[17] Indeed, the legislator has simplified regular adoption by a stepparent in a number of ways. The two most notable are: (1) waiving the requirement of the permission of the family court in cases where the child to be adopted is the child of the adoptive parent's spouse;[18] and (2) waiving the requirement of the consent of the non-residential biological parent.[19]

These two special rules for stepchild adoption have received considerable criticism. With respect to (1) (i.e. the waiving of the requirement of permission from the family court), there is a strong argument that in order to protect the interests of the child, the permission of the family court should be required for *all* adoptions of minors, including those by stepparents.[20] The original reasoning behind (1) was the assumption that there was no reason to assume that adoption by a stepparent would be harmful to the best interests of the child.[21] However, many (rightly) argue that it cannot be assumed that such an adoption is in the best interests of the child, and assert that the court as a neutral third party should always have the opportunity (and, indeed, the duty) to check whether adoption in any particular case really is in the interests of the child.[22]

Concerning (2) (i.e. the waiving of the requirement of the consent of the non-residential parent when a stepparent is adopting the child via regular adoption), the current regulation means that it is relatively easy for the spouse of the residential parent to adopt his/her

17 F. Tokotani, 'Youshihou', *in* H. Nakata (Ed.), *Kazokuhoukaisei – konnin/oyako kankei wo chuushin ni*, Yuhikaku, 2010, p. 85 at 90.

18 Proviso to art. 798. The permission of the family court is, as a rule, required for the (regular) adoption of a minor (art. 798).

19 Art. 797 I. As explained above, in the case of regular adoption, it is sufficient if the parties (i.e. the person being adopted and the person adopting) agree on the adoption. For children under the age of 15, in the stepfamily scenario, the residential biological parent who exercises parental authority (and is therefore the legal representative of the child) may give the consent on behalf of the child, and the consent of the non-residential parent who does not exercise parental authority is not necessary. (The same is true for children who are 15 years old or older and can give the consent themselves.)

20 M. Yamamoto, *Senrei hanrei youshihou*, Nihonkajoshuppan, 1996, p. 73; Tokotani, op cit, n. 17, pp. 90 & 100.

21 T. Matsukawa & A. Kubota (Eds.), *Shin kihonhou konmentaru – shinzoku*, Nihon Hyouronsha, 2015, art. 798, p. 162 (K. Habu).

22 S. Ninomiya, *Kazokuhou*, 4th ed., Shinseisha, 2013, p. 190; Matsukawa & Kubota, ibid, p. 162.

stepchild without the knowledge of the non-residential biological parent.[23] As will be discussed further below, this is problematic in light of, among other things, judicial decisions which have consistently held that the non-residential parent cannot apply for parental authority to be transferred to them if the child has been adopted by their stepparent.[24] Consequently, there are calls for an amendment of the Civil Code to make the consent of the non-residential parent a prerequisite to adoption by a stepparent.[25]

As previously noted, in the case of regular adoption of a stepchild, the non-residential biological parent will still be a legal parent of the child (i.e. the child will have three legal parents, two of whom – the residential biological parent and the stepparent – will exercise parental authority in relation to the child). This means, among other things, that the non-residential parent can still legally apply for contact with the child. In this respect, the current state of the law appears to be rather flexible and allows for a child living in a stepfamily to have three "parents" in the legal sense. However, as will be explained below, case law has tended to deny contact between the non-residential parent and a child living in a stepfamily.

2.2 Special Adoption of a Stepchild

Opinions among academics and judges vary concerning the extent to which special adoption should be allowed in the case of a stepchild adoption. Some academics and most judges (based on decisions in published case law) are of the view that, as a general rule, the conditions set out in article 817-7 are not met when a stepparent is applying for adoption of their stepchild.[26] Article 817-7 stipulates that the court shall make a ruling of special adoption only if (1) both parents of the child to be adopted are incapable or unfit to care for the child or (2) there are other special circumstances, and (3) it is found that special adoption is especially necessary in the interests of the child.

It is generally agreed that condition (1) is not met in cases where the new spouse of the residential biological parent is attempting to adopt his/her stepchild, as the residential biological parent continues to care for the child.[27] With respect to condition (2), opinions differ as to what constitutes "other special circumstances."[28] In practice, interpretation of

23 This, in fact, happens rather frequently, as pointed out by Suzuki in H. Suzuki, 'Doitsuno youshihou – fukushigata youshi to tsurekoyoushi wo chuushin ni', *Minshouhou zasshi*, Vol. 138, No. 4/5, 2008, p. 470 at 492.

24 For example Ninomiya, op cit, n. 22, p. 190.

25 M. Ishikawa, 'Kangokensha mataha hikangokensha taru fubo no doui wo enai daidakuyoushiengumi no kouryoku', *in* A. Numabe et al (Eds.), *Kajishinpan jiken no kenkyu (1)*, Ichiryusha, 1988, p. 216 at 226. Critically also Ninomiya, op cit, n. 22, p. 190.

26 For example rulings of Nagoya Family Court, 23 Aug. 1989 (*Kasai Geppou* 42-5-52) and Tokushima Family Court, 17 Nov. 1989 (*Kasai Geppou* 42-5-92).

27 See Z. Nakagawa & M. Yamahata (Eds.), *Shinpan chyushyaku minpou (24)*, Yuhikaku, 1994, art. 817-7, p. 622 (M. Omori).

28 See M. Tanaka, '817jou no 7 nitsuite – tokubetsu youshiengumi no seiritsuyouken toshite no "youhogosei" to "tokubetsu no hitsuyousei"', *Hou to Seiji*, Vol. 68, No. 2, 2017, p. 343 at 353.

this term has proven to be most problematic precisely in cases where a stepparent is applying to adopt their stepchild.

When special adoption was first introduced in Japanese legislation in the late 1980s, the question of whether special adoption by a stepparent should be allowed was the subject of considerable debate. Several problematic aspects of special adoption by a stepparent were pointed out. One was the probability that many applications for special adoption by stepparents would be made based on the interests of the adults rather than the child (for example, the wish of the stepparent to secure the love of their new spouse by adopting their child). A second was that even if the stepparent and the residential biological parent later divorced, it would be virtually impossible to dissolve special adoption (unlike regular adoption which can easily be dissolved if both parties agree). A further problem was that since the consent of the other biological parent is necessary for special adoption, enmity between the adults might be rekindled.

It was argued that in light of these issues it would not be appropriate to allow special adoption by a stepparent without reservation.[29] Such criticism of special adoption by a stepparent is said to have led to stricter conditions being laid out in article 817-7 for special adoption in general[30] and, as well, to the subsequent cautious approach by the courts in cases involving special adoption by a stepparent, including a rather limited interpretation of "special circumstances."[31] However, some scholars and some of the more recent judicial decisions take the position that a looser interpretation of "special circumstances" should be adopted.[32] It is argued by some, for instance, that "special circumstances" should be understood to exist if the non-residential biological parent is disinterested in the child and its upbringing.[33]

It should be noted that to date there is no published case law where special adoption of a *marital* child by its stepparent has been approved by the courts. There are a number of cases where adoption of a *non-marital* child by its stepparent has been approved, and in these cases the courts appear to have applied a comparatively loose interpretation of the "special circumstances" in article 817-7.[34] For example, in a case where the non-residential biological parent had not acknowledged paternity of the child, the court stated that

29 Hosokawa, op cit, n. 7, pp. 104-5. See also Tanaka, op cit, n. 28, pp. 348ff.

30 Ibid.

31 T. Hayano, 'Mininchi no hichakushutsushi dearu tsureko no tokubetsu youshi engumi wo ninyou shita jirei', *Hakuou Hougaku*, No. 24, 2004, p. 127 at 136.

32 See for example F. Tokotani, 'Chyakushyutsu hinin wo shita "keishi" wo tokubetuyoushi tosuru moushitate wo ninyou shita jirei', *Hanrei Times*, No. 949, 1997, p. 78 at 79; Hayano, ibid, pp. 132ff; Nagoya High Court, 14 Nov. 2003 (*Kasai Geppou* 56-5-143).

33 See for example Hayano, op cit, n. 31, p. 138. The Adjudication of Nagoya High Court, 14 Nov. 2003, ibid, also cited the disinterestedness of the non-residential biological parent among the grounds for allowing special adoption. Older case law tended to judge that mere disinterestedness does not suffice: see for example the ruling of the Osaka Family Court, 29 Sept. 1988 (*Kasai Geppou* 41-3-176).

34 See Matsukawa & Kubota, op cit, n. 21, art. 817-7, p. 196 (K. Nishi).

special adoption by the stepparent was in the best interests of the child, as the child would not only acquire the legal status of a marital child through adoption, but the stability of its (legal) familial relationships would be guaranteed by excluding a (potential future) legal parent-child relationship with the biological father.[35] In addition, some of the case law has stated that in certain situations special adoption is justified if it is in the child's best interests to hide the circumstances surrounding its birth by dissolving the legal relationship between the child and one of its biological parents.[36]

More recent academic literature has asserted that the issue of whether special adoption is generally appropriate in the case of a stepchild adoption should be reviewed carefully in light of findings in psychology and sociology, and that it might be advisable to insert specific stipulations concerning stepchild adoption as a separate and individual category of special adoption into the Civil Code.[37]

C Summary

To summarize, Japanese law presents a stepparent with an all-or-nothing choice. Either the stepparent adopts and becomes the legal parent of their stepchild with the attendant legal effects, or they do not adopt, in which case they will be unable to acquire any of these legal rights and duties.

Furthermore, if a stepparent opts for adoption, in the case of regular adoption the stepparent can adopt the child without the consent (and, indeed, without the knowledge) of the non-residential biological parent and as well, without any check by the courts as to whether the adoption is in the best interests of the child. On the surface, regular adoption by a stepparent appears to be a flexible system in which the child has three legal parents. However, as will be explained below, the courts in fact tend to deny contact in cases where the child is living in a stepfamily.

As for special adoption, although the majority opinion is that special adoption by a stepparent should, as a rule, not be allowed, the lack of agreement regarding the best interests of a child living in a stepfamily (which is the basic standard for allowing or denying adoption) is disconcerting. Furthermore, the differing interpretations of the best

---

35 Adjudication of Miyazaki Family Court, 30 Nov. 1990 (*Kasai Geppou* 43-10-35).

36 For example in circumstances where the child was a result of an extramarital affair of the mother during the mother's first marriage, the first husband had rebutted the presumption of paternity, and the biological father had not acknowledged paternity of the child and could not be expected to show any interest in the child in the future (ruling of Nagoya High Court, 14 Nov. 2003 (*Kasai Geppou* 56-5-143); similarly see ruling of Tokyo High Court, 20 Nov. 1998 (*Kasai Geppou* 49-5-78). For a critical commentary on these two cases see Tanaka, op cit, n. 28, p. 373.

37 Tanaka, op cit, n. 28, p. 375.

interests of the child based on whether the child is marital or non-marital are inappropriate in light of the increasing diversity of family forms and general notions of family.

Underlying the current scheme of legal regulation there appears to be a deeply held belief that replacing the non-residential parent with the stepparent via adoption is naturally best for the child and the stepfamily as a whole. However, there is increasing criticism of this belief and the current regulation of stepchild adoption, together with calls for reform regarding the legal standing of a stepparent who does not adopt. Critics argue, for example, that a stepparent should be able to acquire partial legal obligations and rights in relation to their stepchild (according to the specific needs and circumstances of their particular household and familial situation), even if they do not opt for the "whole package."[38] Thus far, no legislative action has been taken.

III The Legal Position of the Non-Residential Parent

There is a definite tendency in Japanese court practice to exclude the non-residential biological parent and in effect sever the familial ties between the non-residential parent and a child living in a stepfamily. This is most apparent in the tendency of Japanese courts to deny contact between a child living in a stepfamily and the non-residential parent, reasoning that such contact is not in the best interests of such a child. It is also apparent in the persistent pattern of courts ruling that a non-residential parent cannot apply for parental authority to be transferred to them if the stepparent has adopted the child.

A *Contact Between the Non-Residential Parent and the Child*

1 Introduction

The statutory basis for contact between the child and its non-residential parent is article 766 of the Civil Code, which stipulates that contact between the father or the mother and the child, as a matter regarding custody of a child, is to be decided by the divorcing/separating parents, or, if the parents cannot agree, by the court.[39] In contrast to some other jurisdictions, Japanese law does not contain a clear statutory *right* to contact on the part of either a parent or a child.

The Civil Code does state clearly that "the best interests of the child must be the primary consideration" when determining whether and to what extent contact should take place.[40]

38 T. Hayano, 'Suteppufamiri wo meguru houteki kadai to tenbo', *Kazoku (Shakai to hou)*, No. 27, 2011, p. 64 at 70; Suzuki, op cit, n. 23, pp. 470ff; Tanaka, op cit, n. 28, p. 375; Tokotani, op cit, n. 17, p. 90.

39 Art. 766 I sentence 2, II.

40 Art. 766 I sentence 2.

Given that "the best interests of the child" is by nature an ambiguous notion, there is some difference of opinion as to how it should be understood in the context of contact, including contact in the stepfamily scenario. The remarriage of the parent with parental authority (Japanese law does not allow for joint parental authority after divorce) and the possible subsequent adoption of the child by the stepparent have been seen as potential grounds for the restriction or exclusion of contact.

2 Reasoning of the Courts and Opinions in Literature

To date, there are few published rulings of Japanese courts concerning contact between the non-residential parent and a child living in a household with the residential legal parent and that parent's new spouse.[41] However, academic literature generally suggests that until the mid-2000s the courts tended to deny contact in the stepfamily scenario, unless special circumstances were present.[42] Although some form of contact was allowed in some of the published rulings, the scope of the contact was often very limited.[43]

The courts have frequently ruled that, considering that the child had formed (or was in the process of forming) a new parent-child relationship with the stepparent,[44] or had in some cases even been led to believe that the new spouse of the residential (biological)

41 The relevant rulings are:
1. Tokyo Family Court, 14 Dec. 1964 (*Kasai Geppou* 17-4-55);
2. Tokyo High Court, 8 Dec. 1965 (*Kasai Geppou* 18-7-31);
3. Osaka Family Court, 28 May 1968 (*Kasai Geppou* 20-10-68);
4. Oita Family Court, 22 July 1976 (*Kasai Geppou* 29-2-108);
5. Tokyo Family Court, 31 March 1987 (*Kasai Geppou* 39-6-58);
6. Yokohama Family Court, 30 April 1996 (*Kasai Geppou* 49-3-75);
7. Kyoto Family Court, 24 Aug. 2005 (*Kasai Geppou* 58-11-56);
8. Osaka High Court, 3 Feb. 2006 (*Kasai Geppou* 58-11-47);
9. Kyoto Family Court, 31 March 2006 (*Kasai Geppou* 58-11-62);
10. Osaka Family Court, 13 March 2015 (*Katei no Hou to Saiban*, No. 6, p. 89);
11. Osaka Family Court, 17 March 2016 (*Hanrei Times*, No. 1435, p. 170); and
12. Osaka High Court, 31 Aug. 2016 (*Hanrei Times*, No. 1435, p. 169).

42 Examples of such special circumstances include an older child, as in the case of adjudication (6), ibid (contact allowed with the 13-year-old sibling but denied in case of the younger 9-year-old sibling); and a child born to an international couple, as in the case of adjudication (5) (court judged that contact with the non-Japanese parent was necessary for a child of mixed origin).

43 For example in adjudication (9), op cit, n. 41, the court deemed both direct contact in the form of face-to-face meetings, as well as contact via phone calls and exchange of letters inappropriate, but ordered the residential mother and her spouse to send the non-residential father copies of the child's school report cards and two photos of the child per year. In adjudications (5) and (6) direct contact once and twice a year, respectively, was deemed appropriate. Note that Japanese courts most often order contact to be exercised once a month, as opposed to many Western jurisdictions where contact every second weekend appears to be the unofficial norm (M. Yokota et al, 'Menkaikouryu shinpanrei no jisshouteki kenkyu', *Hanrei Times*, No. 1292, 2009, p. 5 at 10.

44 Adjudications (2), (3), (4), (6), (8), (9), and (10), op cit, n. 41.

parent was their biological parent,[45] contact with the non-residential legal parent would "throw the child's peaceful family life into turmoil", confuse the child and "wound her/his innocent young heart", and consequently "hamper its healthy mental development." Much of the case law, including some of the more recent rulings,[46] refers to the need to protect the stability of the new household and the relationship between the child and the stepparent which, according to the logic employed by the courts, should from the point of view of the best interests of the child be prioritized over contact with the non-residential parent.[47] Japanese court practice has, in general, been relatively slow to recognize the benefits of contact with the non-residential parent for the child. (This tendency is not limited to cases where the child is living in a stepfamily.)

However, the long and short term benefits of contact are now widely accepted by practitioners and academics alike.[48] Consequently, with respect to contact in the stepfamily scenario, it is now argued that an appropriate balance should be sought between 'the stability of the new household' and maintaining contact with the non-residential parent, and that contact should not automatically be restricted or excluded simply on the grounds that the residential parent has remarried.[49] The more recent case law concerning contact in the stepfamily scenario also reflects this shift in the attitude of the courts towards greater recognition of the significance of contact for the child.[50]

The academic literature also reveals differing opinions on what constitutes the best interests of a child living in a stepfamily when the non-residential parent applies for contact. Some scholars, as well as practitioners, argue that as second and third marriages of parents of minors are no longer a rarity in Japanese society, formerly dominant negative attitudes

45 Adjudications (1), (2) and (4), op cit. n. 41. These do not appear to be isolated cases. Yokota et al also point out that in domestic relations practice it is not rare to come across a case where the residential parent has told the child that the other biological parent has passed away even though that parent is still living (op cit, n. 43, p. 8). In such instances, the courts have argued that if contact with the non-residential parent were to be allowed, the sudden appearance of a "second mother" or "second father" would unsettle the child and hamper its healthy mental development.

46 In addition to earlier case law see also adjudications (9) and (10), op cit, n. 41.

47 This argument also appears in literature. For example, Otsuka speaks of "the right of the child to build a new family", and refers to contact with the non-residential biological parent as something negative that will unsettle the new household (M. Otsuka, 'Kajichoutei niokeru mensetsukoushou nojisshouteki kenkyu', *Shihoukenshujo ronshu souritsu gojusshunen kinen tokushugou*, Vol. 2, 1997, p. 258 at 259.

48 I. Hosoya et al, 'Menkaikouryu ga souten tonaru chouteijiken no jitsujou oyobi shinri noarikata – minpou 766jou no kaisei wo fumaete', *Kasai Geppou*, Vol. 64, No. 7, 2012, p. 1 at 30ff.

49 S. Yoshimoto, 'Mensetsukoushou to sono seigen – jirei no bunseki wo chuushin toshite', *in* T. Ukon et al (Eds.), *Kajijiken no genjou to kadai*, Hanrei Taimuzusha, 2006, p. 158 at 165; Hosoya et al, op cit, n. 48, p. 81.

50 For example in adjudication (8), op cit, n. 41, the Osaka High Court stated: "Contact between the non-custodial parent and the child is essentially beneficial to the healthy development of the child, and therefore it should, as a rule, be allowed, except in cases where there is a threat that the child's welfare will be harmed through contact". See, similarly adjudications (11) and (12). In adjudication (11) the Osaka Family Court also stated that telling the children of their biological mother contributed in the long run to the stability of the familial relations in general. In contrast, see adjudication (10) (which is from 2015).

towards contact between the child and the non-residential parent are becoming increasingly unacceptable.[51] It has also been asserted that, in the context of the remarriage-adoption scenario, the child is perfectly capable of maintaining a relationship with the non-residential parent alongside relationships with a residential parent or parents (biological or adoptive).[52] Others, however, have argued that especially during the early fragile stage of establishing the "new" family, contact between the child and the non-residential parent would unsettle and possibly break up the new household, and this would be harmful to the child.[53] Some also present the "different culture" argument, that is, they allege that even if in the West the current trend is to embrace "two homes" and "two mothers/fathers", it is doubtful whether an identical way of thinking can be accepted without reservations in Japanese society.[54]

To summarize, although some of the more recent case law has allowed contact between a child living in a stepfamily and her/his non-residential parent, the courts (and some scholars) continue to adhere to the traditional notion that the law should prioritize and protect the "typical" or "ideal" closed nuclear family consisting of one mother, one father and their children, and that allowing contact with the non-residential parent would serve only to undermine the new "proper" household and confuse and unsettle the child. It remains to be seen whether the more recent rulings allowing contact signal a new trend in how the courts interpret the best interests of a child living in a stepfamily, or whether they remain the exception.

B The (Im)Possibility of Transferring Parental Authority to the Non-Residential Parent

In 2014, the Japanese Supreme Court[55] gave its stamp of approval to an interpretation of the law according to which, in cases where a stepparent has adopted the child of their spouse via regular adoption, the non-residential parent cannot apply for a transfer of parental authority. The provision being interpreted was article 819 VI, which gives the

51 M. Yamada, 'Fubo no saikon to menkaikouryu', *Koseki jihou*, Vol. 685, 2012, p. 79.

52 Ninomiya, op cit, n. 22, p. 127; also K. Yamada, 'Mensetsukoushou no torikime ni tsuite', *Kikan Kyouikuhou*, Vol. 153, 2007, p. 72 at 75. See also S. Nozawa et al, *Q&A suteppufamiri no kisochishiki – kodure saikon katei to shiensha no tameni*, Akashi shoten, 2006 (advising the residential parent and stepparent to make the child aware of the non-residential parent's existence as early as possible (pp. 178-179) and stressing that the more "parents" caring for a child, the better (pp. 155-156)).

53 T. Hayano, 'Suteppufamiri ni okeru mensetsukoushou', *in* W. Iwashi et al (Eds.), *Kazoku to hou no chihei*, Shougakusha, 2009, p. 160 (at 182 and 184ff); Yokota et al, op cit, n. 43, p. 8.

54 Yokota et al, ibid.

55 Ruling of 14 Apr. 2014 (*Minshuu* 68-4-279).

Family Court the power to transfer parental authority from one parent to another.[56] Article 819 VI does not explicitly prohibit the non-residential parent from applying for a transfer of parental authority in cases of a stepparent adoption via regular adoption. Prior to the above Supreme Court decision, the opinion of the courts was divided on the issue of whether an application by the non-residential parent for transfer of parental authority of a child living with their residential biological parent and adoptive stepparent (who exercised parental authority jointly) should be allowed. However, the majority opinion in the case law and literature was that such an application should not be allowed.[57]

The reasoning behind these cases was that article 819 VI did not contemplate and was not intended to apply to a situation where a biological parent is exercising parental authority jointly with their new spouse who has adopted the child. More specifically, it was argued that article 819 VI (exclusively) presupposes a situation where the parents of a child have divorced and one parent exercises parental authority alone. (Japanese law only recognizes joint parental authority of a married couple;[58] there is no possibility of joint parental authority after the parents divorce.) Allowing for the transfer of parental authority outside of this context would create a situation where two persons who are not married to each other have parental authority for a child[59] (or, for that matter, a situation where two persons of the same sex might have joint parental authority for a child.[60])

This court practice should be seen in a wider context. It should be kept in mind that since Japanese law does not recognize joint parental authority after divorce, the non-residential parent possibly gave up parental authority since they had no alternative. As well, the way Japanese adoption law stands now, it is not necessary to obtain either the non-residential parent's consent or permission by the family court for the (regular) adoption of a child by the stepparent, and adoption is often undergone without the non-residential parent's knowledge. This regulation in turn has been justified by the (mistaken) notion that, as a general rule, adoption by a stepparent is in the best interest of the child, an assumption clearly proven to be false in the case before the Supreme Court.[61]

The Japanese courts' practice of denying applications by the non-residential parent to transfer parental authority in cases where there has been a stepparent adoption is another

56 Art. 819 VI reads: "The Family Court may, on the application of any relative of the child, rule that the other parent shall have parental authority in relation to the child if it finds it necessary for the interests of the child."

57 K. Habu, 'Tsureko youshiengumi ni okeru shinkensha henkou no moushitate no kyohi', *Geppou Shihou Shoshi*, No. 513, 2014, p. 64 at 67ff; A. Hirata's commentary on the above-mentioned Supreme Court ruling of 14 Apr. 2014 in *Minshouhou Zasshi*, Vol. 150, No. 3, 2014, p. 442 at 448.

58 Art. 818 III.

59 K. Habu, op cit, n. 57, pp. 67 and 68.

60 Note that Japanese law does not recognize marriage or civil partnership between two persons of the same sex.

61 The application for the transfer of paternal authority in that case was motivated by the fact that there was serious physical abuse by the stepfather.

example of the way in which Japanese law, in its present form, rather single-mindedly enforces the notion of 'family' as consisting of two parents who are married to each other, and their (biological or adoptive) children, and excludes the non-residential parent. (The fact that Japanese law does not allow joint parental authority after divorce reflects the same tendency.)

IV STEPFAMILIES IN FAMILY SOCIOLOGICAL RESEARCH

As discussed above, Japanese statutory and case law shows a strong tendency to forcefully approximate a stepfamily to the "traditional" two-parent, first-marriage nuclear family. This tendency appears unjustified, or even unreasonable, in light of recent findings in the field of family sociology, which are introduced briefly below. Indeed, the current state of the law does not correspond to the actual situation and needs of stepfamilies and could even at times be said to be contrary to the best interests of the children living in stepfamilies, as well as the interests of other members of the step- and extended family.

Compared to those in the West, Japanese scholars have been late to embark on research concerning the realities and needs of stepfamilies,[62] but in recent years a number of domestic surveys have been undertaken. Such research has confirmed, first, that stepfamily members in Japan (like their counterparts in the West) experience a high level of stress and unique strains that are not present in first-marriage nuclear families. For instance, stepparents, especially step*mothers*, experience immense pressure from those around them to become replacement parents.[63] The children are often reported to feel resentment towards the stepparent and/or residential biological parent, as a new "parent" who is "forced on" them assumes an unwelcome and, especially from the point of view of the children, excessive disciplinary role (usually with the approval of the residential biological parent), while the non-residential biological parent is being excluded.[64] Indeed, family sociologists both in Japan and the West argue that these and similar childrearing methods adopted by stepparents and residential biological parents, on the assumption that the

62 S. Nozawa, 2015, op cit, n. 1, p. 345.

63 M. Kikuchi, 'Keibo ni naru toiu keiken – kekkon heno kitai to genjitsu no gyappu', *Kazoku Kenkyu Nenpou*, Vol. 30, 2005, p. 49. According to Nozawa, research suggests that, for cultural reasons, stepmothers in Asia suffer even greater strain than their Western counterparts (Nozawa, 2015, op cit, n. 1, p. 348). See also S. Nozawa, 'The social context of emerging stepfamilies in Japan: Stress and support for parents and stepparents', *in* Jan Pryor (Ed.), *The International Handbook of Stepfamilies*, New Jersey, John Wiley & Sons, 2008, p. 79.

64 See for example S. Nozawa & M. Kikuchi, 'Jakunen seijin keishi ga kataru keishinshi kankei no tayousei — suteppufamiri ni okeru keishin no yakuwari to keishi no tekiou', *Shakaigakubu Fuzoku Kenkyujo Nenpou (Meiji Gakuin University)*, Vol. 44, 2014, p. 69; S. Nozawa, 'Suteppufamiri no jakunen seijinshi ga kataru doukyoshin to no kankei – oya no saikon he no tekiou ni okeru juuyousei', *Shakai Inobeshon Kenkyu*, Vol. 10, No. 2, 2015, p. 59.

stepparent is a replacement of a non-residential parent, are one of the main hindrances to the adjustment of children to life in a stepfamily.[65]

Second, research has shown that there is great variation in the nature of relationships forged between stepchildren and stepparents. When surveying young adults who had grown up in stepfamilies, Professors Nozawa and Kikuchi identified five patterns of stepchild-stepparent relationships including patterns such as "continuously accepting as parent", "gradual development with non-parental definition", and "consistent avoidance of relation".[66] Therefore, there seems to be little evidence to back up the assumption (or wish) frequently expressed by residential biological parents (for example in the court cases concerning contact in stepfamilies), and shared by many Japanese judges and some scholars, that a stepparent will naturally (and always) become a substitute parent for the child who the child will unconditionally accept and love. While this might be so in some cases, it is not inevitable.

Lastly, when researchers interviewed young adults who had grown up in stepfamilies, they found some evidence that, if given the chance, children were quite capable of accepting more than two "mothers" or "fathers" or a third parent-like figure in addition to their existing parents. These findings run contrary to the frequently voiced fears that the existence of three "parents" would unduly confuse or hurt the child.[67]

Sociologists conclude that forcefully approximating a stepfamily to a 'traditional' first-marriage nuclear family, by insisting that the stepparent become a substitute parent and by excluding the non-residential biological parent, can place enormous psychological strain on the stepchild and the stepparent.[68]

V Conclusion and Proposals for Reform

Japanese statutory and case law endorses and even enforces a tendency in stepfamilies for the residential parent and stepparent to attempt to reconstruct a first-marriage nuclear family, with the stepparent taking on the role of a replacement parent and the non-residential parent being excluded from the child's life altogether. In light of the actual situation and needs of stepfamilies, this is a highly inappropriate outcome in a considerable number of cases. As a matter of general policy, a legal regime which rather single-mindedly pushes stepparents to adopt their stepchild, and de facto excludes potentially loving and caring

65 Nozawa, op cit, n. 1, p. 354.

66 Nozawa & Kikuchi, op cit, n. 64; in English also in Nozawa, op cit, n. 1, pp. 351ff.

67 Nozawa & Kikuchi, ibid.

68 See for example M. Kikuchi, 'Suteppufamiri niokeru keishinshikan no youshiengumi to bekkyoshinshi kankei – intabyu jirei ni miru rikon/saikongo no kazokukeisei to houseido', *in* E. Matsuoka (Ed.), *Kodomo wo umu, kazoku wo tsukuru jinruigaku – orutanatibu heno sasoi*, Benseishuppan, 2017, p. 128 at 133.

external biological parents with whom the child has a close emotional connection cannot be justified as being in the best interests of the child.

In light of the diversity in the nature of relationships formed in stepfamilies, including the diverse roles that stepparents in reality play in the care and upbringing of their stepchildren, it seems high time to rethink the all-or-nothing approach concerning the legal standing of a stepparent towards their stepchild. In an ideal scenario, the interests of the child, as well as those of other members of a stepfamily (including the non-residential biological parent), would best be protected by creating more options for stepparents to obtain legal rights and obligations in relation to their stepchild without resorting to adoption. Such options might include, for example, allocating some portion of parental authority to the stepparent to allow them to act, without disadvantage, as a de facto carer for their stepchild in everyday situations. At the same time, it is imperative to ensure that when stepchild adoption (whether it be special or regular adoption) is undertaken, the courts have the opportunity to check whether such an adoption would indeed be in the interests of the child and is not simply being employed by the adults as a means of recreating what from the outside would look like the "ideal" and "proper" first-marriage nuclear family, by inserting the stepparent as a substitute for the non-residential biological parent, and severing the ties between the latter and the child.

The question of whether special adoption by a stepparent is ever appropriate, and if so, under what circumstances, needs further consideration. With an increase in the number of stepfamilies, a clearer standard is needed. Here again, the central question should be, what is in the best interests of the child. With the diversification of family forms in Japanese society, a differentiation between marital and non-marital children appears increasingly unjustified.

In Japan, legal reform in the field of family law is notoriously slow. Until legislative reform occurs, the courts can play a role in improving the law in this area. When determining what is in the best interests of a child living in a stepfamily, courts should not cling to an image of a "traditional" two-parent first-marriage nuclear family as being "ideal" and therefore best for any child. Judges should be made more aware of the sociological research concerning the actual dynamics in stepfamilies and should conduct their evaluations regarding the best interests of the child accordingly.

Lastly, in view of the diverse relationships in stepfamilies, ensuring, in a legal sense, that a non-residential parent has the opportunity to participate in the care of a child (and this, obviously, includes not only rights but also duties concerning the child) seems to be called for. This is justified not only by the wishes of the non-residential parent, but also from the point of view of the best interests of the child – the more loving adults caring for the wellbeing of a child, the better. Furthermore, the inclusion of the non-residential parent in the care and upbringing of the child is also likely to benefit the residential biological parent and stepparent, who can take time off for themselves as a couple while the child is with the other biological parent, and are less likely to be resented by the child for excluding the other biological parent and possibly forcing the hitherto unknown stepparent on the child as a "'substitute mother/father".

Your Mum is not Your Mum?! Comments on a Custody Case Concerning Surrogacy in China

Lei Shi[*]

I Introduction

In most people's eyes, it is not difficult to identify the mother of a child. However, this issue was the hot potato that the courts hearing the new custody case in China involving surrogacy had to grapple with.

A custody case involving surrogacy (referred to here as the Chen case) was heard by the Shanghai No. 1 Intermediate People's Court in June 2016. The judgment of the appellate court was very different from that of the trial court. Following an introduction to the current surrogacy and parentage laws in China, the author analyzes the different ways these two courts reasoned about the issue before them and comments upon the two judgments. The author then goes on to raise some of the challenging issues that may face Chinese courts in the aftermath of this case and provides suggestions about how best to deal with these challenges.

II Facts of the Case

Luo, the son of Mr Luo and Madam Xie, married his wife Chen in 2007. This was the second marriage for both spouses. Luo had a son and a daughter from his first marriage, while Chen had no children. During the marriage, they decided that they would like to have their own child. Unfortunately, Chen was infertile. She suggested that they purchase eggs and find a woman to act as a surrogate for them and Luo agreed. With the help of a surrogacy agency, they purchased eggs from a college student and Luo provided his sperm. After a zygote was created in an IVF facility, this commissioning couple found someone to be their surrogate and bear a child for them. Ten months later, a pair of twins were born and they went to live with Luo and Chen. This story would have had a happy ending if Luo

* Doctor of Law, Lecturer, Civil and Commercial Law School, Southwest University of Political Science and Law, China. This paper is the initial product of the research project: 'Comparative Studies on Legislation and Judicial Practice on Surrogacy' (2016BS097) supported by Chongqing Federation of Social Science Circles, China and 'Regulation of Surrogacy and Its Related Problems' (2015XZQN-21) supported by the Southwest University of Political Science and Law, China.

had survived. However, Luo unexpectedly died from severe and acute pancreatitis in February of 2014. Ideally, after the death of their only son, Luo's parents would have raised their two grandchildren in collaboration with their daughter-in-law. However, both sides gradually became estranged and fought over Luo's estate, repetitively filing and then dropping petitions before the People's Court. In December of 2014, after Luo's parents discovered that the twins were not biologically related to Chen, the grandparents filed a petition seeking custody of the children.

III Judgment of the Court of First Instance

The court of first instance used two legal documents to support its conclusion. The first was the "Letter on the legal status of the donor child"[1] issued on 8 July 1991 by the Supreme People's Court (hereinafter Supreme Court Letter), according to which if both spouses to a marriage agree to have a child through artificial insemination, any child produced should be regarded as the legitimate child of both parents. Following such a finding, the relevant provisions of the Marriage Law of the People's Republic of China (PRC) (hereinafter the Marriage Law) would be applied regarding the rights and obligations between parents and children. However, the court of first instance explained that the Supreme Court Letter only applies where artificial insemination procedures have been lawfully carried out in authorized health institutes and where the birth mother is the wife in the marriage. Surrogacy is excluded from the Letter's scope because of the rules stipulated in the Measures on the Administration of Human Assisted Reproductive Technology[2] (hereinafter referred to as the MAHART) which were issued by the Ministry of Health and came into effect on 1 August 2001.[3] This regulation restricts the application of assisted reproductive technology (ART). ART is only permitted in medical institutions approved by the provincial health authorities, can only be for medical purposes, and must be in accordance with national family planning policies, ethical principles and relevant legal provisions. Moreover, article 3 of the MAHART stipulates that the sale of gametes, zygotes and embryos in any form is prohibited and that medical institutions and medical personnel cannot participate in any form of surrogate technology. Therefore, the court found that the twins were not Chen's legitimate children.

The court also provided a further reason for their decision that Chen was not the legal mother of the twins. According to the Marriage Law, a woman is presumed to be the legal mother of a child if she is qualified to be an adoptive parent and has adopted the child in

1 《关于夫妻关系存续期间以人工授精所生子女的法律地位的函》.
2 《人类辅助生殖技术管理办法》.
3 On 17 March 2013 the Ministry of Health was replaced by National Health and Family Planning Commission.

accordance with legal procedures.[4] Additionally, a stepmother who is raising and educating her husband's child can also be recognized as the child's legal mother.[5] The court held that except in these two situations, any woman who does not give birth to a child cannot be presumed to be that child's legal mother in accordance with Chinese law. Obviously, the two exceptions did not apply in this case. The court also determined that there is no presumption that a commissioning mother who raises a child born through surrogacy is that child's legal mother. Surrogacy is illegal in China and, as such, it would be difficult to conclude that a commissioning mother can become the child's legal mother simply by raising it. Simply put, the illegality of surrogacy means that subsequent actions cannot have legal effect.

The court of first instance held that grandparents should be the twins' guardians. Chen appealed the decision to the No. 1 Intermediate People's Court in Shanghai.

IV Judgment of the Shanghai No. 1 Intermediate People's Court

The appeal court gave its judgment on 17 June 2016. The court began by analyzing the legal status of a child born via surrogacy. According to the appellate court, Chinese law has no rules on the determination of legal parentage in this situation. In judicial practice, the People's Court follows a basic rule that the woman who gives birth to a child is that child's legal mother, while the legal father is her husband. Where the birth mother's husband is not the child's biological father and does not wish to be the child's legal father, the biological father is regarded as the legal father, except where the child was conceived by use of donated sperm. The appellate court followed this reasoning and concluded that the twins' legal mother was the surrogate while their legal father was Luo.

The court further concluded that the relationship between Chen and the twins did not constitute a de facto adoption.[6] A contrary conclusion would send a message to society that surrogacy is a legally acceptable practice – an outcome which obviously should be avoided. The court then went on, however, to address the issue of whether the relationship fit into the second exception to the normal rule, whereby a stepmother who is raising and educating her husband's children can be presumed to be their legal mother. Traditional theory holds that, if a spouse is willing to bring up (subjective element) and does bring up the illegitimate child of their spouse born prior to the marriage (objective element), he or she can be regarded as the child's legal parent.[7] The court was of the opinion that the timing

4 Marriage Law, art. 26.

5 Marriage Law, art. 27.

6 Further see W. Chen & L. Shi, 'Present Legislation on Adoption in China and its Reform Proposals' *in* B. Atkin (Ed.), *The International Survey of Family Law*, London, Jordan Publishing, 2012, p. 53.

7 More details on the determination of the relationship between stepparents and stepchildren can be found below in the section of the paper dealing with parentage law in China.

of the illegitimate child's birth is not a determinative factor stipulated in the Marriage Law. Chen and Luo had been raising the two children for more than four years after their birth. Therefore, the court concluded that Chen, as the twins' stepmother, should be presumed to be their legal mother. As a result, she should be the twins' guardian instead of their grandparents, with the grandparents to have visiting rights. The court noted that this result was in accordance with the best interests of the child principle, stipulated in the United Nations Convention on the Rights of the Child.[8]

V Comments

The Chen case raises two issues: surrogacy and parentage. They are independent legal issues, but related to each other. The relevant law on each issue will be discussed separately, followed by an analysis of the appropriate resolution of each of these issues in the Chen case.

A Surrogacy in China

Surrogacy refers to the procedure whereby zygotes are implanted into the womb of a woman who hands the child over to the commissioning parents after it has been born.[9] Or, to put it succinctly, surrogacy involves borrowing a woman's womb in order for a baby to born (Jiefu Shengzi). A general distinction is commonly made between partial and full surrogacy. In full surrogacy (also known as a gestational surrogacy or IVF surrogacy) the eggs of the commissioning mother are fertilized and then implanted in the surrogate. In contrast, partial surrogacy (also known as traditional surrogacy or natural surrogacy) involves use of the surrogate mother's eggs. Therefore, a partial surrogate is both the genetic and gestational mother.[10]

In the Chen case the commissioning mother had neither fertile eggs nor a fertile womb. As a result, two women were involved in the pregnancy: one donated her eggs and the other acted as the surrogate. The surrogate mother in a gestational surrogacy case such as the Chen case has no genetic relationship with the child and therefore they have less of an emotional connection with the child born. Consequently, full/gestational surrogacy is usually the model now preferred by both surrogacy agencies and commissioning parents.

---

8 United Nations, General Assembly, 1989.

9 W. Chen (Ed.), *Marriage, Family and Succession Law*, 2nd ed., Beijing, Qunzhong Press, 2012, p. 191.

10 W.Y. Qu, 'Surrogacy', *Journal of International Reproductive Health/Family Planning*, Vol. 31, No. 1, 2012, pp. 4-5.

According to a survey in 2014, 73.7% of respondents said that they could accept gestational surrogacy.[11]

Surrogacy cases can also be classified into two types based on profitability: altruistic surrogacy and commercial surrogacy. Altruistic surrogacy is where a woman is willing to act as a surrogate without receiving any monetary compensation. In contrast, commercial surrogacy involves paying the surrogate mother. Some people argue that there are actually three types of surrogacy arrangements: altruistic, compensatory and commercial.[12] In cases of compensatory surrogacy, the surrogate is reasonably compensated for expenses incurred as a result of the pregnancy. Compensation usually covers medical expenses and the cost of nutritional supplements needed to help the surrogate recover from the pregnancy.[13]

Aside from the MAHART regulation issued by the Ministry of Health, China has no law which specifically regulates surrogacy. Surrogacy is illegal in many countries and the same is true in China as a result of the MAHART. However, the MAHART is a ministry-level regulation which only regulates doctors' professional conduct and medical institutions.[14] Therefore, in practice, the desire of infertile couples to have their own children (a problem which has grown since China relaxed its family planning policy and allowed second children to be born) and their huge demand for ART has boosted the underground surrogacy market. In big cities like Shanghai, Guangzhou, Shenzhen and Wuhan, the black market for surrogacy is thriving. Thus, problematic cases involving surrogacy, such as Chen case, have arisen.

In recent years, the issue of the legalization of surrogacy has been hotly debated in China. In December 2015 the legislature added a provision banning surrogacy in the draft of the revised Population and Family Planning Law of the PRC. However, this ban on the use of surrogate mothers was removed after some lawmakers objected that it was not directly related to family planning policies and that further research into surrogacy was needed. Zhang Chunsheng, the head of legal affairs for the National Health and Family Planning Commission, explained at a news conference why the ban was being scrapped: "Some members of the standing committee argued that surrogacy cannot be totally forbidden." He added that, even with a law prohibiting surrogacy in place, "rich people would still be able to go abroad to countries where surrogacy is allowed."[15]

---

11 Y.S. Zhi, *On Legal Regulation of the Gestational Surrogacy*, (LLM thesis on file at the Guangxi Normal University, Guilin, 2014), p. 15.

12 For an interesting discussion on this, see Y.L. Zhang, 'The Basis of Surrogate Mother Being Permitted', *Hebei Law Science,* Vol. 24, No. 4, 2006, pp. 137-140.

13 Some people have argued that compensatory surrogacy (or compensated surrogacy) and commercial surrogacy are interchangeable. See A.J. Newson, 'Compensated transnational surrogacy in Australia: time for a comprehensive review', *Medical Journal of Australia,* Vol. 204, No. 1, 2016, pp. 33-35.

14 More discussion can be found in L. Shi, 'Surrogacy System in China: Problems and Suggestions', *in* J. M. Scherpe (Ed.), *Eastern and Western Perspectives on Surrogacy*, Intersentia, forthcoming.

15 X.D. Wang, 'Policymakers drop legal ban on surrogacy', *China Daily,* 28 December 2015, at http://europe.chinadaily.com.cn/china/2015-12/28/content_22835586.htm.

Few of the laws and rules that affect surrogacy lead to difficulties relating to custody disputes about children born through surrogacy arrangements. However, this was the issue that the People's Court needed to resolve in Chen case.

B Parentage Law in China

1 Legal Parents of a Legitimate Child and an Illegitimate Child

In relation to the parent-child relationship, article 25 of the Marriage Law provides that an illegitimate child shall have the same rights as a legitimate child, and that they shall not be harmed or discriminated against by any person. This is the only article that expressly references the rights of a legitimate child. The Marriage Law provides no definition of a legitimate child and includes no rules on the factors which give a legitimate child their legal status. Although the statute offers little detail on parent-child law, judges are, in practice, able to use other guidelines issued by the People's Supreme Court. In 1956 the People's Supreme Court issued the "Reply on How to Determine the Paternity of Xiao Miao born to XU Xiu Mei."[16] This Reply expressly sets out a principle for identifying the legal father of a child: a child born during a marriage is the child of both the husband and the wife. Any putative legal father who wishes to disavow the husband's paternity must prove that he is not the child's biological father.[17]

In this regard, the People's Court may commission paternity tests.[18] Paternity tests are now widely used in China because of their high degrees of accuracy. However, courts sometimes encounter difficulties in practice where respondents refuse to take paternity tests. Thus, article 2 of "Interpretation No. 3 of the Supreme People's Court of Several Issues on Application of the Marriage Law of the PRC", issued in 2011, provides that where the petitioner has provided convincing evidence to prove paternity, and the putative father has no contrary evidence and refuses to take a paternity test, the petitioner's claim about paternity will be confirmed.

In addition to the acquisition of legal parental status through a biological relationship, the law also provides other avenues for the recognition of legal parenthood which will now be discussed.

---

16 《关于徐秀梅所生的小苗应如何断定生父问题的复函》.

17 In the past this was proven by evidence that the husband had not cohabited with the wife at the time of conception.

18 C.Z. Wu (Ed.), *New Research on the Marriage and Family Law*, Beijing, China University of Political Science and Law Press, 2002, p. 237.

2 Legal Parents of an Adopted Child and a Stepchild

In accordance with the Adoption Law of the PRC, adoptive parents are the adopted child's legal parents once the adoption is legally complete and effective. The legal requirements for adoption are as follows: (1) the adoptee must be a minor under the age of 14 who is either an orphan, or an abandoned infant or child whose parents cannot be found, or a child whose parents are unable to rear them due to unusual difficulties;[19] (2) the prospective adoptive parents must be childless, capable of rearing and educating the adoptee, and over 35 years of age;[20] and (3) adoptions of abandoned infants or children whose parents cannot be found or orphans in the care of a social welfare institution must be registered at the civil affairs department.[21] In short, qualified adoptive parents must register the adoption of a qualified adoptee, otherwise the adoption will not be legally valid. These requirements apply to adoptions occurring after 1 April 1994 when the Adoption Law took effect.

The situation is a little different where the intended parents are stepparents. Article 27 of the Marriage Law stipulates:

> The relevant provisions in this Law governing the relationship between parents and children shall be applied to the rights and duties in the relationship between stepfathers or stepmothers and their stepchildren who receive care and education from them.

This means that, where stepfathers or stepmothers raise and educate their stepchildren for a period of time, they acquire legal parental status.[22] The law does not expressly state how long the period of care and education by stepparents must last before a stepparent is recognized as the child's legal parent.[23]

---

19 Adoption Law, art. 4.

20 Adoption Law, art. 16.

21 Adoption Law, art. 15. For further information on conditions for legal adoption, see Chen & Shi, op cit, n. 6, p. 54.

22 There has been some discussion about how to determine whether a stepparent is their stepchild's legal parent. Generally speaking, if the common property of the spouses is used to raise the child and pay for his or her education, the stepparent will be regarded as the legal parent. However, some stepparents who have paid such bills do not want to be the legal parent of their stepchild because they do not want to bear any responsibility for the child support if the marriage breaks down. For further discussion, see Y.N. Ma (Ed.), *The Marriage and Family Law*, Beijing, Beijing University Press, 2012, p. 200. Other writers argue that if a stepparent cohabits with their stepchild and takes care of and educates this child, even if they do not bear the cost of the child's living expenses, this special relationship is sufficient to ground a reasonable claim of legal parenthood. See Chen (Ed.), op cit, n. 9, p. 178.

23 This is regarded as a defect in the present law on stepparent-child relationships in China. The current law raises another question about when this legal parent-child relationship, once confirmed, should be ended. Further see X.J. Wei & T. Tan, 'Thinking on the Legislation of Stepparent-Child Law', *Theoretical Exploitation*, Vol. 23, No. 2, 2006, pp. 155-157.

With respect to children born by means of ART, the relevant principle for determining their legal parents is set out in the Supreme Court's 1991 Letter, referred to above. Therefore, if both spouses decide during the marriage to have a child through artificial insemination, they will be the legal parents of any child born as a result.

C *Which Rule Should Be Applied to This Case?*

To answer this question, it is necessary to first identify the controversy. The Chen case was a custody case. Thus, it was necessary to determine whether Chen was the legal parent of the twins born via surrogacy. Determining the legal parents of a child born via surrogacy is a new problem, and one which could not have been expected when the Marriage Law was first enacted in 1950 nor in 1980 when the second Marriage Law was enacted. As a result, there is obviously a lacuna in the law.[24] Looking back on the judgments of the two courts involved in this case, it is safe to say that the court of first instance and the appellate court used different reasoning to reach their conclusions.

First, the trial court said that none of the rules outlined above could be applied to this case. A careful consideration of the judgment of the trial court suggests that a hidden logic supported its conclusion: the commissioning mother could not acquire legal parental status because of the illegitimacy of surrogacy. As the maxim goes, *nullus commodum capere (potest) de sua iniuria propria.*[25] Therefore, the illegality of surrogacy means that the commissioning mother simply cannot become the legal mother of a child born through surrogacy. As such, it was reasonable for the People's Court to hold that the grandparents should be the twins' guardians. According to legal hermeneutics theory, the court adopted a restrictive interpretation based on a purposive approach;[26] that is to say, it rejected the argument that the commissioning mother was the legal mother recognized by the Marriage Law because surrogacy is an action contrary to public order and an offence against the fundamental dignity of human beings. Protecting public order and human dignity must surely be the priority of the civil law.[27] In judicial practice, whenever the People's Court is required to determine the legality of an act which disturbs the market or public order and

24 In a broad sense, legal hermeneutics covers the following basic tasks: (1) determining the meaning of a given legal text; (2) filling a lacuna in the law; (3) determining ambiguous legal concepts such as gross misunderstanding and adding value to general principles such as honesty or public order and good morals. See H.X. Liang, *Legal Hermeneutics*, 4th ed., Beijing, China Law Press, 2015, p. 215.

25 It means that no man ought to derive any benefit from his own wrong.

26 Further see Liang, op cit, n. 24, p. 276.

27 In China, the Marriage Law is a part of the civil law.

is otherwise unregulated by law, they utilize the principle of respect for public order and good morals to declare such an act invalid.[28]

However, the appellate court saw the case differently. In its judgment, the Chinese adoption rules could not be used to establish a legal parent-child relationship between Chen and the twins. The court further explained that, if de facto adoption were presumed from the facts, the implication would be that surrogacy is legally acceptable – a conclusion that should obviously be avoided. Therefore, the court held that de facto adoption definitely could not be presumed. Furthermore, even if the case did involve de facto adoption, Chen would not be legally recognized as the twins' adoptive mother since the adoption was not registered at the relevant administrative authority.

Instead, the appellate court used the stepparent-child law to conclude that Chen was the twins' legal parent. The court relied on the two elements covered in article 27 of the Marriage Law (subjective and objective) to confirm the existence of a legal parent-child relationship between Chen as a stepparent and the twins as stepchildren. In interpreting this law, the court determined that the best interests of the child principle stipulated in the Convention on the Rights of the Child was applicable in cases concerning children, and applied this paramount principle in support of its conclusion. Thus facing the same case as the trial court, the appeal court interpreted the law in an expansive manner using a purposive approach.[29]

This is a clear example of a theoretically hard case. As one commentator has stated, in hard cases the court needs to take into account substantive (i.e. non-legal) considerations beyond the statutory rules.[30] Cardozo has also pointed out that law ought to be guided by consideration of the effects it will have on social welfare. In his opinion, social welfare is a broad term which could include concepts of public order, shared goods and ethics. Indeed, social welfare requirements are also the requirements of religion, ethics, and social fairness.[31] Balancing different values is a prerequisite for choosing between different legal interpretations.[32] In this case, there were two principles in play that reflected different values. One can infer that the trial court found the public order and good morals principle to be paramount, while the appellate court put the best interests of the child principle first.

---

28 The public policy principle is one of the basic principles stipulated in article 7 in the *General Principles of the Civil Law of PRC*; see W.Y. Zhao, *Ethical Analysis of the Civil Law*, 2nd ed., Beijing, China Law Press, 2011, p. 173.

29 Further see Liang, op cit, n. 24, p. 280.

30 K. Chen, 'Hard Case, Judicial Decision, Substantive-Factors Weight', *Science of Law*, Vol. 362, No. 1, 2012, pp. 1-3.

31 Further see B.N. Cardozo, *The Nature of Judicial Process*, translated by S. Li, Shanghai, Commercial Press, 2000, p. 43.

32 Z.H. Shen, *Balancing Values as a Methodology of Legal Thinking*, Jinan, Jinan University Press, 2014, p. 120.

These two principles and their application in the context of the Chen case will now be discussed.

1 The Public Order and Good Morals Principle

The public order and good morals principle is somewhat vague and indeterminate, like many other principles in China's civil law. Some commentators have argued that the public order and good morals principle should be understood with reference to the religious and ethical values that are highly regarded in society. In China, it is difficult to reconcile the traditional role of a wife or a mother with surrogate motherhood. On this view, surrogacy is clearly aberrant. It both violates traditional ethical and moral codes within Chinese society and disturbs normal societal and family ethics. Surrogacy is a tool for commissioning parents to realize their selfish motives, while completely denigrating the surrogate's human dignity.[33] The ancient maxim – 'No man shall profit from his own wrong' – should thus be applied to safeguard current standards of public order. This reasoning justifies the trial court's conclusion, i.e. that the commissioning mother is unable to become the legal parent of children born via surrogacy.

However, if this problem is viewed from a historical perspective, it is safe to say that the content of the public order principle has actually changed over time.[34] The principle is affected by factors such as economic progress, social improvement, political needs and changing social attitudes.[35] For example, as Chinese divorce law has evolved, the traditional rules governing divorce in ancient China—such as the rule that a husband could divorce his wife on the ground of her infertility—have been abolished. In terms of culture, another example is that discrimination against live-in sons-in-law,[36] prevalent in traditional Chinese society, has been eliminated. Therefore, limiting women's opportunities on the basis of traditional expectations about women and social values that are now obsolete would result in a discordance between theory and reality. When the public order and good morals principle is discussed, it is critical to bear in mind that principle's connotations change in line with reality. As a result, deep exploration of the social implications of particular actions is required. Thus, in this case, the impact of surrogacy on society needs to be explored.

Surrogacy has gradually come to be accepted as a way of resolving a couple's fertility problems. Therefore, the public now tends to be sympathetic to infertile couples and to understand the difficulty of their situation. However, commercial surrogacy usually brings opposing voices into public debate. Despite these mixed responses to surrogacy, it has

33 C.Q. Liu, 'Jurisprudential Criticism of Legalizing Surrogacy Partly and Legislative Choice of Regulating Surrogacy in China', *Research of Rule of Law*, Vol. 34, No. 3, 2016, pp. 140-147.

34 B. Li, 'Surrogacy: Between Jurisprudence and Ethics', *Journal of Hunan Public Security College*, Vol. 22, No. 2, 2010, pp. 113-117.

35 B. Yang, 'The Problem of Enforceability of Surrogacy Contracts: Market, Ethics and Law', *Tribune of Political Science and Law*, Vol. 33, No. 4, 2015, pp. 34-47.

36 This refers to husbands living with their wife's family after marriage.

been used as a standard infertility treatment since the 1990s.[37] In the first five surrogacies that took place at the Beijing University Third Hospital before 2011, when the prohibition on surrogacy came into force, there were no commercial motives. This was because the surrogate in each case was a relative of the infertile commissioning mother. There was no factual evidence that social or family orders were damaged by these pregnancies. These cases showed that the criticism that surrogacy disturbs social and family orders and denigrates human dignity, reflecting a common anxiety about this new technology, is to some extent inaccurate.[38]

Furthermore, the complexity involved in surrogacy arrangements makes it impossible to regulate this practice in a simple unitary way. Even the seemingly plausible claim that surrogacy disturbs social and family orders can be refuted with readily available evidence to the contrary. For example, with regards to altruistic surrogacy, the infertile couple has a reasonable justification for seeking the help of doctors, their relatives and even a third party who is willing to be a surrogate. From an ethical perspective, altruistic surrogacy cannot be criticized as being against morality. Nor can the surrogate be criticized for being willing to make sacrifices for the infertile couple's benefit. On the contrary, her altruistic action deserves social recognition and praise.

However, the Chen case involved commercial surrogacy, which is an entirely different situation. It is difficult to counter the arguments set out above when they are made against commercial surrogacy. However, even if these criticisms of commercial surrogacy are convincing, should the People's Court have concluded that the commissioning mother could not be the legal parent of these two children born via surrogacy? The application of the best interests of the child principle and its conflict with the public order and good morals principle is explored next.

2 The Best Interests of the Child Principle

The best interests of the child is another vague principle, for it is not always clear what the child's best interests are. Some opponents of surrogacy use the best interests principle to support their position, arguing for example that surrogacy should be prohibited because of the unclear status of a child born through surrogacy.[39] However, regardless of whether surrogacy should be legalized, when a child is born through surrogacy a custody issue

37 Surrogacy was first carried out in China at the Beijing University Third Hospital by Professor Zhang Lizhu in 1996. This hospital has the largest and most highly specialized center for ART in China. IVF was first performed there in 1984 by a research team led by Professor Zhang Lizhu and the first test-tube baby was born there in 1988.

38 Actually, this problem is complicated. Commercial surrogacy indeed has shortcomings which have been targeted by feminists and child rights advocates.

39 J.M. Feng, 'Legal Problems on Human Reproduction Technologies', *in* L. Huixing (Ed.), *Civil and Commercial Law Review (8)*, Beijing, China Law Press, 1997, p. 89.

arises. Are the child's best interests protected by the child remaining with the surrogate? It depends.

The basic requirement of best interests principle is found in Article 3 of the Convention on the Rights of the Child (CRC):

> In all actions concerning children, whether undertaken by public or private social welfare institutions, courts of law, administrative authorities or legislative bodies, the best interests of the child shall be a primary consideration.

China is a signatory to the CRC. Therefore, this article should be applied within Chinese law. When a child is born through surrogacy, the child's best interests should become the paramount consideration and should dominate the court's reasoning. Courts should give effect to this principle by examining the situation of the child and giving judgment accordingly.

As such, the judge needs to determine whether the interpretation of a given legal provision should be guided by the best interests of the child principle. In this case (i.e. the Chen case) it is the interpretation of the stepparent-child rule that is of critical importance. Some commentators argue that the rule should be construed broadly so that a stepchild includes a legitimate child from the first marriage, an illegitimate child from a relationship outside of marriage, and an adopted child from the first marriage.[40] Indeed, judicial practice has supported this opinion, based on the recognition that regardless of the timing of the child's birth, whether before or during the current marriage, it is beneficial to the child for the wife of their biological father to be their stepparent.

Turning to whether the relationship between Chen and the children can be presumed to be a legal parent-child relationship, another test must also be applied. That test is whether the stepparent has supported and educated the step child for a period of time. In judicial practice, the following factors are considered: 1) whether the stepparent, either partially or fully, paid relevant support and education bills for the stepchild; 2) whether the stepparent lived with the stepchild, and took care of and educated the child;[41] 3) whether this relationship of support and education lasted for a period of time;[42] and 4) whether the

40 Further see X. Zhang, 'On Stepparent-Child Relationship', *Jilin University Journal Social Science Edition*, Vol. 47, No. 3, 2002, pp. 100-106; S. Fang & Q. Zheng, 'Thinking on the Reasonability of the Succession Right between Stepparent and Stepchild', *Social Science Front*, Vol. 36, No. 6, 2014, pp. 203-207; and R. Sun, 'Research on the Child Custody after Divorce', *Jurist*, Vol. 20, No. 6, 2005, pp. 73-79. In contrast, traditional opinion held that a 'stepchild' only refers to a child born during the first marriage.

41 See Chen (Ed.), op cit, n. 9, p. 178.

42 See Qian and Qian v. Zhu, heard by the 2nd Intermediate People's Court in Shanghai, docket number [(2013)沪二中民一(民)再字第3号]. In this case, the stepmother supported the stepchild for 16 months; Qian v. Zhao and Wang, heard by the Intermediate People's Court in Jiaxing City, Zhejiang Province, docket number[(2011)浙嘉民终字第42号]. In this case, the stepmother actually lived with and supported

stepparent intended to become the stepchild's parent.[43] On the facts of this case, it is clear that Chen supported and educated the twins for more than four years and that she lived with the children. The current law therefore does support the conclusion of the appellate court that Chen was the twins' legal parent.

However, Chen's status as the twins' legal parent did not guarantee that she would hold that position forever. The next question concerned Chen's ability to be the twins' guardian. Chen supported and educated the two children while the surrogate did not. In comparison with her husband's parents, Chen was young and in the prime of her life. Letting her raise the children would not detrimentally affect their interests and would be beneficial to their physical and emotional wellbeing. Moreover, there was no reason to abridge her guardianship right. Awarding Chen guardianship therefore met the requirements of the best interests of the child principle. Following this line of reasoning, the issue of child custody can be separated from the issue of the illegitimacy of surrogacy.

3 Balancing these Two Principles

It is ironic that the law can support the acts of an offender (i.e. acquiring a baby by surrogacy). The application of the best interests of the child principle puts Chen, the commissioning parent, in a favorable position. Therefore, the court faced a dilemma in this case – should Chen be awarded custody of the two children or not? Zhou Qiang, the Chief Justice of the Supreme People's Court, recently pointed out that all of the work of the People's Court is directed at realizing, protecting and promoting the interests of the people. The judiciary endeavors to deliver justice and give people access to fair and just outcomes in every case.[44] It is hard to show that denying Chen the status of being the twins' legal parent would benefit the interests of most people; the present social order could be more justifiably maintained by penalizing surrogacy brokers, who earn a great deal of money regardless of whether the rights and interests of the weak are prejudiced. It is not difficult to conclude that justice would not have been delivered if these children had been ordered to live with their grandparents instead of their de facto mother who had raised them for more than four years. Separating the twins and Chen would not have respected the emotional connection that existed between them and would have harmed the twins.

---

the stepchild for a year and her husband used common property to pay child support from the time of their marriage, when the child was six years old.

43 See article 13 of "The Several Opinions of the Supreme People's Court on Handling Child Support and Custody in hearing Divorce Cases" (1993). It stipulates that, when a biological parent divorces a stepparent and the stepparent does not consent to continuing to support the stepchild, the child should be raised by the biological parent. This shows that the courts use a test of intention to decide whether the stepparent-child relationship has ended. Notably, as some commentators point out, article 27 of the Marriage Law does not include consent as a factor. See Chen (Ed.), op cit, n. 9, p. 179.

44 Q. Zhou, 'Promote the Creative Work of the People's Court under the Guidance of the Speech of President Xi on 1st July', *People's Courts Daily*, 10 October 2016, p. 1.

Analyzing current judicial practice, Professor Wang has summarized the rules for prioritizing different interests when dealing with hard cases. In his opinion, personal interests should be prioritized. Judicial practice should be 'people-oriented, i.e. put personal welfare and dignity as the ultimate goal of the nation and society instead of a means to achieve other targets.'[45] Putting aside differences about the legitimacy of surrogacy, protection of the personal rights of the children required the court, in this case, to prioritize the best interests of the child principle and award custody of the twins to Chen. Judge Jiang from the People's Supreme Court has also given advice about how to hear hard cases by finding the essence of a law: "Stability of law should be regarded as the basic value to apply laws. Meanwhile, the court should take account of how to realize the teleonomy and the fairness value of law."[46] The purpose of the parent-child law has moved away from the family-oriented objectives promoted in ancient China to address modern day child-oriented concerns.[47] Therefore, subject to the requirement to ensure consistency between current laws, i.e. no surrogacy in accordance with the MAHART, it is necessary for courts to consider the purpose of the parent-child law.

From this perspective, it is safe to say that the appeal court did a much better job. It began by declaring that surrogacy is not allowed in China, thereby making a clear break from the hot debate about legalization of surrogacy. This declaration ensured the stability of the present rules. The appeal court then went on to find that Chen was the legal mother in accordance with the stepparent-child law. This finding was made following consideration of the present family structure, the existing relationship between Chen and the two children, and Chen's ability to raise these two children. This judgment also avoided a common problem among courts of first-instance which tend to stick strictly to the text of law so as to avoid mistakes in legal reasoning.[48]

VI Unsettled Questions

Considering that this custody case essentially concerned the rights of the children involved, this writer is in complete agreement that Chen should be their legal parent. Chen and the twins had been living together for more than four years, and Chen had a greater ability to raise and financially support the twins than her parents-in-law. But can one safely conclude

45 L.M. Wang, 'The Hierarchy of Competing Interests in Civil Law', *Jurist,* Vol. 29, No. 1, 2014, pp. 79-90.

46 B.X. Jiang, 'Materialization of Its Social Effect within Law', *China Legal Science,* Vol. 26, No. 3, 2009, pp. 5-14.

47 X.Y. Cao, *Research on the Parentage Law under the Principle of the Best Interests of Child,* Beijing, Qunzhong Press, 2015, pp. 47-53.

48 Because of the large population in China, the People's Supreme Court uses a series of mechanisms to safeguard legal consistency and avoid differences between judges as to the understanding of particular laws. Further see Liang, op cit, n. 24, p. 367.

that the court's application of the stepparent-child law was unproblematic? Did the judgment avoid conveying a message to society that surrogacy is legally acceptable in law? It seems not.

First, the stepparent-child law in China has many problems. Given that the law is problematic, it is difficult to support reasoning relying on it to solve a new legal issue which is intertwined with technology. The stepparent law does not have clear criteria for determining the point in time that a stepparent acquires legal parental status. Thus, this lacuna will bring further difficulties to the People's Court when it hears disputes concerning personal interests. It is expected that courts will reach different decisions about whether stepparents are legal parents in similar cases. This will undermine the predictability and consistency of the law and further confuse the complicated problem of surrogacy.

Second, assuming that the appeal court's judgment is convincing, other courts will follow its decision. As a result, commissioning mothers will become guardians on the same de facto basis which triggered the application of the stepparent-child law in the Chen case. Can one truly say that these judgments will not spread the message that surrogacy is legitimate? If the law does not accept surrogacy, why does it allow commissioning mothers to realize their dreams of motherhood in this manner?

Of course, a better solution to these problems would be to effect a new legal regime governing surrogacy with clear rules about parentage. Considering that public opinions on surrogacy vary greatly, creating a new surrogacy regime might not be an easy task. However, even if a new surrogacy law is not enacted, Chinese rules on parentage need improvement so that disputes like the Chen case can be dealt with.

On the basis of the best interests of the child principle and judicial practice in China, this author recommends that the following provisions on children born via surrogacy and on the stepparent-child relationship should be added into current parentage laws:

- First, a child born through surrogacy should be the child of the surrogate mother, irrespective of whether the surrogate has blood relationship with the child.
- Second, the surrogate should be able to transfer her parentage to a third party if she gives the child to that party and completes any relevant legal procedures (for example, adoption registration). Any surrogate who is not biologically related to the child and who gives their child to the commissioning parents, but fails to register this change of parentage, should remain liable for raising the child and should have the right to reclaim the child until two weeks have passed from the date that the baby was away. At this point, the surrogate's right to reclaim the child ought to be waived.
- Third, a stepparent should acquire legal parental status only if he or she satisfies the following tests: (1) he or she is willing to be a legal parent of this child; (2) he or she has been registered as a legal parent in a civil affairs office or has continuously raised the child for at least two weeks beginning on the date that he or she began living with this child.

Assisted Reproductive Technologies: New Family Forms and Welfare of Offspring in Comparative Family Law*

*Gordana Kovaček Stanić*** and *Sandra Samardžić****

I Introduction

Family law legislation often fails to offer a definition of family. The Family Act[1] of the Republic of Serbia, which dates from 2005, is no different. There are many reasons for this. One is that the Family Act governs family relations, i.e. the relationships between individual family members. As such, even though the family enjoys the protection of the state and society pursuant to the Constitution, the family itself is not regarded as the bearer of rights and obligations. Another reason is that a precise definition would result in the law recognizing only a limited notion of "family". Family relations are changing rapidly and new forms of family, historically unknown, are emerging. These family patterns could be excluded from the legal notion of family if a definition were to determine the persons that constitute family members. For example, unmarried cohabitation only gained legal recognition in the 20th century; equally, recognition is now given to the so-called "binuclear family", where parents who do not live together co-parent. In certain countries, legal significance is also given to same-sex families as same-sex partners are allowed to adopt children or to become parents by using biomedical assistance to conceive.

This paper analyzes new forms of family emerging as a result of the use of assisted reproductive technology (hereinafter referred to as "ART"). For the purposes of this paper, a family encompasses persons regarded as legal parents[2] and their children. The classifica-

* This paper is a contribution to the project "Biomedicine, environmental protection and law" of the Novi Sad Faculty of Law financed by the Ministry of Education, Science and Technological Development of Republic of Serbia. For part of this paper, "Welfare of Offspring and Procreative Liberty", the ISFL Committee for scholarship approved and awarded Sandra Samardžić a scholarship for young researchers. Special thanks go to Isidora Nikolić Savin, attorney at law, court translator for English, for the translation of this paper into English.

** Full Professor of Family Law, Comparative Family Law and Inheritance Law, Faculty of Law, University of Novi Sad, Serbia.

*** Ph.D., Assistant of Family Law, Faculty of Law, University of Novi Sad, Serbia.

1 *Official Gazette of the Republic of Serbia* no. 18/05 (hereinafter "*Official Gazette*").

2 For reasons of length, this paper will not deal in any detail with the issue of the determination of parentage in cases involving use of ART. In the typical case where an opposite-sex couple (married or unmarried)

tory criteria adopted in this jurisprudential research are: the number of legal parents, their gender, and their genetic link to the child. This paper analyzes comparative legal solutions to issues raised by ART, comparing solutions adopted in the Serbian legislation with the respective pieces of legislation of former Yugoslav countries (hereinafter referred to as "the region"), and of other European countries. This paper also analyzes the impact of ART on the welfare of offspring. This analysis is needed as one of the important issues in regulating medically assisted reproduction is ensuring that the best interests and rights of children are weighed against the wishes of adults.

II Number of Legal Parents

The first criterion for assessing new forms of family is the number of legal parents. A family formed through ART may consist of two legal parents and a child, or of one legal parent and a child. The laws of the European countries that regulate ART envisage spouses and partners as the primary beneficiaries of reproductive technologies rather than single persons.

The Serbian Act on Biomedically Assisted Fertilization, which dates from 2017, (hereinafter "Serbian Act") sets out the conditions that must be met in order for *couples* to be eligible for ART. These conditions concern: legal age and legal capacity, cohabitation, and capacity to exercise parental duties.[3] An individual's capacity to exercise parental duties is measured by the requirement that persons should be in such a physical and social state that they can reasonably be expected to be capable of exercising parental duties in conformity with the law and in the best interests of the child. While it is clear that prospective parents should be required to fulfill certain conditions in order to prove that they are capable of exercising parental rights in the best interest of the child, it is uncertain how compliance with those criteria is to be evaluated. It is of the utmost importance that competent persons are authorized to verify fulfillment of the criteria, and that due care is taken not to make the evaluation procedure unduly cumbersome. An additional condition – age – is found in a separate but related piece of legislation dealing with health insurance which grants women, up to the age of 42, the right to an *in vitro* fertilization procedure

---

uses donated gametes, parentage laws in the former Yugoslav countries deem the birth mother and her husband or partner to be the child's legal parents. If the husband or partner did not consent to the use of donated sperm, it is possible for him to contest fatherhood (see arts. 57, 58, Serbian Family Act). In Macedonia, which allows surrogacy, it is stipulated that spouses who started the ART procedure with a gestational carrier will be indicated in the civil register as parents (art. 12-v, Macedonian Act); for more on this see G. Kovaček Stanić, 'State Regulation of Surrogate Motherhood: Liberal or Restrictive Approach', *International Journal of Jurisprudence of the Family*, Vol. 4, 2013, pp. 35-57.

3 Act on Biomedically Assisted Fertilization, *Official Gazette*, no. 40/2017, art. 25(1) [Zakon o biomedicinski potpomognutoj oplodnji, *Službeni glasnik Republike Srbije* 40/2017].

free of charge. The Serbian state finances three attempts of IVF.[4] The Province of Vojvodina finances a free IVF attempt for a second child, and local governments finance a certain number of IVF procedures in line with their respective rules.

The same eligibility criteria – legal age, legal capacity, cohabitation and capacity to exercise parental duties – are also set out in the laws of other countries in the region.[5] Croatian legislation, however, contains an exception related to legal capacity: the right to a medically assisted fertilization is also vested in a person whose legal capacity has been limited (by a court decision) if the limit does not apply to actions concerning personal status (article 10(3)). In addition to these criteria, the laws of Croatia, Macedonia, Slovenia and Montenegro use age as a criterion for capacity to exercise parental duties.[6] Along with age, Croatian law also prescribes overall health as a pre-condition for capacity to parenting, while the laws of Slovenia and Montenegro expressly require prospective parents to be in an adequate physical and social condition.[7] Consequently, capacity to parent requires fulfillment of the following conditions: physical and social condition (Serbia, Slovenia, Montenegro), overall health (Croatia) and age (Croatia, Macedonia, Slovenia and Montenegro).

In Croatia, the Act on Medically Assisted Fertilization states, as in Serbia, that women up to 42 years of age are entitled to medically assisted fertilization at the expense of the Croatian Healthcare Insurance Institution. The Croatian law also contains an exception to this rule, which permits the physician, in cases particularly justified by health-related reasons, to offer medically assisted fertilization to a woman beyond 42 years of age.[8] In

---

4 Regulations on the content and extent of rights to health care protection deriving from mandatory health insurance and participation for 2018, *Official Gazette*, no. 18/2018, art. 10(3). [Pravilnik o sadržaju i obimu prava na zdravstvenu zaštitu iz obaveznog zdravstvenog osiguranja i o participaciji za 2018, *Službeni glasnik Republike Srbije* 18/2018].

5 **Slovenia**: Act on Treatment of Infertility and Fertilization Procedures by Biomedical Assistance, *Official Gazette*, no. 70/2000 and 15/2017, arts. 5 and 6 [Zakon o zdravljenju neplodnosti in postopkih oploditve z biomedicinsko pomočjo, *Uradni list*, 70/2000 i 15/2017, čl. 5, 6] (hereinafter "Slovenian Act").

Croatia: Act on Medically Assisted Fertilization, *Official Gazette*, 86/2012, Arts. 10 and 11 [Zakon o medicinski pomognutoj oplodnji Hrvatske, *Narodne novine*, 86/2012, čl. 10, 11] (hereinafter "Croatian Act").

Macedonia: Act on Amendments and Supplements to the Act on Fertilization Assisted by Biomedicine, *Official Gazette*, no. 149/2014 [Закон за изменување и дополнување на Законот за биомедицинско потпомогнато оплодување Македоније, *Службени весник* 149/2014] (hereinafter "Macedonian Amendment Act") *and* Act on Fertilization Assisted by Biomedicine, *Official Gazette*, no. 3/2008, arts. 11 and 12 [Законот за биомедицинско потпомогнато оплодување Makedonije, *Службени весник* 3/2008 čl. 11, 12] (hereinafter "Macedonian Act").

Montenegro: Act on Treatment of Infertility by Assisted Reproductive Technologies, *Official Gazette, no. 4/2009*, art. 12 [Zakon o liječenju neplodnosti asistiranim reporduktivnim tehnlogijama Crne Gore, *Službeni list*, 4/2009, čl. 12] (hereinafter "Montenegro Act").

Bosnia and Herzegovina: does not, at present, regulate ART.

6 Croatian Act, art. 10(1); Macedonian Act, art. 9(1); Slovenian Act, art. 6(1); Montenegro Act, art. 12(1).

7 Croatian Act, art. 10(1); Slovenian Act, art. 6(1); Montenegro Act, art. 12(1).

8 Croatian Act, art. 10(4).

addition, the laws of Slovenia and Montenegro connect access to ART with the woman's age; a prospective mother must be of an age appropriate for reproduction.[9] It should be noted that age as a criterion for capacity to exercise parental duties and age as a condition of access to ART are two different things. For instance, one could imagine the situation of 50-year-old woman who is considered capable of exercising parental duties, but who is not of an age appropriate for reproduction. It could be said that laws of Slovenia and Montenegro are the strictest with respect to age as a condition of access to ART.

When determining whether *unmarried partners* qualify for medically assisted fertilization, family legislation governing unmarried cohabitation must be consulted to determine whether unmarried couples are legally recognized, and if so, the criteria used to define such relationships.[10] The Serbian Family Act (article 4) defines unmarried cohabitation as the permanent cohabitation of a woman and a man, between whom there are no legal obstacles for entering into marriage (unmarried partners). Unmarried cohabitation is established by factual cohabitation. The factors which prevent legal recognition of unmarried cohabitation are the same as those preventing valid entry into marriage: existing marriage, mental incapacity, kinship, adoption or in-law relation, guardianship, minor age, and lack of free will. It is of the utmost importance to verify, prior to initiating the medically assisted fertilization procedure, whether an unmarried cohabitating couple's relationship fulfils the criteria for legal recognition and, in particular, whether there are any obstacles preventing entry into marriage. In practice, a typical obstacle is a pre-existing marriage. If one of the partners is already married, the unmarried cohabitation is legally invalid and, as a result, the couple has no right to medical assistance in conceiving a child.

A family created using ART may also consist of only one legal parent and a child. This situation occurs where a *single* woman gives birth to a child as result of ART. The current Serbian Act provides that single women have the right to access biomedical fertilization procedures, but only as an exceptional option. The eligibility conditions are the same as those that apply to married couples and unmarried partners.[11] Under the previously applicable law in Serbia – the Act on Treatment of Infertility by Procedures of Biomedically Assisted Fertilization from 2009 – single women were only granted access to biomedically assisted fertilization procedures in the presence of "particularly justified reasons". This was interpreted to mean reasons of a medical nature. Biomedically assisted fertilization was understood to be available exclusively for the treatment of infertility, a practice that was apparent from the very title of the Act and was in line with the principle of medical

9 Slovenian Act, art. 6(2); Montenegro Act, art. 12(2).

10 For more on this issue see G. Kovaček Stanić & S. Samardžić, 'Subjekti artificijelnih reproduktivnih tehnologija i njihova prava u primeni ovih postupaka (preimplantaciona dijagnostika)' ['The Subjects of Artificial Reproductive Technologies and Their Rights with Respect to Application of Such Procedures - the Pre-Implantation Diagnostics'], *Pravni život*, No. 10, 2016, pp. 57-72.

11 Art. 25(2).

justifiability that was expressly set out in the Act.[12] Consequently, the homosexual orientation of a woman or her inability to procreate solely due to her lack of partner were not regarded as justified reasons. Single women were required to obtain the consent of two competent Ministers in order to access the procedure – the Minister in charge of healthcare and the Minister in charge of family relations.[13]

One might question whether this position was intended to continue under the 2017 Act, or whether the right of access to biomedically assisted fertilization now accrues to all single women. On the one hand, the title of the new Act omits the reference to treatment of infertility. On the other, the new Act has retained the principle of medical justifiability of biomedically assisted fertilization. The principle has been formulated in the same manner as in the previous Act, but its application extends to cases of future infertility.[14] The provisions affecting this issue are thus inconsistent. One may assume that the legislator intended, with this Act, to award the right of access to biomedically assisted fertilization to single women for the very reason that they do not have partners. If so, for the sake of clarity and consistency, this intention should have been expressly identified as an exception to the principle of medical justifiability.

The consequence of giving a single woman access to ART is that the resulting child will have only one legal parent – a mother. This raises a question about whether a woman's reproductive rights conflict with the child's interests in being raised by two parents. A solution to this potential conflict exists in UK law. Section 13(5) of the Human Fertilisation and Embryology Act 1990 (HFEA) originally contained the following rule:

> A woman shall not be provided with treatment services unless account has been taken of the welfare of any child who may be born as a result of the treatment (including the need of that child for a father, and of any other child who may be affected by birth).[15]

This section was subsequently amended in 2008 and the phrase "including the need of that child for a father" was replaced by the requirement to consider "the need of that child for supportive parenting".[16] Section 14(2)(b) of the Code of Practice developed under the HFEA provides the following guideline for implementing this requirement:

12 *Official Gazette*, no. 72/2009, art. 4 [Zakonu o lečenju neplodnosti postupcima biomedicinski potpomognutog oplođenja, *Službeni glasnik Republike Srbije*, 72/2009, član 4).

13 Kovaček Stanić & Samardžić, op cit, n. 10.

14 Art. 4.

15 UK Human Fertilization and Embryolgy Act 1990, c. 37, replaced by UK Fertization and Embryology Act 2008, c. 22, available at http://www.legislation.gov.uk/ukpga/2008/22.

16 Discussed in E. Nelson, *Law, Policy and Reproductive Autonomy*, Oxford & Portland, Oregon, Hart Publishing, 2013, p. 275. Nelson comments that this change was very contentious as well.

> Where the child will have no legal father, the centre should assess the prospective mother's ability to meet the child's/children's needs and the ability of other persons within the family or social circle willing to share responsibility for those needs.[17]

In our opinion, such a solution would also be acceptable in Serbia because Serbian society places a high emphasis on the maintenance and nurturing of family relations. As such, it is unlikely that a Serbian woman would have difficulty finding assistance from others willing to partake in the raising of a child.

Other countries in the region – Croatia, Montenegro and Macedonia – also allow women without partners to access biomedically assisted fertilization.[18] In Slovenia, however, single women have no right to access ART. In Croatia a single woman can only access ART for medical reasons and not where she simply lacks a partner.[19] In Montenegro women who are not married or in a legally recognized unmarried union can access ART to treat infertility. However, access requires the consent of the Minister of Healthcare. The Minister's consent is based on an opinion obtained from the Committee for the Application of ART Procedures.[20] In Macedonia single women must meet the same requirements as women who are married or cohabiting with their partner outside of marriage. Macedonia permits access to ART if it can be established that previous treatment for infertility was unsuccessful and that the prospective mother is capable of parenting, given her age and general conditions. These requirements are problematic from the theoretical point of view. As Elena Ignovska has argued, "infertility is not the rationale behind a single woman's attempt to conceive using assisted reproduction." However, as she went on to explain: "Nevertheless, in practice, single women use ART to conceive without conditions."[21]

A family created through ART may also consist of a single legal parent – the father of the child. In these cases, the child has no mother. Surrogacy has made this situation theoretically possible.[22] Within the region, Macedonia is the only country that permits surrogacy.

---

17 As reported by N. Gamble, 'Considering the Need for a Father: The Role of Clinicians in Safeguarding Family Values in UK Fertility Treatment', *Reproductive Medicine Online*, Vol. 19, 2009, pp. 15-17, cited in Nelson, ibid, at p. 277, n. 287. The text of the Code of Practice is taken from Nelson.

18 Croatian Act, art. 10(2); Montenegro Act, art. 11(3),(4); Macedonian Act, art. 9(3).

19 Ibid., p. 90, art. 10(2).

20 This counseling body is comprised of: a representative from the Ministry; an expert in medical ethics; one expert from each healthcare institution involved in using ART procedures; one expert in the respective fields of psychology or psychiatry, embryology and genetics; a representative of the Chamber of Physicians of Montenegro; and a representative of the Ombudsman (art. 8).

21 E. Ignovska, *Sperm Donation, Single Women and Fertilization*, Cambridge, Intersentia, 2015, p. 86. According to Ignovska's research, in practice single women in Macedonia who were requesting ART only because they did not have a partner were able to avoid the infertility condition and were able to access ART.

22 It should be noted that this situation would depend upon the surrogate not being the legal mother under the applicable law. The media have cited the case of the famous football player Cristiano Ronaldo, who is

However, in Macedonia surrogacy is only available to married couples and therefore the situation where a child born through surrogacy only has a legal father does not arise.

Another form of family that can result from ART is where a child has two legal parents, but de facto has only one. This can occur in cases of posthumous fertilization. Serbian law does not expressly state whether posthumous fertilization is permitted or prohibited. Article 41 of the Serbian Act provides: "In the procedure of fertilization assisted by biomedicine, it is only permissible to use reproductive cells and embryos of donors who are alive." However, in cases of posthumous fertilization using sperm of the husband or unmarried partner (homologous fertilization) or an embryo originating from fertilization of an egg by their sperm, the husband or partner is not considered to be the donor of the genetic material. On the contrary, he is considered to be the subject in such procedures alongside his wife or partner. It thus remains unclear whether the legislature intended article 41 to apply to posthumous fertilization. More generally, the condition that donors must be alive is not supported by sound reasoning and, in practice, it would be difficult or impossible to obtain this information.

The remaining countries in the region also fail to expressly deal with posthumous fertilization. In Montenegro and Croatia, as is the case in Serbia, use of a donor's sperm is prohibited after his death.[23] Some European countries, for example the UK and Greece, permit posthumous fertilization.[24] In contrast, posthumous fertilization is prohibited in France,[25] Switzerland[26] and Italy.[27]

III Gender of Legal Parents

The second criterion which can be used to classify families created using ART is the gender of the legal parents. It is possible for a child to have parents of different sexes (a mother and a father) or parents of the same sex. This latter situation arises where persons of the same sex, who are married or in a relationship – typically a registered partnership – become parents by using ART. Same-sex parents could be two women, in which case the child has a mother and another parent, or two men, in which case the child has a father and another

said to have had three children born through surrogacy. No woman is regarded as the legal mother of these children. See *News Platform*, 19 July 2017, p. B92.

23 Montenegro Act, art. 33(4); Croatian Act, art. 33(3).

24 E. Zervogianni, 'The Changing Concept of "Family" and Challenges for Law in Greece', *in* J.M. Scherpe (Ed.), *European Family Law Vol. II: The Changing Concept of 'Family' and Challenges for Domestic Family Law*, Cheltenham, Northampton, Edward Elgar, 2016, p. 97.

25 See L.F. Terminal, 'The Changing Concept of "Family" and Challenges for Family Law in France', *in* Scherpe (Ed.), ibid, p. 39.

26 Artificial Insemination Act (2004), art. 3(4).

27 Federal Law on Medically Assisted Procreation (1998); see also I. Schwenzer & T. Keller, 'The Changing Concept of "Family" and Challenges for Family Law in Switzerland', *in* Scherpe (Ed.), op cit, n. 24, p. 325.

parent. If two women are in a same-sex union, the ART procedures that can be used include heterologous insemination (*in vivo* or *in vitro*) and use of donated embryos. Where two men are in a same-sex union, the relevant ART procedure is surrogacy.

Partners of the same sex are ineligible for ART in Serbia and other countries of the region. Slovenia expressly prohibits same-sex partners from accessing ART as well as from adopting children. This prohibition applies both to partners who have entered into a formal union (registered partnership) and partners who have not formalized their relationship.[28] In Macedonia, the only country in the region which regulates surrogacy, surrogacy can only be accessed by married couples, thus excluding same-sex couples.[29]

Looking to European comparative law, Sweden was one of the first countries to permit lesbian partners to access heterologous artificial insemination and IVF back in 2005. Thus, in accordance with that law, the woman giving birth to the child is its mother, while her partner is the child's other parent.[30] However, not all European countries that permit same-sex marriages allow same-sex couples to access ART. In France, for example, as one author has explained:

> Assisted reproduction is only permitted to overcome "pathological infertility" but forbidden by legal provisions in cases of "structural infertility" (for example, for same-sex couples or where the person seeking assistance is single).[31]

IV Genetic Link between the Child and their Legal Parents

A child born through ART can be genetically related to both of their legal parents, just one of their parents, or have no genetic link with either of its parents. A child born following homologous artificial insemination (insemination with sperm of the husband or partner) will be genetically related to both parents. Homologous artificial insemination is permitted in Serbia and all other countries in the region. A child conceived through embryo transfer will also be genetically related to both parents where the embryo was made by the egg of the legal mother and the sperm of her husband or partner.

---

28 Act on Civil Partnership of Slovenia, *Official Gazette*, no. 35/16, arts. 2(3) and 3(4) [Zakon o partnerski zvezi Slovenije, *Uradni list*, 35/16, čl. 2(3) i čl. 3(4)].

29 Macedonian Amendment Act, op cit, n. 5, art. 6.

30 M. Jänterä-Jarebor, 'Sweden: Lesbian Couples are Entitled to Assisted Fertilization– towards Equal Legal Rights for Homosexual Couples', *Zeitschrift für das gesamte Familienrecht*, Vol. 18, 2006, pp. 1329-1330. The provisions are contained in the Code on Children and Parents (1949/381) (*Föräldrabalken*), in particular in Chapter 1, Part 9, which was amended by the law SFS 2005/434 and by the Act on Insemination (1984/1140, amended in 2005, SFS 2005/443).

31 Terminal, op cit, n. 25, p. 52.

Moreover, a child will have a genetic connection with both of its legal parents in cases of gestational surrogacy where the embryo carried by the surrogate mother is created using the gametes of the commissioning (legal) parents.[32] As has been discussed above, the only country in the region that permits surrogacy is Macedonia. Article 1(5) of the Macedonian Act requires that the commissioning parents be a married couple. Thus, in Macedonia, a child born through gestational surrogacy could be genetically related to both of its legal parents, unless donated gametes or embryos were used.

The child will have a genetic link to one of its legal parents – its mother – where heterologous artificial insemination with donated sperm is used. Similarly, a child created using a donated egg that was fertilized by sperm of the mother's husband or partner will have a genetic link to one of its legal parents – the father. Both procedures are permitted in Serbia and in all countries in the region.

Pursuant to article 29(2) of the Serbian Act, donated gametes can only be used alongside gametes of one of the spouses or partners, or those of a single woman. As a result, children born following egg or sperm donation will always share a genetic connection with one of their legal parents. This limitation also exists in the Slovenian Act (article 8), the Croatian Act (article 8), and the Montenegro Act (article 14(2)). The Macedonian Act does not contain any such provision.

It is possible for children born via surrogacy to have a genetic connection with only one of their legal parents, which can be either their mother or their father. If an embryo is created using the sperm of the commissioning father and a donated egg or the egg of the surrogate mother, the child will have a genetic link only with its legal father. If an embryo is created using an egg of the commissioning mother and donated sperm, the child will have a genetic link only with its legal mother. Under the Macedonian Act, both types of surrogacy procedure are permitted; however, genetic surrogacy, where an egg of the surrogate mother is used, is not permitted.

A child born through ART will have a genetic connection with one of its legal parents where its legal parents are in a same-sex union. Where the couple consists of two women, ART involves fertilizing an egg of one of the women with donor sperm. Where the couple consists of two men, ART involves fertilizing a donor egg with the sperm of one of the men, and the resulting embryo being carried to birth by a surrogate mother. The surrogate mother can also be the egg donor. As noted above, Serbia and the other countries in the region do not allow same-sex partners to access ART.

Finally, it is also possible that a child born through ART will have no genetic connection with either of its legal parents. This scenario occurs in cases of embryo donation and where donated eggs and sperm are used (where allowed). Sometimes, ART procedures result in the creation of spare embryos. A couple might have spare embryos because they have

32 For more on surrogate motherhood see Kovaček Stanić, op cit, n. 2.

successfully had a child or children through ART and have no use for the remaining embryos. Other reasons include the dissolution of the couple's marriage or the end of their unmarried cohabitation. Where spare embryos exist, a decision needs to be taken about what to do with them. One possible solution is to donate the embryos to another infertile couple. Embryo donation is permitted in Serbia (article 29), Croatia (article 18) and Macedonia (article 16), but is prohibited in Slovenia (article 13(1)) and Montenegro (article 40). Article 1(5) of the Macedonian Amendments Act permits donated embryos to be used in cases of surrogacy. Across Europe, embryo donation is a procedure that has not been universally accepted. For example, it is permitted in France, the UK, and Greece, but is not permitted in Austria and Italy.[33] The donation of eggs and sperm in the same ART procedure is not allowed in Serbia (article 29(2)), Croatia (article 28), Montenegro (article 14(2)) or Slovenia (article 8).

V Welfare of Offspring and Procreative Liberty

A Procreative Liberty – Autonomy

> *To be a child is to be at risk, dependent, and without capacity or authority to decide what is "best" for oneself.*
> *To be an adult is to be a risk-taker, independent, and with capacity and authority to decide and to do what is "best" for oneself.*
> *To be an adult who is a parent is to be presumed in law to have the capacity, authority, and responsibility to determine and to do what is good for one's children.*
> *Joseph Goldstein*[34]

As Goldstein indicates, adults should have the autonomy to decide what is good for their children. However, it is clear that children living in today's world are in a different situation from children born in earlier times, and that parents today have responsibility for, rather than rights over, their children. The idea of children being a distinct and special group is no longer controversial.[35] In the past, people found it hard to accept that protection of

33 UK: HFEA, op cit, n. 15; Greece: Application of Medically Assisted Reproduction, *Law 3305/2005;* France: Bioethical Acts 1994, 2004, 2011, discussed in Terminal, op cit, n. 25, p. 52; Italy: Artificial Insemination Act 2004; Austria: The Austrian Reproductive Medicine Act 1992 [*Fortpflanzungsmedizingesetz – FmedG*].

34 J. Goldstein, 'Medical Care for the Child at Risk: On State Supervention of Parental Autonomy', *Yale Law Journal*, Vol. 86, 1977, pp. 645-670 at 645, available at https://digitalcommons.law.yale.edu/cgi/viewcontent.cgi?article=3449&context=fss_papers.

35 A. Ben-Arieh et al, *Measuring and Monitoring Children's Well-Being*, Springer Netherlands, 2001, p. 5.

children's interests might require separate policies that could, and sometimes did, differ from family policy.[36] Today, saying or doing something that could potentially lead to unsatisfactory consequences for children seems almost unthinkable. Children play a central role in society and it is now entirely accepted that children's best interests may be completely different from the interests of their parents and family.

Moreover, today we also talk about children having autonomy. Autonomy, in this context, is used in a much broader sense than it is in relation to adults. Even though autonomy can have different meanings and can be understood as something that we possess in varying degrees, which change over time,[37] its basic connotation is quite familiar. The liberal concept of autonomy refers to the idea that each person has the freedom to act in accordance with their own beliefs and convictions, so long as others are not harmed.[38] But when it comes to children who are too young to exercise their autonomy, another responsible person must represent their interests. Usually parents are the persons who are entitled to make decisions for their children and, as such, there is a presumption that they are able to choose the best solutions for their children.

However, it is not uncommon for parents today to have less freedom or autonomy in respect of their children than in the past. As a result, the principle of the best interests of the child should be a primary consideration when regulating ART. However, the bests interests of children born through ART are not, currently, given priority over other competing interests, such as the interests of adults using ART and the clinics which profit from these procedures. Some ART procedures which can be used by adults raise serious concerns about their impact on children's rights and interests. On the other hand, there are some ART procedures that could save the lives of children but, unfortunately, the freedom of adults to use them is considerably limited.

B *Donor Insemination*

Depending on the nature of the fertility problem, ART can be performed using donated eggs or donated sperm. Furthermore, in some cases, it may be necessary to use both donated eggs and sperm, in which case embryo donation is a possible solution. Each of these procedures raises certain problems and controversial issues, but the focus here will be on sperm donation.

36 J. Qvortrup, 'Childhood Matters: An Introduction', *in* J. Qvortrup et al (Eds.), *Childhood Matters: Social Theory, Practice and Politics*, Vienna, Avebury, 1994.

37 M. Friedman, *Autonomy, Gender, Politics*, Oxford, Oxford University Press, 2003; A. Mullin, 'Children, Paternalism and the Development of Autonomy', *Ethical Theory and Moral Practice*, Vol. 17, No. 3, 2014, pp. 413-426.

38 W. Kymlicka, *Liberalism, Community and Culture*, Oxford, Oxford University Press, 1989.

One concern is with respect to the right of a child to know their genetic origins. In some countries use of donated sperm is allowed, but disclosure of the identity of the donor is forbidden. Preparing a child to deal with this situation could be difficult given the strong need many people have to find out the truth about their genetic parents. We see this need, for example, in many adopted children.

Increasingly legislation across Europe has deemed that the only acceptable solution is to make donor information available and to forbid donors from remaining anonymous. One of the first countries to abolish anonymous donation was Sweden, which did so more than thirty years ago. However, countries that have taken this path have seen a reduction in the number of donors, which has further increased the number of couples (or individuals) travelling abroad in order to become parents. Revealing the identity of donors could also be disadvantageous to children conceived through use of donated sperm. It may be difficult for a child to expect nothing from their biological father and to understand that they cannot have a relationship with him.

Other problems can also occur when donated genetic material is used. The quality of the donated material may be questionable. Some people are willing to take any measure in order to become parents. They may seek assistance outside of licensed clinics and, as a result, endanger themselves and their future children as uncontrolled donations may result in serious diseases and conditions being passed on.[39] There are also examples of children conceived using donated sperm obtained through licensed clinics where the donor's medical history was not fully investigated.[40] The information about donors available to sperm banks can be incomplete and inaccurate. The fact that such risk exist does not necessarily mean that this practice should be banned, rather the testing of the donated material must be more systematic and comprehensive, although how to do so raises many dilemmas.

39 Ari Nagel, a New York mathematics professor donated his sperm over the internet and is now the biological father of 22 children. He has been recognized as the *legal* father of some of these children since the legal provisions regulating parenthood in cases where donated genetic material has been used cannot be applied where the insemination was not performed in a licensed clinic. See A. Genova & M. Towner, 'More than 100 women have contacted married New York professor after it was revealed he has sired 22 children by donating his sperm', *DailyMail*, 25 June 2016 [electronic version], available at http://www.dailymail.co.uk/news/art.-3659777/More-100-women-contacted-married-New-York-professor-revealed-sired-22-children-donating-sperm.html.

40 One such case was that of "Donor 9623". This case concerned Angela Collins and her partner who used reproductive material offered by a sperm bank in Georgia. The sperm bank described Donor 9623 as a "man with an IQ of 160 who was healthy and working toward his Ph.D." However, seven years later Ms Collins discovered the man's identity through a donor sibling group and found out that he had a history of mental illness and a criminal record and had exaggerated his educational accomplishments. See C. Hauser 'Sperm Donor's Profile Hid Mental Illness and Crime, Lawsuits Say', *New York Times*, 17 April 2016 [electronic version], available at https://www.nytimes.com/2016/04/18/world/americas/sperm-donors-profile-hid-mental-illness-and-crime-lawsuits-say.html. For more about this issue see S. Samardzic, 'Paternalism Today and Children's Rights', *in* S. Knežević & M. Nastić (Eds.), *Globalisation and Law: Collection of Papers from the International Scientific Conference*, Faculty of Law, University of Nis, 2017, p. 295.

For some children who were born using donated genetic material, the whole procedure is seen only as a question of money. In the words of one child of anonymous sperm donation: "There is a huge monster of money and people desperate for children, who don't want me to make it harder for them to buy and sell children."[41]

Serbia, Croatia, Slovenia, Macedonia and Montenegro all allow the donation of reproductive cells. However, these countries only permit a child conceived with donated reproductive cells to receive non-identifying information about the donor, for example information of medical significance. Furthermore, children can only obtain this information once they have reached the age of maturity, which is 15 in Serbia, Slovenia and Montenegro,[42] and 18 in Croatia and Macedonia.[43]

C *Savior Siblings*

Some uses of ART pose moral and ethical dilemmas upon which people have diametrically opposite views. One such issue is the use of preimplantation genetic diagnosis ('PGD')[44] in order to create a child who can be a matching donor of bone marrow or stem cells for an existing child who is ill. PGD is primarily used in conjunction with IVF in order to minimize the risk of passing on genetic diseases and disorders. Regulation of this technique has begun only recently and many jurisdictions allow it only in cases when there is a strong likelihood that parents will pass on a genetic disease. However, PGD is also an option for parents who have a child with a condition that requires a donation of bone marrow or stem cells, but neither the parents nor anyone else in the family is a matching donor. Where PGD is used, the parents can select embryos that will be perfect donors for their child.

However, this use of PGD to create "saviour siblings" raises a question about whether it is morally justifiable to conceive and give birth to a child for the purpose of donation. This use of PDG is relatively new[45] and, as with other forms of assisted reproduction, it has been met a great deal of denial and non-acceptance. At this moment, only a few countries, such as the UK, Spain, and Australia, allow this procedure.[46] Three main concerns have been voiced.[47] The first is that saviour siblings will be treated as mere means rather

41 Alana, the child of a sperm donor and the activist behind AnonymousUs.org, in the documentary *Anonymous Father's Day*.

42 Serbian Act, art. 57; Slovenian Act, art. 18; Montenegro Act, art. 24.

43 Croatian Act, art. 15; Macedonian Act, art. 57.

44 Pre-implantation genetic diagnosis (PGD or PIGD) is the genetic profiling of embryos prior to implantation, and sometimes even of oocytes prior to fertilization.

45 Adam Nash, a boy born in the USA in 2000, was the first saviour sibling born with the help of PGD. Blood from his umbilical cord was successfully used to treat his sister Moli, who suffered from a rare form of anemia.

46 In the U.S. the procedure is not yet regulated and is left to the discretion of providers and patients.

47 S. Sheldon & S. Wilkinson, 'Should selecting saviour siblings be banned?' *Journal of Medical Ethics*, Vol. 30, No. 6, 2004, pp. 533-537.

than ends-in-themselves. Second, there is fear that permitting such techniques will lead to the creation of "designer babies". Finally, there are concerns that child's psychological and physical health could be endangered in this way.

However, these concerns seem to be insufficient when weighed against saving the life of a sick child. As one commentator has put it: "you have got to have a very powerful reason to resist the means by which [a child's] life can be saved".[48] Furthermore, the resulting child could be seen as being enormously advantaged by PGD for, without it, the embryo that became that child would never have been selected and the child would not have been born.[49] There is no proof that the parents in this situation will not love the donor child in the same way as their existing child and that the specific conditions under which the child will be born will have effect on its future life. All of the academic objections are not sufficiently powerful to forbid the only possible treatment solution for an existing child.

A comparison of the two procedures – sperm donation and the use of IVF and PGD to create saviour siblings – clearly demonstrates that adults are currently allowed differing degrees of autonomy in the area of medically assisted reproduction. On the one hand, parents can use donated genetic material to create children who are unable to discover the identity of their other biological parent or establish a relationship with them. On the other hand, having a child through IVF and PGD in order to cure an existing child is usually forbidden, even where there is no risk of any harm.

PGD is expressly permitted in Serbia, Macedonia and Montenegro,[50] but only where there is a risk of passing on inherited conditions. The same conclusion can be reached in respect of Macedonia and Croatia[51] on the basis of the provisions that regulate access to ART. In these two countries it is stated that persons who are in danger of transmitting a disease may access ART even though they are not infertile. On this basis, individuals could use PGD to prevent disease transmission, but not for the purpose of selecting a compatible donor embryo. However, as PGD is allowed, there is a basis from which future legalization of this technique for creating saviour siblings could be sought.

VI Closing Remarks

Medically assisted reproduction has transformed the traditional notion of family, which historically consisted of a mother, a father and their children. The family law systems of some European countries permit children who are born by means of ART to have only

48 J. Glover, quoted in 'Doctor plans "designer baby" clinic', BBC News, 11 December 2001 at http://news.bbc.co.uk/1/hi/health/1702854.stm.

49 C. Foster, *Choosing Life, Choosing Death - The Tyranny of Autonomy in Medical Ethics and Law*, Portland, Hart Publishing, 2009, p. 58.

50 Serbian Act, art. 47; Slovenian Act, art. 31; Montenegro Act, art. 37.

51 Croatian Act, art. 4; Macedonian Act, art. 3.

one legal parent or to have parents of the same sex – a mother and another parent, or a father and another parent. Legislation in some countries permits use of ART procedures which result in the child produced having a genetic link with only one parent. Moreover, legislation in other countries enables ART to be used to create a child that is not genetically related to its legal parents. One might argue that the establishment of legal parenthood in family law extends the autonomy of parties beyond the principle of material truth. Persons who want a child can indeed become legal parents, even if they are not parents in genetic terms and are incapable of becoming so. A person may be unable to become a genetic parent because of infertility or because they are in a same-sex relationship.

It is safe to say that Serbian legislation adopts certain liberal solutions when defining legal parenthood in cases of medically assisted reproduction. For example, by providing single women with access to assisted fertilization, Serbia allows children to have only one legal parent. Moreover, by permitting the donation of spare embryos to other couples, Serbia accepts that a child may not have any genetic connection with its parents whatsoever. However, Serbian legislation remains conservative when it comes to same-sex couples using ART. This positions flows from the fact that Serbian family law does not recognize same-sex unions, neither in the form of a factual union or registered partnership, nor in the form of same-sex marriage. We are of the opinion that the Act governing medically assisted reproduction should not be the first legal instrument in Serbia to grant rights to persons of the same sex. However, it should be acknowledged that Serbian legislation remains isolated in its position that same-sex unions have no legal effects. We believe that national legislation should introduce a form of same-sex partnership recognition - the registered partnership. Serbian legislation also adopts a restrictive attitude towards surrogacy and, on this issue, Serbia falls within the group of countries that have conservative regulation.

On the one hand, we agree that people who want to have children should be entitled to all available treatments to enable them to do so.[52] Families know their values, priorities and resources better than anyone else; they are also the ones who will be most affected by ART decisions.[53] Therefore families, in conjunction with doctors, are best placed to take decisions about ART. On the other hand, all societies need to be careful when regulating medically assisted reproduction and must have the best interests and rights of children in mind, not only the wishes of adults and the desire for profit. In order to protect children the law needs to find a balance between parental autonomy, children's welfare and the desire of clinics to make a profit. Some form of control of ART is necessary so that a consistent approach is created. Dworkin's definition of paternalism could be modified and

52 M. Quigley, 'A right to reproduce', *Bioethics*, Vol. 24, No. 8, 2010, p. 410.

53 B. Kelsey 'Shall These Children Live? A Conversation with Dr. Raymond S. Duff', *Reflection* (Yale Divinity School Magazine), Vol. 72, Jan. 1975 at 4, cited in Goldstein, op cit, n. 34, p. 656, n. 25.

used to justify the limitations that are needed. Interference with the liberty of adults and clinics can be "justified by reasons referring exclusively to the welfare, good, happiness, needs, interests, or values of the"[54] present and future children.

54 G. Dworkin, 'Paternalism', *in* R.A. Wasserstrom (Ed.) *Morality and the Law*, Belmont, Calif., Wadsworth Publishing Company, 1971, p. 181, available at http://www.sjsu.edu/people/paul.bashaw/courses/phil186fall2012/s1/Paternalism.pdf.

Part IV
Family Relationships and Financial Obligations

The Child's Right to Maintenance: Criteria for Establishment of the Amount and Form of Maintenance in Lithuania

*Inga Kudinavičiūtė-Michailovienė** *and Vitalija Šimkienė***

I Criteria for Determination of the Amount of Maintenance

The state of Lithuania recognises that the family is the basic element of society and the state, serving as a natural environment for the development and well-being of children, and that children require special protection and care, both before and after birth. The Constitution of the Republic of Lithuania[1] (point 6 of article 38, article 39) establishes that both parents shall be responsible for maintaining their underage children and the state shall provide adequate conditions for them to perform their parental duties.[2]

Determination of the amount of child maintenance is essential to the proper implementation of the child maintenance duty. There is no universal, worldwide system for determining the amount of child maintenance: the amount is selected in accordance with a prescribed system, which varies between in different jurisdictions. Examples include the income percentage system, the system of "balancing needs and opportunities", expense-sharing systems and income-distribution systems. Each of these systems has its own advantages and disadvantages, and so any discussion regarding a "perfect system" may only be relative. Thus, we may assume that the model operated by the legal system of each country should be deemed as appropriate, as long as it reflects the social and economic realities prevailing in that country in the current phase of its public and legal development.

Paragraph 1 of article 81 of the Lithuanian Matrimonial Family Code, which became effective till 01-Jul-2001, established the income percentage system:[3] "Alimony for juvenile children shall be collected from their parents in the following amounts: for one child, one

---

* Professor, Mykolas Romeris University, Lithuania.

** PhD student, Turiba University, Latvia.

1 Constitution of the Republic of Lithuania, 1993. Vilnius: LWUP edition.

2 V. Šimkiene, 'Tėvų pareigs išlaikyti savo vaikus: valdžios ir turinio kontekstas bei teisinis reglamentavimas' ['The obligation of parents to maintain their children: the context of the content of authority and legal regulation'], *Professional studies: theory and practice*, Vol. 8, 2011, pp. 286-291.

3 G. Sagatys, 'The Pre-harmonization Area: A Comparison of Lithuanian, Latvian and Estonian Child Maintenance Laws', *in* K. Boele-Woelki, J. Miles & J.M. Scherpe (Eds.), *The Future of Family Property in Europe,* Antwerp, Intersentia, 2011, p. 311.

fourth; for two children, one third; for three and more children, half of their parents' earnings (income)."[4] However, after the new Civil Code[5] (hereafter CC) became effective, this system was cancelled and a system of "balancing needs and opportunities" was established in its place. Paragraph 2 of article 3.192 of the CC establishes that "the amount of maintenance shall be proportionate to the needs of juvenile children and the financial situation of their parents and the conditions needed for the child to develop". The essential criteria, which affect the amount of maintenance to be awarded, are the child's needs and the financial situation of the parents, whilst a common criterion (which incorporates both the child and the parents, and prevents the court of law from leaning towards one or the other side too much), is the priority principle of protection of the child's rights and interests. We shall proceed by discussing each of these criteria individually.

A Criterion of the Child's Needs

Child's needs is a very broad category, divided into general and individual needs. A *child's general needs* encompass the need for food, clothing, housing, learning and education, health care, and passing leisure time, which have been established on an international and national level and are common to all children, regardless of their age, education, and their acquired and natural abilities.

In establishing a child's need for food, the current practice of the courts refers to the child's right to be provided with a sufficient amount of food, based on the Law on Fundamentals of Protection of the Rights of the Child of the Republic of Lithuania[6] – that is, a child should have the quality and quantity of food which would satisfy his/her full physiological development.[7]

A child's needs for clothing are established on the basis that a child needs clothing to ensure his/her health and dignity. This means that a child's needs for clothing must be met by maintenance that would enable a child to have seasonal clothing and footwear in his/her size, as well as reserving some part of the funds for his/her leisure time activities.[8]

A child's right and simultaneously his need for housing have been established in Lithuania by article 13 of the Law on Fundamentals of Protection of the Rights of the Child. The jurisprudence of the Supreme Court of Lithuania (hereafter SCL) establishes that

---

4 Marriage and Family Code of the Lithuanian Soviet Socialist Republic, *Vyriausybės Žinios [Official Gazette]*, 1969, No. 21-186.

5 Civil Code of the Republic of Lithuania, *Official Gazette*, 2000, No. 74.

6 Law on Child Rights Protection Fundamentals of the Republic of Lithuania, *Official Gazette*, 1996, No. 33-807 9 (as amended).

7 Decision of District Court of Kelmė Local Area of 5 August 2014 in Civil Case No. 2-571-446/2014.

8 Decision of Vilnius Regional Court of 1 March 2018 in Civil Case No. 2A-115-619/2018.

children of different genders should have a separate residential space, such as separate rooms.[9]

Having analysed the jurisprudence, it should be noted that the amount of maintenance is also affected by a child's needs for education, expressed as costs needed to cover expenses related to education at a preschool, school, or a special education establishment. Such expenses mostly include the purchase of school supplies, payment for tutors' services and extra-curricular activities as well as other necessary costs.[10]

A child's right (need) to be healthy has been secured in the United Nations Convention on the Rights of the Child[11] and the Law on Fundamentals of Protection of the Rights of the Child. A child's right to health, to a healthy environment, and to proper health care is of exceptional significance in his/her life, and must therefore be ensured properly. A court assesses each individual case of a child's health care based on the evidence provided for the case and awards an amount of maintenance on this basis, as well as by observing the principles of rationality and good faith.[12]

A child's need to have leisure time is also ensured on the national level: a child must be provided with opportunities to play, take part in cultural activities, to engage in activities he/she likes and corresponds to his/her acquired and natural abilities. Therefore, these needs must be secured for each child without exception, and the amount thereof must be determined by a court based on the evidence presented and the principles of the best interests of the child, as well as rationality, good faith, and justice.[13]

A child's *individual needs* refer to educational and developmental issues specific to the particular child. Having analysed the jurisprudence,[14] we may conclude that the following factors are flagged most often as determining individual needs: 1) a child's natural or acquired talent; 2) health condition; 3) age; and 4) special needs.

Margaret Price, who has analysed determination of the amount of maintenance for children with special needs in the USA, has observed that specific and variable needs should be evaluated when dealing with the issue of maintenance of a child with special needs. Specific, elaborate needs include physicians' (specialists') services and costs for modification

9 Decision of the Supreme Court of Lithuania during the Plenary Session of 20 May 2010 in Civil Case No. 3K-P-186/2010.

10 Ruling of Supreme Court of Lithuania of 28 March 2013 in Civil Case No. 3K-3-209/2013; Resolution of the Senate of the Supreme Court of Lithuania (SCL) No. 54 of 23/06/2005 "On the application of laws regulating parental maintenance obligations in court practice", *Teismų praktika*, 2005 m. Nr. 23 [Case Law, No. 23, 2005].

11 United Nations Convention on the Rights of the Child, *Official Gazette*, 1995, No. 60-1501.

12 Ruling of the Supreme Court of Lithuania of 3 February 2016 in Civil Case No. 3K-3-16-706/2016.

13 Resolution of the Senate of the Supreme Court of Lithuania (SCL) No. 54 of 23/06/2005 "On the application of laws regulating parental maintenance obligations in court practice",*Teismų praktika*, 2005 m. Nr. 23 [Case Law, No. 23, 2005].

14 Decision of Panevėžys Regional Court of 30 August 2018 in Civil Case No. e2A-522-755/2018; Decision of Kaunas Regional Court of 17 October 2016 in Civil Case No. 2A-1605-230/2016.

of home environment (e.g. special stairs to accommodate disability, etc.). It might be impossible to estimate other costs in detail in advance, but they should definitely be included in preliminary calculations, such as transport costs to take a child to medical establishments, the cost of medications (a child might be taking one set of medication at the age of 5, but it is unlikely that these medications would remain effective at the age of 15), etc.[15]

According to Lithuanian case law usually a child's needs must be demonstrated in a court by providing detailed calculations and supporting evidence (receipts, invoices, etc.) reflecting the amounts of money spent monthly to meet those needs.[16] However, the authors believe that this type of evidence should only be regarded as one of many substantiating arguments, and that neither a disproportionate weight should be given to the quantity of such evidence (number of invoices, receipts, etc.), nor should it be mandatory to provide such evidence. This conclusion has been made because persons are able to submit abundant evidence of this kind (it is easily obtainable), and the sheer quantity of these documents would simply complicate the consideration of case. Moreover, the assessment of general needs is usually based on case law established before 2016, according to which maintenance is usually determined by reference to the minimum wage. However, it is reasonable to think that the court, when determining the amount of maintenance, should focus not on the justification of general needs but rather on the presence or absence of individual needs of the child in question that could be supported by a corresponding evidence, such as medical and similar certificates (produced by medical doctors, orthodontists, speech-language pathologists, etc.).

When delivering a decision on awarding maintenance, a court always evaluates both general and individual needs of a child. The jurisprudence consistently adheres to the standpoint that maintenance must meet such needs of the child to ensure material conditions for the child's physical and social development, as well as cultivation and improvement of his/her natural abilities and the acquisition of new skills to aid his/her development into an adult. The amount of maintenance should not be limited only to meeting the minimum (general) needs of a child.[17] In accordance with the law, the duty to pay child maintenance includes not only sharing the costs in meeting the daily needs of a child by parents, but also additional child care expenses of a one-off, temporary, or continuous nature.[18]

15 M.S. Price, 'Divorce Issues and the Special Needs Child', *American Journal of Family Law*, Vol. 25, No. 1, 2011, pp. 28-36.

16 Resolution of the Senate of the Supreme Court of Lithuania (SCL) No. 54 of 23/06/2005 'On the application of laws regulating parental maintenance obligations in court practice', *Teismų praktika*, 2005 m. Nr. 23 [Case Law, No. 23, 2005].

17 Decision Vilnius Regional Court of 10 October 2013 in Civil Case No. 2A-2417-25/2013.

18 Ruling of SCL of 29 June 2016 in Civil Case [No.] 3K-7-231-969/2016.

B Criterion of the Financial Situation of Both Parents

The financial situation of both parents is the second criterion taken into consideration by a court when awarding maintenance to a minor child. This criterion is significant, but not decisive, when determining the amount of maintenance payable.[19] The Supreme Court (the SCL) has also clarified that parents have an equal duty to maintain their children, but this does not mean that each of them must provide an equal amount of maintenance.[20]

Evaluation of the financial situation of both parents includes consideration of: all types of income received by them (wages, royalties, pensions, scholarships, social benefits; income from commercial and economic activities such as rent, dividends, etc.); their bank account balance and other credit establishments; movable property (vehicles, valuable movable property, jewels) and real estate (residential houses, apartments, other buildings, land, forest); stocks (shares, bonds); legal entities (individual companies) and their assets.[21] In evaluating the financial situation of a person obliged to provide maintenance to a minor child, consideration must be given not just to the amount of income at the person's disposal, but also to whether such income is regular or intermittent, and whether that person has any outstanding debts or obligations to third parties.[22] On the other hand, the SCL has noted that for the assessment of a person's financial situation and ability to provide maintenance, only the necessary expenses incurred by that person should be taken into consideration in order to assess whether upon their deduction the remaining income becomes insufficient to provide a certain level of maintenance.[23]

Following a systematic assessment of national legislation and practices, as well as the laws of other jurisdictions, Gediminas Sagatys has noted that the dominant approach in determining the amount of maintenance is establishing parents' actual income (this method is also used in Latvia, Estonia, and Norway), that is, relying on objective criteria, through identifying assets owned by each of the parents and their income. In addition to this, he observes that a different method exists in other countries e.g. in Austria and some US States – imputed income assessment, which involves assessment of not only the assets

19 Ruling of SCL of 28 March 2013 in Civil Case No. 3K-3-209/2013.

20 Ruling of SCL of 3 February 2016 in Civil Case No. 3K-3-16-706/2016.

21 Ruling of SCL of 7 February 2007 in Civil Case No. 3K-7-6/2007 and Ruling of SCL of 27 May 2010 in Civil Case No. 3K-3-243/2010.

22 Ruling of SCL of 20 February 2013 in Civil Case No. 3K-3-37/2013.

23 For instance, on 24 October 2014 in Case No. 3K-3-454/2014, the Court of Cassation agreed with the assessment given in the decision of the Court of Appeal that "purchasing of housing in the USA on a hire-purchase and payment of contributions shall not be regarded as necessary expenses incurred by the appellant. Having such unnecessary expenses is not a sufficient reason for reduction of maintenance for the person's children (which shall be given priority in terms of importance) as he/she can afford paying a proper amount of maintenance based on his/her financial situation".

owned by each of the parents and their current income, but also income expected to be received based on the parents' education and professional training.[24]

Naturally, the amount of maintenance awarded should be proportionate to the child's needs and the parents' financial situation. The Supreme Court has stated that the amount of maintenance directly depends on the child's needs and the parents' financial situation, while the priority principle of protection of the child's rights, established in paragraph 1 of article 3.3 of the CC, helps courts maintain their balance. For example, in cases when the children are divided between both parents but one of the children is more poorly provided for because of the differences between the salaries or wealth of the parents, the court may award maintenance for the benefit of the poorly provided-for child.[25]

In order to analyze the impact of parents' financial situation on the amount of maintenance for a minor child, based on the national jurisprudence, the authors have broken down parents' financial situation into three groups: good, moderate, and difficult.

1 Parents in a Good Financial Situation

When parents' financial situation is *good*, maintenance claimants often seek a bigger sum of money for child maintenance based on the priority principle of protection of children's rights, specifying that not only fundamental (general) needs (the need for food, clothing, housing), but also individual (special needs (e.g. to develop a child's talent, health condition) of a child must be ensured. Moreover, it is stated that a child should not have a lower standard of living merely because the child does not live with both parents. The chamber of judges has noted that the spouses' divorce *per se* does not mean that the child's maintenance conditions must necessarily change for the worse. The child's needs that have developed during the parents' marriage must continue to be met to the same extent after the divorce, provided the material situation of the parents does not change substantially. This means that the court, when taking a decision on the amount of maintenance, cannot use the fact of divorce as a standalone basis for reducing the share of finances and services that was allocated for the child's needs during wedlock. For example, if, while living together and jointly providing for their minor child, the spouses agreed to provide him/her with private education and/or healthcare services and have managed to ensure the fulfilment of the child's needs at such level, the court should have to regard to this agreement when taking a decision regarding the child's needs.[26]

---

24 G. Sagatys, 'Aktualūs vaiko išlaikymo dydžio nustatymo klausimai' ['Relevant issues associated with determination of the amount of a child's maintenance'], *Jurisprudencija*, Vol. 71, No. 63, 2005, pp. 23-33.

25 Ruling of SCL of 23 January 2003 in Civil Case No. 3K-3-80/2003; Ruling of SCL of 20 February 2013 in Civil Case No. 3K-3-37/2013.

26 Ruling of SCL of 10 November 2009 in the civil case No. 3K-3-495/2009.

On the other hand, maximizing the amount of a child's maintenance is not irrefutably the best solution in each and every case.[27] The marriage dissolution case of a famous basketball player S.J. and his spouse V.J., which became a matter of public interest, is an example. In this case, the court applied interim protective measures and obliged S.J. to pay more than LTL 11 000 (3186 EUR) per month for maintenance of the child. But the court's final ruling was that LTL 4 500 (1303 EUR) per month was to be paid until the child attains his/her majority.[28] This suggests that where parents' financial situation is *good*, the maintenance to be awarded should comfortably cover the general and individual needs of the child, but the court is not obliged to grant the maximum amount that could be awarded. Another argument to be acknowledged is that "the purpose of maintenance provided to a child is not accumulation of savings, or acquisition of property which is not necessary for meeting a child's needs".[29] Some others consider that any amount of excess maintenance remaining after meeting the essential needs of the child may be used for other purposes, such as for his/her leisure or expenses incurred in relation to maintenance of his/her housing, etc., whereas any amounts of maintenance that are saved should be invested or deposited on a bank account opened on behalf of the child.[30]

2 Parents in a Moderate Financial Situation

When the parents' financial situation is *moderate*, courts usually award a level of maintenance to meet the minimum needs of the child. The jurisprudence takes the view that maintenance equivalent to one 'minimum monthly salary' (hereafter MMS, equivalent to 400 EUR per month since 1 January 2018) should be taken as a reference point in awarding maintenance to meet a child's minimum needs. However, the specific circumstances of the case should be considered in applying this criterion.[31] Some courts do not seek to identify a sum which would correspond to the actual needs of a child, but would rather award a sum equivalent to MMS instead.[32] In this regard, the MMS should be regarded as a clarification made by courts of law to fill the gap in paragraph 2 of article 3.192 of the CC (because no criterion has been given for determination of maintenance needed to ensure the minimum needs of a child),[33] but this does not mean that a child's parents must reserve a sum precisely equivalent to MMS in order to meet the child's minimum needs.

27 I. Kudinavičiūtė-Michailovienė & J. Vėgelienė, 'Child Maintenance: Several Topical Theoretical and Practical Aspects', *Jurisprudencija*, Vol. 19, No. 1, 2012, pp. 209-29.

28 Vilnius District Court No. 1, Civil Case No. N2-1133-55/2011.

29 Ruling of SCL of 15 April 2005 in Civil Case No. 3K-3-193/2005.

30 V. Mikelėnas, *Lietuvos Respublikos civilinio kodekso komentaras. Trečioji knyga. Šeimos teisė [Comment on the Civil Code of the Republic of Lithuania. Book Three. Family Law]*, Vilnius, Justitia, 2002, p. 386.

31 Ruling of SCL of 2 April 2013 in Civil Case No. 3K-3-276/2013.

32 Ruling of SCL of 2 May 2007 in Civil Case No. 3K-3-177/2007.

33 I. Kudinavičiūtė, 'Civilinio kodekso normų, susijusių su šeimos narių teisių apsauga, įgyvendinimo problemos, Jurisprudencija' ['Realization of Civil Code Norms Related with the Defence of the Family Members' Rights// Jurisprudence'], LTU research work, Vol. 28 (20), 2002, pp. 137-143.

The idea that the amount of maintenance for children living in Lithuania is usually determined by reference to the minimum wage is not a set practice, however, because the amount of maintenance is established individually in each case. Maintenance is allocated to assist with a child's life and development, but the amount of maintenance is established in proportion to parents' existing and potential capacity to pay. The minimum wage often is sufficient to meet the minimum, basic needs of a person. However, as we have already mentioned, comprehensive development of a child requires more than merely meeting the minimum needs.[34] Thus, in 2016 the SCL held that, in general, the amount of maintenance to be awarded to a child should not be associated with a MMS.[35] In February 2016, it stated:

> … the fact that the amount of maintenance is usually determined on the basis of minimum salary is not an established and followed practice, since the amount of maintenance is determined in each individual case.[36]

However, the SCL has not categorically refused to link maintenance amounts with the minimal salary in its rulings. For example, the court found that maintenance lower than what is necessary to satisfy a child's basic needs may be granted in exceptional cases, where parents, despite their honest efforts, have no financial capacity to do so.

3 Parents in a Difficult Financial Situation

Under normal circumstances, the fact that parents are in a *difficult* financial situation is considered a reason to award a smaller amount of maintenance, which should be no less than the basic social benefit in the state (hereinafter BSB; since 1 January 2015 the BSB amount is 38 EUR per month). Lithuanian doctrine suggests that the minimum amount of maintenance should correspond to 1.5 BSB, to be provided by the State if a child fails to receive maintenance from his/her father/mother.[37] If a child's interests are considered as a priority, it is difficult to imagine how such an amount could sufficiently meet a child's needs.

Having analysed the jurisprudence, we may conclude that parents' financial situation may be regarded as *difficult* in the following cases: due to objective reasons; due to parents' negligence; or due to parents' unfair practices. These cases require the court to deal with a complex issue: how to meet a child's basic needs and maintain social justice. In cases when parents are in a difficult situation due to their negligent behaviour (drinking, prodigal expenditure of assets, etc.), courts do not consider this as a valid reason to reduce

34 Ruling of SCL of 3 February 2016 in Civil Case No. 3K-3-16-706/2016.
35 Ruling of SCL of 8 April 2016 in Civil Case No. 3K-3-209-916/2016.
36 Ruling of SCL of 3 February 2016 in Civil Case No. 3K-3-16-706/2016.
37 Kudinavičiūtė-Michailovienė & Vėgelienė, op cit, n. 27, p. 9.

the amount of maintenance. Sometimes the parents seem clearly to be acting dishonestly, such as by hiding their actual financial situation or deliberately refraining from earning a higher income. Their actual financial situation is often concealed by forged certificates, deliberately giving away assets as gifts, and taking other measures to devalue their financial situation. In cases when the actual financial situation of parents raises reasonable doubts, the court awards maintenance by making an assessment for the benefit of the child's interests, i.e. by assuming that the parents' financial situation allows the award of a sum of maintenance to ensure the child's basic needs.[38] In this way, the child's interests and the right to receive fair maintenance are protected. In the authors' opinion, in cases when parents deliberately avoid finding a better-paid job based on their education or training, it would be expedient to apply the abovementioned imputed income estimation method (when parents' income is calculated based not on actual income, but potential income, considering their education, professional training, age, and health),[39] to prevent abusive practices. Of course, this method should be applied with caution, taking into account the existing ratio of supply and demand of the skilled labour force, and the subjective situation of the child maintenance debtor.

4 The Problem of Children who are Relocated Abroad

Another problem related to determination of the amount of maintenance is encountered when a child's place of residence is with a parent who lives abroad, where living costs are greater than in Lithuania. The jurisprudence adopts the following rule:

> when a child departs to a foreign country where the cost of living is higher in comparison to Lithuania in order to live there at the initiative of one of the parents, in that case the parent staying to live in Lithuania should not be obliged to assume any resulting increase in costs incurred on account of meeting the child's needs. A respective part of increased costs required for meeting a child's needs due to his/her departure to a foreign country for residence purposes shall be assumed by the parent who initiated the child's departure from Lithuania, unless the criterion of the financial situation of the parents would justify a different decision.[40]

38 Ruling of SCL of 10 November 2009 in Civil Case No. 3K-3-495/2009.

39 Parents' duty to provide maintenance to the child is imperative, and failure to comply may not be justified by reason of earning minimum income. The jurisprudence of the Supreme Court acknowledges that evaluation of each parent's financial situation in awarding maintenance "shall include evaluation of measures he/she has taken in order to receive income corresponding to his/her age and the parent's professional potential." Ruling of SCL of 21 October 2013 in Civil Case No. 3K-3-491/2013; Ruling of SCL of 22 February 2018 in Civil Case No. e3K-3-70-969/2018

40 Ruling of SCL of 8 April 2015 in Civil Case No. 3K-3-195-915/2015.

This means that, if a child is taken to a foreign country for residence purposes based on parents' mutual agreement, both parents knowingly assume the burden of increased costs, whereas if one of the parents does not approve the child's residence in a foreign country, the parent who initiates the child's departure to a foreign country for residence purposes must take on a certain part of the increased costs in meeting the child's needs.

On a related issue, there is no unanimous opinion of courts on who should bear the financial burden of establishing and maintaining communication between the child and the parent with whom he/she does not primarily live when the parents reside in different countries.[41] The latest jurisprudence of the Supreme Court provides that children who have contact with another parent under a court-ordered regime usually do not stay with that parent (referred to here as the non-resident parent) permanently (they are together a few days per week or during holidays). Moreover, they are already provided with clothes and personal belongings for the daily life and basic needs, therefore the expenses incurred in relation to the child by the non-resident parent cannot be assessed exclusively as being proportionate to the time that the child spends with this parent. When the maintenance is adjudged from the non-resident parent, the amount of maintenance awarded is intended to partly cover the needs of the child without associating them with the time spent with that or another parent.[42]

II Peculiarities in the Determination of the Form of Maintenance

Both Lithuanian and foreign legal systems provide that establishing the material conditions for physical and social growth and development of the child is dependent on the amount and form of maintenance. The court, in awarding maintenance, shall take into consideration the child's needs, age, health condition, talents, interests and shall select such an amount and form of maintenance that would best meet the child's interests. We have discussed the criterion of the amount of maintenance in the previous section, and now turn to its form.

Article 3.196 of the CC establishes that maintenance shall be awarded in (usually) one of the following *forms*: (1) periodical benefits paid on a monthly basis, (2) a specific sum of money, or (3) assets. Each of these forms of maintenance must be evaluated in light of the specific circumstances of the case, which shall help determine the best way to ensure maintenance. In order to determine the disadvantages and advantages of each form, we will discuss them individually.

---

41 Ruling of SCL of 27 May 2010 in Civil Case No. 3K-3-243/2010; Ruling of SCL of 19 December 2011 in Civil Case No. 3K-3-528/2011; Ruling of SCL of 29 May 2014 in Civil Case No. 3K-3-308/2014, etc.

42 Ruling of SCL of 19 September in Civil Case No. 3K-3-393/2014.

A Monthly Periodical Payments

Having analysed the national jurisprudence, we may claim that the most common form of awarding maintenance and the best way to ensure the child's interests is *periodical benefits paid monthly*. This form of maintenance is consistent with a child's need to receive steady maintenance. Periodical payment is the best option when the child's parent has regular income (salary, pension, benefits, etc.). The CC establishes a general rule that maintenance awarded in the form of periodical benefits shall be subject to indexing under the procedure established by the Government, taking inflation into account.[43] Following approval of the resolution by the Government in 2008,[44] maintenance debtors became obliged to index the awarded amounts of maintenance, by recalculating the periodical benefits in order to fully or partially compensate for income lost as a result of increased consumer prices; periodical benefits are indexed by comparing the consumer price index of December of the previous year and the year before, which is calculated and made public by the Department of Statistics of Lithuania. But while the advantage of maintenance awarded in the form of periodical benefits is regular receipt of maintenance of a set amount, whereas a disadvantage of this form is that in the event of the debtor's insolvency, the child might not receive any maintenance whatsoever.

B A Fixed Lump Sum

Maintenance in the form of a *specific sum of money* is available in cases when this is possible considering the financial situation of the parent who is obliged to provide maintenance, particularly when this is expedient in order to protect the child's right to maintenance from the potential insolvency of the child's parent. Maintenance in the form of a specific sum of money is usually awarded where there is a real risk of the maintenance debtor going insolvent, or when extra maintenance costs (for example, in relation to additional hobbies, holiday expenses) are incurred. The total amount of maintenance is calculated by multiplying the amount of one-month maintenance by the number of months until the child attains his/her majority. For instance, if the amount of maintenance needed for the child is EUR 300 per month, and the child turned 16 on 01-Jan-2015, this means that two years (24 months) remain until he/she attains majority on 01-Jan-2017; so the maintenance to be awarded would amount to EUR 7 200 (EUR 300 x 24 months). The main advantage of maintenance in the form of a specific sum of money is that the child receives maintenance at once and is protected from the debtor's insolvency, whereas the disadvantages include

43 CC, article 3.208.

44 Resolution of the Government of the Republic of Lithuania, 'On Approval of the Description of the Procedure Applicable to Indexing of the Amount of Maintenance Awarded in the Form of Periodic Benefits and Compensation of Damages' of 9 July 2008, *Valstybės Žinios [Official Gazette]*, No. 684.

the impact of inflation on meeting the child's needs in future (as the lump sum cannot be index-linked), and the need to rely on the integrity of the child's legal representative in using the awarded sum for meeting the child's needs.

C Maintenance in the Form of Assets

Awarding of a certain part of the parent's *assets* to the child by transferring the title of ownership is possible in cases when the parent owns assets, and such assets could be used or realized to generate maintenance for the child, or to meet the child's needs in other ways.[45] Maintenance in the form of assets is awarded in exceptional cases, as provision is usually made to meet daily, current needs of the dependent minor child. Whenever delivering a decision whether to award maintenance in the form of assets, the court evaluates the child's interests, the type of the assets (asset maintenance costs, asset liquidity) and the parent's capacity to provide this form of maintenance (the parent's indebtedness and ability to manage the awarded assets). The Lithuanian jurisprudence specifies that:

> asset transfer to children means that children shall become owners, whereas the father of the children shall lose a part of the assets. The children shall assume obligations as the owners of the assets (to pay taxes associated with the assets, to have assets needed for maintenance, upkeep thereof, etc.), therefore assets must be transferred upon making detailed considerations, whether it was actually beneficial for the children to receive the assets, considering the resulting new duties. On the other hand, as the parent loses [his/her] assets or a part thereof, it is also necessary to take into consideration, if this did not constitute an excessive violation of his/her rights.[46]

The essential advantage of awarding maintenance in the form of assets is long-term and reliable assurance of the child's needs, because there are two ways of using assets: renting it and receiving regular income from it; or realizing the assets (selling them) and obtaining a specific amount of money. However, this form of maintenance has disadvantages as well: there is always a risk that awarding maintenance in the form of assets would require additional funds to pay for maintenance of these assets. The court has discretion to choose a form of maintenance which is best for the child's interests in a specific case. Therefore, the court must evaluate the compatibility of awarding maintenance in the form of assets with the child's interests. For instance, when the court determines that the income received

45 Ruling of the Supreme Court of Lithuania of 15 December 2011 in Civil Case No. 3K-3-513/2011.
46 Ruling of the Supreme Court of Lithuania of 21 October 2013 in Civil Case No. 3K-3-491/2013.

by the parent will be insufficient to meet the maintenance obligation, maintenance in other forms may be awarded, as a lump-sum, real estate or movable property.

In practice, cases occur in which maintenance for a child in the form of assets is claimed for a child who does not live in Lithuania.[47] In one such case, the Court of Cassation stated that a better way to meet the interests of minor children who live in a foreign country is maintenance provided in the form of periodical benefits, rather than real estate located in Lithuania, so that their needs could be met promptly.

Lastly, we should mention the case of *Koturenka v. Lithuania*[48] which prompted discussion about awarding assets as maintenance. In 2004, the applicant's wife departed from Lithuania to Germany and took their two children to Germany with the applicant's consent. A year later, the applicant's wife filed a claim in the Lithuanian court for divorce. In May 2007, Vilnius City First District Court decided to dissolve their marriage and found the applicant guilty in relation to breakdown of the marriage. On the grounds of the best interests of the children, it determined that the children's residence should be with the applicant's wife, and awarded maintenance for the two children from the claimant in the form of an apartment owned by him. The Vilnius Regional Court upheld that decision. The applicant lodged a cassation appeal with the Supreme Court arguing that the decision to award his apartment as a form of maintenance was unjustified. However the SCL refused to examine the appeal on the ground that it raised no important legal questions.[49]

The applicant complained to the European Court of Human Rights under Article 1 of Protocol No. 1 to the Convention about the domestic courts' decision to award his apartment as a form of maintenance for his two children. He objected that the apartment was his "only personal property" and argued that an order for regular maintenance payments would better protect his children's interests. The claimant also argued that, since the national courts had failed to analyse his wife's financial situation and not required proof of the children's needs, they had failed to ensure a proportionate distribution of the children's maintenance requirements between both parents.

In assessing the argument under Article 1 of Protocol No. 1, the ECtHR established that the deprivation of property was implemented (1) in accordance with the law (as the maintenance was determined in accordance with the provisions of the CC and the SCL's jurisprudence) and (2) in the public interest (the purpose of interfering in the claimant's titles of ownership was provision of maintenance to two minor children). Finally, (3) the ECtHR concluded that the measure applied by the State was also proportionate, achieving

47 In Ruling of SCL of 18 January 2010 in Civil Case No. 3K-3-49/2010, the essential dispute between the parties involved the form of maintenance for two juvenile children. The children's mother asked for the court to award maintenance to two daughters in the form of real estate, i.e. a three-room apartment owned by the defendant by the title of personal ownership.

48 *Koturenka v Lithuania* (Application No. 10646/08), available at http://hudoc.echr.coe.int/eng?i=001-158242.

49 http://lrv-atstovas-eztt.lt/naujienos/teismas-paskelbe-nutarima-kuriuo-peticija-koturenka-pries-lietuva-pripazinta-nepriimtina.

a fair balance between the claimant's rights and community interests. On this issue, the ECtHR noted that the Lithuanian courts had comprehensively analysed both children's needs in their country of residence, as well as the financial situation of both parents. The court noted that the applicant had conceded that his income was limited, allowing him to provide maintenance of only LTL 200 (EUR 58) per month per child, and that the domestic courts had held that this was "clearly insufficient to meet the children's daily needs in Germany", such that awarding the property by way of maintenance was "the only available option" to meet the applicant's maintenance obligation. The Court also took into account the domestic court's finding that even having allocated the apartment to the children as maintenance, the mother "continued to bear a bigger financial burden in the upbringing of their children".[50] Moreover, since the applicant did not live in the apartment, he had not been deprived of his home. In light of all this, the application was declared inadmissible as manifestly ill-founded: the Lithuanian courts' decision had fairly balanced the applicant's rights with the general interests of the community.

The case *Koturenka v. Lithuania* provides a unique precedent in Lithuania, wherein a person challenged before the ECHR the form of maintenance that had been selected, having regard to both the child's best interest and the inviolability of the maintenance-debtor's property rights. National courts had to seek to balance those two interests. Although the Civil Code does not prescribe any hierarchy between the different forms of maintenance that may be used (they are merely presented as alternatives), maintenance in the form of assets should be regarded as an extreme maintenance obligation for two reasons. First, because if assets are allocated to the child by way of maintenance, the debtor-parent's maintenance obligations are deemed to be completed, which precludes any further maintenance claims (except expenses related to the child's health care) during the child's minority (up to the age of 18). This contrasts with regular maintenance payments which can be reduced or increased through later court proceedings. Secondly, the parent who becomes responsible for the administration of the child's property is charged with a huge responsibility to use those assets properly for the fulfilment of the child's needs up to his/her maturity. That parent must manage those assets wisely to ensure that, whether by selling or leasing them, they generate sufficient funds for the child up to the age of maturity.

III Conclusions

In 2017, the number of cases involving maintenance claims in the courts of the first instance was 5979 (in 2016 – 6415 cases, in 2015 – 7185 cases, 2014 -7775 cases, in 2013- 8396

50 Ibid, para. 29.

cases).[51] The number of cases that reach court does not necessarily imply that no maintenance had been provided before the court was involved; the appeal to the court may have been intended to bring legal clarity that can only be provided by the court decision. However, this does not deny the fact that most such cases are launched when parents are unable to reach agreement about the amount or form of child maintenance. A recent survey of the maintenance cases at the district courts of Lithuania's 5 major cities suggests that the average size of maintenance per child was EUR 163.77 in the period of 1 January – 31 June, 2018.[52]

Systematic application of the criteria for determining child maintenance in Lithuania is determined by the priority principle of protection of child's rights and interests, which is established in paragraph 1 of article 3.3 of the CC of the Republic of Lithuania and paragraph 1 of article 3 of the UN Convention on the Rights of the Child, which uphold this principle as one of the most important sureties for securing a child's rights. This means that in passing and applying laws, or dealing with issues not governed by legislation, it is always necessary to evaluate decisions or actions in respect of a child and ensure that the child's rights and interests are protected. This principle has been given exceptional status by the fact that, when dealing with child maintenance issues, courts are required to take into account the child's interests and needs (articles 3.192 – 3.208 of the CC). This means that all doubts regarding award of maintenance, determination of the amount and form thereof must be evaluated for the benefit of the child's interests, and assets owned by children, including maintenance, must be managed and used exclusively for the child's interests. This standpoint is also reflected by the provision established in the article 3.203 of the CC.

As the system of "balancing needs and opportunities" for determining child maintenance awards prevails in the Lithuanian legal system, *the child's needs and the parents' financial situation* are regarded as the essential criteria for awarding maintenance. In order to establish a reasonable and fair amount of maintenance, it is necessary to attain *a balance* between a child's rights and the parents' financial situation. When assessing the parties' financial status, the court has to evaluate not only parents' existing possessions and income, but also the action that mother and father has taken to ensure income commensurate with his or her age and professional capabilities, which could be used to provide maintenance for their children.

---

51 Report on the Hearing of Civil Cases (1st Instance Court). https://www.teismai.lt/en/courts/statistics/654. The dropping number of cases may reflect various demographic changes: in the total population size, divorce and birth rates: see generally *Statistical year book of Lithuania, 2018. Vilnius: Statistics Lithuania,* available at https://osp.stat.gov.lt/en/statistikos-leidiniu-katalogas?eventId=177985.

52 I. Kudinavičiūtė-Michailovienė, 'Establishing the size of child's maintenance in the Lithuanian Case Law', *International Comparative Jurisprudence*, forthcoming.

Ongoing social changes (such as the growing number of families with one parent living abroad) require a new approach and adaptation of legal norms to new phenomena. In awarding maintenance, courts should take into consideration not only well-established criteria, such as the child's needs and parents' financial situation, but also the state of communication between parents and children, as well as modifying the amount of maintenance in cases of residence in different countries, by establishing specific conditions regarding distribution of the amount of maintenance between parents (including extra costs incurred in relation to communications).

The purpose of maintenance is to fulfil the child's daily needs. The amount of maintenance awarded to a minor child by a court decision does not mean that parents may not provide additional maintenance to the child at their own accord, because taking into consideration child's abilities and wishes, he/she must also be provided with material means to participate in various extra-curricular activities, sports and cultural events, to attend theatres, concerts, children's holiday camps, and be supplied with various material for development of his/her talents, for playing, etc. Such parents' behaviour would be consistent with the priority principle of protection and defence of children's rights and interests as established in paragraph 1 of article 3.3 of the CC, as well as the principle of good morals.

Marital Agreements: What's Love Got to Do with it? Challenges and Possibilities of the *Ex Contractu* Conformation of the Patrimonial Effects of Marriage

Rute Teixeira Pedro[*]

> *"[...] I wish there was a treaty Between your love and mine"*
> Treaty,
> Leonard Cohen

I Introduction

This chapter addresses marital agreements as a specific manifestation of private autonomy. The departure point for discussion is the traditional obstacles to acceptance of the legal relevance of private autonomy in the family context (Section II). But the widely-known movement of "contractualisation of family law"[1] (Section III) sets the scene for a different approach to the subject. Discussion of this topic is especially relevant in Portugal, where the immutability principle still applies to prenuptial agreements,[2] under article 1714 of the Civil Code[3] (Section IV).

---

* Assistant Professor, Law Faculty of the University of Porto, Portugal. Researcher at *Centro de Investigação Jurídico-Económica* (CIJE) of the University of Porto, Portugal.

1 This expression is inspired by Maine's characterization of the progressive movement "from Status to Contract": H.J.S. Maine, *Ancient Law. Its connection with the early History of society and its relation to Modern ideas* (originally published 1866), New Jersey, Transaction Publishers, 2002, p. 170. This expression is regularly used to describe the late 20th century's accentuation of that tendency: e.g. as a motto for the reflections in D. Fenouillet & P. De Vareilles-Sommières (dir.), *La contractualisation de la famille*, Paris, Economica, 2001; and in the title of F. Swennen (Ed.), *Contractualisation of Family Law - Global Perspectives*, Cham/Heidelberg/New York/Dordrecht/London, Springer, 2015.

2 Despite academic discussion and lack of unanimity in case law regarding the precise scope of this principle, it is undisputed that the immutability principle means that the marital property regime cannot be changed during marriage, whether it is chosen by the spouses in a prenuptial agreement, the default regime or a mandatory, legally- imposed regime. For further observations, see Section IV.

3 Hereafter the Portuguese Civil Code will be referred to as "PCC", and references to particular articles without reference to the law to which it belongs, refer to articles of the PCC as it is in force at the time of writing, in 2018.

In this reflection on the legal nature of, and the regime applicable, to matrimonial agreements[4] the family context in which they arise must be considered. The fact that matrimonial agreements cover family relationships explains in many ways why the application of an *ius singulare* (a law specific to this context) is needed. This special legal framework often reduces parties' freedom to stipulate their own terms and deviates from the general regime applicable to contracts (Section V).

This reflection considers not only agreements concluded before the wedding, but also agreements concluded during the marriage designed to govern the effects of marriage or the consequences of an actual or anticipated divorce. This chapter only considers the economic effects of marriage.[5]

II The Traditional Obstacles to the Emergence of Agreements as a Contractual Model to Govern the Effects of Marriage

Traditionally, private autonomy had only narrow scope to operate in relation to the effects of marriage, even when marriage was recognized as a contract.[6] Tight restrictions restrained spouses' freedom to stipulate the rules that should apply to their marriage or to its dissolution in the event of divorce (when the indissolubility of marriage was abolished).[7]

The acceptance of prenuptial agreements to define the property regime that should apply to the marital relationship was an exceptional and unique expression of private autonomy regarding the legal effects of marriage, as the principle of immutability of prenuptial agreements commonly applied, preventing the modification or revocation of those agreements during marriage.

As a consequence, despite being based upon a legally relevant act formed by the consensus of two parties (spouses),[8] marriage was mainly governed by mandatory legal rules. Additionally, there were several legal obstacles to concluding legally binding agreements regarding the effects of marriage, four of which are considered in the following paragraphs.

4 For earlier work on marital agreements by the author, see R. Teixeira Pedro, *Convenções Matrimoniais. A autonomia privada na conformação dos efeitos patrimoniais do casamento*, Coimbra, Almedina, 2018.

5 The distinction between the law of the person ("*Personenrecht*") and property law ("*Vermögensrecht*") is common within family law, and has developed particularly regarding matrimonial law ("*Eherecht*"). Despite this distinction, the personal relationship inevitably influences the economic effects of marriage, so the influence of the personal relationship cannot be disregarded when the regime governing the economic effects of marriage is shaped: see O. Von Gierke, *Familienrecht, Deutsches Privatrecht*, Volume 4 (originally published 1895), Berlin, Duncker & Humblot, 2010, pp. 6-7.

6 In Portuguese law, marriage is considered to be a contract: article 1577, "marriage is the contract entered into between two persons intending to form a family through full communion of life".

7 For further observations and additional bibliography, see Teixeira Pedro, op cit, n. 4, pp. 39-104.

8 This consensus – which was constitutive of the marriage – was, in principle, definitive and irrevocable, as divorce was either not accepted or accepted only in particularly limited situations.

Firstly, the role that law played in the regulation of marriage was conditioned by the extra-juridical nature of marriage and by the confluence of multiple normative systems (ethical, religious, moral) governing family and marital relationships. In consequence, legal intervention was marginal[9] and the law's coercive effect was applied only in certain moments and with clearly defined aims. Thus, the law merely performed the function of reinforcing the normativity that transcended it, when it seemed necessary and convenient. In this context, apart from prenuptial agreements, agreements between spouses would belong to a space outside the legal citadel and would hold no binding force.

Secondly, the institutional aspect of marriage was prominent, which accounted for some essential characteristics of the applicable legal regime, namely its mandatory character and the impossibility of renunciation by the spouses. There was an aspect of marriage that was greater than the sum of the individuals such that communitarian interests prevailed over the individual interests of the spouses. Consequently, they could not, even when agreed, modify the effects of the relationship, or even put an end to it, by mere agreement.[10]

Thirdly, the structural difference between spouses – the inequality between men and women – was a major obstacle to the autonomous regulation of marriage. The essence of the contract, as *lex privata*, demands that the parties who enter into it are equals. The equality of spouses was not recognized by law until the 20th century. As a consequence, there were no grounds for contractual regulation of the marital relationship.

Fourthly, the personal component of marriage gives rise to a difficulty in reconciling the need to recognise the freedom of each spouse with the "*pacta sunt servanda*" paradigm that characterizes a contract. Indeed, each individual's right to free development of personality demands that each spouse should be permitted to reconsider his/her decisions within the personal sphere. Such freedom, however, has the potential to undermine the binding force of agreements of spouses.[11]

These obstacles gave rise to a set of legal solutions regarding legally binding agreements within marital relationships: either they were rejected or they were accepted only under special conditions. In the latter case, the special nature of those agreements was stressed, leading to the application of a special regime that deviated from the regime applicable to contracts in general. Sometimes, agreements were accepted under the principle of *numerus clausus* or with strict time limitations. Frequently, only agreements concluded before the

---

9 Italian author A.C. Jemolo adopts a very expressive formulation: that the sea of the law can do no more than touch the island that is the family (*"la famiglia appare sempre, [...], come un'isola ce il mare del diritto può lambire, ma lambire soltanto"*). "La famiglia e il diritto", *in Pagine sparse di diritto e storiografia*, scelte e ordinate da L. Scavo Lombardo, Milan, Giuffrè, 1957, p. 241.

10 On the institutional character of marriage, see G. Renard, *La Théorie de l'institution*, Paris, Librairie du Recueil Sirey, 1930, pp. 105-47: "The family is an institution – the first of the institutions – and marriage is its founding act" (*"La famille est une institution – la première des institutions – et le mariage en est l'acte de fondation"*), p. 124.

11 This obstacle still plays a significant role and demands a special approach by the law: see Section V.

celebration of marriage were accepted as being binding:[12] that was so when pre-nuptiality and immutability principles applied.

III The Trend towards the "Contractualisation of Family Law" and the Expansion of the Concept of Marital Agreements

In the second half of the twentieth century, there was a process of deinstitutionalization of the family. This phenomenon occurred in both practice and law: in relation to the former, significant social changes arose as a consequence of an array of economic, demographic, and political factors; and important amendments to the legal system also occurred. Reciprocal influence between those changes and amendments were noticed.[13]

On the legal level, the process of "*constitutionalization*" of family law was of paramount importance. Indeed, the epicentre of legal change regarding marriage (and the family) was located at the constitutional level. Constitutions in several jurisdictions expressly enshrined the principle of equality between men and women and extended it to marriage.[14] New provisions emphasized the corollaries of freedom and autonomy. The right to free development of personality has played an important role in setting a new tone for the legal approach to personal relationships.

As a consequence, a "personalist" conception of the family emerged and a subjectivist revolution happened within the family. There was an increased attention to the position of the individuals within marriage and as a consequence the model of subjectivity of family positions changed: the model grounded in "status" was gradually replaced by a model grounded in "rights". Central to that replacement was the disappearance – at least, at the legal level – of the structural asymmetry in, and elimination of, the legal assignment of *a priori* designated roles within the family based on a particular view of the wellbeing of the family. Consequently, family relations are also conceived of as a field of tension between individuals' rights ("*Spannungsfeld der Rechte*"),[15] as happens in other fields of private law.

12 Prenuptial agreements were envisaged as the "economic constitutional chart" of the household ("*charte pecuniaire du ménage*"): P. Malaurie & L. Aynes, *Les régimes matrimoniaux*, 4th ed., Paris, LGDG Lextenso Éditions, 2013, p. 83.

13 About this "double deinstitutionalization of the family" with many bibliographical references, see Teixeira Pedro, op cit, n. 4, pp. 105-220.

14 Under the Constitution of the Portuguese Republic, article 13, n. 1 generally proclaims the principle of equality ("All citizens possess the same social dignity and are equal before the law"). The same principle receives special attention in article 36 concerning family – e.g. n. 1: "everyone has the right to form a family and to marry under conditions of full equality"; n. 3: "Spouses have equal rights and duties in relation to their civil and political capacity and to the maintenance and education of their children"; and finally, n. 4: "children born outside wedlock may not be the object of any discrimination for that reason, and neither the law, nor official departments or services may employ discriminatory terms in relation to filiation".

15 J. Gernhuber & D. Coester-Waltjen, *Familienrecht*, 6th ed., Munich, Beck, 2010, p. 31.

Furthermore, there was a clear emergence of two hemispheres in family law:[16] on one side, relations between parents and children and other vulnerable persons – where the need for special protection existed and where the general private law framework did not provide enough protection; and on the other side, relations between adults, where freedom and equality set a new tone for legal solutions.

Within the field of adult relationships, the conjugation of equality and freedom led to the eruption of a new marital legal order with some major consequences. Firstly, the conjugal legal bond became more fragile, as significant amendments lessened the conditions necessary to obtain a divorce decree. Under the "no-fault divorce" model, divorce was grounded on "the irretrievable breakdown of marriage", dissolution of the marriage no longer depending on a spouse's fault. Furthermore, divorce by mutual consent was accepted in certain circumstances, such that the agreement of the spouses was sufficient grounds to dissolve the marriage. But logically, it might be said, if they have the power to put an end to the relationship, they also have the power to shape its effects. The promotion of autonomy within the family thus led to the acceptance of legally binding agreements/contracts within the family.[17]

"From Status to Contract" is the well-known expression coined by Maine[18] to refer to this reality. As a key expression of this phenomenon of contractualization of family law, agreement became an important model for reaching legal solutions within marital relationships. Consequently, marital agreements came into the limelight and their scope significantly broadened, as is clear from the evolution in several legal systems.[19]

In Germany, the narrow notion of "*Eheverträge*" ("marital contracts") derived from § 1408 of the German Civil Code (BGB) was gradually replaced by the notion of "*Eheverträge*" in a broad and functional sense (also known as "*Ehevereinbarungen*", i.e. "marital agree-

16 The movement "from partners to parents" focused on children's well-being: J. Carbone, *From Parents to Partners: the second revolution in family law*, New York, Columbia University Press, 2000, especially pp. 133ff.

17 The personalist notion of the family also explains the emergence and multiplication in recent decades of compensation claims grounded on the lack of performance or imperfect performance of family duties. At the same time that fault is being removed from the law of divorce, compensation claims are emerging based on marital fault. On this trend, concerning breach of duties in marriage, see R. Teixeira Pedro, 'A responsabilidade Civil como (derradeira) manifestação de juridicidade dos deveres conjugais?, Anotação ao Acórdão do Supremo Tribunal de Justiça (2.ª Secção) de 12.5.2016, Proc. 2325/12.3TVLSB.L1.S1', *in Cadernos de Direito Privado* (ISSN: 1645-7242), n. 61, abril/junho de 2018, pp. 33ff.

18 Questions now arise as to whether this development took us beyond contract, namely to a "factual relationship" ("*Realbeziehung*"): I. Schwenzer, *Vom Status zur Realbeziehung. Familienrecht in Wandel*, Baden-Baden, Nomos Verlagsgesellschaft, 1987, pp. 31ff (especially pp. 62 - 64).

19 See further, Teixeira Pedro, op cit, n. 4, pp. 337-426.

ments"),[20] which encompasses the possibility of regulate many more aspects of the marital relationship than those expressly mentioned in that paragraph.[21]

In Spain, traditional "*Capitulaciones matrimoniales*" ("marital agreements") were shaped in accordance with articles 1325 ff of the Spanish Civil Code that referred only to the regulation of the economic regime of the marriage. Recently, many other manifestations of the "private autonomy of spouses" ("*autonomía de la voluntad de los cónyuges*") have been accepted:[22] e.g. "*Convenios reguladores*",[23] "*Convenios reguladores sin aprobación judicial*",[24] "*Acuerdos prematrimoniales en previsíon de ruptura*".[25] Increasing acceptance of self-regulation of the effects of marriage dissolution was decisive here.[26]

In Italian Law, there was a movement away from the "*Convenzioni Matrimoniali*" ("marital agreements") defined in articles 159 ff of the Italian Civil Code towards the broad acceptance of the "*negozialità*" (i.e. the possibility of negotiating) regarding marriage and the effects of its dissolution.[27] As a consequence, growing importance was given to "*accordi di indirizzo della vita familiare*" ("agreements concerning the orientation of family life"),

---

20 The deployment of either the word "*Vertrag*" ("Contract") or the word "*Vereinbarung*" ("Agreement") is relevant as it is linked with the substantial discussion of the nature, scope and legal force of the agreements.

21 See G. Langenfeld & L. Milzer, *Handbuch der Eheverträge und Scheidungs- vereinbarungen,* 7th ed., Munich, C. H. Beck, 2015, pp. 1ff.

22 See E.R. Trias, *Libertad y Familia*, Valencia, Tirant Lo Blanch, 2014 and J. Ferrer-Riba, 'Marital Agreements and Private Autonomy in Spain', *in* J. Scherpe (Ed.), *Marital Agreements and private Autonomy in Comparative Perspective*, Oxford and Portland, Oregon, Hart Publishing, 2012, especially pp. 357-358.

23 "*Convenios reguladores*" are agreements designed to shape the effects of a marital crisis (in case of separation or divorce, or when the marriage is void or voidable). They must meet the legal requirements demanded in articles 90ff of the Spanish Civil Code and must be submitted for judicial assessment. They will be approved by the judge unless harmful to the children or seriously damaging to one spouse (article 90 n. 2). See further A.J. Pérez Martín, *Pactos prematrimoniales. Capitulaciones Matrimoniales. Convenio Regulador. Procedimento Consensual, Tratado de Derecho de Familia,* Valladolid, Lex Nova, 2009, pp. 34ff.

24 These are the same type of agreement referred to in the previous note, but not approved by the judge: see ibid. It was originally considered that before judicial approval these agreements were not binding; but it is increasingly accepted that these agreements may be binding even without (or before) that approval.

25 These agreements regulate the effects of a separation or a divorce. Unlike the "*Convenios reguladores*" (see n. 23), they are concluded before marriage, and so before the marital crisis happens. See S.G. Lera, 'Acuerdos prematrimoniales sobre relaciones personales entre cónyuges y su ruptura: limites a la autonomia de la voluntad', *Anuario de Derecho Civil*, Vol. LXIV, No. III (July-September), 2011, p. 1042

26 The judicial decision of the Spanish *Tribunal Supremo* (Decision n. 217/2011, 31st March 2011, which was considered as a "ground-breaking" decision; see Ferrer-Riba, op cit, n. 22, pp. 350ff) and Catalonian innovative solutions have played an important role in the trend described in the text.

27 For a brief description of the evolution, see F.D. Busnelli & E. Bargelli, 'Convenzione Matrimoniale', *Enciclopedia del Diritto*, Aggiornamento IV, Varese, Giuffrè Editore, 2000, pp. 436-67. For further analysis see E. Russo, *Le Convenzioni matrimoniali. Il codice Civile Commentario. Artt. 159- 166 bis*, Fondato da Piero Schlesinger e diretto da Francesco Busnelli, Milão, Giuffrè Editore, 2004 and B. de Filippis, *Convenzioni Matrimoniali e contratti di convivenza*, Padova, CEDAM, 2014.

"*accordi non omologati*"[28] and "*accordi preventivi sugli effetti economici del divorzio*".[29] General rejection of agreements was replaced by a case-by-case evaluation, in which the idea of "*proporzionalità*" ("proportionality") plays an important role.[30]

In French Law, the movement has been neither as clear nor as broad. Even so, besides the "*contrat de mariage*" ("marital contract") as is regulated in articles 1387 ff of the French Civil Code), agreements governing "*l'entretien de la famille*" and "*la contribution aux charges du mariage*", i.e. "the contribution to family expenses" (article 114)[31] and "*conventions réglant les conséquences du divorce*", i.e. "agreements on the consequences of divorce" (article 230) are being gradually accepted. This more moderate evolution is explained by the existence of a principle of controlled mutability in France.

As far as English law is concerned, a "*presumption of enforcement*" of "*marital property agreements*"[32] was adopted in the 2010 decision of the Supreme Court in *Radmacher v Granatino.*[33] According to this presumption,

> the court should give effect to a nuptial agreement that is freely entered into by each party with a full appreciation of its implications unless in the circumstances prevailing [and the point of application on divorce] it would not be fair to hold the parties to the agreement.[34]

More particularly, the Court suggested that while it would generally be possible for parties by agreement to preclude application of the "sharing" principle (whereby certain property might usually be shared equally on divorce), it would often not be fair to exclude the "need" or "compensation" principles, which would permit adjustment of parties' property rights or payment of maintenance despite any agreement purporting to exclude such claims. Whilst parties' agreements could therefore not entirely exclude judicial intervention in relation to the financial effects of divorce, the *Radmacher* decision effectively gave spouses more potential to *limit* that intervention.

---

28 Like the Spanish "*Convenios reguladores sin aprobación judicial*", these agreements should be judicially approved, but were not (see n. 24).

29 Like the Spanish "*Acuerdos prematrimoniales en previsíon de ruptura*", these agreements regulate the effects of a separation or a divorce, but are concluded before the marital crisis happens (see n. 23).

30 As was stated in Decision of the *Corte Suprema di Cassazione* (Italian Supreme Court) n. 23713, 21 December 2012.

31 See F. Terré & D. Fenouillet, *Droit Civil. La famille*, 8th ed., Collection Précis droit privé, Paris, Dalloz-Sirey, 2011, pp. 151-3.

32 This presumption represents "quite a leap from the pre-existing position where the discretion of the court trumped any such private arrangement": L. Crowley, 'International and European Developments in Family Law 2013', *in* B. Atkin (Ed.), *International Survey of Family Law 2013*, Bristol, Family Law/Jordan Publishing, 2013, p. 25.

33 [2010] UKSC 42.

34 Ibid, para. 75.

The evolution in these legal systems reveals some important trends, which may be summed up as follows:

i. the abandonment of a radical conceptual framework in which contracts in the marital sphere were either rejected or accepted only with strict limitations;
ii. the enlargement of the space for the exercise of private autonomy, concerning not only the effects produced during marriage, but also the effects produced at the time of the dissolution of the relationship. Agreements encompass both the "physiology" of the relationship and its "pathology" and are no longer limited to choices concerning the economic regime of marriage *stricto sensu*;
iii. the removal of chronological limits: agreements are accepted whether they are concluded before or after the wedding;
iv. the prominence of judicial decisions that considerably altered the legality of agreements in the context of marriage, even when no statutory amendments had occurred;[35] and
v. the growing similarity of the legal regimes applicable to contracts in the marital field and to contracts in general, though distinctions remain.

As a consequence of this research, I concluded that marital agreements are characterised by three distinct perspectives: (1) from a subjective perspective – the contracting parties are two persons already married to each other or two persons who want to be bound by wedlock; (2) from a substantive or final perspective – the agreement directly or indirectly concerns the effects of the contract of marriage, especially the development and the "liquidation phase" of the spousal relationship; and (3) from an instrumental perspective – marital agreements find their *causa* in the future or past marriage celebration and their existence depends on the contracted or about-to-be-contracted marriage. The legal regime applicable to marital agreements should be developed bearing in mind these perspectives.

Nonetheless, in Portugal the evolution presented some particularities, described in next section.

IV The State of the Art in the Portuguese Legal System

In 1977, a major reform of the fourth book of the Portuguese Civil Code – dedicated to Family Law – took place in consequence of the entry into force of the new Constitution of the Portuguese Republic, enacted in 1976. The new Constitutional framework, in which

35 To illustrate the role played by Courts, see the decision of the German *Bundesverfassungsgericht* 6 February 2001 and 29 March 2001 and of the *Bundesgerichthof* (XII ZR 265/02) 11 February.2004; the decision of the Spanish Supreme Court (*Tribunal Supremo)* n. 217/2011 31 March 2011; the decision of the Italian Supreme Court (*Corte Suprema di Cassazione)* n. 23.713, 21 December 2012, and Constitutional Court (*Corte Costituzionale*) 27 June 1973, and finally the decision of the UK Supreme Court in *Radmacher (formerly Granatino) v Granatino* [2010] UKSC 42.

the principle of equality played an important role, including within the family, demanded significant amendments to the rules governing the family, which were introduced by Executive-Decree nº 496/77 dated 25 November. Other important reforms have occurred in the following four decades, in particular concerning divorce, which, at present, may result from the spouses' joint application when there is mutual consent, or may result from a unilateral request when there has been "the irretrievable breakdown of marriage" (article 1781 PCC).

Although significant changes occurred regarding the dissolution of marriage, the regime applicable to marital agreements remains largely unchanged. There has been neither legislative reform, nor leading judicial decisions. At present, in Portugal, three different kinds of agreements (not all of them classed as contracts) relating to the marital relationship are legally recognized: "prenuptial agreements" ("*Convenções Antenupciais*") regulated in articles 1710 ff PCC; "agreement concerning the orientation of family life" ("*Acordo sobre a orientação da vida familiar*") considered in article 1672; and "complementary divorce agreements" ("*Acordos complementares de divórcio*") referred to in article 1775.

As far as "prenuptial agreements" are concerned, they are envisaged as an accessory to the marriage contract, through which the economic regime governing the marriage is stipulated.[36] They are the privileged manifestation of the exercise of private autonomy in the marital sphere. There are, however, several limits on the exercise of autonomy: concerning the object of the agreement,[37] the moment of celebration of the "prenuptial agreement", and the possibility of post-nuptial modification. In fact, there is no possibility of modification, as the principle of immutability of both prenuptial agreements and the marital property regime still applies (articles 1712 and 1714, PCC). In consequence, the property regime cannot be changed during marriage, whether it is a regime chosen by the spouses, the default regime or a mandatorily imposed regime. Furthermore, according to

---

36 Before celebrating marriage, the yet-to-be spouses may conclude a "prenuptial agreement" and choose which property regime they want applied to their property relations in order to identify assets and define to whom they belong. If no valid prenuptial agreement is concluded, the community of acquired assets property regime (article 1717) applies. On marital property relations in Portuguese law see F. Pereira Coelho & G. De Oliveira, *Curso de Direito da Família, Tomo I, vol. I: Introdução. Direito Matrimonial,* 5th ed., Coimbra, Imprensa da Universidade de Coimbra, 2016, pp. 558-646; R.L. Xavier, *Limites à autonomia privada na disciplina das relações patrimoniais entre os cônjuges*, Almedina, 2000 and Teixeira Pedro, op cit, n. 4, and comments on articles 1698-1736, in A. Prata (Ed.), *Código Civil Anotado*, Vol. II, Coimbra, Almedina, 2017, pp. 592-646.

37 Some exceptions to the principle of freedom of stipulation aim to prevent marriage from simply becoming a legal device to attain economic benefits, to the detriment of other family members. That is the purpose of the provision inserted in article 1699, n. 2 in which the choice of a full community of property regime (or any other regime with broader community than the one provided by the default regime of community of acquired assets) is forbidden if at the time of the marriage one spouse already has descendants from a previous relationship. See also article 1720, n. 1, where the regime of separation of assets is mandatory (i) whenever a spouse marries over the age of 60; and (ii) whenever marriage is concluded without the spouses' legal ability to marry having been assessed (e.g. as regards age, lack of prohibited degrees, etc).

a broader understanding of this principle,[38] the conclusion by the spouses during marriage of any agreement between them that purports to change the qualification of assets (as common property or personal property of one spouse) is forbidden. The exercise of private autonomy by spouses is, thus, greatly reduced and, as will be argued below, without any valid reason.

"Agreement concerning the orientation of family life" ("*Acordo sobre a orientação da vida familiar*"), regarding the way family life will take place (where to live, how to divide family expenses and tasks, how to spend holidays, to have or not to have a child, number of children) is a significant consequence of the recognition of equality between the spouses (article 1671, 2 PCC). Indeed, the need for spousal agreement to define the major aspects of marital life gives rise to an additional marital duty:[39] the duty to search for a mutually-agreed orientation of family life. There is no specific form to be used in these agreements and mutual consent may be inferred from behaviour. Nonetheless, their contractual nature is not undisputed. It is argued that marital agreements should deviate from contracts owing to the need to recognise a significant "*ius variandi*" (i.e. the possibility to unilaterally modify or terminate the legal effects of the agreement) and the inability to enforce their specific performance in law.

Finally, legal recognition of "complementary divorce agreements" ("*Acordos complementares de divórcio*") is awarded upon divorce by mutual consent. In this kind of divorce, the spouses may present a joint application to the Civil Registrar, provided they also present agreements on certain issues, including the exercise of parental responsibilities for the child(ren), maintenance for the spouse who needs it, use of the family home, and care of any pets. The contractual nature of such agreements is controversial. Reinforcing the non-contractual nature of these agreements, it is argued that their legal enforcement depends not only on the free consent of both spouses, but also on the approval ("ratification") by a public entity – the "Registrar of Civil Registry" or the Court.

Apart from these three types of agreement expressly referred to in the law, the legal regime applicable to other agreements/contracts concluded by spouses before and after marriage is still strongly influenced by the traditional, hostile view of the exercise of private autonomy in the marital context. That perspective may lead to reliance upon the above-mentioned principle of immutability (article 1714 PCC), as well as the irrevocability of contractually-binding donations concluded with a legally relevant link with a future marriage (article 1758), and the free revocability *ad nutum* (i.e. on demand by one party

38 On the meaning and consequences of the principle of immutability of prenuptial agreements, see Pereira Coelho & De Oliveira, op cit, n. 36, pp. 581ff and Lobo Xavier, op cit, n. 36, pp. 233ff and 'Sociedades entre cônjuges. Sociedade de capitais, responsabilidade por dívidas sociais, código das sociedades comerciais, lei interpretativa', *Revista de Direito e de Estudos Sociais*, Ano XXXV, n. 1/2/3/4 (1993), pp. 254 and 255.

39 Article 1672, PCC, identifies five duties: fidelity, respect, cohabitation, (non-economic) cooperation, and (economic) assistance.

without the need to present a ground for the revocation) of donations between spouses (article 1759).

Despite providing an apparently broad scope for the parties to exercise private autonomy, strong limitations exist in Portugal and significant deviations from the common principles of contract law still apply.

V A Critical Perspective on the Portuguese *Status Quo* and a Proposal for Change

As a consequence of my research, with the decisive insights of comparative law, I cannot but express a negative view vis-à-vis the "*status quo*" of the Portuguese legal system, as it reflects an unjustifably hostile perspective towards the exercise of private autonomy within the marital relationship.

On one hand, there are no valid grounds for the application of the immutability principle. The traditional reasons upon which it was grounded no longer exist.[40] Nowadays, prenuptial agreements are the product of the mutual consent of spouses and consequently, it should be possible to change or terminate them if that is their will (either jointly or unilaterally if a legitimate justification is presented). Furthermore, spouses, being equal individuals under the law, may enter into agreements which ought to be accepted provided there are no reasonable doubts about the freedom with which the spouses entered the agreement. In fact, as is the case with other agreements, an *ad hoc* evaluation must take place in order to declare them invalid if a breach of any of the mandatory rules has taken place, namely those that aim to guarantee that the consent of both parties is freely given and informed. Moreover, the legitimate expectations of other individuals who had entered into contracts with the spouses would be protected, as the change of prenuptial agreements and applicable economic regime would produce only future legal effects (*ex nunc*) and after being recorded in the civil register. Finally, it is incongruous to prohibit a change of prenuptial agreements and economic regime of marriage during marriage when spouses may put an end to it by joint request; under the current system, spouses can dissolve the marriage, but cannot dissolve the economic regime applicable to marriage.[41] As a conse-

40 The principle of immutability was justified on three bases: (1) Prenuptial agreements constituted "family agreements" and consequently could not be changed by spouses after the foundation of the family, because the agreement transcended their will. (2) During marriage, it was said that there were good reasons to conclude that the consent of each spouse would not be free as it could be undermined by the other spouse's undue influence. (3) The immutability of the prenuptial agreements and the economic regime would protect other individuals who had entered into contracts with the spouses, as they would have legitimately expected that those prenuptial agreements / economic regime would apply. See Pereira Coelho & de Oliveira, op cit, n. 36, p. 582.

41 Sometimes, spouses do decide to divorce merely to end the marital property regime, even if they do not want to end their marital relationship. Such simulated divorces may cause damage to third parties.

quence, in terms of legal reform, I would endorse the revocation of the principle of immutability and in the meantime, under the existing law, I favour a strict interpretation of article 1714 PCC in order to narrow its scope.[42]

On the other hand, there are good reasons to accept spouses' exercise of private autonomy concerning the economic effects of marriage and divorce before and during the marriage. It enhances "individualized tailoring"[43] of the applicable regime and reduces conflict and so litigation. Besides, it is in accordance with the need for "planning" ("*Planungsdenken*") and "precautionary reasoning" ("*Vorsorgedenken*") in the field of private relations. Agreements represent "risk mitigating strategies" ("*die risikomindernden Strategien*"),[44] considering the exercise of "risky freedoms" ("*riskante Freiheiten*")[45] in the "liquid modernity",[46] and also within the family sphere (the possibility of the occurrence of divorce is a good example of that liquidity). Furthermore, attention must be paid to pluralism as a value protected by law. Indeed, the "polymorphism of marital life" ("*Polymorphismus des Ehelebens*") must be mirrored by a "polymorphic legal regime" ("*polymorphen Eherecht*").[47] Consequently, the heteronomous regulation of the marital relationship should be partially withdrawn and a bigger space for private autonomy should be recognized. The marital relationship should be a relationship that is primarily shaped by the spouses.[48]

However, while the possibility of exercising private autonomy within marriage should be the rule, some particularities must be taken into account.

Acceptance of the exercise of private autonomy in marriage does not eliminate the need for legal intervention, at both the procedural and the substantive levels. The danger

42 The scope of the principle of immutability, as enshrined in article 1714, n. 1 PCC, is highly controversial in Portugal. Portuguese scholars analysing this principle take two main approaches. On the narrower approach, which I support, this principle merely prohibits any change of marital property regime during marriage. Additional restrictions to the private autonomy of the spouses only apply where specific provision exists (e.g. article 1714(2) PCC, concerning the sales of goods contracts and participation in a company). Conversely, on the broader perspective, any change of qualification of assets (as common property or personal property of one spouse) following the conclusion of any agreement between the spouses during marriage is forbidden. On the meaning and consequences of the principle of immutability of prenuptial agreements, see references in n. 36.

43 I. Smith, 'The Law and Economics of Marriage Contracts', *Journal of Economic Surveys*, Vol. 17, No. 2, 2003, pp. 202-3.

44 E. Beck-Gernsheim, *Was kommt nach der Familie? Alte Leitbilder und neue Lebensformen*, 3th ed., Munich, C.H. Beck, 2010, p. 66 and pp. 72 ff.

45 U. Beck & E. Beck-Gernsheim (Eds.), *Riskante Freiheiten: Individualisierung in modernen Gesellschaften*, Frankfurt, Suhrkamp Verlag, 1994.

46 Z. Bauman, *Liquid Modernity*, Cambridge, Polity Press, 2003 and (especially regarding intimate relationships) *Liquid Love: On the Frailty of Human Bonds*, Cambridge, Polity Press, 2003.

47 J. Gernhuber, 'Die geordnete Ehe', *FamRZ* (*Zeitschrift für das gesamte Familienrecht mit Betreuungsrecht, Erbrecht, Verfahrensrecht, Öffentlichem Recht*), Vol. 3, 1979, p. 194, and for further developments, *Eherecht und Ehetypen*, Berlin/ New York, Walter de Gruyter, 1981.

48 Gernhuber expresses this idea, referring to marriage as "*geordnete Ehe*": op cit, n. 47 (first source), p. 12 and (second source) pp. 193ff, especially pp. 196-7.

of asymmetric distribution of power between spouses persists and demands paternalistic intervention to correct imbalances. This protective aim demands a type of revised paternalism. However, universally applicable, abstract protectionism defined by categories (for instance, gender, age, moment of celebration of the agreement and so on) and applied regardless of the actual need for protection should be replaced by proportional protectionism based on a case-by-case assessment of the actual need for protection. Thus, legal intervention limiting autonomy must be shaped in light of principle of proportionality.[49]

As a consequence, the exercise of private autonomy between spouses will be recognised, and the enforceability of agreements will be the rule, as it should be assumed that spouses are able to freely express their will and to assess what is in their best interests and in the best interests of the family. Procedural and substantive requirements should be met in order to guarantee freedom of consent and the fairness of the content of the agreement: some derived from general rules and other from special (family) rules. Restrictions should apply to safeguard protected rights and interests of the spouses (particularly of the vulnerable spouse).[50] Further, if needed in the case, various legal tools may be invoked, just as may occur in relation to any other contract concluded between two persons who are not married to each other. For instance, if one party lacks capacity at the moment of formation of the contract, or if there is any vice that affects contractual consent of one spouse – e.g. undue influence,[51] coercion,[52] mistake or misrepresentation[53] – legal mechanisms that are settled in statute law should be applied, demanding an individual assessment considering the specific conditions of the case, namely the family context. Such an approach would not generate uncertainty, as the protection is governed by strict rules that include a set of specific legal requirements to be met, regarding the procedure and the content of the agreement. In this sense, a radical, status-based and generalist restrictive perspective towards agreements between spouses would be replaced by a case-by-case and individualized perspective governed by the principle of proportionality that would limit spouses' private autonomy only when needed to protect them, and merely to the extent it is strictly necessary for the appropriate support of the spouse who needs protection.

Moreover, given the subject matter of marital agreements, the circumstances in which they are concluded and the long-lasting character of the marital relationship to which they are related, legal intervention and suitable safeguards are needed.[54]

Regarding the object of the agreements, there are mandatory effects of marital status which spouses cannot disregard and from which marital agreements cannot derogate. As

49 For additional observations, see Teixeira Pedro, op cit, n. 4, pp. 225-37.

50 For further observations about these "legal safeguards" see Teixeira Pedro, ibid, pp. 635-712.

51 Article 282 PCC.

52 Articles 255 and 256 PCC.

53 Article 254 PCC.

54 For further observations about these "legal safeguards", see Teixeira Pedro, op cit, n. 4, pp. 615-35 and 713-55.

a consequence, it is necessary to assess whether each aspect of the legal regime dealt with by marital agreements can be changed or excluded. In order to make such an assessment, teleological reasoning should be used and the protective aim of each legal solution ("*Schutzzweck der gesetzlichen Regelung*")[55] and its scope must be identified. For that purpose, the theory of the core of the legal regime ("*Kernbereichlehre*")[56] may play an important role.

Concerning the circumstances in which the agreement is concluded, account must be taken of the consequences of the existential closeness of the parties and the emotional context in which they are acting. Those factors may affect the spouses' freedom of will. Besides that, dependencies are generated over the course of the marital relationship. Marriage produces inequalities between the parties[57] that cannot be disregarded, especially when the marriage is dissolved. These circumstances require the intervention of a public authority (notary, registrar, judge) at the moment of the conclusion of some agreements to assess the actual freedom of the parties when they enter into some contracts (such as those regarding the economic regime of marriage).

Finally, the potentially long-lasting duration of the marital relationship cannot be neglected. Frequently, agreements are concluded a long time in advance of their anticipated effects (for example, preventive agreements for a future and hypothetical divorce). The well-proven lack of accurate "*risk-estimation faculties*"[58] may mean that the will of one or both spouses at the time the agreement was concluded was faulty, or that the contents are unfair in light of the circumstances existing at the relevant time. In this context, the "time-bomb" problem must be highlighted ("*Zeitbombencharakter*"), as within marriage, imbalance develops over the course of time, "as a consequence of the jointly practiced life".[59]

---

55 B. Dauner-Lieb, 'Reichweite und Grenzen der Privatautonomie im Ehevertragsrecht (Zugleich Vortrag vor der Kölner Juristischen Gesellschaft am 26. April 2001)', *AcP (Archiv für die civilistiche Praxis)*, Vol. 201, 2001, pp. 326ff, especially p. 331; and T. Fest, 'Regelungsinhalte von Eheverträgen und Grundlagen der Inhaltskontrolle', *in* H. Hager (Ed.), *Update Familienrecht*, Schriften zum Notarrecht: Band 38, Baden-Baden, Nomos Verlag, 2013, pp. 40 and 41.

56 This theory was applied by the German *Bundesverfassungsgericht* in its well-known decision (BGH XII ZR 265/02) dated 11 February 2004.

57 "Derivative dependency", using M.A. Fineman's expression (in 'Equality, Autonomy, and the Vulnerable Subject in Law and Politics', *in* M.A. Fineman & A. Grear (Eds.), *Vulnerability: Reflections on a new Ethical Foundation for Law and Politics*, Farnham, Ashgate, 2013, p. 18) or "marriage-related imbalances" to use the words of N. Dethloff, 'Contracting in family law: a European perspective', *in* K. Boele-Woelki, J. Miles & J. Scherpe (Eds.), *The future of family property in Europe*, Cambridge-Antwerp-Portland, Intersentia, 2011, pp. 90-1.

58 M.A. Eisenberg, 'The Limits of Cognition and the Limits of Contract', *Stanford Law Review*, Vol. 47, No. 2, Jan. 1995, p. 222.

59 "*die Ungleichgewichtslage entwickelt sich erst im Laufe der Zeit, als Konsequenz der gemeinsam praktizierten Lebensform*": Dauner-Lieb, op cit, n. 53, p. 321.

Consequently, attention must be given to fact that the course of the marriage and the vicissitudes that occur over time may affect the binding force of the agreement. The "*pacta sunt servanda*" principle cannot be applied strictly. A "*ius variandi*" (i.e. the possibility to unilaterally modify or terminate the legal effects of the agreement) which is wider than for contracts in general must be recognized. Sometimes, when the most intimate sphere of the individual is affected, there is the need for recognition of the possibility of unilateral disengagement *ad nutum* (i.e. on demand by one party without the need to present a ground for the revocation). Nonetheless, spouses are bound by behavioural duties to each other. Both must act in good faith and if they fail to comply with that standard of behaviour, a compensation claim[60] may be grounded on the failure to fulfil these duties, in order to protect mutual "trust, which is based on actual behaviour". ("*Vertrauensschutz, der sich an tatsächlichem Verhalten orientiert*").[61] For that reason, the intervention of a public authority (judge) at the moment the agreement is put into effect may be needed to assess the fairness of the agreement, in light of the change of circumstances since the spouses entered into the agreement.

VI Concluding Remarks

In the light of the movement of "contractualisation of family law" that is evident in several legal systems, the traditional obstacles to the acceptance of private autonomy within the family context have diminished in recent years.

A great contrast between the solutions adopted in the Portuguese legal system and the abovementioned trend is apparent. In Portugal, the manifestations of "contractualisation of family law" are still very weak.

This paper advocated a change in the Portuguese legal "status quo". As a kind of Copernican revolution in that legal system, the exercise of private autonomy regarding the economic effects of marriage should be accepted as a rule. Nevertheless, there remains a need for external examination of marital agreements, including the specificity of their object, the circumstances in which the contract was concluded and the length of the marriage to which they are related and changes that have occurred in the parties' circumstances in that time.

---

60 Frequently, legal enforcement of the agreement is not possible due to the personal implications of its content. In such a case, the protection of freedom opposes the coercive implementation of the agreement. As a consequence, claims grounded upon the civil liability regime may be a solution, and the spouse who does not comply with the commitment may have to compensate the other for the damage that he/she has suffered. On the application of civil liability within family relationships in general and spousal relationship in particular, see n. 17.

61 N. Dethloff, *Familienrecht, Ein Studienbuch*, 30th ed., Munich,Verlag C.H. Beck, 2012, p. 3.

Abstractly defined protectionism that exists regardless of the actual need for protection should be replaced by proportional protectionism based on a case-by-case assessment of the actual need for protection. External intervention must be shaped in the light of the principle of proportionality.

In short, the legal regime applicable to agreements concluded between the spouses should serve simultaneously to protect the autonomy of the spouses and to protect the spouses against the unfair effects of the exercise of their autonomy.[62]

62 Referring to mandatory rules, J. Scherpe says that those rules "protect autonomy" and "protect from autonomy": Introduction to J. Scherpe (Ed.), *Marital Agreements and private Autonomy in Comparative Perspective*, Oxford, Portland, Oregon, Hart Publishing, 2012, p. 2.

Evidence-Based and Politics-Driven: Comparing Child Support Law Evaluations Across Welfare-State Models

Elizabeth Stuart Perry[*]

I Introduction

How does child support law evolve today, specifically regarding the simultaneous influences of empirical research evidence and political factors on evaluations of the law? This paper analyzes this issue with comparative examples from one predominantly liberal-market-economy jurisdiction (California) and one more comprehensively social-welfare-insuring jurisdiction (Sweden).

The child-support-lawmaking life cycle is ongoing in many jurisdictions. This paper compares two recent reform processes, each entailing delegated expert evaluation then incremental legislative change. It presents examples of how *legislative intent to find reliable empirical evidence* about what reforms to child support laws would improve outcomes and solve known problems tends to *interact with political factors* and *conflicting legislative priorities* once recommendations are received—or even earlier, at the stage of focusing the evaluators on certain questions and types of evidence.

This chapter also observes how the differing welfare-state models in California and Sweden can be seen to affect the jurisdictions' responses to evidence-based recommendations for reforms to child support law. Swedish assumptions about a more comprehensive role for the state in ensuring that children have their financial needs met and American assumptions about a more limited role for the state lead to different child-support-reform preferences in these examples, even though the stated legislative intents for these child support laws do not differ markedly.

One set of conflicting priorities present in these (and many other) jurisdictions relates to how the respective child-support duties of parents and the state should be defined and enforced. Children have legal rights to sufficient financial support from their parents, *secondarily* guaranteed by the state, under the law in each of the two jurisdictions examined, and parents have *primary* responsibility to support their children to the extent of their abilities. The jurisdictions' legislatures have both stated desires to reduce state expenditure

* LL.D. candidate, Umeå University, Sweden.

on child-support administration, enforcement and social benefits to one-parent households by incentivizing parents only to approach the state for cash assistance if some enforcement of private child support legal obligations has been attempted. Both legislatures also have stated desires not to burden low-income payors unduly and to prioritize the best interests of the child.

The interactions between evidence and politics in the reform examples described appear to moderate not only which reform recommendations are implemented, but also which are requested or discouraged. Lawmakers do not act exclusively in accordance with the recommendations,[1] as might be expected if no other factors than the empirically-based reform priorities were involved. Recommended reforms are not implemented in full and in accordance with the evaluating experts' priorities. Instead, it appears lawmakers have chosen among reform recommendations based on factors including their own political preferences and financial and other constraints. Reforms that had been strongly recommended after earlier review processes, yet not implemented, were again recommended and this time implemented. Simple, cost-saving recommendations were adopted as well. More complicated or costly recommendations, and ones recommending further evaluation, were not implemented, at least not within a few years following the publications of the relevant reviews.

Legal researchers studying empirical evidence and proposing reforms to current laws may therefore want to consider two questions: is a reform proposal likely to be chosen for implementation in its current form, or can it be modified to make it more likely to be favored by the politicians?[2] Can the need for deeper, costlier reforms be communicated differently, acknowledging the pressures on the lawmakers from a welfare-state-model perspective, including society's attitudes on the role of governments and families?

---

1 I avoid making the claim that lawmakers never act exclusively in accordance with review recommendations, although such a conclusion may seem intuitive to some researchers familiar with these processes. The examples presented here are not statistically representative of all review and reform processes affecting child support in these jurisdictions. They are instead demonstrative of how the processes are structured and some results that can occur.

2 Legal scholars sometimes debate whether legal scholarship should venture beyond analysis of what the law "is" into what the law "should be", to effectuate, clarify or even improve its aims. In my view, because family law researchers are invited to make reform proposals, awareness of the utility of various types of reform proposals can assist them with that task. It is also appropriate for legal scholars to critique the fact that lawmakers often demur from using empirical evidence for political reasons, despite the law requiring its collection and use.

II Reform and the Child-Support-Lawmaking Life Cycle

Evaluation and reform of existing law is part of an evolutionary process that I term the child-support-lawmaking life cycle. Illustrated below as linear, it is actually cyclic, as laws are evaluated and reformed periodically over many years.

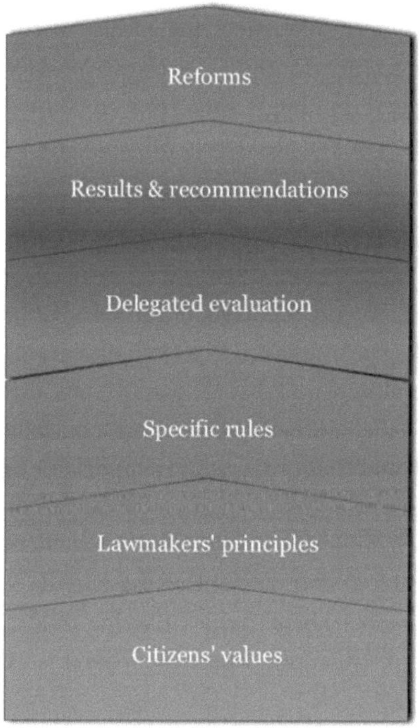

A Values and Beliefs

Society members' values, beliefs and existing customs on how to provide financially for children of parents not living together exist separately from but also in relation to current and earlier law.[3] At the "beginning" of the law-making process, at least theoretically and

3 One line of investigation by child support legal researchers examines how close to actual law are the public's intuitions of what the law should be. See e.g. I.M. Ellman, S.L. Braver & R.J. MacCoun, 'Abstract Principles and Concrete Cases in Intuitive Lawmaking', *Law and Human Behavior*, Vol. 36, No. 2, April 2012, pp. 96-108 and I.M. Ellman & S.L. Braver, 'Child Support and the Custodial Mother's Move or Remarriage: What Citizens Believe the Law Should Be', *Psychology, Public Policy and Law* (Amer. Psych. Assoc'n), Vol. 21, No. 2, 2015, pp. 145-160 (reporting on two of several child support rule public opinion studies).

historically, society members' and leaders' *values and beliefs* about how to provide financially for these children cause lawmakers to define certain *principles* they desire the legal rules to follow. Relevant to this step, researchers in law and legal sociology, among others, have studied public opinions on whether child support orders are needed, in what circumstances, and how much child support is necessary, desirable and fair. Hundreds of years of background culture concerning families, roles of men, women, children and more have contributed to the cacophony of values from which lawmakers must retain or set new principles and then specific child support rules. Evolving ideals, whether among a minority or majority of citizens, create pressures for the law to change progressively, to stay unchanged, or to revert to earlier forms. Troubling results from implementation of the law or new financial constraints on the state can also create pressures for reform.

B Implementing Principles into Child Support Legal Rules

Two principles that lawmakers in California and in Sweden have derived from societal values and lawmakers' policy positions are that (1) both parents should contribute to the financial support of their children, and that (2) parents have the primary responsibility to support their children, while the state has a secondary responsibility. Both of these principles are emphasized in Swedish and Californian child support law or preparatory works.[4] The first leads to legal rules that promote both parents' financial contributions to the costs of raising a child, especially when the parents do not live together. The second leads to legal rules emphasizing and enabling enforcement of the parents' child support duties, and simultaneously to public law social benefit rules insuring children against falling below an acceptable living standard in situations where their parents cannot or will not support them adequately.

Once lawmakers have defined the principles to be promoted by child support law, they engage in detailed *rulemaking* to implement the principles. Lawmakers may be courts, legislatures or administrative agencies, depending on a legal system's child support structure. In California, the makers of child support rules have historically been the legislature for the public-law side of family law – enacting statutes on state-provided relief for the poor including especially many single mother-led families; and the courts for the private-law side – developing rules for allocating the private (parents') child support duty between

4 See e.g. California Family Code § 4053 and Proposition (to Swedish Parliament) 2014/15:145 at pp. 11-14 (citing both the Swedish Children and Parents Code, Föräldrabalken, and the United Nations Convention on the Rights of the Child as sources of these principles in Swedish law). The principles are also represented in the legislative intents of the jurisdictions' public- and private-law versions of child support law, despite the significant difference in welfare state models.

parents, usually upon divorce.[5] Today, Californian legislation regulates both private law child support disputes and public law rules under which the state seeks child support on behalf of custodial parents, often to repay state welfare benefits previously provided for the household.[6] In Sweden, the Swedish Parliament has developed both the current private-law and public-law child support systems, but they have been administered and developed largely separately by public-law-focused versus private-law-focused professionals within several government agencies and the administrative (public-law) and civil (private-law) court systems. The two child support systems largely remain separate, more so than in California.[7]

C Rules and Results, Evaluation and Reform

Legal rules in these jurisdictions concern the legally-required amount of child support to be paid for a given child, how it is calculated, modified, and enforced, by which actors and following which procedures. As the rules are implemented and used over time, lawmakers and politicians often legally must or politically choose to *evaluate* the results of their efforts. At this point in the child-support-lawmaking life cycle, the lawmakers often *delegate* their legislative evaluating duty, the detailed (proposed new) statutory drafting, or both, to expert consultants.

Finally, lawmakers must decide whether, when and how recommendations made pursuant to the evaluations are to become *implemented reforms*, in other words new law. This study focuses on this final step, where empirical evaluations of child support law conducted by experts to whom the evaluative task was partially delegated may or may not result in implementation of the recommendations.

5 See J. tenBroek, 'California's Dual System of Family Law: Its Origin, Development and Present Status: Part 1', *Standford Law Review*, Vol. 16, 1964, pp. 257-317 (comprehensively reviewing the history of child support laws, both public and private, and their origins in England and early American colonies).

6 Though a mandatory statewide "guideline" formula calculates *amounts* of support due for each child, regardless of public-benefit status, California's *enforcement* systems remain significantly distinct, with different actors and courts in charge of setting and enforcing support collection depending on the income levels of the custodial parents, as indicated by whether or not they receive low-income public benefits.

7 For example the public support, *underhållsstöd*, is calculated as to the support amount and the payment obligation of the payor parent under separate rules than those for the private support, *underhållsbidrag*, a confusing situation that has led to parents over-using the public system. The reforms studied herein were partially designed to correct this.

III Two Evidence-Based Child Support Law Evaluations

Multidisciplinary empirical research is today a valued component of child-support-law-making and periodic-review processes in both California and Sweden.[8] In California, it most often occurs pursuant to a legally-mandated review schedule, "at least every four years" since the introduction of a mandatory state child support guideline.[9] In Sweden, it is usually initiated by the government currently in power, which appoints a committee to study an area of law and changes it would like to explore making.[10] The committee issues a research-based preparatory work known as an SOU (*Statens offentliga utredning*), and then the Swedish Parliament considers the government's written *Proposition* for changes to the law, based on the SOU findings and outside experts' commentary on the legal changes proposed therein. This can happen more or less often than every four years in a given policy area. Beyond these reviews that specifically seek law reform proposals, both jurisdictions also demonstrate their commitment to empirical evidence by, for example, collecting statistics about children and parents receiving and paying child support[11] and seeking input from the research community.[12]

8 See e.g. California Family Code § 4054(b), discussed below, and Judicial Council of California, 'Elkins Family Law Task Force, Final Report and Recommendations', 2010, p. 92 (recommending on behalf of a family-court-procedures- review task force of California family law experts that "The Administrative Office of the Courts and local courts should continue to explore best practices by reviewing research and reports from other jurisdictions, both nationally and internationally, that have implemented new programs or services related to the family court. In obtaining such materials, they should emphasize studies that employ rigorous research methods.") In Sweden, see e.g. Sveriges Riksdag, Departementsserie 2014:27, 'Increased Support for Child Maintenance Regulation' (*Ökat stöd för underhållsreglering* in Swedish; translation this author's), p. 27 (citing and summarizing multiple other studies taken into consideration by the government as it prepared to reform child support law).

9 California Family Code § 4054(e). All states must review their child support guidelines at least every four years, per 45 C.F.R. § 302.56. California adopted its schedule to comply with these U.S. federal regulations.

10 See H. Vogel, 'Chapter 2: Sources of Swedish Law', *in* M. Bogdan (Ed.), *Swedish Legal System*, Stockholm, Norstedts Juridik, 2010, p. 30 (summarising the Swedish lawmaking process including a constitutional requirement for public comment on reform proposals).

11 Recent child support statistics can be found at http://www.childsup.ca.gov/reports.aspx for California and https://www.forsakringskassan.se/statistik/barn-familj/underhallsstod, for Sweden. See also Socialförsäkringskassan, *Social Insurance in Figures 2017* (statistics in English, available at www.forsakringskassan.se). Private-law child support agreements and orders are not included in these statistics regarding the public child support benefit, leading to weakened understanding of them in relation to child support cases involving the state social insurance agency.

12 California also annually tracks child-support-law performance, most directly the public family law system's performance, using five "federal performance measures" and eight "state performance measures"; California's Department of Child Support Services Data Performance Analysis Branch submits annual reports to the California Legislature. The federal US government requires states to review child support guidelines and collection data to receive federal contributions to each state's temporary financial assistance to low-income families (welfare) program. As in Sweden, data on private-law child support cases are less comprehensively available.

A The Stated Purpose and Evidentiary Basis Underlying Each Evaluation

1 California

The California Legislature has enacted its "intent ... that the statewide uniform guideline shall be reviewed by the Legislature at least every four years and shall be revised by the Legislature as appropriate to ensure that its application results in the determination of appropriate child support amounts".[13] The law requires the Judicial Council of California, a state administrative agency, to conduct these reviews[14] and to include in each review "economic data on the cost of raising children and analysis of case data, gathered through sampling or other methods, on the actual application of the guideline" as well as "an analysis of guidelines and studies from other [U.S.] states, and other research and studies...".[15] The Judicial Council may also report on other matters; California Family Code § 4054(d) provides a non-exclusive list of other relevant topics.

The purpose of and evidentiary basis for the reviews and their resulting recommendations are thus recurrent in California, and specified in state legislation, based on federal law. The evaluators also are bound by the limitation that "[a]ny recommendations for revisions to the guideline shall be made to ensure that the guideline results in appropriate child support orders, to limit deviations from the guideline, or otherwise to help ensure that the guideline is in compliance with federal law",[16] which (while quite broad) excludes the possibility of any recommendation to hold Californian child support law to a standard *alternative* to federal requirements. Other reviews addressing questions of political interest at a given time may be conducted periodically (as most Swedish reviews are done), but the recurrent § 4054 reviews are the main source of California child support reform suggestions.

This paper analyses the most recent available review report submitted to the California Legislature, entitled Review of Statewide Uniform Child Support Guideline 2010 ("the 2010 Review").[17] The 2010 Review evaluator was the Center for Policy Research (CPR), hired "to provide technical assistance" to the Judicial Council of California by conducting the review.[18] CPR sampled case files from a representative selection of California county courts, did economic and comparative law research, and held focus groups with family-law judges, attorneys, and other stakeholders including fathers' groups and women's groups before it delivered its report to the Judicial Council for submission to the Legislature.[19] In

13 California Family Code § 4067 (further requiring that reviews include consideration of changes required by federal laws and regulations or proposed by the Judicial Council of California).

14 Ibid, § 4054(a).

15 Ibid, § 4054(b).

16 Ibid, §4054(c).

17 Judicial Council of California, *Review of Statewide Uniform Child Support Guideline 2010: A Report to the California Legislature (June 2011)*. A 2017 Review was released in 2018 (nearly six years after the last).

18 Ibid, p. i (within the Executive Summary).

19 Ibid, pp. iv-v, 121-130.

carrying out its review, the CPR aimed primarily (1) "to ensure that the guideline results in the determination of appropriate child support award amounts", and (2) to assess economic data on child-rearing costs plus court-case-file data to determine how the guideline is being applied and ensure that deviations from the guideline are limited,[20] meaning that courts are not granting deviations (exceptions) excessively as they apply the guideline rules. In addition the 2010 Review considered two currently-important topics in depth: "child support orders for low-income families" and "underlying factors affecting statutory provisions for establishing and modifying medical support orders" regarding children's insurance and uninsured medical costs.[21]

2 Sweden

The recent Swedish child support law review entailed two separate investigations, with different yet interrelated purposes and evidentiary bases. These two reviews became the preparatory-works basis for, inter alia, Proposition 2014/15:145 on "Increased Regulation of Children's Support Outside the Governmental Child-Support-Benefit System".[22]

In June 2009, the Government tasked the Swedish Ministry of Health and Social Affairs (*Socialdepartementet*) with appointing an expert committee to review how laws providing economic support to families with children affect cooperation between separately-living parents.[23] The experts were to review laws concerning the public child-support-like benefit for such children (*underhållsstöd*), but also laws on several other economic supports that Sweden's social-democratic welfare state provides to families via public law, including means-tested housing assistance, a non-means-tested, universal child benefit paid to all families monthly for each child, parental leave benefits, financial supports for care for children with special needs, and others. The expert committee was to gather empirical evidence, both quantitative and qualitative, to report on: how separately-living parents cooperate on financial issues; how they divide incomes and costs related to their children;

---

20 Ibid, pp. 1, 121. This language mirrors the statute mandating the periodic reviews, California Family Code § 4054(c). A "deviation" occurs when a court calculates child support according to the mandatory guideline but then deviates from that amount for a reason permitted in statute or case law and not forbidden by statute. See California Family Code § 5057(b). Deviations are discouraged.

21 Judicial Council of California, op cit, n. 17, pp. 121, 128. Discretionary topics may be reviewed and reported on, per California Family Code § 4054(d). Two primary recommendations of the 2005 Review had been to review two discretionary topics. They both became central to the 2010 Review, specifically "the impact of support orders among low-income families in concert with efforts by the courts, DCSS, and other state entities to assist low-income families" and possible increases to "the income threshold for applying the low-income adjustment". Judicial Council of California, p. 6.

22 Proposition 2014/15:145, op cit, n. 4, (*Ökad reglering av barns underhåll utanför underhållsstödet*; author's translation above).

23 *See* SOU 2011:51, 'Co-parenting: On Responsibility, Economics and Cooperation for the Child's Sake' (*Forsatt föräldrar – om ansvar, ekonomi och samarbete för barnets skull* in Swedish), pp. 49-50 (citing Direktiv 2009:56 and Direktiv 2011:8, attached as its Addendums 1 and 3, and detailing the experts' assigned areas of inquiry).

what needs, rights, and typical costs associated with their upbringing children have at different ages; how their time with each parent and the division of costs are associated in practice; how parents view the conditions necessary for, and how they practice a balance between, work and care for their children; what effects the public benefits rules have on parents' ability to cooperate well; and what help and support from the government might be needed to assist separately-living parents, towards the aim of reducing conflict and supporting parents' ability to assure the best interests of their children.[24] The committee was also to consider possible ways to offer separating parents co-parenting conversation sessions concerning how they would fulfill their shared child-support duties, potentially by adding economic issues to the existing local-municipality-led co-parenting conversation sessions on custody and visitation issues.[25]

Significantly, the committee was *required to abstain* from suggesting any changes to the Swedish Children and Parents Code (*Föräldrabalken*), the private-law rules governing the parents' duty to pay child support that serves as the basis for requiring parents to repay the public-law child support benefit. The committee was specifically to indicate whether their reform suggestions would directly or indirectly affect the *Föräldrabalken* rules.[26]

In June 2011, the expert committee released its report "Co-parenting: On Responsibility, Economics and Cooperation for the Child's Sake".[27] This report was followed by the second, partially-empirical review studied here. The Government assigned an inter-departmental group led by Swedish Ministry of Health and Social Affairs to investigate how best to improve state administrative-agency support to parents, specifically in order to get more parents to use the private-law child support system instead of turning first to the public child support benefit system. This assignment was based upon the first report's findings that child support under the private-law rules would often provide significantly-higher monthly payments, especially for children in the lowest-income households, than the state-guaranteed, one-size-fits-all amount available when a private child support agreement or judgment has not been reached.[28] The group was also to recommend which government agency could best support parents learning about the two systems and attempting to agree to appropriate (individualized, private-law) child support based on their incomes and the

24 SOU 2011: 51, ibid, pp. 49-50.

25 Ibid.

26 Ibid, again citing Addendum 1, the Direktiv 2009:56. This is remarkable given this chapter's thesis. Perhaps the government was simply satisfied with the private-law rules and wished to preserve them and focus on the public-law rules, yet once again public and private child support laws were treated as less than fundamentally intertwined. The review committee itself found this a difficult limitation, as reflected in their recommendations, discussed below. Perhaps this limitation on their focus reflected instead the government's desire to keep public-law and private-law rulemaking processes distinct, another example of the difficulties in many jurisdictions due to the historically-based separation of these two areas of family law.

27 Ibid, pp. 17-18 (summarizing the investigative committee's aims and limits to its scope, including that it was not to suggest changes to the civil-law child support rules).

28 Departmentsserie 2014:27, op cit, n. 8, p. 21.

children's needs, and to estimate what financial consequences moving to the private system might have for children presently receiving a public-law child support benefit.[29] The group's stated purposes also included proposing what kinds of assistance an agency could give parents, for example if the agency should help to collect income information rather than rely on parents' reports; what the economic costs to the agency might be; to what extent supports could be provided in electronic form; and the secrecy law and budgetary consequences of any proposed legal changes.[30] This group was also discouraged from proposing any changes to the *Föräldrabalken*; it was to compare public-law and private-law child support rules, yet only propose private-law reforms if the group decided that those rules hindered parents in getting the new agency's help to reach a private agreement.[31]

Neither Swedish review was assigned a specific empirical methodology as was assigned to the California review, although all three reviews did examine economic data, applications in practice, and input from multiple stakeholders.

B Recommendations Made and Reforms Implemented

The following overview of the empirically-based review recommendations, some adopted and some rejected, is not comprehensive. The multiple legislative bills introduced in recent years that partially respond to the reviews described above go beyond the scope of this article's purpose. This section highlights the most central conclusions and recommendations of the reviews, and some legislative responses to them.

The Swedish evaluations found several difficulties, both with social benefit laws that still assumed one custodial parent after separation despite a dramatic recent rise in alternating residence, and with the existence of two child-support systems. The 2011 report emphasized that the state sends double messages ("*skickar dubbla budskap*") to parents by providing two different sets of rules.[32] It recommended *further research* into making the public support an advance of support in the amount set by the private system's rules, and meanwhile that an *agency become responsible* for advising parents on the current rules to reduce their conflicts (ideally *Försäkringskassan*, the Swedish Social Insurance Agency), plus *incentives* be introduced to steer parents towards cooperating in using the private system (including making the public support time-limited), among other detailed changes such as creating a new website and needs-calculation tool plus collecting statistics on

29 Ibid, p. 6 (reporting that they replicated a study done by the committee discussed above and found similar benefits to the private-law calculation rules, e.g. that some children could receive 80% more in private child support than through the public system, if parents would agree to a child support amount under the private-law rules).

30 See ibid, pp. 22-23 (defining its tasks).

31 See ibid, p. 24.

32 SOU 2011:51, op cit, n. 23, p. 27.

children alternating residence and investigating indebted parents' situations.[33] The 2014 report concluded that *Försäkringskassan* would be the most appropriate and effective agency to perform the responsibilities proposed in the SOU and Proposition; it proposed more specifically what those responsibilities to support parents could entail.[34] It further proposed certain changes to the public-child-support-benefit laws to incentivise parents to agree to a private child support amount, including that the public benefit be made unavailable until the second month after a separation, and that the right to receive the benefit would expire if the child-support-owing payor paid, in full and on time for six months, the amount he (or she) was calculated to owe as a payment to the state, because this would this would indicate that a private-child-support agreement (reliably paid directly to the custodial parent) was possible.[35] The evaluating group expressed uncertainty whether parents would switch systems, if the public system were still available to them without time limits, and recommended a different time-limitation strategy than had the SOU, namely the six-months rule defined above.[36]

The legal reforms proposed by Proposition 2014/15:145 were enacted as Swedish law effective April 1, 2016. Proposition 2014/15:145 included several but not all recommendations from each review introduced above.[37] Some priority recommendations made by the two reviews have not yet been implemented, most notably the larger reform (or further research towards it) recommended by SOU 2011:51 that the public child-support benefit amount be replaced by a system advancing payment of a child support amount calculated under the individualized private-law rules. The government's drafters of new *public (social*

33 See ibid, pp. 28-34.

34 See Departmentsserie 2014:27, op cit, n 8, pp. 5-6.

35 See ibid, pp. 6-7. The leap in logic here, that a payor reliably repaying the government at most 100% of the one-size-fits-all public guarantee benefit amount of child support would then voluntarily agree to pay to the custodial parent significantly more per month under the private-law rules, has been noted by some expert commentators including family law academics. See e.g. Proposition 2014/15:145, op cit, n. 4, pp. 35-36 (giving the response by the government that they hope the public-benefit amount will become less normalized and parents, especially newly-separating parents, will indeed be incentivized voluntarily to use the private-law rules including to pay more than the public amount but indicating that stronger incentivizing measures will be considered if the hoped-for results do not occur). The public-law benefit, approximately $180 USD per month, is intended to cover approximately one-half of an average child's costs after consideration of the universal child support paid as state child support assistance for every child. A payor parent repays 0-100% of that amount to the government. In contrast, the private-law rules allocate a child's costs in proportion to the relative incomes of the parents. See e.g. A. Singer, *Barns rätt*, Uppsala, Iustus Förlag AB, 2017, pp. 138-157 (summarizing the Swedish child support systems).

36 See e.g. Departmentsserie 2014:27, op cit, n. 8, p. 82.

37 Other legislative bills made several other of the recommended changes. See e.g. Proposition (to Swedish Parliament) 2012/13:189 (implementing the recommendation within SOU 2011:51 that local municipality-run co-parenting talks begin to include economic issues relating to the child or children, available at https://www.riksdagen.se/sv/dokument-lagar/dokument/proposition/forstarkta-samarbetssamtal_H003189) *and* Proposition 2016/17:216 (partially implementing another recommendation from SOU 2011:51 that the public child-support benefit begin to be paid in different amounts depending on the age of the child, available at http://www.regeringen.se/rattsdokument/proposition/2017/07/prop.-201617216/).

benefits) law thus received empirical evidence and recommendations from their own expert reviewers that the lawmakers should strongly consider integrating the two child support systems by removing from law the public child support benefit. They instead passed law retaining the two systems but incentivizing parents to use the private system whenever possible.

In summary, empirical evidence in Sweden showed that having two child-support systems was causing conflict and confusion, plus normalizing a one-sized child support amount that acted against the private system's requirement that child support amounts be individually tailored. Some children could receive more child support if parents stopped using the public benefit option (and its one-size-fits-all amount) simply to have a middle-man between them, the experts found, especially those living with the lowest-income custodial parents since then the non-custodial parent's higher income would be expected to pay *more* than one half of the child's needs remaining, not just to repay the public benefit amount designed to cover one-half of an average child's needs. Lawmakers responded with legislation dependent on a (politically-driven?) assumption, which they did not ask researchers to test and which the SOU 2011:51 expert committee *expressly disagreed with*: payors would willingly pay higher child support, even if the public-benefit amount was retained (albeit for unlimited use in fewer situations). This hesitation to scale back the state's role via this social benefit in assuring children's wellbeing could reflect social-democratic welfare state priorities, as introduced in the next section.

The evidence also showed that the rules on one parent receiving social benefits for the child could lead to conflict between parents whose children alternate residence, living approximately half-time with each parent, and those laws *were* largely reformed.[38] An expert-recommended removal from law of a repayment amount reduction for visitation time spent with the payor parent was implemented too,[39] though parents paying a private child support still have an analogous visitation reduction, so the change added another disparity. That recommendation was a simplifying and cost-saving one.

In California, the 2010 Review proposed no specific modifications to statutory wording, as the Swedish reviews did, so subsequent changes were introduced on the initiative of individual legislators or legislative committees. This may be because California's review was led by a private team of social science researchers less expert in statutory drafting than the Swedish reviewers, yet perhaps more expert than Sweden's reviewers at economic

38 See e.g. Proposition 2013/14:6 (concerning dividing certain benefits in response to SOU 2011:51).

39 See Proposition 2014/15:145, op cit n. 4, pp. 12-13 (describing nettoberäkning whereby a payor can have his or her repayment amount owed to the state each month reduced because he has a custody judgment or legally validated agreement for the child to spend a certain number of days in his care, and umgängesavdrag whereby a payor can have his repayment liability for the child's underhållsstöd payment reduced in a given month by reporting visitation that would allow a child support duty reduction under the private family law rules, and proposing only the latter be removed from the law as expensive and ineffective). The Proposition became law, as discussed supra.

analyses relevant to the complicated California guideline formula for calculating individualized child support amounts.

California's 2010 Review's "Recommendation 1" was to update the monthly income limit that payors may earn before they are is deemed ineligible for a "low-income adjustment", reducing the guideline child support payable due to their need to self-support. The reviewing experts deemed the existing limit, $1000 per month, outdated, not indexed to federal poverty guidelines as such limits are in other U.S. states and "inadequate". They noted research findings suggesting that "it inadvertently could reduce the obligor's incentive to work in the legitimate economy, pay support, and maintain contact with the child, potentially resulting in other adverse effects on child outcomes".[40] Evaluators also deemed the change necessary because a payor making minimum wage would otherwise be unable to live at subsistence level and pay child support.

The California Legislature implemented this reform recommendation. Politically, it could be viewed by the public as favoring payors (largely fathers in both California and Sweden) over payees (largely mothers with primary custody of the children, in both jurisdictions). The lawmaker introducing the bill publicized it carefully, for example in this local newspaper interview: "In light of Father's Day, AB [Assembly Bill] 2393 will enable fathers to successfully meet their obligations and provide more consistent child support payments, improving the income stream for families, promoting family self-sufficiency and improving the overall wellbeing of children living in single-parent households."[41]

This political message reflects the liberal-market-economy emphasis in the U.S. on more private support of children, and on families being "self-sufficient", meaning not receiving public benefits that might, from a Swedish perspective, enable the individuals within the family to enjoy better life possibilities than if they remained more dependent on the private resources of their family.[42] The reform, reducing the monthly amount a payor may be ordered to pay as child support thereby increasing the likelihood that his

40 Judicial Council of California, op cit, n. 17, p. ix.

41 'In Time For Father's Day – Child Support Adjustment Bill Passes', *L.A. Watts Times*,14 June 2012 (available at http://www.lawattstimes.com and quoting California Legislature Assemblyman Mike Davis, the bill's sponsor).

42 While certain universal public supports to children exist in the U.S., such as public schools for students from approximately age 5 through 17 and tax deductions for parents, and while there is a relatively strong commitment to social benefits for families and children in California, it remains a U.S. state. The public supports generally and the safety net for struggling families are relatively weak in the U.S. compared to those in economically-comparable countries. See e.g. C. Skinner & J. Davidson, 'Recent Trends in Child Maintenance Schemes in 14 Countries', *International Journal of Law, Policy and the Family*, Vol. 23, 2009, pp. 25-52 (describing models and principles for child support policy across countries including most of the Nordic and Anglo-American countries). See also 'Is California the welfare capital?', *San Diego Tribune*, 28 July 2012 (available at http://www.sandiegouniontribune.com/news/politics/sdut-welfare-capital-of-the-us-2012jul28-htmlstory.html and discussing with researchers California's social safety net in comparison to other states).

child will require public benefits, is promoted as a way for the state to save taxpayer money in the long run, by supporting fairness and public trust in the child-support system.

Children's "overall wellbeing" seems to refer to the experts' conclusion that fathers who cannot pay an unreasonably-high child support order have strained relationships with their children, which is harmful for the children, but this is not spelled out and emphasized in the lawmaker's communication to the public. Instead the article comments on his behalf that the "low-income adjustment has not been increased since it was first introduced in 1993, even though the cost of living increased by 50% during that same period. According to the U.S. Bureau of Labor Statistics, if $1,000 in 1993 was adjusted for inflation, it would represent $1,576 in today's dollars. This bill's increase to $1,500 is entirely consistent with inflation." This communicates to the public that lawmakers were not generous with payor parents, but rather simply fair. Legal experts making recommendations to lawmakers may wish to take note.

Other recommendations made within the 2010 Review included (2) to evaluate the current income-attribution policies as they apply to both parents and in light of case law on imputing incomes, to determine if they continue to be consistent with legislative child-support principles; (3) to educate and engage stakeholders such as parents, so that they will be able better to use the guideline rules; (4) to adopt any necessary changes for California to comply with 2008 federal medical support rules, although 2010 legal changes could complicate this; and (5) to encourage better, more detailed information in court case files, so that the basis for calculations of child support are available in case parents need a modification.[43] The second recommendation (for further evaluation of imputing income) has been followed by the experts who conducted the 2017 periodic review of California's child-support guideline and practices, seemingly because the same issue was addressed nationwide in a new federal child-support-agency rule requiring state law adjustments.[44] Court administrators or others may act on recommendations 3 and 5 (for better education and court practices), without them being enacted as legislation, or new legislation soon required for federal rule compliance and recommended by the 2017 Review's experts may

43 Judicial Council of California, op cit, n. 17, pp. ix-x.

44 Per President Obama's Executive Order 13563 seeking improvements and scientific integrity in federal regulations and regulatory review, the federal Office of Child Support Enforcement published comprehensively-revised rules governing the Child Support Enforcement Program it regulates nationwide. The rules were significantly revised for the first time in 35 years, in part due to the U.S. Supreme Court decision *Turner v. Rogers, et al.*, 564 U.S. 431 (2011), regarding constitutional due-process rights of child-support payors. The final rule, 'Flexibility, Efficiency, and Modernization in Child Support Enforcement Programs', was published December 20, 2016, at 81 Fed. Reg. 93492. *See* National Conference of State Legislatures, 'Final Rule Resources' (available at http://www.ncsl.org/research/health/office-of-child-support-enforcement-ocse-final-rules-governing-child-support-enforcement-programs.aspx. See also the 2017 Review report as made available for public comment before delivery to the California Legislature, pp. 161-62 (available at http://www.courts.ca.gov/documents/SP17-05.pdf).

address them. To date, however, none but the first of the 2010 Review recommendations has clearly been enacted into law.[45]

IV Political and Economic Factors: Two Welfare State Models

The two jurisdictions studied share various features, not least the gaps identified between the empirical results and the steps taken by lawmakers. However, one significant dissimilarity – that can explain several other dissimilarities in the child support laws and their implementation in practice in California and Sweden – is the welfare state model that their respective legal systems exist within and create.

Welfare state variants internationally can be classified as clusters of states that share qualitatively similar "arrangements between state, market and the family".[46] California's liberal-market welfare state model is one in which: private resources and the market economy are relatively prominent over, and less regulated by, governmental resources and actors; a safety net of social benefits is primarily reserved for the very poor and, to a certain extent, senior citizens; and there are relatively large economic class stratifications.[47]

In contrast, Sweden's social-democratic welfare state model is characterized by governmental resources and regulations being more prominent, in a deliberate effort to prevent economic class divisions and to keep capitalism balanced with as broad an equality among citizens as possible. Danish sociologist Gøsta Esping-Andersen described the approach to social benefits for families in a social-democratic welfare state like Sweden:

> In contrast to the corporatist-subsidiarity model [followed by France and Germany], the principle is not to wait until the family's capacity to aid is exhausted, but to preemptively socialize the costs of familyhood. The ideal is not to maximize dependence on the family, but capacities for individual inde-

45 See e.g. National Conference of State Legislatures, 'Child Support and Family Law Legislation Database' (available at http://www.ncsl.org/research/human-services/child-support-and-family-law-database.aspx and tracking legislative changes in all U.S. states).

46 G. Esping-Anderson, *The Three Worlds Of Welfare Capitalism*, Cambridge, Polity Press, 1990, p. 26 (describing further, at pp. 26-29, the three welfare state models observable within capitalist societies: "liberal", for example the United States, Canada and Australia; "corporate", for example France, Austria and Germany; and "social democratic", the smallest group, comprised of the Scandinavian countries including Sweden).

47 Ibid, p. 26, (describing the liberal welfare state cluster, "in which means-tested assistance, modest universal transfers, or modest social-insurance plans predominate. Benefits cater mainly to a clientele of low-income, usually working-class, state dependents. In this model, the progress of social reform has been severely circumscribed by traditional, liberal work-ethic norms: it is one where the limits of welfare equal the marginal propensity to opt for welfare instead of work. Entitlement rules are therefore strict and often associated with stigma; benefits are typically modest. In turn, the state encourages the market…").

> pendence. … Perhaps the most salient characteristic of the social democratic regime is its fusion of welfare and work.[48]

It is within this model that the well-known long, paid parental leave, low-cost government-provided daycare for preschool children, universal healthcare and no-cost higher education with students paid a monthly living grant exist. Less well-known is the fact that Sweden had previously, as recently as the 1930s, a welfare state model more closely resembling the liberal model that the U.S. also had then, and retains now. Sweden, through political and lawmaking processes, developed from a liberal model to a social-democratic model between 1937 and 1947.[49]

Compared to California, social supports available today in Sweden are relatively generous when an individual earns zero income. Social supports diminish with increasing incomes, as in California, but lower-income earners in Sweden are taxed relatively highly to pay for the comprehensive social benefits they and all other Swedes receive. The broad middle class is included in social benefits, with lower and higher income earners less included in some benefits.[50] These differences can be explained in large part by the frequent link, in Sweden, between social insurance benefits and marketplace participation. Those on parental leave from a well-paying job, for example, receive replacement income based on their most recent salary level, while those who become parents while unemployed cannot receive as high a monthly income-replacement social insurance benefit. The differences are also explained in large part, in California, by the society's concern that social benefits at higher levels would discourage workforce participation and lead to benefit reliance. This concern seemed to affect, as analysed above, how and when an empirically-based child-support reform proposal could be adopted: politically, it was crucial to emphasize that, according to the empirical research, the reform would increase and not decrease payors' participation in work and in paying timely child support. Concern that social benefits will reduce workforce participation and lead instead to reliance on safety-net social benefits is much less prominent in Sweden. Swedish workers are *all* recipients of social benefits at higher levels than in California. Some (such as healthcare and education) are universal but many others (such as parental and sick leave) are framed as "insurances" tied to workforce participation, strengthening the employment norm. Benefits offering higher levels of social protection to workers at times in life when they are not working, and benefits (such as adequate supports to children) that will strengthen the workforce of

48 Ibid, p. 28.

49 Ibid, p. 28. The change in Sweden from a mean-tested child benefit (*barnbidrag*), introduced in 1937, which could stigmatize its recipients, to a universal one introduced in 1947 is one example of Sweden's development from a liberal to an early social democratic model during that decade.

50 See A. Bergh, *Den kapitalistiska välfärdsstaten*, 3rd ed., Lund, Studentlitteratur, 2013. Broader participation in both receiving benefits from and paying taxes to the state seems to strengthen positive public attitudes towards the welfare state.

the future, are seen in Sweden as more likely to increase than to decrease broad workforce participation and minimal reliance on need-based social benefits.

V Concluding Remarks

These two child support legal jurisdictions share an emphasis on parents' primary responsibility, yet when viewed in the context of the jurisdictions' differing welfare state models, the willingness of the state to step in to avoid financial hardship for children is much stronger in Sweden, and the living standard Sweden provides via public benefits significantly higher.

Both jurisdictions also emphasize encouraging private settlements of child support issues between parents, yet Sweden's comprehensive public benefits and social insurance legal regimes can be seen in the child support legal area to have dissuaded parents from private settlements using private, civil-law child support rules. Sweden may also have over-emphasized avoiding litigation between parents on child support issues, to the extent that the empirical reviews studied here made recommendations dependent on parents engaging in private agreement-making, without much mention of the civil-law possibility these parents have to litigate the issue. As prohibitively expensive as that option may be today, given relatively low support amounts (including as ordered by courts), reform recommendations or the governmental requests for review could have regarded possible private-law improvements encouraging settlements backed by the threat of litigation somehow made more accessible, but this was unlikely given the heavy focus on the public-law side of child support.

Compelling non-residential parents to pay their fair share of the costs of raising children seems more emphasized in California, and not simply for reasons of children having higher needs for private support. There is also the liberal-model-related emphasis on holding parents responsible for fulfilling their child support obligations, even when they have very low incomes on which to live, and this becomes a political barrier to more effective child-support rules for low-income situations.

This research demonstrates how political and practical legislative contexts, including welfare-state orientations, impact the effectiveness of evidence-based family law evaluation processes, at least with respect to their reform-proposing functions, even when lawmakers have stated an intent to seek objective, evidence-based expert advice as a basis on which to make reform decisions.[51]

---

51 Evaluations also have several latent functions, of course, such as to document the "successes" or "failures" of legislators, courts, agencies and other stakeholders in child support law, and to comply with laws and expectations requiring periodic review of the law in practice, whether or not the results lead to reform.

Is Post-Divorce Spousal Maintenance in Bulgarian Law Obsolete?

*Dimitar Topuzov**

I Introduction[1]

The Bulgarian Family Code (in force since 1 October 2009) essentially adopts a very restrictive regulation of maintenance between former spouses, continuing the position adopted by the law prior to that date. A historical review of this regulation shows that it was established as a concept during the period of early socialism. However, social relations during that period significantly differ from contemporary ones. The present study aims to assess whether the Bulgarian regulation of post-divorce maintenance matches the new social and economic realities and family models. The starting point of the study is the understanding that legislative decisions should, above all, correlate with present-day patterns of marital relationships.

After a brief presentation of the current regime of maintenance between former spouses, the article will focus on social conditions and relationships during the socialist era. This approach is necessary because it is important to understand the environment in which the legislation concerning maintenance between former spouses (now contained in the Family Code) was established. The article will analyse the family model (considering the distribution of responsibilities between the spouses – financial support of the family, housekeeping and child care) that was shaped by living conditions during the socialist regime.

Next, the study will discuss the way in which socio-economic changes after 1989 affected the Bulgarian family and the model for reconciliation of work and family life.

The study will compare the Bulgarian regulation on post-divorce spousal maintenance with that in other European jurisdictions, seeking to give an account of the differences in socio-economic conditions and established family models. The reason for the legislation adopted in Bulgaria will also be sought in the light of the Principles of European Family Law regarding divorce and maintenance between former spouses (PEFL).

---

* Chief Professor Assistant, Law Faculty of Plovdiv University, Bulgaria.

1 This article is part of the author's work on a scientific project funded by the "Scientific Research" Fund at Plovdiv University, "Paisii Hilendarski" (ФП17-ЮФ-003/2017). The author would like also to thank the Robert Anderson Research Charitable Trust, United Kingdom.

Finally, the article will propose an alternative approach to the arrangement of maintenance between former spouses, in order to bring it more closely in line with the socio-economic reality in Bulgaria and the contemporary models of Bulgarian family life.

II A Brief Overview of the Current Regulation

Bulgarian legislation regulates maintenance between former spouses as a special type of support. Article 155 of the Family Code (hereafter "FC") is dedicated to this maintenance. However, article 155 does not exhaust the preconditions under which a former spouse is entitled to receive maintenance. Along with the requirements established in article 155 FC, maintenance is due only if the basic criteria determining the right to maintenance according to Bulgarian law are both met, namely: the claimant has an employment disability (inability to engage in paid work because of some illness, disability, pregnancy or childbirth), and the claimant is unable to provide for himself/herself from assets/property (article 139 FC).

The special requirements for a spouse's right to maintenance are positive and negative. The main positive requirement is that the spouse who is in need of maintenance must be innocent in relation to the marriage's breakdown (i.e. either neither parties were at fault, or only the respondent was at fault in relation to the divorce).[2] The negative requirements are that no more than three years must have elapsed since the termination of the marriage and that the claimant must not have entered into another marriage.

Some authors also maintain the existence of an additional requirement when employment disability occurs after the divorce, namely: a causal relationship between this disability and the terminated marriage must be shown.[3]

Along with all the preconditions laid down, the place of the former spouse in the line of the persons entitled to maintenance from the defendant must be considered (see article 141 FC). A claim for maintenance against a former spouse will be upheld only if the defendant has enough means to provide this maintenance after providing for his or her own needs and the needs of the persons who are within the first two lines of persons entitled to maintenance – children, current spouse and parents.

---

2 See generally V. Todorova, *Grounds for Divorce and Maintenance between Former Spouses*, p. 39, http://ceflonline.net/wp-content/uploads/Bulgaria-Divorce.pdf.

3 B. Barov, *The Maintenance Obligation*, Sofia, Bulgarian Academy of Science, 1956, pp. 107-8; M. Markov's revision of L. Nenova, *Family Law*, 3th ed., Book Two, Sofia, SOFI-R, 2010, pp. 548-9; M. Markov, 'Maintenance Obligation', *in* T. Tsankova, M. Markov, A. Staneva & V. Todorova, *Commentary on the New Family Code*, Sofia, Trud i pravo Publishing House, 2009, p. 428; contrast D. Konstantinov, *Maintenance obligations*, Sofia, Nauka i izkustvo Publishing House, 1954, pp. 94-6; E. Mateeva, *Family Law of the Republic of Bulgaria*, Sofia, Varna Free University Press, 2010, p. 518.

III The Legal History and the Socio-Political Justification of the Adopted Regulation

The existing restrictive legislation governing the right to maintenance of an ex-spouse dates back to the period of socialism. The legal conception was established with the Ordinance on Marriage Act of 1945 (the provisions of which silently amended the former regulation on the right to maintenance after divorce, as stipulated in article 4 of the Ordinance on Alimony Obligation Act of 1937). According to the established principle of equality in Bulgarian family law, both ex-spouses have the right of maintenance after the termination of their marriage only insofar as their income is not sufficient to provide them fully.[4] By virtue of the Persons and Family Act of 1949, the legislature expressly provides as a general precondition for the right to maintenance the requirement for employment disability. This prerequisite also applies when an ex-spouse exercises his/her right to maintenance.[5] Pursuant to an established rule, maintenance paid to an ex-spouse is due for a maximum of three years after termination of the marriage. The three FCs of 1968, 1985 and 2009 essentially reproduced these prerequisites for the right to post-divorce maintenance, but the legislation allows the court to extend the three-year period if the ex-spouse is in a particularly grave condition and the other is able to make the maintenance payment without any particular difficulties.

The regime of the right of maintenance between former spouses, recognised by the 2009 FC, can only be fully understood in light of the socio-political processes that occurred during its formation. Consideration of some of the processes helps to reveal the philosophy behind the adopted legal provisions.

The regime of socialism in Bulgaria, established after 1944, followed the soviet model. This gave prominence to Marxist-Leninist philosophy that formed the basis for Bulgarian state policies, including those on employment and family issues.

According to classical Marxist-Leninist theory, the true equality of a woman can be achieved only if the woman is involved in social production.[6] The care and upbringing of children therefore must be taken over by the state. Building public canteens and children's nurseries and kindergartens was the key to release women from domestic slavery.[7] The woman had to be "taken out" of the home and engaged predominantly in community service.[8] Consistent with this viewpoint, after 1944, a family model in which both spouses

4 P. Venedikov, *Commentary on the Marriage Act*, Sofia, 947, p. 322.

5 See Konstantinov, op cit, n. 3, pp. 94ff, and Barov, op cit, n. 3, pp. 102ff.

6 K. Marx, F. Engels & V. Lenin, *On Women and the Family*, Sofia, Otechestven front Publishing House, 1978, pp. 146-7.

7 Ibid, pp. 176-7.

8 See detailed analysis by A. Luleva, '"Women's Question" in Socialist Bulgaria – Ideology, Politics, Reality', *in* R. Ivanova (Ed.), *Socialism – Reality and Illusions. Etiological Aspects of Everyday Culture*, Sofia, Bulgarian

worked outside the household was deliberately imposed. This model was a matter of state policy, and the existence of alternative models was impossible. The consequences of that hard-and-fast state policy became evident in the destruction of the bourgeois and patriarchal families that belonged to the previous system.[9]

The *ratio legis* (rationale) of the maintenance provision follows this socialist philosophy. Each spouse was obliged to do socially useful work, save where disabled. The State was only obligated to provide alimony protection in case of disability. Otherwise, the person had to meet his/her needs with the income from his/her work. The acquisition of income by able-bodied individuals from sources other than labour (passive income) was considered to be unacceptable[10] and so could not be guaranteed, here by the State making provision for a maintenance claim in such circumstances.

Since labour was compulsory and the employment was secured by the State, the able-bodied person would not need alimony. Moreover, with regard to maintenance after marriage termination, the enforced family model of two working spouses created the conditions for their greater economic independence from each other. This, in turn, led to a less disruptive divorce in which there would be no need for any maintenance claims between the ex-spouses in most cases.

Nevertheless, during the period of socialism women worked in spheres where the salaries were lower,[11] and hence earned lower income than men. This was partly due to the fact that women continued to bear the burden of child care and housekeeping.[12] To some extent, this could be reason enough to subject the regulation of maintenance after divorce to criticism even before the democratic changes. Today, however, there is a far greater justification for criticism.

IV The Changed Social and Economic Circumstances

After the democratic changes, the social and political environment became different. Women's rights could not be guaranteed through forced engagement with community service: labour became voluntary. The principle of freedom of labour and the ban on forced

Academy of Science, 2003, pp. 160-1. See also I. Pachamanova, *The Woman in the Bulgarian Family (the mid-1940s – late 80s of the 20th century)* (Abstract of PhD thesis, Sofia, 2012, p. 20 et seq.).

9 P. Kubadinsky, *On the Socialist Family*, Sofia, Otechestven front Publishing House, 1986, p. 38.

10 Public policy required that all able-bodied persons should work; income from sources other than labour might disincentivise this.

11 K. Vladimirova, 'Gender Equality in the Transition of Bulgaria to a Market Economy and European Integration: Change of Policies - From Inclusion and Development of Women to Achievement of Factual Equality between Men and Women', *in* T. Turlakova (Ed.), *Studies on the History of Socialism in Bulgaria. The Transition – II*, Sofia, Center for Political and Historical Studies, 2013, p. 493.

12 Ibid, pp. 492-3. See further Pachamanova, op cit, n. 8, pp. 22ff.

labour, provided for in article 48, paras. 3 and 4 of the Constitution, became key principles of labour law.[13]

The principle of freedom of labour and the development of the private sector has led to the establishment of different family models.[14] There are signs of a slight tendency to return to the traditional family model, where one of the spouses, usually the husband, provides financial support for the family, while the other spouse, usually the wife, maintains the household and takes care of the children.[15] Free economic initiative has provided opportunities for acquisition of a significant amount of revenue, allowing the maintenance of some Bulgarian families to be taken over by one spouse. However, the income of the average Bulgarian citizen remains one of the lowest in Europe, which usually makes it necessary for both spouses to maintain the family.[16]

On the other hand, the new realities have led to greater insecurity in labour relations. A number of labour market risks have appeared – such as unemployment, competition, income inequality, precarious transitions in individual career development, employment in the "black" economy – without employment contracts and insurance.[17] At the same time, women continue to bear the burden of raising children and working in the household, doing so-called unpaid labour. The lack of a more equal partnership between the genders in sharing the responsibilities for housekeeping and taking care of the children makes it harder for Bulgarian women to adapt to the new economic environment than their husbands. Their opportunities for finding employment and earning income remain more limited.[18] Indeed, finding employment depends exclusively on qualifications, but for women

13 For this principle, see V. Mrachkov, *Labour Law*, Sofia, Sibi Publishing House, 2010, pp. 67-8.

14 For the main types of family models, see S. Kovacheva, 'Models For Reconcilation of Work and Family Life', *in* V. Todorova, Gr. Grigorov & A. Shopov (Eds.), *Family Relations in a Changing World. Legal, Sociological and Economic Dimensions*, Sofia, Sibi Publishing House, 2014, pp. 134-5.

15 According to data from the National Statistical Institute, women constitute 71.0 thousand of the 102.1 thousand unemployed persons between 15 and 64 years old who would work under suitable conditions in the childcare sector: see data here https://tinyurl.com/y98luq3q.

16 According to Eurostat data, in 2015 in eight EU Member States, namely Romania (25.4%), Latvia (22.5%), Lithuania (22.2%), Spain (22.1%), Bulgaria (22.0%), Greece (21.4%) and Croatia (20.0%), one fifth or more of the population is at risk of falling into poverty – https://ec.europa.eu/eurostat/statistics-explained/index.php?title=Income_poverty_statistics/bg#.

17 R. Stoilova, *Gender and stratification. Socio-structural dimensions of gender inequalities in the Bulgarian society after 1989* (Abstract of DSc Thesis, Sofia, 2011, p. 5).

18 Vladimirova, op cit, n. 11, pp. 499-500. According to Eurostat data, in Bulgaria as well as in other EU member states, the employment rate among men is higher in 2014 than that among women. See more at http://ec.europa.eu/eurostat/statistics-explained/index.php/File:Employment_rates_by_sex,_age_group_15%E2% 80%9364,_2014_(%C2%B9)_(%25)_YB16.png. There are considerable, though slightly lower than the EU-28 average, differences between the average earnings of men and women. Women's earnings are about 14% lower than that of men. The smallest differences in average pay for women and men are observed in Slovenia, Malta, Italy, Poland, Luxembourg and Belgium (below 10.0%). See further http://ec.europa.eu/eurostat/statistics-explained/images/b/b7/Gender_pay_gap%2C_2014_%28%C2%B9%29_%28%25_difference_between_average_gross_hourly_earnings_of_male_and_female_employees%2C_as_%25_of_male_gross_earnings%2C_unadjusted_form%29_YB16.png.

the return on education is lower. All this reflects the fact that obligations at home are traditionally ascribed to women.[19]

Private sector employers often do not want to employ women owing to interruptions due to pregnancy and child care, given the greater emphasis on competitiveness and efficiency. Given these expectations and the inevitable career breaks that they take for family reasons, women often prefer employment in the public sphere, despite the lower payment, in search for income security and job stability.[20] Because of the inequality in the sharing of household care and child care, the egalitarian family model in Bulgaria is rather fictitious, even when both spouses are working.[21]

V EVALUATION OF THE CURRENT LAW

In the light of the foregoing discussion, I will try to assess the current regulation of maintenance between former spouses in Bulgaria.

Some of the requirements for an ex-spouse's right to maintenance are justified and unobjectionable, such as the requirement that the claimant ought to be unable to support him/herself from assets/property.[22] The very essence of maintenance presupposes the presence of a person in need.

There is no objection to the special negative precondition for the right to maintenance – the claimant (the recipient of the maintenance) must not have entered into a new marriage. Here the explanation can be found in moral requirements: it would not be acceptable from a moral-ethical point of view for the receiving spouse, who has created a new family, to be able to claim for maintenance from his/her ex-spouse. Instead, the new marriage obliges the current spouse to maintain his/her partner, and so there is a new person obliged to take care of the claimant.

Whilst many jurisdictions today do not take this approach, the requirement that the claimant must not be at fault in relation to the divorce could arguably also be accepted. To require an ex-partner to demonstrate solidarity toward the guilty spouse under the fear

19 Stoilova, op cit, n. 17, pp. 7, 8-9, 30-32. The prevailing understanding in Bulgarian society is that "… the mother has to take on greater part of the responsibilities in the long run and agree to delay her career development to take care of young children; while the father's responsibility mainly concerns the financial security of the family." Kovacheva, op cit, n. 14, p. 147.

20 Stoilova, op cit, n. 17, pp. 23-4.

21 Kovacheva, op cit, n. 14, pp. 141, 152-4.

22 The term "property" as a prerequisite for the right to maintenance is understood only as an aggregate of income and pecuniary rights except those that "should not to be transformed into means of subsistence" - the individual's necessary dwelling and household goods: Decree of the Plenum of Supreme Court No. 5-70, item 1.

of state coercion and sanction might be considered morally unacceptable.[23] Of course, recognising the importance of fault does not mean that the maintenance obligation is deemed as a sanction.[24]

However, other requirements for maintenance between former spouses – the principal focus of the argument I wish to make in this chapter – are more difficult to accept. One of the most challenging legal requirements is that of the claimant's employment disability. In practice, it almost makes maintenance between former spouses nonsensical, because it imposes too tight a framework of solidarity upon their relations. This requirement limits the right to maintenance to persons who objectively are, completely or partially, unable to work. This inability must be related either to the health of the claimant or to natural biological processes and conditions that affect their ability to earn income (old age, pregnancy, childbirth). In all other cases, regardless of the market situation, the ex-spouse does not have the right to maintenance, although he/she cannot be reproached for not looking for a job if there are no jobs available. As far as maintenance between former spouses is concerned, this legislative solution is unjustified because it does not take into account the spouses' marital partnership – the distribution of responsibilities between them – and so the economic difficulties that divorce usually generates for the economically weaker spouse.

Even more unacceptable, in my view, is the requirement asserted by some legal scholars that a link must be established between the terminated marriage and the maintenance claimant's employment disability in cases where that disability arose after the divorce. These scholars argue that if the disability has arisen after the divorce and it is not related to the marriage, the right to maintenance remains unjustified.[25] However, this requirement has no basis in the law and does not suit the legal nature of maintenance of a former spouse. A terminated marriage is the legal ground for claiming support from a former spouse, just as the existence of a continuing marriage is the ground for claiming support from a current spouse, and kinship is the ground for claiming support between parents and children, brothers and sisters and so on. In all these cases, the ground for maintenance does not depend on the reasons for employment disability. Maintenance is not compensation.[26]

---

23 This should not be seen as an expression of support for claiming fault in relation to the irretrievable breakdown of marriage under Bulgarian family law, and were fault removed from divorce law, it would then lose its importance as a factor regarding maintenance.

24 It has been a leading concept for many years: Barov, op cit, n. 3, pp. 99-101.

25 Ibid, pp. 107-8.

26 Compensation arises in response to causing unlawful harm. The purpose of maintenance is different. The reason for the right to maintenance is the justified need. Indeed, in a number of cases, one of the spouses abandons their professional development for the sake of the family and so misses opportunities which would guarantee their economic independence. However, such pecuniary damage is not the basis of this spouse's claim for maintenance. This is so at least because a right to maintenance equally involves a spouse in need who has not suffered any such damage. Dissolving boundaries between legal concepts is dangerous; the more unclear they are, the more difficult enforcement of the law becomes. It should be noted, however, that under certain legal systems maintenance between ex-spouses is given compensatory functions as well;

Under Bulgarian Law, the regulation of maintenance between former spouses does not seek to provide redress of the "rightful" party or to restore the economic balance between the spouses after divorce. Its functions are different, so it should not be necessary to identify a link between the disability and the terminated marriage. The important thing is that there once was a marriage between the parties, in light of which the legislature requires solidarity even after the divorce, albeit of a narrower scope. This principle, which we can conditionally call the principle of post-divorce solidarity, is the basis of Bulgarian regulation of maintenance between former spouses.[27]

The limited time-period for maintenance between former spouses – up to 3 years from the termination of the marriage – also raises certain objections. Although the court can extend this period in where the claimant suffers from a particularly grave condition, and the defendant can provide maintenance without particular difficulty, the normal statutory deadline for maintenance (which is a relatively short one) is not the best normative solution. Of course, it cannot be denied that such a time limit pursues a legitimate aim – to release the ex-spouses as soon as possible from any obligations founded on the terminated marriage and so to permit a "clean break".[28] However, this is contrary to the principle of solidarity, which, as previously stated, outlasts the marriage. It also contradicts the need to protect those who are unable to provide for themselves.

Finally, the decision by the current FC to move former spouses from the first to the third line of persons obliged to provide maintenance (and respectively entitled to such) is also problematic.

VI Proposals for Law Reform

In view of the new social and economic circumstances and family models, the principle of solidarity in family relations generally and between ex-spouses becomes increasingly important. The Bulgarian legislature should take this into account in regulating maintenance

---

see K. Boele-Woelki, B. Braat & I. Sumner (Eds.), *European Family Law in Action. Volume II: Maintenance Between Former Spouses*, Antwerpen-Oxford-New York, Intersentia, 2003, pp. 75ff; P. Parkinson, *Family Law and the Indissolubility of Parenthood*, Cambridge: Cambridge University Press, 2011, pp. 250ff; C. Rogerson, 'The Causal Connection Test in Spousal Support Law', *Canadian Journal of Family Law*, Vol. 8, 1989, pp. 95-132. Some authors maintain that maintenance between former spouses has a compensatory nature under Bulgarian law too: Venedikov, op cit, n. 4, pp. 233-324.

27 The principle of "post-divorce solidarity" is unwritten but may be derived from the regulation of post-divorce spouses relations. In particular, this principle can be derived from the regulation of maintenance and for use of the family home after divorce – see art. 56, para. 1 FC: "In granting a divorce where the family home cannot be used by the two spouses separately the court should award its use to one of the spouses provided he or she has requested and that and is in need of housing." In German legal doctrine, the principle is referred to by the term "nacheheliche Solidarität": see D. Martiny & E.D. Schawb, 'Germany' *in* Boele-Woelki et al (Eds.), op cit, n. 26, p. 46.

28 Further on this aim and the clean break principle, see Parkinson, op cit, n. 26, p. 238.

between former spouses. Perhaps owing to inertia, the current FC has adopted a regime of maintenance between former spouses that was originally created to serve abandoned political and philosophical doctrines under the conditions of a planned economy, in the framework of a virtually non-alternative family model imposed by the state, and the lack of unemployment. There is now a compelling need for a change in legislation.

It is unacceptable that employment disability is a prerequisite for obtaining maintenance from a former spouse. As already discussed, there are sufficient grounds for not applying the general requirement for work-incapacity as a precondition for this particular type of maintenance. Maintenance payments can be justified on several other hypotheses – such as inability to earn income due to child care, lack of competitiveness and the need for adaptation due to long-term commitment to housework and children during marriage. The former spouse should be obliged to pay maintenance in these cases, provided he or she has enough means.

A comparative law review also supports the thesis defended. Most European legal systems do not require the former spouse who claims maintenance to be disabled. Maintenance may be granted to an ex-spouse after divorce on a number of other bases as well. Only the legislation of the Russian Federation and some other former Soviet republics make an exception.[29]

The Principles of European Family Law on Divorce and Maintenance between Former Spouses (PEFL) also do not require the receiving spouse to be unable to work. The general conditions for maintenance according to the PEFL are limited to a lack of sufficient resources for the claimant to meet his or her needs, and the other ex-spouse's ability to satisfy those needs (Principle 2:3). Additional criteria, such as inability to work, age, health, child care, division of duties during the marriage, etc. are only considered for assessment of the need and the maintenance debtor's ability to pay.[30]

The latter approach deserves support in light of the considerations set out earlier in this paper. Therefore, I propose by way of law reform that the Bulgarian legislature ensure that the right to maintenance of a former spouse does not dependent on his/her disability. As regards legislative technique, different approaches are possible. If the importance of

29 M. Antokolskaia, 'Russia', *in* Boele-Woelki et al (Eds.), op cit, n. 26, pp. 121-122. The Ukrainian Family Code (UFC), on the one hand, retains the requirement for employment disability as a precondition for maintenance between former spouses (art. 76, para. 2) but on the other hand, tries to "escape" from it (art. 76, para. 4), giving a right to receive post-divorce maintenance to a former spouse who has been unable to receive education or perform work because of his/her engagement with childcare, housework and other relevant circumstances. In this widely recognised hypothesis, maintenance is due regardless of the employment disability of the person in need. The Code of the Republic of Belarus on marriage and the family more consistently imposes this prerequisite as a general rule (see art. 30).

30 See Principle 2:4 PEFL and the commentary on the provision in K. Boele-Woelki et al (Eds.), *Principles of European Family Law Regarding Divorce and Maintenance Between Former Spouses*, Antwerp-Oxford: Intersentia, 2004, p. 92.

claiming fault is not reconsidered, the provision of article 145, para. 1 FC could read as follows:

> The spouse innocent of the divorce shall be entitled to maintenance even if he or she is able to work, if the provision of such a maintenance is justified considering the circumstances of the case, such as:
> 1. the parties' age and state of health;
> 2. the care of children;
> 3. the distribution of duties during the marriage;
> 4. the duration of marriage and other relevant circumstances.

As already stated, the normative decision to fix a maximum period of 3 years during which the maintenance will be due is also unacceptable. The court should be able to award maintenance for a longer period, and not only under the conditions of article 145 para. 2, second sentence FC: i.e. if the ex-spouse is in a particularly grave condition and the other is able to make the maintenance payment without any particular difficulty. In a number of cases, this is necessitated by the circumstances from which the need arises. The following two examples will help illustrate the practical dimensions of the problem.

Spouses are divorcing after having been married for 30 years or more during which they maintained a traditional family model. After the termination of the marriage, the spouse who cared for the household remains without income. Additionally, he/she is of or near retirement age and is not insured. In contrast, the other spouse, who has had the opportunity for professional development throughout his/her life (partially thanks to the way that the family responsibilities were distributed) is in a good financial position at the end of the marriage and able to secure his/her needs at present and in the future.

In another example, parental rights in relation to a minor child have been granted to the wife post-divorce. The child suffers from a disease that requires constant and immediate care, which prevents the wife from working full time or at all. Conversely, the husband maintains full potential to develop his professional skills and to earn income.

In the above examples and in similar cases, it appears obvious that maintenance needs to be established for a period longer than three years. As a rule, the need is likely to persist for longer in such cases, and cannot be expected to cease after a certain period of adaptation to the new environment.

In most European legal systems, although the "self-sufficiency" principle after divorce is explicitly or implicitly accepted, maintenance between former spouses is not limited in time. This is the approach in the Czech Republic, England and Wales, Finland, Germany, Hungary, the Republic of Ireland, Italy, Portugal, Russia, Spain and others.[31] However, it

31 See Boele-Woelki et al (Eds.), op cit, n. 26, pp. 159, 161, 164-5, 170-3.

cannot be denied that the alternative model of fixed-term maintenance has been adopted in a few countries, such as Denmark (up to 10 years from marriage termination, except for some special cases, where it is indefinite), the Netherlands (up to 12 years, but up to 5 years for short-term marriages without children) etc.[32] The PEFL also do not fix a time-period for the right to maintenance, but raise this issue for the court's consideration.

It would be more justified to have a non-fixed term to ex-spouse maintenance, which is why I proposed amendment of article 145, para. 2 FC, repealing the maximum term for the right to post-divorce maintenance.

One could object to this proposal because the modern trend is to terminate financial relations between former spouses as soon as possible after the dissolution of the marriage. More and more jurisdictions are attempting to impose a time limit on the right to post-divorce maintenance.[33] The concept of the marriage as an act which gives rise to a lifelong commitment is withering away. Development of social relations and especially the high divorce rate today gives reason to encourage financial independence of ex-spouses from each other. However, the time limits in the FC do not allow the judge to take into account the peculiarities of the case in determining the period during which the post-divorce spousal maintenance will be provided. This often leads to unfair results. It is also important to bear in mind that under Bulgarian law, maintenance is designed to cover only essential needs of the former spouse, not to maintain the standard of living he or she had during the marriage. Contrast the laws of those jurisdictions which have imposed a time limitation on the right to post-divorce maintenance but where the amount of maintenance is determined according to the standard of living of the spouses before the termination of their marriage.[34]

Of course, it is worthwhile considering whether there should be a time limit after divorce by which the former spouse should *claim* maintenance. It is not acceptable for ex-spouses to have (new) claims against each other several years after the dissolution of marriage and after the consequences of the divorce have been overcome. It would be unjustified to reinstate in such a way the relations between ex-spouses which have been terminated not only on legal but also on factual terms.[35]

Finally, in order avoid rendering the proposed changes pointless, future law reform must place the former spouse in the first line of persons entitled to maintenance, and respectively, the persons obliged to provide such maintenance. This was the decision of the two repealed FCs of 1968 and 1985. The current statutory solution, in which the ex-

32 Ibid, pp. 159-61, 165-9.

33 See J. Scherpe, *The Present and Future of European Family Law*, Cheltenham-Northampton: Edward Elgar Publishing, 2016, pp. 59-60.

34 For Belgium, the Netherlands (in which the importance of this factor decreases) and Scotland, see Boele-Woelk et al (Eds.), op cit, n. 26, pp. 176, 179, 183.

35 Such a view, but in defence of a different thesis, is also found in Markov & Nenova, op cit, n. 2, p. 549.

spouse is third in the line of persons entitled to claim maintenance (and respectively, obliged to provide such maintenance) has been reasonably criticised in the Bulgarian legal doctrine.[36] It is unjustified for the needy spouse who has been contributing to the welfare of the family up to the divorce (a fact which is not undermined by the marriage having broken down irretrievably) to be obliged to seek maintenance not from his former spouse, but from his/her children and parents.[37]

VII Conclusion

The current law of maintenance between former spouses fails to match current social conditions and there is a great need for its thorough revision in order to protect the economically weaker spouse. Failure to reform post-divorce maintenance is likely the result of the uncritical perception of the idea that equality has been achieved between men and women in society and in marriage – a guarantee of their economic independence. However, realities often differ from ideologies. While equality in law between men and women in Bulgaria appears to have been achieved, we are still far from equality in fact.

36 V. Todorova, 'The new family code and contemporary values in the family, marriage and child care' *in* R. Dimitrova (Ed.), *The New Family Code. The family – a nest or a cage?*, Sofia, Apis, 2009, p. 132.

37 Ibid.

The Dissolution of Marriage: Law versus Real Needs

*Cinzia Valente**

I The Italian Context

In the last few years, after a long period of inactivity, the Italian legislature has been obliged to take into account social changes that have important repercussions in family law, resulting in a sudden acceleration in family law reforms. Examples include the legal recognition of homosexual relationships and the regulation of some issues concerning unmarried couples; the reduction of the period between separation and the beginning of divorce proceedings to accelerate the dissolution of marriage; the introduction of alternative dispute resolution for consensual separation and divorce proceedings, such as the "administrative" procedure before the Registrar of the Public Registry Office, or the assisted negotiation with the support of a lawyer to reach an agreement; and the equalisation of the status of legitimate and illegitimate children.

Although the legislation may appear definitive, the Courts' interpretative role has sometimes generated novel results, such as occurred with respect to the right of maternal anonymity in opposition to the adoptees' right to know.[1] Furthermore, intervention by European Union and the ECHR in certain sensitive areas further contributes to the overall picture of the Italian system, along with the growing importance of foreign influences that have stimulated reform in particular fields, such as the regulation of assisted reproduction.[2] Some other critical aspects of regulation of the "private" life are still being evaluated by the legislature, such as the legal recognition of maintenance agreements.[3]

The objective of this short paper is to analyse, within this complex context, the maintenance rights of the economically weaker party in Italian divorce proceedings. This topic has been discussed at length and the courts have offered various solutions suited to the specific characteristics of different cases, providing us with guidelines. Two recent

* Lecturer for Jean Monnet Module, University of Modena and Reggio Emilia, Italy.

1 See M.G. Stanzione, *Identità del figlio e diritto di conoscere le proprie origini*, Turin, Giappichelli, 2015.

2 See B. Liberali, *Problematiche costituzionali nelle scelte procreative: riflessioni intorno alla fecondazione medicalmente assistita ed all'interruzione volontaria di gravidanza*, Milan, Giuffrè, 2017.

3 See draft laws (n. 2129/2012; n. 2669/2014) on the limited recognition of prenuptial agreements: http://www.camera.it/leg17/126?tab=&leg=17&idDocumento=2669; http://www.senato.it/leg/16/BGT/Schede/Ddliter/36596.htm.

important decisions by the Italian Supreme Court have modified the traditional balance between the interests of the economically weaker party and the self-sufficiency principle following divorce. Where traditionally the standard of living had guided the Judge resolving disputes about maintenance, a new trend risks eliminating this "privilege", instead supporting the principle of financial self-sufficiency. A second intervention of the Supreme Court, in Plenary Session, clarified the criteria governing this delicate issue.

II MAINTENANCE ON MARITAL BREAKDOWN IN CONTEXT

Before proceeding with a more detailed analysis of the remedies available to the economically weaker party after divorce, this section explains some aspects of the Italian patrimonial regime (maintenance and matrimonial property laws) and the procedure concerning the regulation of marital breakdown.[4]

In Italy, the award of maintenance is historically linked to the two processes inherent to the dissolution of marriage, involving a stage of legal separation prior to divorce. During separation, the effects of marriage are "suspended" (as the Italian system encourages reunification when possible), which often led to the prolongation of marital solidarity.[5] In this context, while the duties of moral assistance and cooperation no longer apply, the duty of material assistance remains intact. This duty determines the right to maintenance for the spouse in need of support due to a lack of sufficient income to meet their needs and maintain a standard of living similar to that of marital life.[6]

Furthermore, the Italian legal system provides for the community of property regime as the standard regime for married couples, although parties are entitled instead to opt for separation of property. On both separation and divorce, the court is bound to apply the relevant property rules in dividing the couple's assets.[7] The standard community property regime is designed to level out the parties' different income capacities and protect the economically weaker spouse on divorce. When the parties depart from the standard regime and opt for separation of assets (which is becoming increasingly common), the divorce

4 G. Autorino Stanzione, *Manuale di diritto di famiglia*, Milan, Giappichelli, 2016; M. Sesta, *Manuale di diritto di famiglia*, Milan, Cedam, 2019, pp. 95ff.

5 On the consequences of separation proceedings, see the reform introduced by Law 6 May 2015 n. 55, discussed by G. Oberto, 'Il divorzio breve: separazione legale e comunione legale tra coniugi', *Famiglia e Diritto*, Vol. 6, 2015, pp. 615-47.

6 Cass. 4 December 2017 n. 28938.

7 The standard regime is the community of property that provided for a joint ownership of all assets purchased after the marriage and the spouses' earnings, art. 177 CC, with some exceptions. The parties can expressly choose the separation of property regime, in which the assets and earnings remain in the sole property of each spouse. The property regime has an important role on separation and divorce; in the case of community of property, the weaker party has the right to share all the assets, while in the separation regime he/she only retains his/her own assets. In both cases, the weaker party is entitled to ask for a maintenance payment if the legal requirements are met.

ends up penalising the economically weaker spouse. The judge has no discretionary power (without the parties' agreement), and formal ownership of the property in such cases cannot be overruled. And so the maintenance allowance has long been used to make up for this imbalance. Restricting the scope of the maintenance allowance is therefore potentially problematic.

As mentioned, the separation procedure is generally the first step in the dissolution of marriage. The Italian Civil Code ("CC"), in article 156, confers maintenance rights when the applicant is not responsible for the separation and lacks sufficient income. Article 156 provides, in very general terms, that the amount of maintenance is to be shaped by the circumstances of the case and the earnings of the obliged party. The wording of article 156 provides no further details, so the Supreme Court[8] had to furnish more guidance. Lack of sufficient income does not mean a condition of poverty, but insufficient resources to maintain the accustomed standard of living.[9]

On separation, the marital standard of living has become the main parameter for maintenance decisions. Establishing the standard of living is not a simple matter, as it requires the evaluation of all financial aspects, including the professional position of each member of the family, the costs of living, career advancement; some other factors could include the ownership of the family home or a second home, a mortgage, rental costs, all the assets, savings, etc.

In calculating maintenance, the term "circumstances" in article 156 is understood to include any financial aspect relevant to the final arrangement; in general, this includes the assignment of the family home, the duration of the marriage, child custody, the financial resources of each person, etc. One very important point is the income earning capacity and the employment prospects of the unemployed spouse (generally the wife). The financial conditions of the paying spouse refer generally to his/her income and assets. Because the criteria indicated by legislators are so generalised, a complex and wide range of factors are potentially relevant.[10]

The dissolution of a marriage by divorce has consequences for both members of the couple on both a personal and an economic level. Apart from determining a loss of conjugal affection and the status of spouse, when certain conditions are met, dissolution also imposes financial obligations that establish a continuing, albeit weakened, conjugal solidarity.

---

8 Cass. 24 April 2007 n. 9915.

9 See Cass. 4 April 2016 n. 6427.

10 See A. Zaccaria, *Commentario breve al diritto della famiglia*, Milan, Cedam, 2016; G. Ferrando & L. Lenti, 'La separazione personale dei coniugi' *in* G. Alpa and S. Patti (Eds.), *Trattato teorico pratico di diritto privato*, Milan, Cedam, 2011; G. Oberto, *Gli aspetti patrimoniali della famiglia. I rapporti tra coniugi e conviventi nella fase fisiologica ed in quella patologica*, Milan, Cedam, 2011.

The right to a maintenance payment[11] for the weaker party on divorce is established in article 5, Law 1 December 1970 n. 898 (Divorce Law), as amended by Law 6 March 1987 n. 74.[12] (The text before the reform is set out in this footnote.[13]) Italian divorce law lists a series of considerations to determine the maintenance right and its amount when the claimant does not have sufficient income or earning capacity. The sixth section of article 5 provides:

> with the final decision regarding the dissolution or termination of the civil effects of marriage, the Court orders a periodical payment in favour of the person who does not have an adequate income or is not able to procure it for objective reasons; the Court has to take into account: the financial conditions of the spouses, the reasons for the divorce, the personal and financial contributions provided by each person to the management of the family, including personal assets and those in common, and the length of the marriage.

Moreover, the Courts have indicated several other factors could be taken into account, namely the parties' social background, their health,[14] their professional position, each spouse's contribution to the marriage and family welfare, including any contribution made to care of the home and family, etc. A judge may prioritise certain criteria and overlook others.

Recent Supreme Court decisions, overruled in 2018, have held that there are two stages to the decision about maintenance on divorce: entitlement and quantification, dealt with in the same proceedings.[15] The aim of the first is to establish whether either party is entitled to the payment (*an debeatur*) on the basis of the existence or inexistence of sufficient means, or the applicant's incapacity to obtain such means (based on comparison of the

---

11 Italian legislation refers to a "divorce allowance", rather than "maintenance" (unlike in legal separation proceedings), differences in wording differentiating between the two situations (see M.G. Cubeddu, 'Il divorzio', *in* S. Patti & M.G. Cubeddu (Eds.), *Diritto della famiglia*, Milan, Giuffrè, 2011, p. 626). This paper uses the term "maintenance" interchangeably with "divorce allowance".

12 Prior to the reform, Italian law allowed courts to grant a maintenance right taking into account, overall, the parties' conditions, the reasons for the divorce, and each party's contribution to their family life. The presence of one of these factors could be sufficient for an allowance to be granted, even if there were no imbalance in the parties' financial conditions (among others: Cass. 10 July 1987 n. 6016).

13 With the final decision regarding the dissolution or termination of the civil effects of the marriage, the Court orders a periodical payment, taking into account the economic conditions of the spouses and the reasons for the divorce; the amount is proportioned to assets and income of the obliged spouse. In determining the payment, the judge takes into account the personal and economic contribution given by each of the spouses to family management and to the formation of the patrimony of both. Upon agreement of the parties, the payment can be made in a sole solution.

14 A spouse's substance abuse problem, for example alcohol or drugs, can negatively impact the spouse's right to claim maintenance: Cass. 27 December 2011 n. 28892.

15 See Cass. 9 June 2015 n. 11870.

parties' financial conditions and lifestyles). The aim of the second (if entitlement is established) is to quantify the amount of the payment (*quantum debeatur*). The principle of post-marital solidarity only applies if it is established during the first stage that the former spouse has insufficient means (thus 'passing' the first stage); otherwise, there would be an undue enrichment of the maintenance beneficiary at the expense of the maintenance payer, unjustified as based on a relationship (marriage) which has since become extinct (through the divorce).

However, the absence of clearer guidelines has generated a myriad of potential different solutions due to the range of possible scenarios. The starting point was that, as in separation proceedings, the standard of living during the marriage was the decisive criterion for maintenance rights. However, in the last two years a revolutionary development has occurred, as will be discussed below.

III From the Standard of Living Principle ...

The wording of article 5 (Divorce Law), set out above, is ambiguous, with numerous factors mentioned but not listed in any specific order of importance; and the legislation does not specify which factors or criteria are relevant to stage 2, quantification of the payment amount.

The intention of the reformed law, as clarified (not without difficulty) by the evolution of the case law from 1987 to 2017, is to link the maintenance payment to applicants' temporary or permanent incapacity to provide for themselves. It is designed to be of mere "supporting" nature. The references to the parties' financial conditions, the reasons for the divorce, the contribution made by each spouse to their married life, and the duration of the marriage were, for a long time, used only at the *quantification* stage (stage 2).

Case law has taken different positions over time on the maintenance right. The first few decisions[16] (preceding the 1987 reform) favoured a compound approach in which the function of divorce maintenance was to meet all the following fundamental needs: for support, (if innocent in the divorce) for compensation, and for redressing the balance between the parties following divorce. In other words, a person without sufficient income could be deemed entitled to a maintenance payment, to be compensated for the breakdown of the marriage, and also to balance out the effect of the breakdown of the relationship, based on his or her personal and financial contribution to the family when he/she was not responsible for the divorce. These same factors were deployed at both stages: to determine entitlement to maintenance and to quantify the amount to be paid.

16 Cass. 26 April 1974 n. 1194.

Other elements stated in article 5 were used, in specific cases, to preserve the position of the economically weaker party and justify entitlement to maintenance even when that party had his or her own income. Relevant factors, resulting from judicial interpretation of the article 5 included: any form of deterioration in that party's financial condition, comparison of the couple's wealth during the marriage and both spouses' subsequent position; the legitimate expectations of the weaker party of a share in an increase in the couple's financial assets is also relevant, as the improvement of each party's financial condition could be considered a consequence of joint decisions made during the marriage.

The absence of a set list identifying priority factors has led to valid criticism of the discretion used by the courts in resolving similar cases. However, the dominance of the "support" function of maintenance became undisputed,[17] taking priority over the previous triple aspect of maintenance (to support, to compensate and to redress balance). This trend began in the 1990s, when the Supreme Court,[18] in plenary session, established entitlement to maintenance in all cases in which the weaker party lacked sufficient means to maintain the marital standard of living. In other words, the judge was required to guarantee the weaker spouse the same financial conditions as enjoyed during marital life if he/she was not financially self-sufficient. That party was not required to be "in need" for the payment to be granted, but simply in an appreciably worse position than when married, which would justify a redressing of the balance between the two parties' situations. The lifestyle to which the spouses had become accustomed and their future financial expectations were relevant to the decision about maintenance. However, the obligation would cease when the beneficiary spouse entered into a new marriage or in the event of a significant change in the circumstances of either party.[19]

Case law was almost unanimous in this approach.[20] It clarified that the divorce allowance could be granted by comparing the applicant's[21] financial circumstances and earning potential (taking into account any objective reasons why the applicant may be unable to obtain financial means) with the marital standard of living. It was also necessary to consider

---

17 G. Bonilini & A. Natale, 'L'assegno post- matrimoniale', *in* G. Bonilini (Ed.), *Trattato di diritto di famiglia, III*, Milano, Utet, 2016, p. 2876.

18 Cass. Plenary Session, 29 November 1990 n. 11490 in Giur. It., 1991, 1410; see also Cass. Plenary Session, 29 November 1990 n. 11492.

19 The issue of whether the right to receive maintenance is lost if the recipient cohabits with a new partner is much debated. The Italian Supreme Court (Cass., 12 March 2012, n. 3923) decided that no allowance will be granted in such instances; other rulings have even denied an allowance merely because the beneficiary was in a stable relationship without cohabitation (Trib. La Spezia, 1 June 2016, n. 2133).

20 Cass. 17 December 2014 n. 26635 stated that the parties' financial conditions following the end of the divorce procedure may be relevant; the parties' earnings and assets, after the divorce, are considered to be the result of the choices made during the marriage.

21 In one recent case (Cass. 8 January 2014 n. 129), the maintenance payment was denied on the grounds of a finance agreement entered into by the applicant for the purchase of a Mercedes SLK car (considered indicative of a position of wealth), combined with the applicant's decision not to remain employed (deemed incompatible with a position of financial hardship).

any economic imbalance between the parties arising from an improvement in the financial situation or prospects of one spouse during the marriage, for example, thanks to the acquisition of professional qualifications or progression at work.[22] In practice, it was not infrequent that an allowance of this kind was granted, although some resistance was displayed in certain lower courts and in a few isolated cases before the Supreme Court.[23]

For a considerable time, the application of this approach led to the declaration of the right to a monthly payment for the weaker spouse whenever that party was unemployed or had a lower level of income than the other spouse. The courts sought to guarantee the weaker spouse "recognition" for the dedication shown to the family, in the form of caring for the children and the home, or abandoning career prospects to allow the other spouse to concentrate on his or her own career.

The intention was to determine the value of the "invisible"[24] contribution made by the weaker spouse to the family in financial terms, so that that party would not be adversely affected when a marriage (which may have been long-standing) came to an end. This requirement held even more importance in what is known as the "big money cases", where the wife risked losing the "privileges" linked to a particular position of wealth that she had helped create indirectly over the course of her married life.

Although the purpose of divorce, as formally declared by the legislature, was to dissolve any bonds between the spouses, the link between the "supporting" nature of the right to maintenance and the marital standard of living effectively ensured that the bond to the previous relationship was maintained. This position was based on the principle of solidarity (also guaranteed by the Italian Constitution), which is also reflected in other areas, such as the right of a former spouse to a survivor's pension, to a portion of employee severance pay, etc. All this gave the dissolved relationship some continuing, albeit limited, legal effect.

The most persistent criticism of the approach described in this section emphasised how the "standard of living to which one has become accustomed" criterion maintained a de facto "indissolubility" of the marital bond following divorce, cancelling out the effects of the dissolution of the marriage. Critics were also concerned that the court's discretionary powers were increasing uncontrollably, as judges were free to adapt the law according to individual circumstances.[25] [26]

---

22 Cass. 17 September 2014 n. 19529.

23 See also M. Palazzo, 'Le progressive aperture della Suprema Corte al principio di autoresponsabilità nella configurazione dell'assegno post-matrimoniale', *Rass. Dir. Civ.*, 2013, pp. 423-60.

24 E. Al Mureden, 'Assegno post-matrimoniale: è possibile valutare il "capitale invisibile" ed attuare una equa condivisione delle risorse della famiglia?', *Famiglia e diritto*, Vol. 3, 2006, pp. 302-308.

25 B. De Filippis & M. Pisapia, *Mantenimento per il coniuge e per i figli nella separazione e nel divorzio. Nuovi orientamenti della giurisprudenza: verso il concetto europeo di autosufficienza dei divorziati*, Milan, Cedam, 2017, p. 158.

26 A ruling by the Constitutional Court (following application by the Court of Florence) (Constitutional Court, 11 February 2015, No. 11) made it clear that there was no constitutional illegitimacy in the construction of rules on divorce that acknowledge the importance of living standards. It was stated that the judges assigned

IV ... to the Self-Sufficiency Approach

Social changes and trends (also recorded in other European legal systems) prompting a revised view of marital solidarity in favour of encouraging financial self-sufficiency have recently led to the overruling of the case law discussed above by rulings destined to cause a stir, in particular a decision of the Supreme Court in 2017 (Cass. 10 May 2017 n. 11504).[27]

As mentioned above, there are two stages in the decision about the maintenance of the former spouse on divorce: entitlement and quantification. The Court's 2017 decision changed the criterion used for the first stage. Sufficiency of means had long been assessed by reference to marital standard of living as a determining factor, generating similar results in divorce and separation proceedings. The novelty of the 2017 ruling consisted in the acknowledgment that this approach risked extending the financial effects of a marriage that had been dissolved. The core of the decision lay in the court's confirmation of the following principles:

- maintenance has the specific aim of supporting the former spouse;
- a former spouse who is financially independent is not entitled to periodical payments;
- maintenance is designed to help the former spouse for a limited period, until he/she is self-sufficient.

The view of marriage as a life-long financial arrangement accordingly gave way to a vision thought to be more in line with social reality, not afraid of breaking tradition and recognising marriage:

> as an act of freedom and self-responsibility as well as a place of affection and effective communion of life, as such dissoluble (today, marriage in Italy can be "dissolved", subject to agreement, through a simple declaration by the parties to the registrar of marriages, pursuant to Decree Law 12 September 2014 n.

---

these cases could, if necessary, reach several decisions, which could even be contrary to consolidated opinion. In other words, while not taking any position on the evolution of law in this area, by defending, in practice, an approach based on the standard of living, the Constitutional Court implicitly authorised possible departure from precedent. The decision states "While, in the event of construction of a law that has been consolidated - as in the case in hand - within the context of 'living law', the same judge has the power to either comply with it or not (rulings no. 117 dated 2012 and no. 91 dated 2004), therefore remaining free, in the second case, to exercise the very 'living right' applicable to their complaints (order n. 253 dated 2012)". See also: A. Astone, 'Assegno post matrimoniale ed autoresponsabilità degli ex coniugi', *Dir. fam. e persone*, 2017, pp. 1208ff.

27 See F. Danovi, 'La Cassazione e l'assegno di divorzio: en attendant Godot (or Combined Chambers)', *Famiglia e diritto*, 2018, pp. 51-64; D. Piantanida, 'L'assegno di divorzio dopo la svolta della Cassazione: orientamenti (e disorientamenti) nella giurisprudenza di merito', *Diritto e famiglia*, 2018, pp. 65-78.

132, Article 12, converted into law, with amendments, by Law 10 November 2014, n. 162, cf. Article 1, paragraph 1).[28]

Sufficiency of means must therefore be related to the applicant's prospects of financial independence, which must be inferred from a series of indicators, such as the possession of income of any kind and/or of real and personal property, the applicant's actual employability and employment prospects (in relation to health, age, sex and the labour market), and stable rights to a home. Indeed, a principle which aims to prevent a former spouse becoming "parasitic" on the other by rendering the beneficiary responsible for their own self-sufficiency is gaining ground in family law, whether that beneficiary is an adult child or a former spouse. In the case of maintenance for adult children, the same criterion requires the adult child to become independent, despite enjoying special protection arising from the provisions governing filiation status, such that maintenance is limited where the dependent adult child is found to be intentionally inactive. If the rule that a person must take action to be self-sufficient applies to an adult child (who enjoys a special status which can never be lost), *a fortiori*, this approach must also apply to a person who has permanently lost the status of spouse as declared in the decision of the Supreme Court in 2017. On the other hand, the two positions (adult child and former spouse) are not at all similar; an adult child is in a particular situation, with long-term prospects, in which he or she must take action to achieve their own independence; a divorcee, meanwhile, has very different employment prospects and has already "invested" his or her life in a life plan, albeit failed.[29]

The starting point of the 2017 decision is that divorce is characterised by the principle of self-responsibility. The supporting function of maintenance must therefore serve to allow the former spouse to acquire financial independence and no longer burden the previous partner. The dissolution of the marital bond, in this interpretation, ends the parties' marital status. If divorce is based on the fact that spiritual and physical communion has ceased and has likewise ceased on a personal and financial/property level, the former spouses take on a "single" status (without this affecting any obligations towards their children). To allow the marital standard of living to impact on the appraisal of the right to maintenance would undermine the divorce, allowing economic effects of a dissolved marriage to survive. The aim is not to redress the balance of the parties' financial positions but rather to give the financially weaker party the chance to become self-sufficient. Only in this way are all the obstacles to the reconstruction of a new life removed and with them, possibly, the obstacles to the constitution of a new family without any burdens on the "stronger" spouse arising from the previous relationship.

28 Cass. 10 May 2017 n. 11504.

29 E. Al Mureden, 'L'assegno divorzile tra solidarietà e autoresponsabilità: dal parametro del tenore di vita coniugale a quello dell'indipendenza economica del richiedente?', *Giustizia Civile. Com*, 2017, 15 May 2017, pp. 1-10.

This approach[30] upset the former *modus operandi*, finding broad consensus in lower-level court decisions[31] and led to a series of cases which overruled decisions based on the previous principle, with the aim of "freeing" (generally) former husbands from any financial burden. The trend set by the 2017 decision was taken up by the majority of the lower-level courts, where application of the new principle has generated results that are rather tough for the economically weaker party, to such an extent that recognition of divorce allowances have been rejected and existing orders have even been revoked. One of the first courts to take action in support of the "new trend" was the court of Milan,[32] which established a parameter of independence corresponding to the income threshold that the State applies for access to legal aid (i.e. gross monthly income of just under €1,000). This decision did not consider some essential circumstances, including the impact on children under the age of eighteen or the costs to pay home rent.

Establishing the criteria according to which the former spouse may be deemed financially self-sufficient is problematic. The possession of sufficient means or the capacity to obtain such resources refers to not only the state of not being in need, but in a broader sense, being above mere subsistence level.[33] The 2017 decision identified four prerequisites which can suggest self-sufficiency, namely: possession of income of any kind, personal and real property assets, employability and actual employment prospects, and rights to a home.

This formula is very general and not very effective. While the presence of income facilitates the assessment of financial independence, the other elements are less readily assessed and likely to lead to unfair arrangements. Consider, for example, cases in which the party requesting the allowance, while having no earnings, has substantial real property assets which do not provide income and would not easily be liquidated; or a former spouse who, while being employable, has no real prospects of joining the workforce due to their age. The abstract possibility of becoming self-sufficient does not correspond to reality in many situations. Insufficient attention is given to relevant factors such as the applicant's age and the duration of the marriage, which would allow the rule to be applied in a way more suited to the circumstances of individual cases.

---

30 Confirmed by Cass. 7 February 2018 n. 3016; Cass. 22 June 2017 n. 15481; Cass. 9 October 2017 n. 23602; Cass. 25 October 2017 n. 25321.

31 See Trib. Bologna, 1 February 2018 n. 331; Trib. Forlì, 29 January 2018 n. 66; Court of Appeal Milan, 16 November 2017 n. 4793.

32 Trib. Milan, 22 May 2017, available on jurisdata online 2018.

33 This element serves to distinguish between the divorce allowance and alimony, which is governed by art. 433 CC and the function of which is to guarantee the beneficiary a dignified life (food, shelter, medical care). Alimony is a general institute of family law; the essential prerequisites for alimony are: the objective need of the beneficiary (i.e. the lack or insufficiency of means to satisfy the basic everyday needs) and who is unable, partly or entirely, to be financially self-sufficient; any parental of that person is legally required to fulfil this obligation. See M. Dogliotti, A. Figone & S. Giuliano, *Obblighi di contribuzione, mantenimento e alimenti. Nuovi modelli di famiglia, etero ed omosessuale (La nuova famiglia)*, Milan, Giuffrè, 2016, p. 181.

Few decisions[34] opposed the principle stated in by the Court in 2017. These decisions, while abolishing the standard of living criteria, demonstrated the need to establish a different criterion by which to anchor entitlement to maintenance in order to alleviate the effects of such a drastic change. The exclusive use of the "sufficient means" criterion, without taking other factors into consideration, is likely to generate unfair results and limit the resources of the weaker party, especially after long-lasting marriages.

Therefore, attempts have been made to highlight the applicant's "social status"; in other words reference to "sufficient means" risks penalizing the party who despite having earnings is nevertheless unable to maintain the previous lifestyle leaving an imbalance between the parties.[35] This issue has been raised by many authors[36] who have criticised the approach adopted by the Supreme Court in 2017.

The dissolution of the marriage, and its associated financial consequences, seem fair in the case of short-lived marriages in which the spouses are relatively young and childless (and therefore have the possibility to rebuild independent lives for themselves). However, the same cannot be said for long-standing marriages in which most of the spouses' life was spent as part of the couple, investing resources (even if not amenable to financial valuation) and building expectations; or cases where one spouse has dedicated him or herself to the care of the couple's children, a circumstance which clearly affects the "employability" of the carer spouse.

V Looking for a Fair Solution

As a result of the 2017 decision, financial independence and self-sufficiency replaced the standard of living criteria in the evaluation of each case. The decision, in theory, took a modern approach, reflecting some European trends which severely limited the right to receive a periodic payment. However, as will be explored in the conclusion, the new approach failed to take account of the actual situation in Italy, and as outlined above, numerous problems with the Court's interpretation of the legislative criteria can be identified.

There followed a further intervention by the Supreme Court (in Plenary Session, 11 July 2018 n. 18287) which aimed to prevent its general statements in the 2017 decision from being misinterpreted and misapplied. The decision evaluated the legislative and jurispru-

---

34 Trib. Rome, 11 September 2017 n. 16887. See criticism by F. Danovi, 'Assegno di divorzio e irrilevanza del tenore di vita matrimoniale: il valore del precedente per i giudizi futuri e l'impatto sui divorzi già definiti', *Famiglia e diritto*, Vol. 7, 2017, pp. 655-668; D. Buzzelli, 'L'assegno di divorzio, ventisette anni dopo', *Jus civile*, Vol. 6, 2017, pp. 538-554.

35 Trib. Rome, 21 July 2017, available on jurisdata online, 2018.

36 See C.M. Bianca, 'L'ultima sentenza della Cassazione in tema di assegno divorzile: ciao Europa?', GiustiziaCiv.com, editorial 9 June 2017.

dential development of family law in the field of maintenance rights that led to the historical and constitutional reconstruction of the area in 2017. The result is a partial overruling of the previous standard, including the 2017 Court's decisions and substitution of specific principles guiding the dissolution of marriage.

A compromise between the position privileging the self-sufficiency and the solidarity approach became necessary, and so the Court in 2018 declared that post-divorce maintenance is both supportive and compensative in nature, designed to reach a balanced solution. Rather than distinguishing sharply between the factors necessary to establish an entitlement to maintenance and the criteria used to quantify the amount, the Supreme Court held that all of the conditions listed in the law (article 5 Divorce Law) are relevant at both stages. Accordingly, the economically weaker party's lack of adequate means has to be evaluated in the context of the marriage. The financial conditions of the parties on divorce are often the result of joint decisions made during the marriage; in this sense, the imbalance between the former spouses is a consequence of those decisions and cannot be irrelevant at the point of dissolution when maintenance is available to restore a condition of "parity". In this context, the Court declared the importance of adequately evaluating the spouses' contributions. The responsibilities acquired by each spouse during the marriage and the identification of specific roles in the family life could not remain without consequences, as the previous interpretation of the 2017 decision had permitted.

Family solidarity and the self-responsibility principle cannot be considered in opposition. Both must be considered, both during marriage and following its demise. A fair solution aims to grant dignity and this means "distributing" the burden arising from the parties' agreed choices. The decision to invest in the career of the husband to a detriment of the wife cannot be disregarded as it could have an irreversible effect on the wife. The resulting gap has to be filled on divorce.

The Supreme Court decision in 2018 accordingly requires attention to the specific facts of individual cases in order to balance the needs and responsibilities of both parties, given their joint decisions, the length of the marriage, the age of the family members, and the economically weaker party's job prospects and realistic chances of self-sufficiency. This assures that the constitutional solidarity principle is respected in all its aspects. By contrast, elevation of the self-responsibility principle by the 2017 decision ignores that fact that financial imbalance on divorce is shaped by an objective gap between woman and wife, including their career possibilities, access to the world of work, pay levels, and so on.

The 2018 decision seems to come back to the "origins" of maintenance as being, at the same time, a means of providing support, compensating and redressing economic imbalance. The Court introduced some important innovations, including abandonment of the distinction between the entitlement and quantification stages, and recognition that all the factors listed in article 5 of the Divorce Law have equal value. Moreover, this approach reflects the rule enunciated in article 143 CC and article 29 of the Constitution, according to which the spouses have the same duties and rights and are obliged to contribute to the common life with their own assets and professional capacities; divorce has to take into account this arrangement.

The Court's principles remain on an abstract level as the Court did not take the opportunity to give more specific guidance. The risk is the return to the "standard of living" criterion, because analysis of the former spouses' financial position and the reasons for that could in turn revert to an evaluation of the parties' financial condition during the marriage.[37] For the time being, we must wait for the decisions of the trial judges applying this principle to evaluate its impact.

VI Discussion and Closing Remarks

For a long time, on divorce as on separation, the standard of living was used as the basis for entitlement to maintenance. The recent focus on self-sufficiency, as a result of influences from foreign legal systems in which the right to receive a periodic payment is severely limited, has produced important consequences in the Italian system.

The right to post-divorce maintenance is a complex issue as it addresses different opposing goals, all deserving of attention (as the Supreme Court stated in 2018):[38] on the one hand, the need to guarantee both spouses the possibility of rebuilding their lives, and on the other, the necessity to protect the position of the weaker party, who made life and employment choices based on the existence and stability of the marriage.

Given the characteristics of the Italian system briefly described earlier, applying a self-sufficiency principle of the sort adopted by the Court in 2017 indiscriminately to all situations could lead to grossly unfair results. Family life often involves an asymmetric distribution of duties within marriage and of the parties' financial roles, and consequently family dissolution requires the law to redress the resulting imbalance. Due importance must be given to both the parties' financial contributions and the "invisible" contribution to the family made by the spouse who gave up or reduced paid employment for the benefit of the family.

Consider a situation in which the spouses agreed that the wife should leave her job. She will find herself, perhaps at a senior age, faced with the difficulties of the labour market, within which seeking financial independence in compliance with the 2017 interpretation of the law would become an arduous, if not impossible, task. This situation risks becoming dangerous given the tendency, stimulated by the Court's 2017 decision, by lower-level courts to acknowledge the amount of €1,000 per month as the threshold to guarantee a

37 M. Dogliotti, 'L'assegno di divorzio tra innovazione e restaurazione', *Famiglia e diritto*, Vol. 11, 2018, pp. 964-970.

38 Cass. Plenary Session, 11 July 2018 n. 18287.

dignified life.[39] This encourages a belief that wherever the applicant has income above that amount, she or he will not require any other payment from the former spouse, and a belief that this amount also dictates the maximum that can ever be granted where maintenance is awarded.

Moreover, this approach clashes with other general principles of family law, in particular those that attribute caring for the home the same value as employment, and require spouses to contribute to the family life according to their abilities.[40] In short, the wife is asked to choose to share a life plan with her husband which, if it fails, will leave her disadvantaged a priori on divorce. This would be a veritable act of faith if the support available via social security/social assistance under Italian law are insufficient to redress the resulting economic imbalance that was not remedied by maintenance. While it is undoubtedly vital to encourage the independence and responsibility of the family members with the aim to avoid parasitic situations and to allow the beginning of an autonomous life for both former spouses, we have to remember that self-sufficiency must not mean discrimination, and marriage must not become a "risk", as it would end up undermining the emotional nature[41] of the union by accentuating its financial aspects.

In addition, the Italian legal system still prohibits couples from entering into agreements that would manage a future divorce, thereby preventing them from governing in advance the consequences of the dissolution of their marriage, and depriving sometimes the weaker party of a chance to provide for a form of early protection.[42]

Moreover, the possibility of obtaining a divorce increases following the grant of legal separation (six months in the event of consensual separation or one year for separation sought by one spouse only). Instead of allowing the weaker party an opportunity to establish a better financial situation, the short period of time before divorce makes the situation of the economically weaker spouse precarious while privileging the other. Although maintenance payments are frequently granted at separation, the later ruling in divorce proceedings (which can be reached shortly after) – based on the "sufficient means" prerequisite – removes the protection afforded in the separation proceedings.

Reconstruction of a family occurs after the dissolution of a marriage; the general emancipation of wives is undoubtedly occurring; the increase in divorces and family breakdowns are confirmed by statistics; and life expectancy is increasing. All these factors contribute to the declaration in the Court's 2017 decision regarding the self-sufficiency principle. On this view, marriage cannot be viewed either as simply a route for wives to

39 Trib. Milano, 22 May 2017, available on jurisdata online.

40 On this point, see criticism by G. Savi, 'La rilevanza del "tenore di vita" nel regolamento delle crisi del rapporto coniugale', *Dir. di famiglia e delle persone*, 2017, Vol. 3, pp. 793-826.

41 On the evolution of the concept of "family", see R. Picaro, 'Le famiglie e la loro regolazione', *Rassegna di diritto civile*, Vol. 4, 2017, pp. 1419-64.

42 See n. 1 above.

improve their financial situation or a life-long status; the reality is different now. The promotion of the principle of autonomy/independence is both a guideline for resolving the breakdown of a marriage and a goal to be reached, taking into account the specific needs of the parties and the development of family life. In this context, a fair solution might depend upon public support being made available to mothers (in particular) following divorce, including to assist those re-entering the workforce, in order to help balance out the effect of more limited maintenance being paid in private law, in pursuit of the self-sufficiency objective.

But, in the field of family law, due consideration must also be given to out-of-court factors, such as local traditions, as well as the philosophical and religious influences that often affect this sphere as well as social and "political" aspects that could affect the efficiency of legal solutions.[43] Moreover, data published by ISTAT[44] show that, while husbands and wives share similar levels of education and number of double-income couples has increased, the pay gap between women and men remains significant. In recent years, only 20% of families registered equal pay between the man and the woman; in other words, the traditional model in which the man represents the main income producer of the family still prevails.

It is important also to bear in mind the broader legal context in which the maintenance question is determined. In a system in which the courts have no power to adjust the parties' property rights, maintenance can perform a redressing function, in which the marital standard of living plays an essential role. Limiting this right without providing for other forms of redress leaves a significant proportion of the community without protection (thereby burdening the entire community). On the other hand, if the principle of equality between spouses applies during the marriage, it cannot be simply disregarded when the relationship is ailing, and there is a very real need for its protection.

In contexts such as family law, standardisation does not always guarantee a fair result. The goal must be for the law and the courts to find a balance between the principles of responsibility, equality, self-determination and dignity for the applicant. The judges' task may sometimes be "creative" but must always be carried out with the aim of providing justice in the particular case – involving the exercise of some discretion – rather than "justice" based on entirely generic and abstract reasoning. While family law is increasingly oriented towards freedom from any form of interference by the state, it is also necessary to take action, in some cases, to protect the vulnerable.[45]

---

43 See J. Eekelaar, 'Law and Community Practices', *in* M. Maclean & J. Eekelaar, *Managing Family Justice in Diverse Societies*, Oxford, Hart Publishing, 2015.

44 http://www.istat.it/it/popolazione-e-famiglie.

45 On the relationship between autonomy and state intervention, see A. 'Diduck, Autonomy and family justice', *Child and Family Law Quarterly*, Vol. 28, No. 2, 2016, pp. 133-49, at p. 144; P. Murat, *Droit de la famille*, 7th ed., Paris, Dalloz, 2017.

Part V
Regulating the Parent-Child Relationship When Parents Live Apart

A Family Impact Analysis of the Proposed Children Proceedings (Parental Responsibility) Bill in Hong Kong

*Yuk King Lau**

I The Existing Law on Child Custody and Access in Hong Kong

Divorces rates have risen dramatically in recent decades in Hong Kong. The crude divorce rate increased from 1.1 per 1,000 people in 1991 to a historic high of 3.1 per 1,000 people in 2013.[1] Hong Kong's substantive laws on child custody and access, contained in different ordinances, are seriously fragmented.[2] The laws define the parent-child relationship on the 'rights and authority' of each parent to their children.[3] Sole custody to the mother remains the norm, with the father granted access to the children.[4] Although a parent is always entitled, regardless of his/her custodial status, to know and be consulted about major matters regarding the children, "sole custody" is persistently taken to imply exclusive control by the custodial parent and exclusion of the non-custodial parent.[5]

The same legal model on custody and access was formerly adopted in some other common law jurisdictions.[6] This custody model is described as a clean-break model, which presupposes "that divorce could end the relationship between parents in such a way that people could get on with their lives with only residual ties to their former partners".[7] On this model, parents (mostly mothers) with sole custody have very limited legal obligations

* Professional Consultant, Department of Social Work, Chinese University of Hong Kong.

1 Census and Statistics Department, 'Marriage and divorce trends in Hong Kong, 1991 to 2013', *Hong Kong Monthly Digest of Statistics*, 1st August 2018, pp. FA1-FA14.

2 K. Lynch, 'Reform of family justice: Children's dispute resolution in Hong Kong', *Cardozo Journal of Conflict Resolution*, Vol. 19, 2015, pp. 909-36.

3 Labour and Welfare Bureau, *The proposed legislation to implement the recommendations of the Law Reform Commission report on child custody and access: Public consultation*, Hong Kong, Labour and Welfare Bureau, 2015, p. 1.

4 Jockey Club Centre of Suicide Research and Prevention, *A study on the phenomenon of divorce in Hong Kong*, Hong Kong, University of Hong Kong, 2014, pp. 55-65.

5 Hong Kong Bar Association, *Response on the Children Proceedings (Parental Responsibility) Bill*, Hong Kong, Hong Kong Bar Association, 2016, p. 8.

6 Law Reform Commission of Hong Kong, *The Law Reform Commission of Hong Kong report: Child custody and access*, Hong Kong, Law Reform Commission of Hong Kong, 2005, p. 4.

7 P. Parkinson, *Family law and the indissolubility of parenthood*, New York, Cambridge University Press, 2011, p. 12.

to the other parent beyond organizing the logistics of visits. The sharp differentiation in the respective roles of custodial and non-custodial parents has led to a win/lose adversarial sentiment that polarizes divorcing parties and the legal practitioners, and causes greater harm to children by escalating existing conflicts.[8] It also creates gender inequality for parents of both sexes. While most custodial mothers hold the parental rights and are thus saddled with the assumption of sole responsibility of their children, non-residential fathers suffer a disadvantaged and peripheral parental role in their children's lives. Over time, this can lead to non-residential fathers having diminishing contact or even drifting out of the children's lives altogether.[9]

II AN INTERNATIONAL TREND OF MOVEMENT TOWARDS "JOINT PARENTAL RESPONSIBILITY"

Over the last forty years, there is a growing realization that while marriage may be freely dissoluble, parenthood creates enduring connections that outlive the marriage.[10] Along with the changing ideals in men's roles in families, many men are now more prepared to play an active, nurturing role in the lives of their children.[11] In post-divorce families, there is also a significant cultural change in attitude of fathers toward contact with their children after separation and divorce.[12] When each parent wants to retain a close connection with the child, the parents' lives continue to be entwined through their continuous parental responsibilities and the continuing need to negotiate co-parenting arrangements.[13]

To facilitate post-divorce co-parenting and provide space for fathers' involvement in children's lives, many European countries and common law jurisdictions shifted away from the emphasis on parents' rights to *children's* rights to have contact with both parents and parents' continuing parental *responsibility*.[14] For instance, England & Wales abolished the language of custody, guardianship, and access, the Children Act 1989 providing instead that each parent has "parental responsibility", which continues after the dissolution of a marriage. Instead of making a custody ruling to allocate a bundle of rights and powers to

---

8 G. Firestone & J. Weinstein, 'In the best interests of children—A proposal to transform the adversarial system', *Family Court Review*, Vol. 42, No. 2, 2004, pp. 203-15.

9 Law Reform Commission of Hong Kong, op cit, n. 6, p. 5.

10 Parkinson, op cit, n. 7, p. 277.

11 S. Mintz, 'From patriarchy to androgyny and other myths: Placing men's family roles in historical perspective', *in* A. Booth & A.C. Crouter (Eds.), *Men in families: When do they get involved? What difference does it make?*, New York, Psychology Press, 2016, pp. 3-28.

12 J. Cheadle, P. Amato & V. King, 'Patterns of non-residential father contact', *Demography*, Vol. 47, No. 1, 2010, pp. 205-25.

13 Parkinson, op cit, n. 7.

14 P. Parkinson, 'The payoffs and pitfalls of laws that encourage shared parenting: Lessons from the Australian experience', *Dalhousie Law Journal*, Vol. 1, 2014, pp. 301-43.

make decisions about the child's welfare to only one parent, the court orders resolve any practical disputes that arise, for example about where the child is to live.[15] Scotland and Australia legislated similar reforms in 1995.

In line with the concept of joint parental responsibilities, child support is now vigorously enforced in many countries.[16] For child-care arrangements, common legislative approaches are joint custody orders and the non-intervention principle that the courts make no order unless the arrangement contradicts the child's best interests or in case of dispute. Without an order, joint custody and joint parental responsibility are deemed to continue after separation. The non-intervention principle is now the norm in many European countries.[17]

A further step in this movement is a legislative support for courts to give serious consideration to shared-time parenting in disputed cases, except those in which there are issues of domestic violence or child abuse.[18] Australia made a radical reform by adopting a rebuttable presumption on "equal shared parental responsibility" in the Family Law Amendment (Shared Parental Responsibility) Act 2006. It is stated in the Act that if this is in the best interests of the child and reasonably practicable, the court must "consider making an order to provide (or including a provision in the order) for the child to spend equal time with each of the parents".[19] There is a similar legislative requirement for courts in Belgium and also in some states of the United States.[20]

The presumption of "equal shared parental responsibility" gave rise to the confusion that equal time share or shared care was the default presumption. It ignited many fathers' requests for equal time or equal shared residency in post-divorce parenting arrangements.[21] Many fathers were furious with the court system, as their expectations of an equal share in the children's time and residency had not been actualized.[22] Realizing the confusion and the evidence that the empathetic endorsement of parental involvement might have exposed some children to violence or abuse, the Australian government decided that the emphasis on parental involvement should be balanced with greater protection against abuse. Legislative reform in 2011 accordingly adopted an expanded definition of "family

15 Parkinson, op cit, n. 7.

16 P. Parkinson 'Forty years of family law: A retrospective', *Victoria University of Wellington Law Review*, Vol. 46, No. 3, 2015, pp. 611-26.

17 D.M. Blair & M.H. Weiner, 'Resolving parental custody disputes – a comparative exploration', *Family Law Quarterly*, Vol. 39, No. 2, 2005, pp. 247-65.

18 R. Graycar, 'Family law reform in Australia, or frozen chooks revisited again?', *Theoretical Inquires in Law*, Vol. 13, No. 1, 2012, pp. 241-69; B. Smyth, R. Chisholm, B. Rodgers & V. Son, 'Legislating for shared-time parenting after parental separation: Insights from Australia?', *Law and Contemporary Problems*, Vol. 77, 2014, pp. 109-49.

19 Family Law Amendment (Shared Parental Responsibility) Act 2006, s. 65DAA.

20 Parkinson, op cit, n. 14, pp. 313-14.

21 Smyth et al, op cit, n. 18. pp. 119-120.

22 B. Fehlberg, B. Smyth, M. Maclean & C. Roberts, 'Legislating for shared time parenting after separation: A research review', *International Journal of Law, Policy and the Family*, Vol. 25, No. 3, 2011, pp. 318-37.

violence", provisions to increase the chances that violence concerns would come to the courts' attention, and a provision mandating that courts attach "greater weight" to child protection when determining what is in a child's best interests.[23]

Australia is not alone in making such a readjustment. In the United States, Bartlett has observed "the most significant development of custody law in the past five to ten years is an increasing legal protection for parents and their children from domestic violence".[24] Learning from the Australian experience, the Children and Families Act 2014 in England & Wales clearly rejects an equal share notion when making an amendment to promote shared care among separated and divorced parents. The amendment added a rebuttable presumption that parents' involvement will further the child's welfare while clearly stating that involvement means "involvement of some kind, either direct or indirect, but not on any particular division of child's time".[25] Aware of about the challenges of shared parenting after divorce, most countries have resisted a one-size-fits-all approach, instead, retaining flexibility in the preferred parenting arrangement according to what is in the best interests of each child.[26]

Recent Australian research evidence showed "a general decline in parental conflict among separated families, including shared-time families".[27] This positive change is attributed to the provision of child-sensitive dispute-resolution processes and well-integrated legal and relationship support services, instead of legislative change. The Australian government not only changed the law in 2006, but also introduced comprehensive reforms to the entire family law system. Parents were mandated to attempt "family dispute resolution"—that is, mediation—before being permitted to file applications for parenting orders in court, unless exempted from doing so owing to violence or abuse or because the case was otherwise deemed unsuitable for mediation.[28] A network of Family Relationship Centres was introduced throughout Australia, providing information, referrals and affordable mediation service. They act as an early intervention strategy to help separating parents to work out their parenting arrangements.[29]

Observing the reforms in these common law jurisdictions, the Law Reform Commission of Hong Kong proposed the concept of "parental responsibility" for consultation in 1998

23 J. McIntosh, B. Smyth, M. Kelaher, Y. Wells & C. Long, *Post-separation parenting arrangements and developmental outcomes for infants and children*, Victoria, Australia, Family Transitions, 2010.
24 K.T. Bartlett, 'U.S. custody law and trends in the context of the all principles of the law of family dissolution', *Virginia Journal of Social Policy and the Law*, Vol. 10, No. 1, 2002, pp. 5-53, 26.
25 See Children Act 1989, ss. 1(2A) and (2B).
26 Parkinson, op cit, n. 14.
27 Smyth et al, op cit, n. 18, p. 145.
28 Parkinson, op cit, n. 14.
29 Smyth et al, op cit, n. 18, p. 145.

and recommended its adoption in 2005.[30] A consultation on whether to implement the recommendation through legislative means was conducted from December 2011 to March 2012. Though major stakeholders generally support or do not dispute the concept, there are divided responses about implementing the concept in legislation: there is strong support from legal professionals, strong opposition from single parents (mostly resident mothers), and reservation from social workers and welfare NGOs. [31]

III The Children Proceedings (Parental Responsibility) Bill

After the prolonged consideration and consultation process, the Children Proceedings (Parental Responsibility) Bill was proposed for consultation in 2015.[32] The Bill consolidates the relevant existing legislative provisions and incorporates new provisions into one ordinance. The consultation paper accompanying the Bill states that the

> parental responsibility model... emphasizes the obligations rather than the rights of the parents, and stresses the rights of the children to maintain a continuing relationship with both parents after divorce if it is in the child's best interests (p. 1).

The Bill is broadly based on England's Children Act 1989, as amended by the Children and Families Act 2014, together with Australian law's Family Law Act 1975 (as amended) and the Children (Scotland) Act 1995.

The Bill abolishes the outmoded common law right of the father to be natural guardian and replaces "guardianship" with "parental responsibility". Based on the Children (Scotland) Act 1995, the concept of parental responsibility under the Bill encompasses all parental duties and rights towards the child. The function of "parental right" is to help the parents fulfil "parental responsibility". The proposed responsibilities and rights of a parent are as follows:

Parental Responsibilities
(a) Safeguard the child's best interests.

---

30 Law Reform Commission of Hong Kong, *Subcommittee on Guardian and Custody—Consultation paper*, Hong Kong, The Law Reform Commission of Hong Kong, 1998; Law Reform Commission of Hong Kong, op cit, n. 6.

31 Labour and Welfare Bureau, LC Paper No. CB(2)1483/12-13(02), *Information paper for Legislative Council Panel on Welfare Services: Hong Kong Law Reform Commission report on child custody and access*, Hong Kong, Legislative Council Panel on Welfare Services, 2013, pp. 4-5.

32 Labour and Welfare Bureau, op cit, n. 3.

(b) Provide direction and guidance to the child in a manner appropriate to the child's development.
(c) Maintain personal relations and direct contact with the child on a regular basis.
(d) Act as the child's legal representative.

Parental Rights
(a) Live with the child or otherwise regulate the child's residence.
(b) Control, direct or guide the child's upbringing in a manner appropriate to the child's stage of development.
(c) Maintain personal relations and direct contact with the child on a regular basis.
(d) Act as the child's legal representative.

The Bill allows for parents' independent decision-making on daily matters, but requires mutual notification for major medical, educational and religious decisions for the child. It requires written consent of the other parent or a court order for a change of the child's surname, removing the child out of Hong Kong for more than one month, or permanently removing the child from Hong Kong.

Echoing the 2014 amendments to the Children Act 1989, the Bill abolishes custody and access orders, replacing them with: "Child Arrangement Orders", which address arrangements relating to the person with whom the child is to live, spend time or have contact; "Prohibited Steps Orders", which prohibit the exercise of certain aspects of parental responsibility, for example to prevent a parent from relocating the child outside the jurisdiction; and "Specific Issue Orders", which allow the court to determine a specific question that has arisen or may arise (e.g. schooling) in connection with any aspect of parental responsibility for a child. To assist the court in determining what is in the best interests of the child, a statutory checklist of factors was proposed, borrowing from both the Children Act 1989 and the Family Law Act 1975 (the latter providing the references to family violence and practical difficulties of the child maintaining contact with a parent). The checklist includes:
(1) The ascertainable views of the child concerned (considered in light of the child's age and understanding);
(2) The child's physical, emotional and educational needs;
(3) The nature of the relationship of the child with each of the child's parents and with other persons;
(4) The likely effect of any change in the child's circumstances;
(5 The child's age, maturity, sex and social and cultural background, as well as any other relevant characteristics;
(6) Any harm that the child has suffered or is at risk of suffering;
(7) Any family violence involving the child or a member of the child's family;

(8) How capable each of the child's parents, and any other person in relation to whom the court considers the question to be relevant, is of meeting the child's needs;
(9) The practical difficulty and expense of the child's maintaining contact with a parent.

As well as requiring reference to the child's views, the Bill specified how those views should be ascertained by the court, given that a child should not be required to express views, and set out a list of circumstances to determine when it is appropriate to appoint a separate representative for a child in children's proceedings. Other significant reforms include: the acquisition of parental responsibility for an unmarried father by signing the birth register; and the removal of the limitation (e.g. to apply for leave) on third parties (such as grand-parents) to apply for court orders (including maintenance orders against either or both parents) in relation to the child, as long as the child has been living with the third party for a total of one year out of the previous three years.

Words such as "joint", "shared" and "equal" in the models adopted in other jurisdictions suggested, to some extent, that parents had rights to shared time or shared rights to the child.[33] Given the difficulties encountered elsewhere, these words are totally omitted in the Bill. Furthermore, a non-prescriptive approach has been adopted to encourage the continuous involvement of both parents, particularly non-residential parents, without a presumption on the proportion of shared care or the extent of minimum contact. It takes a flexible legal framework to determine the preferred parenting arrangement according to what is in each child's best interests.[34]

In conjunction with the proposed legislative reform, specialized financial and Children's Dispute Resolution (CDR) procedures were formally introduced in 2016. The CDR procedures involve a preliminary hearing during the Children's Appointment, followed by a substantive CDR Hearing. At the Children's Appointment, the judge may adjourn any matters relating to the children for mediation or collaborative practice and instruct the parties to attend counselling or parent education programs. The Children's Appointment also gives an opportunity for the child to voice his/her views. Before the CDR hearing, a standard form is used to guide parents to think through what is the best arrangement for the children. In brief, the procedures address the children's best interests, aiming to reduce acrimony among family members and facilitate the settlement of parental differences outside the adversarial trial process.[35] The matter proceeds to trial only if a settlement is not achieved at the CDR hearing.

---

33 Law Society of Hong Kong, *Law Society's submissions: Labour and Welfare Bureau's consultation paper, children custody and access: Whether to implement the 'Joint Parental Responsibility Model' by legislative means*, Hong Kong, Law Society of Hong Kong, 2012, http://www.hklawsoc.org.hk/pub_e/news/submissions/20120424.pdf.

34 Labour and Welfare Bureau, op cit, n. 31, pp. 9-10.

35 Lynch, op cit, n. 2.

In addition to family justice system reforms, the Social Welfare Department has been undertaking publicity and public education work to promote the concept of continuing parental responsibility. These include a territory-wide program entitled *Marriage May End, but Parenthood Goes on*, including a set of DVDs, information sheets for social workers and parents, and handbooks providing more detailed information and guidance to separated/divorced parents and their children on co-parenting. A two-year pilot project on child contact services was launched in late 2016. Five specialised co-parenting support centres will be set up in 2019 to be operated by NGOs for five clusters over the territory:

> Services to be provided for divorced parents and their children include co-parenting counselling and parenting coordination service, structured parenting groups or programmes, child-focused counselling, groups or programmes, as well as children contact service.[36]

IV The Controversy on the Possible Impacts of the Law Reform on Families Involved

Despite the forthcoming legislation, possible impacts of the planned reform remain controversial. Those who support reform expect that parental hostility during divorce proceedings will be reduced by the prospect of both parents being involved in their children's lives post-divorce. The parents would see no need to battle for their parental rights through "winning" custody.[37] Women's groups and single parents' groups do not subscribe to the model. With concrete experience in the difficulty of managing relationships between partners before and after divorce, they consider that the model dictates demanding, if not unrealistic, expectations on separated/divorced parents. There are concerns that it may provide more excuses and opportunities for abusive parents to continue harassing their former spouses and children after separation/divorce. Furthermore, those parents who remain angry or hostile may abuse the new model to cause trouble (short of violence) for the former spouse and children.[38]

These concerns indicate the need for thoughtful scrutiny of the possible impacts of the proposed legislation for members of affected families. The following sections present a

36 Legislative Council Panel on Welfare Services, *Follow-up on the Law Reform Commission Report on Child Custody and Access and related* support *measures*, Hong Kong, Social Welfare Department, 12 March 2018, p. 4.

37 A. Scully-Hill, 'A critical evaluation of the draft Children Proceedings (Parental Responsibility) Bill', *Hong Kong Law Journal*, Vol. 46, No. 2, 2016, pp. 387-404.

38 Y.K. Lau, 'The debate over the joint parental responsibility model in Hong Kog', *China Journal of Social Work*, Vol. 7, No. 2, 2014, pp. 145-60.

comprehensive family impact assessment of the bill, and identify the measures necessary to maximize the potential benefits of the law reform and minimize its negative impacts.

V Family Impact Analysis

Family impact analysis (FIA) is informed by a growing vision of incorporating a family perspective or family impact lens in policymaking.[39] It examines how policy or legislation may benefit families or produce unintended negative consequences. Based on an ecological-systemic perspective, FIA envisions that policies, legislations and programs constitute and shape the environmental context in which families function, thus affecting family well-being.[40] The law of divorce is a social and psychological process, in addition to a legal one. Decisions by parents and courts to have impacts on the parties concerned years after the legal divorce.[41]

The most common approach for conducting a FIA adopts a checklist. A key step of this approach is the selection of a suitable checklist and checklist questions.[42] After careful scrutiny, the UK's Family Test provides the most direct and relevant questions that address the family impacts of the proposed bill.[43] There are five questions in the test:

(1) What kind(s) of impact might the policy have on family formation?
(2) What kind(s) of impact will the policy have on families going through key transitions, such as becoming parents, getting married, fostering or adopting, bereavement, redundancy, new caring responsibilities or the onset of a long-term health condition?
(3) What impacts will the policy have on all family members' ability to play a full role in family life, including parenting and other caring responsibilities?
(4) How does the policy impact families before, during and after couple separation?
(5) How does the policy impact those families most at risk of deterioration of relationship quality and breakdown?

39 K. Bogenschneider, O.M. Little, T. Ooms, S. Benning, K. Cadigan & T. Corebett, 'The family impact lens: A family-focused evidence-informed approach to policy and practice', *Family Relations*, Vol. 61, 2012, pp. 514-31; Families Commission, *Methodologies for analyzing the impact of public policy on families*, Wellington, Families Commission, 2005.

40 Bogenschneider et al, op cit, n. 39; Families Commission, op cit, n. 39; C.K. Law, *Family impact analysis and two case studies: Public rental housing and comprehensive social security assistance*, Hong Kong, Central Policy Unit, 2008; D.Wong, *Family proofing policy—A review of international experience of family impact assessment*, Cambridge, UK, Relationships Foundation, 2010.

41 Law Reform Commission of Hong Kong, op cit, n. 6, p. 4

42 Family Impact Institute, *Conducting a family impact analysis of rules, legislation, laws, or programs*, West Lafayette, Indiana, Purdue University, 2017.

43 Department for Work and Pension, *Family Test—Guidance for government departments*, UK, Department for Work and Pension, 2014.

These questions are interrelated rather than discrete, so questions 2 to 4 will be combined to facilitate the analysis. The first question will be expanded to address family preservation. The following analysis is based on research evidence on the impacts of similar law reforms in other countries and some research findings in Hong Kong.

VI Possible Family Impacts of the Bill

A *Impacts on Family Formation and Preservation*

The Bill aims to preserve the parent-child relationship and parents' commitment to the welfare of the children despite the dissolution of the couple's relationship. In addition to the paradigm shift from the emphasis on "parental rights and authority" to "parental responsibility", the reform conveys a strong message on the "indissolubility of parenthood" and the "enduring family".[44] Divorce ends the marriage but not necessarily the family, though it does introduce significant family transitions. Ahrons proposed the concept of "binuclear family" as parents living apart but continuing to be parents of their children and parental partners to one another.[45] In other words, the parental responsibility model may preserve the family and facilitate its transformation into a cross-household family system. But Smart and Neale warn that by legitimizing post-divorce families as binuclear families and emphasizing the need for both parents' involvement in the healthy development of the children, we may reinforce a pathological perspective on single parenthood.[46] In the Chinese context of Hong Kong, there is a strong emphasis on family integrity. Single-parent families are perceived as "broken families" and single parents as deficient parents.[47] Unnecessary and unverified postulations have frequently been made linking suicide and other family tragedies to single parenthood and the families of divorced parents.[48] Further reinforcement of this deficit perspective may harm families in alternative arrangements, such as single-parent families and grand-parenting families.

---

44 Parkinson, op cit, n. 7; Parkinson, op cit, n. 16, pp. 611-26.

45 C.R. Ahrons, *Good divorce: Keeping your family together when your marriage comes apart*, New York, Harper Collins, 1994.

46 C. Smart, & B. Neale, *Family Fragments?*, Cambridge, Polity Press, 1999.

47 Caritas-Hong Kong, *Report on public opinion on single parent families*, Hong Kong, Caritas-Hong Kong, 2000; Y.K. Lau, 'Social welfare services for single parent families in Hong Kong: A paradox', *Family and Child Social Work*, Vol. 8, No. 1, 2003, pp. 47-52.

48 C.K. Law, *Study on newspaper report on single parents and divorcees*, Hong Kong, Office of Law Chi Kong, Hong Kong Legislative Council, 2000.

B *Impacts on Families Going through the Transition of Separation/Divorce and Family Members' Ability to Play a Full Role in Family Life*

1 Reinstatement of Non-Residential Parents' Parenthood

Separation and divorce are stressful life events and family transition.[49] Continued contact with both parents after divorce may minimize the children's loss of important relationships. The Bill conveys a clear social expectation of ongoing contact for both parents with the children and of cooperative parenting. In England & Wales, Neale and Smart perceived similar reform as a move towards restoring the status of fatherhood.[50] As in that jurisdiction, most non-residential parents in Hong Kong are fathers. There is also an increasing trend in fathers' involvement in childcare,[51] and so the proposed bill may similarly restore fathers' position. The parenthood of unmarried fathers would be similarly reinforced through the acquisition of parental responsibility by signing the birth register.

Studies in the United States have identified a trend towards an increase in fathers' post-divorce involvement with their children alongside changes in the law governing child custody.[52] Systemic meta-analysis found the benefits of an ongoing, meaningful relationship between non-residential parents and children. It is the quality of contact rather than the frequency of contact that matters.[53] Consistently, studies in Hong Kong found that non-residential parents' involvement in quality parenting was positively associated with children's well-being.[54]

2 The Mixed Impacts when Complicated Family Dynamics Arise from Post-Divorce Co-Parenting

Nevertheless, empirical studies found that non-residential parents' involvement is not always beneficial to children's well-being. Its effects are very much a function of the broader

49 T.H. Holmes & R.H. Rahe, 'The social readjustment rating scale', *Journal of Psychosomatic Research*, Vol. 11, No. 2, 1967, pp. 213-18.

50 B. Neale & C. Smart, 'Experiments with parenthood?', *Sociology*, Vol. 31, No. 2, 1997, pp. 201-19.

51 M. Liong, *Chinese fatherhood, gender and family*, London, U.K., Palgrave Macmillan, 2017.

52 E.E. Maccoby, C.E. Depner & R.H. Mnookin, 'Custody of children following divorce', *in* E.M. Hetherington & J.D. Arasteh (Eds.), *Impact of divorce, single parenting, and stepparenting on children*, New York, London: Psychological Press, 2014.

53 K. Adamsons & S.K. Johnson, 'An updated and expanded meta-analysis of non-residential fathering and child well-being', *Journal of Family Psychology*, Vol. 27, No. 4, 2013, pp. 589-99; P.R. Amato & J. G. Gilbreth, 'Non-resident fathers and children's well-being: A meta-analysis', *Journal of Marriage and the Family*, Vol. 61, No. 3, 1999, pp. 557-73.

54 Y.K. Lau, 'Parent-child relationship, parental relationship and children's self-esteem in post-divorce families in Hong Kong', *Marriage and Family Review*, Vol. 42, No. 4, 2008, pp. 87-103; Y.K. Lau, T.H. Lam & F.K. Cheung, *Impact of co-parenting approaches on children's well-being in post-divorce families in Hong Kong*, Hong Kong, Hong Kong Family Welfare Society, 2016.

family context.[55] There is strong evidence that continuing and regular contact with both parents is beneficial to children when parents cooperate and communicate and have low levels of conflict. It is equally evidenced that ongoing post-separation parental conflict is damaging for children.[56]

A report of resident parents who were users of a family services agency in Hong Kong found that post-divorce co-parenting is a demanding task for parents with continuing relational difficulties, often generating complicated family dynamics.[57] More active parental involvement by non-residential parents exposed children to greater risk of being triangulated within parental conflicts and of a lower degree of residential parent-child intimacy.[58] Furthermore, conforming to social expectations for post-divorce co-parenting was correlated with more parental communication and inter-parental support, and simultaneously more inter-parental conflict.[59] Barnett also commented that similar law reform in England & Wales seems to sustain the post-separation family by constraining resident parents' autonomy (mostly women) and placing an invisible burden on them to facilitate and sustain post-separation contact between children and fathers.[60] These complicated family dynamics suggest that the proposed reform might be a mixed blessing to children and parents in those families.

3 A Comprehensive Package of Reforms May Facilitate the Family Transitions

Fortunately, studies in the US and Australia found that the majority of parents in shared care expressed satisfaction with their parenting arrangements.[61] In Australia, the comprehensive package of reform has induced a cultural change with reduced court applications and increased use of mediation.[62] It is recognized that many of the disputes over children following separation are driven by relationship problems rather than legal ones. These disputes are better suited to community-based, child-focused interventions that assist

55 K.K. Elam, I. Sandler, S. Wolchik & J.Y. Tein, 'Non-residential father–child involvement, interparental conflict and mental health of children following divorce: A person-focused approach', *Journal of Youth and Adolescence*, Vol. 45, 2016, pp. 581-93.

56 Fehlberg et al, op cit, n. 22.

57 Lau et al, op cit, n. 54.

58 Y.K. Lau, 'Post-divorce co-parenting and children's well-being in Hong Kong', paper presented in the International Conference on Shared Parenting (ICSP) in Boston, MA, USA on 29 May 2017.

59 Lau et al, op cit, n. 54.

60 A.E. Barnett, *Contact at all costs? Domestic violence, child contact and the practices of the courts and professionals* (PhD thesis), London, UK, Brunel University, 2014.

61 R. Kaspiew, M. Gray, R. Weston, L. Moloney, K. Hand & L. Qu, *Evaluation of the 2006 Family Law Reforms*, Melbourne, Australian Institute of Family Studies, 2009; N.S. Melli & P.R. Brown, 'Exploring a new family form – The shared time family', *International Journal of Law, Policy and the Family*, Vol. 22, No. 2, 2008, pp. 231-69; P. Parkinson & B. Smyth, 'Satisfaction and dissatisfaction with father-child contact arrangements in Australia research', *Child and Family Law Quarterly*, Vol. 6, No. 1, 2004, pp. 289-304.

62 Parkinson, op cit, n. 14.

parents to resolve the relationship problems. Most of the parents attempting family dispute resolution were able to sort out their arrangement.[63] Jamison, Coleman, Ganong, and Feistman's qualitative study in the US showed that successful transition to amicable and civilized post-divorce co-parenting is possible. Empathetic support services to facilitate the reorganization of inner life and behaviours, as well as a workable parenting plan, may help.[64] For parents who are willing but struggling in managing conflicts, parallel parenting plans may reduce conflict by addressing the specifics and providing a structure that reduces the parents' need for contact.[65] These studies underscore the importance of a good services system.

4 The Need for a Well-Integrated Legal and Relationship Services System in Hong Kong

In Hong Kong, separating/divorcing parents are encouraged to use mediation on a voluntary basis.[66] The service is under-utilized, as reflected in the relatively low number of mediation cases compared with the number of divorces granted. There is no evaluation of the compliance rate of agreement and re-litigation after mediation.[67] The only existing project on parental coordination and the project on child contact service are under operation with short-term funding. The services' long-term future depends on further funding. Furthermore, after reviewing the recent reforms in Hong Kong's family justice system, Lynch pointed out that, despite the various reform efforts at different levels, there is a lack of coordination to ensure consistent and cost-effective reform.[68]

The setting up of specialised co-parenting support centres is an encouraging development. It reflects an enhanced attention to challenges that co-parenting imposes on parents with relational difficulties and on their children. However, the service's quality, adequacy of manpower, and its integration and coordination with the family justice system will significantly determine its effectiveness. If the service innovation facilitates the development of well-integrated, coordinated legal and relationship services, the positive trend of declining disputes in Australia would be more likely to happen in Hong Kong.

63 Kaspiew et al, op cit, n. 61.
64 T.B. Jamison, M. Coleman, L.H. Ganong & R.E. Feistman, 'Transitioning to postdivorce family life: A grounded theory investigation of resilience in coparenting', *Family Relations*, Vol. 63, No. 3, 2014, pp. 411-23.
65 L. Nielsen, 'Shared residential custody: Review of the research (Part I of II)', *American Journal of Family Law*, Vol. 27, No. 1, 2013, pp. 61-72.
66 Y.K. Lee & A. Lakhani, 'The case for mandatory mediation to effectively address child custody issues in Hong Kong', *International Journal of Law, Policy and the Family*, Vol. 26, No. 3, 2012, pp. 327-50.
67 Department of Social Work, The Chinese University of Hong Kong, 'A study on family mediation services in Hong Kong—Final report', Hong Kong, Central Policy Unit, 2017.
68 Lynch, op cit, n. 2.

C Impacts on those Families Most at Risk of Deterioration of Relationship Quality

The greatest concern about the impacts of the law reform relates to families with domestic abuse or an imbalance in the parties' respective dominance or control. The results of a recent study in Hong Kong highlight the power issues inherent in divorcing and post-divorce families with domestic violence.[69] The study found that physical violence before divorce or separation increases the likelihood of both an unequal co-parental relationship and conflict later on. It seemed to coerce residential parents to make more concession in the post-divorce childcare and visitation arrangements. While a presumption of continuing parental responsibilities may empower caring non-residential parents to negotiate greater parental involvement, it may also strengthen the hand of a non-residential parent wishing to manipulate or harass the other parent.[70]

To balance the emphasis of parent-child contacts and parental involvement with adequate protection against abuse, the proposed Bill has included a history of family violence and abuse in the checklist as a consideration in determining the best interests of the child. By contrast, the "friendly parent" provision—a parent's willingness and effort to facilitate the parental involvement of the other parent[71]—is not a consideration in determining the child's best interests. This may reduce the risk of a parent hesitating to disclose family violence or resist contact owing to the fear of being perceived as an "unfriendly parent". A non-prescriptive parenting arrangement framework may help to reduce the risk of harassment and abuse. However, some respondents in the previous consultations expressed concerns that the legislation was not sufficiently flexible to provide for individual cases.[72] Such worries reflect the confusion of the Hong Kong legislation with laws in jurisdictions that adopted a presumption of shared care or even equal share of time.

The concern about better protection of children and parents subjected to domestic violence has also been addressed with the amendment of the Domestic Violence Ordinance (scheduled to become the Domestic and Cohabitation Relationship Violence Ordinance) in 2009. The ordinance was expanded to persons formerly in spousal/cohabitation relationships with their children. However, the legislation is under-utilized owing to lack of awareness and knowledge about the law, as well as sociocultural factors, such as reluctance to talk about violence.[73]

69 Lau et al, op cit, n. 54.

70 F. Kaganas, 'A presumption that 'involvement' of both parents is best: Deciphering law's messages', *Child and Family Law Quarterly*, Vol. 25, 2013, pp. 270-96.

71 Graycar, op cit, n. 18; Smyth et al, op cit, n. 18.

72 Labour and Welfare Bureau, op cit, n. 31, p. 6.

73 A. Barrow & A. Scully-Hill, 'Failing to implement CEDAW in Hong Kong: Why isn't anyone using the Domestic Cohabitation Relationships Violence Ordinance?' *International Journal of Law, Policy and the Family*, Vol. 30, 2016, pp. 50-78.

VII Conclusion and Recommendations

The preceding analysis points to the possible positive impacts of the Bill on family preservation and restoration of fatherhood in families that have undergone parental separation or divorce. However, for families in which parents have continuous relational difficulties – to whom the law is most likely to apply in litigation in practice – existing research evidence suggests that the Bill may have mixed impacts. The greatest concern about the impacts of the reform relates to families with domestic violence and abuse. Though efforts have been made in the proposed Bill to balance the emphasis on parent-child contacts and parental involvement with adequate protection against abuse, it is necessary to promote the existing ordinance on domestic violence and its integration with the legal and relationship services in the family law system.

It is evident from the Australian experience that change to the legislative framework in family law risks being interpreted differently by various interest groups and professionals.[74] Misunderstanding of the presumption of the legislation should be addressed via a clear statement in the bill to clarify its non-prescriptive approach in contact and parenting arrangements. The statement on the meaning of "involvement" in English law's Children and Families Act 2014 (s1(2B)) is a useful precedent.[75] To maximize the potential benefits of the law reform in Hong Kong and minimize its negative impacts for all family members, the setting up of co-parenting support centres is hopefully a start of the establishment of a holistic well-integrated services system. Without active case management and well-organized and supported family courts, disputed cases usually drift endlessly through the legal system as different alternative dispute resolution measures are attempted with mounted expenses and escalated negative emotions.[76]

Jaffe, Ashbourne and Mamo proposed a family justice system with a case management paradigm based on a principled approach to promoting appropriate dispute resolution.[77] The principled approach emphasizes different intervention strategies ranging from non-intervention to court-mandated intense interventions. The foundation of the approach is a careful screening of the nature and degree of conflict between the parents and early interventions of the judges and clinicians to minimize post-separation/divorce parenting disputes. Schepard stated the importance of integrating violence sensitivity into parent education and mediation. Rather than emphasizing that "parents should cooperate for the

74 Family Law Committee, *Final federal-provincial-territorial report on custody and access and child support—Putting children first*, Ottawa, Canada, Department of Justice Canada, 2002.

75 See Families Act 2014, ss. 1(2B).

76 A.A. Mamo, P.G. Jaffe & D.G. Chiodo, *Recapturing and renewing the vision of the family court*, Toronto, Canada, Ministry of the Attorney General, 2008.

77 P.G. Jaffe, D. Ashbourne & A.A. Mamo, 'Early identification and prevention of parent-child alienation: A framework for balancing risks and benefits of intervention', *Family Court Review*, Vol. 48, No. 1, 2010, pp. 136-52.

benefit of the children", parent education programs have to make the message clear that "parents should cooperate if it is safe for parents and children to do so". Mediators should be trained to recognize domestic violence before and during the mediation process.[78]

The family law system should also carefully screen for different types of violence, for instance, "conflict-instigated violence" that is physical violence used as a tool of conflict resolution and "control-instigated violence" that is part of a larger and planned pattern of domination. The former is more amenable to positive intervention, while the latter is based on a deeply rooted personality trait that is much more taxing to change.[79] Though all domestic violence is unacceptable, individualized consideration is necessary when helping families with domestic violence to develop post-divorce parenting plans with a greater focus on protection of victims and children, with less emphasis on speedy, cooperative outcomes:[80]

> Only an effective screening program can provide high conflict families with special treatment without overly burdening the reasonably cooperative majority of divorcing parents whose children do not need extensive state intervention for their protection.[81]

In summary, a holistic, well-integrated services system requires the development of differentiated services that can benefit the multiple needs of separating/divorcing and post-separation/post-divorce families. It also requires a multidisciplinary partnership with close orchestration of the family court's interventions and interventions provided by community-based services.[82] Hopefully, the services system could be developed in Hong Kong as a package with the law reform. The effectiveness of these service system innovations and the actual impacts of the law reform should be rigorously evaluated to inform any necessary remedies and further innovations.

---

78 A. Schepard, 'The evolving judicial role in child custody dispute: From fault finder to conflict manager to differential case management', *University of Arkansas at Little Rock Law Review*, Vol. 22, No. 3, 2000, pp. 395-428.

79 Jaffe et al, op cit, n. 77.

80 Jaffe et al, op cit, n. 77; J.R. Johnston, 'Domestic violence and parent-child relationships in families disputing custody', *Australian Journal of Family Law*, Vol. 9, 1995, pp. 12-25.

81 Schepard, op cit, n. 78, p. 422.

82 J.R. Johnston, 'Building multidisciplinary professional partnerships with the court on behalf of high-conflict divorcing families and their children: Who needs what kind of help', *University of Arkansas at Little Rock Law Review*, Vol. 22, No. 3, 2000, pp. 453-79.

Parental Alienation, Contact Refusal and Maladaptive Gatekeeping: a Multidisciplinary Approach to Prevention of Contact Failure

Philip Marcus[*]

I Introduction

This paper proposes a multidisciplinary approach, based in part on a quasi-medical analogy, for prevention of one of the most difficult situations facing family courts and therapists – when contact between a child and a parent does not take place: contact failure.

At present, these situations are handled by professionals in three fields: mental health, social work, and the court system. The issues are dealt with only when the problem has become acute – when contact between the child and a parent has already been or is about to be severed. Little or nothing is done to prevent contact failure, and by the time the parents or one of them ask for help, much damage has already been done, and the situation may be irrevocable. There is, therefore, a need for early identification, both of the populations of children and parents who are at-risk of contact failure, and the first signs of distress which point to the possibility of a child ceasing to have contact with one of his parents. This requires the harnessing of members of many professions in a coordinated effort.

This paper describes, on the basis of published research and personal experience, as a family lawyer and family court judge, the factors which may lead to failure of contact, and suggests methods of preventing it.

II The Quasi-Medical Analogy

In our lifetime, poliomyelitis has been almost completely eradicated. The eradication took place in stages: First, the medical world treated the symptoms, but not the cause, and only when the disease became acute; they called the disease by its symptom – infantile paralysis. The second stage was the identification of the poliomyelitis virus leading to a specific diagnosis. The third stage was recognition of the method of transmission of the virus. As a result, the public was made aware of the risk factors and encouraged to take appropriate

* Judge (retired), Jerusalem Family Court, Israel.

precautions (including handwashing after using the lavatory) for prevention. Finally, a vaccine was developed, by Dr Jonas Salk; the WHO recommended universal vaccination; governments made vaccination compulsory; and lives are saved in their hundreds of thousands.

This medical victory has the following components:

- identifying the phenomenon;
- identifying the causes;
- identifying at-risk populations; and
- raising public awareness of the disease and its causes, and development of preventive techniques.

This paper seeks to apply the lessons learned from the eradication of polio to a phenomenon which affects millions of children, and in many cases causes them lasting emotional and psychological damage: the cessation of contact between a child and his parent. It looks to the fields of epidemiology and public health, and suggests how educational and health professionals and others should be involved in prevention and early intervention.

Adoption of the epidemiology/public health model would include:

- increasing public awareness of the phenomenon and its causes;
- enabling identification of at-risk populations and of the first signs which point to behaviours which are liable to cause a child to resist contact with a parent and outright refusal of contact; and
- taking steps to prevent contact failure.

The medical analogy is of course not a perfect fit. However, where there is a possibility that a child will – without good cause – stop having any contact with one of his parents, it is possible to educate about the risk factors and dangers of contact failure, and about the first signs which point to the possibility of the development of alienation, and thereby prevent deterioration.

Identification of the early signs is crucial; the period of time between the first signs of resistance to contact and the total breakdown of contact may be as little as 3-4 months.[1] Restoration of contact later is exceptionally difficult.

1 Mordechai Sheri (Clinical Psychologist, expert witness in Family Court cases involving children, Israel), (personal communication, 2017).

III Contact Failure, Parental Alienation, Refusal, Resistance and Gatekeeping

Parents are the adults who are primarily responsible for raising their children, and whose basic concern should be the best interests of the child (see, for example, article 18 of the 1990 UN Convention on the Rights of the Child, hereinafter "CRC"). The Convention imposes duties on the States parties to it to ensure performance of certain obligations. Among these are, that parents protect their children from harm (article 3), and encourage and enable them to develop normal inter-personal relationships. This includes the duty to allow the child to be the child of two active and involved parents (article 9 of the CRC establishes that a child who is separated from one or both parents shall maintain personal relations and direct contact with both parents, except if it is contrary to the child's best interests) and to encourage him to love both of them (articles 24 and 27 of the CRC provide that the child's health and physical, mental, spiritual, moral and social development be assured). In biblical terms, we speak of giving the child the opportunity to honour both parents. This brings with it the duty of each parent not to interfere with the development and keeping of good relationships.[2]

When the parents of children are at odds, even when divorce or separation proceedings have not yet started, their children are inevitably affected by the changes in their lifestyle; the foundations on which their lives have been built are shaking, and they will have to live, at best, in two homes rather than one. Where the parents are preoccupied with the dispute, they may have less time to attend to the children's needs. When the dispute develops into open conflict, the children very often find themselves exposed to arguments and verbal and physical fights; this undermines their sense of safety and stability. They hear things that one parent says to, or about, the other parent. Where one parent opposes the separation, the child, who also fears the breakup of the family, may identify with that parent. The child may feel angry, abandoned, and injured, and he may find himself taking sides in the dispute or being enlisted by one parent against the other.[3] This is exacerbated when the parents separate and disagree as to where the children are going to live and who is going to make decisions about them, and the best interests of the child have to be determined by the court.[4]

---

2 P. Marcus, 'Parental Responsibilities: Reformulating the Paradigm for Parent–Child Relationships', *Journal of Child Custody*, Vol. 14, No. 2-3, 2017, pp. 83-105 and 106-33. In this two-part article, I deal with the responsibilities of parents to children, not in terms of the rights of the child, nor on the basis of parental rights, but on a foundation of duties and responsibilities.

3 Z.B. Bergman & E. Witztum, 'Parental Kidnapping and Parental Alienation Syndrome' *Sichot (Hebrew)* Vol. 9, No. 2, 1995, pp. 115-130; D. Gottlieb, 'Parental Alienation Syndrome', *Medicine and Law (Hebrew)*, Vol. 31, 2004, pp. 106-116.

4 In my article, op cit, n. 2, I criticize the use of terms such as custody and visitation, which exacerbate the legal confrontation between the parents. Even where these terms have been replaced by parental responsi-

Sooner or later, especially in situations of high conflict between the parents, some children stop seeing one of the parents. This is referred to in this paper as "**contact failure**". There may be many reasons for contact failure:

- Where the child has been physically or sexually abused by a parent, or a parent has abused or killed the other parent, the child (or resident parent on the child's behalf) may be justified in breaking off contact with the perpetrator.
- Sometimes a child will choose to break off relations with one of his parents, so as to resolve (he thinks) the impossible conflict of loyalties that he feels.
- In other cases both parents may bear part of the responsibility.
- However, in many cases one of the parents has acted or said things to the child which have caused the breakdown of contact.

The term "**parental alienation"** became popular in the late 1980's, principally as a result of the work of Richard Gardner, who described contact failure as the parental alienation syndrome.[5] He suggested that one parent was always to blame when contact failed, and suggested methods, some of them quite radical and alarming, to change the situation.

Others place the blame, or at least part of it, on the child. There are cases in which children, and particularly adolescents, refuse contact, and both the parents and their advisors are sure that the parents bear no responsibility. This is the basic understanding of the terms "**contact refusal**" or "**contact resistance**", or the **refuse-reject dynamic** (RRD).[6]

In some jurisdictions (such as England and Wales[7]), the failure of contact is sometimes described as being the result of an **intractable dispute** between the parents. The word "intractable" implies pessimism about the possibility of resolving the issues, and carries with it a negation of the parents' joint responsibility to act in their children's best interests, as if they may continue their fight regardless of the effect it has on their children.

All of the terms usually used to describe the situation in which arrangements for a child to have contact with a parent do not take place – parental alienation, contact resistance or refusal, intractable dispute, and the like – imply blame, which requires a judicial finding of fault, with the child or with a parent.

---

bility, or joint or shared custody, the parents feel compelled to fight about recognition as the dominant or more important parent. The reality is that parents often argue over these issues, instead of looking hard and clearly at the needs of the specific child and the ability and availability of each parent to supply these needs, so as to reach an agreed arrangement for the benefit of the child.

5 R.A. Gardner, *The Parental Alienation Syndrome*, 2nd ed., Creskill (New Jersey), Creative Therapies Inc., 1998.

6 M.G. Walters & S. Friedlander, 'When a Child Rejects a Parent: Working with the Intractable Resist/Refuse Dynamic', *Family Court Review*, Vol. 54, No. 3, 2016, pp. 424-55.

7 See, for example, *Q v R (intractable contact)* [2017] EWFC B35.

It is regrettable that in many circles, *all* cases in which a child ceases to have contact with a parent are attributed to parental alienation, that is, to the acts or omissions of one parent only. This encourages high conflict disputes, in which the child is the inevitable victim, wounded, often critically, by the incessant crossfire between the parents. It is perhaps because of the indiscriminate use of the term "parental alienation syndrome" that lawyers and others contend that there is no such thing.

Use of this type of emotionally loaded blaming terminology has two effects, both of which obstruct the finding of solutions. One effect is that the use of a quasi-scientific terms diverts the discussion away from looking at the individual child and his family. Instead, the parents, their lawyers and expert witnesses spend time and resources fighting over whether the facts of the case fit or do not fit the criteria for the existence of the syndrome, or over who is at fault. In the meantime, the child's feelings of guilt, and/or his conviction that his hostility to one parent and alliance with the other parent are justified, only become more embedded. As Walters and Friedlander have observed:

> Time is a major enemy in RRD cases. The dynamic becomes increasingly entrenched the longer it remains unaddressed and the longer the period of no contact between the rejected parent and the child. The excruciatingly slow pace at which the court system moves also delays efforts to resolve the problem and may be exacerbated by a prolonged evaluation, and as well as litigation over intervention. In fact, delay has often been employed as a legal tactic in such cases, especially in cases of older adolescents, as the court is less inclined to intervene as the adolescent gets older, and once the adolescent turns eighteen the court no longer has jurisdiction.[8]

The second effect is the false impression that until there is total absence of contact, and sometimes even then, nothing should be done (or perhaps can be done) about a family in which relations between the parents, or between a parent and a child, are at risk. This is exacerbated by the classification of contact failure as *mild* – where the child is reluctant to have contact but still sees the targeted parent and enjoys his stay; *medium* – where the child resists visiting and if he does see the targeted parent, curses him or accuses him, and may destroy property; and *severe* – when no contact is possible.[9] As this article demonstrates, there is a need for intervention at the first signs of reluctance, since the speed of deterioration is very swift. While the description of the child's behaviour is accurate, the classification of mild may give the impression that intervention is as yet unnecessary.

8 Walters & Friedlander, op cit, n. 6, p. 429.

9 https://psychlaw.net/are-there-different-degrees-of-parental-alienation/.

There are still therapists who refuse to take on helping a child who is in the throes of a high-conflict battle between the parents until there is a final judicial decision about custody and related matters. Their rationalizations include an unwillingness to taint any evidence of the suffering of the child, or fear of manipulation by one or other parent of the treatment or findings. To the contrary, any signs of reluctance of a child to have contact with a parent must be tackled immediately, and it is unfortunate that there are professionals who are prepared to justify non-involvement for reasons that are irrelevant to the issues at stake.

IV Why Does Contact Fail?

Most researchers and practitioners dispute the need to use the terminology of a syndrome, and prefer to identify the causes of the problem on a case-by-case basis.[10] 'Contact failure' is a neutral description of these situations, and avoids allocating blame. Quite simply, the fact is that contact, ordinarily the natural connection between child and parent, is not taking place.

In what follows, this paper will principally discuss the fourth of the causes of "contact failure" identified above, what might be called true parental alienation, where one parent behaves or speaks in a way which distances a child from the other parents. However, many of the recommendations and suggestions for early identification of distress in a child and for immediate intervention are equally applicable to cases in which the child himself, without pressure from one of the parents, becomes reluctant to have contact or breaks off contact, or cases in which *both* parents bear some level of responsibility

It is rare for one parent to say directly to the child that he must have no contact with the other. The reasons why a child stops seeing a parent usually build up over time. But where one of the parents has, by words or actions, made it more difficult for the child to enjoy contact with the other parent, or has encouraged the child, by action or default, to form an unjustifiably negative view of the other parent, this is a manifest breach of his obligation, identified above, to encourage correct and loving relations between the child and the other parent.[11]

A Gatekeeping

Much of this behaviour falls within the category of "parental gatekeeping". Parental gatekeeping refers to how parents' attitudes and actions affect the involvement and quality of

10 B.J. Fidler, N. Bala & M. Saini, *Children Who Resist Post-separation Parental Contact,* Oxford, OUP, 2013; S. Friedlander & M.G. Walters, 'When a Child Rejects a Parent', *Family Court Review*, Vol. 48, No. 1, 2010, pp. 98-111.

11 Text to n. 2 supra.

the relationship between the other parent and child, whether positively or negatively. Gatekeeping takes many forms, and is not necessary inappropriate; it may be facilitative or restrictive. Facilitative gatekeeping occurs when a parent acts to support continuing involvement and maintenance of a meaningful relationship with the child. 'Facilitating' behaviours are proactive, inclusive, and demonstrate to the child that the parent values the other parent's contributions. "Restrictive" gatekeeping entails parental actions intended to interfere with the other parent's involvement with the child and that would predictably undermine the quality of their relationship. Sometimes restrictive gatekeeping is essential, for example where there has been a history of abusive or inappropriate behaviour of the parent toward the child or in his presence; but if gatekeeping is damaging to the child, it is 'maladaptive': it unnecessarily damages the quality of the other parent's relationship or restricts the level of his involvement with the child.[12]

For this reason, the appropriate question to ask in any case is not just whether gatekeeping is restrictive. The issue is whether, in the particular circumstances of the specific child, the gatekeeping is appropriate or maladaptive.[13] that is, whether it serves the child's interests or deprives the child of the contact he needs, for his healthy development, with the other parent.

B Maladaptive Gatekeeping and Alienation

According to Darnall,[14] alienating parents (including parents who engage in maladaptive gatekeeping) fall into three main categories:

- Those who do it consciously out of spite and/or hatred; they know it is wrong but seek vengeance and "justice", or payback for the perceived responsibility of the targeted parent for failure of the marriage, etc. They may make false accusations of abuse of the child. This is described as conscious, malicious, direct and active behaviour.
- Those who do it because of a personality defect or disorder; they do not see it as being wrong. They have no insight, and externalize responsibility.
- Those who do it carelessly, almost passively, because they do not understand what they are doing or the effects of what they are doing on the child, or they do not understand that the child's refusal is an inadequate way of coping with a very difficult situation,

12 W.G. Austin, L. Fieldstone & M.K. Pruett, 'Bench book for assessing parental gatekeeping in parenting disputes: understanding the dynamics of gate closing and opening for the best interests of children', *Journal of Child Custody*, Vol. 10, 2013, pp. 1-16.

13 M.A. Saini, L.M. Drozd & N.W. Olesen, 'Adaptive and Maladaptive Gatekeeping Behaviors and Attitudes: Implications for Child Outcomes after Separation and Divorce', *Family Court Review*, Vol. 55, No. 2, 2017, pp. 260-72.

14 D. Darnall *Divorce Casualties: Protecting Your Child from Parental Alienation,* Lanham (Maryland), Taylor Publishing Co., 1998.

and thus do not try to stop it. This is described as naïve, unconscious, or manipulative alienation (or gatekeeping).

The first and third categories of maladaptive gatekeeping and alienation may be preventable, by suitable education and intervention at the first signs. This paper suggests suitable techniques below. However, the second category needs to be dealt with by the court as soon as possible, since the perpetrators are susceptible to neither education nor persuasion, and will manipulate or sabotage attempts at mediation or treatment.

In the current state of the literature, good progress has been made in identifying the reasons for contact failure, and in particular in honing the definition of gatekeeping and its typology. Maladaptive gatekeeping is a precursor, and also a predictor, of alienation of a child from the parent. To this extent, we are, as regards contact failure, at the same point as the second stage in the fight against polio: the symptoms have been described, and the causes of the phenomenon have been identified. The challenge is to proceed to the next stages: arousing public awareness and developing measures that prevent the problem from becoming pathological.

It is unlikely that contact failure can be prevented in all cases: for example, where there are false allegations of abuse, including sexual abuse (as part of a programme of alienation[15]) and when the child is convinced that he was abused as an infant. It is unlikely that such cases would be susceptible to the measures proposed here. However, prevention of contact failure will generally be to the great benefit each child.

V Why We Need to Prevent Contact Failure

Understanding the short- and long-term effects of alienation on children is crucial when considering if, when and how there should be intervention. There is a wealth of literature about the effects of alienation and maladaptive gatekeeping that consistently reports that alienated children are at risk of emotional distress and adjustment difficulties, far more than children from litigating families where there has been no alienation.

A *Alienated Children Suffer*

Children who stop having contact with a parent often express fear of that parent, even though the fear may have no rational basis. Clinical observations, case reviews and both qualitative and empirical studies uniformly indicate that alienated children may exhibit:

- poor reality testing;

15 Fidler, Bala & Saini, op cit, n. 10, p. 40.

- illogical cognitive operations;
- simplistic and rigid information processing;
- inaccurate or distorted interpersonal perceptions;
- disturbed and compromised interpersonal functioning;
- self-hatred;
- low self-esteem, or inflated self-esteem or feelings of omnipotence;
- pseudo-maturity;
- identity and self-image problems;
- poor differentiation of self (enmeshment, parentification);
- aggression and conduct disorders;
- disregard for social norms and authority;
- poor impulse control;
- emotional constriction, passivity, or dependency; and
- lack of remorse or guilt.[16]

B Adults who Were Alienated as Children Suffer

In a qualitative retrospective study of adults alienated as children, it was discovered that these adults suffered from:

- low self-esteem, having internalized the negative characterization by the alienating parent of their rejected parent;
- self-hatred, self-blame and guilt for abandoning younger siblings;
- significant episodes of depression (seventy percent of those interviewed);
- use of drugs or alcohol during adolescence, to cope with painful feelings arising from loss and parental conflict (one third of the sample);
- self-doubt about their own perceptions and feelings about themselves and others;
- difficulty trusting other people, and fear that they will never be loved;
- high rates of divorce (two-thirds had been divorced once and one quarter more than once);
- anger and resentment about being emotionally manipulated and controlled;
- negative effect on their relationship with the alienating parent;
- alienation from their own children.[17]

Where therapeutic interventions were tried, poorer outcomes were described when the reactions began in earlier childhood than in adolescence. Further, in a follow-up study,

---

16 Ibid, p. 99.

17 A. Baker, *Adult children of parental alienation syndrome: Breaking the ties that bind,* New York, W.W. Norton, 2007.

highly successful outcomes occurred only in a minority of cases, and these successes were more likely with early intervention and prevention when alienation was first alleged.[18] This shows clearly the importance of early identification, intervention and prevention for this younger age group. Better long-term outcomes were found when the predominantly negative feelings for one parent developed during adolescence (12 to 15 years), when primarily in reaction to the recent divorce, compared to earlier in childhood. The adolescent's resistance or rejection was a developmentally expected coping mechanism.

C *Alienation Is Maltreatment*

Child abuse and neglect are child maltreatment, which has been defined by the World Health Organisation as:

> All forms of physical and/or emotional ill-treatment, sexual abuse, neglect or negligent treatment or commercial or other exploitation, resulting in actual or potential harm to the child's health, survival, development or dignity in the context of a relationship of responsibility, trust or power.[19]

High levels of parental conflict, maladaptive gatekeeping and alienation should be identified by child protection agencies as emotional abuse and neglect.[20] A child who exhibits serious symptoms such as anxiety, depression, withdrawal, self-destructive or aggressive behaviour or delayed development[21] may have been subjected to maltreatment by a parent. Of course, any professional observing such symptoms must carefully explore the possibility of other reasons for the child's distress, with or without family stresses.

Child protection workers must therefore keep in mind the possibility of contact failure. They may be the first people outside the family to see the beginnings of contact failure, including maladaptive gatekeeping and alienation by one of the parents. Failure of a parent to cooperate with treatment that has been recommended for helping the child, for example by failing to bring the child to therapeutic appointments or to attend relevant appointments themselves, strongly indicates maladaptivity. Child protection personnel should regard such behaviour as abuse, and act accordingly, according to their powers.

---

18 J.R. Johnston, & J.R. Goldman, 'Outcomes of family counseling interventions with children who resist visitation: An addendum to Friedlander and Walters', *Family Court Review*, Vol. 48, No. 1, 2010, pp. 112-15.

19 A. Butchart, A. Harvey, M. Mian & T. Kahane, *Preventing Child Maltreatment: A guide to taking action and generating evidence*, Geneva, World Health Organization, 2006.

20 A.N. Joyce, 'High Conflict Divorce: A Form of Child Neglect', *Family Court Review*, Vol. 54, No. 4, 2016, pp. 642-56.

21 B.J. Fidler, N. Bala, R. Birnbaum & K. Kavassalis, *Challenging Issues in Child Custody Disputes: A Guide for Legal and Mental Health Professionals*, Toronto, Thomson Carswell, 2008.

However, in most jurisdictions, child protection agencies do not intervene if they believe that one of the parents is adequate, as they consider that the family assessments and court proceedings between the parents are enough to address any protection concerns. This is caused or exacerbated by the dichotomic approach to the needs of the child. This may be manifested by the splitting of judicial authority in many jurisdictions between different courts (Family Courts and Juvenile Courts), or the different procedures for handling public law and private law cases involving children, or by separate agencies, each with its own procedures and approach, such as child protection agencies and general social services. There is a need for synchronization and a holistic approach; all of the issues regarding a specific family should be allocated to one judge, who can bring together all the judicial disputes and all the investigative therapeutic services relating to a specific child.

D A Public Health and Child Protection Issue

We have to understand that contact failure, in particular in the context of high conflict and alienation, is a public health[22] issue of great importance. At this point, however, the focus of research and programming has been on the legal proceedings, and trying to help the parties and their children in individual cases where contact has already failed or is on the brink of doing so.

There is a compelling state interest in preventing the development of full blown contact failure, in terms of savings in the budgets of court systems in handling these cases, and reductions in spending on social services and medical facilities in treating the child-victims long-term. Short-term intervention at the outset and avoidance of contact failure will be far less costly than the huge expense of investigations, court proceedings, and the involvement of social and mental health services to try to help those who have been damaged by alienation from a parent.

VI At Present, Cases Are Dealt With when the Contact Has Already Failed

In the vast majority of cases, the parents come to court only after they move physically to live separately. But the conflict between them, characterized by arguments and silences, if not worse, is apparent to children long before this. Children start to react to stress immediately, from the outset. This has visible symptoms, but there is also strong evidence of

22 V.C. Vezzetti, 'New approaches to divorce with children: A problem of public health', *Health Psychology Open*, July-December 2016, pp. 1-13.

epigenetic damage – that is, delayed or arrested brain development – whose effects may only become apparent in the long term.[23]

Judges in Family Courts are frequently asked to deal with cases in which contact has already failed. The alienated parent may not have been aware of maladaptive and alienating behaviour of the other parent; for this reason, in many cases, a claim is filed in court only when contact has failed altogether.

Where contact has failed the court needs to act promptly to reinstate contact, unless there is substantial proof that the protection of the child cannot be ensured except by preventing any contact – and where this is alleged, the allegation must be adjudicated immediately. This is an emergency, and it is often essential to take immediate steps, even before a full diagnosis, and make clear and unequivocal orders for the reinstatement of contact and therapeutic assistance.[24] But experience shows that in many cases, there is no way to turn back the clock.

Once contact has stopped, it is extremely difficult to reinstate. In my experience, specific orders for contact may be unsuccessful. Often the parent with whom the child lives is obstructive, and can be dealt with by imposition of sanctions on the alienating parent, like a financial fine, or reduction of child support, or imprisonment.[25] But no progress can be made in cases where both parents say that they genuinely want the child to have contact but the child is intransigent, despite referrals to psychologist and social workers, and despite meetings with the judge.

Some judges become frustrated and angry with children who unreasonably (in the eyes of the judge) refuse contact. Just two years ago, a judge in Michigan, USA, threatened children (one of whom was nine years old) with imprisonment because they refused to see their father, and ordered the 13 year old to be handcuffed and led away to the Children's Village, forbidden contact with his mother and siblings. When that happened, the 9 year old, who had previously agreed to see his father, changed his mind and said he wanted to be with his older brother.[26] (The judge was found to have committed no less than 15

23 J.L. Hanson et al, 'Behavior Problems After Early Life Stress: Contributions of the Hippocampus and Amygdala', *Biological Psychiatry*, Vol. 77, No. 4, 2015, pp. 314-23.

24 "For the non-intractable RRD cases, the damaging effect of time can be mitigated through educational efforts aimed at prevention, identification of at-risk cases early in the legal process, and early intervention. However, as it is not usually clear in the beginning whether a family will become intractable, having a more sharply focused awareness of the potential for intractability can lead to early implementation of court orders that include the structures necessary for effective treatment. Having these structures already in place can expedite the process of holding family members accountable for their part in unraveling and resolving the RRD. This, in itself, creates momentum for change." Walters & Friedlander, op cit, n. 6, p. 429.

25 The Jerusalem Family Court imposed the following sanctions on a father who refused (despite court orders to do so) to take part in treatment of the children whose contact with the mother was failing because of his actions: restraining the father from leaving the country and banning him from using debit cards: F.C. 4287-07-15 *Anon v. Anon* (20 April 2017).

26 *Eibschitz-Tsimhoni v Tsimhoni*, Case No. 09-76649-DM, 6th Circuit.

breaches of her judicial duties.[27]) This is, of course, an egregious case, but it exemplifies the inability of the court to force a child to see a parent from whom he has been alienated.

Various programs for re-establishing contact have been set up, and some of them appear to be quite successful.[28] However these programs often involve an intensive sleep-away camp, and are very expensive. Some programs have been devised for early intervention. The Child-Centered Conjoint Therapy, which is aimed at children from pre-school age focuses on the child's need to master developmental skills and appropriate behaviour despite parental conflict, has been adapted to respond to resistance or refusal by the child to have contact with a parent.[29] However, these valuable programs receive referrals from the court or mental health or social work professionals only when the child has exhibited signs of resistance to contact or has already ceased to have any contact with one of the parents. In many cases, the therapy and persuasion are unsuccessful, and the parent and the court have no alternative but to suspend efforts to reestablish contact, and have to "let go".[30]

For this reason, it is of particular importance that there be prompt judicial action to nip in the bud actions by one of the parties unjustifiably to reduce the level of contact between the child and the other parent. For example, moving the child from his residence to a place far from the home one of the parents without that parent's consent must be met with immediate and strong action to keep the child in his accustomed location or to return the child after the non-consensual move. Any attempts to breach an order of the court must be faced with strong sanctions. There are, unfortunately, judges who, after the child has been improperly moved, will take account only of the "need" of the child not to be moved again and not take notice of the cumulative effect of reducing contact with the parent who stayed put; thus, the unscrupulous parent takes advantage of his own wrongdoing.

VII Where Do We Stand?

Applying the quasi-medical approach, it is clear that the present state of judicial and therapeutic play regarding contact failure is at the stage before Jonas Salk invented the vaccination against polio in the early 1950's. The phenomenon of contact failure is recognized (symptoms), although there is insufficient awareness of the existence of the phe-

27 D.P. Ryan, *Report of Hon. Daniel P. Ryan, Master Appointed by the Michigan Judicial Tenure Commission*, Formal Complaint No. 98, July 1, 2016.

28 See, for example, R.A. Warshak, 'Family Bridges: Using Insights from Social Science to Reconnect Parents and Alienated Children', *Family Court Review*, Vol. 48, No. 1, 2010, pp. 48-80.

29 L.R. Greenberg, L.D. Fick & R.A. Schnider, 'Catching them before Too Much Damage is Done: Early Intervention with Resistance-Refusal Dynamics', *Family Court Review*, Vol. 54, No. 4, 2016, pp. 548-63.

30 This is taken from the title of chapter 5.3 at page 103 of Fidler et al, op cit, n. 10.

nomenon and its severity; the causes are known (the virus); attempts are made to deal with alienated children (treatment); but little or nothing is being done to prevent the occurrence of the phenomenon (vaccination). In short, at this stage the literature and case law deal in the main with identifying the situations in which alienation and gatekeeping have already caused contact failure, and judges and mental health and social work professionals try to reverse contact refusal. They are usually unsuccessful.

For this reason, we must look for ways of preventing parental alienation, or at least reducing its incidence. Making maladaptive gatekeeping and alienation into a crime, or defining it as abuse so as to invoke child protection measures, will not by themselves prevent parents from doing these things, any more than laws against child sexual abuse prevent abusers from their reprehensible acts. We need to enlist members of all those professions whose activities can make a difference. This includes enhancing public awareness of the existence of maladaptive gatekeeping and parental alienation and the damage they cause, and teaching those who come into contact with children about ways to identify distress in children and intervene in a timely fashion, to prevent the damage from happening.

VIII A Multidisciplinary Approach to Advancing Knowledge of Contact Failure, its Symptoms and Results

The existence of gatekeeping and parental alienation is unknown to wide sections of the public. Only those families (a minority, in most countries) who have experienced a breakdown between the parents in which one of the parents, consciously or otherwise, tries to turn a child away from proper contact with the other parent will be aware of the phenomenon.

A Public Awareness

Prevention of a disease or any other negative phenomenon requires that all those who may be at risk have the necessary knowledge. The prevention of polio was impossible until the public was made aware that a virus was responsible, that preventive steps could be taken, and that the vaccine was available. Such programming requires collaboration between the therapeutic community, educators and media people.

Fidler, Bala and Saini speak of primary prevention: focusing on "the entire population who may be at risk of parent-child contact problems after separation"; and then of secondary prevention, targeting "children and parents who have been identified at greater risk of becoming involved in alienation"; and tertiary prevention, where there are severe levels of alienating behaviors.[31]

On primary prevention, Pickar and Kauffman say the following:

> Psycho-educational programs are helpful before people decide to have children together and when raising children, and are especially valuable if they find themselves having relationship difficulties or are in the very early stages of separation. These programs can assist parents to develop effective communication, problem solving and conflict resolution skills, and effective parenting and co-parenting, including learning about the importance for their children of maintaining positive relationships with both parents and about the harm of alienation. Programs explaining the various methods of non-adversarial dispute resolution and the negative effects of parental hostility and litigation are imperative. While such programs may not prevent the most severe cases of alienation from occurring, they have positive value for many parents and children.[32]

Similarly, as examples of primary prevention, Fidler and her colleagues propose public announcements, awareness campaigns, and presentations in the community and at schools about the risks. In short, the public needs to be informed of the possibility that parental separation may cause serious and long term problems for children. This should take the form of education, in the latter years of high school, in the context of life skills and relationship classes, which include (or should include) courses on parenthood. These classes have for some years included material on interpersonal violence and abuse; our characterization of alienating behaviour as maltreatment that is abusive of the child makes the case for inclusion of programming on gatekeeping and alienation.

In addition, when prospective marriage partners meet with counsellors, those counsellors should include reference to the adverse effects on children if the marriage gets into difficulties. There is also a need for a movie or a television series about parental alienation and its effects.[33] The press and other media need to be alerted to the cases of contact failure, and not only by disgruntled parents in specific sensational cases; journalists and editors should be provided with suitable background material.

31 Fidler et al, op cit, n. 10, p. 106.

32 D.B. Pickar & R.L. Kaufman, 'Parenting Plans for Special Needs Children: Applying a Risk-Assessment Model', *Family Court Review*, Vol. 53, No. 1, 2015, pp. 113-33.

33 The Michigan case mentioned above (n. 26) would need little dramatization; it involved court proceedings over several years. Untold suffering, not to speak of wastage of resources – court time and lawyers' fees - could have been avoided by identification of the personalities of the parents and the children, and of the high intensity of the conflict between the parents, together with resolute court action mandating therapeutic intervention and zero tolerance for alienating behaviours.

Without awareness of the potential problems, people will have little incentive to join educational relationship programs. The emphasis here is on reaching the entire population of children and parents, including people who have children outside marriage or commitment to any long-term couple relationship; the responsibility of both parents to the child starts from conception and subsists throughout the child's minority, regardless of any legal relationship between the parents.[34]

Fidler and her colleagues are not convinced that such campaigns will be effective with those parents in high conflict cases, many of them exhibiting signs of personality disorders or mental illness, who will be least able to identify and address their alienating behaviours.[35] With respect, I agree: mere publicity about the existence of the phenomenon and its dangers will be ineffective in many cases, and needs to be backed by the involvement of those who come into frequent contact with children, and who can tell the parents that something is wrong and refer them to counseling and treatment.

This paper does not ignore the many excellent programs for separating and divorcing couples and their children, including classes to which parents are referred at the outset of court proceedings, and we have already mentioned intervention processes when gatekeeping and alienation have been established. However, the thrust of this article is to try to prevent the occurrence of these phenomena altogether: stretching the medical metaphor maybe beyond its tensile strength, to "vaccinate" the public.

B *Early Identification of At-Risk Populations and of Behaviour which May Lead to Contact Failure*

Any child whose parents are going through a rough patch in their relationship may be exposed to arguments and disputes, and will in all likelihood suffer some consequences. However, a majority of children will weather the storm, as a result of the child's personality and/or as a result of adequate actions and explanations by the parents together, the presence of loving grandparents, or other protective factors.[36] However, as the level of conflict becomes higher, or as the child is more susceptible, the danger of lasting damage increases. So this paper proposes identification of those children who may be especially susceptible to damage, and of those parents who are liable to behave in such a way as to endanger their children.

34 See Marcus, op cit, n. 2.

35 On the prevalence of personality disorders in parents involved in high conflict disputes, see B. Eddy, *The Future of Family Court*, Scottsdale AZ, High Conflict Press, 2012, pp. 2ff. At p. 20, he says the following: "How does the judge know that it is a potentially high-conflict case? When one or both parents seek to restrict the other's parenting time".

36 "Invincible kids", in the words of Professor Gerald Caplan (personal communication, 1991).

C *The Role of Professionals*

All those whose profession brings them into contact with children should be encouraged to identify the signs that behaviour by a parent, which may endanger the child's ties with the other parent and so be problematic. This will require alerting both parents to the situation – of whose existence, or of whose problematic nature, one or both of the parents may be unaware – and advising them that they might need counseling or other help.

In the past few decades, medical and educational professionals have become more aware of the existence of parental child maltreatment, physical, emotional and sexual, and are taught to spot the signs in their pupil/patient populations. In many jurisdictions, they are required to report their suspicions and findings to the child protection authorities. It is important to put in train a similar process in the case of mental-emotional abuse and neglect by maladaptive gatekeeping and alienation. Lawyers and judges should also be made aware of the need for immediate, authoritative and detailed orders where contact failure is liable to happen, in light of the urgency of these cases and the potential for lasting harm to a child if contact with a parent fails completely.

This will require training of these professionals, and setting up appropriate therapeutic services for advice and counselling for parents and help for the children. The cost of such short-term intensive services will be far less than the cost of providing legal, judicial, social work and mental health services if the maladaptive and alienating behaviour is allowed to continue and cause contact failure.

In a workshop presented at the Annual Conference of the Association of Family and Conciliation Courts, in June 2018, Dr Tirtza Joels and I presented a detailed analysis of the signs of distress in children that might be reactions to parental disputes, and described the types of services which need to be made available to children and their parents for immediate intervention, since, as we have shown, time is of the essence. The workshop included recommendations, adapted to specific professions, for early detection of children and parents who are in this context at risk, and of maladaptive gatekeeping and alienating behaviour by one of the parents. The intention is to equip teachers and kindergarten staffers, school counsellors, pediatricians, family doctors and nurses with the information they need, and recommendations how they can approach parents and guide them to obtain help, advice and, where necessary, treatment, for themselves and their child, so as to ward off the possibility of further harm by contact failure.

IX Conclusion: Prevention

Parental alienation, and its precursor or predictor – maladaptive gatekeeping – are known to the legal and mental health professions. At-risk populations have been identified, and the results of contact failure are recognized. But little or nothing is being done to prevent the development of these highly damaging phenomena. This issue is almost unknown outside the welfare, mental health and legal professions and those families who are directly involved. Its results are very serious, and cause damage, often permanently, to the children involved. It is a child protection and public health issue, over and above the need to help those directly involved.

Using a systemic, multidisciplinary approach, this paper has argued that preventive steps can and should be taken. These include:

- making the general public aware of the existence of maladaptive gatekeeping and parental alienation and their destructive results;
- enlisting all agencies, public and private, that educate for family life, including schools, youth movements, religious and communal organizations, to include programming about the vulnerability of children to marital strife and the dangers of contact failure;
- alerting and educating personnel in the professions that come into contact with children and their parents about the warning signs and indicators that alienation is possible;
- coordination between these professions and counseling and treatment services in the community;
- setting up services – a one-stop-shop – for immediate counselling and intervention when contact failure is perceived as a possible outcome of disputes in the family; and
- encouraging courts to tackle these situations in a speedy and effective fashion.

It is for each community and jurisdiction to work out how to best act to prevent children from becoming cut off from their parents.

Growing Numbers of Parental Responsibility Agreements following Divorce Reform in Croatia

Branka Rešetar[*]

I Introduction

The new Croatian Family Act (hereinafter FA 2015),[1] which came into force on 1 November 2015, has changed divorce procedure where minor children are involved. The new Act has introduced two extrajudicial procedures which precede the initiation of divorce proceedings: mandatory counselling and a mandatory first meeting with a family mediator. If parents reach an agreement on parental responsibility[2] and child maintenance (hereinafter "agreement on parental responsibility"[3]), either by themselves or through the mandatory counselling or family mediation procedure, a divorce can then be obtained very quickly. Spouses (parents) file a consensual divorce application, supplemented by the agreement on parental responsibility. The Court will scrutinize the agreement to ensure that it is consistent with the best interest of the child and, if so, will then order a divorce by mutual consent. If the extrajudicial procedures do not produce an agreement about parental responsibility, the spouses are required to initiate divorce proceedings before the court by filing a suit (divorce without consent). In such case the court is then *ex officio* obliged to decide on the exercise of parental responsibility, child contact and child maintenance as well as ordering the divorce.[4]

---

* Associate Professor, Faculty of Law University of Josip Juraj Strossmayer, Osijek, Croatia.

1 *Official Gazette* no. 103/2015.

2 According to art. 92, FA 2015, parental responsibilities are a collection of rights and duties aimed at promoting and safeguarding the welfare of the child. They encompass in particular: (1) care, health and protection; (2) education; (3) contact with the child; (4) determination of residence; (5) administration of property, and (6) legal representation.

3 An agreement on parental responsibility is a written agreement between parents on the manner in which their parental responsibilities will be exercised after divorce. Such agreements will deal with residence, contact with the child as well as on the way information about the child is to be exchanged, modes of communication and how possible disputes relating to parental responsibility are to be resolved. Child maintenance, which is separate obligation of a non-resident parent, must also be determined under the agreement on parental responsibility (art. 106, FA 2015).

4 B. Rešetar & J. Berdica, 'Divorce in Croatia: The Principles of No-Fault Divorce, Parental Responsibility, Parental Education and Children', *Family Court Review*, Vol. 51. No. 4, October, 2013, pp. 568-577 and B.

One year after the FA 2015 came into force, figures showed a large increase in the number of divorces by mutual consent (supplemented by agreements on parental responsibility) and a decrease of in the number of *ex officio* court decisions on divorce and parental responsibility. The first research into effects of the FA 2015 was conducted by a journalist, Kristina Turčin.[5] Turčin compared numbers of divorce petitions filed at Croatian courts by mutual consent (with a parental agreement) with those that were contested (those without such an agreement) at two points in time: first under the former Family Act (hereinafter FA 2003),[6] and then under the current FA 2015. Her findings were extraordinary. When the FA 2003 was in force, the ratio of divorces by mutual consent (with agreements on parental responsibility and child maintenance) to divorce petitions heard by the court (divorce without an agreement on parental responsibility) was 30 to 70. Since the new FA 2015 has been in force, this ratio has been reversed in favour of divorces by mutual consent, with the result that today only 30% of marriages are dissolved through divorce proceedings at court.

This article will provide a comparison of Croatia's former and current divorce procedures in order to explain why agreements on parental responsibility are increasing under the FA 2015. The article proceeds in four parts. Part II depicts Croatian divorce law under the FA 2003, revealing how the state (through the court) played a central role in organising family life with children after divorce. Part III presents the new approach, following the reforms to divorce procedure by the FA 2015, which gives parents the responsibility of organising family life after divorce, but with the support and assistance of the state. Part IV sets out and explains the first study of the reformed divorce process. The study, as noted above, compared the divorce procedure under the FA 2003 with the procedure under the FA 2015, concluding that parents are more likely to make an agreement on parental responsibility (leading to divorce by mutual consent) if they have an obligation to participate in an appropriate supportive process before initiating court proceedings. Part V concludes the article with comments on the limitations of the first study on the new divorce procedure in Croatia and indicates possible avenues for further research in this field.

II Divorce under the Family Act 2003

Croatian family law defines divorce as the termination of marriage pursuant to a court decision. The basic principle of the FA 2003 was "no-fault divorce", fault-based divorce

Rešetar, 'New Divorce in the Republic of Croatia under the Influence of Psychology, Sociology and International Law', *International Journal of Law, Policy and Family*, Vol. 32, No. 1, 2018, pp. 63-79.

5 https://www.jutarnji.hr/vijesti/hrvatska/analiza-jutarnjeg-prosla-je-prva-godina-primjene-obiteljskog-zakona-koji-je-donijela-kukuriku-vlada-je-li-uistinu-doslo-do-pada-sudskih-razvoda/5339203/.

6 *Official Gazette* no. 116/2003, 17/2004, 136/2004, 107/2007, 57/2011, 61/2011, 25/2013, 5/2015.

having been abandoned in Croatia with the enactment of the 1978 Marriage and Family Act.[7] Pursuant to the FA 2003, divorce had to be obtained through judicial proceedings, regardless of whether the divorce was contested. A divorce could be only be granted where issues relating to children had been resolved.

A Substantive Law

According to the FA 2003, a single spouse could initiate the divorce procedure by filing a suit (divorce without consent) or both spouses could file a consensual divorce application (divorce by mutual consent).[8] Mutual consent was implied in situations where one spouse initiated the divorce procedure and the other subsequently joined the divorce application.[9] Divorce by mutual consent was permitted by the court if it found that the marriage had been gravely and irretrievably damaged (irretrievable breakdown of marriage), or if the spouses had, in fact, been separated for one year.[10]

The court was not obliged to examine the quality of the marital relationship or the reasoning behind the spouses' mutual consent to the divorce. However, if only one spouse initiated the divorce procedure on the grounds that the marriage had irretrievably broken down, the court was obliged to determine whether such a deterioration had occurred. One of the primary aims of the divorce regime under the FA 2003 was to promote the reconciliation of the spouses. However, in cases where the spouses had been separated for one year, the court was not obliged to examine the reasoning behind the separation and could issue a decision on divorce simply on the ground of factual separation.[11]

Where the spouses had minor children, the FA 2003 obliged the court to make decisions on the parent the child would live with, contact arrangements for the child, and the child maintenance obligations of the non-resident parent.[12] The court was required, however, to take into account a parental agreement on the above consequences of divorce, provided that the agreement was consistent with the best interests of the child. If the parents'

7 See M. Alinčić, 'Rastava i razvod u 21. Stoljeću' ['Judicial Separation and Divorce in the 20th Century'], *Collection of Works of the Faculty of Law of the University of Zagreb*, Vol. 52, No. 6, 2002, pp. 1159-1180 (dealing with judicial separation and divorce in their historical and contemporary form and meaning in Europe).

8 Art. 42(1), FA 2003.

9 Art. 280(3), FA 2003.

10 Art. 43, FA 2003.

11 N. Hlača, 'Divorce in Family Law in Croatia', *in* P. Šarčević et al, *Family Law in Croatia*, Wolters Kluwer International, the Netherlands, 2011, pp. 115-117.

12 Art. 294(1), FA 2003. See B. Rešetar, 'Roditeljska skrb u Prijedlogu Obiteljskog zakona 2013: očuvanje pravnog kontinuiteta i osuvremenjivanje eurospkim i međunarodnim standardima' ['Parental Responsibility in Draft of Family Act 2013: Legal Continuity and Modernization by European and International Standards'] *in* I. Kunda (Ed.), *Obitelj i djeca: europska očekivanja i nacionalna stvarnost*, Rijeka, Pravni fakultet u Rijeci, 2014, pp. 29-49.

agreement failed, the FA 2003 obliged the court to make the necessary decisions itself, with reference to the custody evaluation and recommendations of the social welfare centre.[13]

It should be noted that the FA 2003 automatically gave both parents parental responsibility, irrespective of whether they lived together or apart.[14] A single parent could have parental responsibility alone where the other had died, been deprived of parental responsibility, been pronounced legally incompetent or partially legal incompetent in respect of parental responsibility, or was otherwise incapable of caring for the child.[15]

B Divorce Procedure

Under the FA 2003, once divorce proceedings had been initiated at court, spouses were obliged to attend mandatory conciliation classes at a competent social welfare centre. This requirement, which was carried over from the 1978 Marriage and Family Act, existed regardless of whether the spouses had minor or adult children or no children at all. In addition to social welfare centres, an authorized person (conciliator) or family advisory service could conduct conciliation.[16] During the first court hearing, even if the divorce was brought by mutual consent, the judge would inform the spouses of their right to choose an institution or person to conduct the mandatory conciliation. If no choice was made, the judge would appoint a conciliator and would order the spouses to participate in the mandatory conciliation.[17]

Social welfare centres had a limited number of duties to perform during the mandatory conciliation: (1) to inquire about the reason for the marriage's deterioration and to try to reconcile the spouses; (2) to inform the spouses about the psychosocial impact of divorce; and (3) depending on the circumstances of the case, to undertake any necessary measures for child protection.[18] The conciliator was required to conduct the conciliation within three months and to deliver an expert opinion on the conciliation, accompanied by a conclusion about the possibility of reconciliation.[19] The expert opinion would be sent to the court and spouses. The content of the expert opinion was regulated by the "Regulation on the Essential Elements of the Expert Opinion in the Process of Mandatory Conciliation" (hereinafter the Regulation on Mandatory Conciliation).[20] The Regulation on Mandatory

13 Art. 298 in conjunction with art. 295(1), FA 2003.

14 Art. 99(1), FA 2003.

15 Art. 99(2), FA 2003. See Rešetar & Berdica, op cit, n. 4, pp. 568-577.

16 Despite the fact that other institutions or persons could conduct mandatory conciliation, these services were not taken up at all in the period from 2003 to 2015, when the new FA 2015 came into force. In other words, only social welfare centres provided conciliation.

17 Art. 46, FA 2003.

18 Art. 48, FA 2003.

19 Art. 49, FA 2003.

20 *Official Gazette* no. 32/2005.

Conciliation provided that the expert opinion should include an evaluation of the marital relationship and family dynamics, and an assessment of the likelihood of the marriage being saved.

The scope of the mandatory conciliation, regulated by the FA 2003, and the content of the expert opinion, prescribed by the Regulation on Mandatory Conciliation, reveal that the goal of the legislator, as it had been for decades, was the preservation of the institution of marriage.[21] After more than 30 years, the family conciliation procedure (which has been mandatory since 1978) turned out to be unsuccessful in practice. This point is evidenced by the fact that while 10% of marriages were preserved when this measure was first implemented, the figure had dropped to only 2% by 2004.[22]

III DIVORCE UNDER THE FAMILY ACT 2015

A growing recognition of the complexity of marital relationships and family therapy, combined with the demonstrated inefficiency of the mandatory conciliation procedure, led the Croatian legislator to seek a new approach to divorce. In that regard, the new Family Act 2015 does not require either an investigation into the causes of marriage breakdown or spousal conciliation. Under the new regime, divorcing spouses without minor children deal directly with the court (by means of a consensual proposal or petition), while divorcing spouses with minor children are encouraged to be autonomous and take responsibility for organising, outside of court, the exercise of post-divorce parental responsibility.

A *Substantive Law*

The substantive divorce law in Croatia has essentially remained unchanged under the FA 2015, including the basic principle of no-fault divorce. When the FA 2015 was being drafted and the substantive grounds for divorce were being reviewed, the Croatian legislator took into account the *Principles of European Family Law Regarding Divorce.*[23] In accordance

21 M. Alinčić, 'Divorce Law' *in* Alinčić et al, *Family Law*, Narodne novine, Zagreb, 2007, p. 96.

22 M. Alinčić, 'Institut mirenja bračnih drugova' ['Family Conciliation'], *Collection of the Works of the Faculty of Law of the University of Zagreb*, Vol. 42, Nos. 5-6, pp. 859-861. According to official data, the conciliation success rate (marriage preservation) totalled 4% in 2002 and only 2% in 2004, I. Majstorović, Posredovanje prije razvoda braka: hrvatsko pravo i europska rješenja ['Pre-divorce Mediation: Croatian Law and European Solutions], *Collection of Works the Faculty of Law of the University of Zagreb*, Vol. 57, No. 2, pp. 414 and 447, A. Korać, 'Obiteljsko posredovanje – Prilog alternativnom rješavanju obiteljskih sporova' ['Family Mediation – a Contribution to an Alternative Resolution of Family Disputes'], *Croatian Legal Journal*, Vol. 5, February 2005, p. 77.

23 K. Boele-Woelki et al (Eds.), *The Principles of European Family Law Regarding Divorce and Maintenance between Former Spouses*, Interesentia, Antwerp-Oxford, 2004, issued by the Commission on European

with those principles, a divorce must still be granted by the court, regardless of whether it is contested or uncontested.[24] A divorce must also be granted with or without consent of both spouses if they have been factually separated for one year.[25] Divorce by mutual consent is divorce based on an agreement between the spouses to end their marriage. Such an agreement may be found in a joint application by the spouses or in an application by one spouse which has been confirmed and accepted by the other spouse.[26] The spouses may agree on their parental responsibility, their child's residence, contact concerning children, child maintenance, division of matrimonial property and spousal maintenance. The agreement must be in writing.[27] If spouses (parents) cannot reach an agreement about their parental responsibility, the child's residence, or contact with the children and child maintenance, the court should decide these issues. Agreements which are consistent with the best interests of the child are to be taken into account by the court.[28]

There are two issues on which substantive divorce law under the Croatian FA 2015 and the *Principles of European Family Law Regarding Divorce* differ: reflection periods and exceptional hardship to the petitioner.[29] Croatian family law regulates neither issue.

B Divorce Procedure

The central reform to divorce law by the FA 2015 is the new divorce procedure. In light of the psychosocial impact of divorce on children, the Croatian legislator has attempted, through changes to the divorce procedure, to develop a new approach to divorce. This approach emphasises the autonomy of divorcing parents by empowering them to organise their parental responsibility, limiting the need for court involvement.[30]

Accordingly, if spouses have minor children and agree on arrangements for their children after divorce, then the divorce procedure becomes "easier" and cheaper. Spouses (parents) file a consensual divorce petition supplemented by an agreement on parental responsibility. The court scrutinizes the agreement on parental responsibility to determine if such is in the best interests of the child and if so, it pronounces divorce by mutual consent. However, if parents fail to reach an agreement on these matters, the divorce procedure

Family Law (CEFL). The main objective of the CEFL is to launch a pioneering theoretical and practical exercise in relation to the harmonization of family law in Europe.

24 Art. 50, FA 2015 and principles 1:2 and 1:3.

25 Art. 51(3), FA 2015 and principle 1:8.

26 Arts. 51(1) and 369(3), FA 2015 and principle 1:4.

27 Art. 52, FA 2015 and principle 1:6.

28 Art. 53 in conjunction with arts. 56 and 107, FA 2015 and principles 1:7 and 1:10.

29 Principle 1:5 requires a period of reflection before divorce. Principle 1:9 prescribes exceptional hardship to the petitioner that covers cases of family violence and allows a spouse to initiate divorce proceedings without a previous period of separation.

30 Rešetar, 2018, op cit, n. 4.

becomes "harder" and more expensive as fees for an attorney are needed. Furthermore, the child is explicitly regarded as a party in divorce proceedings. The exercise of the right of the child to be heard is clearly regulated and the child is provided with a special guardian who is obliged to represent child's interests in divorce proceedings.[31]

The enactment of the FA 2015 has introduced a new divorce procedure which aims to encourage spouses with minor children to cooperate with one another in making future arrangements for their children. As a starting point, the FA 2015 obliges spouses with minor children to take two mandatory steps prior to initiating divorce proceedings before the court: attending mandatory counselling at a social welfare centre and having one meeting with a family mediator.

Just like the former FA 2003, the new FA 2015 requires experts providing mandatory counselling in social welfare centres to inform the spouses about the legal and psychosocial consequences of divorce for themselves and their children and to advise them to undergo marriage therapy or undertake measures for child protection depending on the circumstances of the case. However, the FA 2015 imposes additional obligations on the team of experts that works with parents as part of mandatory counselling. This team must also: provide spouses with assistance in reaching an agreement about their future family life (agreement on parental responsibility); refer spouses to family mediation or to the court in cases with high levels of conflict; and protect victims of domestic violence.[32]

Prior to the FA 2015, spouses were required to attend counselling at the competent social welfare centre within the framework of pending divorce proceedings and regardless of any agreement, they might have reached. Unlike the former FA 2003, the FA 2015 regards mandatory counselling as the first step before divorce proceedings are initiated in cases involving minor children.[33] While the primary function of the new mandatory counselling under the FA 2015 is to assist divorcing parents in reaching an agreement on parental responsibility after divorce, it is also concerned, depending on the circumstances, with protecting children and victims of domestic violence.[34]

If there is no agreement between parents on their future arrangements for their children, parents are informed of their duty to attend an informative meeting with a family mediator and are given information about the subsequent divorce procedure at court. Parents are told that the child has an independent role during the court procedure, as well as the right to an independent representative and the right to express their views.[35]

Family mediation, a procedure through which parties attempt to resolve a family dispute with the assistance of one or more family mediators, is one of the most important changes

---

31 Ibid, p. 1.

32 Art. 325, FA 2015.

33 Art. 54 (1), FA 2015.

34 Art. 321(1), FA 2015.

35 Art. 325(1) in conjunction with art. 327, FA 2015.

introduced by the FA 2015. The aim of family mediation is not only to encourage parents to reach an agreement about their future family life, but also to agree upon property division and maintenance.[36] However, only the first meeting with the family mediator is obligatory. During that meeting, parents are informed of the benefits of family mediation and the advantages of reaching an agreement. An emphasis is placed, throughout, on the best interests of the child.[37]

If no agreement is reached between parents on the legal arrangements for their children after divorce (through either mandatory counselling or family mediation), the court will make determinations about parental responsibility, the residence of the child, contact with the child and child maintenance following the divorce.[38] Divorce proceedings involving minor children under the FA 2015 are now more focused than in the past on protecting the procedural rights of children to be heard and to be represented by an independent representative (special guardian).

The court must establish the consequences of the divorce for the child in accordance with the guidelines proposed by the FA 2015. In relation to parental responsibility post-divorce, the court is obliged to take into account the child's wishes, pre-divorce parenting routines, the parents' ability to provide parental care, the willingness of a parent to cooperate, and the parents' willingness to encourage contact with the child.[39] Above all, the court is to apply the best interests of the child principle.[40]

The aforementioned divorce procedures regulated by the current FA 2015 have resulted in a growing number of agreements on parental responsibility. As discussed in the next section of this paper, the first study of divorce cases before the Croatian courts since the adoption of the FA 2015 shows that the number of agreements has increased significantly under the new Act.

IV Divorce Cases before the Croatian Courts – Impact of the New Divorce Procedure

A Research Objectives

The first research into effects of the FA 2015 was conducted by a journalist, Kristina Turčin.[41] She compared numbers of divorce petitions filed at Croatian courts by mutual

36 Art. 331, FA 2015.
37 Art. 320(3), FA 2015.
38 Art. 413(1), FA 2015.
39 Art. 416, FA 2015.
40 Art. 5, FA 2015.
41 Turčin, op cit, n. 5.

consent (with a parental agreement) with those that were contested (those without such an agreement) at two points in time: first under the former Family Act (FA 2003) and then under the current FA 2015.[42] This comparison was intended to serve as an objective metric for evaluating the effectiveness of the FA 2015 in resolving divorce cases. This part of the paper describes and analyses in detail the data obtained Turčin in order to bring her findings out of obscurity and present them to a broader circle of family law experts.[43]

B Research Methodology

1 Method

In order to objectively evaluate the differing approaches to divorce in the schemes found in the FA 2003 and the FA 2015, both schemes were first described and then compared using the number of divorces by agreement and the number of divorces resolved at court (divorce by court order).[44] The data obtained was analysed both at court level and cumulatively.

2 Sample

The research looked at divorce cases before 21 out of 24 courts in Croatia. The sample therefore covered 88% of the courts in Croatia, which means that the sample-size was sufficient to meet quantitative requirements. From a qualitative perspective, the sample was representative as it included the biggest cities in Croatia where most divorces take place.

3 Time Period

The data used to support this study's findings were from two consecutive years: the period February – November 2015 (as a sample for divorces managed under the FA 2003), and the period February – November 2016 (as a sample for divorces managed under the FA 2015).

42 The pool of divorces on which the study was based only involved divorces with minor children.

43 Turčin collected the data and published it only in the daily press. The author was given the data by Turčin and further analyzed and elaborated upon her findings.

44 Technically every divorce in Croatia requires a court order. However, for the purposes of presenting the data from Turčin's study, "divorce by court order" refers to a divorce not based on mutual consent where there was no agreement on parental responsibility and the court was thus required to make its own determinations.

4 Research Results

Table 1 shows the total number of divorces in the observed periods (2015 and 2016), classified according to the type of divorce. This figure reveals that in 2016 there were 331 fewer divorces than in the preceding year.

Table 1 Number of Divorces By Type and Time Period

Divorces	Agreements (by Mutual Consent)	Court Order (without mutual consent)	Total
Period 1 Feb 2015 – 1 Nov 2015 (According to the FA 2003)	1114	2095	3209
Period 1 Feb 2016 – 1 Nov 2016 (According to the FA 2015)	2019	859	2878
Total	3133	2954	6087

In order to get the bigger picture from the analysed data, the type of divorce needs to be shown as a percentage of total divorces. Table 2 demonstrates that, out of all the analysed cases, 53% of them occurred in 2015 and 47% took place in 2016. The analysed divorces are therefore time-comparable.

Table 2 Relative Structure of Total Divorces in the Observed Period

Divorces	Agreement	Court Order	Total
Period 1 Feb 2015 – 1 Nov 2015 (FA 2003)	18.3%	34.4%	52.7%
Period 1 Feb 2016 – 1 Nov 2016 (FA 2015)	33.2%	14.1%	47.3%
Total	51.5%	48.5%	100%

The key comparison, as shown in Table 3, is the comparison between types of divorce within the reference period. 35% of the divorces observed in 2015 were based on an agreement (by mutual consent) and 65% were initiated via a contested divorce petition. In 2016, the opposite was true: 70% of divorces were agreed upon by divorcing spouses.

Table 3 Relative Structure of Divorces by Time Period

Divorces	Agreement	Court Order	Total
Period 1 Feb 2015 – 1 Nov 2015 (FA 2003)	34.7%	65.3%	100%
Period 1 Feb 2016 – 1 Nov 2016 (FA 2015)	70.2%	29.8%	100%
Total	51.5%	48.5%	100%

When the above percentages are translated into real numbers and proportions, as shown in Table 4, it can be seen that the total number of divorces by agreement (2015 + 2016) almost matches the total number of divorces by court order during the same period. More precisely, the respective ratio is 1.1:1. However, these overall figures are derived from completely different situations: in 2015, for every 100 divorces there were 53 divorces based on an agreement, while in 2016, for every 100 divorces there were 235 divorces based on an agreement.

Table 4 Relative Coordination Number

Divorces	Agreement	Court Order	RCN
Period 1 Feb 2015 – 1 Nov 2015 (FA 2003)	1114	2095	0.5
Period 1 Feb 2016 – 1 Nov 2016 (FA 2015)	2019	859	2.4
Total	3133	2954	1-1

In order to complete the study, analysis of the type of divorce over both periods is needed. As shown by Table 5, 64% of all consensual divorces (based on an agreement) in the observed periods (2015 + 2016) relate to the year 2016, whereas the opposite is true in respect of divorces initiated by divorce petitions, where 70.9% relate to 2015. Such a rise in uncontested divorces (or a drop in contested divorces) in 2016 can be directly related to the amendment of the Family Act or in other words, to the legal regulation of the divorce procedure.

Table 5 Relative Structure of Divorces by Type

Divorces	Agreement	Court Order	Total
Period 1 Feb 2015 – 1 Nov 2015 (FA 2003)	35.6%	70.9%	52.7%
Period 1 Feb 2016 – 1 Nov 2016 (FA 2015)	64.4%	14.1%	47.3%
Total	100%	100%	100%

A more detailed view emerges when one analyses changes by individual courts, as shown in Table 6.

Table 6 Number of Divorces by type and Time Period

	Period 1 Feb 2015 – 1 Nov 2015 (FA 2003)		Period 1 Feb 2016 – 1 Nov 2016 (FA 2015)	
Municipal court	**Agreement**	**Court Order**	**Agreement**	**Court Order**
Bjelovar	58	88	90	43
Čakovec	0	74	53	21
Dubrovnik	52	58	30	32
Gospić	5	23	10	12
Karlovac	9	75	47	26
Koprivnica	5	39	52	16
Osijek	173	156	171	50
Požega	0	13	29	18
Pula	128	113	120	40
Rijeka	184	133	149	50
Sisak	58	83	66	49
Slavonski Brod	1	13	54	43
Split	39	201	137	69
Šibenik	40	68	39	8
Varaždin	8	112	117	35
Velika Gorica	63	77	63	27
Virovitica	50	69	23	24
Vukovar	2	191	88	34
Zadar	72	85	76	21
Zagreb	117	137	433	169
Novi Zagreb	10	204	120	46

	Period 1 Feb 2015 – 1 Nov 2015 (FA 2003)		Period 1 Feb 2016 – 1 Nov 2016 (FA 2015)	
Municipal court	**Agreement**	**Court Order**	**Agreement**	**Court Order**
Zlatar	40	83	52	26
Total:	**1114**	**2095**	**2019**	**859**

In terms of relative shift, as shown by Table 7, the difference in the share of divorces by agreement between 2015 and 2016 was about 35%. In some courts this difference was significantly larger (in 10 courts the difference was up to 72%). No court experienced a decline in the number of divorces by agreement.

Table 7 Relative Structure of Divorces by Type and Time Period

	Period 1 Feb 2015 – 1 Nov 2015 (FA 2003)		Period 1 Feb 2016 – 1 Nov 2016 (FA 2015)		Difference in the share of divorces by agreement
Municipal court	**Agreement**	**Court Order**	**Agreement**	**Court order**	**Difference**
Bjelovar	39.7%	60.3%	67.7%	32.3%	27.9%
Čakovec	0.0%	100.0%	71.6%	28.4%	71.6%
Dubrovnik	47.3%	52.7%	48.4%	51.6%	1.1%
Gospić	17,9%	82,1%	45,5%	54,5%	27,6%
Karlovac	10,7%	89,3%	64,4%	35,6%	53,7%
Koprivnica	11,4%	88,6%	76,5%	23,5%	65,1%
Osijek	52,6%	47,4%	77,4%	22,6%	24,8%
Požega	0,0%	100,0%	61,7%	38,3%	61,7%
Pula	53,1%	46,9%	75.0%	25.0%	21.9%
Rijeka	58.0%	42.0%	74.9%	25.1%	16.8%
Sisak	41.1%	58.9%	57.4%	42.6%	16.3%
Slavonski Brod	7.1%	92.9%	55.7%	44.3%	48.5%
Split	16.3%	83.8%	66.5%	33.5%	50.3%
Šibenik	37.0%	63.0%	83.0%	17.0%	45.9%
Varaždin	6.7%	93.3%	77.0%	23.0%	70.3%
Velika Gorica	45.0%	55.0%	70.0%	30.0%	25.0%
Virovitica	42,0%	58,0%	48,9%	51,1%	6,9%
Vukovar	1,0%	99,0%	72,1%	27,9%	71,1%
Zadar	45,9%	54,1%	78,4%	21,6%	32,5%
Zagreb	46,1%	53,9%	71,9%	28,1%	25,9%

	Period 1 Feb 2015 – 1 Nov 2015 (FA 2003)		Period 1 Feb 2016 – 1 Nov 2016 (FA 2015)		Difference in the share of divorces by agreement
Municipal court	**Agreement**	**Court Order**	**Agreement**	**Court order**	**Difference**
Novi Zagreb	4,7%	95,3%	72.3%	27.7%	67.6%
Zlatar	32.5%	67.5%	66.7%	33.3%	34.1%
Total:	34.7%	65.3%	70.2%	29.8%	**35.4%**

5 Conclusion

The analysis of divorce by type in the above two periods clearly shows that the enactment of the FA 2015 resulted in a considerable increase in both the actual number and percentage of divorces by agreement in 2016 as compared to 2015.

V CONCLUSION ON THE NEW DIVORCE PROCEDURE IN CROATIA

The reform of divorce procedure in Croatia was focused, one the one hand, on abolishing "spousal conciliation" and the objective of saving marriages and, on the other hand, on encouraging divorcing spouses with minor children to take responsibility for planning family life after divorce. The Croatian legislator has not weakened the significance of marriage as the prevailing form of family life in Croatia through this reform. Rather, it has embraced reality by suggesting that "saving marriage by professionals" requires more subtle mechanisms, such as marital therapy. There is no room for saving a marriage once divorce proceedings have been initiated.

The Croatian legislator intended that the FA 2015 would protect children by helping their parents reach an agreement on issues which affect family life after divorce (parental responsibility, the residence of the child, contact, and child maintenance). Among the key changes, one can single out the introduction of two extrajudicial procedures – mandatory counselling and a mandatory first meeting with a family mediator – which aim to provide parents with interdisciplinary assistance where the divorce involves children.

Divorce cases before the Croatian municipal courts indicate a rise in the number of consensual divorces in relation to the number of divorces initiated by a divorce petition by only one spouse. When the FA 2003 was in force, 35% of all divorces were consensual, while 65% of divorces were initiated by a divorce petition by one spouse. In 2016, after the FA 2015 had entered into force, the situation changed completely; 70% of divorces were agreed upon by divorcing spouses whereas only 30% of divorcing spouses needed active court involvement in ending their marriage.

However, further multidisciplinary studies are needed in order to reach a final conclusion on the quality of the new divorce procedure in Croatia. Studies could examine: the re-litigation of divorce issues; enforcement of agreements or orders relating to children; the operation of child and domestic violence protection measures within divorce proceedings; and child participation in all stages of divorce proceedings – before Croatian courts, in social welfare centres or family mediation.

Legal Rules on the Exercise of Joint Parental Responsibility by Parents Living Apart: A Comparative Approach to the Law and its Impact on Bargaining Power

Kirsten Scheiwe[*]

I Introduction

How is joint parental responsibility to be exercised - individually or consensually? Is there a distinction between "daily matters" that can be settled alone and "important matters" that have to be decided together? Is what will be referred to in this chapter as the "legal representation"[1] of a child to be conducted jointly or individually? What differences are there in the rules for parents with joint parental responsibility who live together and those that live apart?

Legal rules on these matters differ between countries. Some jurisdictions make individual exercise the rule (if the other parent disagrees, they can apply to have the decision revised by a court) and require joint exercise of parental responsibility only in exceptional cases. Other jurisdictions have joint exercise as the rule (each parent can also go to court if they cannot reach an agreement on an important matter) and only allow parental responsibility to be individually exercised for matters of minor importance (such as "daily matters"). There is little comparative research on this issue. Making legal comparisons is interesting as it enables us to better understand what differences these two types of regulation make in practice, and how they affect the relative bargaining power of each parent (especially if parents with joint parental responsibility are separated or divorced).

For example, German law strictly emphasizes the joint exercise of parental responsibility and parental legal representation of a child, even where parents are separated. Separated parents can only make individual decisions about daily matters concerning care for the child when the child is with that parent. This model generates a strong pressure to cooperate and reach agreement, but gives a dissenting or unwilling parent a veto. In contrast, the

* Professor of Law, University of Hildesheim, Germany.

1 In continental law jurisdictions, "legal representation" refers not only to representation of the child in court procedures, but also to the authority to stipulate contracts and agree to legal acts binding upon the child.

basic rule in English law is independent exercise of parental responsibility. Each parent may act alone and without the agreement of the other in meeting that responsibility, subject only to court orders. Only a few important issues (such as permanent removal of the child from the UK or change of surname) are excluded from the individual exercise of parental responsibility. Under this model of individual exercise, a dissenting parent can apply to the court to revise the other parent's decision, but cannot veto that decision themselves. Can other jurisdictions be classified as having an individualistic or a joint model for the exercise of parental responsibility? What particular rules exist to regulate the exercise of joint parental responsibility by parents living apart, particularly in cases of separation or divorce? These questions are investigated in relation to a number of European countries.

A theoretical and empirical question is how different types of regulation affect the relative bargaining power of parents that live apart, an issue which might have relevant gender dimensions. But answering the empirical aspect of this question requires socio-legal research. It could be that differences in practice are not as big as one might expect, possibly because people do not know the law in detail or simply ignore it.

II Some Questions for the Identification and Comparison of Basic Models for Regulating the Exercise of Joint Parental Responsibility

How is parental responsibility to be exercised when parents are living apart - jointly or individually? Who can take what decisions, when can parents act alone and when do they have to act jointly? These main questions are discussed from a comparative perspective, with the goal of identifying commonalities and differences. The legal comparison is between the following jurisdictions: Belgium, Germany, England and Wales, the Netherlands, Norway, Poland, Sweden and Switzerland. However, as space precludes a full description of these countries' laws,[2] they are predominantly used to illustrate the main points of this paper's argument. Moreover, the rules on the exercise of parental responsibility where parents live apart are the main focus of this paper; the legal conditions for granting sole custody to one parent are not discussed here.

---

2 For detailed accounts of the national law on parental responsibility, see the country reports and statutes in A. Bergmann, M. Ferid & D. Henrich (Eds.), *Internationales Ehe- und Kindschaftsrecht mit Staatsangehörigkeitsrecht*, Frankfurt a. M.- Berlin, Verlag für Standesamtswesen, 2017; and K. Boele-Woelki, B. Braat & I. Curry-Sumner (Eds.), *European Family Law in Action, Vol. III: Parental Responsibilities*, Antwerpen - Oxford, Intersentia, 2005 (see also http://ceflonline.net/parental-responsibility-reports-by-jurisdiction/ (30.11.2018); K. Boele-Woelki et al (Eds.), *Principles of European Family Law Regarding Parental Responsibilities*, Antwerpen – Oxford, Intersentia, 2007; C. Mecke & K. Scheiwe, *Gemeinsame Elternverantwortung: Eine rechtvergleichende Studie zu Grundfragen und Problemen beim Elternkonflikt getrennt lebender Eltern*, Göttingen, Universitätsverlag Göttingen, 2018.

Nowadays, the *basic rule* for parental responsibility after divorce is that, where parents already held joint parental responsibility, this joint responsibility usually continues after separation or divorce. No distinction is made between married or unmarried parents.[3] (The legal conditions for granting sole custody to one parent are not discussed here.) Thus, the general rules on *exercising* joint parental responsibility also have to be applied to parents that live apart, subject to certain exceptions which are made for reasons of practicability. Comparing jurisdictions makes it clear that the general regimes governing exercise of joint parental responsibility differ; in essence, *three models* can be distinguished (these models are explained in detail in section III). Countries that have different approaches are compared and then grouped into the three models. But what are the central features of these models?

Model A:
The power to act alone is the general rule: each person with parental responsibility is authorized to exercise it individually (with some exceptions). This model stresses parental independence and the right to act alone. Dissenting parents can apply for a court order. A key example is England and Wales, but the model also applies to a lesser extent for certain groups in Poland and Spain (divorced parents) and Norway (the parent with whom the child lives permanently).

Model B:
Joint exercise is the general rule, but it is presumed that each parent acts with the other's consent. A parent is entitled to act alone within the scope of this presumption; however, the field of application of this presumed consent differs between countries. Examples are Belgium, France, Russia and Switzerland.

Model C:
Joint exercise is stressed; a parent can act alone only in 'daily matters', 'usual matters' or in relation to unimportant decisions. Joint exercise is the general rule for important decisions and legal representation of the child, while solo decision-making is rather limited. If no consent can be reached, a parent needs to go to court in order for his or her view to prevail. Germany provides the foremost example of this model.

3 Boele-Woelki et al, 2007, ibid, p. 84; J. Ferrer-Riba, 'Parental responsibility in a European perspective', *in* J.M. Scherpe (Ed.), *European Family Law, Vol. III: Family Law in a European Perspective*, Oxford, Edward Elgar Publisher, 2016, pp. 284-310 at 308.

There are some general issues to bear in mind when thinking about the regulation of the joint exercise of parental responsibility by parents living apart. *First,* it may be impracticable to stress the joint exercise of parental responsibility after separation or divorce too much, since the living situation of parents who live apart is considerably different from that of two parents who live in one household with the child. Where a lot of cooperation is required, an opportunity is created for one parent to block or to veto decisions of the other. This risk is particularly high where there is a high level of conflict between parents or if one of them wants to cause trouble. If no agreement can be reached, a parent will need to go to court before they can legally act alone. The more the parents have to cooperate with one another and act together, the more scope for conflict is created and the more the courts might have to do. The question then becomes this: how should conflicts be settled, and what role should family courts or other institutions have in reducing conflict? However, if instead independent exercise of parental responsibility is encouraged and a parent has wide powers to act alone, there is a risk that the other parent may be excluded from certain decisions about the child in which he or she wants to be involved.

Second, the model of joint exercise of parental responsibility is based on the formal equality of parents, whereas experience of real life shows that substantial inequality exists. This is especially the case in the context of childcare provided by parents who live apart, where mothers are far more involved than fathers. In the overwhelming majority of cases, the child mainly lives with the mother who is the primary carer. Besides this arrangement, a variety of parental arrangements for the distribution of care exist, ranging from more or less equal sharing of childcare (a small proportion of separated parents do so) to asymmetric distribution of care up to and including little or no contact between one parent and the child.[4] Formal equality may often not be able to deal with these differences.[5] I will argue in this paper that legal regulation of the exercise of joint parental responsibility should deal with these differences in an appropriate manner and should provide a gradation of rights reflecting the division of care between parents. This would allow the parent who

4 In Germany, 6% of all children of separated parents had no further contact with the non-resident parent even though the parents had joint parental responsibility; furthermore, 25% of children reported that contact was rare (A.N. Langmeyer, *Sorgerecht, Coparenting und Kindeswohl*, Heidelberg, VS Verlag für Sozialwissenschaften, 2015, p. 35). In Switzerland, contact with the non-resident father who retained joint parental responsibility had decreased for 31% of children and had ended for 7% of these children (A. Büchler & H. Simoni (Eds.), *Kinder und Scheidung – Der Einfluss der Rechtspraxis auf familiale Übergänge*, Zürich, Rüegger Verlag, 2009, pp. 225, 294). These data highlight the fact that for about one third of the children of separated parents with joint parental responsibility contact is rare or non-existent and therefore joint exercise of parental responsibility exists more on paper than in reality.

5 See S.B. Boyd, 'Equality: An Uncomfortable Fit in Parenting Law', *in* R. Leckey (Ed.), *After Legal Equality: After Legal Equality: Family, Sex, Kinship*, Abingdon, New York, Routledge, 2015, pp. 42-58; C. Smart & B. Neale, *Family Fragments*, Cambridge, Polity Press, 1999; P. England & N. Folbre, 'Involving Dads: Parental Bargaining and Family Well-being', *in* C.S. Tamis-LeMonda & N. Cabrera (Eds.), *Handbook of Father Involvement: Multidisciplinary Perspectives*, Mahwah-New Jersey, Erlbaum Associates, 2002, pp. 387-408.

has to take most day-to-day decisions and legal actions in to do so without hindrances. Different jurisdictions allow gradation in parental responsibility to varying extents.

Third, how do rules on the exercise of parental responsibility affect behaviour and daily life? Do different rules bring about different outcomes? These rules could affect bargaining power between parents and lead to strategic behaviour. Some rules generate situations of veto (where one parent can block the other from taking certain decisions, since the agreement of both is needed or a court order has to be substituted in the absence of consensus). The rules could also impact, to differing degrees, upon the main carer's life – for example, they may prevent her from moving with the child to another town – and have a gendered impact. Moreover, they can allow for more or less independence in decision-making about and legal representation of the child. What level of involvement do courts have in settling conflicts? Are overall outcomes similar despite differences between these models because people do not properly know the rules or choose to ignore them? This final question is an open question which can only be answered by empirical research.

III Commonalities and Differences between Jurisdictions in Detail

In all jurisdictions considered in this piece the following are core issues upon which parents must act jointly: adoption of the child, a change to its name or surname, and a prolonged stay abroad with the child. A change of residence within the home country, the choice of school education, religious affiliation and major health treatments and medical interventions are often, but not always, matters for joint decision-making. Some jurisdictions require the consent of both parents as a rule, even for acts such as travelling abroad with the child for short periods, for routine vaccinations and for choice of kindergarten. Details and modifications of each model and a few of the jurisdictions in which they are used are now explored.

A The Power to Act alone as the Basic Rule - Model A

Under model A, the power to act alone is the general rule, with certain exceptions for decisions of major importance. The prototype for this model is *England and Wales*. The Children Act 1989 clearly states: "Where more than one person has parental responsibility for a child, each of them may act alone and without the other (or others) in meeting that responsibility."[6] The reason given by the Law Commission for England and Wales (the architect of the Children Act 1989) for the basic rule of independent exercise of parental

6 Section 2(7) Children Act 1989, England and Wales (CA). Note that in some situations a person who is not the child's parent can have parental responsibility in English law.

responsibility was that a duty to cooperate or consult would be neither desirable nor practical.[7] However, limits upon the authority to act independently are set by statute[8] and case law,[9] effectively requiring, in a number of situations, that parental responsibility be exercised jointly or in accordance with any court order. A parent is not allowed to act contrary to a court order concerning the child,[10] a rule which is particularly important in the context of the child's residence where their parents live apart, and where the child lives with a third party pursuant to a residence order of the court.[11] Save in those situations where joint decision is effectively required, a parent with parental responsibility who disagrees with the other parent's decision has to go to court and apply for an order determining the particular issue or prohibiting a certain action. There is no general statutory duty in England and Wales to consult or inform the other parent about important decisions concerning the child, save in those situations identified by statute and case law noted above – and there, the onus to bring the matter to court rests with the person who wishes to effect the relevant change.

In other jurisdictions, the power to act alone only applies in certain situations, such as where the parents are separated or divorced, or where the child permanently lives with just one parent. In *Spain* parental responsibility generally has to be exercised by both parents, but in cases of separation the rule is that it is exercised solely by the parent with whom the child lives.[12] A non-resident parent with parental responsibility can apply to the court, on the basis of the child's best interests, requesting the joint exercise of parental responsibility or another distribution of functions between both parental responsibility holders.

---

7 Law Commission (Law Com No 172), *Family Law Review of Child Law Guardianship and Custody*, London, HMSO, July 1988, para. 2.07.

8 As expressly acknowledged by the second part of s. 2(7) CA. For example, the consent of both parents with parental responsibility is (effectively) required when: consenting to the child's adoption – though the need for either parent's consent may be dispensed with by the court (s. 52 Adoption and Children Act 2002); placing the child with foster parents on a voluntary basis (s. 20(7)(8) CA); taking the child abroad for more than one month, so as to avoid a child abduction offence (s. 1 Child Abduction Act 1984); and consenting to the marriage of a minor of 16 or 17 years (s. 3(1A) Marriage Act 1949).

9 Courts have identified a duty to consult (and corresponding veto) in some important situations, e.g. on choice of school *Re G (Parental Responsibility: Education)* [1995] 3 FCR 569); change of the child's name *Re PC (Change of Surname)* [1997 2 FLR 730], Re T (Change of Surname) [1998] 2 FLR 620 (EWCA); religious circumcision *Re J (SIO Muslim Upbringing and Circumcision* [2000] 1 FLR 571 (EWCA); and vaccination *Re B (A Child) (Immunisation)* [2003] 3 FLR 156. Against a duty to consult, see J. Eekelaar, 'Do parents have a duty to consult?', *Law Quarterly Review*, Vol. 114, 1998, pp. 337-4 at 337; critical also J. Herring, *Family Law*, 7th ed., Harlow, Pearson Education Limited, 2015, p. 443.

10 Section 2(8) CA.

11 Even persons who do not hold parental responsibility may have relatively wide decision-making competency: see s. 2(9) CA regarding delegated exercise of parental responsibility, and s. 3(5) which more generally provides that an adult "caring for a child, may ... do what is reasonable in all the circumstances of the case for the purpose of safeguarding or promoting the child's welfare". This statutory provision grants competency beyond decision-making in respect of only 'daily matters' in appropriate circumstances.

12 Art. 156 Spanish Civil Code.

In practice, joint exercise of parental responsibility by both parents after separation is rare in Spain.[13]

In *Poland* joint exercise of parental responsibility only continues after divorce where both parents have applied for it to do so in court.[14] Statistically, this is a rare occurrence. Normally, the parent with whom the child lives can generally act alone and legally represent the child by his or herself. In the overwhelming majority of divorce cases, Polish courts transfer the right to exercise parental responsibility to one parent and assign only partial rights to joint decision-making and legal representation to the other parent. The particular issues upon which joint decisions are required have to be expressly listed in the court decision. If the court order fails to identify decisions on which joint decision is required, the other parent can legally take decisions and action alone,[15] even if the matter is important and should generally be decided jointly.[16]

In *Norway* there is a special right to act alone where a child permanently lives with only one of their parents. The parent with whom the child permanently resides has powers to take a range of important decisions about care for the child by themselves. The other parent with parental responsibility cannot challenge these decisions, which include whether the child will attend a day-care centre, where the child will live in Norway as well as other major decisions affecting everyday life.[17] However, both parents have to consent to a change of residence to another country.[18]

B Joint Exercise as the Rule, but a Legal Presumption of Consent Allows one Party to Act Alone - Model B

Even though joint exercise is the rule in model B, this rule is limited by a presumption that each parent consents to the other's decisions. Therefore, jurisdictions that use model B are similar to those of model A in practice, despite their different legal starting points. However, the similarity depends on how far the presumption reaches and the type of legal acts to which it applies, and this differs considerably between countries. In *Belgium* the presumption applies to all acts,[19] while in *France* it is restricted to "routine decisions".[20]

13 C. Gonzales Beilfuss, *National Report: Spain* [http://ceflonline.net/wp-content/uploads/Spain-Parental-Responsibilities.pdf] (updated to 30.3.2018).

14 Art. 58 § 1a s. 2, Kodeks rodzinny i opiekuńczy as amended on 9 March 2017.

15 J. Słyk, "Rozstrzyganie o istotnych sprawach dziecka w przypadku braku porozumienia rodziców (art. 97 § 2 k.r.o.)", *in Prawo w działaniu. Sprawy cywilne*, Vol. 14, 2013, pp. 77-120.

16 Art. 97 §§ 1 and 2, Polish Family and Guardianship Code states important decisions should be taken jointly.

17 Art. 37 Norwegian Children Act 1981 *Decisions that may be taken by the person with whom the child lives permanently*.

18 Art. 40(1), ibid.

19 Art. 373 para. 2 Belgian Civil Code for acts concerning the person of the child and art. 376 para. 2 CC for other acts.

20 It applies to all "usual" and ordinary acts, art. 372-2 French CC.

In *Portugal* the presumption of the other parent's agreement[21] is valid in all cases except those where statute expressly requires the consent of both parents or where the act is of special importance.[22] In *Russia* the presumption applies to all bar a few listed major decisions,[23] whereas in Switzerland the presumption only applies to the legal representation of the child.[24] The presumption is rebuttable, although it can usually only be rebutted where it is shown that the third party acted *mala fide*. However, this is not the case in Spain where the presumption is not rebuttable.[25]

In summary, the authority to act alone under the legal presumption that the other parent consents can be far-reaching and come close to the power to act alone seen in model A. Under model B, a dissenting parent can apply to the court for assistance.

C *Joint Exercise of Parental Responsibility is Stressed, Supplemented by a Limited Right to Act Alone in "Daily Matters", but with no Presumed Consent - Model C*

Under model C, joint exercise of parental responsibility is the general rule for important decisions and for the legal representation of the child. Parents can act alone in matters that are unimportant, sometimes referred to as "daily matters" or "usual matters". This model applies in Germany, Greece, Italy, Lithuania, the Netherlands and Sweden. In German law, "daily matters" are defined by statute as those matters that happen frequently and without consequences for the child that are hard to reverse.[26] In Sweden, there is no statutory definition of "daily matters" (a definition was explicitly rejected during the legislative process), and there is only limited recourse to the courts if parents cannot agree on how parental responsibility is to be exercised. When Swedish law was being reformed in 1998, it was decided not to define the decision-making power of the residential parent in greater detail. Family courts will not settle conflicts about "daily matters", but the parties can apply for sole custody and try to persuade the court to reverse joint parental responsibility. Otherwise, parents must settle their conflicts themselves, or seek advice by the social welfare committee or undergo mediation under supervision of the administrative social welfare committee.[27] Courts can only determine applications for sole custody, conflicts

21 Art. 1902 No. 1 Port. CC.

22 Art. 1902 No. 2, ibid.

23 Art. 65 Russian Family Code. Consent is required to take the child abroad, to change the child's name or family name, change the child's nationality or allow the adoption of the child.

24 Art. 304 phrase 2 Swiss Civil Code.

25 Boele-Woelki et al, 2005, op cit, n. 2, p. 498.

26 § 1687 German Civil Code.

27 Chapter 6 Sec. 18 Swedish Children and Parents Code.

about contact or residence, and cases where domestic violence or maltreatment might be involved.

This model strongly emphasizes parental consent and unanimity: parents should come to an agreement. The requirement of joint exercise of parental responsibility creates a strong pressure to cooperate. As a result, a dissenting parent has more room to block or veto the decisions or legal actions of the other parent. Catalan law includes an interesting clause to prevent such deadlock where communication between parental responsibility holders is difficult. While they generally have to decide jointly on important matters, the alternative in a difficult situation is for the parent intending to take a given decision to inform the other one, and the latter parent, upon being informed of the other's intention, has a veto right; but if this right is not exercised within thirty days of having been informed, the other parent is allowed to proceed alone.[28]

One might also expect to see more litigation and case law than in jurisdictions that do not use model C, since under this model parents who have their decisions or actions blocked have to apply to the courts. Moreover, the distinction between "important" and "non-important" and "usual" and "unusual" decisions, and the application of the legal term "daily matters" (which one parent can decide alone) to concrete cases, keep the courts busy, as the German example shows.

The German rules on the exercise of shared parental responsibility highlight the joint nature of this exercise[29] and require the joint legal representation of the child.[30] If parents disagree on matters of major significance for their child, the only solution is to turn to the family courts. Only matters of everyday life can be decided by a parent on her own, so separated parents must agree upon important issues.[31] The legislator defined "decisions in daily matters" as those which happen frequently and do not have consequences for the development of the child which are hard to reverse.[32] The current rules are rarely questioned even though they were originally designed for married parents and, since 1958, were intended to provide equal rights to married mothers, who used to be discriminated against in family law. But the same rules apply to separated parents. The rules used to cause few problems in practice, as, in the past, parental responsibility was assigned to one of the parents after divorce. But this practice changed in 1998 when joint parental responsibility became the norm. Since then, disagreements between separated parents over decision-making and what counts as a "daily matter" have been increasingly debated in family courts.

28 Art. 139 Catalan Family Code; see Boele-Woelki et al 2007, op cit, n. 2, pp. 88ff.

29 § 1627 German Civil Code.

30 § 1629 s. 1 phrase 2, ibid.

31 § 1687, ibid.

32 Ibid, s. 1 phrase 3.

The legal concept of "daily matters" was controversial from the beginning and criticized on the grounds that a child's daily routines might be of major importance (for example, nutritional or healthcare decisions), while some more important decisions are reversible (for example, choice of school or religious affiliation). Nowadays, family courts are regularly confronted with litigation by parents about issues such as short foreign holidays, enrolment in kindergarten, and healthcare choices such as dental retainers and vaccinations etc.[33] Quarrels between separated parents who are unable take a common decision or who fight over the construction of "daily matters" are frequent; courtrooms offer a prominent stage for ongoing fights between warring parents.

Take the example of a mother, who is the primary carer, who wishes to take her child on a short foreign holiday – a decision that the child's father opposes. She wants to go to Antalya in Turkey, and therefore applies to renew the child's passport which has expired. The father refuses to accept the decision and to sign the passport application form, and as both parents' signatures are required this means the mother will not be able to take the child away. The mother could claim that this is a short holiday trip and, as such, a "daily matter" which she can decide alone. The father could apply to the family court arguing that this planned trip is not a daily matter, but rather an important decision which requires his consent. If the family court determines that this is an important decision, it will permit the parent who is most able to take a decision in the child's best interests to decide the matter alone.[34] It is likely that the dates of the planned holiday will have passed before the court reaches a decision. Interestingly, contradictory case law arises in relation to short holidays and travel abroad; these cases trigger discussion of and prejudices about whether particular destinations are safe or risky. Currently, travel to Antalya is not considered a "daily matter" by some German courts due to the state of emergency in Turkey. However, there were no problems with travelling with a child to France during the two years that it declared a state of emergency. These conflicting cases create room for prejudice and do not enhance legal certainty. In 2003, travelling to the US with a child was not a daily matter, but an "important matter" that was not to be decided by one parent alone. This was because the US was a "country in war" at the time. A child's participation in a language class in the UK was also an "important issue" because of terror threat posed by the Iraq war. Moreover, a trip to Egypt was held not to be a daily matter that could be decided by one parent alone due to the risk of infected water and the 'foreign culture group' in Egypt.[35] As these acts were categorized as important issues by the court, both parents had to give their consent

33 For details of the case law, see J. v. Staudinger, *Staudingers Kommentar zum Bürgerlichen Gesetzbuch mit Einführungsgesetz und Nebengesetzen. Buch 4. Familienrecht*; §§ 1626-1633; RKEG (Elterliche Sorge 1 – Inhaberschaft und Inhalt), Berlin, Sellier- de Gruyter, 2015/16, § 1687 and § 1628 BGB.

34 Para. 1628 German Civil Code.

35 These family court decisions were about: a trip to the US (AG Freising 10.04.2003 – Az.: 2 F 00292/03, FamRZ 2004, 968); language study travel to the UK (AG Heidenheim 09.04.2003 – Az. 2 F 271/03, FamRZ 2003, 1404); and a holiday to Egypt (OLG Köln 26.10.1998 – Az. 14 UF 170/98, FamRZ 1999, 249).

to the child travelling and, in cases which involved further litigation, the court transferred the right to decide to the parent it considered most appropriate to take the decision.

D A Critique of Model C

I am rather skeptical about model C, which places a strong emphasis on the joint exercise of parental responsibility even where parents live apart, as it creates complexity through its firm enforcement of the duty upon parents to agree. It is not easy for third parties to know who has to consent to acts involving the child, especially when parents live apart. Model C unduly restricts the ability of parents to act alone. The German legal definition of 'daily matters' does not help identify situations where a parent can act alone and so defuse conflicts. In cases where the level of conflict between parents is high and cooperation low, courts must resolve numerous minor issues which could and should be otherwise settled out of court (see, for example, the Swedish system). Another disadvantage of model C is that it makes it difficult for third parties (social parents, step-parents) to participate in the exercise of parental responsibility, since three or more persons, instead of two, would have to reach a consensus. In times where social parents play an important role in the lives of many children, models A and B can more flexibly accommodate social parents. Where both parents cannot reach an agreement the consequences disproportionately burden the main carer, the person who has to take most decisions for the child.

IV Commonalities, Differences, Problems and Reform Proposals

As shown above, all jurisdictions identify some core issues that have to be decided jointly. Jurisdictions differ as to the manner in which these issues are identified: some jurisdictions provide a detailed statutory list of the issues, others have a general clause which is then interpreted through case law. All jurisdictions also provide parents with a right to act alone in emergencies and in situations where the other parent cannot be contacted in due time.

A Advantages and Disadvantages of the Different Models

A wide authority to act alone is given *explicitly* in model A and *implicitly* through a legal presumption in model B (although the scope of the presumption differs between countries using model B). A parent acting alone can be subject to court control following an application by the dissenting parent, and the authority to act alone can be restricted by court order. An important difference between model A (a far-reaching power to act alone) and model C (a strong emphasis on consensual action and joint legal representation of the child) is *the point in time* when action can be taken. Under *model A* (and *model B* within the scope of presumed consent) a parent's decision will not generally be blocked by the other parent's dissent, but their decision can be constrained by a court order (which may be handed down after the decision has been taken or, if the other parent is informed about the intention to take the decision, before it takes place). In contrast, under *model C* the action or decision can be vetoed without a court order, since under this model parents are legally obliged to reach an agreement and represent the child jointly. Although *model C* allows one parent to act alone in unimportant, "usual", or "daily matters", a parent may still be blocked where the other parent claims that the issue is important (not a usual or daily matter) and goes to court. As the discussion above has shown, the definition of 'daily matters' as unimportant is highly problematic. This has the consequence that, under *model C*, the main carer can be burdened and restrained much more than the other one by dissent and legal procedures.[36] However, *model A* carries the risk that the parent who is less involved in the day-to-day care and life of the child could be cut out from important decisions about the child's life if not informed or consulted by the other parent. Therefore, the right of one parent to information and a corresponding duty on the other to supply that information seems to be an important complement to the authority to act alone. From a comparative perspective, the law in England and Wales is exceptional in not giving a right to be informed or imposing a duty to consult.

B *The CEFL Proposal on the Exercise of Joint Parental Responsibility*

In 2007, the Commission on European Family Law (CEFL) developed its "Principles of European Family Law regarding parental responsibilities".[37] Principles 3:11 to 3:18 in chapter IV deal with the exercise of parental responsibility. Principle 3:11 suggests that parents who have parental responsibility should have an equal right and duty to exercise it and, whenever possible, should do so jointly. For reasons of practicability, this principle does not mean that parents have to act together in all circumstances.[38] Therefore, principle 3:12 grants parents the authority to act alone in daily matters. The CEFL decided not to adopt the model of a general right to act alone, as in model A, but debated the alternatives described herein as model B and model C. After comparing systems which authorize each holder of parental responsibility to act alone in relation to daily matters with those that

36 For a discussion of these inequalities from an economic perspective on law and other theoretical angles see K. Scheiwe, 'Zwischen Autonomie und Kooperationszwang - Die Ausübung der gemeinsamen elterlichen Sorge getrennt lebender Eltern im Rechtsvergleich', *in* R. Fankhauser & A. Büchler (Eds.), *Neunte Schweizer Familienrecht §Tage*, Bern, FAMPRA, 2018, pp. 39-58.

37 See the document in six languages in Boele-Woelki et al, 2007, op cit, n. 2, pp. 281ff and principles 3:11 to 3:18 in the appendix below.

38 Ibid, p. 85.

establish a presumption that each parent acts with the consent of the other, the CEFL decided that they preferred the limited right to act alone in respect of daily matters. Why? The CEFL concluded that a presumption would be technically more difficult and could result in uncertainty if rebuttable: "It seems clearer and more close to reality to establish an individual right to act alone in daily matters."[39] Thus, CEFL adopted model C.

In my view, a presumption of consent (model B) is instead preferable for a number of reasons. First, it is easier for a third party to act on the basis of presumed consent rather than always having to investigate whether the other person with parental responsibility should be involved in the decision or not. Moreover, model B avoids arguments about whether a certain issue is a daily matter or not. Second, a presumption is more practical where parents live apart as it allows a separated parent to act alone, but sticks to the basic principle that parents should try to agree upon important issues. A presumption also avoids the intricacies involved in defining what is "daily" or "usual", as opposed to "important". "Usual" or "daily matters" are not always easily defined because daily issues concerning care and education can have considerable importance.[40]

C The Case for a Graduated Approach

Within model C and its strong requirement for separated parents to cooperate, the rules on the exercise of joint parental responsibility should at least distinguish between parents who both participate in the daily care of their child and those where the child primarily lives with only one parent. The Norwegian approach, that "decisions concerning important aspects of the child's care" and "major decisions concerning everyday life" can be decided by the person with whom the child lives permanently, is convincing. This rule takes into account the substantial inequalities between parents and gives the parent with whom the child lives permanently a broader competence to act and take decisions on their own.

Rules on exercising joint parental responsibility should also take into account factual differences in childcare arrangements and allow for gradation of rights in accordance with the caring situation and residence of the child. A situation where both parents share the childcare more or less equally and the child's residence alternates (a practice of a minority of separated parents) is different from one where one parent has no or rare contact with the child (the case for about 30 percent of children in some countries). Both situations are different again from that where the child mainly lives with one parent (typically, the mother) and regularly visits the other parent. While joint parental responsibility may in principle

39 Ibid, p. 89.

40 "Parental responsibility is chopped up artificially (…) Daily matters can be of considerable importance for the child. (…) Intervening into the everyday life of the child - what can be more fundamental?" (Salgo, Comment on § 1687 Rn. 27, cited in Staudinger, op cit, n. 33, author's translation).

continue under all of these different arrangements, rules on how it is to be exercised should take into account these differences and accommodate parental arrangements.

Examples of systems which graduate rights have already been given, such as the Norwegian rule that allows the permanent carer of a child to take certain important decisions by themselves. In the Swiss debate preceding reform in 2014, detailed proposals for graduated rules on the exercise of joint parental responsibility were made,[41] but were not implemented. The basic idea is to set out in statute decisions that necessarily have to be taken by both parents, but widen the range of decisions that a parent with whom the child permanently resides can take alone. If both parents are substantially involved in caring for the child and the child lives with both of them, rules on the exercise of parental responsibility should adapt to this situation too. The purpose of graduating rules on the exercise joint parental responsibility is to bring decision-making and legal representation competence closer to the reality of the child's daily life, care and residence and to grant parents the legal competences they need given the factual situation of care and residence. Important issues where joint decision-making and judicial control are appropriate could include: the choice of a school or professional education, a change of residence, major medical interventions, the religious affiliation of the child, placing the child into third party care (foster parents or boarding school), and even the participation in dangerous sports.[42]

These issues also seem to be common subjects of conflict between separated parents across those jurisdictions which frequently see litigation. A major source of conflict is where one parent (the main carer) wants to move within the country with the child and change their residence. Going abroad with the child is another contested issue. Health care and vaccination decisions, as well as decisions on circumcision, frequently occupy the courts or competent administrative bodies. Choice of school, or even preschool and kindergarten, as well as decisions about religious affiliation or religious acts are other prominent subjects of conflict. Courts have also intervened in respect of other legal acts and the legal representation of the child, as well as the administration of property. Despite similarities in the issues contested across jurisdictions, one would expect to see differences arising from the disparate approaches to regulation summarized in the three models. However, there is not much comparative research on the frequency of litigation, and it is also difficult to compare statistics and judicial data in this area. Further research into this topic would be desirable.

---

41 L. Cantieni, *Gemeinsame elterliche Sorge nach Scheidung: eine empirische Untersuchung*, Bern, Stämpfli Verlag AG, 2007, pp. 278-284; Büchler & Simoni 2009, op cit, n. 4, pp. 305ff.

42 Büchler & Simoni 2009, ibid, p. 313.

V Do Different Legal Rules Really Make a Difference in Practice? The Need for Empirical Research

The question is whether different rules on the exercise of joint parental responsibility really make a difference in practice and daily life. This question arises as it is well known that *law in books* may differ from *law in action*. Further questions follow: how do different sets of rules affect the bargaining power between parents? What, if any, gender dimensions are there?

Empirical research is also needed to understand how important these different rules are in practice to the parents, and also to third parties who have to check whether one parent can legally act alone or whether both parents have to act jointly. It maybe that the differences outlined above make no difference in practice, perhaps because parents and third parties do not know about the legal requirements, or because they do not bother with them. As far as I am aware, there is little empirical research on these issues; however, there is some evidence from England. In research conducted by Pickford on step-parents, she discovered, through her interviews, that many unmarried fathers thought they had parental responsibility even though they had not applied to the court to acquire it or made an agreement with the other legal parent.[43] Why were these fathers subject to this misunderstanding? The apparent reason was that nobody – neither schools nor doctors nor other institutions – asked about parental responsibility in day-to-day life.

We need to design a model, underpinned by a theoretical framework, for comparative research of these questions, and undertake further empirical research to understand the effects of different regulation of joint exercise of parental responsibility in practice. Questions that need answering include which issues are most contested, whether and how courts are involved, and how regulation affects gender inequalities between parents who live apart.[44]

43 R. Pickford, *Fathers, Marriage and the Law*, Family Policy Studies Center for the Joseph Rowntree Foundation, 1999, p. 32. Note that since 2002 unmarried fathers in England and Wales have been able to acquire parental responsibility if registered as the child's father on birth registration.

44 This is one task of an ongoing research project at Hildesheim University on the power and powerlessness of motherhood, https://www.uni-hildesheim.de/mom-projekt/.

CEFL Principles 3.11 to 3.18 Regarding the Exercise of Joint Parental Responsibilities[45]

A PARENTS

Principle 3:11 Joint exercise
Parents having parental responsibilities should have an equal right and duty to exercise such responsibilities and whenever possible they should exercise them jointly.

Principle 3:12 Daily matters, important and urgent decisions
1. Parents having joint parental responsibilities should have the right to act alone with respect to daily matters.
2. Important decisions concerning matters such as education, medical treatment, the child's residence, or the administration of his or her property should be taken jointly. In urgent cases a parent should have the right to act alone. The other parent should be informed without undue delay.

Principle 3:13 Agreement on exercise
1. Subject to the best interests of the child, parents having joint parental responsibilities may agree on the exercise of parental responsibilities.
2. The competent authority may scrutinize the agreement.

Principle 3:14 Disagreement on exercise
1. Where parents having joint parental responsibilities cannot agree on an important matter they may apply to the competent authority.
2. The competent authority should promote agreement between the parents.
3. Where agreement cannot be reached the competent authority should divide the exercise of parental responsibilities between the parents or decide the dispute.

Principle 3:15 Sole exercise upon agreement or decision
Subject to the best interests of the child a parent may exercise parental responsibilities alone

a. upon agreement between the parents according to Principle 3:13, or
b. upon a decision of the competent authority.

45 Boele-Woelki et al, 2007, op cit, n. 2, pp. 82ff.

Principle 3:16 Exercise by one parent
If only one parent has parental responsibilities he or she should exercise them alone.

B THIRD PERSONS

Principle 3:17 Exercise in addition to or instead of the parents

A person other than a parent may exercise some or all parental responsibilities in addition to or instead of the parents.

Principle 3:18 Decisions in daily matters
The parent's partner living with the child may take part in decisions with respect to daily matters unless the other parent having parental responsibilities objects.

Part VI
Protecting Children's Rights and Interests: New Challenges

"Vulnerable" Children, Cultural and Social Realities and Regulation: Moving Towards Early Intervention in New Zealand

*Bill Atkin**

I Introduction

Child abuse is an endemic problem in most jurisdictions. While abuse can occur in institutions and sadly in otherwise respected organisations such as churches, it is a major problem within what should be the kind and nurturing framework of the family. It thus challenges the solidarity of the family and the orthodox views about the private sphere in which the family is supposedly located. While the State has long been recognised as having a role as parens patriae, this is usually regarded as a residual power. However, since the work of Kempe in the early 1960s,[1] it has been accepted that child abuse is a matter for the community to address on a much wider scale. The State in most countries now has a vast machinery aimed at protecting children from abuse and neglect within the family structure. Nevertheless, the tension remains between the family and the State. If the State intervenes improperly, this can be very disruptive in people's ordinary lives; if the State fails to intervene a child can be seriously harmed or even die. It is not easy matching the social realities of child abuse with legal regulation.

Despite being an affluent country, New Zealand has some of the worst child abuse statistics in the Western world. In 1989, its approach to the problem was novel and world-leading. Nevertheless, the amount of abuse and, sadly, of child fatalities remains far too high. In this decade, moves have been made at what could be called the macro level, involving high-powered planning and inter-agency co-operation, and others at the micro level, involving quite specific changes to the law. Also, there have been developments sitting outside the legislative framework, the exact legal status of which remains unclear. These various moves have occurred at different stages with the latest being substantial and con-

---

* Professor of Law, Victoria University of Wellington, New Zealand. Special thanks to Fuzz Shahbaz, my research assistant for this project.

1 C.H. Kempe, 'The Battered Child Syndrome', *JAMA*, Vol. 18, 1962, p. 17, noted, for example, by S. Katz, 'Protecting Children Through State and Federal Laws', *in* B. Atkin (Ed.), *The International Survey of Family Law 2007 Edition*, Jordans, Bristol, 2007, p. 309 at 321.

troversial legislation passed Parliament in 2017 by one vote. In many respects, the current response to child abuse in New Zealand is stuttering.

The author first sets out some of the statistical background to child abuse in New Zealand, then the cultural factors that play a major part in the law in New Zealand. The current legal basis for intervention is explained, i.e. where a child is determined to be "in need of care or protection". We then come to the recent move towards "early intervention", i.e. where the State intervenes at an early stage before the threshold of being "in need of care or protection" has been crossed. A critical examination of this is undertaken. The ostensible benefits of early intervention belie some underlying concerns.

II The Social Context

New Zealand is a small country in the South Pacific. As of 31 December 2017, Statistics New Zealand estimated the resident population to be 4,844,400.[2] Despite its small population New Zealand consistently ranks amongst the worst offenders in terms of child maltreatment amongst OECD countries. Indeed, child maltreatment has been a prevalent problem in New Zealand for a long time. Despite constituting merely 15.3 per cent of the total population (734,300),[3] the incidence of abuse, sadly, is disproportionately greater among the indigenous Māori.

From 1994 to 1998, New Zealand exhibited the third highest rate of homicide from maltreatment among children under the age of 15 years old – 1.2 children per 100,000 children – exceeded only by the United States and Mexico. This number was six times higher than the average for leading countries.[4] Another report reviewed hospital admissions and mortality rates from injuries arising from maltreatment of children under the age of 15 years from 2000 to 2013. It found that hospital admissions declined gradually while the mortality rate remained static.[5] For example, from 2012 to 2013, 15 children per 1,000 were admitted to hospital and 1.5 children per 100,000 died from injuries arising from maltreatment.[6] Admissions from injuries arising from maltreatment were consistently higher for Māori and Pacific children.[7] For example, from 2009 to 2013, 31.24 per 100,000

2 https://www.stats.govt.nz/assets/Uploads/National-population-estimates/National-population-estimates-At-30-June-2018/Download-data/national-population-estimates-at-30-june-2018-components-of-population-change-csv.csv.

3 https://www.stats.govt.nz/information-releases/maori-population-estimates-mean-year-ended-31-december-2017.

4 *A League Table of Child Maltreatment Deaths in Rich Nations*, Innocenti Report Card 5, UNICEF Innocenti Research Centre, Florence, 2003, pp. 2 and 4-5.

5 J. Simpson et al, *The Determinants of Health for Children and Young People in New Zealand*, NZ Child and Youth Epidemiology Service, University of Otago, Dunedin, 2016, pp. 389-390.

6 Figure 125.

7 At p. 390.

Māori children and 23.39 per 100,000 Pacific children were admitted to hospital compared to 12.01 per 100,000 and 6.51 per 100,000 for European/other and Asian/Indian children respectively.[8]

Statistics provided by Child, Youth, and Family ("CYF")[9] continue to paint a grim picture in relation to child maltreatment and preventative and protective services in New Zealand. A Treasury Analytical Paper identified an increased rate of mortality for children and young people between the ages of 10 and 22 years with some level of care and protection contact with CYF. Children with such contact had a mortality risk 1.7 to 2 times higher than the rest of the cohort.[10] In 2015, the Expert Panel Final Report, which prompted the previous government's reform in setting up the Ministry for Vulnerable Children, Oranga Tamariki, estimated that approximately 230,000 children may have been vulnerable at some point during their childhood.[11] Of this group, 6 out of 10 children were likely to be Māori.[12]

In 2016, there were 84,228 care and protection reports of concern and 58,021 police family violence referrals.[13] Of the care and protection reports of concern, CYF took further action in 44,689 cases or 53 per cent. The total number of substantiated abuse findings was 16,394. The number of children and young people involved in care and protection family group conferences reached 7,757. Further, 5,453 children and young people have been removed from their homes and are in the care of the Chief Executive. Of this number, 3,354 children or 62 per cent are Māori.[14] Finally, more generally, Māori children and young people are twice as likely to be referred to the authorities compared to the rest of the population.[15] These figures are likely to be even higher given the degree of underreporting that exists.

The statistics paint an unenviable picture. The reality is that far too many children are abused or neglected. However, when we dig a bit deeper, we find the position to be complicated by an increasingly amorphous set of demographics, differing world views, and a cultural context that makes it much harder to develop consistent legal policies.

---

8 At p. 392.

9 CYF was part of the Ministry of Social Development until the creation of the Ministry for Vulnerable Children, Oranga Tamariki on I April 2017 (discussed later). The new government following the September 2017 election dropped the word "vulnerable" from the name.

10 R. Templeton et al, *Research Using Administrative Data to Support the Work of the Expert Panel on Modernising Child, Youth and Family*, Analytical Paper 16/03, Treasury, Wellington, May 2016, p. 25.

11 Expert Panel Final Report, *Investing in New Zealand's Children and Their Families*, Ministry of Social Development, Wellington, December 2015, p. 41. "Oranga" means welfare and "tamariki" means children.

12 At p. 41.

13 For an earlier discussion of "the sad realities", see M. Henaghan & R. Ballantyne, 'Legal Responses to Violence in the Home in New Zealand', *UNSWLJ*, Vol. 33, 2010, p. 870, Part I.

14 Child, Youth, and Family, 'Key Statistics from 1 July to 31 December 2016', (2016) <www.msd.govt.nz and *Annual Report 2015/2016* (Ministry of Social Development, Wellington, October 2016) p. 21.

15 Expert Panel Final Report, op cit, n. 11, p. 43.

III The Cultural Context

New Zealand is a country where the dominant population is derived from its colonial settlement days. The law reflects the common law that came with colonialism. The indigenous Māori population is in the minority, representing approximately 15.3 per cent as noted above, but increasing. A growing sector is made up of people whose families have immigrated from the Pacific Islands. More recent immigration has seen an increase in Asian citizens. Māori and Pacific peoples tend to be Christian, with Māori having some Christian denominations of their own and a spirituality that draws deeply on their historical roots. Pacific peoples tend to belong to orthodox and conservative denominations. This is highly relevant to a fundamental question: how is the law to respond to the variety of cultural and religious beliefs and practices, especially where the underpinnings of the law are based on the very different Western models? As Barbara Atwood, talking of the United States situation, has said, judgment calls about child abuse "are even more difficult in a pluralist society when the decision maker is confronted with markedly different lifestyles, cultural beliefs, and religious practices".[16]

The history of the Māori people has not always been a kind one. This is found in the way in which family law reflects European rather than Māori perspectives.[17] However, the one major area where this is far less true is child abuse. The principal statute governing child protection is the Children, Young Persons, and Their Families Act 1989, which from 14 July 2017 had its name changed to the Oranga Tamariki Act 1989 or the Children's and Young People's Well-being Act 1989.[18] This is not to be confused with the very different Care of Children Act 2004, which deals inter alia with parenting issues on separation.

The history of the 1989 Act is quite remarkable. The original proposal was Eurocentric: the centrepiece was decision-making by child protection teams comprised of "experts" and officials. The approach was paternalistic and monocultural. This view was reinforced by the contemporaneous publication of a report called *Puao-Te-Ata-Tu*, which evaluated the relevant department of state, then called the Department of Social Welfare.[19] The report was damning in finding that the Department largely ignored the Māori perspective.

---

16 B. Atwood, 'Child Protection in a Pluralist Society: Challenges and Opportunities' *in* B. Atkin (Ed.), *The International Survey of Family Law 2009 Edition*, Jordans, Bristol, 2009, p. 492.

17 See J. Ruru 'Kua tutū te puehu, kia mau' *in* M. Henaghan & B. Atkin (Eds.), *Family Law Policy in New Zealand*, 4th ed, LexisNexis, Wellington, 2013, ch. 2.

18 Children, Young Persons, and Their Families (Oranga Tamariki) Legislation Act 2017, s. 5. The bulk of this Act will be in force no later than 1 July 2019. However, some amendments, including the change to the name of the statute, came into force immediately. It is not clear which of the two alternatives will commonly be used: the author uses the Māori version. It is noteworthy that the reference to "families" has been dropped, which could signal a disturbing anti-Māori and Pacific attitude.

19 J. Rangihau (Chair), *Puao-Te-Ata-Tu (Day Break) The Report of the Ministerial Advisory Committee on a Maori Perspective for the Department of Social Welfare*, Wellington, Government Printer, 1988.

The Māori perspective cannot be described easily in a few words, but in summary it is a more communitarian approach than that found in much of family law.[20] It emphasises not so much the parent/child relationship but rather the relationship of the child to the "whānau" or the family in a much wider sense, involving several generations and other kin, and beyond that to the tribe and subtribe ("iwi" and "hapū"). Another vital aspect of the sense of personhood and belonging is "whakapapa", or ancestry. Pacific peoples tend to have a similar understanding. So, when the first version of the 1980s legislation was being debated, Māori and Pacific spokespeople objected very forcefully. The result was a policy u-turn. A new Bill was drafted modelled on Māori and Pacific approaches and it became law. Instead of the proposed child protection teams, the centrepiece is the "family group conference" ("FGC"). If, following notification of possible abuse, a social worker investigation determines that a child is "in need of care or protection", an FGC must be called. This will be attended by members of the family/whānau, along with the social worker, any advocate for the child, and others whom the family wishes to be present.[21] The child attends, unless attendance would not be in the child's welfare and best interests or is undesirable for some other reason (for example, it may be traumatic if the abuser is present). At certain points, the family on its own can deliberate without the presence of outsiders.

The advantage of the FGC process, apart from its cultural alignment, is that the wider family group can often work through issues and explore options in a way that outsiders would not be able to do. It also enables the culturally appropriate methods to be followed – "tikanga" to use the Māori word. The disadvantage is that some families are dysfunctional and harbour tensions. FGCs for these families can boil over into abuse, though inflammatory exchanges remain subject to the privilege that governs FGCs, unless for example they involve a genuine threat to harm someone.[22] Another downside is that the conference may decide that the child should be returned to the abusive environment that gave rise to the issues in the first place. A check on FGC plans that are not in the child's interests is that the social worker has in effect a veto, in which case the matter may end up going to court. The Family Court's role is however a residual one: in general an application cannot be made unless an FGC has been held and no declaration that a child "is in need of care or protection" can be made without an FGC first.[23]

A policy position in the Act that reflects the emphasis on culture is the first priority that is to be given to placing a child with the family. As the original Act put it: "wherever practicable, the child or young person should be returned to, and protected from harm

---

20 See Ruru, op cit, n. 16.

21 Oranga Tamariki Act 1989, s. 22.

22 *H v. H [Family group conference: privilege]* [2010] NZFLR 821. On privilege, see Oranga Tamariki Act 1989, s. 37.

23 Oranga Tamariki Act 1989, ss. 70 and 72.

within, that family, whanau, hapu, iwi, and family group".[24] Placement outside the cultural network is of secondary priority, and only where family placement is not practicable. Controversially, the Children, Young Persons, and Their Families (Oranga Tamariki) Legislation Bill 2016, when first introduced into Parliament, proposed to remove the priority in favour of the family. Instead, placement decisions were to be guided by a range of factors, including the welfare and best interests of the child and also the maintenance of "personal identity and cultural identity".[25] The judgment call evident in the original Act - that placement within the wide family is prima facie in the best interests of the child – was to disappear.

The change in policy just described brought a very strong reaction from various quarters,[26] most notably the Māori Party, which had two Members of Parliament and officially supported the centre-right government that ruled until the September 2017 election. The Party threatened to withdraw its support from the government unless the policy was reversed. The Minister announced a u-turn and the Bill as enacted contains the following:[27]

> ... preference should be *given* to placing the child or young person with a member of the child's or young person's wider family, whānau, hapū, iwi, or family group who is able to meet their needs, including for a safe, stable, and loving home.

Despite this, the Māori Party and the then Opposition Labour and Green Parties opposed the legislation. The Labour Party considered that the Bill still did not place sufficient emphasis on the "whānau first" principle and on other rights such as access to language and cultural practices. In the end, Parliament passed the Bill by just one vote.

Meanwhile, other provisions in the 2017 Act endeavour to reflect the important role that Māori must play in child abuse policies and practices. For example, a new section 7AA requires the chief executive of the relevant government department "to recognise and provide a practical commitment to the principles of the Treaty of Waitangi", and, in this context, refers to "measurable outcomes" and "strategic partnerships" including the power to delegate functions to appropriate Māori people and organisations. The Treaty is

24 Oranga Tamariki Act 1989, s. 13(2)(f)(i). Note that the use of the macron, the stroke over a vowel (as in ā), was not common in 1989 but is now parliamentary drafting practice.

25 Children, Young Persons, and Their Families (Oranga Tamariki) Legislation Bill 2016, cl 13 as originally introduced, amending s. 13 of the original 1989 Act.

26 See for example H. Kaimarama & K. Scarlet, 'A Critical Analysis of the Children, Young Persons, and Their Families Act (Oranga Tamariki) Legislation Bill', *Council Brief*, February 2017, p. 6, and the New Zealand Law Society's submissions on the Bill, at paras. [114] and [115], which described the proposal as "a radical departure", clashing with the United Nations Convention on the Rights of the Child.

27 Children, Young Persons, and Their Families (Oranga Tamariki) Legislation Act 2017, inserting new s. 13(2)(i)(iii)(A) into the 1989 Act.

one signed in 1840 between Māori chiefs and representatives of the British Crown, and today is regarded as establishing a partnership between the indigenous people and the government. Its explicit inclusion is unique in family law legislation.

This excursus into legal policies involving Māori is designed to show that the cultural context and ethnic realities are fundamental to the development of legal policy on child abuse. Arguably, this is a universal truth, though obviously how this is worked out will depend on the particular jurisdiction and balance of ethnicities found in different countries. In New Zealand the non-European cultures are minority groups, and so majoritarian forces need to be persuaded to enact laws that not only accommodate but also embrace the variety of beliefs, mores and practices that are evident in the country, subject of course to core principles such as making sure children are safe. In other countries, where the indigenous population is the majority, the dynamics may be different, but nevertheless not ignorant of culture.

IV Intervention

A *Controversy Surrounding Intervention*

The power of the State to intervene into family life in order to protect children is a considerable intrusion. It is justified on the basis of the vulnerability of children and the interest of society to see its children prosper and grow into worthy citizens. However, for some, the rhetoric of "parental rights" is a rallying cry. In New Zealand as elsewhere it came to the fore in a debate over corporal punishment of children. A Green Party Member of Parliament's Bill proposed to repeal s. 59 of the Crimes Act 1961, which gave parents a defence to assault charges on the basis of using reasonable force for the purposes of correction.[28] In the end, the Crimes (Substituted Section 59) Amendment Act 2007 was passed by an overwhelming majority of Members of Parliament, but only after a vigorous and at times unruly debate had occurred in the community. It is reported that, even today, a third of children are still "smacked" by their parents, but the Children's Commissioner, Judge Andrew Becroft, stated that the 2007 Act has no doubt worked to protect children.[29]

The parental discipline saga is not isolated. The original 1989 Act itself contained a principle of minimal intervention in s. 13(2)(b)(ii) (amended as discussed below):

28 See B. Atkin, 'Physical Punishment by Parents: The New Zealand Law Reform', *in* A. Buchler & M. Muller-Chen (Eds.), *Festschrift für Ingeborg Schwenzer zum 60. Geburtstag*, Staempfli Verlag, Bern, 2011, pp. 99-113.

29 https://www.stuff.co.nz/national/94166691/many-kiwi-parents-still-consider-smacking-as-an-acceptable-way-to-parent.

"...intervention into family life should be the minimum necessary to ensure a child's or young person's safety and protection".

This provision in an interventionist piece of legislation is partly redolent of its time in the late 1980s: neo-liberal ideologies were prevalent in New Zealand, impacting markedly on economic policies but, as in this example, on social policies as well.

B *The Conventional Test for Intervention*

Under the current law, the process of intervention starts with a report of a belief of ill-treatment or neglect to a police officer or a social worker.[30] Anyone can make a report and, if bona fide, attracts immunity from liability. Under the 2017 legislation, reporting goes beyond a belief that a child is being harmed to "concerns about the well-being of a child", which is wider phraseology presumably designed to attract a wider range of notifications.[31] A report must be investigated to see whether there is a basis for intervention, in which case a family group conference will be convened.

The test for intervention, originally found in s. 14, was redrafted under the 2017 Act. It has become more complex and spread over two sections, ss. 14 and 14AA. For situations of abuse and neglect (as opposed to situations where the parents lack the ability to care for a child, where the child is uncontrollable, or is engaging in criminal activity) the new version of s. 14 uses the overarching words that "the child ...is suffering, or is likely to suffer, serious harm" and then refers to relevant circumstances in s 14AA. These circumstances are not unlike those in the original law but reshuffled:

> (a) the child or young person is being, or is likely to be, abused (whether physically, emotionally, or sexually), deprived, ill-treated, or neglected; or
> (b) the parents or guardians or other persons who have the care of the child or young person are unwilling to care for, or have abandoned, them.

Then, rather awkwardly, a further set of four circumstances are set out in s 14AA(2):

> (a) a child's or young person's development or physical or mental or emotional well-being is being, or is likely to be, impaired or neglected, and that impairment or neglect is, or is likely to be, avoidable:
> (b) the child or young person has been exposed to domestic violence (within the meaning of section 3 of the Domestic Violence Act 1995):

30 Oranga Tamariki Act 1989, s. 15 and following.
31 Children, Young Persons, and Their Families (Oranga Tamariki) Legislation Act 2017, inserting new s. 15.

(c) serious differences exist between the child or young person and the parents or guardians or other persons who have the care of them:
(d) serious differences exist between a parent, guardian, or other person who has the care of the child or young person and any other parent, guardian, or other person who has the care of them.

Under the new s. 14AA(3), "serious harm" may occur as a result of "an incident", "2 or more incidents ... the cumulative effect of which is serious enough to cause serious harm" or "the co-existence of different circumstances". Thus a series of similar or different incidents may amount to serious harm as well as one-off instances of serious harm.

In an early judgment, McGechan J, on appeal in the High Court, held that "harm must be of sufficient degree to warrant Court intervention".[32] In other words, although the wording of s 14 appears very broad and all embracing, it has by implication some constraints. Indeed, the umbrella use of the word "serious" under the new formulation reinforces the approach taken by McGechan J. Furthermore, if a parent meets "minimum acceptable standards" of parenting, which obviously allows for a considerable amount of variation in approaches to parenting, then a child is not in need of care or protection.[33] There is thus a degree of leeway before intervention will occur.

A new basis for intervention enacted in 2017 is in s 14AA(2)(b): where a child has been exposed to domestic violence, typically where one parent has abused the other. It has been long recognised that exposure to adult abuse may in itself be psychological abuse of the child (see for example s 3(3)(a) of the Domestic Violence Act 1995). This can even extend to psychological and emotional abuse generated by the way in which a party has involved a child in litigation and dealings with the other parent.[34]

Earlier, in 2016, another new ground was added: where the child is a "subsequent child".[35] A subsequent child is one born to a parent who has previously been convicted of the homicide of a child or has had a child removed, in other words a parent who has already been shown to be abusive. Although it was possible to remove a child at birth or shortly thereafter prior to the addition of the "subsequent child" ground, a key element now is the introduction of a "reverse onus". This means that the burden is on the parent to convince either a social worker or a judge that the child will be safe, rather than the onus being on the authorities to prove that the child is in need of care or protection. The policy justification

32 *Director-General of Social Welfare v. S* [1992] NZFLR 309 at p. 312.

33 *Re ITA* [1997] NZFLR 385 at p. 394, where Judge Green referred to the High Court decision of Anderson J in *E v. Department of Social Welfare* (1989) 5 FRNZ 332. Judge Green was dealing though with non-accidental injuries that she described as "physical abuse at the most serious end of the scale" (p. 393).

34 *C v. B* [2018] NZCA 322. The psychological abuse by the mother was linked to her fixed belief that the father had physically and sexually abused the children.

35 Oranga Tamariki Act 1989, s. 14(1)(ba), as added by the Children, Young Persons, and Their Families (Vulnerable Children) Amendment Act 2014), changed to s. 14(1)(c) under the 2017 amending legislation.

is "safety first" for the child, which is easy to agree with, but it is, arguably justifiably, inconsistent with conventional legal principles about the burden of proof. It is also a sign of a move away from minimal intervention and segues into the next topic of early intervention.

C *From Minimal to Early Intervention*

The changes referred to in the last section are not really controversial. However, the Children, Young Persons, and Their Families (Oranga Tamariki) Legislation Act 2017 heralds a swing to far greater intervention than in the past by its inclusion of what we may label "early intervention". It is indeed a massive shift in policy that had already been put into practice prior to the enactment of the 2017 amendments. In other words, the executive arm of government moved ahead of the legislative arm, a trend that constitutionally is worrying but ultimately beyond the scope of the present discussion.

The following are the main provisions of the 2017 Act on early intervention, all amending the 1989 Act:

(i) In the section dealing with the *duties of the chief executive*, s. 7(2)(bab) reads:

> ensure, where practicable, that any services funded by the department to reduce the impact of early risk factors for future involvement in the care, protection, or youth justice systems under this Act are co-ordinated with other government-funded activities for improving outcomes for children, young persons, and families, or reducing the impact of those early risk factors...

This paragraph flags several important concepts: first, that "early risk factors" can be identified, sometimes referred to as "predictive risk modelling"; that funding will be directed to the "impact" or negative consequences of early risk factors; that government and government-supported agencies will co-ordinate their work or "services", which implies information sharing on a personal level; and that the goal relates to "outcomes", which presumably are measurable short-term improvements or reductions in the risks of abuse. Described this way, a lot is good here, but also various aspects may be described as tendentious.

(ii) In the section setting out *principles for care and protection*, s. 13(2)(a)(ii), which contained the minimum intervention principle, has been amended to state:

> (a) it is desirable to provide early support and services to—
>
> (i) improve the safety and well-being of a child or young person at risk of harm;

(ii) reduce the risk of future harm to that child or young person...

There is a note of irony that the new legislation, promoted by a right-wing government, removes the minimum intervention principle, and emphasises "early support and services". On the other hand, and somewhat contrariwise, new s. 13 also contains another principle, which to an extent echoes the notion of least intervention:

> (d) a power under this Part that can be exercised without the consent of the persons concerned is to be exercised only to the extent necessary to protect a child or young person from harm or likely harm...

Nevertheless, the principle in (a) is a broad one that is picked up in two other new provisions as follows.

(iii) Section 17 is amended. Section 17 empowers the *investigation of a report of abuse* to take place. Under the pre-existing law, a case could proceed to an FGC only if the investigation resulted in a reasonable belief that a child was in need of care or protection. A new subsection changes this and enables the State to continue to intervene despite the primary criteria for intervention not being satisfied:

> (2A) If, after an investigation under subsection (1), a care and protection co-ordinator is not notified under subsection (2), the chief executive may, nevertheless,—
> (a) undertake a further assessment or provide services to the child or young person, their family, or other persons having the care of the child or young person; or
> (b) refer the child or young person, their family, or other persons having the care of the child or young person to other services provided by agencies or in the community; or
> (c) take no further action ....

In other words, even if there is no proven harm, action can be taken on the basis that some risk of future harm can be identified, perhaps as a result of "predictive risk modelling" or some other tool that is not specified in the legislation. While support and services should be undertaken "wherever possible ... on a consensual basis",[36] ultimately the point of s. 17(2A) is that coercive intervention can nevertheless take place.

(iv) A *new s. 18AAA* (the capital letters represent a recent and confusing drafting practice) enables a family group conference to be held even when the threshold for ordinary intervention has not been met:

> (18AAA) If the chief executive is not satisfied that a child or young person is in need of care or protection but believes that holding a family group conference would best assist in formulating a plan to help the child or young person, the chief executive may refer the case to a care and protection co-ordinator, who must convene a family group conference under section 20.

(v) For the sake of completeness, we should note provisions in the Vulnerable Children Act 2014 requiring the *creation by the government of an overall vulnerable children's plan.* Under s. 9(2)(a), the content of the plan must include "outcomes" in relation to children "who have early risk factors for future involvement in the statutory care, protection, and youth justice systems under the Oranga Tamariki Act 1989." As discussed later, following the change of government at the end of 2017, significant changes are being made to the Vulnerable Children Act, including the deletion of reference to "vulnerable" children. However, the language of "early risk factors" is retained and indeed extended to the official government "strategy" relating to the well-being of children.[37]

(vi) In *summary* New Zealand now has a hotchpotch of provisions on early intervention slotted into the legislation at sundry points. Would a more coherent and principled approach have been preferable?

D Children's Teams

As part of the swing to early intervention, the government has established children's teams around the country operating at a local level.[38] They are made up of professionals and members of agencies from the social service sector. They have a "lead professional" who is in charge of a team.[39] Their aim is to offer a co-ordinated approach for children in need. In essence, they are the way in which the government is responding to risk indicators for children who are nevertheless not legally in need of care or protection under s 14. Their aim is to prevent harm before it happens, which is surely a good thing.

Yet, from the legal point of view, there are at least two particular concerns about the development:

---

36 Oranga Tamariki Act 1989, s. 13(2)(b)(iii).

37 Child Poverty Reduction Bill 2018, inserting new ss. 6(1)(d) and 9(1)(a) into the renamed Children's Act 2014.

38 https://www.mvcot.govt.nz/working-with-children/childrens-teams/.

39 https://www.mvcot.govt.nz/working-with-children/childrens-teams/how-they-work/.

(i) These teams are the very model that was so forthrightly criticised and abandoned in the 1980s. FGCs replaced teams in the ultimate form of the legislation. It was pointed out above that this had a great deal to do with removing monoculturalism from the system. The FGC system still operates where a child crosses the s. 14 threshold and, as noted in the previous section of this discussion, under the new amendment Act they may operate as part of early intervention as well. However, the teams appear to be playing a significant interventionist function, not in the serious situations of actual harm, but in the situations of possible future risk. When the legal history of the 1989 Act is recalled, the irony is strong.

(ii) The White Paper that preceded the 2017 Act and the earlier Vulnerable Children Act 2014 indicated that children's teams would be legislated for.[40] This however has not happened. There is no express statutory mandate for children's teams - for their constitution, appointment, powers, or accountability. One key question is whether they can intervene in a coercive way, i.e. without the consent of the family concerned. These issues are unanswered in terms of the law. The existence of teams is regarded as an "operational" matter, which enables the government to act without parliamentary authorisation. Yet the teams' de facto role is, as far as one can really tell, a major one and a key element in the new strategy. Is this the right way to address even the most benevolent of aims?

V A BENIGN EXPERIMENT?

If early intervention means that a child is saved from abuse or even death, then it is hard to question it. However, we need to drill more deeply to see whether the picture is as simple as this. Are there downsides that make us hesitate?

New Zealand is not the only country to have proactive policies but it may be the first to have a scheme along the lines that we have been discussing which uses prediction tools and teams. In that sense it may be described as an experiment. Scotland has recently developed a scheme where every child would be assigned a "named person", possibly a health professional or teacher, who would play a role in the child's life to promote, support and safeguard the child's well-being.[41] The proposal ran into a great deal of opposition and was partly challenged by the United Kingdom Supreme Court, although the general concept was upheld.[42] The Scottish legislation also provides for the issuing of guidance for

40 Ministry of Social Development, *The White Paper for Vulnerable Children*, MSD, Wellington, 2012, Vol. II, p. 165.

41 Children and Young People (Scotland) Act 2014, ss. 19-32. See E. Sutherland, 'More Proactive Child Protection: A Step Too Far?' *in* M. Brinig (Ed.), *The International Survey of Family Law 2017 Edition*, Jordans, Bristol, 2017, p. 287 especially p. 304 and following.

42 *Christian Institute v. Lord Advocate* 2016 SLT 805.

the purpose of assessing the wellbeing of a child, with appropriate consultation requirements before such guidance is issued.[43] In other words, a system of early risk indictors has been built into the Scottish law, though with flexibility for modification.

The Scottish approach of "named person" is a universal one. That is both its virtue and its vice. All children are covered without discrimination. All children are thought to benefit from the scheme as opposed to some who may be labelled "vulnerable" because they happen to tick too many boxes on a list of risk indicators.

In New Zealand, the tale is a somewhat volatile one that is influenced by changes in political fortunes. The approach of the previous National-led Government was one where intervention and support were addressed essentially to a narrowly identified class of children. Following a general election in September 2017, a new coalition government was formed from the Labour, Green and New Zealand First Parties. It moved in a more universalist direction, while retaining a focus on children with high needs.

On 31 March 2017, a new Ministry came into being, named Oranga Tamariki Ministry for Vulnerable Children. There is a sense in which all children are "vulnerable" but the children referred to in the name of the new Ministry (the English part of the name as opposed to the Māori part) singled out a selected group of children who in a negative sense are different from others. When the name of the Ministry was first announced, the Children's Commissioner described it as "cripplingly disappointing"[44] and his views were widely echoed. The government of the day however stuck with the tendentious title. Who exactly is a vulnerable child remains hard to determine. In s. 5(1) of the Vulnerable Children Act 2014, "vulnerable children means children of the kind or kinds (that may be or, as the case requires, have been and are currently) identified as vulnerable in the setting of Government priorities under section 7". Section 7 states that the government must set "priorities for improving the well-being of vulnerable children" and so, the definition of "vulnerable children" is circular and unenlightening. We can surmise however that it is linked to early intervention as described earlier.

One of the first acts of the government formed after the 2017 election was to drop the word "vulnerable" from the name of the Ministry. In other words, the Ministry is for all children, not just those labelled "vulnerable". Further, the government introduced legislation into Parliament that also dropped the word "vulnerable" from the Vulnerable Children Act (noted above), which became the Children's Act 2014.[45] Perhaps more significantly, the Child Poverty Reduction Bill 2018 requires the relevant Minister to adopt a "strategy" of which the first aim is to improve "the well-being of *all* children".[46] Although the

43 Children and Young People (Scotland) Act 2014, s. 96.

44 http://www.stuff.co.nz/national/faces-of-innocents/85577096/Who-named-the-Ministry-for-Vulnerable-Children-Oranga-Tamariki.

45 Child Poverty Reduction Bill 2018, cl 41, which became the Children's Amendment Act 2018, s. 4.

46 Clause 45, inserting new s. 6 into the 2014 Act. Emphasis added.

remaining items that the strategy must address refer to children with greater needs, child poverty, and children such as "those with early risk factors", the movement towards a broader canvass is apparent.

The Scottish approach avoids the perils of the earlier New Zealand one with its emphasis on vulnerability but it then runs up against the other side of the coin. Many children are in loving homes and progress to adulthood perfectly satisfactorily. Why should the paternalistic arm of the State extend to them, adding to costs, time and energy of those involved, including the State, and intervening unnecessarily in the lives of good families? Baroness Hale has made the point rather bluntly:[47]

> In a totalitarian society, uniformity and conformity are valued. Hence the totalitarian state tries to separate the child from her family and mould her to its own design. Families in all their subversive variety are the breeding ground of diversity and individuality. In a free and democratic society we value diversity and individuality. Hence the family is given special protection in all modern human rights instruments ...

On the other hand, the same complaint may be made against policies that are targeted at early intervention as in New Zealand. We need to be reminded that early intervention applies, not where a child is suffering harm, but where a child *may possibly* do so according to a set of criteria. Intervention in these families may in reality challenge "the diversity and individuality" of families, to use Baroness Hale's words, and thus be paternalistic in a more insidious way because of discrimination against certain families. Where services and support are offered with the consent of the family there can hardly be objection. However, the idea of early intervention under the new New Zealand legislation (as drafted) means that action can be taken to "help" families and children without their agreement. Contrast this with a different model of long standing. For over 100 years, a non-profit organisation called Plunket (named after Lady Plunket, the wife of the then Governor-General) has offered services to all newborns. Plunket sees about 90 per cent of newborns on a voluntary basis, and is a greatly admired part of the New Zealand culture. It does not discriminate on the basis of vulnerability. So, it is not targeted and it is consensual, with government financial backing.

Some further points should be made about early intervention.[48] First, significant weight is placed on the effectiveness and appropriateness of the factors that predict risk. Ethnicity

---

47 *In re B* [2009] 1 AC 11 at para. [20] cited by Sutherland, op cit, n. 41.

48 Some of these points are found in T. Dare, 'The Ethics of Predictive Risk Modelling' *in* L. Waterhouse & J. McGhee (Eds.), *Challenging Child Protection New Directions in Safeguarding Children*, Jessica Kingsley Publishers, London, 2015, p. 64 and following, and E. Keddell 'The Ethics of Predictive Risk Modelling in

is not explicitly one such factor, even though, as discussed above, it is significant in the New Zealand social and cultural context. It would be extremely unwise to tar children because of the colour of their skin. However, it has been pointed out that, because some ethnicities such as Māori tend to figure low in terms of socio-economic status, they are indirectly targeted.[49] Further, how often will the assessment produce false positives and false negatives? False positives are less worrying if the process of intervention is reliant on consent but consent is not mandatory under the New Zealand scheme. False negatives mean that other traditional methods of identifying and dealing with child abuse remain essential and of the highest priority.

A key aspect of the risk assessment process is obtaining the necessary data about individual families. A corollary of this is that government agencies need access to personal information. Information sharing provisions are found in the Children, Young Persons, and Their Families (Oranga Tamariki) Legislation Act 2017,[50] and non-government agencies contracted to assist the government have been pressured to hand over personal information in order to retain their contracts. These developments raise important questions about the value placed on privacy (in New Zealand partly legislated for in the Privacy Act 1993) and the confidential nature of the relationship between professionals, such as counsellors and doctors, and their clients.

Although the goals of early intervention are positive, the perception may be the opposite. If a family is a candidate for intervention, stigma may attach because of the high risk label. In some instances, this may involve stigma on top of stigma, for example where a social security beneficiary, who faces bad press because of that status, is also treated as a high-risk parent.

Early intervention depends on effective measures to address the issues. Children's teams and some problematic aspects about them have already been discussed. What kinds of help are to be expected? If the real reason for a child's being at risk is poverty, what exactly would be done to alleviate this and how far will the resources stretch? Inevitably this gets into much bigger political questions about redistribution of wealth, government budgets and the philosophy of big government versus small government. Prima facie early intervention will cost the government more, and it is ironical that a right wing government advanced the policy. On the other hand, because of the targeting involved and perhaps the belief that ultimately the number of incidents and hence costs of actual abuse will fall, the scheme has been described as a "residualist, neo-liberal" approach.[51] Perhaps it is sig-

---

the Aotearoa/New Zealand Child Welfare Context: Child abuse prevention or neo-liberal tool?', *Critical Social Policy*, Vol. 35, 2014, p. 69.

49 Keddell, op cit, n. 48, p. 76.

50 Children, Young Persons, and Their Families (Oranga Tamariki) Legislation Act 2017, s. 41.

51 Keddell, op cit, n. 48, p. 71.

nificant that some of the new government's policies are in a Bill called Child Poverty Reduction.

One further angle on this is what is known in New Zealand and elsewhere as "social investment".[52] This is an approach that goes much wider than child abuse and can involve most government social spending, exemplified by the previous government's establishment of a new Social Investment Agency. The word "social" accepts that there are legitimate community concerns and as such it is contrary to neo-liberal ideology.[53] It involves the need for "outcomes" from the money that the government spends. This means that government money should be spent in a way that is an investment that brings returns, or successfully addresses issues. Like early intervention, this sounds worthwhile especially when accompanied by the need for evidence-based initiatives, i.e. policy not made on the basis of hunches, intuition or lobbying but solid evidence. If we relate social investment to early intervention, we would look for sound reasons to act and spend money, with results that lead to improved lives for children and less abuse. Again, this sounds good.

On the other hand, "social investment" may also be problematic. As Harris has said "[t]he focus on government as investor may place insufficient emphasis on the benefits to society and other actors that might come from government spending".[54] "Excessive reliance on evidence can be a way to uphold a problematic status quo, when a lack of evidence is given as a reason for inaction". More importantly, Harris suggests that the approach may distract from the task of determining what values and hence outcomes are the right ones for the community to aspire to.

VI Summary

We must applaud measures aimed at reducing child abuse. Intervening early where children are "vulnerable" may be a good "investment". Early intervention indeed sounds positive and may make a real difference. However, it is experimental with problematic concepts, methodologies and consequences. In the end, is it truly benign?

52 For example S. Qualtieri, 'Social Investment in Children', *Canadian Social Work*, Vol. 14, 2012, p. 27 and N. Parton, 'Comparing child protection systems: towards a global perspective', *in* P. Dolan & N. Frost, *The Routledge Handbook of Global Child Welfare*, Routledge, Abingdon, 2017, especially p. 235. See also J. Boston & D. Gill (Eds.), *Social Investment New Zealand Policy Experiment*, Bridget Williams Books, Wellington, 2017.

53 See M. Harris, *The New Zealand Project*, Bridget Williams Books, Wellington, 2017, p. 67.

54 Ibid, p. 68.

The Legal Impact of Article 3 CRC as a Corrective Remedy – Is Article 3 CRC to Youth Law What Article 8 ECHR Was/Is to Family Law?

Coby de Graaf[*]

I Introduction

In this paper I would like to focus on the role of the court in cases regarding the establishment of children's rights, particularly where it concerns the meaning of article 3 of the United Nations Convention on the Rights of the Child ("CRC"): the child's best interests as a primary concern. Article 3 seems to play – or has the potential to play – a significant role as a corrective factor in family-law legislation in which parent's rights easily gain the upper hand.[1]

Whereas previously, it could be asserted that the criteria for the child's best interests were or could be defined at the discretion of adults, on the basis of the current "documents", this is definitely no longer the case.[2] Not only is article 3 itself "enshrined" in children's rights as a whole – along with articles 2, 6 and 12, it defines the framework for interpretation of all articles of the CRC – it is also elaborated upon in a General Comment. General Comment no. 14 gives important concrete directions as to what the child's best interests require.

The significance of this set of regulations and directions is even greater against a backdrop of social developments in which 'individual self-determination and freedom of choice' – in the words of Pessers – are keywords.[3] The CRC in its entirety provides the moral framework, in which terminology such as self-determination and freedom of choice

* Guest lecturer at Leiden University and University of Amsterdam and executive director of the Centre for Children's Rights Amsterdam.

1 When determining the structure of this paper I was inspired by the layout of the inaugural lecture by professor Chantal Mak, which also included a number of examples from legal practice. This choice was also determined by two CCRA studies into the application of the CRC in Dutch case law and by the fact that I am editor of the Dutch case law magazine *JPF*.

2 J. de Ruiter *in* J.A.M. Schouten, *Hulp en Recht*, Deventer, Kluwer 1972, pp. 17-19.

3 D.W.J.M. Pessers, *Verdwaalde seksen: over sperminators, metrosekseksuelen en autocopien*, Thijmessay, Valkhof pers, 2003, p. 26.

are placed at the heart of parental responsibility, the latter being a fundamental concept within the CRC. Parental responsibility is the guiding principle of the CRC, forming the foundation on which children's rights can be and must be established. After all, children are – and always will be – dependent on their parents for the implementation of their rights. From the perspective of children's rights, this is often referred to as the right to have responsible parents. In the CRC the child is recognized as rights holder – in which sense the child is autonomous. However, the establishment of that autonomy depends on the parenting style of the parents – the child as a dependent being.

In the courtroom, article 3 CRC in particular, has fulfilled a significant role, often in combination with other articles. In order to shed light on its meaning, a few cases will be discussed in which article 3 CRC has been an important factor. The first case study is the most recent and also the most fundamental one. It concerns the right of the child to be informed about his biological origins. In this case, the Supreme Court of the Netherlands reaffirmed a decision by the Court of Appeal which, with reference to the CRC, ordered the parents to provide the information. The second example, or set of examples, concerns cases in which the judge – with a reference to article 3 in combination with articles 18 and 20 CRC – ruled on the placement of children in care and termination of parental authority. Here the court played a primary role in the matter of the child's right to continuity and stability in care. This ruling has in fact led to a change in the law. After this new regulation came into effect as of 1 January 2015, the court has once more become more active in nuancing judgements deemed to be too stringent in this direction. The third example concerns the right of the child to be heard, a right formulated in article 12 CRC, which – in combination with article 3 – is one of the core provisions of the CRC. In that particular case, the Supreme Court quashed the decision of the Court of Appeal, which stated that it was not necessary to invite the child to a second hearing, because, in a nutshell, it would not have led to a different decision.

Subsequently, I will comment on the CRC and its direct legal effect, and in particular, its application in accordance with the Convention and General Comment no. 14. This Comment has contributed to a clear definition of 'the child's best interest', application of which is still in its initial phase/infancy. With good reason the expectations are high, especially considering the clear, well-applicable elements it contains, all of which will become apparent in the discussion of the Comment.

Finally, the desirability of judicial activity will be discussed. The broader provisions under international law provides the possibility to incorporate more moral notions when arriving at an opinion, in this case supported by the CRC.

II Case Studies

A *The Right to be Informed about One's Biological Origin*

The first case relates to the ruling by the Supreme Court of the Netherlands on the child's right to be informed about their biological origin. Although the District Court ruled that an adult male had no cause of action regarding his request for a parental access arrangement, both the Court of Appeal and the Supreme Court ruled that it was the obligation of the mothers to inform the child during the next parental contact that the man in question was in fact his biological father. For a deeper understanding of the case, let us focus on the facts.

The male party had responded to an advertisement placed by the mothers, who desired to have children and were in search of a sperm donor. The mothers were registered partners. A sperm-donor agreement was reached between the biological mother and the male party, which was also signed by the co-mother. In 2008 the biological mother gave birth to the child. The pregnancy was accomplished through self-insemination with the sperm of the male party. The co-mother adopted the child with the male party's approval. The mothers obtained joint parental responsibility. From the birth of the child up to and including June 2009, there had been parental contact between the male party and the child once a month on average, each time lasting three hours on average. Since June 2009, there had been less and less contact, and in January 2010 all contact came to a halt altogether. Subsequently, as a result of a petition filed by the male party, a settlement agreement was drawn up in which parental access arrangements were made for the years 2011 and 2012. In late February 2013, the mothers cut all ties between the male party and the child.

The biological father then requested the court, *inter alia*, to determine a parental access arrangement between himself and the child, pursuant to article 1:377a (2) Dutch Civil Code. After the District Court rejected his request, the Court of Appeal made its final decision – after an investigation by the Child Care and Protection Board of the Netherlands – which included a ruling that the male party and the child should have parental contact once a year, the first parental contact being in May 2016. Furthermore, the Court of Appeal ruled that the mothers were required to provide the child with "status information" – information on the identity of the donor – before 30 April 2016, which meant telling the child about his biological origin.[4]

---

4 The Court of Appeal has taken the following into consideration. From the very start it was the intention of all parties to include the biological father in the life of the child. If and insofar as a close personal relationship within the meaning of article 1:377a (1) Dutch Civil Code did not exist already between the male party and the child before the birth of the child, it is likely that this bond has developed based on a number of occasions of contact.

In an appeal in cassation before the Supreme Court only the legal remedy of the incidental appeal was scrutinized, in this case the judgement in the final decision and the provision in the dictum that the mothers had to provide the child with status information by 30 April 2016. The legal remedy had pointed out that there is no legal rule in place that can oblige parents to inform their child about his biological origin before a specific date. Pursuant to article 8 of the European Convention on Human Rights (ECHR), the parent's right to family life specifically means that it is up to the parents themselves to decide on the appropriate moment to inform a child, who is conceived through a donor, on who his biological father is. The male party is not a parent and has no say in the upbringing of the child. The extent of family life that he is entitled to does not entitle him to determine how the parents raise their child or the choices they make. And, according to the mothers, the court cannot unilaterally interfere.

The Supreme Court of the Netherlands disagreed. It is especially interesting how the Supreme Court construed the right of the child to status information, namely based on the definition of what parental authority entails in article 1:247 (1) Dutch Civil Code: "The care of and responsibility for the mental well-being and personal development of a child includes giving information (notification of his biological origin)". And: "Even though parental authority is a 'right' falling to the parents, this right is granted in the best interest of the child, and can therefore not be separated from the obligation to serve this interest." Reference is made to a decision by the Supreme Court dated 25 September 1998, in which parental authority is not primarily referred to in terms of a right, but in terms of authority in the child's best interests.[5] Because, according to the Supreme Court,

> in cases such as the present case, in which the child has been conceived with sperm from a donor who does not exercise parental authority, the child's best interests in view of effectuating the right of parental contact with his biological father may imply that the child will be informed that the person who will have parental contact with him is indeed his father. If the court takes the view that this is indeed the issue at hand, it may determine that the child will be informed of his biological descent prior to the next parental contact moment. In this regard the court's opinion concerning the child's best interests in view of the parental contact when it comes to knowing his biological origin, will prevail over the right of the parents to determine when the child will receive that information.

The question of whether the child needs to receive status information about his biological origin is beyond dispute as such, nor is it brought up by the mothers. In principle they

5 Supreme Court of the Netherlands, 25 September 1998, ECLI:NL:HR:1998:ZC2714, NJ 1999/379.

recognize the child's right to status information. This question has already been answered in an affirmative sense, both on a national level – for instance the Valkenhorst ruling – and within the scope of the right of protection of private life pursuant to article 8 ECHR. The Advocate General also refers to this in 3.3, in which reference is made, *inter alia*, to *Gaskin v. the United Kingdom* and to *Mikulic v. Croatia*.[6]

The Supreme Court only refers indirectly to the CRC, notably to article 7 (the right to a name, including but not limited to the right to know his or her parents) and to article 8 (the right to respect for one's identity). First, the right to private life under article 8 ECHR is brought forward, in particular the right to personal identity. According to the Supreme Court, this right also implies that a child has the right to know from whom he descends. This does not mean the moment that the child asks for it himself – as the mothers had thought – but rather at an earlier stage, and in conjunction with the parental contact with the biological father, which is what the Child Care and Protection Board had advised, as becomes evident from the statement of the Attorney General, the Public Prosecutor at the Supreme Court.[7] Incidentally, it is remarkable that the Attorney General does not define the legal ground for the obligation to provide status information as "the right of the child to know who he descends from, which also arises from article 8 ECHR", as is asserted, but construes this based on the male party's right of protection of his private life within the meaning of article 8 ECHR.[8] In other words, the Supreme Court clearly deviates here, by taking the right of the child to know who he descends from as a basis, and does not only refer to the child's right of private life pursuant to article 8 ECHR, but, in order to emphasize it even more, also to articles 7 and 8 CRC.

How fundamental the right to information on the biological origin is, also becomes evident from the General Comment to article 3 CRC. Within the seven elements, it is named second when determining what the child's best interests require. Under the heading "The Child's Identity", a direct connection is made between "the opportunity to access information about their biological family" and "the child's best interests".[9]

B *The Right to Continuity in Upbringing*

Following this interpretation by the Supreme Court concerning the notion of parental responsibility, it is illuminating to look more closely to its link to child protection measures. This is particularly fitting because in cases where these measures come into play, it is clearly about the exercise of parental authority as a form of authority in the child's best interests

6 Statement by the Advocate General, ECLI:NL:HR:2015:2287, under 3.3.
7 Refer to statement by the Advocate General, ECLI:NL:HR:2015:2287, under 2.15.
8 Statement by the Advocate General, ECLI:NL:HR:2015:2287, under 3.6.
9 Committee on the Rights of the Children, 'General Comment No. 14 (2013) on the right of the child to have his or her best interests taken as a primary consideration', no. 53, p. 13.

(*doelbevoegdheid*): a view of parental authority that also resonates in the ruling of the Supreme Court on the right to status information.

This leads to the second set of examples of judicial activity, where article 3 CRC has had a corrective effect on the legal system. In the scope of child protection measures, article 3 CRC is often referred to, in many cases in combination with article 18 (parental responsibility) and article 20 CRC (protection of children without parental care). The link between parental responsibility and the best interests of the child is expressed in article 18 CRC. It reads:

> 1. States Parties shall use their best efforts to ensure recognition of the principle that both parents have common responsibilities for the upbringing and development of the child. Parents or, as the case may be, legal guardians, have the primary responsibility for the upbringing and development of the child. The best interests of the child will be their basic concern.

This guarding of the best interests of the child, however, also shows another side of the coin. When parents do not adhere to what is expected of them regarding their parental responsibility, the right of the child could prevail over the right of the parents to exercise that responsibility, and therefore can result in a child protection measure. This could be in the form of a lengthening of a placement in care or the termination of parental authority as a measure when the renewed lengthening of the placement into care is not considered to be in the best interests of the child. In the latter case, the view is that a child in care outside of the home has – after a period of time – the right to know where it is up to, which in certain cases leads to the termination of parental authority. With a combined reference to articles 3, 18 and 20 CRC, there have been many judgments in which the court has thus ruled.[10] Keywords in this context have steadily been the right to continuity in upbringing and the right to clarity regarding the childrearing perspective, all of which represents stability in upbringing. A representative case is the ruling of the District Court of Groningen dated 13 March 2012 which is also referred to in the study into the application of the CRC in Dutch Courts:

> Regarding the best interests of children, the Court considers that although the rights and obligations of parents have to be taken into account pursuant to article 8 ECHR and articles 9 and 18 CRC, the right of children to continuity of care and undisturbed attachment with the foster family in accordance with articles 3 and 20 CRC must be given more weight than the interests of the

10 J.H. de Graaf et al, *De toepassing van het Internationale Verdrag inzake de Rechten van het Kind*, Deel II, De Boekdrukker, 2015, p. 11.

parents concerning the restoration of family life between them and the children.[11]

In this respect the question of whether parents can invoke the CRC seems appropriate. This only appears to be justified if and when this appeal is founded on the rights of the child. Against the backdrop of the principle of parental responsibility, in the child's best interests and the weighing up of the rights of the child and those of their parents within the scope of child protection measures, it seems inappropriate to speak of an 'infringement' on parental responsibility. It would be preferable to speak of a violation of a principle, following the example of the Court of Appeal Leeuwarden. The Court of Appeal asserts that: "the principle of honouring of responsibilities, rights and duties of parents pursuant to article 5 (the role of the parent) and article 9 (separation from parents and the right to contact) can be interrupted if and when the grounds for the continuation of the placement into care are still present."[12]

This development whereby parental authority is terminated[13] with reference to articles 3, 18 and 20 CRC at an earlier stage than before, has been continuing for some time in case law.[14] Recently this development came to its completion in the revision of the child protection measures, which came into effect on 1 January 2015. It has been stipulated that there has to be clarity about the care perspective (permanency planning) within a "reasonable period of time". This is clarified in the explanatory memorandum regarding article 1:266 (1) Civil Code, which provides the grounds for the new measures concerning termination of authority: "As well as with the family supervision order, when it comes to the determination in which family he will grow up in, the standard for determining the acceptable time limit for a child is the period of uncertainty that the child will be able to overcome without any further serious developmental damage." And a little further down: "The implementation of this principle requires a tailor-made approach, a precise term cannot be determined."[15] In reference to this passage in the explanatory note, the Court of Appeal Arnhem-Leeuwarden recently terminated parental authority in two cases. Also in reference to this explanatory memorandum, the Court of Appeal offers the following building blocks:

(a) the importance of clarity regarding the child-rearing and developmental perspectives of the child;

11 District Court (Rb.) Groningen, 13 March 2012, ECLI:NL:RBGRO:2011:3640.

12 Court of Appeal-Leeuwarden, 19 June 2012, ECLI:NL:GHLEE:2012:BX0430.

13 Previously this was called relief of authority.

14 E.g. the judgment from the Court of Appeal-Hertogenbosch, 6 June 2006, LJN AY6904, where the Court, with reference to articles 3 and 20 CRC, ruled that compelling meaning is given to the best interests of the child in cases of continuity of care and the uninterrupted attachment process, and the parental authority of the mother was terminated.

15 Dutch Parliamentary papers II, TK 2008/2009, 32015, no. 3, p. 34.

(b) the extension of a family supervision order/placement in care over a number of years is in principle an incorrect measure;
(c) the importance of continuity in upbringing and an undisturbed attachment process for the child; and
(d) the bare willingness of the parent with authority not to resist the placing into care of the child should not be decisive in the granting of the request for termination of parental authority.[16]

The necessity of a tailored approach becomes clear in a judgment of the Court of Appeal-Hertogenbosch, in which the Court annulled a decision of the Youth Court and ordered a family supervision order despite the fact that the prospect of a healthy upbringing was not with the mother, but with the grandmother. In this case the provisions of article 1:255 (1 sub b) Civil Code would not be met. This article determines that family supervision can only be ordered when, pursuant to article 1:247 (2) Civil Code, there is a chance that the parents will be able to take on the responsibility for the care and raising of the child for an acceptable period of time as far as his or her person and development is concerned. The Court of Appeal has a different view and considers the family supervision order as a means to repair the relationship between the mother and the grandmother. This could result in a situation in which the mother can resume her role as caregiver by giving her approval to her child being cared for by the grandmother so that the provision of article 1:255 (1 sub b) Civil Code would be met.[17] With this explanation the Court of Appeal circumvents this far-reaching provision and offers an opening for a less rigid implementation. When a family supervision order is not appropriate, the next step after all would be termination of authority.

C *The Right to be Heard*

The third and last example of the application of article 3 CRC as a corrective factor is the right to be heard pursuant to article 12 CRC. In the introduction it was already mentioned that article 3, in conjunction with articles 2, 6 and 12, forms one of the four key provisions of the CRC. In particular the right to be heard is crucial when it comes to representing the child's best interests. This is also reflected in the General Comment to article 3 CRC, in which the right to be heard is named as one of the key pillars and even the first element

16 Court of Appeal Arnhem-Leeuwarden, 14 June 2016, ECLI:NL:GHARL:2016:4933 and Court of Appeal Arnhem-Leeuwarden 21 June 2016, ECLI:NL:GHARL:2016:5119.

17 Court of Appeal-Hertogenbosch, 27 August 2015, ECLI:NL:GHSHE:2015:3336, JPF 2015/131 with a comment by J.H. de Graaf.

when it comes to "the assessing of the child's best interests", in the words of the comment. The Comment reads:

> Article 12 of the Convention provides for the right of children to express their views in every decision that affects them. Any decision that does not take into account the child's views does not give due weight in accordance with their age and maturity, does not respect the possibility for the child or children to influence the determination of their best interests.[18]

The impact of article 12 CRC is also clearly visible in case law. A clear example is a ruling by the Supreme Court of the Netherlands of 1 November 2013.[19] This case involved the following facts. The father filed an appeal in cassation before the Supreme Court concerning the right of the minor to be heard pursuant to article 809 (1) Dutch Code of Civil Procedure. The issue at hand was a court order issued by the Youth Court regarding parental contact arrangements as well as alternative consent for medical treatment. The Court of Appeal confirmed this court order, without however hearing the minor once more. The Court of Appeal did send the minor an invitation for an interview, but this invitation did not reach the minor, because Child and Youth Care felt that such a conversation would be too stressful for the minor. In other words, the minor was unaware of this invitation and therefore did not appear in court. In its decision not to invite the minor a second time, the Court of Appeal seems to have considered that the opinion of the minor would not have led to a different decision.

The legal remedy now raises the question of whether the Court of Appeal was justified in refraining from inviting the minor for an interview, when it became clear that the invitation had not reached the minor.

The judgement of the Supreme Court, in reference to article 12 CRC, is loud and clear. The decision that the minor did not need to be invited again, because hearing the child would not lead to a different decision, is based on an erroneous interpretation of the law. After all, as the Supreme Court takes into consideration:

> In view of the best interests of the minor to express his opinion in matters that concern him – which interest is not only reflected in Section 809 (1) Dutch Code of Civil Procedure, but also in article 12 CRC – the unsubstantiated opinion of Child and Youth Care that the minor is suffering from an anxiety disorder and will get confused when confronted with choices, forms an inadequate basis for the contested judgment.

---

18 Op cit, n. 9.

19 ECLI:NL:HR:2013:1084, JPF 2014/101.

The Supreme Court therefore annulled the decision of the Court of Appeal.

This judgment is all the more significant because it shows a clear change compared to a previous decision by the Supreme Court on 23 November 2012[20], in which the Advocate General argued that involving the minor would lead to 'too much mental stress'. But isn't it in cases like these that the importance of professional legal counsel becomes apparent? It is interesting that De Ruiter already emphasized the importance thereof as early as 1972. In a preliminary expert opinion titled 'Law and Assistance', De Ruiter argued in favour of a legal counsel who is able to "unilaterally put the child's best interests first as these interests are experienced by the child itself".[21] This is fundamentally necessary, as he puts it, 'in order to prevent the child – under the pretext of being heard – from being subjected to manipulation'. In this context it is also useful to quote Van Zutphen's views on the role of the lawyer. Van Zutphen refers to the legal counsel as a "spokesperson, guide and interpreter" for the child.[22]

That the General Comment certainly can lead to further improvement is evident in another ruling by the Supreme Court in 2014 as well.[23] Here, the question at stake was whether or not a behavioural scientist, in a statement of consent required for a detention, must demonstrate that he had given due consideration to the information made available to him by or on behalf of the minor. The Supreme Court did not agree, and maintained the legalistic position that, pursuant to article 3:2 Dutch General Administrative Law Act, the behavioural scientist was not obligated to do so. However, there is something to be said against this, especially based on the wording of the General Comment quoted above: after all, what matters is to give due consideration to the opinion of the minor 'in every step of the proceedings'.

III The CRC and General Comment No. 14

And so this decision leads us directly to General Comment no. 14, which gives a deeper definition of article 3 CRC. But before going into more detail, let us first give careful consideration to the meaning of the CRC. How does the CRC work? How is it put into practice? Can the CRC have the same significance to child law/children's rights as the ECHR had – and still has – to family law? It is an eye opener in this respect to remember what was brought forward in Dutch Parliament during the negotiations on the CRC Ratification Act. During the parliamentary hearing, it was argued, for instance by MP Schutte, that the

20 Supreme Court of the Netherlands 23 November 2012, ECLI:NL:HR:2012:BY3968, JPF 2013/132, with comment by J.H. de Graaf.

21 De Ruiter, op cit, n. 2.

22 A.C. Enkelaar *in* M.E. van Zutphen, *De autonomie van de minderjaroge in de rechtszaal', in 'Rechten van het kind en autonomie*, Nijmegen, Ars Aequi, 2010, p. 183.

23 Supreme Court of the Netherlands, 18 April 2014, ECLI:NL:HR:2014:951.

CRC could well have far more impact than the Minister had asserted in his replies to relevant questions. People who say: "We will hardly notice it" might be in for an unpleasant surprise, as he puts it in reference to the ECHR, where people at the time were of the same opinion: Dutch legislation complied already with the ECHR.[24] After all, under the influence of the ECHR, our entire family law has undergone drastic changes. It is now crystal clear that Schutte was absolutely right. The two subsequent studies carried out by the Centre for Children's Rights Amsterdam into the application of the CRC demonstrate how much influence the CRC has had.[25] This is not only in regard to the number of cases in which the CRC was invoked, but also to the number of cases in which it has led to a positive result.

At the time, I too, took the view that the CRC would have little effect. I based this opinion on the fact that many provisions hardly have any normative value and no direct legal effect.[26] But it turns out that the question of whether or not it had any direct legal effect – did not in practice have the impact that was attributed to it. The main reason for this is that the courts often use the so-called application in accordance with the CRC, the use of the CRC supporting the interpretation of a national provision, or acting in the spirit of the CRC. Both studies show that the courts often prefer to apply the CRC in this manner, thus circumventing the question of whether or not a provision has direct legal effect. After all, by doing so the court leaves the primacy of the legislator intact. And as far as "the limited normative value" is concerned: the more often the CRC is applied, the more tools are available to actually implement it. In this regard, both studies provide ample leads for further application.[27]

In addition to the examples provided by legal practice, the General Comments – as drawn up by the Committee on the Rights of the Child – provide more than a few reference points. Seen from the perspective of the subject of this paper, this applies in particular to General Comment no. 14. This Comment explicitly states that only the first paragraph of article 3 is commented on: "In all actions concerning children, whether undertaken by public or private social welfare institutions, courts of law, administrative authorities or legislative bodies, the child's best interests shall be a primary consideration". It is emphasized that the child's best interest is "a right, a principle and a rule of procedure". This is a clear expression of the fact that the concept is "rights based", meaning that it is the right of the

24 Dutch Parliamentary papers II, TK 81-5559, 23 June 199. Refer also to J.H. de Graaf, 'Rechten van het kind en ouderlijke verantwoordelijkheid, een Inleiding' *in* J.H. de Graaf et al, *Rechten van het Kind en ouderlijke verantwoordelijkheid*, Nijmegen, Ars Aequi, 2008, p. 17.

25 J.H. de Graaf et al, *De toepassing van het Internationale Verdrag inzake de Rechten van het Kind*, Nijmegen, Ars Aequi, 2012 and J.H. de Graaf et al, *De toepassing van het Internationale Verdag inzake de Rechten van het Kind*, Deel II, Amsterdam, De Boekdrukker, 2015.

26 J.H. de Graaf, 'De betekenis van de Ontwerp-Conventie inzake de rechten van het Kind', *in* M. de Langen, J.H. de Graaf & F.B.M. Kunneman, *Kinderen en Recht*, Deventer, Kluwer, 1989, pp. 14-24.

27 J.H. de Graaf et al op cit, n. 25, p. 285.

child that his or her best interests are served and that for the definition of those best interests, the other rights in the convention have to be taken into consideration as well. There is no better way to express the shift from thinking of the rights of the child as *object* of law towards thinking in terms of *subject* of law.

Worth mentioning is that in the General Comment, the elements concerning the implementation of "the best interests of the child" derive from a joint study by Kalverboer and Zijlstra, who developed the so-called BIC model (otherwise known as the "Best Interests of the Child model"). In the words of Kalverboer, this model consists of: "14 parenting conditions that in the life of children need to be of adequate quality to allow children to have a happy childhood and to safeguard their development. Together, these conditions stand for the quality of the upbringing environment".[28] This model is integrated into the wording of chapter V of the General Comment, which reads: "V. Implementation: assessing and determining the child's best interests", in which "assessing" stands for assessment of such best interests and "determining" stands for defining it. Or, as it is put in paragraph 50 in the Comment: "The Committee considers it useful to draw up a non-exhaustive and non-hierarchical list of elements that could be included in a best-interests assessment by any decision-maker having to determine a child's bests interests".[29] The elements that need to be observed are subsequently listed and elaborated on in the Comment, where the elements from the BIC model are clearly identifiable, as becomes clear from Kalverboer's article.[30] For the BIC model itself and the reference made by Kalverboer to the corresponding elements in the Comment, please refer to the article by Kalverboer.

IV Conclusion

The fact that the courts have played an active role in family law is inherent to this area of law. Family and child law are par excellence areas of law in which general legal concepts are applied. This does not only include concepts such as the child's best interests, but also the highly fundamental concept of parental responsibility, which plays a central role in family law and child law as well. In defining this concept, the legislator has exercised appropriate constraint. For instance, article 1: 247 Dutch Civil Code determines that parents have the obligation and the right to take care of the child and to raise it. Pursuant to article 1: 247 (2) Dutch Civil Code this duty of due care also means: "the care of and responsibility for the mental and physical well-being and safety of the child, as well as stimulation of the

28 M. Kalverboer, 'De visie van het Kinderechtencomite op hoe het belang van het kind onderzocht en vastgesteld moet worden; een uitwerking voor zaken betreffende kindermishandeling en verwaarlozing', *Pedagogiek,* 2014/34, afl. 3, pp. 222-236. For the elaborated/full BIC model please refer to diagram 1 – p. 225.

29 Op cit, n. 9, p. 12.

30 M. Kalverboer, op cit, n. 28, p. 227.

development of his personality". For example, parents are not under any legal obligation to love their children, though this could certainly qualify as a fundamental precondition for the development of the child.

Family law is however quintessentially an area of law that reflects social developments and the relationship between partners, in which the rights of parents – as already discussed in the introduction – may easily get the upper hand, thus moving children's rights – also easily – to the background. The legislator does not seem to sufficiently counter this effect, or seems to be unable to counter the force of "the tyranny of the democratic majority". What is the power of law indeed, if social developments and the relationship between partners develop in a direction in which "individual self-determination and freedom of choice" are the keywords of choice? The law cannot do this in the form of legislation, or so it seems, even though the legislator could be – and should be – asked not to get so easily carried away by numerous lobbyists.

It seems, in a way, that the Court could seek more guidance within this area of political tension in the form of a moral authority in which the CRC is an important source of inspiration. Keeping this in mind, the Court may exert a corrective influence. As I have demonstrated with these three cases – convincingly, I hope! -, the Court indeed does so already.

Protecting Children Affected by Atypical Gender Identity Organization: A Comparative Legal Perspective

*Elena Falletti**

I "Atypical Gender Identity Organization"

Recently, several news sources[1] have emphasized that even pre-pubescent children have been subjected to hormonal treatment to slow down the appearance of puberty in order to "choose" their sex[2] or sexual orientation.[3] However, such sources do not specify that there exist individuals who, even from an early stage of life, feel that at the core of their self-perception[4] they belong to the opposite sex, despite their absolute normality in the biological sphere. According to medical literature, these children are affected by "Atypical Gender Identity Organization" (AGIO).[5] This is a disorder that emerges when children, even at a very young age[6], display "cross-sex" behaviors that need to be understood and "helped in the maturation of their gender identity".[7]

---

* Lecturer in Private Comparative Law at Università Carlo Cattaneo, Castellanza, Italy. Each Internet source was accessed on 4 October 2018.

1 E. Day, 'Transgender kids: "Everyone was calling me Sebastian, but I knew I was a girl"', *The Guardian*, 5 April 2015, https://www.theguardian.com/society/2015/apr/05/transgender-kids-children-change-sex-families; J. Leake, 'NHS helps children choose their sex', *The Sunday Times*, 17 November 2013, https://www.thetimes.co.uk/article/nhs-helps-children-choose-their-sex-r3vw0fx9r38; H. Devlin, 'Children aged 9 with gender issues can delay puberty', *The Times*, 19 May 2014, https://www.thetimes.co.uk/article/children-aged-9-with-gender-issues-can-delay-puberty-jv2wcqpvrn8.

2 B. Frigerio, 'Arriva in Italia il trattamento ormonale per cambiare sesso ai bambini. "Delirio di onnipotenza"', *Tempi*, 24 October 2013, https://www.tempi.it/arriva-anche-in-italia-il-trattamento-ormonale-per-cambiare-sesso-ai-bambini/.

3 O. Vetri, 'Sospendere la pubertà per scegliere l'orientamento sessuale', *Famiglia Cristiana*, 25 February 2015, http://m.famigliacristiana.it/articolo/olanda-fermare-la-puberta-per-scegliere-l-orientamento-sessuale.htm.

4 E. Schneider, *An insight into respect for the rights of trans and intersex children in Europe*, Strasbourg, Council of Europe, 2013, p. 7.

5 A. Lorenzetti, *Diritti in transito*, Milano, Franco Angeli, 2013, p. 49, n. 2; C. Manieri, & S. Einaudi, *Orientamento sessuale e disturbi dell'identità di genere in epoca adolescenziale*, 2014. (courtesy of the authors).

6 E. Skougard, 'The Best Interests of Transgender Children', *Utah Law Review*, 2011, No. 3, p. 1165.

7 C. Manieri, 'Assistenza a soggetti in età evolutiva con "Organizzazione Atipica dell'identità di Genere" (AGIO)', (courtesy of the author), p. 2.

Until recently, there has been controversy among experts about the diagnosis, terminology and treatment of AGIO,[8] and the debate carries on.[9] DSM-5 2013 provides different criteria for the diagnosis of gender dysphoria in children compared to adolescents and adults.[10] Children must display a marked inconsistency between the experienced/expressed gender and the assigned sex over a duration of at least 6 months. This inconsistency is manifested by the presence of at least six of the following criteria (one of which must be Criterion A1):

A1. A strong desire to be of the other gender or an insistence that one is the other gender (or some alternative gender different from one's assigned gender).
2. In boys (assigned gender), a strong preference for cross-dressing or simulating female attire: or in girls (assigned gender), a strong preference for wearing only typical masculine clothing and a strong resistance to the wearing of typical feminine clothing.
3. A strong preference for cross-gender roles in make-believe play or fantasy play.
4. A strong preference for the toys, games, or activities stereotypically used or engaged in by the other gender.
5. A strong preference for playmates of the other gender.
6. In boys (assigned gender), a strong rejection of typically masculine toys, games, and activities and a strong avoidance of rough-and-tumble play; or in girls (assigned gender), a strong rejection of typically feminine toys, games, and activities.
7. A strong dislike of one's sexual anatomy.
8. A strong desire for the primary and/or secondary sex characteristics that match one's experienced gender.

B. The condition is associated with clinically significant distress or impairment in social, school, or other important areas of functioning.

In adolescents and adults, however, an inconsistency between the experienced/expressed gender and the assigned sex, over a duration of at least 6 months, must be manifested by at least two of the following criteria:[11]

---

8 J. Drescher, P.T. Cohen-Kettenis & G.M. Reed, 'Gender incongruence of childhood in the ICD-11: controversies, proposal, and rationale', *Lancet Psychiatry*, Vol. 3, 2016, p. 428.

9 Ibid.

10 C. Manieri, 'La Disforia di Genere: aspetti psico-endocrini', 2015 (courtesy of the author).

11 American Psychiatric Association, Diagnostic and Statistical Manual of Mental Disorders, V, 2013. A different classification is provided by International Statistical Classification of Diseases and Related Health Problems 10th Revision (ICD-10)-2016-WHO Version for 2016, that defines AGIO as "A disorder, usually first manifest during early childhood (and always well before puberty), characterized by a persistent and intense distress about assigned sex, together with a desire to be (or insistence that one is) of the other sex. There is a persistent preoccupation with the dress and activities of the opposite sex and repudiation of the individual's own sex. The diagnosis requires a profound disturbance of the normal gender identity; mere tomboyishness in girls or girlish behaviour in boys is not sufficient." Available on http://apps.who.int/classifications/icd10/browse/2016/en#/F64.2.

A1 A marked incongruence between one's experienced/expressed gender and primary and/or secondary sex characteristics (or in young adolescents, the anticipated secondary sex characteristics).
2. A strong desire to be rid of one's primary and/or secondary sex characteristics because of a marked incongruence with one's experienced/expressed gender (or in young adolescents, a desire to prevent the development of the anticipated secondary sex characteristics).
3. A strong desire for the primary and/or secondary sex characteristics of the other gender.
4. A strong desire to be of the other gender (or some alternative gender different from one's assigned gender).
5. A strong desire to be treated as the other gender (or some alternative gender different from one's assigned gender).
6. A strong conviction that one has the typical feelings and reactions of the other gender (or some alternative gender different from one's assigned gender).
B. The condition is associated with clinically significant distress or impairment in social, occupational or other important areas of functioning.

Such a condition is associated with significant suffering or disturbance in the social and educational environment or in other areas of functioning, with an increased risk of negative responsiveness or disability. It can be a condition of its own, or be associated with a "Sexual Difference Disorder".[12] In this regard, variance of gender identity can be defined as the state in which gender identity is organized atypically during the period of psycho-sexual development of a child.[13] In these cases, children and adolescents perceive their sexual identity as being inadequate to their body, and as a result, their biological sex. They may feel unhappy about their physical characteristics and sexual functions and express a desire to be recognized as belonging to the other gender. They may prefer clothes, toys and games commonly associated with the other gender, as well as friendships with people of the other gender. Such situations may be accompanied by both emotional and behavioral difficulties, and the resulting suffering associated with their condition.[14]

---

12 Manieri & Einaudi, op cit, n. 5.

13 P. Valerio, I. Parisi & F. Santamaria, *Puberty Blocking During Developmental Years: Issues and Dilemmas for Gender-Variant Adolescents, Bioethical Issues, by the Interuniversity Center for Bioethics Research*, Editoriale Scientifica, Napoli, 2014, p. 144.

14 Ibid.

II Assistance and Treatment of AGIO-Affected Children

There are three main centers in the world that have the most relevant experience in managing children suffering from AGIO: Amsterdam (formerly coordinated by Prof. Peggy Kettenis), London (formerly coordinated by Prof. Di Ceglie, now by P. Carmichael), and Toronto (coordinated by Prof. Zucker). The scientific research conducted at these centers indicates that psychological support for AGIO children and their families is indispensable to provide a space for re-elaborating and understanding the variant gender experience, and for incorporating it into a socio-family context that promotes egosyntonic development. These outcomes were confirmed in an international study by Dutch scholars who first applied the hormonal suspension of puberty over a prolonged period of time.[15]

Cases dealing with these children have shown that about one-third of them will have a gender dysphoria experience that will require medical-surgical adjustment, while the other two-thirds will completely overcome dysphoria over the stages of their puberty development, accepting the identity of their biological sex. In adulthood, half of the latter will have a heterosexual orientation and the other half will evolve towards a homosexual orientation.[16]

In rare cases, after extensive psychological evaluation, international literature would propose a process of puberty blockage and subsequent "cross-sex puberty". In these cases, it is considered appropriate to take a longer time to decide on a possible pharmacological treatment in accordance with the guidelines issued by the Endocrine Society in 2009 and ratified by the WPATH (World Professional Association for Transgender Health) in 2011. Such criteria for treatment are well-defined in DSM 5 TR, which states that the patients should be subjects who have started pubertal development (at least at stage II-III of Tanner), are able to fully understand the meaning of the treatment, and are well-supported in their family and social environment. These patients would display increased gender dysphoria with the first signs of puberty, and would not show signs of psychiatric comorbidity. They would have access to adequate psychological and social support during the treatment, and demonstrate knowledge and understanding of the results and risks of GnRHA treatment, cross-sex hormone treatment, and specific surgical treatment, as well as the risks and social benefits of sex reassignment.[17]

The protocol treatment includes a monthly administration of GnRHA, which blocks the production of puberty hormones. The treatment may only start from the Tanner II-III stage, generally around 12 years of age. Only after 16 years of age is it possible to administer increasing doses of estradiol for MtF individuals, and increasing doses of

15 A.L.C. de Vries et al, 'Young Adult Psychological Outcome After Puberty Suppression and Gender Reassignment, *Pediatrics*, Vol. 134, No. 4, 2014, pp. 696-704.

16 Manieri, op cit, n. 7.

17 Manieri & Einaudi, op cit, n. 5.

testosterone for FtM persons. Individuals would also simultaneously receive supportive psychotherapy, and have hormonal, clinical and hematochemical parameters checked every 3-4 months.[18]

Treatments dispensed during the first step are completely reversible, while those during the second step are only partially reversible. Such treatments must always be carried out with psychological and social support in the presence of a "supportive" family.[19]

These therapies pursue specific goals, namely:

- to provide more time for professionals and children to better understand what to do without the assessment of the development of puberty, allowing the children and their families to make a thorough psychotherapeutic investment;
- to prevent sex characteristics (of the biological sex) from developing so far as to be render them difficult to manage, resulting in disruptive "cross" social insertion; and
- to be able to live in the desired role by making the adolescent's social inclusion more fluid so as to prevent the risk of social and school exclusion, a widespread phenomenon among these juveniles.[20]

However, specialized medical literature does not shy away from the fears and potential problems that could arise from undergoing such therapies, particularly in regards to diagnostic mistakes made in such a "fluid" time as puberty. Examples include interference with physical development by creating abnormal conditions in cognitive and endocrine maturation, especially with regards to statural growth and bone density. Others such as insufficiently mature and uninformed consent, and fertility difficulties, may also be encountered.[21]

III The Relevant Juridical Issue: Consent to Treatment

The condition of children affected by AGIO directly involves the relationship between parenting choices and the protection of the child's best interests, primarily for his or her well-being. Medical knowledge has taught us that gender dysphoria can be primary when

18 Ibid.

19 Ibid.

20 Manieri & Einaudi, op cit, n. 5; I. Wilson, C. Griffin & B. Wren, 'The interaction between young people with atypical gender identity organization and their peers', *Journal of Health Psychology,* Vol. 10, No. 3, 2005, pp. 307-15.

21 Manieri & Einaudi, op cit n 5; S. Giordano, 'Ethics of Management of Gender Atypical Organization in Children and Adolescents', *in International Library of Ethics, Law, and the New Medicine,* Vol. 42, 2008, Springer Netherlands, Dordrecht, p. 258ff; D.A. Perkiss, 'Boy or Girl: Who Gets to Decide? Gender-Non-conforming Children in Child Custody Cases', *Hastings Women's Law Journal,* 2014, Vol. 25, No. 2, pp. 57-79.

it appears during childhood or adolescence, or secondary when manifested later during adulthood.

During childhood, AGIO does not evoke a desire to seek physical alterations[22] and playing allows children to manifest their sexual identity. Indeed, children sense their identity very early on, identifying themselves as either male or female independently of the gender attributed to them at birth.[23] Since they are disinterested in social, environmental, or family implications until they reach puberty, their social environment allows them to manifest their own inclinations through play.

To do this, children require a safe and supportive environment. From this time and up until puberty - when hormonal development inevitably overcomes play - support, observation and protection from parents is vital.

However, there are cases in which the child who "deviates" from socially accepted and stereotyped gender behavior can be subjected to numerous forms of social pressure or "corrections", such as oral reprimands, punishment, and psychological or physical abuse, which can be imposed by parents, other family members, schoolmates, educators, healthcare professionals, and even strangers in public. This has led many authors to argue that transgender children may be in danger. Even though scientific literature is scarce at the European level, studies focusing on the experience of AGIO children confirm that such mechanisms exist and have a significant impact on both the affected children and their families.[24]

As far as therapeutic treatment is concerned, child transsexuality is dealt with by personality development experts under a psychosexual and psychiatric perspective to understand the context in which the DSM-5 criteria emerged. This begins with a deeper psychological analysis over a period of six months, while psychiatric support is given to handle the personological aspects of gender identity, in at least three meetings over the same period. The psychiatrist must ensure that the gender disorder in the examined patient, who must be a primary transsexual, is not confused with other psychopathologies or identity disturbances.[25] The psychiatrist then presents the contraindications to the treatment, which could be either physical or psychiatric, or both. An endocrinologist must examine

22 Giordano, op cit, n. 21.

23 K.R. Olson, A.C. Key & N.R. Eaton, 'Gender Cognition in Transgender Children', *Psychological Science,* 2015 Vol. 26, No. 4, pp. 467-474.

24 Schneider, op cit, n. 4. For a recent study on the sex-reassignment in communities of Gender dysphoria/transgender adolescents, M. Sumia et al, 'Current and recalled childhood gender identity in community youth in comparison to referred adolescents seeking sex reassignment', *Journal of Adolescence*, 2017, Vol. 56, pp. 34-39.

25 A. Prunas, D. Hartmann & M. Bini, 'Disforia di genere e diffusione dell'identità: quale relazione?' *in* R. Vitelli et al (Eds.), *XV Congresso nazionale della sezione di psicologia clinica e dinamica, Napoli, 27-29 settembre 2013,* Fridericiana Editrice Universitaria, Napoli, 2013, p. 106; P. Meyenburg, 'Gender dysphoria in adolescents: difficulties in treatment', *Prax Kinderpsychol Kinderpsychiatr.*, Vol. 63, No. 3, 2014, pp. 510-522.

the patient at least twice, observing the entire medical history of the person, who must be in good health. The physician must also consider whether there are any medical problems, especially obesity and related pathologies, which would contraindicate the completion of the hormonal treatment. This is a teamwork approach between psychologists and doctors. However, the doctors' opinion will not be binding and they must adhere to the agreed treatment, while the eligibility of the patient for treatment is confirmed by psychologists.

In this context, the protection of the child's best interests is of great importance, especially concerning manifestation of consent for the administration of hormone therapy. In the psychiatric field, AGIO is still considered a mental pathology, while some scholars argue that it is a medical convention that violates the personalistic principle of self-determination.[26] Other scholars wonder whether only parental consent or legal authorization is sufficient to start hormonal treatment.

Article 315 bis, par. 3, of the Italian Civil Code,[27] states that minors, and even children under twelve years of age, have the right to be heard in all matters and procedures concerning themselves. Therefore, listening to the child seems to be indispensable when the judge's decision concerns a treatment of his or her condition. If his or her family supports the choice, he or she will undergo the hormonal therapy. On the contrary, if his or her parents are in conflict with each other, or with the child, court intervention would be required, especially if there is urgency to protect the child's life, such as in cases where the child is in danger of death or threatens suicide.[28]

In Italian case law there is only one published decision by the Tribunale di Roma which authorized a sex reassignment surgery in the following terms: "the right to effective sexual identity is a clear specification of the broader right to health, according to article 32 of the Constitution. This right can no longer be confined to physical integrity alone, but also to general physical and relational well-being. Sexual reconstruction surgery is a medical treatment aimed at achieving psychophysical integrity with the consequence, therefore, that when it is to be performed on a child, the principle of parental representation applies. The application for authorization is a complex act, which is an expression of the concurring will of the minor and that of the parent. Under the child's perspective, his or her age and

---

26 Lorenzetti, op cit, n. 5.

27 R. Pesce, 'L'ascolto del minore tra riforme legislative e recenti applicazioni giurisprudenziali', *Famiglia e Diritto*, No 3, 2015, p. 242; F. Tommaseo, 'La tutela dell'interesse dei minori dalla riforma della filiazione alla negoziazione assistita delle crisi coniugali', *Familia e diritto*, 2015, No. 2, p. 157; P. Virgadamo, 'L'ascolto del minore in famiglia e nelle procedure che lo riguardano', *Il diritto di famiglia e delle persone*, 2014, p. 1656; C. Ricco, 'Il diritto del figlio e di ogni minore di ascolto nelle procedure e la funzione riparativa del buon ascolto', *MinoriGiustizia*, 2014, p. 51.

28 Schneider, op cit, n. 4.

degree of intellectual maturity must be considered, as well as the need to protect his/her personality".[29]

IV TREATMENT OF AGIO. TREATMENT IN INTERNATIONAL AND COMPARATIVE EXPERIENCE

The most important international sources regarding gender issues in transsexual minors are, on the one hand, The Yogyakarta Principles on the Application of International Human Rights Law in Relation to Sexual Orientation and Gender Identity[30] (the Principles of Yogyakarta), which is a soft law source protecting LGBTIQ people's rights. On the other hand, there is the United Nations Convention on the Rights of the Child,[31] which was implemented in hard law sources, such as Law 27 May 1991, No. 176 in Italy.

Article 3 of the Principles of Yogyakarta seems to be relevant to this perspective. It is entitled "the right of recognition before the law" and states:

> Everyone has the right to recognition everywhere as a person before the law. Persons of diverse sexual orientations and gender identities shall enjoy legal capacity in all aspects of life. Each person's self-defined sexual orientation and gender identity is integral to their personality and is one of the most basic aspects of self-determination, dignity and freedom. No one shall be forced to undergo medical procedures, including sex reassignment surgery, sterilization or hormonal therapy, as a requirement for legal recognition of their gender identity. No status, such as marriage or parenthood, may be invoked as such to prevent the legal recognition of a person's gender identity. No one shall be subjected to pressure to conceal, suppress or deny their sexual orientation or gender identity.

Although there are no specific references to children in the text, it seems sensible to affirm that the right of children define their own sexual identity and their dignity, and not to be forced into hormonal treatments or the surgical reassignment of sex, is being recognized.

The United Nations Convention on the Rights of the Child does not contain specific rules on the subject discussed here, but it does contain provisions of immediate interest

29 Tribunale di Roma Sez. I, 11 March 2011. M.G. Ruo, 'Persone minori di età e cambiamento di identita sessuale', *Famiglia e Diritto*, 2012, p. 499.

30 Principles established at Yogyakarta Conference from 6 to 9 November 2006 by International Commission of Jurists, International Service for Human Rights and other international committee, see at: http://www.yogyakartaprinciples.org/principles-en/.

31 UN Convention on the Rights of the Child, 20 November 1989, ratified in Italy with Law 27 May 1991, No. 176.

to minors suffering from AGIO. For instance, Article 7 contains important references to the right of the child to be immediately registered at birth with his or her own name, but without reference to the sexual attributes at birth. Article 8.1 stipulates that:

> States Parties undertake to respect the right of the child to preserve his or her identity, including nationality, name and family relations as recognized by law without unlawful interference.

while Article 12 acknowledges that:

> States Parties shall assure to the child who is capable of forming his or her own views the right to express those views freely in all matters affecting the child, the views of the child being given due weight in accordance with the age and maturity of the child.

Article 16 protects the child from arbitrary or unlawful interferences in his or her private life in his or her family and establishes in favor of the child the right to protection of law against such interference. Finally, States Parties recognize the right of the child to enjoy the best possible state of health and to benefit from medical and rehabilitation services. They strive to ensure that no child is deprived of the right to have access to such services.

A Australia

From a comparative perspective, Australia has a larger number of legal cases concerning AGIO, specifically with regards to the authorization of hormone therapy. In the cases here analyzed,[32] the focus was firstly on whether the reversible hormone treatment in Phase 1, and the partially irreversible treatment in Phase 2, were both considered a "special medical treatment". Secondly, the requirements for consent to these treatments were evaluated: could the minor be considered "competent" to express consent for treatment for him/herself, is it the parents' duty, or should treatment be authorized by the judicial authority? It should be noted that both of these points were read by Australian judges under the lens of the "best interest of the child" standard. In this regard, Australian case

32 *Re Alex: Hormonal treatment for gender identity dysphoria* [2004] FamCA 297; *Re Brodie (Special Medical Procedures: Jurisdiction)* [2007] FamCA 776; *Re Sean and Russell (Special Medical Procedures)* (2010) 44 Fam LR 210; *Re Jamie (Special Medical Procedure)* [2011] FamCA 248, *Re Jamie* [2013] FLC 93-547; *Re Lucy*, [2013] Fam CA 518, *Re Jodie* [2013] FamCA 62, *Re Colin* [2014] Fam CA 449, *Re Spencer* [2014] Fam CA 310; *Re Jordan* [2015] FamCA 175. M.K. Smith & B. Mathews, 'Treatment for gender dysphoria in children: the new legal, ethical and clinical landscape', *Medical Journal of Australia*, Vol. 202, No. 2, 2015, pp. 102-104 (source: http://www7.austlii.edu.au/databases.html).

law first established that, in the case of agreement between all parties involved in initiating the 1st phase of reversible hormonal treatment of AGIO, (i.e. the child,[33] parents and health experts), no judicial authorization is necessary,[34] even if the child undergoing therapy is orphaned and cared for by foster parents.[35] It was at one time held that judicial authorization was necessary to continue the therapy at Phase 2, since it has irreversible effects.[36] However, in a subsequent decision of a specially enlarged bench of the appeal court, the Family Court has decided that there is no need for judicial authorization at all, where parents and doctors are in agreement with the medical intervention.[37]

The rule applied by the Australian courts to self-determine medical treatment is borrowed from English common law and the case of *Gillick v West Norfolk and Wisbech Area Health Authority*.[38] In this decision Lord Scarman stated at paragraphs 188-189:

> I would hold that as a matter of law the parental right to determine whether or not their minor child ... will have medical treatment terminates if and when the child achieves a sufficient understanding and intelligence to enable him or her to understand fully what is proposed. It will be a question of fact whether a child seeking advice has sufficient understanding of what is involved to give a consent valid in law. Until the child achieves the capacity to consent, the parental right to make the decision continues save only in exceptional circumstances.

Based on the above, the House of Lords held that a child under 16 "had the legal competence to consent to medical examination and treatment if they had sufficient maturity and intelligence to understand the nature and implications of that treatment".[39]

This point is relevant from a comparative law perspective, since in common law legal principles circulate independently of the legal system from which it has originated. In fact, in Australia, the *Gillick* rule has been followed in legal cases of children suffering gender dysphoria, while the English legal system is still discussing this rule.[40] For instance, in

33 *Gillick v West Norfolk and Wisbech Area Health Authority* [1986] AC 112 HL. N.J. Lennings, 'Forward, Gillick: Are competent children autonomous medical decision makers?' *Journal of Law and theBbiosciences*, Vol. 2, No. 2, 2015, pp. 459–468.

34 *Re Jamie* [2013] FLC 93-547.

35 *Re Lucy* [2013] Fam CA 518.

36 *Re Jamie* [2013] FLC 93-547.

37 *Re Kelvin* [2017] FamCAFC 258.

38 [1985] UKHL 7.

39 R. Griffith, 'What is Gillick competence?', *Human Vaccines & Immunotherapeutics*, Vol. 12, No. 1, 2016, p. 244.

40 E. Cave, 'Goodbye Gillick? Identifying and resolving problems with the concept of child competence', *Legal Studies*, Vol. 34, No. 1, 2014, pp. 103-122.

recent cases[41] the Family Court of Australia affirmed that Kerry[42] (a MtF adolescent who at the time of making the order was aged 17 years and six months), Dale[43] (a FtM adolescent who at the time of making the order was 16 years of age), and Darryl[44] (a FtM adolescent who at the time of making the order was 17 years and five months of age) were competent to consent to their own medical treatment, commonly known as Stage Two treatment for Gender Dysphoria, in the form of hormone treatments.

B United States of America

In the United States, there are only three reported cases[45] related to transsexual children. However, these involved complex disputes which were focused mainly on the separation of the parents and the custody of the children, some of whom were minors experiencing gender dysphoria. These are *Smith v. Smith*,[46] *Shrader v. Spain*[47] and *Johnson v. Johnson*.[48] Family disputes do not seem to make it easier for transgender minors to face their status serenely.

US decisions concerning minor transgenders do not, as opposed to Australian ones, address the issue of informed consent, but center on the assignment of custody and, consequently, recognition of the manifestation of their gender identity. Indeed, in the reported cases, it is noted that judges have assigned the custody of minors to parents who held a negative attitude to AGIO.

Since these are complex disputes, they should be analyzed, at least partially. *Smith v. Smith* concerned the separation of the parents of two children, one of whom was already in the early stages of a gender disorder, wanting to be treated "as a girl". The mother supported the child's gender identity, agreed to call her "Christine", shared her experiences in support groups, and recognised the commencement of hormone therapy for suspending puberty. Instead, the father treated the child as a male. In 2001, the couple divorced, and

41 *Re Elliott* [2017] FamCA 1008; *Re Eddie (No 2)* [2017] FamCA 100; *Re Kelvin (No 2)* [2017] FamCA 1000; *Re Kelvin* [2017] FamCAFC 258; *Re Bobbie* [2017] FamCA 974; *Re Rae* [2017] FamCA 958; *Re Andy* [2017] FamCA 966; *Re Hudson* [2017] FamCA 938; *Re Adrian* [2017] FamCA 957; *Re Frances* [2017] FamCA 904; *Re Sage* [2017] FamCA 910; *Re Eddie* [2017] FamCA 822; *Re Ryan* [2017] FamCA 821; *Re Tahlia* [2017] FamCA 715; *Re Dana* [2017] FamCA 686; *Re Blaine* [2017] FamCA 647; *Re Julian* [2017] FamCA 621; *Fletcher (an infant by her litigation guardian Rylands) v Northern Territory of Australia* [2017] NTSC 62; *DPP v Leverton* [2017] VCC 1652; *Re Corey* [2017] FamCA 595 (source: http://www7.austlii.edu.au/databases.html).

42 *Re Kerry* [2016] FamCA 970.

43 *Re Dale* [2015] FamCA 473.

44 *Re Darryl* [2016] FamCA 720.

45 Perkiss, op cit n. 21; Skougard, op cit, n. 6.

46 *Smith v. Smith*, No. 05-JE-42, 2007 LEXIS 1282 (Ohio Ct. App. Mar. 23, 2007).

47 *Shrader v. Spain*, No. 05-95-01649, 1998 WL 40632 (Tex. App. Feb. 4, 1998).

48 *Johnson v. Johnson*, No. RF09-463371, at 1 (Superior Ct. of Calif. Cnty. of Alameda, Oct. 10, 2009).

an agreement between the parents stated that the mother obtain custody of the children, while the father was granted the right of visit. In 2004, the mother moved and enrolled Christine in a new school, identifying her as a girl. However, the father turned to court and obtained custody of both children, and despite the mother's appeal, the decision was confirmed on appeal. While the first instance decision was pending, the father obtained an emergency temporary order mandating that the mother stop any treatment or consultation related to the child's gender disorder, and that she stop addressing the child as "Christine", or with any other female name, and to stop dressing her in female attire. However, her mother violated that order by accompanying Christine to a swimming pool dressed as a girl. The court of first instance was very severely opposed to the disobedient mother, sanctioning her for not having shown neutrality or support for the male identity of the child and highlighting the importance of traditional gender roles.[49]

Although Christine continued to refer to herself as a female, three of the five experts at trial refuted the diagnosis of gender dysphoria. Consequently, the Court decided that the child was not suffering from gender dysphoria and forbade hormone therapy to block puberty. Scholars who examined the case severely criticized this decision by pointing out the weakness of Christine's lawyer's requests and, in addition, the lack of meetings which occurred between Christine and the therapist, whose sworn opinion was decisive for the solution of the case. In addition, scholars highlighted the role of the first instance judge in this case: despite the lack of specific experience in evaluating such cases, the judge supported the overwhelming prevalence of male identity in the child, on the conviction that Christine could become more certain of her gender identity as she grew. Further, by prohibiting the manifestation of her gender identity and forcing her to live with her opposing father and attending school as a male, the Court expressed the view that a minor's disphoria may be more acceptable in society by maintaining his or her biological gender. In fact, this was a misconception, especially based on the fact that Christine at the time of the decision was 12 years old, had already entered the Tanner II pubic phase and could have benefited from the hormone-blocking treatment without taking on the male characteristics she felt did not belong to her.

In the case of *Shrader v. Spain*, the custody of Nicholas, an MtF transsexual child, was awarded to his father, who had a negative attitude to the child's gender disorder, instead of to his mother, who supported his gender view. This decision was based on the circumstance that it was in the child's best interests to live more with his father in order to diminish his dependence on his mother, to favor the success of psychology therapy, and to facilitate the separation of Nicholas's identity from that of his mother.[50]

---

49 Perkiss, op cit, n. 21.

50 Nicholas, the parties' son, was diagnosed with gender identity disorder, a serious mental condition. The recommended treatment was for Nicholas to spend more time with his father, and to lessen his dependence on his mother. Dr. Doyle, Nicholas's psychologist, testified that he had not made as much progress in

Finally, in *Johnson v. Johnson*, the cooperative approach of both parents helped resolve the question of custody for MtF Sarah. Indeed, in spite of the strong differences between the parents, the mother and her lawyer prepared informative materials for the judge, explaining her support for her MtF daughter. The Court therefore considered that best interest was the priority of a plan that was supported by a psychologist and dedicated to the investigation of Sarah's female personality before the authorization for the treatment was to be granted.

C *United Kingdom*

The UK's recent published cases concern, on the one hand, a 17-year-old adopted FtM child,[51] and, on the other, the case of a 7-year-old child, who according to his mother, suffered from gender variance.[52]

The child in the first case was adopted when he was 6 years old. His adoptive parents did not accept his gender dysphoria. In these circumstances, P (the child) came to the very clear and very firm conclusion that he no longer wished his parents to be involved in his life and did not wish them to receive any information about his day-to-day life, nor about his assessment and possible treatment at the Tavistock Clinic or other medical facilities. In *Re C (Care: Consultation with Parents not in Child's Best Interests)*[53] Justice Keehan agreed to his request because the facts of the case "are very exceptional, (...) he should instead focus on the competing Article 8 ECHR rights of P and his parents".[54] Because of the extreme conflict between the child and the adoptive parents, the child was admitted to a foster care center. However, it is apparent from the judgment that the adoptive parents were in contact with the Tavistock Clinic in order to get close to the child and accompany him to transition therapy.

---

therapy as she had hoped, and that Nicholas's home environment would be important to his therapy. Dr. Otis, a psychologist who evaluated Husband, Wife, and both children, testified that Wife was unable to admit that Nicholas had a problem, and that Nicholas needed to separate his identity from his mother's. The trial court was within its discretion in deciding that, given Nicholas's gender identity disorder, it was in the children's best interest to live with their father (*Shrader v. Spain*, cit.).

51 *PD v SD and Others* [2015] EWHC 4103 (Fam).

52 *Re J (A Minor),* [2016] EWHC 2430 (Fam).

53 [2006] 2 FLR 867.

54 A. Laing, commenting on *PD v SD and Others* [2015] EWHC 4103 (Fam), http://www.family-lawweek.co.uk/site.aspx?i=ed159735 affirms that: "the ECHR and UNC[RC] show why the duty of confidence owed by a medical professional to a competent young person is a high one and which therefore should not be overridden except for a very powerful reason. In my view, although family factors are significant and cogent, they should not override the duty of confidentiality owed to the child", and: "Parental right to family life does not continue after the time when the child is able to make his own decisions. So parents do not have Article 8 rights to be notified of any advice of the medical profession after the young person is able to look after himself or herself and make his or her own decisions" (para. 28).

The second case[55] concerns a 7-year-old boy (named "J") who was forced by his mother to live as a girl because the mother was convinced that the child, who lived with her after his parents divorced in the year following his birth, suffered from gender variance; so she cared for him as if he were a female, making him wear a "pink headband and nail polish", taking care of him as if he were a girl with feminine recreational activities and planning for him to have treatment at a gender reassignment clinic. His mother showed signs of real anxiety over this aspect of the child's welfare. The judge noted that local authorities, such as school and social services, had consistently failed to "take appropriate action where there were strong grounds for believing that a child was at risk of serious emotional harm. It was "striking" that the local authority had moved into wholesale acceptance that J should be considered as a girl".[56] In addition, the judge noted that although the mother was very well prepared for child gender dysphoria, she did not recognize the child's actual personality and desires. Therefore, the child was entrusted to the father, with whom he has since "flourished", abandoning any reference to problems of gender disparities.

D Canada

The Supreme Court of British Columbia heard a case where the parents of an 11-year-old FtM child were divorced and later remarried, although with problematic issues concerning their child.[57] According to the judge:

> What has not gone well is the relationship between the parties, particularly in respect of J.K. (the child). A.H. (his mother) has been supportive of J.K. and has helped guide him through the appointments with the various physicians and the commencement of the Lupron treatment. A.H. says that she has kept N.K. (the father) informed throughout but that N.K. has been angry and resistant to J.K.'s stated wishes. In contrast, N.K. believes that steps have been taken without his consent and again he is concerned that J.K. has not been properly assessed.

The interesting point in this judgment is the significance that the judge reserved to the child involved. Even though the child was very young, and no other child of such a young age had been granted independent party status in litigation without a litigation guardian, the judge underlined that:

55 [2016] EWHC 2430 (Fam).

56 R. English, 'Mother's determination that child was "gender variant" did him significant harm' – Family Court, UK Human Rights Blog, 1 November 2016.

57 *K(N) v H(A)* [2016] BCSC 744.

> While the issue concerning J.K. is focused on his rights and determining his future, that issue nonetheless arises in the context of a broader, ongoing dispute between J.K.'s parents and I am concerned about the impact on J.K. of placing him squarely in the middle of that dispute.

The judge allowed the child to take part in the litigation through a litigation guardian. According to the judge, the "guardian can guide J.K. through the process and help him formulate the views that he would like to put before the court. The guardian can also deal with the parties on matters relating to the litigation and provide J.K. with something of a buffer from the acrimony existing between his parents."

The Superior Court of Justice of Ontario has dealt with a complex divorce case where the basic element concerned parents who lost their mutual trust for each other.[58] One of the main topics of discussion was the gender dysphoria of their younger child, the nine-year-old James, now referred to as Rosie, by his/her request. The judge established a rigorous child custody and support plan for both their children, which included experienced professionals to help the parents in their education and growth, while for James/Rosie, the judge determined that all professionals and family members involved follow a specific medical and psychological path for the child by specialists of a Gender Diversity center. The judge suggested mediation as a solution, with the help of specialists in the field of gender dysphoria. Any further contentious solutions would be attempted only after mediation fails.

The Court determined that if there are further disputes between the parties or the mediation does not work, the parties must return to court.

V Conclusion

The brief analysis of some comparative case law experiences illustrates that sensitivity to AGIO differs between the medical perspective (in the treatment of AGIO) and the juridical view (regarding the recognition of the gender change process of the child).

The cases studied show that in Australia, the medical and juridical institutions are very supportive of the minor affected by gender dysphoria, and they now leave it up to parents and medical practitioners to determine issues of treatment gender transition treatment if there is no dispute.

In the other jurisdictions, the courts are much more cautious and take further detailed steps to verify if the gender dysphoria suffered by the child is linked to with situations of family or social distress.

58 *Davies v. Murdock*, 2017 ONSC 4763 (CanLII).

In any case, it seems clear that medical experts and judges must coordinate and cooperate from a multidisciplinary perspective in order to protect, as much as possible, the child/adolescent suffering from AGIO and his/her future personal development.

Tell Me Your Surname and I'll Tell You Where You're From: Focus on the Negative Implications of Domestic Surname Policies on Minors with Dual Citizenship

Isabella Ferrari[*]

I The Right to Personal Identity and the Freedom of Movement in Connection to Surnames

The surname represents a core element of everyone's personal identity, mirroring their uniqueness and distinctiveness. Different persons may bear the same name-surname compound, but no person should carry a different name or surname depending on his place of residence or citizenship. This basic principle, however, is not always respected in reality.

As a matter of fact, cross-border situations may put a person's right to surname at stake, denying its unicity. In various cases (described *infra*), different surnames were bestowed upon the same person by two Member States of which they were citizen and resident.

Events like these obviously impede the free movement of interested persons around Europe and the entire world: they may lead to incompatibility between the personal data written on the academic degree and on the *curriculum vitae*; they may hinder the traceability of personal health files; they could hamper boarding on a plane or train, due to the difference between the surname printed on the identification document and the ticket.

The scope of this overall problem is steadily increasing and worsening, in direct proportion to the rise in the number of cross-border families. According to Eurostat, people living in a different Member State from that of their citizenship numbered 19 million in 2000, and 31.9 million in 2009. The 2015 Annual Report on Labour Mobility released by the EU Commission[1] observed a constant increase in the movement of working age persons

---

* Adj. Prof. in Comparative Private Law, University of Studies of Modena and Reggio Emilia, Italy.

1 E. Fries Tersch & V. Mabilia, *2015 Annual Report on Labour Mobility-Final Report*, European Commission 2015.

across the EU-28 States (an increase of around 1.4% compared to 2013), with flows mainly directed towards Western and Northern countries.

In 2013, 55% of movers were between 15 and 35 years of age: thus, the migration trends involve not only university students or young workers, but also teenagers, presumably the offspring of moving families. In fact, cross-border families are a well established entity in today's European Union, giving rise to a compelling and urgent need for harmonization of family law. Among the various sectors of family law requiring harmonization, that of surnames stands out, for its pivotal role in determining the lives and identities of everyone.

This paper analyzes surname policies across Europe, focusing on the current rules in force and on EU decisions already issued on the topic, in order to highlight the negative impact that the current lack of a uniform set of rules has on the right to identity and free movement within EU borders.

II SURNAMES WITHIN THE DOMESTIC FRAME

The discipline on surnames has always been the prerogative of domestic laws, typically reflecting the cultural-historical tradition of each country.

Within most conservative EU countries, and especially in those with solid Christian roots, the offspring is usually entrusted with the father's surname: the historical reasons for this rule may be traced down to Canon law and the so-called *patria potestas*. Like Roman law, Canon law also bestowed parental rights exclusively on the father.[2]

Other countries, which may be considered the modern and liberal ones, allow parents to freely choose the offspring's surname, with the possibility to opt for the surname of the mother, the father or their surnames together, with or without hyphen, with the option to choose the surnames' order.

Given these two situations, the majority of European laws on surnames sit in the middle, following various rules that can be summarized in the following three macro-categories (which may overlap, given that one does not exclude the other).

The first category includes systems which provide different rules for children born in or out of wedlock, as opposed to systems fully respecting the principle of equality among all minors.

2 The origins of surnames date back to the XV century, when registration for all baptism certificates was introduced in France, Italy and Spain. Before that, surnames were a prerogative of the aristocracy, to connect a person with the family or land of origin. For a special focus on surname through centuries see E. Spagnesi, 'Storia', *Enciclopedia del Diritto*, Vol. XXVIII, 1978, pp. 290-304. On the role of the *pater familias* see D. Ceccarelli Morolli, *A Brief Outline of Roman Law*, Roma, Gangemi, 2012, p. 57ff.

The second category includes systems which assign surnames to children in accordance with predetermined rules, contrary to systems providing parents with the freedom of choice.

Finally, the third category includes systems which allow parents various degrees of freedom in the choice of their children's surname.

The following sections will examine these three categories in detail, with a specific focus on EU Member States.

A The Various Surname Approaches in Regard to Natural and Legitimate Children

In the first category described above, systems providing for the unequal treatment of natural and legitimate children clash with systems according equal treatment to all minors. Italy stands among the discriminating systems, whereas France and Spain respect the principle of equality.

In fact, in Italy children born in wedlock automatically acquire the father's surname or the double surname,[3] whereas, if born out of wedlock, they are given the surname of the parent who first recognized them at birth, and, in case of contextual recognition, the paternal or double surname.[4] Therefore, whereas children born out of wedlock can receive the mother's or father's surname, depending on the timing of the parental recognition, the offspring of married parents can only be assigned the paternal or double surname, with the exclusion of the maternal one. This is obviously a discipline rooted in a strongly patriarchal family understanding, of ancient historical origins.[5] Even if various changes have recently been introduced in the field of Italian family law,[6] actual rules on surnames still date back to the Italian Civil Code of 1942. In recent years the Italian legislator attempted to align rules for children born in and out of marriage, abolishing every lexical

3 After the decision No. 286/2016 of the Italian Constitutional Court declared illegitimate the imposition of the only paternal surname on the offspring, the Ministry of the Interior with its circular No. 1/2017 allowed parents to choose between the paternal or double surname. This is an express derogation introduced by the Ministry, provided that the civil code has not been updated.

4 For a collection of Italian rules and cases on surnames see: V. Cappello, *Il nome e il cognome nel diritto di famiglia*, Santarcangelo di Romagna, Maggioli, 2006; F. De Scrilli, 'Il cognome dei figli', *Trattato di diritto di famiglia*, Vol. 2-Filiazione, 2012, pp. 523-550. See also E. Pazè, 'Verso un diritto all'attribuzione del cognome materno', *Diritto di Famiglia e delle Persone*, Vol. 1, 1998, pp. 324-361, on the Italian case-law in favor of the assignation of the mother's surname.

5 See above on *pater familias*.

6 See the so-called "speedy divorce", the introduction of parental responsibility in place of parental power, the 2016 law on civil unions and stable cohabitations, and above all the abolition of the juridical term "natural and legitimate children" by D.Lgs. 154/2013. It must be noted that Law No. 76/2016 on civil unions introduced a special paragraph dedicated to the surname of partners civilly united (M.N. Bugetti, 'Il cognome comune delle persone unite civilmente', *Famiglia e Diritto*, Vol. 10, 2016, pp. 911-918), but the law decree required for the enforcement of the law is not in force as of today.

differentiation in the matter of minors, but he did not take surnames into account: this omission differentiates minors because of their parents' marital status, with a direct impact on the children's identity.

Contrary to the Italian system stand Spain and France, among others. Spain compels all minors to take the double-surname (*appellido paterno y appellido materno*), regardless of the union linking their parents.[7] If the minor is recognized at birth by only one parent, he takes both surnames of that parent.

Thus, given that each Spanish parent has a double-surname, in order to avoid excessively long surnames, the offspring's surname can only be composed of the first part of the father and the mother's surnames. The order between the two parties can be freely chosen by the parents, with the possibility for the child to request reversal when they become of age. In 2000, the mother's surname could be placed first with the father's consent,[8] and since June 30, 2017, regardless of the father's consent.[9] It is noteworthy that, because the second surname of each parent is always discarded, the order of the two parental surnames establishes which surname will be transmitted to the following generation, to grandchildren.

Loi No. 2003-516[10] introduced the double-surname for all minors in France, letting parents bestow on the offspring the surname of the father, the mother or the double-surname.[11] In 2004, a double dash for the double-surname of children born after 2004 was prescribed,[12] but this typographic choice, intended to distinguish a compounded name from double-surnames, was eliminated by the State Council in 2009.

In conclusion, Spain and France grant the same treatment to children born in and out of wedlock, on the obvious assumption that the offspring should not be affected by the parents' relational choices, while Italy remains anchored to a paternalistic vision of society, which is traditionalistic and archaic.

7 Thus, in the Spanish system women never lose their surname. See art. 53, *Ley de 8 de junio de 1957 del Registro Civil*, amended by *Ley 13/2005* (changing the Civil Code with regard to the right to marry and related issues) in force since 3 July 2005.

8 Art. 55, *Ley 40/1999* (*Boletín Oficial del Estado*, 6 November 1999), states that in case of dispute, the father's surname was automatically registered as the first one.

9 Art. 49, *Ley 20/2011*.

10 In line with art. 54, *Loi No. 54/2002*.

11 It is interesting to briefly examine the French surname discipline for adults as well. The *Arrêté du 29 Juillet 2011 du Code Civil* states that "The marriage has no effect on the surnames of the spouses, who continue to have only the official surname, written in the birth certificate...both spouses can, if they wish, use the surname of the partner, adding it or substituting it to their own". Thus, after getting married, both spouses can decide to use the surname of the partner or both surnames. The surname change is not automatic, but follows a request filed at the registrar office. In France there is in fact a substantial difference between surname (*nom*) and surname of use (*nom d'usage*). The surname appearing on birth records always remains the same, even after getting married, whereas the surname of use, that may be chosen for use after marriage at the discretion of the couple, is not imposed by law and can be either the surname of one of the two spouses or the double-surname.

12 Pursuant to Decree No. 2004-1159.

The comparison between the three countries above raises a clear question regarding the legitimacy of the Italian choice, which at first sight seems to stand in stark contrast with the principles of equality not only among minors (born in and out of wedlock), but also between men and women, or rather, between fathers and mothers. Yet, very few cases have been brought to date in front of the European Court of Human Rights by Italian families, given that such anachronistic traditions are still much respected in the country, due to unwritten social laws.

B The Surname Transmission Between Rigidity and Freedom of Choice

The second category distinguishes between systems with predetermined rules for the transmission of the surname, contrary to systems allowing parental free choice.

Parents are compelled by fixed rules in the choice of the offspring's surname in Italy, where, as described above, the father's surname is preferred by law over the mother's one, and in Spain, where the double-surname rule cannot be bypassed.

In Germany, instead, spouses must choose their family surname, which may be that of the husband or of the wife, with the exclusion of the double-surname.[13] However, in the event that parents have not chosen any family surname, or are not entitled to the family surname (if unmarried), they must choose which surname (maternal or paternal) to assign to the offspring, and, without their choice, the court appoints one of the two parents with the right-duty to choose. After one month, in the absence of any party's choice, the offspring automatically acquires the surname of the parent charged with the duty to choose. Alternatively, if the minor is recognized by one parent only, he will exclusively receive the surname of that same parent.

In this schematization, which contrasts with systems that rigidly identify the surname of the children with complete indifference towards the principles of gender equality and equality between legitimate and natural children, and with free choice systems, it emerges clearly that the latter are the only ones in line with international treaties and conventions to protect minors. However, even these systems do not guarantee full protection to minors, since they do not automatically recognize the surname assigned abroad by the foreign country of birth or residence. Thus, even in these States, it may happen that a child named "XY" according to the law of the country of birth or residence, is then forced by the country of citizenship to choose either the surname "X" or "Y", dropping part of the legal double-surname. Such a violation of the personal right to identity affects the single individual and the overall system, clashes with the principles of equality, justice, freedom and respect, and denies the improvements achieved through the battles of the twentieth century for universal equality and tolerance.

---

13 BGB, § 1617.

C Various Degrees of Freedom in the Choice of the Surname

Finally, the third category above concerns free systems which provide parents with various degrees of freedom in regard to the choice of the offspring's surname.

The country which allows parents the highest level of freedom is the United Kingdom. For many centuries the UK highly discriminated against women who, by marriage, would lose their surname together with the possibility of transmitting it to the offspring.[14] Current rules, instead, grant absolute freedom to UK parents, who may opt for the surname of the wife or mother, husband or father or second female parent, or even a third person, void of any link to the two parents.[15]

On the other hand, there is the German system which, although it proved to be avant-garde when in 1994 it introduced the possibility of giving children the maternal surname, was recently convicted by the Court of Justice of the European Union (CJEU) for unjust denial of the foreign double-surname to German nationals residing abroad.[16]

Freedom, but under restricted terms as opposed to the UK, also characterizes the French (freedom to choose the father's, mother's or double-surname), Spanish (freedom in relation to the order of the surnames within the compulsory double-surname), and Portuguese systems (where the only limit upon the choice of surname is the length, which cannot be no longer than six words).

D Novelties within European Domestic Laws on Surnames

It is interesting to note that many countries around Europe have recently modernized their surname policies.

Years ago, the Netherlands devoted special attention to conflicts of laws with regard to surnames, enforcing the so-called International Names Act in 1989,[17] which recognizes the right for any foreign surname officially registered abroad to be used in the country. Yet, the Dutch domestic policy on the matter until not long ago was out of date, violating gender equality: in the event of no choice by the parents, the child was entitled to the

14 On the recent reform on the joint registration of birth in the UK, which necessarily involves the choice of surname, see A. Bainham, 'What is the point of birth registration?', *Child and Family Law Quarterly*, Vol. 20, No. 4, 2008, pp. 49-474. A historical study of the English rules on surnames sheds light on the modernizing drive that, though held back by centuries-old customs and traditions, has often emerged in case-law, as shown in T. Falconer, *On Surnames and the Rules of law affecting their change*, London, Reynell, 1862.

15 *Re T (Otherwise H) (An Infant)* [1962] 3 All ER 970. On the "social task" (in regard to making someone's identification possible) carried out by the surname in UK, see G. Bilò, 'I problemi della famiglia ricostituita e le soluzioni dell'ordinamento inglese', *Familia*, Vol. 4-5, 2004, pp. 855-857.

16 See *infra* sub paragraph 5.

17 *Wet Conflictenrecht Names*, Stb. 1989, 288. See Th.M. De Boer & L. Strikwerda, 'Private International Law', *in* J. Chorus, E. Hondius & W. Voermans (Eds.), *Introduction to Dutch Law*, Alphen aan den Rijn, Kluwer Law International, 2006, p. 271.

paternal surname if legitimate and to the mother's surname if natural.[18] This same rule (set in Book 1 of the Civil Code) is still in force and delegates an automatic surname if parents do not choose any; but parents are now free to bestow on their children either the father's or mother's family name,[19] at their own discretion.[20]

Also, countries where patronymics have been used in the past, such as Sweden, Poland, Lithuania, and Hungary, have recently updated their rules. In these countries, the family traditionally took on the husband's or father's surname, with the addition of various suffixes depending on the language (i.e. -son/-dotter, -ova, -ska, -iené or -ne).[21] Needless to say, systems with such a preference for the paternal surname, and even more so for the patronymic, were giving rise to a serious breach of the principle of gender equality. Thus all these countries have changed and updated their laws.

As for Sweden, a new law on personal names was enforced on 1 July 2017,[22] providing two great novelties: under § 20, the law introduces the possibility for parents to choose the surname of the offspring from either parent's current or previous surname, a combination of the parents' surnames (double-surname), the parents' first name with the addition of -son or -daughter (in Swedish: -son or -dotter), or the surname of a sibling with the same mother and father. The law also allows people to freely change their surnames an unlimited number of times (previously the limit was once, apart from at the time of marriage).

Thus, the Swedish system represents a perfect combination of traditions (set in patronymics) and novelties, to match the contemporary need for a set of rules capable of coexisting internationally with various disciplines, that may be called to work jointly with the domestic ones involved in cross-border situations.

In Poland the offspring can receive the joint surname or the surname of one of either parents. Also Poland has recently taken into account cross-border families, by means of the Registry Office Records Act of 2014: this Act states that the registrar must transfer the content of a foreign document by transcribing foreign register office records without changes to the spelling of names and surnames, and adjusting the spelling to the Polish language only if requested by the parents.

In Lithuania, article 3.167 of the Civil Code[23] states that every child shall be given the mother's or the father's surname according to a mutual agreement of the parents. If the

18 I. Sumner & H. Warendorf, *Family legislation of the Netherlands*, Intersentia, Antwerp, 2003, p. 4.

19 This rule applies to married parents, registered partners or parents who have both acknowledged the child.

20 The father's surname is automatically given at birth. In order to opt for the mother's surname, parents must register their choice at the Registrar of Births, Deaths, Marriages and Registered Partnerships before the birth or when registering the birth.

21 F.R. Fantetti, 'La prevalenza del patronimico ed il valore costituzionale dell'uguaglianza tra generi', *Fam. Pers. Succ.*, Vol. 11, 2008, p. 881ff.; G. Crisi, 'L'aporia della norma che impone il patronimico', *Eur. Dir. Priv.*, 2010, p. 649.

22 *Sveriges Riksdag*, promulgated on November 17, 2016.

23 The Lithuanian Civil Code was introduced by Law No. VIII-1864 of 18 July 2000 (last amended by Law No. XI-1312 of 12 April 2011).

parents cannot agree, the child shall be given the surname of one of the parents by a judicial order.[24] Thus, Lithuania has also recently (2011) moved from a patrilineal transmission of surnames in line with centenary traditions, to a more modern rule on surnames. Yet, as it will be analyzed better *infra*, Lithuania still struggles with rules on the spelling of names and surnames, which according to the domestic alphabet, may include letters or signs derived neither from foreign languages nor from the languages used by national minorities. As of today, an attempt to change the law to permit a separate entry in the Lithuanian passport stating the original form of the surname (in its official language) has failed and foreign surnames are translated by law or transformed into Lithuanian characters. This situation affects not only cross-border families, but also families of different national minorities around the country.

In Hungary, the Act No. IV of 1952 on Marriage, Family and Guardianship (amended in 1974 and 1986) was declared unconstitutional because of the gender discrimination contained therein. The new Hungarian Civil Code 2013, with its fourth book entitled "Family Law Book"[25] has completely revised its surname policy, changing the rules in force in order to respect the principle of gender equality.

The ensuing rule now states that the family surname can be either that of the husband, that of the wife (with a change due to the addition of a suffix), or the double-surname with hyphenation (with a maximum of two last names). At the time of marriage, the spouses must choose the family surname (used by the spouses themselves) and that to be passed down to the offspring (with the possibility of changing it any time before the birth of the first child). The surname for the children can be either parent's surname, if it appears on the marriage certificate, or the double (hyphenated) surname.

This overview of the most recent reforms enacted in Europe on surnames shows how the issue is relevant and well known to national legislators. With this, it appears that the lack of a European discipline on the matter is to be ascribed to a targeted choice rather than a mere forgetfulness.

III Cross-Border Families in the European Frame

The brief overview above on European laws on surnames[26] gives an understanding of the relevant difficulties that may be faced by individuals having dual citizenship, or persons

24 http://ceflonline.net/wp-content/uploads/Lithuania-Parental-Responsibilities-Legislation.pdf.

25 The new Code entered into force on March 15, 2014. See O. Szeibert, 'Marriage and cohabitation in the New Hungarian Civil Code - Answering the new challenges', *in* A. Menyhárd & Emöd Veress (Eds.), *New Civil Codes in Hungary and Romania*, Cham, Springer International Publishing, 2017, p. 173ff.

26 G. Autorino Stanzione, 'Autonomia familiare e attribuzione del cognome: i dubbi in Italia e le certezze in Europa', *Corriere giur.*, 2009, pp. 496-507; R.M. Bova, 'Il cognome del figlio legittimo con doppia cittadinanza:

born or residing in a country other than that of their citizenship, in the event that the two States to which these persons are linked to provide for different and incompatible rules on surnames.

It is patent that the conflict between domestic surname rules, requiring the same person to use different surnames in the country of residence and in that of their citizenship, violates the right to personal identity, which should always be one and protected as such. Moreover, the lack of uniqueness of the surname impedes the concrete exercise of freedom of movement across Europe and on the global scale.

In fact, being identified with different surnames in various countries can lead to very difficult personal and professional issues, with obvious repercussions on the very essence of the personality. Having two different surnames means having different passports, different tax codes, different European health cards, etc.: the identity is affected in its own nature, which by definition must be personal, unique and irreplaceable. On the contrary, having two surnames, both valid and legitimate, to be used in different countries, means enjoying two disjointed identities that are autonomous, independent and unrelated, with the risk of continuous and unnecessary reporting to public authorities.

Taking into account the increasing number of cross-border transactions and negotiations,[27] it is clear that the need for a single surname, to be used in the country of citizenship and in the eventual different ones of residence and business, is essential. Failing that, it will give rise to misunderstandings and even to the complete arrest of the overall business, with consequent probable economic losses. Not to mention the serious prejudice that may be suffered while being subject to inquiries in regard to the authenticity and veracity of all the dual documents.

IV The International Setting

Gender equality and the superior protection of minors are based not only on domestic laws and constitutions, but also on international treaties and protocols.[28]

Article 16 of the 1979 UN Convention on the Elimination of All Forms of Discrimination Against Women, Article 14 of the European Convention on Human Rights of 4 November 1950 on "Equality", the Treaty of Rome of 1957,[29] the Treaty of Amsterdam of 1997, the EU Charter of Fundamental Rights of 2000 and the Women's Charter of 2010: all these

confronto tra l'ordinamento interno, il diritto sovranazionale e le legislazioni degli Stati europei', *Famiglia e Diritto*, 2010, p. 1044.

27 International sales and conveyances, cross-border money transfer, on-line purchases, etc.

28 For an overview on fundamental rights' issues see G. Comandé, G. Brüggemeier & A. Colombi Ciacchi, *Fundamental Rights and Private Law in the European Union*, Vol. I-II, Cambridge, Cambridge University Press, 2010.

29 In regard to equal pay.

acts support the principle of equality between men and women, which is also among the fundamental principles of Community law. Thus no law, domestic or international, should recognize the prevalence of a parent's surname over that of the other parent, based on gender considerations.

On the other hand, the international protection of minors' is based on the 1989 UN Convention on the Rights of the Child,[30] which promotes equal and stable wardship for all minors, regardless of their country of origin, sex, race, religion or status as natural or legitimate.

It is clear that the imposition by law of the father's surname on the offspring, and even more so, exclusively to children born in marriage with the exclusion of those born out of wedlock, furthers unjust inequalities: it is unjust to treat minors differently because of the marital or non-marital relationship of the parents. The patrilineal transmission of the surname, because of the gender discrimination among the two parents that such a rule involves, is also inadmissible.

Several decisions have already been issued on this topic by the European Court of Human Rights and the Court of Justice of the European Union, in order to condemn those systems which do not recognize the surname acquired by their citizens under the rules in force in the country of birth and residence, and to provide adequate respect to the principles of equality between natural and legitimate children and between parents.

V The CJEU in Stefan Grunkin and Dorothee Regina Paul against Standesamt Niebüll

In 2008, in the case of *Stefan Grunkin and Dorothee Regina Paul against Standesamt Niebüll*,[31] Germany was condemned by the Court of Justice of the European Union for refusing to recognize the double-surname of the son of a German couple, who was born in Denmark and was also a Danish resident.

The child had been assigned the double-surname (compound surname, including the two parental ones) under the Danish law of his country of birth, and had used it continuously, having always resided in Denmark. But no double-surname was indicated on the

30 Protection of minors is also ensured by domestic provisions applying the *favor filiationis* criterion (the interest of the minor shall prevail on all others): see M. Romani & D. Liakopoulos, *Giustizia materiale nel diritto internazionale privato e comunitario*, Milano, Giuffré, 2009, p. 151. On the practical application and actual implementation of children's rights in today's society, with a specific focus on UK, see J. Fortin, 'Children's rights-flattering to deceive?', *Child and Family Law Quarterly*, Vol. 26, No. 1, 2014, pp. 51-63.

31 Case C-353/06, ECLI:EU:C:2008:559: "In circumstances such as those of the case in the main proceedings, Article 18 EC precludes the authorities of a Member State, in applying national law, from refusing to recognise a child's surname, as determined and registered in a second Member State in which the child – who, like his parents, has only the nationality of the first Member State – was born and has been resident since birth."

German passport he requested at the age of ten, with the absurd consequence of being identified with two different surnames, one in Germany (his country of citizenship) and one in Denmark (his country of residence).

It is obvious that national legislation cannot force a EU citizen to carry different surnames within the Member States, as this would hinder the right to personal identity and also the exercise of the right of free movement and residence in Europe. Thus, although the rules governing a person's surname fall within the competence of domestic parliaments, they must respect European law. The Member States should take action to ensure that their citizens are not hindered in the exercise of their fundamental rights, and that they fully enjoy the Union's freedoms.

Free movement and the possibility to reside in any EU State and therein receive health care and school education, are among the many goals achieved as a result of the creation of the Union for the benefit of all European citizens; results that should not be denied because of the inexcusable omission, or even forgetfulness, in the regulation of surnames through European regulations.

Therefore, as the Grand Chamber of the CJEU has established in the *Grunkin* case, pursuant to article 258 TFEU, Germany was declared in default and ordered to end the infringement of the Treaties' obligations, by recognizing the validity of the child's Belgian surname. Despite the duties which Germany must carry out as a result of this decision, it should however be noted that to date the recognition of foreign surnames in favor of citizens with dual citizenship, one of which is German, is not automatic nor always guaranteed.

VI Case-law on Articles 8 and 14 of the European Convention on Human Rights

EU case-law on surnames is not in compliance. While the ECHR has repeatedly ascertained violations by the Member States in the context of disputes concerning surnames, the Court of Justice has taken opposing decisions. The outcome is a confused and chaotic situation, which allows the continuation of divergent policies in Europe, to the disadvantage of citizens.

Several decisions of the European Court of Human Rights involve the choice of the family surname: *Cusan and Fazzo v. Italy*[32] ascertained that, because of domestic mandatory rules on surnames the mother was unable to transmit her surname to the child notwith-

32 ECHR, 77/07, 7 January 2014, II Section: European Court of Human Rights, *Information Note on the Court's Case-law*, Strasbourg, 170, pp. 16-17. It should be noted that the Italian discipline has often been updated by means of case-law, as in the decision of the Court of Bologna on 9 June 2009 (this decision was examined in comparison to *Carlos Garcia Avello v. Belgian State*, in *M.N. Bugetti*, 'Lattribuzione del cognome tra normativa interna e principi comunitari', *Famiglia e Diritto*, Vol. 5, 2004, pp. 442-450).

standing the father's agreement. The Court defined the Italian rule on surnames as 'rigid and discriminatory towards women', because of the violation of Articles 8 and 14.

In *Burgharz v. Switzerland*,[33] the Court believed there had been an infringement of Articles 8 and 14 (resulting in discrimination on the ground of sex) by Switzerland, since the Swiss authorities had denied the applicant, Mr Burgharz, the right to put his own surname before the family name (which was that of the wife), although Swiss law afforded that possibility to married women who had chosen their husbands' surname as their family name.

Again, the Court announced a violation of the same Articles 8 and 14 by Switzerland in *Losonci Rose and Rose v. Switzerland*[34], in a case involving a cross-border family: the family had chosen the surname of the Swiss wife as that of the family; then the Hungarian husband had requested to use only his original surname, without the double-barrelled surname, but his request had been rejected. The couple contested a violation of the European Convention on Human Rights, given that if the parties had been inverted (a Swiss husband and a foreign wife), the wife could have chosen to have her surname governed by her national law.

In *Ünal Tekeli v. Turkey*[35], taking into account the impossibility for Turkish married women to use exclusively their maiden name in official documents, the Court declared there had been a violation of Article 8 and recommended the Turkish State to allow both spouses to keep their own surnames or to have an equal say in the choice of the family name.

In conclusion, the ECHR called for the elimination of all discrimination on grounds of sex in the choice of surname within the cases above, out of respect of gender equality among spouses and parents.

At present, the ECHR has not yet considered any cases concerning surnames, which directly involves a minor. And nevertheless, all the decisions mentioned above concerning the choice of the family surname, extend their effects well beyond the parties in court, necessarily including the children born or to-be-born of the applicants. There is therefore an obvious problem of protection against gender discrimination, under Articles 8 and 14 of the European Convention on Human Rights. But there is also the further issue of protecting minors, indirectly and necessarily involved in the disputes by parents in regard to the choice of the family surname in cross-border situations. Because minors are legally incapable of acting in court to assert their fundamental rights, it is then up to national legislators to ensure full protection to all minors.

33 ECHR, 16213/90, 22 February 1994.

34 ECHR, 664/06, 9 November 2010.

35 ECHR, 29865/96, 16 November 2004, IV Section.

The ways that such a goal could be achieved are many, ranging from bilateral or multilateral agreements between States, to EU regulations.

Beyond the operational techniques that could be applied in practice in the choice of the surname for a cross-border minor, what is most important is the pressing need to subtract the discipline in question from the sphere of private international law which, with its referrals, prevents parents from being able to choose *ex ante* the surname of the family and of the offspring with full knowledge and certainty. In fact, except for experts in comparative private law and private international law, who have the necessary tools to be able to predict which surname can be granted based on the place of birth, the citizenship of the parents and the timing in the parental acknowledgement of the child, all other parents, on the other hand, can only face *ex post* an arduous, difficult, long path with an uncertain outcome to bestow on their children the surname they have chosen. In fact, even an eventual favorable decision of the ECHR, recognizing the infringement of Articles 8 and 14 by the resisting States, would not help such parents, given that the Court lacks the executive powers necessary to make its decisions effective.[36]

VII Malgožata Runevič-Vardyn and Łukasz Paweł Wardyn v Vilniaus

The Court of Justice of the European Union, invested in 2009 with a case similar to those discussed at the ECHR and described in the paragraph above, dismissed the decision, sending the case back to the domestic court, thus denying the existence of any issue in regard to freedom of movement or freedom of identity as a result of different surnames for the same individual.

In detail, in *Malgožata Runevič-Vardyn and Łukasz Paweł Wardyn v Vilniaus miesto savivaldybės administration and a.*,[37] the Court examined a case involving a mixed marriage between a Lithuanian and a Polish citizen.

On the Lithuanian marriage certificate there were only Lithuanian characters, not including the letter "W", which was instead in the Polish surname of the husband. After getting married, the spouses moved to Belgium, where their son was born. The mother requested Vilnius's civil services to change her surname on her marriage certificate with the replacement of the letter "V" with "W", and asked for the same change in regard to her son's surname.

---

36 On the "limited binding effects" of the ECHR's decisions, see C. Busch, 'Fundamental Rights and Private Law in the EU Member States, *in* C. Busch & H. Schulte-Nölke (Eds.), *Fundamental Rights and Private Law*, Munich, Sellier, 2011, pp. 1-25. The author attributes to the Court the role of being an "important source for the continuous development of the European fundamental rights", but at the same time underlines the *inter partes* effect of its decisions.

37 ECLI:EU:C:2011:291 (judgment); Case C-391/09. In European Court Reports 2011 I-03787.

The Lithuanian judge invested of the case referred it back to the Court of Justice for a preliminary ruling, requesting a decision on whether the law of the Union precludes legislation of a Member State from imposing the registration of names and surnames in the civil status records of that same State in a form which complies with the official national language rules.

The Court did not rule out the possible inconvenience to the persons concerned as a result of the surname written with and without the letter "W" in Belgium (country of residence of the family) and in Lithuania (country of citizenship of the wife and the son). However, in order to constitute a restriction against the freedoms recognized by the Treaty, the Court held that it had to be a matter of "*serious inconvenience*" of administrative, professional and private nature, and it is for the national court to determine whether the refusal to modify the surname as required may give rise to disadvantages definable as serious inconveniences.

Thus, the case went back to the national court, which had to balance the interests at stake: the right of spouses to respect for their private and family identity and, on the other hand, the interest of Lithuania to safeguard its national official language.[38] In the end, the Lithuanian judge considered the prevalence of the national interest.

Although this decision has led to a defeat for the applicants directly involved, it has in any case shed light on the now essential need to adopt a uniform discipline in Europe, so as to subtract the matter from the discretionary assessments of the individual courts concerned.[39] It should be noted that the same Court years before, in *Carlos Garcia Avello v. Belgian State*[40] had instead decided in favor of the surname change requested by the applicant

> on behalf of minor children resident in that State and having dual nationality of that State and of another Member State, in the case where the purpose of that application is to enable those children to bear the surname to which they are entitled according to the law and tradition of the second Member State.

Thus, even the jurisprudence of the same court is discordant, and therefore calls for a reform of the matter.

38 Similar problems arose in regard to the different spelling of the surname of the applicant in two Member States (Greece and Germany) in *Konstantinidis v Stadt Altensteig and Landratsamt Calw*, C-168/91; see E. Jayme, 'Cognome e diritto di famiglia nella recente riforma tedesca (con spunti di diritto comparato)', *Riv. Dir. Civ.*, 1995, p. 71; W. Pitens, 'Von Konstantidinis bis Grant - Europa und das Familienrecht', *ZEuP*, 1998, p. 843.

39 Criticizing the domestic courts' lack of "impartiality and vision to resolve a binational child custody dispute", see G.P. Romano, 'Conflicts in Respect of Parental Responsibility', *Yearbook of Private International Law*, Vol. XVI, 2014/2015, pp. 146-154.

40 C-148/02 (ECLI:EU:C:2003:539).

VIII Is Harmonization Possible?

The rulings issued by the CJEU and the ECHR show that the heterogeneity of the rules in force in Europe and, above all, their incompatibility, open up conflicts to be solved in court. However, it is unthinkable for contemporary Europe, with an ever-growing number of cross-border couples and mixed families, to maintain such significant divergences, requiring court action to resolve problems that will unavoidably arise, with the further and aggravating unknown about the outcome of similar discretionary judgments.

Thus, it is necessary to rethink rules on surnames, detaching them from the domestic monopolies and trying to create an harmonious European discipline,[41] to avoid discrimination, gender inequalities and unjust treatment against children born in or out of wedlock, offering an appropriate acceleration to the development of rules on surnames, giving a real and concrete dimension to the principle of equality and guaranteeing the protection of the personal and professional identity of European citizens throughout the Union and abroad.

Various procedures to reform surname policies across Europe could be undertaken. By means of a EU regulation, establishing which law should prevail in cross-border cases among the law of the country of residence, that of citizenship, the law chosen by the spouses at the time of marriage, or by the parents at the first child's birth.

By means of bilateral or multilateral agreements, establishing standard criteria in the choice of the surname in cross-border cases (e.g. prevalence of the surname identified on the basis of the law of the country of birth, or that of citizenship, or the one chosen by the parents).[42]

Beyond the concrete methods that will be used to settle the issue, from what has been described above emerges the urgent need to examine the matter and to take effective measures.

41 On the "harmonization debate" in Europe and the role of the Commission on European Family Law see M. Antokolskaia, 'Harmonisation of substantive family law in Europe: myths and reality', *Child and Family Law Quarterly*, Vol. 22, No. 4, 2010, pp. 397-421. The author defines the "national differences in the balance of political power between the proponents and opponents of modernising family law" as the main obstacle to the harmonization of the law. For a critical view of "cross-border family life" and applicable rules see N. Dethloff, 'Arguments for the unification and harmonisation of family law in Europe', *in* K. Boele-Woelki (Ed.), *Perspectives for the Unification and Harmonisation of Family Law in Europe*, Antwerp, Intersentia, 2003, pp. 37-64.

42 The Convention on the law applicable to surnames and forenames, signed in Munich on 5 September 1980 and binding Spain, Italy, the Netherlands and Portugal, connects the choice of the applicable law to the citizenship of the interested person; thus, it does not give any indication re the surnames of individuals with dual citizenships. No other convention has regulated surname policies to the present date. See M.N. Bugetti, op cit, n. 32, p. 444.

The close correlation between surname, right to personal identity and right of free movement is not manifestly obvious.[43] For this reason it has so far been ignored by Member States and also by the Union; or perhaps it has been deliberately neglected, for the precise purpose of firmly anchoring the whole matter of surnames to national secular traditions.[44]

Any appraisal of the origin of the current state, and in particular the assessment of whether the lack of a uniform discipline in the surname field (and even the absence of attempts at standardization) is the result of mere negligence or of deliberate omission (to the advantage of the residual jurisdiction of the internal States) is irrelevant. The overall evaluation has been overcome by the urgent need to provide as soon as possible rules for over 30 million cross-border families in Europe. This should be an immediate task for the EU and its Member States.

To say that from the surname it is possible to determine the place of origin of an individual, as reported in the initial title, is certainly an exaggerated provocation. However, there is no doubt that domestic rules on surname are too preponderant, too many and too conflicting, and therefore it is time for widespread reforms, to be adopted on the basis of a uniform guideline.

43 On the surname as a core element of a child's personality see A. Conti, 'Note intorno all'attribuzione del cognome paterno', *Giurisprudenza di Merito*, Vol. 10, 2011, p. 318. See also Italian Court Cassation No. 2751/2008; Italian Constitutional Court 286/2016. The link between the name-surname compound and personal identity, as protected by art. 2 of the Italian Constitution, is analyzed in connection with the rejection by the Court of Venice of the requested change of name in R.P. Depinguente, 'Immacolata: un nome da cambiare?, *Famiglia e Diritto*, Vol. 3, 2000, pp. 279-283.

44 It should be noted, incidentally, that nationalistic pressures in some countries (e.g. Iceland, Portugal, Saudi Arabia, etc.) are pushing to impose by law an exhaustive list of forenames to choose from for children.

Legal Aspects and Parents' Perception of the Protection of Children on the Internet in the Republic of Serbia

Nadežda Ljubojev[*], *Dragana Glušac and Dragica Radosav*[**]

I Introduction

We live in a time in which information and communication technologies (ICT) have become an integral part of children's lives around the world. About one-third of global Internet users are younger than 18 years of age.[1] The data suggests that the Republic of Serbia has become an information society. The introduction of the Internet and mobile telephony has well surpassed 50% of the total population, and more than 75% of the internet population uses the Internet on a daily basis. Statistical data for the Republic of Serbia indicates that the presence of a computer in households has increased from 55.2% to 64.4% in the period from 2012 to 2015. In the same period, the penetration of Internet in households was even more intense (from 47.5% to 63.8%), while in mobile phones, the situation in the Republic of Serbia is within the framework of European trends (85.8% in 2012, 91.4% in 2015).[2]

The above data indicates that children now live in a modern, technological environment where they have easy access to Internet-enabled devices, either at home or on their personal mobile devices.[3] As the results of the research demonstrates show, children start using ICT at an earlier age, and the number of children and young people who use the Internet every day is constantly increasing, globally and in the Republic of Serbia.[4] For generations that have been born and bred in the digital age, digital communication is a common and even

* Associate Professor, University of Novi Sad,Technical Faculty "Mihajlo Pupin", Zrenjanin, Serbia.

** Full Professors, University of Novi Sad, Technical Faculty "Mihajlo Pupin", Zrenjanin, Serbia.

1 S. Livingstone, J. Carr & J. Byrne, 'One in Three: Internet Governance and Children's Rights', *Innocenti Discussion Paper,* No. 2016-01, Florence, UNICEF Office of Research, 2016.

2 Republic Institute for Statistics - Use of Information and Communication Technologies in RS, 2015.

3 "Youth (ages 15-24) is the most connected age group. Worldwide, 71% are online compared with 48% of the total population. African youth are the least connected: UNICEF, 'The State of the World's Children 2017: Children in the Digital World', https://www.unicef.org/publications/files/SOWC_2017_ENG_WEB.pdf.

4 S. Livingstone et al, *Risks and safety on the internet: The perspective of European children*, London, EU Kids Online, 2011; D. Popadic & D. Kuzmanovic, *Korišćenje digitalne tehnologije, rizici i zastupljenost digitalnog nasilja među učenicima u Srbiji*, UNICEF/Institut za psihologiju Filozofskog fakulteta Univerziteta u Beogradu, 2013, http://sbn.mpn.gov.rs/clientpub/uploads/Digitalno%20nasilje-Izvestaj%202013.pdf.

dominant form of communication. Children today represent a "digital generation", as well as a vulnerable group of the Internet users, who face potential risks.[5] According to UNICEF estimates one third of Internet users globally are children, with the proportion of Internet users likely to be higher in lower income countries where the Internet is rapidly penetrating all spheres of public life.[6]

The use of the Internet provides many opportunities for the psychosocial development of children: from finding information, communication, entertainment, to acquiring the skills of digital, information and critical literacy, essential for life in the 21st century. However, the results of the research data show that children on the Internet, experience negative experiences and risks.[7] But not all risks result in harm, and research also suggests that use of ICTs can help children cope with the problems they encounter.[8]

Research in Europe shows that social networks are very popular among children and adolescents in Europe. It seems to be their favorite Internet activity, as 77% of children aged 13 – 16 and 38% of children aged 9 – 12 have their profiles on social networks.[9] Research in the Republic of Serbia shows that younger children use the Internet for entertainment (playing games, listening to music, watching videos, and movies), while the older ones mostly use social networks.[10] The most popular social networks are Facebook, Instagram, and Snapchat, and most students use several social networks, which is a trend registered in some other areas.[11] At the end of 2013, profiles listed on some social networks (mostly Facebook) accounted for 89% of students and 92% of secondary school students from the Republic of Serbia. Moreover, videos, series, and films on the Internet were watched daily by 50% of elementary students and 62% of high school students, while 41% of elementary and high school students were chatting online on a daily basis.[12]

---

5 S. Livingstone & M. Bober, 'Regulating the Internet at Home: Contrasting the Perspective of Children and Parents', *in* D. Buckingham & R. Willett (Eds.), *Digital Generations: Children, Young People, and the New Media*, New York, Routledge, 2013, pp. 93-113.

6 S. Livingstone, J. Carr & J. Byrne, 'One in Three: Internet Governance and Children's Rights,' Paper Series No 22, Centre for International Governance Innovation and The Royal Institute of International Affairs, Waterloo, Ontario, 2015; J. Byrne & P. Burton, 'Children as Internet users: how can evidence better inform policy debate?', *Journal of Cyber Policy*, Vol. 2, No. 1, 2017, http://dx.doi.org/10.1080/23738871.2017.1291698.

7 K. Subrahmanyam & D. Smahel, *Digital Youth: The Role of Media in Development*, New York, Springer, 2011; D. Kuzmanovic et al, *Digitalno nasilje - prevencija i reagovanje*, Ministarstvo prosvete, nauke i tehnološkog razvoja Republike Srbije i Pedagoško društvo Srbije, Beograd, 2016.

8 S. Livingstone, L. Haddon & A. Gorzig (Eds.), *Children, risk and safety online: Research and policy challenges in comparative perspective*, Bristol, The Policy Press, 2012.

9 S. Livingstone, K. Olafsson & E. Staksrud, *Social networking, age and privacy*, London, EU Kids Online, 2011.

10 M. Stevanovic et al, "Internet navike dece školskog uzrasta u nekim selima borske opštine", Konferencija "*Sinteza*", Beograd, Singidunum Univerzitet, 2014, p. 354.

11 A. Lenhart, *Teen, Social Media and Technology – Overview 2015*, Washington, Pew Research Center, 2015.

12 At the end of 2012, organized by the Ministry of Education, Science and Technological Development, UNICEF and Telenor, within the project Stop Digital Violence, the first research on the use of ICT, risks and digital violence among primary and secondary school students from the RS was conducted. The research

With the increasing availability of ICT and the increasing involvement of children in the world of communications and the Internet, the risks of their potential exposure to various inappropriate content (sexual, pornographic, violent), manipulation, abuse, and exploitation are also increasing. The data collected in the research on this subject can have a great influence on recognizing the individual and social importance of this issue. It is important to realize the level of parents' perception of the safety of children on the Internet. In this regard, data from the research from 2017 is included in this work, and the sample of 83 parents of school children aged 11 – 15 from the Autonomous Province of Vojvodina, a northern region of the Republic of Serbia. Parents' perceptions about the necessity of legal protection of children on the Internet and the attitude of parents regarding the safety of their children on the Internet were examined because the influence of the 'human factor' in this kind of relationship on how children live and operate in the real world cannot be ignored. While global research on digital violence has been very prominent especially in the last two decades, there is still a small amount of research on the subject in the Republic of Serbia. However, the evidence on how use of the Internet impacts child rights and well-being is still scattered and patchy in most countries, with some unsatisfactory measures, fast-outdated findings and uncertainties regarding reliability, validity and generalisability.[13]

II The Risks of Internet Use by Children

Considering the value and the educational potential of the Internet, which are probably not using enough the fact is that the topic of the dangers and risks associated with internet use is often publicly discussed, in order to bring attention to protecting and ensuring the safe use of these ways of communication. Although European research shows that online opportunities and risks are positively correlated,[14] in most of the research so far, the emphasis has been on the negative aspects of the Internet (various forms of risk behavior and digital violence). There are no significant differences in the experiences between students from the so-called general population and students with disabilities or students from the Roma population regardless of whether the experience was positive or negative.[15] For

was based on a survey and it included 34 schools (17 elementary and 17 high schools), i.e. 3786 pupils (2272 elementary and i 1514 high schools), 3078 parents and 1379 teachers. There was a higher presence of women in the parent and teacher sample. See Popadic & Kuzmanovic, op cit, n. 4.

13 M. Stoilova, S. Livingstone & D. Kardefelt-Winther, 'Global Kids Online: researching children's rights globally in the digital age', *Global Studies of Childhood*, Vol. 6, No. 4, 2016, pp. 455-466.

14 S. Livingstone & E. Helsper, 'Balancing opportunities and risks in teenagers' use of the internet: The role of online skills and family context', *New Media & Society*, No. 12, 2010, pp. 309-329; S. Livingstone & M. Bulger, A 'Global Research Agenda for Children's Rights in the Digital Age', *Journal of Children and Media*, Vol. 8, No. 4, 2014, pp. 317-335.

15 D. Kuzmanovic, Z. Pavlovic & D. Popadic, 'Mladi i internet: šta im je zabavno i korisno, a šta ih uznemirava?', Naučna konferencija *Dijalozi u obrazovanju*, Beograd, Filozofski fakultet u Beogradu, 2016a.

minority groups and smaller language communities, digital technologies offer particular networking benefits and economies of scale that could provide positive opportunities and help overcome social exclusion but could also, without them, leave such groups further behind.[16]

Internet and mobile communications have become an indispensable part of active time for many children aged 7 to 18 - within the household, in educational institutions, in peer groups, etc. Consequently, Internet risks and the exposure of children to disturbing content is evident. Research shows that exposure to risks is directly related to the time spent on the Internet.[17] Among youth who use the Internet on a daily basis, 62% of elementary school students and 84% of high school students were at risk.[18] Also, the same research found that the more students were prone to risky behavior, the more often they were involved in digital violence, or suffered, committed or have witnessed such behavior.[19]

Children are exposed to various risks in cyberspace: from sexual and pornographic content, misuse of personal data and privacy, to contact with strangers, and other risks.[20] Exposure to sexual and pornographic content is a problem that is becoming more and more common among children at a global level, even more so than digital violence.[21] In theory, the author considers that in the 1990s, the development of a worldwide Internet network, apart from a number of benefits it provided to users, set this medium as a key variable through which sexual abuse[22] of children emerged beyond the "traditional" criminality, with the demands of radical modification of techniques of suppression and prevention.[23] However, given that exploiting and abusing children for pornographic purposes, as well as data privacy, have been recognized as the main risks of children using the Internet, the work of entities that are dealing with other risks on the Internet has been marginalized.[24]

---

16 Stoilova, op cit, n. 16.

17 D. Kuzmanovic & D. Popadic, 'Use of the Internet by Youth in Serbia: Opportunities and Risks', Beograd, 2013.

18 Popadić & Kuzmanovic, op cit, n. 4.

19 Ibid.

20 U. Hasebrink et al, *Comparing children's online opportunities and risks across Europe: Cross-national comparisons for EU Kids Online.* LSE, London, EU Kids Online, 2009.

21 D. Smahel & M.F. Wright (Eds.), *Meaning of online problematic situations for children. Results of qualitative cross-cultural investigation in nine European countries*, London, EU Kids Online, London School of Economics and Political Science, NSPCC, 2015; *"Always there when I need you": Child Line review: what's affected children in April 2014 - March 2015*, London, NSPCC, 2014.

22 'More than 9 in 10 child sexual abuse URLs identified globally are hosted in five countries – Canada, France, the Netherlands, the Russian Federation and the United States,' Lancet Commission on Adolescent Health and Wellbeing, *Children in the Digital Age.* https://adolescentsourfuture.com/2017/12/children-in-a-digital-age/.

23 Y. Akdeniz, *Internet child pornography and the law: national and international responses*, UK, University of Leeds, 2008.

24 J. Sapic, *Bezbednost dece na internetu u Srbiji: Izloženost bez koordinisane zaštite*, Centar za istaživanje javnih politika, 2016.

Risky behavior on the Internet also includes other risks for children on internet and social networks. For example, the development of the Internet and social networks has led to increased levels of addiction, due to the increased time spent on the Internet.[25] In recent years, the growing dependence on the Internet and social networks has been the subject of research both globally and in the Republic of Serbia.[26] In a relatively short period, the Internet has become the most popular media among children. They gain excellent ICT knowledge at an early age and because of that, they are prone to the influence of this new media. It is also troubling that young Internet users entrust their personal information to strangers.[27] A potential consequence of revealing personal information on the Internet can lead to unwanted contacts out of the network, which could expose a child to physical danger. Some authors argue that it is not empirically confirmed that the sharing of personal data is directly related to the risk of victimization, but other risky behavior is usually included.[28] Also, social networks could be used for promotion of violence. Results research showed that verbal violence forms were the most dominant in peer violence and victimization interactions, which is in accordance with previously research. This forms included aggressive behaviors such as harsh jokes or making fun of someone, insulting others and being abusive to someone. [29]

The definition of cyberbullying is even more unstable, partly because it is a newer phenomenon, occurring on still-evolving technological devices and platforms.[30] While at core it concerns aggression expressed by peers through digital (online or mobile) technolo-

25 S. Kiesler,*Culture of the internet*, Mahwah, Lawrence Erlbaum Associates, 1997.

26 D. Christakis et al, 'Problematic internet usage in US college students: a pilot study', *BMC Medicine*, Vol. 9, No. 77, 2011, pp. 2-6; B. Bodroza, M. Jovanovic & B. Popov, 'Latentna struktura ponašanja u virtuelnim društvenim zajednicama i njegove relacije sa socijalnom anksioznošću', *Primenjena psihologija*, Vol. 1, No. 1-2, 2008, pp. 19-35.

27 According to research, 31.1% of boys and 27% of girls aged from 9 to 15, point out that they have shared their personal data on the Internet (e-mail address, phone number, and even their home address). See E. Dowell, A. Burgess & D. Cavanaugh, 'Clustering of Internet Risk Behaviors in a Middle School Student Population', *Journal of School Health*, Vol. 79, No. 11, 2009, pp. 547-553.

28 M. Ybarra et al, 'Internet prevention messages – targeting the right online behaviors', *Archives of Pediatrics & Adolescent Medicine*, Vol. 161, No, 2, 2007, pp. 138-145.

29 This study aimed at examining different forms of violence and victimization among high school students from urban areas, including relevant factors such as testing period, gender, class and school achivement. The sample included 947 high school students of which 489 were examined in 2013. and 458 in 2014. year. Students were from the second, the third and the fourth class of different high schools from city of Novi Sad (Republic of Serbia). Peer violence and victimization was measured by Peer Violence and Victimization Questionnaire (PVVQ) which contains questions about different forms of physical, verbal and relational violence and victimization in the last school year. V. Sokolovska, B. Dinic & D. Marinkovic, 'Nasilništvo i viktimizacija kod učenika srednjih škola: efekti perioda ispitivanja, pola razreda i uspeha', *Teme*, No. 2, 2015, pp. 617-630.

30 R.S. Tokunaga, 'Following You Home from School: A Critical Review and Synthesis of Research on Cyberbullying Victimization', *Computers in Human Behavior*, Vol. 26, No. 3, 2010, pp. 277-287.

gies targeting a child victim,[31] some assert that the aggression need not be repeated, since cyberbullying messages are easily and widely shared, multiplying the harm by multiplying the number of bystanders and the persistent possibility of future sharing.[32] When it comes to risky contact, it is important to point out that "cyberbullying", i.e. harassment and bullying on the Internet, deserves special attention because of the negative consequences it has on the individual, especially their emotional and social functioning.[33] Cyberbullying is the use of ICT in order to harass, humiliate and harm the other person. According to expert knowledge in this field, the fact that this type of bullying can also happen in contact with peers and school friends is why it is harder to control this type of risk on the Internet by using Internet filters. ICT is often used by adults who falsely present themselves and communicate with young people for the purpose of sexual abuse. There has been an increasing discussion about sexual abuse via the Internet.[34] The Internet (via social networks, and online messaging) allows for various forms of sexual abuse.

Another type of risky contact is grooming, which is a series of procedures and, preparatory actions aimed at establishing contact, maintaining communication, and physically approaching the child, for the purpose of sexual abuse. Sexual predators on the Internet do not have a clear profile. Their professions and age vary, although research shows that they more often than not male.[35] In theory, some authors explores the phenomenon of distribution of amateur photographs and video materials via SMS or MMS messages, through sexting, which has become a common and popular phenomenon among the teenage population.[36] Sexting means sending or uploading of photos, messages or videos with explicit sexual content to the Internet. Some authors warn that the exchange of photos or messages with sexual content can act as harmless flirting or entertainment, but for young people, sexting has serious social and legal consequences.[37] Possession and dissemination of photographs or videos with sexual content of minors, according to the Republic of Serbia Criminal Code (CC), represents the possession of child pornography, and is punishable by imprisonment.[38]

---

31 N. Levy et al, 'Bullying in a Networked Era: A Literature Review', Berkman Center Research Publication, 2012, available at: http://papers.ssrn.com/sol3/papers.cfm?abstract_id=2146877.

32 S. Livingstone, M. Stoilova & A. Kelly, 'Cyberbullying: incidence, trends and consequences', *in Ending the Torment: Tackling Bullying from the Schoolyard to Cyberspace,* New York, United Nations Office of the Special Representative of the Secretary-General on Violence against Children, 2016, pp. 115-120.

33 S. Zukovic & S. Slijapcevic, 'Parental control the behavior of children on the Internet and social networks', *Nastava i vaspitanje,* Vol. 64, No. 2, 2015, pp. 3.

34 Lj. Bogavac & S. Otaševic, *Nacionalna studija o društvenom problemu seksualnog zlostavljanja dece,* Beograd, Incest trauma centar, 2015.

35 J. Wolak et al, 'Online Predators and Their Victims: Myths, Realities, and Implications for Prevention and Treatment', *American Psychologist,* Vol. 63, No. 2, 2008, pp. 111–128.

36 R. Moore, *Cybercrime: Investigating High-Technology Computer Crime,* New York, Elsevier, 2010.

37 J. Ringrose, R. Gill, S. Livingstone & L. Harvey, *A qualitative study of children, young people and 'sexting': a report prepared for the NSPCC,* London, NSPCC, 2012.

38 Art. 185 CC.

Research on Internet risks related to children and their protection on the Internet are very numerous and frequent across the EU and the globe. The first systematic research of this type related to children in the Republic of Serbia was conducted in 2012, at the Institute for Psychology, University of Belgrade, with the support of UNICEF and Telenor.[39] According to the survey data collected, 62% of older elementary school students and 84% of high school students were exposed to risks in cyberspace in 2012.[40] Boys encounter more online risks than girls. [41] Based on this research, it was determined that the most common risk behavior was the acceptance of a friend request on social networks from unknown people (46% of elementary school students and 71% of secondary school students), followed by online messaging, also with unknown people (28% of elementary school students and 56% of high school students), responding to messages from unknown people (27% of elementary school students and 47% of secondary school students), and some accepting to meet up with people they met via the Internet (6% of elementary school students and 15% of secondary school students). The survey also shows that they shared personal data (address of residence, phone number, email) with unknown people (13% of elementary school students and 21% of secondary school students). [42]

Therefore, it is necessary to have adequate and efficient measures of prevention and protection from cyber-bullying and violence, and because of that, numerous laws and regulations have been adopted, both within domestic and international legislation. Parents, as the most powerful source of influence in the education of children, need to be aware of their children's behavior on the Internet, so they could ensure the benefits of its usage. "But only collective action – by governments, the private sector, children's organizations, academia, families and children themselves – can help level the digital playing field and make the internet safer and more accessible for children", UNICEF said in a report.[43]

III Child Protection on The Internet In The Republic Of Serbia

The harmonization of legislation in the Republic of Serbia with the European Union is in progress, through the process of accession of the Republic of Serbia to the European Union. Although significant progress in the protection of children on the Internet in the Republic of Serbia began with the process of European Union integration and harmonization of the national legislation with the European Union, there still exists a need for further improvement of the institutional and legal frameworks at both the local and the national

39 Popadic & Kuzmanovic, op cit, n. 4.
40 Ibid.
41 Kuzmanovic & Popadic, op cit, n. 17.
42 Popadic & Kuzmanovic, op cit, n. 4.
43 'Children exposed to digital risks: UNICEF', *The Independent*, 12 December 2017, available at http://www.theindependentbd.com/arcprint/details/127675/2017-12-12.

levels. The Republic of Serbia established a special service responsible for combating high-tech crime within the Ministry of Interior, as well as the Special Prosecutor's Office for the Combat against High-Tech Crime, ratified by the Council of Europe Convention on High-Tech Crime and largely aligned with the EU Directive on attacks on Information Systems.[44] In addition, it was concluded that further amendments to the regulations are necessary in order to fully align with the EU *acquis communautaire* in the area of combating cybercrime.[45]

By enacting the Law on the Ratification of the UN Convention on the Rights of the Child, Republic of Serbia committed itself to taking measures to prevent and ensure the protection of children from all forms of domestic violence and institutional violence, as well as, the broader social environment.[46] The Convention on the Rights of the Child (CRC) is the first international legal document which is a summary of all children's rights.[47] Article 1 of the CRC defines "child" as any person "below the age of eighteen years unless, under the law applicable to the child, the majority is attained earlier." Importantly, the CRC allows States to adopt lower or higher ages of majority, thus giving States Parties some leeway in defining childhood. CRC prescribes all member states a duty to protect the child from all forms of sexual exploitation and sexual abuse.[48]

The Republic of Serbia is a signatory to two European Council conventions: the Convention on Cybercrime (adopted in Budapest in 2001)[49] and the Convention on Protection of Children against Sexual Exploitation and Sexual Abuse (Lanzarote Convention).[50] After the ratification of the Convention on Cybercrime and the Additional Protocol, the Republic of Serbia amended the Criminal Procedure Code,[51] the Law on Organization and

44 Directive 2013/40/EU of the European Parliament and of the Council of 12 August 2013 on attacks against information systems replacing Council Framework Decision 2005/222/JHA. 14.8.2013. L 218/8.

45 Available at: http://www.bezbednost.org/upload/document/akcioni_plan_za_poglavlje_24_-_mart_2016_.pdf.

46 UN Convention on the Rights of the Child (*Official Gazette of SFRY - International Agreements*, No. 5, 1990 and" *Official Gazette of the FRY - International Treaties*, No. 4, 1996 and 2, 1997).

47 Convention on the Rights of the Child, New York, 20 November 1989, United Nations, *Treaty Series*, vol. 1577. To date, the CRC has 194 States Parties, making it one of the most widely ratified international treaties.

48 Article 34 CRC.

49 The Convention on Cybercrime came into force in 2004. The Republic of Serbia in 2005 signed, and in 2009 ratified the Convention and Additional Protocol to go with it: Law on the Ratification of the Convention on Cybercrime (*Official Gazette of Republic of Serbia*, No. 19, 2009). The Convention on Cybercrime, 2001 is the first international document to explicitly link child pornography and computer systems.

50 In 2005, the Expert Committee of the European Council started drafting the Convention on Protection of Children against Sexual Exploitation and Sexual Abuse and in October 2007 in Lanzarote (Spain) there was a signing ceremony of this convention which represents the first international instrument referring to all forms of sexual violence over children. The Lanzarote Convention came into force in 2010 and the Republic of Serbia, by its ratification in the same year, became a contracting state, which means it has taken on very clear obligations in implementing the Convention and in overall child protection from all forms of sexual exploitation.

51 Criminal Procedure Code (*Official Gazette of Republic of Serbia*, No. 72/2011, 101/2011, 121/2012, 32/2013, 45/2013 and 55/2014).

Jurisdiction of the Government Authorities in Suppression of Cybercrime[52] and the Criminal Code (CC)[53] The Special Prosecutor's Office for Combating High-Tech Crime (Special Prosecutor's Office) was established by the Law on Organization and Competence of State Authorities for Combating High-Tech Crime in 2005. In particular, the Special Prosecutor's Office is responsible for the prosecution of perpetrators of criminal offenses of high-tech crime and has authority over the entire territory of the Republic of Serbia. Pursuant to the provisions of this law, the High Court in Belgrade responsible for dealing with high-tech crimes, while the second instance court in charge is the Appellate Court in Belgrade. Also, by the provision of the Law on Organization and Jurisdiction of State Authorities for Combating High-Tech Crime, within the Ministry of the Interior, a High-Tech Crimes Service has been established, which acts on the orders of the Special Prosecutor. At the beginning of 2016, the Republic of Serbia adopted the Law on Information Security (LIS),[54] Body for the Coordination of Information Security and a workgroup for writing the Strategy for the Development of Information Security. This created a space for improving the relevant legal and institutional frameworks. One of the relevant documents for protecting children from violence is the General Protocol on Protection of Children from Abuse and Neglect, which was adopted by the Government of the Republic of Serbia.[55]

According to changes in the CC, article 185b stipulates that it is a criminal act "using computer network or communicating via other technical means, in order to commit sexual assaults against minors". The one who intended to commit a crime, using a computer network or another method of communication via other technical means in order to arrange a meeting with a minor and actually show up at the agreed place, will face a sentence of six months to five years in prison.[56] If this act was committed against a child, the resulting sentence would be from one to eight years.[57] The most important change is that the CC, for the first time, considers the act of owning and obtaining photos, audio-visual recordings or other items of pornographic content created by exploiting minors as criminal. Legal regulation of cyberbullying, as the most characteristic and frequent form of peer violence through ICT among children, is important for two reasons: firstly, to provide

52 Law on Organization and Jurisdiction of the Government Authorities in Suppression of Cybercrime (*Official Gazette of Republic of Serbia*, No. 61/2005 and 104/2009).

53 Criminal Code (CC) (*Official Gazette of RS*, No. 85/2005, 88/2005 - 107/2005 - 72/2009, 111/2009, 121/2012, 104/2013, 108/2014).

54 Law on Information Security (LIS) (*Official Gazette of RS*, No. 6/2016).

55 General Protocol on Protection of Children from Abuse and Neglect, http://www.pravadeteta.com/attachments/653_286_OPSTI%20PROTOKOL.pdf.

56 Rap (art. 178, para. 4), sexual intercourse with a helpless person (art. 189, para. 3), sexual intercourse with a child (art. 180, paras. 1 and 2), sexual intercourse by abuse of position (art. 181, paras. 2 and 3), illicit sexual acts (art. 182, para. 1), procuring or enabling sexual intercourse (art. 183, para. 2), facilitating prostitution (art. 184, para. 3), dissimulating, obtaining and owning pornographic material and exploiting children for pornography (art. 185, para. 2) persuading minors to witness sexual intercourse (art. 185a).

57 Art. 185 CC.

children with information and education, and to prevent cyberbullying: but also to provide direct and indirect victims with adequate assistance and protection. In this regard, to prevent and protect against violence towards children through ICT, it is necessary to improve the existing legal and regulatory framework of the Republic of Serbia to implement obligations under international treaties that the Republic of Serbia has entered into, as well as to further align the RS with EU *acquis communautaire* in this area.

Progress has been made by adopting the Decree on the Safety of Children based on the National Contact Center for Child Safety, which was established through the Internet.[58] The Decree is in accordance with the Law on the ratification of the United Nations Convention on the Rights of the Child, the General Protocol of the Government of Serbia for the Protection of Children against Ill-treatment and Neglect, and the European Strategy for a Better Internet for Children in 2012.[59] For the first time in the Republic of Serbia, this Decree ets out preventive measures for the safety and protection of children in the use of ICT and appropriate responses in case of violations or the endangerment of children on the Internet. The aim of the Decree is to raise the level of awareness and knowledge about the advantages and risks of using the Internet and how to use it in a safe way to improve the digital literacy of children, that is, students, parents, teachers, and promote inter-sectoral cooperation in this domain.

However, the Commissioner for Information of Public Importance and Protection of Personal Information of the Republic of Serbia has asked whether in the absence of the Law on Children's Rights, the Regulation can ensure the protection and safety of children.[60] He states that the Constitution exclusively stipulates that processing personal information is determined by the law and not by lower acts and a decision made by Constitutional Court confirmed that collecting, keeping and using personal information must be determined only by the law. He also stresses that the importance of the Government taking adequate measures regards to this issue is not questioned.[61]

IV Parents as Entities that Protect Children on the Internet

On the one hand, parents tend to improve their children's educational perspective by using the Internet and, on the other hand, they are worried because of the risks that follow the

58 Citizens can report abuse and behavior that endangers the safety of children on the Internet - to the Center (phone number 19833, email bit@mtt.gov.rs. or via an electronic application on the portal www.pametnoibezbedno.gov.rs.)

59 European Strategy for a Better Internet for Children. (COM 2012): 196 Final.

60 Commissioner for Information of Public Importance and Protection of Personal Information of the Republic of Serbia. https://www.poverenik.rs/en/.

61 P. Tanjug, 'da li se zaštita dece a internetu može braniti uredbom?' *Blic*, 26 Dec. 2016. https://www.blic.rs/vesti/drustvo/poverenik-da-li-se-zastita-dece-na-internetu-moze-braniti-uredbom/48r6dle.

use of the Internet and social networks.[62] Namely, a noteworthy study by the Belgrade Institute of Psychology found that almost 65% of parents of children aged 8 to 17 believe that the Internet and mobile communications are an unsafe and dangerous place for their children.[63]

The fact is that children are often bigger experts than their parents in this field.[64] In this regard, research shows that almost two-thirds of students report that their parents have lesser skills in using computers and the Internet than they do.[65] In the Republic of Serbia there are no studies which evaluate digital literacy of children and youth. Research shows that if digital literacy is defined as a set of simple and procedural skills, or basic technical knowledge, then it can be said that young people are digitally literate. However, if digital literacy is, according to the contemporary concept of literacy, assessed based on more complex cognitive skills (e.g. comparison of information, critical evaluation of site reliability, drawing conclusions from information found on the Internet), it can be concluded that digital skills of young people are not at a satisfactory (and expected) level.[66] Therefore, in theory, today's young people, regardless of their frequent use of ICT, cannot be considered digitally literate.[67]

Some authors believe that setting rules and increasing parental supervision result in a lower degree of exposure to Internet risks and less involvement of young people in digital violence.[68] When it comes to children, the role of parents in the safe use of the Internet and its content is significant. The research of the Institute for Psychology, University of Belgrade, 2012, showed that children are aware of the fact that there are ways to protect their privacy on the Internet, which should serve as a starting point for further steps.[69] The same research indicated that girls and older students are more interested in learning about the ways of protection on the Internet, comparing to the boys and younger students. A lack of awareness in parents and teaching staff about concrete measures of prevention and protection from the risks was also identified.

The ability of children to work on a computer is an important factor in ensuring security in social networking. This applies in particular to the knowledge of privacy protection procedures and the risks they may be exposed to on the Internet. However, with

62 S. Livingstone & M. Bober, 'Regulating the Internet at Home: Contrasting the Perspective of Children and Parents', *in* Buckingham & Willett (Eds.), op cit, n. 5, pp. 93-113.

63 Popadic & Kuzmanovic, op cit, n. 4.

64 Some authors are worried about the percentage (67%) of children who have said that they know more than their parents about the Internet. Livingstone, op cit, n 3.

65 Kuzmanovic, op cit, n. 15.

66 Y. Punie & K. Ala-Mutka, 'Future Learning Spaces: new ways of learning and new digital skills to learn', *Nordic Journal of Digital Literacy*, Vol. 2, No. 4, 2007, pp. 210–225.

67 A. Calvani, A. Fini, M. Ranieri & P. Picci, 'Are young generations in secondary school digitally competent? A study on Italian teenagers', *Computers & Education*, Vol. 58, No. 2, 2012, pp. 797-807.

68 Popadic & Kuzmanovic, op cit, n. 4.

69 Ibid.

experience and time spent on the network, the competence and awareness of Internet users is growing as well as their capacity to protect themselves from potential threats.[70]

Besides parents, it is very important that relevant educational policy subjects within formal education further develop the digital competencies of children, and teach them how to use the Internet in a constructive and critical way, but also how to act safely on the Internet. Given the fact that internet use in children is mainly related to recreational and out-of-school activities, it is necessary to provide better access to the Internet in the school context and to encourage children to use the Internet for educational purposes.[71] Safe behavior on the Internet is one of the key aspects of digital literacy.

One good example of support to parents and teachers in preventing digital violence in school, developed in the Republic of Serbia, views such violence in the context of the deeper social causes of peer violence.[72] Additionally, it offers strategies that include systematic, preventative measures and close collaboration with teachers and parents.[73]

V Methodology and Research Results

Interdisciplinary research was carried out in the spring of 2017 on this issue, which found that legal and technical aspects of the issue were united. The research tried to determine parents' perception on the possible vulnerability of their children and their personal readiness to participate to prevent some negative consequences. A survey of parents of primary school children in the Autonomous Province of Vojvodina, a northern region of the Republic of Serbia, was carried out.

The quantitative method used to conduct the research was a survey in a narrow sense, on the attitudes and opinions of the examinees' parents. Conducting this quantitative research allowed for a precise measuring and quantifying of the relevant indicators. However, the reliability of this survey can be limited because the data collected depends on the examinees' parents and their ability to provide honest answers. It is possible that the survey method is subject to epistemological and social limitations, in the sense that the examinees may not give honest answers, but answers that accord to their social values or their unawareness of the matter.[74] This is why a survey is only one of the phases in the

70 S. Livingston & D. Brake, 'On the rapid rise of social networking sites: new findings and policy implications', *Children & Society*, Vol. 24, No. 1, 2010, pp. 75-83.

71 Kuzmanovic, op cit, n. 15.

72 S. Livingstone & J. Byrne, 'Challenges of parental responsibility in a global perspective' *in* U. Gasser & S. Cortesi (Eds.), *Digitally Connected: Global Perspectives on Youth and Digital Media*, Berkman Center Research Publication, 2015, pp. 26–29.

73 Popadic & Kuzmanovic, op cit, n. 4. Livingstone and Byrne, op cit, n. 24.

74 N. Ljubojev, D. Glusac & D. Radosav, 'Children in the Internet: Protection and Parents' Perception', *in* B. Katalinic (Ed.), *DAAAM International Scientific Book*, Vienna, DAAAM International, 2017, ch. 9, pp. 105-120.

research process, without neglecting other aspects of the research. The information was collected in an indirect survey, or a questionnaire in paper form. The parents were asked if they knew what activities their children did on the Internet and if they considered these activities risky. Also, the parents were asked if they knew the legal and institutional frameworks for protecting their children on the Internet.

This interdisciplinary research brought together, experts in the field of legal and information sciences, but it became evident that there is a need to involve other experts to expand the research. The research confirmed the need for more interdisciplinary research in this field and demonstrated the benefits and challenges of close cooperation of legal professionals and IT experts.

The survey measured the attitudes of parents regarding their knowledge of children's behaviour on the Internet, and their perception of the possible dangers. In the legal sense, the aim of the survey was to determine the existence of parents' consciousness about the need for institutionalized protection of their children. Moreover, the parents were asked if they were informed about the existing legal and institutionalized framework regarding children's protection on the Internet. The results were partially presented in publications and it became clear that parents were facing a new type of fear different from traditional fears related to children's safety - the fear and the perceived danger of, the unknown world of the Internet.[75]

These results are in correlation with some other research from this field, one of them being UNICEF research from 2016 on the level of consciousness of potential Internet risks and abuse among the parents of children aged 8 to 17. [76] What we consider important is the fact that there is a significant percentage of parents who said that they **did not know** if their children had had an unpleasant experience on the Internet and about 20% of the parents stated that their children had not had an unpleasant experience of any kind. However, such answers are opposite to their attitudes as a majority of the interviewed parents said that their children were in danger on the Internet and as parents, they were in need of help. The results imply that parents are confused or ignorant in regards to the ways of protection and need help in being educated on the potential dangers on the Internet, and the measures for prevention and protection and about legal aspects of Cyber crime.

The obtained results show that most parents are not familiar with the legal and institutional frameworks for protecting their children on the Internet. This points to the need

75 Ibid.

76 In August 2015 the Republic of Serbia joined the Global Kids Online international research, organized by the UNICEF Research Office - Innocenti, in partnership with the London School of Economics and Political Science. The Children World Project on the Internet was derived from the EU Kids Online project. Within both projects, the opportunities and rights of children and young people (ages 9 to 17) on the Internet, as well as the risks of digital communication, were explored. The research involved both students and their parents.

for an institutional and organized training of parents about the dangers on the Internet and the necessity of parental involvement.[77] In the survey, the majority of the parents decided to use the help the school would provide mostly in terms of educating parents.

VI Conclusion

Serbian legislation should regulate the protection of children on the Internet as a vulnerable group. Also, it is important to include child protection on the Internet in the future Strategy for Development of Information Security of Serbia, which would lead to the strengthening of the legal framework and the capacity of institutions that deal with children. The changes to the Criminal Code in 2003 stipulated that exploiting the computer network or communicating in other technical means for the commission of criminal offenses against sexual freedom against a minor person (article 185 b) is defined as a criminal offense punishable by law. The shift was made by the adoption of the Decree on the Safety of Children in the use of ICT, on the basis of which the National Contact Center for Child Safety was established on the Internet. For the first time, in the Republic of Serbia, by this Decree some preventive measures for childrens' security and protection at using ICT are being implemented. In this regard, in order to prevent and protect children from violence through ICT, the reforms improve the existing legal framework and positive legal regulations of the Republic of Serbia to implement obligations in the international treaties that the Republic of Serbia has entered into, as well as further align the legal system of the Republic of Serbia with EU *acquis communautaire* in this area.

When it comes to children, the role of parents in the safe use of the Internet and its content is significant. The spread of the Internet is requiring parents to direct their children in the right way to ensure they use this virtual space safely.

---

77 Only 11% of them check that the child behaves on the Internet, and as many as 48% say that they do not know if they are able to help their child protect him or herself from Internet dangers. D. Glusac, N. Ljubojev & D. Radosav, 'Parents' perception of the needs for implementing measures for child protection on the Internet', Proceedings of International Conference of Information Technology and Development of Education VIII (ITRO 2017), Zrenjanin, Serbia, June 22, 2017.

Domestic Violence against Children: Legislation, Practice and Prospects in China

*Ran Qiyu** *and Peng Wanran***

I Introduction

Domestic violence is a global problem, and China is no exception. Recognition of the illegality of domestic violence and the legitimacy of public powers to intervene in domestic violence only occurred in the late 20th century. Indeed, academic attention towards domestic violence only began in the 1980s, much like the rest of the world.[1] Due to traditional ideas such as that "children are the private property of their parents", and the saying "spare the rod and spoil the child", domestic violence against children is a common phenomenon in reality. Although domestic violence prevention in recent years has aroused great concern, the attention has mainly been focused on women as victims, whereas children have attracted far less attention in society.[2] Research demonstrates that child abuse must be prevented, to save not only this generation of children, but also the next generation, as far too often, an abused child in turn becomes the abusing parent of his or her own child.[3] With a gradual, deepened understanding of the damaging impact of domestic violence on children, more and more people are realizing that violence against children must be prevented in families.

The Convention on the Rights of the Child, adopted in 1989 by the United Nations, played a crucial role in promoting the enactment of laws on domestic violence against children, which became binding in China in 1992. Article 3 of this Convention stipulates that in all actions concerning children, whether undertaken by public or private social welfare institutions, courts of law, administrative authorities or legislative bodies, the best

* Dr Ran Qiyu, associate professor at Southwest University of Political Science and Law, Chongqing, China.

** Peng Wanran, undergraduate student at Chongqing Technology and Business University, Chongqing, China.

1 Chinese scholars' attention to domestic violence began with the translation of foreign articles. The first article consulted by the National Knowledge Infrastructure Network on domestic violence was 'Children and Women Abuse Crimes in the United States', which was published in the *Global Law Review*, excerpted and translated by Zhou Yeqian from *The Times* in 1983. Since then, more attention was paid to domestic violence among Chinese sociologists and legal scholars.

2 G. Ying, 'Damages of Family Violence to Children and Its Social Intervention', *Study of Contemporary Youth*, Vol. 5, 2006, p. 22.

3 J.D. Payne & M.A. Payne, *Canadian Family Law*, 6th ed., Irwin Law, Toronto, 2015, p. 115.

interests of the child shall be a primary consideration. China has agreed to be bound by its provisions. To fulfill its promise to the international community under the Convention and other instruments, the Chinese government quickly implemented measures to protect the rights and interests of children, including enacting laws to prevent children from family violence.

The first domestic violence prevention association was established by the Women's Federation in Tangshan City, Hebei Province in 1996.[4] In response to calls for the fight against domestic violence, Changsha City of Hu'nan Province took the lead in formulating Certain Provisions on the Prevention of Domestic Violence in 1996, on the basis of which, the first local regulation to prevent domestic violence was passed in March 2000 by Hu'nan Provincial People's Congress. Hence, the concept of domestic violence was introduced into the Chinese legal system for the first time.[5]

Domestic violence first appeared in national legislation in the 2001 amendment of the Marriage Law of the PRC, in which "prohibition of domestic violence" was written into the Act. The Judicial Interpretation I of Several Problems on the Application of the Marriage Law of the PRC (hereinafter the Judicial Interpretation I of Marriage Law) issued in 2001 by the Supreme People's Court defines domestic violence. Furthermore, violence against children is expressly prohibited in the Protection of Rights and Interests of Children Act of the PRC 1991. Following this, the People's Supreme Court and other departments issued several opinions on the Prevention of Domestic Violence one after another. On July 31, 2008, the All-China Women's Federation, the Central Propaganda Department, the Supreme People's Procuratorate, the Ministry of Public Security, the Ministry of Civil Affairs, the Ministry of Justice and the Ministry of Health jointly released the Opinions on the Prevention of Domestic Violence in 2008 (hereinafter referred to as the Domestic Violence Opinions 2008).

The Supreme Court, the Supreme People's Procuratorate, the Ministry of Public Security, and the Ministry of Justice jointly issued the "Opinions on Handling Cases of Domestic Violence by Law" in 2015 (hereinafter referred to as Opinions on Domestic Violence 2015). Relevant Chinese departments issued "Opinions on Several Issues Concerning the Handling of Guardians' Violations of the Rights and Interests of Minors" in 2014 (effective on January 1st, 2015, hereinafter referred to as the Guardianship Opinions 2015).

However, the abovementioned provisions on family violence are far from systematic – some are promulgated by the legislature, and some are released by the Supreme People's Court or other departments. These provisions are scattered in different acts, opinions or

4 'The First Anti-Domestic Violence Association Was Set up in Tangshan', *Morality and Civilization*, Vol. 3, 1996, p. 40.

5 J. Yue'e, 'The Process of Legislation against Domestic Violence in China', *Chinese Women's Movement*, Vol. 6, 2014, p. 38.

judicial interpretations, and some of them are either in conflict or are inconsistent with each other. Some provisions are ambiguous and abstract, lacking practicability. In addition, these provisions are mainly applied to sanctions imposed after violence, the punishment threshold to the offender is too high, and the intervention by public authorities is unsatisfactory.[6] Hence, there is a need for specific, specialized, systematic and uniform legislation against family violence.[7]

To further prevent domestic violence and enact a uniform act, the Standing Committee of the National People's Congress passed the Domestic Violence Prevention Act of the PRC on December 27, 2015 (in effect on March 1, 2016, hereinafter referred to as the Domestic Violence Act 2015). The promulgation of this Act is the result of joint efforts of legislatures, governments, the judiciary, people's organizations, social organizations, experts and scholars, and the public. It is also the result of many years of activism and promotion by women and women workers.[8] The Domestic Violence Act 2015 symbolizes the establishment of a legal system to prevent domestic violence, which is of milestone significance in the process of structuring the legal system in China.[9] As a uniform Act against domestic violence, the Act builds an all-round line of protection for victims by providing a variety of relief measures and placing corresponding responsibilities on the perpetrators. Most provisions in the Act are applicable to violence both against adults and children, but some special provisions are only applied to the latter.

II Legislative Characteristics of the Domestic Violence Act 2015 to Prevent Violence Against Children

The Domestic Violence Act 2015 adopts the following legislative measures to prevent violence against children: it establishes the principle of special protection to minor children; it increases the types of domestic violence and expands legislative applicability to members living together; it introduces mandatory reporting of relevant organs; it adopts various relief measures; and guardianship can be terminated under legitimate circumstances.

6 X. Hui & X. Yumin, 'Theory and System on Domestic Violence against Women Refereeing from Foreign Countries', *Seeker*, Vol. 7, 2006, pp. 106-107.

7 Z. Gonglin, 'Legislative Integration and Trend of Domestic Violence Prevention Law', *The Science of Law*, Vol. 2, 2012, p. 51.

8 S. Yueyue, 'Speech at the Forum to Study and Publicize Domestic Violence Prevention Act Held by National Women's Federation', *Chinese Women's Movement*, Vol. 2, 2016.

9 L. Mingshun, 'The Domestic Violence Prevention Act as a Good Law Playing Multiple Significant Roles', *Collection of Women's Studies*, Vol. 1, 2016, p. 5.

A Principle of Special Protection of Children

The Domestic Violence Act 2015 establishes principles to prevent domestic violence, including the principle of protecting the interests of vulnerable members, the principle of privacy protection, respect for the wishes of victims and the principle of prevention and precaution. With regards to the principle of protecting the interests of vulnerable members, the Domestic Violence Act 2015 stipulates special protection principles to minor children, the elderly, the disabled, women who are pregnant or breastfeeding, and seriously ill patients who are suffering from domestic violence.[10]

Hence, the Domestic Violence Act 2015 expressly states that family members should help each other, care for each other, live in harmony and fulfill their family obligations.[11] It is the common responsibility of the state, society and every family to prevent domestic violence. The Domestic Violence Act 2015 stipulates that the guardian of a minor child shall carry out family education in a civilized manner, perform his or her guardianship obligations and educational duties according to law, and shall not commit domestic violence.[12] This provision has had a positive influence on changing the traditional ideas held by parents on education.[13]

B Definition of Domestic Violence

Article 1 of the Judicial Interpretation I of the Marriage Law provides that the term "domestic violence" as used in the 2001 amended Marriage Law means that "the perpetrator, by beating, bundling, body injury, forced confinement or by other means, causes certain physical, mental or other damage to their family members". On the basis of this interpretation, the Domestic Violence Act 2015 has improved its definition, article 2 of which stipulates that the term "domestic violence" refers to the physical, mental and other infringements committed by family members in the form of beating, bundling, body injury, forced confinement and frequent verbal abuse and intimidation and other acts.[14]

Article 37 of the Domestic Violence Act 2015 also provides that: "Violence committed between persons other than family members who live together shall be regulated by the

10 Art. 5 of the Domestic Violence Act 2015.

11 Art. 3, ibid.

12 Art. 12, ibid.

13 Z. Xuemei, 'Interpretation of the Special Protection to Special Groups in the Domestic Violence Prevention Act', *Chinese Lawyer*, Vol. 4, 2016, p. 73.

14 As for the relationship between family violence and abuse, in China, definitions treat domestic violence different from abuse. Article 1 of Interpretation I on the Application of the Marriage Law of the PRC describes persistent and regular domestic violence as abuse. Moreover, according to legislation in China, economically abusive behaviour such as providing no adequate food, housing, clothing, or medical care etc. can constitute child abuse, but not violence against children.

provisions of this Act". Compared with the definition of domestic violence in the Judicial Interpretation I of the Marriage Law, the Domestic Violence Act 2015 possesses three striking characteristics. Firstly, it insists on a de-familialized definition of domestic violence. The definition of domestic violence has shifted from "Family Member-focused Orientation" to one encompassing family members as well as other people that live together, such as those in a relationship of custody, support, foster care, or cohabitation. This concept is consistent with the legislative spirit in Amendment IX to the Criminal Law of the PRC on August 29, 2015, in which maltreatment constitutes an abuse crime – not only of a family member, but also persons who are in a relationship of custody or care with the abuser.

This shift indicates that the value orientation of the legislature is no longer confined to traditional philosophy, but more attention is being paid to the normative functions played by the law on human rights equality, legal protection etc., and the space for public powers to intervene in domestic violence has been expanded as well.[15] It is not only necessary but also reasonable to legislate to incorporate persons other than members of the family who live together into the domestic violence framework as perpetrators and victims, which is great progress in protecting the dignity, health and lives of individuals[16] Secondly, compared with the Judicial Interpretation I of Marriage Law, which only refers to physical violence, the Domestic Violence Act 2015 lists forms of mental and psychological abuse to constitute domestic violence as well.[17] Thirdly, evidence of victims' suffering or damage is no longer the requisite for domestic violence, which reduces the proof burden for victims, strengthens the intervention in domestic violence by public powers and protection of the legitimate rights and interests of victims.

15 Q. Song, 'The Choice and Optimization of the Criminal Relief Path of Domestic Violent Crimes', *Issues on Juvenile Crimes and Delinquency*, Vol. 4, 2016, p. 12.

16 J. Yue, 'An Interpretation of the Concept and Connotation of Domestic Violence', *Collection of Women's Studies*, Vol. 1, 2016, p. 7.

17 For the first case concerning mental violence decided by the Chinese courts, see the divorce case of Zheng Mouli v. Ni Moubin. In the case, the plaintiff Zheng Mouli and the defendant Ni Moubin registered to marry on February 11, 2009. The court held that the plaintiff and the defendant entered into a hasty marriage without fully understanding their decision. During the time the plaintiff and the defendant lived together, the defendant wrapped a basketball with white cloth hanging on the balcony of the residence, and on the white cloth, the defendant wrote aggressive and threatening words to the plaintiff such as, "I want to kill, kill Zheng Mouli", which was fear-inducing for the plaintiff. The court found that the defendant's actions constituted mental/spiritual violence, and ruled for the defendant to compensate the plaintiff 30,000 yuan for damages. See China Court Network: 'Zheng Mouli v. Ni Moubin Divorce Dispute Case—Threat as a Means of Domestic Violence in Judicial Determination' at http://www.chinacourt.org/article/detail/2014/02/id/1220836.shtml.

C Mandatory Reporting Obligations of Relevant Organs

Because of the relationship between children and their close relatives and the limited capacity of children themselves, the percentage of reported cases on domestic violence against children is very low. According to a survey, only 2% of minor respondents suffering from domestic violence reported their abuse.[18]

The Domestic Violence Act 2015 provides for mandatory reporting obligations of relevant organizations when persons with no or limited capacity for civil conduct encounter domestic violence. Mandatory reporting laws are the product of the medical community's recognition of child abuse as a social problem in the early 1960s in the United States. Today, mandatory reporting laws are widely accepted as an integral component in the fight against child abuse.[19] Mandatory reporting obligations have been in legislation for more than 50 years in the United States. By 1965, 46 states in the United States had enacted mandatory reporting laws on domestic violence against children.[20]

Based on the experience of foreign legislation, the Domestic Violence Act 2015 established a mandatory reporting system for persons with no or limited capacity for civil conduct, embodying the international vision of Chinese legislation. The 2015 Act places a mandatory reporting obligation upon bodies such as schools, kindergartens, medical institutions, Neighborhood Committees, Villagers' Committees, social work services, relief management agencies, welfare agencies and their staff members. If they find that persons of no civil capacity or limited civil capacity have suffered/are suffering from domestic violence or suspected violence, they should promptly report to the public security organs. Moreover, the Act prescribes legal responsibilities for organs or their staff members who are obligated to perform their mandatory reporting obligations, but failed to fulfill the obligations, resulting in serious consequences. In such cases, the department at the next level of hierarchy or the obligated organ itself, shall punish the directly responsible persons in charge, or other directly liable persons according to law.

D Relief Measures

The Domestic Violence Act 2015 provides various measures to protect children in domestic violence cases, such as civil monitory (a system of monitoring and warning of citizens), shelters for victims and protection orders.

18 Z. Lei, 'Children's Perspective Cannot be Absent in Domestic Violence Prevention Legislation ', *Legal Daily*, 16 April 2011, p. 003.

19 A. Hinshaw, 'Mediators As Mandatory Reporters Of Child Abuse: Preserving Mediation's Core Values', *Florida State University Law Review*, Vol. 34, 2007, p. 285.

20 M. Oswald, 'Mandatory reporting of child abuse—necessary medicine for "nervous Nellies" or a remedy too far?', *International Data Privacy Law*, Vol. 3, No. 4, 2013, p. 270.

Firstly, a civil monitory is a striking system in the new Act.[21] The civil monitory originated from the "Implementation Measures of Monitory System in Domestic Violence Cases (for Interim Implementation)" promulgated by Jiangsu Province in 2013. It was the first time to establish administrative education guidelines for domestic violence perpetrators in China under local legislation.[22] Then, this system was legalized in the Domestic Violence Act 2015.

Secondly, the Domestic Violence Act 2015 requires the establishment of temporary shelters for victims as temporary relief measures. Legal relief agencies should provide legal aid to victims of domestic violence according to law. It stipulates that the municipal people's governments at the county or district levels may establish temporary shelters for victims of domestic violence, on its own or depending on relief management agencies, providing temporary living assistance for victims of domestic violence. When a person without civil capacity or with limited capacity for civil conduct suffers from serious physical injury for domestic violence, faces personal safety threats or is in an unattended dangerous state, the public security organ shall notify the civil affairs department and relocate the battered victims to temporary shelters and relief agencies or social welfare institutions.

In addition, The Domestic Violence Act 2015 provides for protection orders for children victims. After the Domestic Violence Guidelines issued by the Supreme People's Court in March 2008, protection orders were experimentally utilized in local judicial practices. In August 2008, the People's Court of Wuxi City issued the first "protection order" to stop beating and threatening the victim, so as to protect the personal safety of the victim.[23] The People's Court in Changsha city, Hunan province, issued more than 30 protection orders in May 2009.[24] For more than 1 year after the implementation of the Domestic Violence Guidelines, the People's Courts in Hunan Province had made 25 protection orders in total.[25] By 2010, more than 100 protection orders had been issued by courts across China.[26]

21 Art. 16 of the Domestic Violence Prevention Act stipulates that if the domestic violence is slight and the act is not punished by public security administrative institutions according to law, the public security organ shall criticize the perpetrator or issue a warning document. The warning statement shall include the identity of the perpetrator, a statement of facts regarding the domestic violence, and a prohibition on domestic violence imposed upon the perpetrator. The public security organ shall send the warning document to the perpetrator and the victim, and inform the Neighborhood Committee and the Villagers' Committee.

22 X. Ninglan, 'The Warning System in Domestic Violence is an Institutional Innovation with Chinese Characteristics', *Collection of Women's Studies*, Vol. 1, 2016, p. 14.

23 J. Lou Yinsheng, 'Exploring the Judicial Basis of Anti-Domestic Violence', *People's Court Daily*, 24 January 2011, p. 7.

24 Y. Qian & L. Li, 'Reflections on the System of Protection Order Being Established in the Law — From the Perspective of Anti-domestic Violence Trial Practice in Changsha City', *People's Judicature*, Vol. 7, 2014, p. 17.

25 D. Zhiwei, 'Looking Back and Prospect of the Applicability of the Personal Protection Order—Taking the Practice of Hunan Court as an Example', *People's Judicature*, Vol. 5, 2011, p. 9.

26 More than one hundred Personal Protection Orders have been issued. http://sxfy.chinacourt.org/article/detail/2010/10/id/2273513.shtml.

By February 2016, courts had issued a total of 738 personal safety protection orders referring to the "Domestic Violence Guidelines".[27] Based on the practical experience of local courts, the Domestic Violence Act 2015 further clarifies the involvement of public powers in domestic violence cases from the following aspects. Firstly, it has strengthened the precautionary measures against domestic violence. A protection order can be applied for when domestic violence is happening, or when the applicant is in danger of domestic violence. Secondly, the Act emphasizes the principle of facilitating applicants and protecting victims, which stipulates that the application for a protection order can be submitted without applying for divorce, free from litigation costs and offering no guarantee in litigation.[28] Protection orders are divided into Emergency Protection Orders and Ordinary Protection Orders. [29] A protection order can be submitted orally or in writing and can be applied for in person or by others on behalf of the applicant in specific circumstances. If the applicant is one with no or limited capacity for civil conduct or is prevented from applying for a protection order because of coercion or intimidation, his close relatives, public security organs, women's federations, the Neighborhood Committees, Villagers' Committees and relief administrative agencies can apply for a protection order on behalf of the victim.[30] Thirdly, measures that not only protect the physical safety of the victim, but also others, may be taken.[31]

According to the "exchange / social control theory", violence against family members is more likely to occur when there is few or no social or legal costs to pay. Hence, increasing the legal costs of antisocial behaviors can reduce the rate of violence.[32] Where the obligated persons fail to perform the obligation in protection orders, dual-level criminal relief is provided to victims.[33] That is, in addition to the provisions of criminal law that can be applied to the perpetrators, the Domestic Violence Act 2015 also describes criminal liability

27 W. Chunxia, 'Personal Protection Order Should be Enforced by the Public Security Organ ', *China Women's Daily*, July 15, 2016, p. A04.

28 Reply of the Supreme People's Court on Relevant Procedural Issues Concerning the Case of Personal Protection Order (Adopted at the 1686th Session of the Judicial Committee of the Supreme People' s Court on June 6, 2016, effective as of July 13, 2016).

29 Art. 28 of the Domestic Violence Act 2015 describes that after accepting an application, the People's Court shall make a personal protection order or reject the application within 72 hours. If the situation is urgent, it shall be made within 24 hours.

30 Art. 23 of the Domestic Violence Act 2015 stipulates that if a party is a person without civil capacity or with limited capacity for civil conduct, or cannot apply for a personal protection order due to coercion or intimidation, his or her close relatives, public security organs, women's federations, Neighborhood Committees, Villagers' Committees and relief administrative organs may apply on behalf of him or her.

31 Article 29 of the Domestic Violence Act 2015 provides that a personal protection order may include the following measures: (1) restraining the respondent from committing domestic violence; (2) restraining the respondent from harassing, tracing or contacting the applicant and his close relatives; (3) ordering the respondent to move out of the applicant's residence; and (4) other measures to protect the personal safety of the applicant.

32 H. Lie, 'Theoretical Research on Domestic Violence ', *Collection of Women's Studies*, Vol. 3, 2002, p. 61.

33 Qian, op cit, n. 15, p. 12.

for violation of civil protection orders. If the violation of a civil protection order does not constitute a crime, the People's Court may impose a fine of not more than ¥1,000 or a detention of less than 15 days on the perpetrator depending on the circumstances of the case.

E Termination of Custodianship

Although the "Protection Law of Minor Children" stipulates termination of guardianship, its provisions are so rarely applied in practice that they are regarded as "zombie clauses" or "sleeping clauses". The Domestic Violence Act 2015 further details the provision for the termination and resumption of guardianship. It provides that where the guardian violates seriously the lawful rights and interests of the person under guardianship, the People's Court may make a decision to terminate the guardianship, upon receipt of an application from the close relatives of the child, or from relevant institutions, such as Neighborhood Committees, Villagers' Committees and the civil affairs departments of the people's governments at the county level.[34] If it is terminated, the circumstances of the case will determine whether guardianship will be resumed or not.

The "General Rules of Civil Law" 2017 also sets out that the People's Court may, according to an application by relevant persons or organs, revoke guardianship, take necessary measures to arrange temporary custody, and designate guardians in accordance with the principle of being best in favor of persons under guardianship, in any of the following circumstances: (a) conducting acts causing serious damage to the physical and mental health of persons under guardianship; (b) failing to fulfill the duty of guardianship, or being unable to perform the duties of guardianship and refusing to delegate part or all of the duties of guardianship to others so that the person under guardianship was in a state of danger; (c) conducting any other act that seriously infringes upon the lawful rights and interests of persons under guardianship.[35] After the guardianship has been revoked, on application from the guardians, the People's court may allow them to resume the guardianship unless the guardians have intentionally committed a crime against the persons under guardianship.[36] The guardian shall not normally be allowed to resume his or her guardianship, if any of the following has occurred: (1) sexual assault, or the selling of minors; (2) abusing or abandoning minors for more than six months, or repeated abandonment of minors which has caused severe damage or more severe consequences; (3)

34 Art. 21 of the Domestic Violence Act 2015.
35 Art. 36 of General Rules of Civil Law 2017.
36 Ibid.

those who have been sentenced to imprisonment for five years' or more because of their acts of infringement on guardianship.[37]

After the termination of guardianship, other guardians shall perform the responsibilities. Where there are no other guardians, the People's Court shall appoint a guardian on the principle of being most beneficial to the minors. If a person is appointed to act as a guardian, his or her wishes, conduct, state of health, economic position, emotional connection with the child, and the wishes of a child who can express opinions, shall be taken into consideration. Where there is no suitable person or agency to act as the guardian, the People's Court shall designate the civil affairs department to act as the guardian, and the children's welfare agencies attached to the civil affairs department shall take the children in and foster them.[38] The child may be adopted from the welfare agencies that bear the custodial duty 1 year after the termination of guardianship except in one of the following circumstances in the above-mentioned article 40(2) of the Guardianship Opinions 2015.[39]

III Practical Problems of the Domestic Violence Act 2015

A unified legislative model has been adopted in Chinese legislation to encompass most provisions applicable to both adult and child victims. In addition, the Guardianship Opinions 2015 and the Domestic Violence Act 2015 adopt a series of special measures to prevent domestic violence against children. However, only some of these provisions specifically target family violence against children, which means that the current legislation cannot adequately deal with family violence against children. The following problems arise in practice.

A Difficulty in Determining whether or when Public Powers Shall Intervene in Families

The Domestic Violence Act 2015 clearly stipulates the intervention of public powers in targeting domestic violence, as well as the responsibility of the state, society and families to prevent domestic violence. Any form of domestic violence is prohibited. The Act also stipulates that victims of domestic violence, their legal representatives and close relatives may report the case to public security organs or institute a suit in the People's Court in accordance with the law. Agencies and individuals have the right to prevent domestic violence on time where it is happening. Since coming into force with the Domestic Violence

37 Article 40(2) of the Guardianship Opinions 2015.

38 Ibid, art. 36.

39 Ibid, art. 44.

Act 2015, public powers have been actively carrying out their duties and safeguarding the legitimate rights and interests of children. However, although the Domestic Violence Act 2015 establishes the basic principles for dealing with cases of domestic violence, these are general principles applicable to all cases of domestic violence, not well targeted at cases of domestic violence against minors, except for the principle of special protection to children. Minors are at a special stage of psychological and physiological development, the relationship between a perpetrator and victim is one between a guardian and a child under guardianship, and therefore, dealing with such a case is different from other domestic violence cases. It is not the final purpose of the law to disqualify the guardianship of guardians. Rather, the ultimate goal is to protect minor children and guarantee them a life in non-violent circumstances. When public powers intervene in domestic violence matters, parental guardianship shall be considered as a matter of priority, in accordance with the interests of minors. However, it is a pity that the relevant legislation does not distinguish between violence against adults as opposed to children, nor does it clarify the priority of parental custody over alternative care by the government or other relief agencies. Therefore, when public powers become involved in minor cases of domestic violence, how can the autonomy of the family and intervention of the state be balanced? What can be done to guarantee the priority of family guardianship over social alternative care? What principles should we adhere to when it is necessary for public power to involve itself with families? What are the factors to consider? These issues are not clearly addressed in the existing law, so its operability is deficient.

B *Problems in Relocating Children*

In cases of domestic violence against children, the Domestic Violence Act 2015 stipulates that governments at a county or district-level may provide temporary shelters for victims. The Guardianship Opinions 2015 stipulates that when parental guardianship is disqualified, relief agencies of minors can adopt the methods of family fostering, voluntary support, agency support or government-appointed boarding schools to relocate the child, and stipulates the circumstances under which the guardianship cannot be resumed.[40] It also stipulates that relief and protection agencies of minors may organize social work service agencies to offer guidance, psychological counseling and other assistance to the guardians, and conduct an investigation and evaluation into the circumstances of the minors, the repentance of the guardians, and child's wishes as well as his/her physical and mental wellbeing. (Civil Affairs Departments may set up relief and protection agencies for minors, including relief management stations and centers).

---

40 Ibid, arts. 16, 40.

In the case of a guardian's application for resumption of guardianship, the People's Court may also authorize relief or protection agencies at the applicant's residence to conduct an investigation into relevant factors, such as the child's wishes, the guardian's contrition, guardianship ability, physical and mental health, and the guardian's work and living conditions, and produce an investigation and evaluation report.[41] Unfortunately, the Opinions Act 2015 only stipulates that the minors' relief and protection agencies may organize social service agencies to carry out the above acts, but not as a routine statutory obligation, nor does it require the mandatory use of such a report to determine whether the guardianship of guardians can be resumed. In addition, how will these judgments be made and who can decide whether custodians are eligible to continue serving as guardians? Current legislation offers no answers to these questions.

C *Unsatisfactory Effects of the Compulsory Reporting System*

In reality, it is rare for cases of domestic violence to be discovered as a result of mandatory reporting obligations regarding family violence against children. A study on the implementation of the Domestic Violence Act 2015 by several public welfare organizations concerning women's rights in Beijing, carried out in Changsha and Xiangxiang in Hunan Province, and Qiuxian in Hebei Province, showed that the mandatory reporting system to protect persons without civil capacity or with limited capacity for civil conduct has hardly started to work.[42]

One of the main reasons why compulsory reporting system does not work well may be the influence of the traditional idea that the child is the private property of parents, and therefore public authorities should not intervene in families. Although the Domestic Violence Act 2015 imposes a mandatory reporting obligation on relevant persons or agencies, punishment for failing to fulfill the mandatory reporting obligation only applies to individuals, while no punishment is imposed on agencies, especially private enterprises.

D *Difficulty in Issuing and Enforcing Protection Orders*

Before the enactment of the Domestic Violence Act 2015, protective orders were enforced by the People's Courts or public security organs differently.[43] The Domestic Violence Act 2015 stipulates that the protection of personal safety shall be carried out by the People's Court, the public security organs or Neighborhood Committees, and Villagers' Committees

41 Ibid, art. 18.

42 Beijing Yuanzhong, 'Gender Development Center, Research Report on the Implementation of Anti-Domestic Violence Act', http://www.360doc.com/content/17/0315/12/31530813_637045613.shtml.

43 C. Min, 'Trial Skills in Domestic Violence Cases', *People's Court Press*, 2013, p. 78.

are obligated to assist. Since the implementation of the Domestic Violence Act 2015, protection orders issued by courts at different levels varied in numbers. Some issued more, and some rarely issued orders. Protection orders issued for violence against children were even rarer. For example, a study found that, on the first day that the Domestic Violence Act 2015 came into force, five protection orders were issued by basic courts throughout China, but during March, only a total of 33 orders were issued nationally.[44] Meanwhile, feedback from many courts shows that it is difficult to enforce protection orders.[45] In addition, the question of whether protection orders should be enforced by the trial court or executive board depends on the different courts.[46]

The reasons for this phenomenon may be as follows: firstly, only a small number of protection orders are issued, not because it is unnecessary, but because courts have different understanding of legal application. As the severity of domestic violence differs in various situations, and there is no specific guideline on assessing the level of violence, it is difficult to decide whether or when public powers should intervene in family affairs by issuing a protection order. Secondly, the allocation of power in the enforcement of protection orders has been poorly placed. The People's Court cannot enforce civil judgments involving personal rights, as the judicial police cannot perform the functions of the public security police. Meanwhile, the People's Court has no mechanism to adequately supervise the perpetrator.[47] Hence, the enforcement power should be reallocated and measures should be taken to strengthen the practicability of the current law.

E *Poor Effects of Relief Measures*

Psychological interventions for minors suffering from domestic violence are difficult to carry out. The Domestic Violence Act 2015 provides comprehensive measures to prevent domestic violence, including people's governments at all levels, which should support social work services and other social organizations to carry out mental health counseling, family relations guidance, education on family violence and its prevention, and other services. Other bodies such as trade unions, Communist Youth Leagues, Women's Federation, Disabled Persons' Federation, Neighborhood Committees and Villagers' Committees should educate perpetrators of domestic violence and provide psychological counseling to the perpetrators and victims if necessary. The Guardian Opinions 2015 also provides

44 C. Min, 'Situations, Challenges and Solutions to the Enforcement of Personal Protection Order', *Juvenile Delinquency Prevention Research*, Vol. 3, 2016.

45 L. Zhangguang, 'Dilemma of Enforcing Personal Protective Order', *Democracy and the Rule of Law*, May 15, 2016, 008 Version; W. Chunxia, 'Personal Protection Order Should be Enforced by the Public Security Organ', *Chinese Women Newspaper*, 15 July 2016, p. A04.

46 i. Zhangguang, ibid, p. 008.

47 Chen Min, op cit, n. 44, pp. 38-40.

that relief agencies can provide psychological counseling, emotional comfort and other services to minors. Article 34 of the Guardian Opinions 2015 also stipulates that the People's Court may provide psychological counseling and evaluation services for minors and the perpetrator, as part of its work in hearing cases of termination of guardianship, or relocation of minors. However, the above provisions state that the relevant departments "may" provide psychological counseling for minors, but it is not a statutory obligation. More importantly, factors such as funding, specific staff members and agencies to offer mental health counseling, family relations guidance, education and other services have not been clearly established. The same problem confronts us in the shelters system.

IV Improvements To The Domestic Violence Act 2015

Although the uniform legislation on Domestic Violence in China has made remarkable progress in many aspects, the legal reform of even the most thoughtfully developed legislation can be problematic[48] due to the complexity of domestic violence itself and the deep-rooted causes for violence. Based on the above analyzed problems that confront us, some improvements will be suggested.

A Specifying the Principles and Relevant Matters Considered in Determining whether or when to Intervene in Domestic Violence against Children

Principles should be established for the involvement of public powers in cases of domestic violence against children. It is proposed that the ability for public authorities to intervene in family affairs be limited, and instead establish state intervention on the basis of the principles of "Best Interests of the Child", "Original Family Nurturing" and "Minimum Damage". A variety of measures will be taken to ensure that parents maintain custody of their children, to minimize the destruction of children's parenting environment when public powers intervene in family affairs. Meanwhile, relevant matters to be considered in determining whether or when to intervene in domestic violence against children shall be stipulated. Legislative experience can be drawn from other jurisdictions, such as the legislation in Alberta, Canada, which stipulates that if a child is in need of intervention, a Court, an Appeal Panel and all persons who exercise any authority or make any decision relating to the child must do so in the best interests of the child and must consider relevant matters. Examples of such factors include: the family as the basic unit of society, well-being

48 A. M. Schneider, 'Domestic Violence Law Reform in the Twenty-First Century: Looking Back and Looking Forward', *Family Law Quarterly*, Vol. 42, No. 3, 2008, p. 362.

of which should be supported and preserved; the importance of stable, permanent and nurturing relationships for the child; the intervention services needed by the child, which should be provided in a manner that ensures the least disruption to the child; and a child should be removed from the child's family only when other less disruptive measures are insufficient to protect the survival, security or development of the child, etc.[49]

B Detailing Provisions on the Relocation of Children

Firstly, a mechanism of statutory assessment should be established as a means for the People's Court or protection agencies to determine whether the original guardians can resume the care of their children. It is suggested that welfare institutions in protection agencies of minors should make an investigation and submit an evaluation report on factors such as the willingness, contrition and competence of the original guardians, their physical and mental health and their work situation, to determine whether original guardianship can be resumed or not.

Secondly, considering that the native family is the best living environment for minor children, community correction and mandatory counseling could be used to assist dysfunctional custodians to become eligible ones. Where it is not suitable for the original guardian to resume guardianship, the custody of the child can be handled by family fostering, voluntary support, agency support or government-appointed boarding schools, as well as adoption. Fewer restrictions will be imposed on the requirements to adopt such a child.

In addition, it is recommended that domestic violence be treated as a factor in the determination of child custody in divorce cases and as a statutory reason for divorced couples to modify the custody to the child.

C Strengthening the Role of Civil Protection Orders

At present, enforcement of protection orders encounters resistance in practice. Protection orders concerning property can be enforced by the People's Court, but it is suitable for public security organs to enforce protection orders concerning behavior prohibition. Once a perpetrator does not comply with the protection order, immediate action should be taken by the public security organs to enforce the protection order and protect the personal safety of the applicant, in a quick, flexible and responsive way. This is different from enforcement of property cases.[50] At the same time, a mechanism for classifying and evalu-

49 Child, Youth and Family Enhancement Act, RSA 2000, c C-12, s. 2, in force since Nov. 17, 2014.

50 J. Fengjian 'Discussion on the Enforcement of Personal Safety Protection Order', *People's Justice*, Vol. 10, 2016, p. 15.

ating domestic violence is helpful in deciding whether a protection order is needed. By doing so, protection orders can better play its role to protect victims.

D Establishing Dual-Punishments to Compulsory Reporting Obligation

It is recommended to strengthen the role of compulsory reporting obligations, by establishing dual-punishments for failure to comply. If obligated individuals or agencies or enterprises fail to report domestic violence against children, punishment may be applied to individuals and to the agencies or enterprises. Punishments such as warnings, demerit recordings or major demerit recordings, demotion of rank, dismissal from post or expulsion can be applied to individuals. Punishments such as fines or license revocation can be applied to the agencies or enterprises.

E Improving Relief Measures to Children

It is suggested to provide fiscal support and specialized personnel for the provision of statutory psychological counseling, family guidance, education and shelters. Children's relief agencies and the local People's Court should set up a statutory psychological counseling department with specialized personnel and funds to offer psychological counseling to children victims. Special fiscal support and specialized personnel should be included in local People's governments' budgets to facilitate mental health counseling, family relations guidance, education on prevention of family violence and other services to the perpetrators. Children's relief agencies in the Civil Affairs Department should establish a certain number of shelters with specialized personnel and funds to provide temporary living assistance for victims.

Perspectives on the South African Statutory Regulation of Child-Headed Households

*J.A. Robinson** *and Ronelle Prinsloo***

I Introduction

The phenomenon of child-headed households has been increasing in sub-Saharan Africa in recent years. It is predominantly in countries with growing populations infected and affected by HIV/AIDS where it has manifested.[1] Research shows that children in such households are typically more vulnerable to harassment, exploitation, discrimination and physical and sexual abuse. Due to their living conditions, they are in vital need of protection and support.[2] Legal recognition, provision of support and supervision of such households consequently are themes continuously resonating in various international fora.[3]

The South African Children's Act 38 of 2005[4] is the first national legislation in Africa which comprehensively deals with child-headed households. Most importantly, this legislation recognises these households as a form of alternative care.[5] Essentially the recognition aims to protect families and households without an adult caregiver by providing access to social grants, social services and adult supervision, and also by protection of property rights.[6] South Africa ratified the United Nations Convention on the Rights of the Child[7] and the African Charter on the Rights and Welfare of the Child[8] (hereinafter "CRC" and "ACRWC" respectively) and realised its obligations under these international instruments

* North-West University, South Africa.

** Vaal University of Technology, South Africa.

1 M. Van Donk, '"Positive" urban futures in sub-Saharan Africa: HIV/AIDS and the need for ABC (A Broader Conceptualization)', *Environment and Urbanization*, Vol. 18, No. 1, 2006, pp. 155-175 at 156.

2 S. Rosa, 'Counting on children: realising the right to social assistance for child-headed households in South Africa', Working paper Number 3 produced by the Child Rights Programme of the Children's Institute, University of Cape Town, (August) 2004, pp. 1-39 at 31.

3 D. Van Dijk & F. van Driel, 'Supporting Child-Headed Households in South Africa: Whose Best Interests?', *Journal of Southern African Studies*, Vol. 35, No. 4, 2009, pp. 915-927 at 915.

4 Hereinafter the "Children's Act".

5 C. Phillips, *Child-Headed Households: A Feasible Way Forward, or an Infringement of Children's Right to Alternative Care* (Ph.D thesis, Leiden University, 2011), p. 208.

6 J. Sloth-Nielsen, *Realising the rights of children growing up in child-headed households: A guide to laws, policies and social advocacy* (Ph.D. thesis, Leiden University, 2008), p. 77.

7 This convention was passed by the General Assembly of the United Nations in 1989 and was ratified by South Africa in June 1994.

8 The Charter was adopted in 1990 but came into force only on 29 November 1999.

by providing *inter alia* that the child's voice be heard and his/her best interests be considered as a paramount consideration in the Bill of Rights contained in the Constitution of the Republic of South Africa, 1996[9] ("the Constitution") and the Children's Act.

The Children's Amendment Act 41 of 2007[10] specifically provides that child-headed households may legally be recognised as a placement option for children. It also ensures suitable support by a supervising adult who may arrange assistance be provided. Such support may include access to financial grants on behalf of the children.[11] However, the supervising adult may not take any decisions concerning such household and the children in the household without consulting the child heading the household; and bearing in mind the age, maturity and stage of development of the other children, also those other children.[12] Despite this requirement, the children are generally in a subordinate position vis-à-vis the adult supervisor, and anecdotal evidence shows that they do not openly question or dispute the adult supervisor's opinions or decisions.[13]

Various issues are raised by the appointment of the supervising adult. Such include, *inter alia,* the nature of the legal relationship between the child heading the household *qua* primary care-giver and the supervising adult. The extent to which the voice of the child is heard on the one hand but also whether the supervising adult is bound to give effect to the child's voice are issues that come to the fore. Extensive qualitative research among child-headed households in the Port Elizabeth area shows that adult support does not greatly contribute to the well-being of children and young people[14] – children often are not consulted about the administration of grants which were collected on their behalf, are not taken seriously or are even worse off after adult interventions. As a result, many of these children experience a sense of helplessness over their situation.

---

9 Hereinafter the "Constitution".

10 Hereinafter the "Amendment Act".

11 Section 137(5):
(a) The child heading the household, or the adult contemplated in subsection (2) may collect and administer for the child-headed household any social security grant or other grant in terms of the Social Assistance Act, 2004 (Act No. 13 of 2004) or other assistance to which the household is entitled.
(b) An adult that collects and administers money for a child-headed household as contemplated in paragraph (a) is accountable in the prescribed manner to the organ of state or the non-governmental organisation that designated him or her to supervise the household.
See also Van Dijk & Van Driel, op cit, n. 3, p. 283.

12 Section 137(6): The adult referred to in subsection (2) may not take any decisions concerning such household and the children in the household without consulting:
(a) the child heading the household; and
(b) given the age, maturity and stage of development of the other children, also those other children.

13 S.M. Mogotlane, M.E., Chauke, G.H. van Rensburg, S.P. Human & C.M. Kganakga, 'A situational analysis of child-headed households in South Africa', *Curationis*, Vol. 33, No. 3, 2010, pp. 24-32 at 26.

14 D.A. Van Dijk, *Beyond their age. Coping of children and young people in child-headed households in South Africa.* Leiden: African Studies Centre (Ph.D. thesis, Leiden University, 2008), p. 275.

II BACKGROUND

In Africa, orphaned and vulnerable children are traditionally cared for by family members, but the vastly increasing number of children in need of alternative care has become an overwhelming burden for many families.[15] With a total of 22.5 million people infected towards the end of 2009, sub-Saharan Africa remains the region most seriously affected by HIV/AIDS, with the highest number of AIDS-related deaths. The majority of these deaths result in children being deprived of one or both parents and as a result in need of alternative care. By 2009, more than 56 million children in sub-Saharan Africa had lost one or both parents due to a variety of causes and the number of children without parental care is currently still on the increase, predominantly in Eastern and Southern Africa.[16] In some households, alternative care is being increasingly provided not solely by adult members of the extended family, but also by children.[17] Unfortunately most African states do not have resources to provide conventional forms of alternative care as recognised by the CRC and the ACRWC.

A child-headed household essentially is one in which a child has taken on the core of parental responsibilities over a longer period of time. Such responsibility may even include care for an incapacitated caregiver. The responsibilities of a child heading a household are significant and far reaching, in that he/she is in charge of taking the day-to-day decisions in addition to being the decision-maker in important matters concerning the household. The onus of providing necessary material and immaterial support rests solely on that child. It is clear that in a child-headed household the role of the caregiver is being assumed by a child as the head of the household.[18]

Both in research reports and in policy documents, the definitions of child-headed households vary widely. A household may be defined as a group of people (irrespective of

15 Phillips, op cit, n. 5, p. 10.

16 H. Meintjes, 'Orphans of the AIDS epidemic? The extent, nature and circumstances of child-headed households in South Africa', *AIDS Care*, Vol. 22, No. 1, 2010, pp. 40-49 at 40.

17 Sloth-Nielsen points to the finer distinction made in the relevant literature: "Some authors distinguish between child-headed households and adolescent headed households." An appropriate response to the situation would depend on whether the person heading the household needs more intensive support or less. Sometimes children still have caregivers, who are terminally ill with HIV/AIDS, though not strictly speaking orphans would be in the category of child-headed households. When parent(s) become too sick to do what is necessary, these children assume the responsibility of heading the household. As Sloth-Nielsen puts it: "child headed households in which there is no effective adult caregiver generally do the same as families: work to support siblings, get food, clothing and shelter, and deal with the emotional well-being of their members". J. Sloth-Nielsen, *Realising the rights of children growing up in child-headed households: A guide to laws, policies and social advocacy*, Community Law Centre, University of the Western Cape, 2004.

18 D. Donald & G. Clacherty, 'Developmental vulnerabilities and strengths of children living in child-headed households: a comparison with children in adult-headed households in equivalent impoverished communities', *African Journal of AIDS Research*, Vol. 4, No. 1, 2005, pp. 21-28 at 21.

whether they are related by blood, marriage or adoption)[19] sharing shelter and food, who are involved in continuous social interaction based on loyalty and authority[20] and where there is a division of tasks and roles. Apart from a group of people sharing a housing unit, a single person occupying a dwelling on his own may also be regarded as a household.[21]

To date, the United Nations Committee on the Rights of the Child's General Guidelines[22] forms the only international instrument to refer specifically to child-headed households. The definition provided in paragraph 37 defines such a household as a living arrangement consisting of two or more siblings who have lost their parents or other caregivers, in which no adults are present and where the oldest child is to be "[b]oth willing and deemed capable of acting as the household head".[23]

South Africa is the first country in Africa to regulate the subject of child-headed households in national legislation and to make provision for legal recognition of these households as a form of alternative care.[24] Characteristics that are required for such a household to be recognised by the Department of Social Development[25] include: the parent or primary caregiver of the household being terminally ill or deceased; no adult family member being available to provide care and support; and a child having assumed the role of primary caregiver in respect of a child or children in the household by taking responsibility for the provision of food, clothing, and psycho-social support.[26] This exposition accepts the fact that a child-headed household may have adult members, but the key issue is that a child is the one responsible for the day-to-day upkeep of the household.

Statistics South Africa defines a household as a person or a group of persons who occupy a common dwelling for at least four days a week and who provide themselves jointly with food and other essentials for living.[27]

A definition of a child-headed household by the Children's Amendment Act reads as follows:

---

19 H. Meintjes, K. Hall, D.H. Marera, & A. Boulle, 'Orphans of the AIDS epidemic? The extent, nature and circumstances of child-headed households in South Africa', *AIDS Care*, Vol. 22, No. 1, 2010, pp. 40-49.

20 Z. Mkhize, *Social functioning of a child-headed household and the role of social work* (Unpublished DPhil Dissertation, Pretoria, University of South Africa, 2006).

21 US Census Bureau 2003, p. 14.

22 Hereafter the "UN General Guidelines".

23 Phillips, op cit, n. 5.

24 M. Couzens & F.N. Zaal, 'Legal Recognition for Child-Headed Households: An Evaluation of the Emerging South African Framework', *International Journal of Children's Rights*, Vol. 17, No. 2, 2009, pp. 299-320.

25 Hereafter the "DSD".

26 E.R. Munro et al, 'The contribution of the United Nations Convention on the Rights of the Child to understanding and promoting the interests of young people making the transition from care to adulthood', *Children and Youth Services Review*, Vol. 33, No. 12, 2011, pp. 2417-2423.

27 Stats SA, 1998:12.

137. (1) A provincial head of social development may recognise a household as a child-headed household if—

(a) the parent, guardian or care-giver of the household is terminally ill, has died or has abandoned the children in the household;
(b) no adult family member is available to provide care for the children in the household;
(c) a child over the age of 16 years has assumed the role of care-giver in respect of the children in the household; and
(d) it is in the best interest of the children in the household.

It is suggested that this definition is comprehensive and in line with the Guidelines for the Alternative Care of Children adopted recently by the United Nations General Assembly.[28] The Act furthermore makes it clear that this legal recognition is aimed at the protection of families without an adult caregiver through access to grants, provision of social services and the appointment of adult supervision, as well as protection of property rights[29] for them.

III LEGAL FRAMEWORK

A *Care in Terms of the Constitution, the Children's Act and International Instruments*

A child's right to care is constitutionally enshrined in the Bill of Rights. Care is also extensively defined in the Children's Act. The Constitution contains a dedicated children's rights clause in the Bill of Rights[30] and several rights[31] contained in section 28 are relevant to children growing up in child-headed households. True to their constitutional nature, these rights also relate to the state's obligations towards children growing up in, and heading such a household.[32] Section 28(1)(b) of the Constitution stipulates that anyone below the age of 18 is considered to be a child[33] and that children have the right to family

28 UN Committee on the Rights of the Child, CRC/C/38, 1996 UN Committee on the Rights of the Child, General Guidelines regarding the Form and Contents of Periodic Reports to be submitted by States Parties under article 44, paragraph 1(b), of the Convention, 1996, CRC/C/38, 1996.

29 Sloth-Nielsen, op cit, n. 17, p. 77.

30 Hereinafter "the Bill".

31 *Bhe and Others v. Khayelitsha Magistrate and Others*, 2005 1 BCLR 1 (CC) para. 52.

32 L. Stewart, 'Interpreting and Limiting the Basic Socio-Economic Rights of Children in Cases Where They Overlap with the Socioeconomic Rights of Others', *South African Journal on Human Rights*, Vol. 24, No. 3, 2017, pp. 472-492 at 473.

33 Section 28(3) of the Constitution.

or alternative care.[34] Where family or parental care is inadequate[35] or non-existent, or where a child has been removed from the family environment, section 28(1)(b)[36] indicates that children have the right to alternative care.[37] Section 28 of the Constitution provides an important benchmark for the protection of children, with the child's best interests being of paramount importance and based on principles derived from international law on children's rights.[38]

Section 1 of the Children's Act elaborates on the concept of care by providing as follows:

> "care", in relation to a child, includes, where appropriate -
> (a) within available means, providing the child with –
> (i) a suitable place to live;
> (ii) living conditions that are conducive to the child's health, well-being and development; and
> (iii) the necessary financial support;
> (b) safeguarding and promoting the well-being of the child;
> (c) protecting the child from maltreatment, abuse, neglect, degradation, discrimination, exploitation and other physical, emotional or moral harm or hazards;
> (d) respecting, protecting, promoting and securing the fulfillment of, and guarding against any infringement of, the child's right set out in the Bill of Rights and the principles set out in Chapter 2 of this Act;

34 Means the care of a child in accordance with section 6 of the *Children's Act.*

35 *The Government of the Republic of South Africa v. Grootboom*, 2001 1 SA 46 (CC). As confirmed in the *Grootboom* case, the right to alternative care only arises where existing parental and family care is seriously deficient or non-existent.

36 Section 28(1)(b) of the Constitution provides as follows:
1. Every child has the right –
(a) ...
(b) to family care or parental care, or to appropriate alternative care when removed from the family environment; ...

37 The failure of the CRC Committee and the African Committee of Experts on the Rights and Welfare of the Child to adopt any explicit general comment or explanation regarding the interpretation and implementation of the right to alternative care, and special protection and assistance, may also have contributed to the lack of understanding of state obligations under the relevant articles. The exponential increase of children who are deprived of their family environment in various parts of Africa, and, especially, the recent movement to recognise various new forms of alternative care of children, including child-headed households, require greater importance to be given to properly understanding and implementing the right to alternative care, and special protection and assistance of children who are deprived of their family environment. F.N. Zaal & C.R. Matthias, 'Children in need of care and maintenance order', *in* C.J. Davel & A. Skelton (Eds.), *Commentary on the Children's Act*, Cape Town, Juta, 2007, pp. 9-3.

38 *Minister of Welfare and Population Development v. Fitzpatrick*, 2000 3 SA 422 (CC) and *S v. M* (Centre for Child Law as Amicus Curiae), 2008 3 SA 232 (CC).

(e) guiding, directing and securing the child's education and upbringing, including religious and cultural education and upbringing, in a manner appropriate to the child's age, maturity and stage of development;
(f) guiding, advising and assisting the child in decisions to be taken by the child in a manner appropriate to the child's age, maturity and stage of development.

The provisions of the Constitution and the Children's Act leave little doubt that the duty to care for a child no longer arises from common law principles but from the Children's Act instead.[39] Any measures to provide care and protection to children deprived of their family environment must be designed to fulfil the purpose of article 20[40] of the CRC and article 25[41] of the ACRWC, which is to realise the full range of the rights of children in particularly vulnerable situations due to their lack of family environment. The social reality that a child has essentially taken on the care of other children in a child-headed household brings this phenomenon in line with the exposition respectively in article 20 of the CRC and 25 of the ACRWC of alternative care. This viewpoint is further supported by legal reviews of South Africa and Namibia that recognise child-headed households as a form of alternative care. The Children's Act defines a caregiver as any person other than a parent or guardian who factually cares for a child and includes a foster parent; a person who cares for a child with the implied or expressed consent of a parent or guardian of the child; a person who cares for a child whilst the child is in temporary safe care; the person at the head of a child and youth care centre where a child has been placed; the person at the head of a shelter; a child and youth care worker who cares for a child who is without appropriate family care in the community; and the child as head of a child-headed household. Section 137(1)(c)[42] specifically provides that a household headed by a child may statutorily be recognised as such if a child over the age of sixteen years has assumed the role of primary

39 *Heystek v. Heystek*, 2002 2 SA 754 (T) 757E-G. The new position was explained as follows: "The Constitutional notion of parental care and the paramountcy of the best interest of the child require an attitudinal shift from an antiquated Germanic parent and child relationship, which formed the substratum of the common law, to the rights of the child, which includes parental care and family care. Common law needs to be aligned to serve the constitutional imperatives of the child in a heterogeneous society."
40 Article 20 (children deprived of family environment): Children who cannot be looked after by their own family have a right to special care and must be looked after properly, by people who respect their ethnic group, religion, culture and language.
41 Article 25: Children who are separated from their parents should get special protection and should be provided with alternative family care. States should also take all possible steps to trace and re-unite children with parents.
42 A child over the age of 16 years has assumed the role of care-giver in respect of the children in the household; Children's Amendment Act No. 41 of 2007.

care-giver.[43] It is clear that the child assumes the role as primary caregiver and not a supervisor.

1 The Role of the Supervisor

The Children's Act requires that children in a child-headed household be supported by an adult acting as a supervisor and who is appointed by a children's court, an organ of state or a non-governmental organisation as determined by the provincial head of social development. The mandate of the supervisor is to ensure the children's best interests. The adult should possess the requisite competence to provide the household with supervision and carry out his responsibilities[44] in accordance with the court's instructions. The duties[45] of the adult supervisor are clear and it appears that the functions these supervising adults fulfil can also be considered as care in terms of the Children's Act although it seems that the definition of caregiver does not make a provision to include the supervising adult. Therefore one can assume that the supervising adult is acting solely as supervisor.

Sections 137(5) and (6) stipulate:

> (5) (b) An adult that collects and administers money for a child-headed household as contemplated in paragraph (a) is accountable in the prescribed manner to the organ of state or the non-governmental organisation that designated him or her to supervise the household.
>
> (6) The adult referred to in subsection (2) may not take any decisions concerning such household and the children in the household without consulting—

---

43 For purposes hereof, no attention will be paid to the position where the child heading the household is less than sixteen years old.

44 National Guidelines for Statutory Services to Child-Headed Households: The guidelines should be read together with the Children's Act No. 38 of 2005 as amended and the Policy Framework for Orphans and Other Children Made Vulnerable by HIV and AIDS in South Africa. The guidelines clarifies the responsibilities of a supervising adult as follows. The supervising adult must be made aware of his or her statutory responsibilities, which include: the collection and administration of money (social security and other grants) and other assistance to which the child-headed household is entitled; being accountable to the organ of state or non-governmental organisation that designated him or her to supervise the household; consulting the child heading the household and other children in the household provided they are of sufficient age, maturity and stage of development. The supervising adult does not have to reside in the household with the children but should be accessible to the household and visit the household periodically (not less than once every 2 weeks) to support the children and to fulfil the duties prescribed in the regulations to the Act.

45 Regulation 55 of the Children's Act list the various duties that a supervising adult must fulfil. Section 137 provides:
(3) The supervising adult must
  (a) perform the duties as prescribed in relation to the household; and
  (b) be a fit and proper person to supervise a child-headed household.
(4) A person unsuitable to work with children is not a fit and proper person to supervise a child-headed household.

(a) the child heading the household; and (b) given the age, maturity and stage of development of the other children, also those other children.

2 The Child as Care-Giver

The Amendment Act and the regulations place certain responsibilities specifically on the child as caregiver. These include:

- the responsibility to collect and administer any social security grants for the child-headed household or grants in terms of the Social Assistance Act 13 of 2004 or any other assistance to which the household is entitled in terms of section 137(5)(a);[46]
- to make day-to-day decisions relating to the household and the children in the household according to section 137(7);[47] and
- to report, together with other children in the child-headed household and bearing in mind their age and maturity, the supervising adult to the organ of state or non-governmental organisation if the child or children are not satisfied with the manner in which the supervising adult is performing his or her duties in terms of section 137(8).

3 Conclusion

Sociological reality leads to the inevitable conclusion that the formation of child-headed households is unavoidable and that with appropriate support these households should be accepted as a care option. They are deemed to have positive characteristics in that siblings are able to remain together. Remaining in such households apparently also coincides with the wishes of the children involved. Despite the risks these children are exposed to, the overburdening of traditional social safety nets and the unavailability of other alternative care options increasingly lead to these households being viewed as a viable solution. Within a child-headed household a child has taken on the care for other children. Factually this role falls within the ambit of the statutory exposition of alternative care. The child heading the household acts as a caregiver and falls within the definition of primary caregiver as stipulated in the Children's Act – he/she is therefore considered to be any person other than the parent or guardian, who de facto provides a(nother) child with day-to-day care. The supervising adult on the other hand performs the duties as prescribed in relation to the household and must be a fit and proper person to supervise a child-headed household. The role of the supervisor is confined to collecting and administering money for the child-

46 Section 5(a): "The child heading the household, or the adult contemplated in subsection (2) may collect and administer for the child-headed household any social security grant or other grant in terms of the Social Assistance Act, 2004 (Act No. 13 of 2004) or other assistance to which the household is entitled."

47 The Children's Act defines the Primary Caregiver: This is a person who has the parental responsibility or right to care for the child and who exercises that responsibility and right. A person older than 16 years, whether or not related to a child, who takes primary responsibility for meeting the daily care needs of that child (Social Assistance Act, No. 13 of 2004).

headed household and only to act as supervisor. He/she may not take any decisions concerning such household and the children in the household without consulting the child heading the household as primary caregiver and also, bearing in mind the age, maturity and stage of development of the other children, also those other children.

B Financial Grants

As a way of alleviating poverty among orphans, child-headed households and other children who qualify in terms of certain criteria, the government has allocated social assistance in the form of grants. Section 27(1)(c) of the Bill of Rights provides that "[e]veryone has the right to access social security, including, if they are unable to support themselves and their dependants". It obliges the State to take reasonable legislative and other measures within its available resources to achieve the progressive realisation of each of these rights. Children in child-headed households are equally entitled to social assistance in much the same way as children living with adult caregivers. The equality clause contained in section 9 of the Bill of Rights[48] and the dignity clause contained in section 10[49] provide the constitutional framework against which to measure socio-legal problems associated with child poverty. These constitutional provisions also serve as impetus for further legislative measures to protect the rights of children living in child-headed households. The provision of grants by the Department of Social Development in terms of section 137 of the Social Assistance Act 13 of 2004 which may be accessed by children in child-headed households flows from this constitutional and legislative obligation upon the State. There are general qualifying requirements for these grants, however.[50]

---

48 Section 9 of the Constitution provides:
(1) Everyone is equal before the law and has the right to equal protection and benefit of the law.
(2) Equality includes the full and equal enjoyment of all rights and freedoms. To promote the achievement of equality, legislative and other measures designed to protect or advance persons, or categories of persons, disadvantaged by unfair discrimination may be taken.
(3) The state may not unfairly discriminate directly or indirectly against anyone on one or more grounds, including race, gender, sex, pregnancy, marital status, ethnic or social origin, colour, sexual orientation, age, disability, religion, conscience, belief, culture, language and birth.
(4) No person may unfairly discriminate directly or indirectly against anyone on one or more grounds in terms of subsection (3). National legislation must be enacted to prevent or prohibit unfair discrimination.
(5) Discrimination on one or more of the grounds listed in subsection (3) is unfair unless it is established that the discrimination is fair …

49 This provision in the Constitution reads that everyone has inherent dignity and the right to have their dignity respected and protected.

50 Regulation 8(c) added by regulation 2 of Government Notice R556 of 2011 of the Social Assistance Act. The applicant must be a South African citizen, permanent resident or refugee (when applying for Foster Care, Disability and Care Dependency grants); be resident in South Africa at the time of application; not be maintained in an institution funded by the state; and not be in receipt of another social grant in respect of him/herself.

In terms of the legislation, a child heading a household who is over 16 years of age can apply for a Child Support Grant or a Care Dependency Grant[51] on behalf of younger children in the household, provided that he/she has a bar-coded identity document. The supervising adult[52] may however in terms of section 137 of the Children's Amendment Act collect and administer any social security grant or other grant provided for by the Social Assistance Act[53] or other assistance to which the household is entitled, when it is not possible for the child who heads the household to do so.[54] However, as indicated above, he/she may not take any decisions concerning such household and the children in the household without consulting the child heading the household and other children in the household bearing in mind their maturity and stage of development.[55]

As mentioned, the child heading the family and the supervising adult may apply for and administer any grant or assistance the household is eligible for. Where the designated adult performs the statutory prescribed tasks, he/she is accountable to a relevant NGO or a government organ. For the purposes of accountability, the supervising adult must, in consultation with the members of the household:

- develop a monthly expenditure plan reflecting the available financial resources and the payments;
- ensure that the monthly expenditure plan is signed by the child at the head of the household; and
- submit the monthly expenditure plan, duly signed by the organ of state or the non-governmental organisation, as the case may be, together with original documentation, receipts, invoices and other documentation that may serve as proof of the expenditure incurred.

---

51 The Social Assistance Act defines social grants as: "a child support grant, a care dependency grant, a foster child grant, a disability grant, an older person's grant, a war veteran's grant and a grant-in-aid".

52 Section 137(2) stipulates that the supervising adult must be appointed by (a) a children's court; or (b) an organ of state or a non-governmental organisation determined by the provincial head of social development.

53 Hereinafter the "Social Assistance Act".

54 Section 137(5)(a): "The child heading the household or the adult contemplated in subsection (2) may collect and administer for the child-headed household any social security grant or other grant in terms of the Social Assistance Act, 2004 (Act No. 13 of 2004) or other assistance to which the household is entitled."

55 This provision once again enhances the principle of child participation in matters affecting children as is provided for in the Children's Act.

In addition to the exposition of the statutory obligations set out above, the UN Guidelines[56] should also be borne in mind.[57] They prescribe that all individuals providing formal alternative care for children should be monitored and reviewed by the competent authorities: "[a]uthorities should develop appropriate criteria for assessing the professional and ethical fitness of care providers and for their accreditation, monitoring and supervision".[58]

It is clear from the legislative provisions referred to, that the role of the supervising adult *qua* supervisor is primarily to collect and assist in administering the grant, together with the head of the household as caregiver, and in the best interests of the children. However, qualitative research among child-headed households in the Port Elizabeth area shows that so-called "adult support" does not greatly contribute to the well-being of children and young people, despite them supposedly being monitored and reviewed by competent authorities.

Research among 20 child-headed households in Port Elizabeth by Van Dijk and Van Driel[59] mentioned the above outlined methods of adult intervention and their actual contribution to the well-being of children and young people, and whether their needs, wishes and interests are of paramount importance and are being adhered to. An example referred to in the research relates to Marc and Janine, who were both 13 years old in 2004. They had lived alone since their grandmother had died six months earlier. They did not know any relatives but a "Granny" who was their grandmother's sister and who was living in another town with her boyfriend. A few months after the first meeting, "Granny" moved in and applied for a Foster Care Grant[60] (hereafter FCG) for both children. By 2006 "Granny" had been regularly receiving these grants. However, Janine claimed that they were not cared for properly and claimed that "Granny" had spent the money on outstanding debts and alcohol. Hence it seems that "Granny's" motives for moving in with Marc and Janine were not to care for them but rather to receive the FCGs.

In other cases, children went to live with relatives or neighbours. In one specific case, the child (Mona, aged 16) moved in with the family that had been supporting her. However, she was treated differently from the other (biological) children in the household and ceased to receive any support from the family. Although the family received a FCG, they did not

56 In 2004, the International Social Service and UNICEF expressed their concern about the fact that a number of States Parties fail to provide suitable alternatives for children without parental care. The CRC Committee was briefed on the dire need for and the feasibility of global standards for the protection and well-being of children in need of alternative care. The Committee called for guidelines to be developed to ensure the protection of children who do not or who cannot live with their parents. On 20 November 2009 – the 20th anniversary of the CRC – the Guidelines were welcomed by the UN General Assembly. Phillips, 2011.

57 Although not legally binding, the UN Guidelines should be seen as a reference text for governments, policymakers and those involved in alternative care for children. Phillips, op cit, n. 5.

58 Phillips, op cit, n. 5.

59 Van Dijk & Van Driel, op cit, n. 3, p. 283.

60 Hereinafter "FGC".

spend any money on Mona and told her she should not expect to be treated the same as the other children. This ended in altercations and Mona left that family.

It is clear that the quality of adult support is sometimes uncertain and not always in the particular child's best interests. The influence of generational constructions of subordination (children must be seen, not heard) can negatively impact on children's ability to cope; they are not supposed to oppose or directly confront an adult. They are often silenced and denied an opportunity to negotiate with adults on matters that can have a direct bearing on their lives despite having the competency. It is especially the child heading the household who may suffer negative consequences – he/she is the primary caregiver, yet has to yield to decisions of the supervisor who per the provisions of the Children's Act is not a caregiver.

C Conclusion

The Children's Amendment Act stipulates that the supervisor may not take decisions without consulting the child who is heading the household, and when relevant, other children within the household too. Despite this progressive stipulation however, children generally are in subordinate positions vis-à-vis and it is incorrect to assume that they will openly question or dispute adult opinions. Lundy's model is suggested as a roadmap to conceptualise the child's right to participation aid in negotiating with adults.[61]

61 However, Laura Lundy, Professor of International Children's Rights at the School of Education at the Queen's University of Belfast developed a participation model as an aid to having the child's voice heard. Her model provides a way of conceptualising a child's right to participation, as laid down in article 12 of the *CRC*. Lundy cautions that these references to article 12 of the *CRC* can create the impression that it is sufficient to give children an opportunity to voice their opinions, but that there is no duty actually to listen to them and give their views due weight. Furthermore, article 13 of the *CRC*, which deals with the child's right to freedom of expression, is separated from article 12 dealing with the child's right to be heard. The latter right is not about providing children with a right to self-determination or merely to voice their opinion but is concerned with the involvement of children in decision making. Owing to the risk of unduly diluting the content of the right to participate, measures should be in place to ensure that, in implementing this right, attention is given to all its dimensions. Lundy proposes a new model to conceptualise the right. It is Lundy's opinion that the two key elements of the right to participate - the right to express a view and the right to have the view - must be given due weight. She avers that, to implement article 12 of the *CRC*, attention should be given to four factors, namely space, voice, audience and influence. The Lundy model outlines four chronological steps in the realisation of a child's right to participate. First, "space": children must be provided with the opportunity to express a view in a space that is safe and inclusive. Second, "voice": children must be facilitated to express their view. Third, "audience": the view must be listened to. Fourth, "influence": the view must be acted upon as appropriate, and the reasons for the decision taken must be communicated to the child. Children do not have the definitive say in the decision-making process, but their views should be given due weight, having regard to their age and maturity.

IV Conclusion

Although there are issues in relation to the statutory regulation of child-headed households in South Africa, it should still be viewed as progressive in nature and of relevance in a society where a child being the head of a household is not a foreign phenomenon. It is clear that the voice of the child heading the household as primary caregiver should be heard by the supervising adult. The necessary reporting structures are provided for in the Children's Act as amended, should the supervising adult neglect his/her duties and not act in the best interests of the child. The concern is that reporting the supervising adult might not be realistic in a society where children are generally in subordinate positions vis-à-vis adults. The procedure to bring the supervising adult to task should be simplistic – keeping in mind that the child as head of the household and as primary caregiver is not able to perform his/her statutory duties as a result of the supervising adults' obstruction.

Guardianship for Children: Challenges in the Context of Migration

*Velina Todorova**

I Children and Current International Migration

The protection of the rights of children affected by international migration[1] has become an increasingly topical issue[2] in Europe.[3] The "refugee crisis" of 2015-17 has been defined as "the greatest humanitarian challenge to have faced the European Union since its foundation" and "that children, many of them unaccompanied by a parent, relative or guardian, are in the forefront of the crisis".[4] There is a consensus[5] that in the context of international

---

* Associate Professor, Civil and Family Law, Law Faculty, Plovdiv University 'P. Hilendarski', Member to CRC Committee.

1 Since there is no agreed definition of the term "international migrant", for definitions see: International Organization for Migration (IOM), Key Migration Terms at: https://www.iom.int/key-migration-terms.

2 As the UN Secretary General stated in his report 'Making migration work for all': "Migration is an expanding global reality. There are an estimated 258 million international migrants (which includes 25.9 million refugees and asylum seekers, representing 10.1 per cent of all international migrants). The United Nations calculates that the total number of international migrants has grown by 49 per cent since 2000, surpassing the global population growth rate of 23 per cent. As a result, migrants have gone from 2.8 per cent to 3.4 per cent of the world's population." (A/72/643 of 12 December 2017, para 3).

3 A tototal of 4.7 million people immigrated to one of the EU-28 Member States during 2015, of which an estimated 2.4 million were citizens of non-member countries, 1.4 million people with citizenship of a different EU Member State from the one to which they immigrated, around 860 thousand people who migrated to an EU Member State of which they had the citizenship (for example, returning nationals or nationals born abroad), and some 19 thousand stateless people. At least 2.8 million emigrants were reported to have left an EU Member State. Germany reported the largest total number of immigrants (1 543.8 thousand) in 2015, followed by the United Kingdom (631.5 thousand), France (363.9 thousand), Spain (342.1 thousand) and Italy (280.1 thousand). Germany reported the highest number of emigrants in 2015 (347.2 thousand), followed by Spain (343.9 thousand), the United Kingdom (299.2 thousand), France (298 thousand) and Poland (258.8 thousand). A total of 17 of the EU Member States reported more immigration than emigration in 2015, but in Bulgaria, Ireland, Greece, Spain, Croatia, Cyprus, Poland, Portugal, Romania, Latvia and Lithuania, the number of emigrants outnumbered the number of immigrants. In 2016 the situation changed. The number of asylum seekers among migrant decreased from 1,322,825 in 215 to 1,260,910 in 2016. EUROSTAT At: http://ec.europa.eu/eurostat/statistics-explained/index.php/Migration_and_migrant_population_statistics and http://appsso.eurostat.ec.europa.eu/nui/show.do?dataset=migr_asyappctza&lang=en.

4 *Children in crisis: unaccompanied migrant children in the EU*. House of Lords (Parliament of the UK), European Union Committee, 2nd Report of Session 2016–17, published on 26 July 2016, p. 3.

5 See A/72/643 of 12.12.2017, para. 17: "Child migrants also deserve special attention. A great many migrant children who experience violence, abuse and exploitation, are held in detention centres and deprived of education. Those who are separated from their families are often let down by weak guardianship systems

migration, children may be in a situation of double vulnerability, as children, and as children affected by migration who (a) are migrants themselves, either alone or with their families, (b) were born to migrant parents in countries of destination or (c) remain in their country of origin while one or both parents have migrated to another country. Additional vulnerabilities could relate to their national, ethnic or social origin; gender; sexual orientation or gender identity; religion; disability; migration or residence status; citizenship status; age; economic status; political or other opinion; or other status.[6]

The U.N. Convention on the Rights of the Child (CRC) stipulates clear legal obligations of the States Parties to respect and ensure the rights of every child within the State's territory and to all children subject to its jurisdiction (art. 2). The enjoyment of rights is not limited to children who are citizens of a State party and must therefore, if not explicitly stated otherwise in the Convention, also be available to all children - including asylum-seeking, refugee and migrant children - irrespective of their nationality, immigration status or statelessness.[7] Against these standards, various sources provide evidence of numerous protection gaps in the treatment of children in the context of international migration and of unaccompanied ones, in particular.[8]

This paper explores briefly the legal institute of "guardianship" as one of the means to assist unaccompanied migrant children in realisation of their rights. It aims also to observe the legal problems that impede the implementation of international and EU standards on guardianship at the national level, as well as to ascertain the feasibility of applying a harmonised approach to the institute, Europe-wide. My assumption is that the common historical roots of guardianship as well as the shared modern values and obligations under the CRC and the new EU asylum law package should provide a favourable basis for creating a new paradigm of guardianship in Europe. The paper starts with Roman law on guardianship and briefly presents some of the current domestic legislation of EU member states (MS) in a comparative perspective and in light of the EU acquis on asylum that is again under revision.[9] It also discusses the protection gaps in some countries resulting

and a lack of other options to protect them. Authorities can be slow to determine their status or assess their best interests, and sometimes they fail to do so altogether"; and UN GA resolution 71/1, 3 para. 32.

6 See Joint general comment No. 3 (2017) of the Committee on the Protection of the Rights of All Migrant Workers and Members of Their Families and No. 22 (2017) of the Committee on the Rights of the Child on the general principles regarding the human rights of children in the context of international migration. CMW/C/GC/3-CRC/C/GC/22, para. 3.

7 See Committee on the Rights of the Child, general comment No. 6 on Treatment of Unaccompanied and Separated Children Outside their Country of Origin. CRC/GC/2005/6, para. 12 and CMW/C/GC/3-CRC/C/GC/22, paras. 11-18.

8 See http://www.corestandardsforguardians.com/images/11/279.pdf.

9 On 4 May and 13 July 2016, the Commission submitted seven legislative proposals aimed at reforming the Common European Asylum System. This package included the recast of the Dublin Regulation and of the Eurodac Regulation, a proposal for a Regulation on the establishment of the European Union Agency for Asylum (EUAA), a proposal for a Regulation establishing a common procedure in the EU, a proposal for a Qualification Regulation, the recast of the Reception Conditions Directive and a proposal for a Regulation

from weak and insufficiently resourced migration and child protection systems attempting to handle the recent massive migration flows. One such example is Bulgaria, having faced the challenges of international migration only recently. This paper will focus on the opportunities created by the current situation of international migration in order to reinvent the old legal institution of guardianship and to modernise it in accordance with new demands.

One further preliminary remark: research has shown that there is little academic interest in the law of guardianship for children. Until very recently, it was a neglected subject of research. The recent migration flows, however, have increased enormously the volume of information and expertize on guardianship for children that could provoke a good academic perspective on the issue.

A *Guardian or a Representative*

The need for a guardian arises always in the absence of a parent or another carer from the extended family. The specific situation of some children traveling alone in the migration context was recognised and defined in 2001 under the EU acquis.[10] Soon after, the CRC Committee adopted a similar definition: "Unaccompanied children" (also called unaccompanied minors) are children (as defined in art. 1 CRC), who have been separated from both parents and other relatives and are not being cared for by an adult who, by law or custom, is responsible for doing so. 'Separated children' are children (as defined in art. 1 CRC), who have been separated from both parents, or from their previous legal or customary primary caregiver, but not necessarily from other relatives. These may, therefore, include children accompanied by other adult family members.[11]

---

establishing a Union Resettlement Framework, at: http://www.asylumineurope.org/useful-documents-and-links.

10 See Council Directive/2001/55/EC of 20.07.2001 (temporary protection), art. 2/f - "unaccompanied minors" means third-country nationals or stateless persons below the age of eighteen, who arrive on the territory of the Member States unaccompanied by an adult *responsible for them whether by law or custom*, and for as long as they are not effectively taken into the care of such a person, or minors who are left unaccompanied after they have entered the territory of the Member States. This definition was further developed mainly in order to clarify the meaning of 'law and custom'. Directive 2011/95/ of 13.12.2011 – (qualification directive), complements the definition as follows: 'unaccompanied minor' means a minor who arrives on the territory of the Member States unaccompanied by an adult responsible for him or her whether *by law or by the practice of the Member State concerned*, and for as long as he or she is not effectively taken into the care of such a person; it includes a minor who is left unaccompanied after he or she has entered the territory of the Member States' (art. 2/l). The definition is applied by the following: Directive 2013/32/EU of 26.06.2013 – (procedures directive), Directive 2013/33/EU of 26.06.2013 (reception conditions) and by Regulation (EU) No 604/2013 of 26.06.2013- Dublin 3.

11 See CRC/GC/2005/6, paras. 7-8. The Guidelines for the Alternative Care of Children, A/Res/64/142, para. 29/a/ i, ii, considers unaccompanied children as a specific subgroup of children without parental care: ".... who are outside their country of habitual residence or victims of emergency situations may be designated

Although a consensus exists on the definition of an "unaccompanied child", a commonly agreed definition of a guardian seems difficult to achieve. In addition to "guardian", the EU acquis since 2001 uses the terms "legal or other representative" and "special representative" to describe the person appointed to assist and support unaccompanied children.[12] The EU asylum pack (recast) of 2013 uses the term "representative" more consistently. This perhaps reflects the difficulty in achieving a shared notion among EU MS about the role of the guardian, the reason being that the systems involved mainly designate guardians to national children and therefore lack available guardians that have been trained to support children from different cultural and linguistic backgrounds, who have experienced trauma over the course of their journeys. Thus the representative meets the minimum required standard, ensuring at least the due process rights of children seeking asylum.

The guardian substitutes the child's parents, not so much in their caring responsibilities (which are vested on the systems for alternative care) but rather in ensuring that the best interests of the child will be given primary consideration in all decisions affecting the child.

This shift in responsibilities from care to representation of the child is also reflected in the terminology of the CRC Committee:

> [t]he appointment of a competent guardian as expeditiously as possible, serves as a key *procedural* safeguard to ensure respect for the best interests of an unaccompanied or separated child. .... [S]uch a child should only be referred to asylum or other [administrative or judicial] procedures after the appointment of ... a legal representative in addition to a guardian.[13]

The proposed new asylum EU pack (2016), however, goes back to the term "guardian".

II OLD REGULATION OF GUARDIANSHIP

The institution of guardianship known to the European legal system originates from Roman legal traditions.[14] Classical and post-classical Roman law reveals two types of guardianship

---

as: 'Unaccompanied' if they are not cared for by another relative or an adult who by law or custom is responsible for doing so; or 'Separated' if they are separated from a previous legal or customary primary caregiver, but who may nevertheless be accompanied by another relative".

12 Council Directive/ 2001/55/EC of 20.07.2001, art. 16. For more on this, see *Guardianship for children deprived of parental care - A handbook to reinforce guardianship systems to cater for the specific needs of child victims of trafficking*, FRA, 2015, pp. 13-14.

13 See CRC/GC/2005/6, para. 21 and CMW/C/GC/3-CRC/C/GC/22, para. 32/h.

14 Research claims that the influence of some aspects of Roman law can be traced also in the common law systems and this early history has had a significant impact on the development of the common law of guardianship. See A. Buti, 'The Early History of the Law of Guardianship of Children: From Rome to the

with regard to a child who is not under the authority of the *pater familias*: *tutela impuberum* (tutelage of minors[15]) and *cura minorum* (curatorship of children[16]).[17] Research also suggests that although guardianship under Roman law is intended to protect the child, the regulation focuses more on the interests of the family and of society at large.[18] *Tutela impuberum* was considered a family relation of public interest.[19] Rather, its major functions were to protect the family property, or to control girls or young women,[20] but not so much the well-being of the child concerned.

The Napoleonic Code integrated this Roman law concept and transferred it to other civil law systems, such as the Italian Civil Code followed by other legislatures (e.g. Bulgaria after 1878). The Roman law tradition was also influential in shaping early German and Austrian guardianship laws.[21] Their regulations have accepted some features of the old institution of guardianship: for example, the types of guardianship (for minors and adolescent children), the priority of testamentary guardianship, the extended family acting as guardians (with a preference for male relatives), the mother appointed as a guardian in special circumstances, voluntary guardianship, and the focus on the protection of property of the child with a special focus on the land in medieval common law.[22]

Despite its focus on the interests of the public or the adult, the guardianship still remains historically the first legal construct to provide individual protection of a child left without

Tenures Abolition Act 1660', *University of Western Sydney Law Review*, Vol. 7, No. 1, 2003, pp. 91-108 at 92.

15 Puberty was fixed in the Justinian law at fourteen for males and twelve for females. C. Sherman, *Debt of the Modern Law of Guardianship to Roman Law*, Yale Law School Legal Scholarship Repository, 1913, p. 125.

16 An individual aged 14 to 25 is fully *sui juris*, but needs counsel and help to prudently manage his affairs. Curators are special or general. Example of a special curator is the *guardian at litem* in England, ibid, p. 129.

17 For more on guardianship and its early forms, see R. Shom, *The Institutes of Roman Law*, Oxford, Clarendon Press, 1892, pp. 388-399, available at: https://archive.org/stream/institutesroman01gruegoog#page/n4/mode/2up.

18 Tutor and curator are both charged with the care of the person as well as the property of the ward. The distinction, however, lies in the position which they respectively occupy in regards to the ward's property. ... The essence of tutela is the assistance of the tutor which is required for the conclusion of juristic acts. Under the Justinian Law, the institute of the guardianship has changed in accordance with the changes in the Inheritance law, and guardians become the nearest cognates of the ward. Ibid, p. 395.

19 Guardianship in chivalry (when a tenant of land held under knight service died leaving an infant heir) did not concern itself with the welfare of vulnerable heirs. Rather, it treated them as an adjunct to their land, seeing in them not a child to be protected, but a valuable proprietary right to be exploited. Buti, op cit, n. 14, p. 5.

20 Ibid, pp. 397-398. Tutela Mulierum, although it is not found at all in the Justinianean Roman law, nor does it exist in the modern law. See also Sherman, op cit, n. 15, p. 129.

21 Buti, op cit, n. 14, pp. 9-10.

22 In contrast to early English medieval feudal law, where guardianship applied only to infants of property, the *potestas* concept in Roman times applied to all minors *sui juris*, whether they had property or not. This is also the case today, where a guardian has responsibility for a child regardless of whether they have property or not. Ibid, pp. 9-10.

the care of his/her parents, by its twofold functions – to protect the child's property (not so much their welfare), as well as to exercise the legal capacity for the child.

III Modern Developments in Guardianship Law

The Roman paradigm of guardianship has been confronted by the changing societal values and contexts in Europe for many years. For example, industrialisation paired with rising internal migration, poverty and loosened social structures, as well as the transformations of the family forms, have led to an increased public engagement with guardianship (also due to unavailability of relatives to be appointed as guardians), integration of the institute in the mandates of public authorities, as well as modification of the functions of the guardians.[23] The guardians are no longer expected to provide physical, everyday care for children as well as the care of their property. Their major role is the legal care of the child –legal representation and assistance to children in the elaborated legal procedures concerning their welfare and human rights.[24] This created a greater concern about the profile and the training of the guardians and the quality of their performance.

Another serious impact on the institution of the guardianship has come from the transfer of the function of care for children with no parental care to the state, and in particular from the development of child protection legislation, policies and practices.[25] The values context as well as international human rights commitments are also decisive factors for the past and current developments.

The specific needs of a foreign child travelling across borders unaccompanied posed a new challenge to the national systems. The systems had to adjust in order to account for relevant factors, such as background, language, culture, religion, traumatic experiences, distrust of the authorities in the host country and others.[26] This has gradually created a need for more guardians with special training.

Shaping of the modern legal institute of guardianship started at different times across Europe - for instance, in the early nineties in Germany and at the start of the 21st century in countries such as Bulgaria, Romania, Poland, and Hungary. The process is still ongoing.

23 See B. Noske, *Closing a Protection Gap. Core Standards for guardians of separated children*, German Report, 2010-2011, p. 8, at http://www.corestandardsforguardians.com/p/1/172.

24 See *Guardianship for children deprived of parental care*, op cit, n. 12, p. 15 and Noske, ibid.

25 In Germany, during the 20th century, it became common practice that the guardian merely was in charge of the ward's legal representation. Other actors carried out the actual care; see op cit, n. 24.

26 See *A tool for guardians and other actors working for the best interest of the child*, NIDOS, 2014, pp. 9-14, and *Children in crisis: unaccompanied migrant children in the EU*, p. 6.

Some countries maintain one system for all children,[27] while others have created parallel systems for national and foreign children.[28]

The regulation of guardianship is part of the civil codes of many European states. In countries that do not have civil codifications, like Bulgaria, guardianship is part of family law or of the law on persons. In addition, almost every EU MS have enacted specific regulations on guardianship for unaccompanied migrant children either as part of asylum law or of child protection legislation.

The system in **Germany** is complex and fragmented. It is established by the Civil Code (BGB, 1900) and complemented by the Youth Welfare Act,[29] the Family Act and the Asylum Proceedings Act and is currently under revision. A Draft on the Reform of Guardianship Law was published in 2016 which aimed to change the current focus from the property to the person of the child.[30] Guardianship authority was decentralised as a duty of the local governments in 1924,[31] various forms of guardians for minors became subject to regulation and the service was largely becoming professional and employment-based, rather than family-based.[32] The trend is to separate the legal care of the child (representation) from custody (care) although this is still being debated.[33] All guardians are appointed by the court following proposals from the Youth office. Because guardian and social services are merged, competences and responsibilities are becoming blurred.

The system in **Austria** is also inclusive for all children, not only for national ones. Responsibility for guardianship lies with the Children and Youth Service Authorities (art. 207 Civil Code).[34] The asylum-seeking unaccompanied children are appointed a legal

27 For example, Germany and Italy. See a study coordinated by France Terre d'asile: *Right to asylum for unaccompanied minors in the European Union, Comparative study in the 27 EU countries*, 2012, pp. 25-36.

28 Sweden, the Netherlands, Belgium and the countries from Central and Eastern Europe. Ibid.

29 The German Youth Welfare Act explicitly includes the specific group of separated children: "The Youth Welfare Office is authorized and obligated to take over custodial care if [...] an alien child or an alien youth comes to Germany unaccompanied and if neither the person having the care and custody of the child nor the legal guardian sojourn in Germany." Op cit, n 23, p. 8.

30 See H. Oberloskamp, 'Plans of the German Government to Reform the Law of Guardianship for Minors: A presentation of the present and the future law in Germany,' *LeXonomica*, Vol. 9, No. 1, June 2017, pp. 52-54.

31 As a consequence, youth welfare can differ significantly from federal state to federal state and even from municipality to municipality. Ibid.

32 Although until the 19th century mostly relatives took over guardianship for orphans, after the change of the Civil Code (1900) in 1924, the newly established Jugendamt (Youth Office) has taken the duty over the guardianship and the institution could even have become a guardian of a child in the absence of other options. See op cit, n. 26, p. 8 and Oberloskamp, op cit, n. 30, p. 52.

33 Legal care (curatorship) (§ 1915 BGB) does not mean physical and mental care, but the care concerning legal questions of a person. Legal care has various aspects. It usually distinguishes between the legal care of the person and the legal care of a person's property. Oberloskamp, op cit, n. 30, p. 53.

34 As the Austrian Supreme Court clarified in its decision on 19 October 2005, the system applies to all minors irrespective of their age and no differentiation can be made between Austrian citizens and foreign nationals. See S. Koppenberg, *Unaccompanied Minors in Austria – legislation, practices and statistics*, IOM, 2014, pp. 36-37.

advisor who acts as a temporary legal representative with regard to the asylum procedure and the Youth Welfare Authorities manage the guardianship (i.e. responsibility for care and education, asset management and legal representation in areas other than the asylum procedure).

Spain also has a system based on the Civil Code, involving a decentralised appointment of a guardian by the administration, and reliance on NGOs or religious institutions which are financed by Minors' Protection Services. It implies the responsibility of protecting and promoting the child's best interests, guaranteeing the minor's access to education and proper training, legal assistance or interpretation services when necessary, enabling the child's social integration and providing him or her with adequate care.[35]

The Civil Code is the legal basis of guardianship in **the Netherlands.** The country is unique in the EU with its special guardianship authority for separated children - Foundation NIDOS,[36] which is a quasi-autonomous non-governmental organisation, which executes governmental tasks and is funded by the government. Officially, NIDOS is the only guardian of all separated children in the Netherlands, since the custody of all these children is granted to the organization.

Belgium has a separate law governing guardianship for unaccompanied children, and like the Netherlands, has a centralised, but government based, system - a National Guardianship Office to the Ministry of Justice.[37] The Office is responsible for the identification of unaccompanied minors, the selection and assignment of guardians, and monitoring and coordination of their work. Guardians can be either "volunteer-guardians" (the majority of guardians) or "employee-guardians" (for example, employees of NGOs such as Caritas International or Flemish Red Cross). After special training, the guardians are tasked to search for a "durable solution" for the minor's situation (i.e. family reunification, return to the country of origin or another country, prolonged stay in Belgium), looking after the minor's interests in all aspects of life (concerning the minor's residence permit, the asylum procedure, reception of the child, care, education), and representing the minor in all legal matters (e.g. accompanying the minor during the interviews of the asylum

35 At http://www.asylumineurope.org/reports/country/spain/legal-representation-unaccompanied-children.

36 Article 1:253 CC provides the basis for the appointment of temporary custody to NIDOS over separated children who are awaiting a decision on their asylum application. The court appoints a guardian when the parents are (temporarily) incapable of executing their authority or when there is uncertainty about the existence and/or residence of the parents. After the Child Care and Protection Board (Raad voor de Kinderbescherming) sends a certificate of "no objection" to the court, temporary custody will be granted to NIDOS. See M. Goeman & C. van Os, *Closing a Protection Gap*, op cit, n. 23, Dutch Report, DCI-ECPAT the Netherlands, 2010, at http://www.corestandardsforguardians.com/images/11/292.pdf.

37 See K. Fournier, *Closing a Protection Gap*, op cit, n 23, Belgian Report, Service Droit des Jeunes, 2010-2011, at http://www.corestandardsforguardians.com/images/22/321.pdf and *Implementing the Core Standards for Guardians of Separated Children in Europe Country Assessment*: Belgium, at https://ec.europa.eu/justice/grants/results/daphne-toolkit/en/content/closing-protection-gap-20-implementing-core-standards-guardians-separated-children-europe.

procedure). Their task is complete when the minor leaves Belgium or when he/she attains the age of majority.[38]

In **Italy**, although guardianship is generally governed by the Civil Code,[39] the appointment of guardians for separated children is partly regulated by common child protection law (which applies also to Italian children), and partly by immigration and asylum laws.[40] Upon notification, a guardian is appointed by the Tribunal-Guardianship Judge who is also responsible for the supervision and monitoring of the guardians. Guardians are usually social workers from municipalities.

The legal development in **France** has followed a similar trajectory. Competent to appoint a guardian is the guardianship judge, but the Public Prosecutor, once notified by the Prefecture, should appoint an *ad hoc* administrator (legal representative), often provided by Red Cross and other voluntary associations.[41] The *ad hoc* administrator is appointed to represent the child only in administrative and judicial procedures related to the asylum claim. This person is not tasked to ensure the child's welfare the way a guardian would be.[42]

Sweden, like Belgium, has a separate law on guardianship for unaccompanied children that has developed along with the asylum law.[43] The system of guardians is volunteer based and decentralised – it is coordinated at the local level[44] but is monitored by the National Board of Health and Welfare. Separated children are entitled to be represented by an appointed guardian soon after their arrival into Sweden throughout the asylum process until they receive a residence permit, need to leave the country or turn 18. Some children keep their guardian although they have gotten a residence permit, as the municipality can ask the guardian to continue his or her assignment until a Special Appointed Custodian has been appointed.[45]

---

38 I. Derluyn & E. Broekaert, 'Unaccompanied refugee children and adolescents: The glaring contrast between a legal and a psychological perspective', *International Journal of Law and Psychiatry*, Vol. 31, 2008, pp. 319-330.

39 The guardianship is a legal institution aimed at protecting personal and economic interests of the child when both his/her parents are dead or when for some other reason they cannot fulfil their parental responsibility art. 343, Italian Civil Code).

40 See A. Furia & G. Gallizia, *Closing a Protection Gap*, op cit, n. 23, Italian Report, DCI –Italy, 2010-2011, pp. 13-18.

41 See CRC/C/FRA/5, paras. 544 – 546.

42 At http://www.asylumineurope.org/reports/country/france/asylum-procedure/guarantees-vulnerable-groups-asylum-seekers/age-assessment.

43 The Reception of Asylum Seekers and Others Act (1994), the Social Service Act (SoL 2001), and the Act on Guardians for Separated Children (2005). See *Closing the Protection Gap*, op cit, n. 23, Swedish Report on Guardianship, 2010-2011, at http://www.corestandardsforguardians.com/images/11/294.pdf.

44 The guardian should be appointed by the office of the Chief Guardian in the municipality where the child is living. Ibid.

45 The guardian should be involved in all decisions affecting the child – accommodation, care plan, schooling and finances for separated children, etc. Ibid.

The **Central and Eastern Europe** (CEE) MS have similar experiences in developing laws and practices for guardianship. To develop the mere concept of guardianship for a child who has parents but has been separated by them in the context of international migration has been a major difficulty in the region. These states have faced migration only recently and have tried to accommodate the new demands within the traditional guardianship institution. The weak child protection systems and especially the heated political debates and the resistance of political leaders to accept migrants have slowed down the changes.[46] The decisive push factors have been the need to adhere to the EU acquis as well as the pressure from experts and civil society advocating for the implementation of the international human rights standards.

The **Czech** Civil Code (2012) links the appointment of a guardian to the legal or physical absence of parents (section 928 and subsequent). The tutor or the guardian is an individual, or if such a person is not available, the court appoints an appropriate institution – usually an authority responsible for the social and legal protection of children. There are two types of guardians for children seeking international protection. A temporary guardian is appointed for the period of administrative proceedings, whose role ends with the court's appointment of a so-called "residency guardian".[47] It is suggested that in practice, the function of a guardian is administered by the social workers of the institution for social and legal protection of children with various levels of experience, but could also be entrusted onto volunteers, or staff at NGOs or placement centres.[48] The absence of conflict of interest is one criteria taken into consideration regarding the appointment of a guardian. There is no procedure for recruitment, placement and supervision of guardians.

In **Poland**, a legal guardian can be appointed by the family court for a foreign child whose parents are unknown dead, or deprived of parental rights, but not if the parents reside in the territory of another country.[49] The notion of an unaccompanied child has become part of asylum law. It provides for appointment of a representative, rather than a guardian, on the legal grounds for an application for international protection and participation in the procedures. The regulation and practice of guardianship and care is complex – carers and social workers could be in both positions as social guardians and legal guardians.

The **Bulgarian** guardianship law as part of family law accommodates a concept that dates back at 1949. It sets out an exhaustive list of grounds related to parents that must be satisfied in order to establish guardianship, (the same as in Czechia and Poland). This

46 Silent in some countries like Bulgaria, and outspoken in others like Hungary.

47 See I. Štorková, *Reception of Children on the move in the Czech Republic*, Kids Empowerment, 2017, pp. 6-8.

48 IOM, *Overview of guardianship systems for unaccompanied minor asylum-seekers in Central Europe*, Synthesis report, 2012, pp. 11-12.

49 See Nobody's Children Foundation, *Situation Analysis of Children on the Move in Poland regarding International and National Migration. Children in Foster Care*, 2013, pp. 23-24.

makes it impossible under family law to appoint a guardian for an unaccompanied migrant child. The mayor of the municipality has the guardianship authority.[50] After years of hesitation a representative figure was installed into the Law on Asylum and Refugees in 2015 transposing Directive 2011/95/EU (Qualification Directive). The representative seems to have functions limited to the asylum procedure.[51]

In **Hungary**, the Civil Code (2014) does not change the paradigm of guardianship of children. The notion of unaccompanied children has been integrated into the Child Protection Act (1997, amended in 2011). The institution responsible for guardianship is centralised and two types of guardians are possible (for the procedure or for the care) but there is no clear distinction between care and guardianship. In order to prevent eventual conflicts of interests between the child and the head of the child protection facility previously appointed as guardian, the law was amended in 2014 to allow the child protection guardian to take over the guardianship.[52]

The comparison between the national systems suggests that the "old democracies" in EU are maintaining traditional guardianship to accommodate the new demands, relying on their experience with migration, established child protection systems and democratic culture.[53] Their systems have the flexibility to entrust the function of guardian to various subjects, such as persons (volunteers, professionals) or NGOs, in the factual absence of a parent. In countries such as Germany, the Netherlands, Belgium, Finland, Sweden, and Austria, the law stipulates that every foreign unaccompanied child coming into the territory, irrespective of their migratory status, is entitled to have a guardian. The Netherlands and Belgium established new specialised central structures.[54] The timely appointment of a trained guardian and his/her functions still remain problematic, though. To find a balance between full-fledged guardians appointed to national children and a representative for an unaccompanied child seems to be a common difficulty too (with a few exceptions, e.g. Sweden).

50 Arts. 153-154 Family Code (2009) at https://www.mlsp.government.bg/ckfinder/userfiles/files/admobs/Family_Code.pdf.

51 See more in Bulgarian Helsinki Committee, *Annual Report on Status Determination Procedure in Bulgaria*, 2016, pp. 12-13.

52 See European commission and the Ministry of Interior, Hungary, *Policies, practices and data on unaccompanied minors in 2014.*

53 See European Migration Network Synthesis Report for the EMN, Focussed Study 2014, and *Policies, practices and data on unaccompanied minors in the EU Member States and Norway*, Synthesis Report: May 2015, p. 18.

54 NIDOS, the Dutch Guardianship Authority for unaccompanied children, has long recognised the need for cross-border cooperation at a European level and has previously made efforts to set up the European Network of Guardianship Institutions (ENGI). The NIDOS model is recognised for its expertise and experience, and for its considerable efforts to improve capacity in Europe and in EU neighbourhood countries, through sharing of expertise and training activities. NIDOS/ENGI has already coordinated some European-level (and EU funded) projects that have contributed to more effective guardianship and works on a regular basis with EASO on capacity-building. See Brussels, 20.12.2017 C (2017) 8518 final.

Adapting the systems to be inclusive for all children, but also for national ones, is still in process in other states, such as Bulgaria and Poland where only asylum-seeking children are entitled to guardianship (or to a representative). In those states it seems that appointing a guardian is still conditional on the status of the child[55] but not on his/her best interests when in need of a close responsible adult. Thus, children left behind by their migrant parents, for example in Romania and Bulgaria, cannot be entrusted to guardians, which affects many of their rights. It is also common for some states (Bulgaria and Czechia), to seek easy solutions – to appoint as a guardian a person accompanying the separated child, which could be problematic if the best interests of the child are considered.[56]

IV Some Current Problems with Guardianship

The uneven legal and institutional developments in the EU MS in the field of child protection and asylum, have resulted in fragmented systems of guardianship for unaccompanied foreign children. Although all EU MS have established specific regulation (except for the UK[57]), there is a shared understanding that a minimum common core exists at least in two specific areas that are vital for the effective functioning of the systems: the structure (the type of system and the appointment procedures), and the profile and functions of guardians.[58]

A key aspect of effective guardianship is the **timely appointment** of a trained guardian who keeps personal contact with the child and provides not only representation but is also responsible for ensuring a durable solution for the child. The systems in the Netherlands and Belgium are widely admired in this respect but are also considered as good examples for resource management and efficient cooperation with NGOs. Such developments establishes the guardian's position as a new type of child-rights profession – based on clear capacities and training, quality standards and monitoring. Other MS have built upon their decentralised systems, trying to overcome some of their shortcomings in their treatment

55 The parent should be proved missing (dead, unknown or deprived of parental rights).

56 See CRC/GC/2005/6, para. 40.

57 Despite the UN CRC Committee's recommendation (CRC/C/GBR/CO/4, §71c) to the UK to "consider the appointment of guardians to unaccompanied asylum-seekers and migrant children", the Government declared that the implementation of such a guardianship system was not planned because "in England local authorities have a statutory duty to safeguard and promote the welfare of all children regardless of their immigration status or nationality. Unaccompanied asylum seekers and migrant children have the same status and benefits as children in care and have access to an independent advocate who can represent their wishes and feelings. In Scotland, targeted and intensive support is provided for asylum seeking children-through the Scottish Guardianship Service" (CRC/C/GBR/5, paras. 224-225).

58 See *Tenth European Forum on the rights of the child - the protection of children in migration*, Report, 29-30.11.2016, pp. 45-63. Also at http://ec.europa.eu/newsroom/document.cfm? doc_id=44074.

of migrant children. The changes in Germany and Sweden are targeting management improvement and resource mobilisation for their systems.

However, almost all studies illustrate the inconsistency between the law and the realities that affects the effectiveness of the guardianship. Neither a clear timeline for the appointment of guardians exists nor a practice in consistency with the standards regarding their mandate. The legislation in all MS points out that appointment is to be made "as soon as possible", as stipulated in EU law.[59] Yet, the insufficient administrative capacity at the border and the prolonged age assessment procedures (where undertaken) cause delays. Frequently a temporary (ad hoc) guardian is appointed first. The CRC Committee states in this regard, that:

> States should appoint a guardian or adviser as soon as the unaccompanied or separated child is identified and maintain such guardianship arrangements until the child has either reached the age of majority or has permanently left the territory and/or jurisdiction of the State.[60]

The profile of guardians also varies among MS. In some jurisdictions the function is undertaken by social workers from child protection authorities or by employees of municipalities that create a risk of conflict of interests between the care provider and the individual child (CEE MS, Italy, France). Guardians may be volunteers but also professionals - a practice in place in the Netherlands, Germany, Sweden and in Belgium but not yet established in the CEE MS. Appointment of independent guardians from the employees of NGOs or other organisations (Red Cross) is considered to be good practice and is encouraged by the EU law.

The new EU asylum pack aims to harmonise not so much the structure but rather the functions of guardianship systems for unaccompanied minors and to standardise the practices. It proposes a concrete time frame:

> Responsible authorities shall, as soon as possible and not later than *five working days* from the moment when an unaccompanied minor makes an application, appoint a person or an organisation as a guardian....[61]

The proposal for EU Reception Conditions Directive (recast, 2016) lays down common criteria for the profile of the guardian: "these shall not have a verified record of child-related

59 See Directive 2013/32/EU of 26 June 2013 on common procedures (recast), art. 25, para. 1/a.

60 CRC/GC/2005/6, para. 33.

61 See Proposal for a Regulation of the European Parliament and of the Council to establish a common procedure for international protection in the Union and repealing Directive 2013/32/EU, art. 22, Brussels, 13.7.2016 COM (2016) 467final.

crimes or offenses and shall receive continuous and appropriate training ... and shall be bound by the confidentiality rules". Possible conflicts of interests should be carefully observed and "a guardian [should] not be placed in charge of a disproportionate number of unaccompanied minors at the same time that would render him or her unable to perform his or her tasks effectively".[62] Standards for performance, monitoring and complaints are also proposed.

With regard to the functions of the guardian, majority of the national laws define these in relation to parental rights and duties, which is in line with the classical notion of the institute of guardianship. This suggests that historical roots and the international law could serve as a basis for a common approach in establishing the guardian's role. In Sweden, for example, the guardian has the responsibility to decide all matters that concern the personal, financial and legal interests of the child and to represent the child in all situations in the place of the parent, while having no financial maintenance obligation or responsibility for the daily care and supervision of the child. The guardian has to approve the education and accommodation arrangements based on how well they correspond to the needs of the child.

In the Netherlands, the legal guardian has the same competencies and obligations as the natural guardian (parent). The guardian supervises the asylum procedure and is the legal representative of the separated child, taking responsibility for the upbringing and care of the minor in his/her capacity. The guardian is the case manager and contact person for everyone involved in the life of the separated child, such as the mentor, the lawyer, the teachers, foster family, etc. The clear regulation of the functions empowers guardians to interact with the range of authorities involved on an equal basis: asylum, migration, education, care and health as well as the child protection authorities. Thus the guardian could be a factor in integrating and coordinating the governmental and NGO structures in the area of child protection, with one focus (the best interests of a child). In Belgium, the tasks and responsibilities of the guardian are extensively defined by the Guardianship act in a similar way.[63]

The position of the current EU asylum law with regard to the role of the guardian is ambiguous. Its main concern is the representation of the child in asylum procedures which ensures the due process rights of the child. The representative though, in many cases has limited functions, which may lead to downsizing the legal protection of these children. The CRC Committee clearly differentiates the positions of the guardian and of the representative: "In cases where children are involved in asylum procedures or administrative

62 Proposal for a Directive of the European Parliament and of the Council laying down standards for the reception of applicants for international protection (recast), art. 23, Brussels, 13.7.2016, COM (2016) 465 final.

63 See Fournier, op cit, n. 37.

or judicial proceedings, they should, in addition to the appointment of a guardian, be provided with legal representation".[64]

The proposed revised EU asylum law (2016) replaces the term and the notion of "representative" with "guardian" as was the case in the earlier EU asylum law. This shift is commendable. The proposed Asylum Procedures Regulation defines for the first time the guardian's role as:

> to assist and represent an unaccompanied minor with a view to safeguarding the best interests of the child and his or her general well-being in asylum procedures and exercising legal capacity for the minor where necessary.[65]

An important task of the guardian, debated recently, is to assist in finding a durable solution for the child including a safe return to the country of origin, to be reintegrated into his/her family, if it is in the best interests of the child. The EU law refers to at least four factors that could be taken into account in assessing the best interests of the child: (1) family reunification possibilities; (2) the child's well-being and social development; (3) safety and security considerations, particularly for victims of trafficking; and (4) the views of the child, in accordance with his or her age and maturity.[66]

To conclude, it seems that a desired level of coordination could be reached regarding the functions of the guardian in Europe's new realities. The protection of children deprived of parental care is a state obligation under the CRC. Thus, there is no reason not to treat effective guardianship as part of a modern inclusive child protection system which is responsible also for children in the context of international migration, including in countries of origin, transit, destination and return.[67] This perspective reveals also that the recent "refugee crisis" accelerated the paradigm shift in many EU MS to treat children as full fledged rights holders rather than as parent's belongings. Guardianship should be a service for all children and should be better adapted to ensure not only their representation, but also their rights guaranteed by CRC.

---

64 CRC/GC/2005/6, para. 36.

65 Op cit, n. 60, art. 4, para. 2/f/ and art. 22.

66 See CRC/C/GC/14 (2013) on the right of the child to have his or her best interests taken as a primary consideration (art. 3, para. 1).

67 Directive 2013/32/EU of 26 June 2013 on common procedures (recast), § 33 and art. 25, para. 6; CMW/C/GC/3-CRC/C/GC/22, para. 14 and UNHCR Guidelines on Determining the Best Interests of the Child, 2008.

Part VII
Families and Care for Dependants

Eldercare in Belgian Public and Private Law: Who Cares?

Elisabeth Alofs, Frederik Swennen** and Anne-Sophie Vandenbosch****

I Introduction

In Western welfare states, the responsibility to care for the elderly is shared between the family, the State and the market. The allocation of responsibilities between those care actors differs between societies and across time, according to the needs and resources of the elderly, the family and the State.[1] More fundamentally, however, this care model is currently questioned due to demographic trends, such as the double ageing of the population. Double ageing in Belgium, and by extension the EU, comprises the combined effect of: (i) the increasing old-age dependency ratio (people aged 67+ relative to those aged 18-66) due to a declining fertility rate, and (ii) a prolonged average life expectancy resulting in an increase of the *very* aged (85+).[2]

According to the latest projections of the Belgian Federal Planning Bureau, the share of elderly (67+) in the total population will rise from around 16.30% in 2017 to 22.30% in 2070. It is estimated that the percentage of the population aged 18-66 will decline from 63.40% in 2017 to 57.10% in 2070. As a result of these trends, the demographic old-age dependency ratio will increase from 25.70% in 2017 to 39.10% in 2070.[3]

Double ageing poses different challenges to our societies and economies. Concerns exist regarding the sustainability of social security systems wherein a decreasing group of active persons are to guarantee the care of an increasing number of elderly persons. The

* Associated Professor of Family Law and Managing Director of the Master of Laws in Notarial Studies at the Faculty of Law and Criminology of the Free University of Brussels; researcher at the Faculty of Law of the University of Antwerp.

** Full Professor of Family Law at the Faculty of Law of the University of Antwerp.

*** Doctoral student at the Faculty of Law and Criminology, Free University of Brussels. With special thanks to Lieselot Beerens (alumna of the Faculty of Law and Criminology, Free University of Brussels).

1 H. Fulchiron, 'Summary report: Which solidarities for tomorrow?' *in* H. Fulchiron (Ed.), *Les solidarités entre générations – Solidarities between generations*, Brussels, Bruylant, 2013, p. 1119; F. Swennen & L. Verhaert, 'Intergenerational solidarity and allocation of elderly care in the Low Countries', *Child and Family Law Quarterly*, Vol. 27, No. 3, 2015, p. 285 at 285.

2 Swennen & Verhaert, ibid, at p. 286.

3 Federal Planning Bureau, *Demografische vooruitzichten 2017-2070 [Democratic forecasts 2017-2070]*, 2017, pp. 26-27, www.plan.be (consulted on 29 March 2018).

lack of public resources, in particular, puts pressure on public pensions and the healthcare system.[4]

As ageing gives rise to financial, physical, psychological, and social dependency,[5] issues of eldercare need to be addressed in all those areas.

Financial care is aimed, among others, at increasing the elderly person's available income allowing him to buy care on the market. Such increase can be achieved both *directly* through the allocation of income (e.g. pensions, social assistance, maintenance, etc.) and *indirectly* through tax and other exemptions.

Functional or in-kind care comprises practical support and assistance. In the formal care system, professional caregivers are paid to provide care (e.g. a nurse). Formal care is organised on the market, directly by the State or through public-private partnerships (e.g. subsidised services for professional home care). Informal care, particularly by members of the family or social network, comprises unpaid, non-professional care. The State may indirectly encourage informal care through its policy and legal framework (e.g. care leaves, career break schemes, and tax benefits).

The question arises whether a fundamental reallocation of eldercare between the family, the State and the market is needed in light of the recent demographic trends and public expenditure cuts.[6] This paper aims to contribute to answering this question, by elaborating on some public and private law schemes providing direct or indirect financial support to the elderly.

First, an overview will be provided of the Belgian labour market policies aimed at keeping or reintegrating the elderly into the labour force, and thus providing a source of employment income (Section II). Then, a description will be made of the direct financial benefits granted to the elderly in the social security system, such as the unemployment scheme with company supplement, the pension scheme and social assistance benefits for the elderly (Section III). Thirdly, the existing care leaves and career break schemes that support informal care by family members will be discussed (Section IV). The family solidarity mechanisms in private law, particularly the maintenance obligations of adult children

4 S.O. Daatland, M. Veenstra & K. Herlofson, 'Age and intergenerational attitudes in the family and the welfare state', *Advances in Life Course Research*, Vol. 17, 2012, p. 133; E. Eggink, E. Pommer & I. Woittiez, 'Collectieve uitgaven aan verpleging en verzorging in tijden van vergrijzing' ['Public spending on nursing and care in ageing populations'], *Beleid en Maatschappij*, No. 4, 2008, p. 299; J. Ribot, 'Refamilialisation of care and support: scope and limits of family solidarity in ageing societies' *in* Fulchiron (Ed.), op cit, n. 1, p. 709; J.J. Schippers, P.A. Dykstra, T. Fokkema & M. Munderlein, 'Participatiebevordering: werken aan draagvlak voor de sociale zekerheid' ['Promoting participation: working towards support for social security'], *Beleid en Maatschappij*, 2013, p. 296; Swennen & Verhaert, op cit, n. 1, at p. 286; F. Van Istendael, 'De vergrijzingsmaatschappij, het leven (her)begint op 65' ['The ageing society, life starts (over) at 65'], *Jura Falconis*, Vol. 45, No. 1, 2008-09, p. 3.

5 B.H. Casey, 'How will we provide and pay for long-term care?', *European Journal of Social Security*, Vol. 5, No. 1, 2003, p. 67 at 67.

6 Swennen & Verhaert, op cit, n. 1.

(-in-law) towards their parents (-in-law), will be analysed in Section V. Lastly, conclusions will be drawn on the allocation of eldercare in Belgium (Section VI).

II Employment Policies for Older Persons

In Belgium, the effective retirement age, i.e. the average age of labour market exit, is almost 61 years.[7] This is significantly lower than the statutory retirement age of 65 years, which will even be gradually increased to 67 years for pensions taking effect from 2030 (*infra* Section III). Different measures have been taken to increase the effective retirement age and to achieve a 50% participation rate of workers aged 55-65,[8] pursuant to the Europe 2020 strategy.[9]

A first category of measures encourages employers to hire older workers. Under the "target group reduction for older workers",[10] employers in the private sector that hire older workers benefit from a reduction in employers' contributions[11] for two years. The reduction depends on the worker's age (55+) and on whether s/he is currently employed or not. Furthermore, each company that employs more than 20 workers has an obligation to draw an employment plan for older workers,[12] containing all measures taken to maintain or increase the number of workers aged 45+ through training, prospects of occupying a more suitable position, adjusted working hours and conditions etc.

7 According to the OECD statistics (2017), the average age of labour market exit in OECD countries was almost 64,5 years; http://www.oecd.org/els/emp/average-effective-age-of-retirement.htm (consulted on 21 November 2018).

8 https://ec.europa.eu/info/sites/info/files/2017-european-semester-national-reform-programme-belgique-en.pdf; https://ec.europa.eu/info/sites/info/files/2017-european-semester-stability-programme-belgique-en_0.pdf (consulted on 30 March 2018).

9 http://ec.europa.eu/eu2020/pdf/COMPLET%20EN%20BARROSO%20%20%20007%20-%20Europe%202020%20-%20EN%20version.pdf (consulted on 30 March 2018).

10 This Flemish target group reduction replaces the federal target group reduction for older workers. Since it is a regionalised matter, applicability conditions may vary according to the region concerned.

11 Programme act I of 24 December 2002, *Belgian Official Gazette* 31 December 2002; Royal decree of 16 May 2003 issued pursuant to Chapter 7 of Title IV of the Programme act of 24 December 2002 (I), to align and simplify the reduction schemes of social security contributions, *Belgian Official Gazette* 6 June 2003; Decree of 4 March 2016 on the Flemish target group policy, *Belgian Official Gazette* 4 April 2016; Decree of 10 June 2016 of the Flemish Government implementing the Decree of 4 March 2016 on the Flemish target group policy, *Belgian Official Gazette* 28 June 2016.

12 Collective Labour Agreement No. 104 of 27 June 2012, concluded in the National Labour Council, on the implementation of an employment plan for older workers in the company, *Belgian Official Gazette* 8 November 2012.

A second category of measures encourages older workers to maintain or resume their employment. An "end-of-career time-credit"[13] entitles workers[14] in the private sector aged 55+[15] to reduce their employment to a part-time employment until retirement. To compensate the loss of salary, workers aged 60+[16] receive a career break benefit from the National Employment Office. Next, a "soft-end-of-career-system" has been put in to place to encourage workers in the private sector aged 58+ to accept a less burdensome workload (e.g. different job, working days instead of nights), by granting them a premium, that is free of employer's contributions, to compensate for the loss of salary caused by their new position.[17] Lastly, the "Senior-holidays-system"[18] aims to supplement the number of statutory holidays of workers aged 50+ who resume work after a period of full unemployment or disability. Having been (partially) absent during the previous year, and therefore not being entitled to four full weeks of annual vacation, these workers receive additional holidays and they benefit from an additional holiday pay[19] from the National Employment Office.

In the context of pension scheme reforms, the government has introduced a third category of measures, to increase the employment rate and the effective retirement age. These measures will be discussed further in Section III.B.

III Public (Care) Schemes for Older Persons

Three social security mechanisms mitigate the risks of old age by providing direct financial support to elderly persons. Firstly, the unemployment scheme with company supplement constitutes a safety net for dismissed older persons (A). Secondly, the three-pillar pension system (B) encompasses the State pension (1), the non-statutory or supplementary pension

---

13 Collective Labour Agreement No. 103 of 27 June 2012, concluded in the National Labour Council, establishing a system of time-credit, career reduction and end-of-career employment, *Belgian Official Gazette* 31 August 2012. Regarding career break allowances: Royal Decree of 12 December 2001 implementing Chapter IV of the Act of 10 August 2001 on work-life balance concerning the time-credit system, career reduction and reduction of part-time employment, *Belgian Official Gazette* 18 December 2001.

14 To benefit from this end-of-career time credit, s/he must have worked for the employer for at least 24 months and possess a career of 25 years as an employee.

15 However, this age requirement has been lowered to 50 years for certain conditions, e.g. workers employed by a company in difficulty or undergoing restructuring.

16 As of 1 January 2019, there are no longer exceptions to this age threshold.

17 Royal decree of 9 January 2018 on the modification of article 19 of the Royal Decree of 28 November 1969 on the implementation of the Act of 27 June 1969 revising the legislative decree of 28 December 1944 regarding the social security of workers, *Belgian Official Gazette,* 25 January 2018.

18 Art. 54-55 of the Act of 23 December 2005 on the generation pact, *Belgian Official Gazette* 30 December 2005; Royal decree of 25 November 1991 on regulating unemployment, *Belgian Official Gazette* 31 December 1991.

19 This allowance is considered to be an unemployment benefit; the worker may not benefit from any professional income, nor from another replacement income during these holidays.

(2), and the individual supplementary pension through personal pension savings (3). In recent years, several aspects of the Belgian pension scheme have been reformed in order to increase the employment rate of elderly persons and their effective age of retirement (*supra* Section II), and thus to reduce the budgetary costs of an ageing society. These reforms will be highlighted below. Thirdly, social assistance benefits for elderly persons (C) comprise the income guarantee for the elderly (1) and the allowance for assistance to the elderly (2).

A Unemployment Scheme with Company Supplement

The unemployment scheme with company supplement[20] protects workers of a certain age who have been dismissed, by entitling them to both State unemployment benefits, and a "company supplement" paid by their former employer.[21] This scheme is not an early retirement pension but is part of the unemployment insurance. To benefit from it, the dismissed worker must satisfy the conditions[22] relating to age and length of employment laid down in a collective labour agreement entered into at an interprofessional, sectoral or company level.

20 Act of 12 April 2011 amending the Act of 1 February 2011 on the extension of anti-crisis measures in execution of the interprofessional agreement, and to implement the mediation of the federal government with regard to the draft Interprofessional Agreement, as amended by the Act of 29 March 2012 on various provisions, *Belgian Official Gazette* 28 April 2011; Royal Decree of 3 May 2007 determining the unemployment scheme with company supplement, *Belgian Official Gazette* 8 June 2007; Collective Labour Agreement No. 17 of 19 December 1974 establishing a system of additional allowance for some older workers, if they are made redundant, *Belgian Official Gazette* 31 January 1975; Collective Labour Agreement No. 105 of 28 March 2013 determining the conditions for granting an additional allowance in the framework of unemployment with company supplement for some older workers with disabilities or serious physical problems, if they are made redundant, *Belgian Official Gazette* 24 October 2013.

21 Companies recognised as being in difficulty or undergoing restructuring by the Minister of Employment may obtain certain exemptions from the rules that apply to the unemployment scheme with company supplement (e.g. lowering of the required minimum age).

22 In accordance with the Collective Labour Agreement No. 17 of 19 December 1974, the worker dismissed at 62 years of age, for example, must prove a working career of 41 years for a man and 35 years for a woman, to be gradually increased to 41 years in 2025. However, there are age conditions that are more flexible than others, such as for heavy professions.

B *Pension system*

1 **First Pillar: Statutory Pension Scheme**

The statutory pension is organised in the mandatory social insurance systems dependent on the professional status of the older person:[23] salaried worker,[24] self-employed person[25] or civil servant.[26] The first two systems are funded on a pay-as-you-go-basis: current pensions are financed with contributions by current workers, as opposed to a system in which current contributions are invested to finance future pensions. The system for civil servants is a deferred remuneration.

There is no retirement obligation in Belgium: to qualify for a pension, the insured person must submit an application,[27] either to the Federal Pension Service (FPD/SFP) for

23 A differential treatment based on the professional category of the pension recipient is justified according to the European Court of Human Rights (European Court of Human Rights, 25 October 2011, No. 2033/44) and the Belgian Constitutional Court (Court of Arbitration, 4 July 1991, No. 17/91; Court of Arbitration, 9 July 1992, No. 54/92; Court of Arbitration, 22 December 1993, No. 88/93; Court of Arbitration, 6 June 1995, No. 48/95; Court of Arbitration, 20 September 2001, No. 112/2201; Constitutional Court, 10 February 2011, No. 205/2011).

24 Including persons who work in the private sector and those who work as contract staff in the public service. For the most important laws regarding the salaried workers' pension scheme: Royal Decree No. 50 of 24 October 1967 on the retirement and survival pension of salaried workers, *Belgian Official Gazette* 27 October 1967; Royal Decree of 21 December 1967 laying down general rules concerning retirement and survivor's pensions for salaried persons, *Belgian Official Gazette*, 16 January 1968; Act of 5 August 1978 on economic and budgetary reforms, *Belgian Official Gazette* 17 August 1978; Amending Act of 10 February 1981 on social sector pensions, *Belgian Official Gazette* 14 February 1981; Act of 20 July 1990 introducing a flexible retirement age for salaried workers and adapting their pensions to trends in general well-being, *Belgian Official Gazette* 15 August 1990; Act of 26 July 1996 modernising social security and ensuring the viability of the statutory pension schemes, *Belgian Official Gazette* 1 August 1996; Royal Decree of 23 December 1996 implementing articles 15, 16 and 17 of the Act of 26 July 1996 on modernising social security and ensuring the viability of the statutory pension schemes, *Belgian Official Gazette* 17 January 1997.

25 Including persons who are self-employed and their helpers. For the most important laws regarding self-employed persons' pension scheme: Royal Decree No. 72 of 10 November 1967 on the retirement and survival pension of self-employed workers, *Belgian Official Gazette* 14 November 1967; Royal Decree of 22 December 1967 laying down general rules concerning retirement and survivors' pensions for self-employed persons, *Belgian Official Gazette* 10 January 1968; Royal Decree of 30 January 1997 on independent workers' pension schemes in application of articles 15 and 27 of the Act of 26 July 1996 modernising social security and ensuring the viability of the statutory pension schemes and of article 3, § 1, 4° of the Act of 26 July 1996 aimed at achieving budgetary conditions for the participation of Belgium in the European Economic and Monetary Union, *Belgian Official Gazette* 6 March 1997.

26 Including civil servants who are appointed in a public service position at federal, regional, provincial or municipal levels. For the most important laws regarding public servants' pension scheme: General Act of 21 July 1844 on civil and ecclesiastical pensions, *Belgian Official Gazette* 30 July 1844; Act of 5 August 1978 on economic and budgetary reforms, *Belgian Official Gazette* 17 August 1978; Act of 15 May 1984 on measures to harmonise pension schemes, *Belgian Official Gazette* 22 May 1984.

27 Pension rights are increasingly reviewed ex officio without the beneficiary's explicit application (see Royal Decree of 4 September 2002 on the automatic review of pension rights within the pension schemes for salaried and self-employed persons, *Belgian Official Gazette* 25 September 2002).

salaried workers and civil servants, or to the National social insurance institute for the self-employed. As long as an application has not been submitted, the insured person of pensionable age may pursue or complete his/her career, e.g. to replace less well remunerated years with better remunerated years for the calculation of the pension.

1.1 Conditions

Obtaining a statutory pension is subject to three conditions. Firstly, the older person may not pursue a professional activity beyond the legal limits. A restricted accumulation of pension and earned income is allowed, dependent on the older person's age, type of professional activity and the fact of having dependent children or not. These limits do not apply to persons aged 65+ or with a proven working career of minimum 45 years. In addition, the older person may not receive a replacement income for professional activity, such as an illness, disability or involuntary unemployment benefit, a career interruption or diminished working activities allowance, or a supplementary allowance paid under a conventional early retirement arrangement.

Secondly, the older person must have reached the age of retirement.[28] For salaried and self-employed persons, this is currently 65 years for both men and women, but will be increased to 66 for pensions in 2025 and 67 for pensions in 2030. A civil servant can obtain a pension from the age of 65, if s/he has worked in the public sector for a period of five years. All three pension schemes do offer the possibility of an early retirement pension. The age of early retirement will be 63 years, after a career of 40 to 42 years dependent on the retiree's professional status.[29]

Thirdly, pension beneficiaries of foreign nationality should have their actual residence in Belgium. There is an exemption for stateless, recognised refugees, members of international organisations, and citizens of countries with an international agreement with Belgium.

1.2 Amount

The statutory pension is calculated on the basis of three parameters: career length, remuneration, and family situation.

Firstly, a complete career is considered to last 45 years or 1404 career days. For pensions taking effect from 2019, all days worked will be taken into account and not only the 1404 career days. Furthermore, only *worked* days will be taken into account, and periods of illness or disability will be excluded.

---

28 Act of 10 August 2015 aimed at increasing the legal retirement age, conditions for the early retirement pension and the minimum age for the survivor's pension, *Belgian Official Gazette* 21 August 2015.

29 As of 2019, for salaried workers, civil servants and self-employed persons, this is possible from 63 after a career of 42 years.

Secondly, effective wages, fictitious wages for periods assimilated to employment periods, and flat-rate wages for employment periods during which effective wages are not registered or are below the flat-rate wage are taken into account for the pension calculation.

Thirdly, the amount varies depending on the older person's family situation. The pension amount is presented as a percentage - either at the household rate of 75% or the one-person rate of 60% - of the sum of the annual pension entitlements that equate to 1/45 of the pensioner's average indexed, limited and reassessed gross income. The household rate of 75% is granted if the retiree has a dependent spouse. Spouses are considered to be dependent in case they have ceased all professional activity beyond the legal limits of authorised activity and in case they do not benefit a replacement income. Since the one-person rate of 60% is a residual rate, it applies to all retirees who cannot benefit from the household rate. This rate thus applies to single beneficiaries, married beneficiaries whose spouse is not dependent, and beneficiaries in a non-marital relationship. The retirement pension of civil servants does not depend on their family situation. They are however entitled to a pension amounting to 75% of their income, which is equal to a pension at the household rate of the other professional categories.

The pension of salaried and self-employed persons is capped in two ways: in relation to the remuneration amount, and in relation to career length. Pensions of civil servants may not exceed 3/4 of the income relevant for the calculation of the pension.

Finally, the Belgian system grants retirees the right to a guaranteed minimum pension,[30] the level of which depends on his or her professional category.

1.3 Special statutory pension rights

The statutory pension scheme provides for special pension rights, based on the (male) breadwinner model.

Firstly, in case of separation, a spouse's pension at the household rate will be divided, under certain conditions, between the two separated spouses, i.e. a derived right for the dependent spouse.

Secondly, in case of divorce, the ex-spouse who has insufficient pension rights may be entitled to an individual and personal retirement pension amounting to 37.5% of the income of the other ex-spouse. This scheme ceases to apply in case of remarriage of the dependent ex-spouse.

Thirdly, the Belgian statutory pension scheme provides for a survivor's pension, paid monthly under certain conditions to the surviving spouse of a deceased insured person. To qualify for a survivor's pension, the beneficiary must, in principle, have been married

30 The right can be granted to salaried or self-employed persons who can demonstrate a career of a minimum two-thirds of a full career and to civil servants with a career of minimum 20 years.

to the deceased for at least one year at the time of death.[31] S/he must also have reached the minimum age of 47, which will gradually increase to 55 by 2030. If the surviving spouse does not fulfil this age requirement, s/he is entitled to a transitional allowance for 12 months (without dependent children) or 24 months (with dependent children). The survivor's pension amounts to 60% of the income of the deceased spouse. This survivor's pension is suspended in case of remarriage and is not granted in case certain crimes were committed against the deceased spouse.

2 Second Pillar: Non-statutory Pension Scheme

Supplementary pensions[32] are non-statutory insurance benefits either proposed by the employer, or mandatory under a collective labour agreement entered into at a interprofessional, sectoral or company level. Under this scheme, the employer pays (most of) the premiums. The system is based on capitalisation and aims to build up capital, a retirement annuity, or a survivor's annuity to be paid to a designated beneficiary in case of death of the insured. Group insurances and life insurances are two types of supplementary pensions. Group insurance regulations or life insurance contracts determine the age ≥ 60 at which the capital or annuity will become available. The self-employed can also subscribe to a supplementary pension.

3 Third Pillar: Personal Pension Savings Scheme

The personal pension savings scheme creates incentives for persons to voluntarily build up capital or a retirement annuity in their personal capacity. Under certain conditions, the retirement annuity gives rise to a tax deduction calculated on the sum paid. The two types of pension savings are pension savings insurance from an insurance company and pension savings accounts from a bank.

C Social Assistance Benefits for Older Persons

Under two social welfare schemes, direct financial assistance is provided to elderly persons: the guaranteed income for elderly persons (IGO/GRAPA), and the allowance for help to the elderly (THAB /APA). These schemes are funded through taxes rather than through social security contributions. The two allowances are subsidiary in nature and are only

31 This condition is also met if the marriage is directly preceded by legal cohabitation and if these two periods together add up to at least one year. The requirement to be married for one year is not applicable if a child is born, if there is a dependent child at the time of death or if the death is due to an accident or an occupational disease.

32 In Belgium, there are pension funds (also called institutions for occupational retirement provision), which are institutions created by one or more companies or one or several professional sectors in order to manage their supplementary pension plans in the framework of the second pension pillar.

granted to applicants whose income is inadequate, as determined after assessing the income of the older person and of those with whom s/he forms a household.

The guaranteed income for elderly persons[33] is a guaranteed minimum income allocated to persons[34] aged ≥ 65 who have their main residence in Belgium and who are not entitled to a pension or whose pension is inadequate. Its amount is set at a flat rate and depends on the household composition of the beneficiary: the older person obtains either a basic amount if s/he shares his or her main residence with one or several persons,[35] or an increased amount if s/he lives alone. His or her resources and those of his or her cohabitants also affect the calculation: the average total amount of all household income is deducted from the maximum amount of this allowance. The Federal Pension Service is responsible for payment of the guaranteed income for elderly persons.

The allowance for help to the elderly[36] is a supplementary allowance for disabled persons[37] aged ≥ 65 who suffer a loss of autonomy. This allowance compensates additional costs incurred, due to either high healthcare expenses, or the need to rely on services or third parties. Unlike the federal pensions and the federal guaranteed income for elderly persons, the allowance for help to the elderly is a competence of municipalities and Belgian regions. Its amount is determined according to the elderly person's degree of autonomy, which is evaluated on the basis of points awarded on a medico-social scale. However, an allowance will only be granted to the elderly person if his or her income and that of those with whom s/he forms a household are inadequate.

33 Act of 22 March 2001 instituting the Guaranteed income for elderly persons, *Belgian Official Gazette* 29 March 2001.

34 Belgians, foreign nationals of the European Union, recognised refugees or stateless persons and nationals of a country with which Belgium has concluded a reciprocal convention on guaranteed income or in relation to which it has recognised that de facto reciprocity exists, are entitled to the IGO/GRAPA. Other persons of foreign nationality are also entitled to the benefit, provided that they are entitled to a retirement or survivor's pension under a Belgian scheme. If the IGO/GRAPA has taken effect after 31 August 2017, the beneficiary must have been officially domiciled in Belgium for at least 10 years with a period of actual and continuous residence for at least 5 years. If a person stays abroad for more than 6 months, s/he loses the entitlement to the IGO/GRAPA. The Federal Pension Service regularly sends a residence certificate to the beneficiaries to check their residence status.

35 Minors, adult children for whom family allowances are received, people living in the same nursing home, care centre or mental health care home as the applicant and parents or relatives in ascending or descending line and their legal cohabitants are presumed not to share the same main residence as the applicant.

36 Act of 27 February 1987 concerning allowances for persons with disabilities, *Belgian Official Gazette* 1 April 1987; Royal Decree of 5 March 1990 concerning an allowance for help for the elderly, *Belgian Official Gazette* 5 April 1990. For Flemish regulations: Decree of 24 June 2016 relating to Flemish welfare protection, *Belgian Official Gazette* 6 September 2016; Decree of the Flemish Government of 14 October 2016 on the implementation of the Decree of 24 June 2016, *Belgian Official Gazette* 16 December 2016.

37 This allowance is granted to persons registered in the population register (as a Belgian or foreigner), being domiciled and actually residing in Belgium.

IV PUBLIC SYSTEMS FOR FACILITATING (FAMILY) CARE FOR OLDER PERSONS

The State also offers indirect financial or other support for the elderly by encouraging family members to take care of their elderly relatives, allowing them to (partially) suspend their professional activities whilst receiving a limited replacement income.[38] Noteworthy within the field of eldercare are three thematic care leaves: the leave for palliative care (A), the leave for medical assistance (B), and the career break scheme with cause, also called the time-credit on specific grounds (C). The thematic care leaves for palliative care and for medical assistance and the time-credit on specific grounds can be accumulated.

A *Leave for Palliative Care*

Leave for palliative care[39] allows an employee to fully or partially suspend his or her professional activities in order to dedicate palliative care to a person who is in the final stages of a terminal incurable illness and who is not necessarily a family member. Palliative care includes all the care aiming to accompany the patient at the end of life, including medical, social, administrative and psychological care. The leave may be obtained for a maximum period of one month with two possible extensions. During this interruption, the employee may obtain an allowance from the National Employment Office.

B *Leave for Medical Assistance*

Leave for medical assistance[40] allows an employee to fully or partially suspend his or her professional activities in order to assist, or provide care to, a member of his or her household or family who is suffering from a serious illness. Assistance of care includes any form of medical, social, familial or mental assistance which a physician considers to be a necessary contribution to the patient's convalescence, in addition to formal care. The leave can be

---

38 See https://www.rva.be/nl/documentatie/infobladen/infobladen-voor-werknemers?theme=6695&number=&=Filter#results (consulted on 24 March 2019).

39 Act of 27 June 1969 revising the legislative decree of 28 December 1944 regarding the social security of workers, *Belgian Official Gazette* 25 July 1969; Act of 22 January 1985 on social provisions, *Belgian Official Gazette* 24 January 1985; Royal Decree of 2 January 1991 on granting career break allowances, *Belgian Official Gazette* 12 January 1991; Royal decree of 22 March 1995 regarding leave for palliative care, on the implementation of article 100bis, § 4 of the redress Act of 22 January 1985 regarding social provisions and amending the Royal Decree of 2 January 1991 on granting career break allowances, *Belgian Official Gazette* May 5, 1995.

40 Act of 22 January 1985 on social provisions, *Belgian Official Gazette* 24 January 1985; Royal Decree of 2 January 1991 on granting career break allowances, *Belgian Official Gazette* 12 January 1991; Royal decree of 10 August 1998 introducing a right to a career break to assist or provide care to a seriously ill member of the household or family, *Belgian Official Gazette* 8 September 1998.

obtained for periods of minimum one month to maximum three months, and in total for a maximum of 12 months (full suspension) or 24 months (partial suspension). The worker can obtain an allowance from the National Employment Office.

C *Time-credit on Specific Grounds*

Time-credit on specific grounds[41] entitles[42] the employee in the private sector,[43] with a seniority of ≥ 24 months with the employer, to fully or partially suspend his or her professional activity on one of the grounds provided by the regulations. Time-credit for granting palliative care[44] entitles the employee to provide palliative care to a person at the end of life who is in the final stages of a terminal incurable illness. This type of time-credit can be obtained for a fixed period of one month per patient, with the possibility of an additional one-month extension. Time-credit to provide care to a seriously ill person[45] entitles the employee to provide care or assistance to a seriously ill member of his or her household or family. This type of time-credit can be obtained for one to three months. With regard to both grounds, the worker may reduce his or her professional services for a maximum period of 51 months over his or her entire career, whichever the form of career break requested (full-time, part-time or a fifth). During the time-credit period, the worker can receive a monthly replacement income from the National Employment Office.

V Family Solidarity for Older Persons in Private Law

Articles 205 to 207 of the Civil Code establish an intergenerational reciprocal maintenance obligation between descendants and ascendants on the one hand, and between parents-in-law and children-in-law on the other. The basis of this obligation is family solidarity.

41 Collective Labour Agreement No. 103 of 27 June 2012, concluded within the National Labour Council, establishing a system of time-credit, career reduction and end-of-career employment, *Belgian Official Gazette* 31 August 2012. Regarding income replacement: Royal Decree of 12 December 2001 implementing Chapter IV of the Act of 10 August 2001 on work-life balance concerning the time-credit system, career reduction and reduction of part-time employment, *Belgian Official Gazette* 18 December 2001.

42 This is a *right* which does not require the employer's agreement if s/he employs more than ten workers; nevertheless, this right is limited to a quota of concurrent absences. However, if the employer has 10 or fewer workers, this is not considered a right, and the employer's agreement is therefore required.

43 The public sector has a similar system: the career break.

44 As defined in article 100 of the Act of 22 January 1985 on social provisions, *Belgian Official Gazette* 24 January 1985.

45 As defined in articles 3 and 4 of the Royal decree of 10 August 1998 introducing a right to a career break to assist or provide care to a seriously ill member of the household or family, *Belgian Official Gazette* 8 September 1998.

Obligations between (ex-)spouses nevertheless take precedence over obligations to relatives or in-laws.[46]

On the one hand, children owe maintenance to their parents and other ascendants, in case the latter are in need (article 205 of the Civil Code), and vice versa (article 207 of the Civil Code). This obligation applies without limitation of proximity in degrees of kinship (by descent or adoption) but applies only to direct lines. The majority doctrine furthermore considers that persons with the closest degree of kinship should be solicited first, as should the descendants be sought before ascendants with the same degree.[47] Finally, all relatives are held before the in-laws.[48]

On the other hand, there is a reciprocal maintenance obligation between children-in-law and parents-in-law. The above-mentioned priority of relatives over in-laws as maintenance debtors, however, is difficult to apply because the married relative's joint income with his or her spouse will be taken into account to determine the amount of his or her obligation. The maintenance obligation between in-laws exists only in case of marriage and not in case of a registered partnership ("legal cohabitation"), let alone de facto cohabitation. It also ceases in case the marriage is dissolved or declared void, i.e. reciprocally between the child and child-in-law in the event of divorce of either of them; towards parents-in-law, in the event of (re)marriage of a parent-in-law; reciprocally in the event of death of the child whose marriage created in-lawship, in case s/he had no common children with the child-in-law.

The maintenance obligation exists only in case of need. This notion is broader than a standard of living based on the minimum wage or minimum welfare allowances. To the Court of Cassation, the need of a maintenance creditor is evaluated on the basis of normal living conditions which his or her social situation enabled him or her to enjoy.[49] The voluntarily arisen need shall not give rise to maintenance. However, there are no causes for disqualification by conduct, except due to deprivation of parental responsibility. Deprivation may even be imposed on an elderly parent of an adult child, precisely to exclude his or her maintenance claim.[50]

The debtor is only held to the obligation if s/he is able to provide support (article 208 Civil Code). Of course, s/he cannot voluntarily place him/herself in a situation that would enable him or her to evade the legal obligation.[51] In the event of several debtors in the same degree, each one is only responsible for his or her share (*contributio*); they are not jointly and severally liable (*obligation in solidum*).[52] A debtor who has paid more than his or her

46 Court of Cassation, 7 April 1995, C.94.61.N, www.cass.be.
47 Court of Cassation, 15 March 1995, C.94.333.F, www.cass.be.
48 Court of Cassation, 15 March 1995, C.94.333.F, www.cass.be.
49 Court of Cassation, 12 October 2009, C.08.0524.F, www.cass.be.
50 Court of Cassation, 6 May 1987, AR 5796, www.cass.be.
51 Court of Cassation, 17 October 2005, C.04.0057.F, www.cass.be.
52 Court of Cassation, 15 March 1995, C.94.333.F, www.cass.be.

share, shall have a right of recourse against the other debtors. A right of recourse against maintenance debtors also exists for the support provided by the Public Centre for Social Welfare. Indirect action by the maintenance creditor's creditors – e.g. a hospital or elderly home – against the maintenance debtors is not permitted.

Maintenance support is usually paid in the form of a monthly allowance. In case the debtor is unable to execute his or her obligation in cash, the family court may allow him or her to accommodate, feed and care for the creditor in his or her home (article 210 of the Civil Code). Parents can provide in kind in any case (article 211 Civil Code). The maintenance obligation exists *rebus sic stantibus* and can be modified on request of the debtor or creditor (article 209 of the Civil Code).

The provisions on maintenance obligations between relatives and in-laws are imperative and hence the creditor is not allowed to waive future rights.

Very little case-law relating to the maintenance obligation between ascendants and descendants has been published. This could be because there is no societal need or because social security benefits are sufficient to meet the elderly's needs.[53] More realistically, families might be willing to provide the maintenance support voluntarily.[54] In any event, elderly persons are expected to be reluctant to claim maintenance support, so as to avoid counter-productive effects such as the withdrawal of contact with their grandchildren.[55]

VI Conclusion

This paper has offered an overview of public and private law instruments that install direct or indirect financial support to the elderly. It was demonstrated that the Belgian eldercare system is mostly dominated by a myriad of public-law-driven care measures, such as the various labour market policies aimed at integrating or keeping older employees in the labour force for as long as possible, the unemployment scheme with company supplement, the three-tiered pension scheme, the social assistance benefits for the elderly and the publicly financed thematic care leaves and career break schemes for facilitating family care.

53 K. Haberkern & M. Szydlik, 'State care provision, societal opinion and children's care of older parents in 11 European countries', *Ageing & Society*, Vol. 30, 2010, p. 299; M. Kornel, 'Dawn or Twilight of Rights and Duties between Grandparents and Grandchildren in Central Europe', *in* Fulchiron (Ed.), op cit, n. 1, p. 435.

54 Ribot, op cit, n. 4.

55 J. De Jong Gierveld et al, 'Living arrangements, intergenerational support types and older adult loneliness in Eastern and Western Europe', *Demographic Research*, Vol. 27, 2012, p. 167; F. Maisonnasse, 'L'articulation des solidarités familiales et collectives: entre subsidiarité et socialisation du droit aux aliments' ['Articulation of family and collective solidarity: between subsidiarity and socialisation of the right to maintenance'], *in* Fulchiron (Ed.), op cit, n. 1, p. 747; J. Ribot, op cit, n. 4.

The above analysis of the public law measures makes clear that the government has, on the one hand, taken several measures to keep or reintegrate elderly people into the labour force. Yet on the other hand, it has tightened access to a number of eldercare measures and social benefits so as to reduce budgetary costs linked to the ageing society. Further measures have been or will be introduced under an agreement reached by the Belgian federal government in 2017 and 2018: the possibility to take up part-time retirement from 2019 or 2020,[56] the possibility for retirees to earn a supplemental salary[57] of up to 6.000 EUR per year without having to pay charges or social contributions on this income,[58] and the introduction of tax measures designed to increase professional income, such as an increase of the non-taxable income, a reform of tax rates, a higher bonus for the lowest wages and a higher standard abatement for occupational expenses.

Private law mechanisms govern the Belgian eldercare system to a much lesser extent. The maintenance obligations of children (-in-law) towards their parents (-in-law) in fact do seem to have little practical relevance. The responsibility of family members, however, should not be minimalised either. As was pointed out, informal care by family members is encouraged throughout public care systems that offer a limited replacement income in the event of a thematic care leave or career break. However, this financial compensation only partially covers the real cost of the provided care and the loss of income from work, which leaves the family member with no choice but to personally take up responsibility to bear this cost of care.

56 Provided that the retiree has reached the age of 63 and s/he can give proof of a professional career of 42 years.

57 Supplemental activities are allowed, for example, in the non-profit sector.

58 Act of 18 July 2018 on the economic recovery and the strengthening of social cohesion, *Belgian Official Gazette* 26 July 2018.

Care for People with Disabilities in Italy: A Critical Analysis of Act 112/2016 on Assistance for People with Serious Disabilities Lacking Family Support

*Letizia Palumbo**

I Introduction

Although it is a "fundamental aspect of human life",[1] essential for the well-being and reproduction of a society itself, care has traditionally been viewed as a private issue, whose burden, according to a male breadwinner model, is "naturally" and mainly on women's shoulders. As feminist scholars on the ethics of care have stressed, the exclusion of care from the political sphere is rooted in a liberal conception of the (male) subject as an autonomous, self-determining and independent agent which has built on the relegation of body, emotion and needs issues to behind the walls of private households.[2] Dependency and vulnerability have been seen as deficits to be removed and hidden, rather than aspects characterising the human condition, and accordingly requiring adequate and efficacious political responses.[3]

The overlooking of care as a public and political issue and also as work is particularly true in countries such as Italy,[4] where the welfare system builds on a "familistic" model characterised by a lack of structural and long-term public services and the delegation of care activities to families.[5] Care work is a family affair: families – and, within these, especially women – are the main actors responsible for providing care to members who need assistance, receiving from the state only modest monetary contributions (in particular, the so-

---

* Post-Doctoral Researcher in Comparative Law, University of Palermo and Research Fellow, European University Institute, Florence.

1 J.C. Tronto, *Moral boundaries, Political arguments for an ethic of care*, London, Routledge, 1993.

2 E.F. Kittay, *Love's labor: Essays on women, equality and dependency*, New York, Routledge, 1999; B. Casalini, 'Schiavitu domestica e mercificazione del lavoro di cura', *in* T. Casadei & S. Mattarelli (Eds.), *Schiavitu*, Milan, FrancoAngeli, 2009, pp. 195-214; Tronto, op cit, n. 1.

3 Kittay, op cit, n. 2.

4 R. Sarti (Ed.), *Lavoro domestico e di cura: Quali diritti?*, Rome, Ediesse, 2010; A. Sciurba, *La cura servile, la cura che serve*, Pisa, Pacini Editore, 2015.

5 C. Saraceno, *Mutamenti della Famiglia e Politiche Sociali in Italia*, Bologna, Il Mulino, 2007.

called *indennità di accompagnamento* (attendance allowances), which are cash benefits for dependent people, comprising a standard exiguous sum – around €516 per month in 2018 – which is distributed without control upon its use).

In recent years, the shortcomings of the Italian welfare system have emerged in their seriousness due to an increase in the ageing of the population, the shortening of hospitalisation periods in medical institutions, and the concomitant weakening of informal family support, mainly produced by a growth in female participation in the labour market and changes to family structure – i.e. a greater number of one parent families, a decrease in the size of families and an increase in their geographical mobility.[6] The combined effect of all these factors has led to the outsourcing of domestic/care work, mostly through the employment of migrant workers who are often willing, for lack of alternatives, to "accept" substandard and exploitative working conditions in relation to salaries, working hours and protection.[7] This has led to a transition from a family to a "migrant in the family" model of care, in which (female) migrant workers have "met unsatisfied needs for care while ensuring the continuity of a family-based long-term care model".[8]

This paper focuses on the issue of care assistance for people with disabilities in Italy, examining the recent Act n. 112 adopted by the Italian Parliament in June 2016 and entitled "Measures in the field of assistance for people with serious disabilities lacking family support" (*Disposizioni in materia di assistenza in favore delle persone con disabilità grave prive del sostegno familiare*). In particular, I explore whether and how this legislative intervention effectively meets the needs of people with disabilities, especially with regard to their right to live independently and be included in the community as provided by Article 19 of the 2006 UN Convention on the Rights of Persons with Disabilities. I hold that while Act 112/2016 constitutes a significant advance in ensuring people with disabilities the opportunity to live independently and be included and participate in society, it does not however really challenge the national family-centred welfare system, which continues to view families as the main subjects in charge of providing care and assistance to their dependent members.

6 Casalini, op cit, n. 2.

7 R. Maioni & G. Zucca, *Viaggio nel lavoro di cura. Chi sono, cosa fanno e come vivono le badanti che lavorano nelle famiglie italiane*, Roma, Ediesse, 2016; L. Palumbo, 'Exploitating for Care: Trafficking and Abuse in domestic work in Italy', *Journal of Immigrant & Refugee Studies*, Vol. 15, No. 2, 2017, pp. 171-186; L. Palumbo, *Addressing demand in the context of THB in the domestic work sector in Italy*, Report, DemandAT Country Study No. 5, 2016.

8 F. Bettio, A. Simonazzi & P. Villa, 'Change in care regimes and female migration: The "care drain" in the Mediterranean', *Journal of European Social Policy*, Vol. I, No. 3, 2006, pp. 271–285, p. 278.

II National Legislation on the Right of People with Disabilities to Live Independently and be Included in the Community

The adoption of the 2006 UN Convention on the Rights of Persons with Disabilities (UNCRPD) has significantly marked the abandonment in the international scenario of a medical approach to disability – built on the idea that disability is a state of impairment and accordingly that people of disability require primarily therapeutic support – in favour of an approach that recognises people with disabilities as subjects enjoying the same standards of equality, rights and dignity as all other persons.[9] From this perspective, the condition of disability is viewed as originating from a complex interaction between health conditions, personal factors and barriers in the physical and social context that impede the full participation and inclusion of people with disabilities in society.[10]

Italy ratified the UNCRPD in 2009 (Act 18/2009). Yet, already since the 1990s, several laws have been adopted to address, even if with some noteworthy gaps and limitations, the rights of people with disabilities with respect to the issues of accessibility, work, school, integration, non-discrimination, access to justice, and the right to independent living and inclusion in society.[11]

Before illustrating the main national laws concerning the right to live independently and be included in the community, it should be noted that this right[12] is found in Article 19 of the UNCRPD, which affirms that States Parties shall:

> recognize the equal right of all persons with disabilities to live in the community, with choices equal to others, and shall take effective and appropriate measures

9 S. Marchisio, R. Cera & V. Della Fina (Eds.), *La Convenzione delle nazioni unite sui diritti delle persone con disabilità. Commentario*, Roma, Aracne, 2010.

10 Art. 1(2) of the UNCRPD affirms that: "Persons with disabilities include those who have long-term physical, mental, intellectual or sensory impairments which in interaction with various barriers may hinder their full and effective participation in society on an equal basis with others". The inspiring model of the UNCRPD is the so-called social model, which has been being developed in Britain since the 1970s. Yet, as many scholars have noted, the model implemented by the UN Convention seems closer to the bio-psycho-social approach to disability adopted by the WHO's International Classification of Functioning, Disability and Health (ICF) and that – unlike the social model which considers individual impairment as irrelevant to the experience of disability – takes also into account the interaction between impairment and the social and physical context. See K. Kazou, 'Analysing the Definition of Disability in the UN Convention on the Rights of Persons with Disabilities: is it really based on a 'Social Model' approach?', *International Journal of Mental Health and Capacity Law*, No. 23, 2017, pp. 25-48; M.G. Bernardini, *Disabilità, Giustizia, Diritto: Itinerari tra filosofia del Diritto e Disability Studies*, Turin, Giappichelli Editore, 2016, pp. 64-73.

11 See E. Longo, 'Unitarietà del bisogno di cura. Riflessioni sugli effetti giuridici conseguenti al passaggio dal modello medico al modello sociale di disabilità', *Non profit*, Vol. 2, 2011. Longo has also highlighted that, since the 90s, the Italian Constitutional Court, in several of its judgements, has abandoned the medical approach to disability in favour of an approach that views people with disability as subjects of rights.

12 The right to live independently and be included in the community is also protected under EU law in particular through Article 26 of the 2000 EU Charter of Fundamental Rights.

> to facilitate full enjoyment by persons with disabilities of this right and their full inclusion and participation in the community

Article 19 does not provide a definition of the notion "living independently" contained in its title. Yet, this term should not be interpreted solely as the capacity of individuals to carry out daily activities by themselves. Rather, it should be understood as "the freedom to choose and control, in line with the respect for inherent dignity and individual autonomy as enshrined in Article 3" of the UNCRPD.[13] In other words, independent living refers to the individual's ability to choose and control personal daily activities and lifestyle:

> [It] occurs if, in whatever living scheme one chooses to live one's life, which [...] could be one within the extended family, separate from it, or some other arrangement, one retains autonomy and control over one's life and decisions while accessing the individualised supports needed to do so.[14]

Closely linked to independent living, the right to be included in the community relates to the principle of full and effective inclusion and participation in society set out in Article 3 of the UNCRPD. This right includes having access to services that enable people with disabilities to effectively participate in all spheres of social life, including actively participating in the decision-making process of interventions related to disability issues.

Article 19 of the UNCRPD identifies three key elements of the right to live independently and be included in the community: *choice* (paragraph a: "the opportunity to choose their place of residence and where and with whom they live on an equal basis with others and [to not be] obliged to live in a particular living arrangement"); *personalised support* (paragraph b: "access to a range of in-home, residential and other community support services, including personal assistance necessary to support living and inclusion in the community, and to prevent isolation or segregation from the community"); and *access to community services and facilities for the general population* (paragraph c: "ensuring these services and facilities "are available on an equal basis to persons with disabilities and are responsive to their needs").[15]

In Italy, one of the first national legislative interventions concerning the independent living and social inclusion of people with disabilities was Act 104/1992 for the "Assistance, social integration and rights of people with a handicap". This Act identifies among its priorities respect for the human dignity, freedom and autonomy of people with disabilities,

---

13 Committee on the Rights of Persons with Disabilities, *General Comment No. 5 – Article 19: Living independently and being included in the community*, CRPD/C/18/1, 2017, para. 16(c).

14 Council of Europe Commissioner for Human Rights, *The right of people with disabilities to live independently and be included in the community*, Strasbourg, Council of Europe, 2012, p. 16.

15 Ibid.

removing all invalidating conditions that prevent the full development of the person and the achievement of his/her autonomy. It promotes the integration of people with disabilities in families, schools, work and society. Significantly, the Act also provides some specific benefits for workers with disabilities and the relatives who assist them (e.g. the opportunity to choose a workplace closer to home and allows relatives to have paid days of leave from work to assist people with disabilities).[16]

Act 104/1992 has been revised by Act 162/1998 on the "Measures of support in favour of people with serious disabilities", by providing the implementation of programmes of support for people with disabilities, even through the creation of personalised plans.

Act 104/1992 has been welcomed as the first organic legal response addressing the protection of human dignity, freedom and autonomy of people with disabilities. Yet, it provides a definition of disability which relies on a "medical-individualist approach". More specifically, in addition to using a politically incorrect terminology, Act 104/1992 defines a person with a disability as someone "having a permanent or a progressive physical, mental or sensory impairment that determines difficulties in learning, social relations and work integration, in such a way as to determine a process of social disadvantage or marginalization" (article 3). The Act also affirms that there is a situation of serious handicap when the impairment (single or numerous) has caused a reduction in age-related personal autonomy, to the extent that it makes necessary a permanent, continuous and global assistance intervention both in the individual and social spheres. This definition of disability tends to identify disabled people according to their impairment and social disadvantage. Attention is not paid to the context in which the person lives and through which they interact.

On the basis on these considerations, and given the lack in Italian legislation of a definition of disability in line with the 2006 UNCRPD, the UN Committee on the Rights of Persons with Disabilities has recommended that Italy adopt a notion of disability, and an approach to this issue, which is aligned to the UN Convention.[17] This need has also been highlighted in the Second National Biennial Programme of Action for the Promotion of the Rights and the Integration of Persons with Disabilities adopted in 2017.[18]

Another important legislative intervention concerning independent living and inclusion in society for people with disabilities is Framework Act 328/2000 for the "Creation of an integrated system of interventions and social services". This Act provides for the realization of individualised projects for people with disabilities that identify the needs and services necessary for their full inclusion in society and the fulfilment of their rights (article 14).

16 Because of the frequent abuse of this provision, Act 104/1992 has been the object of diverse judgments by the Italian Court of Cassation.

17 Committee on the Rights of Persons with Disabilities, *Concluding observation on the initial report of Italy*, 6 October 2016.

18 The text of the Biennal Programma is available at: http://www.handylex.org/stato/d121017.shtml#cap3.

These projects shall be defined by the municipalities, together with local health units, and on request of the person concerned. The projects shall include: economic measures to support the autonomy of totally dependent people and their ability to remain at home; the creation of social rehabilitation centres and of community accommodations as well as services for temporary replacement of families during their absence; interventions for the elderly and people with disabilities aimed to encourage their staying at home; interventions aimed at facilitating the staying and inclusion in residential and semi-residential centres for those who cannot be assisted at home (article 22).[19]

III Act 112/2016 on Assistance for People with Serious Disabilities Lacking Family Support

In line with the legislative interventions illustrated above, in 2016 the Italian Parliament adopted, almost 17 years after the presentation of its first draft, Act n. 112 of 2016, known by the name *dopo di noi* ("after us", with "us" referring to the families), which addresses the issue of care and assistance for people with disabilities when the essential support provided by families fails or ceases to exist.

Act 112/2016 is aimed at promoting the well-being, full social inclusion, and autonomy of persons with disabilities, implementing the principles established by the Italian Constitution (Articles 2, 3, 30, 32 and 38), the EU Charter of Fundamental Rights (Articles 24 and 26) and the UNCRPD (Articles 3 and 19). In particular, the Act introduces public and civil law measures for the assistance, care and protection of people with serious disabilities not caused by natural ageing or by diseases related to senility, and who lack family support because they are missing both parents or their parents are not able to provide adequate support. These measures, which are illustrated below, may also be implemented in view of a lack of family support, through the progressive taking charge of the person with a serious disability during the time that the parents are still present. As the Act specified, the measures are integrated, with the involvement of the people concerned, into the above-mentioned individualised projects established by Act 328/2000.

19 Over recent years even on the regional level there have been some significant legal interventions concerning independent living and inclusion in the community. V. Zambrano, 'Articolo 19. Vita Indipendente ed inclusione nella società', *in* S. Marchisio et al, op cit, n. 9, pp. 239-251.

A Fund for the Assistance of Persons with Serious Disabilities

Act 112/2016 (article 4) establishes a Fund for the Assistance of Persons with Serious Disabilities Lacking Family Support. The resources of the Fund can be used for the realisation of measures in four ambits:

(1) interventions aimed at facilitating paths of deinstitutionalisation and supporting home assistance by reproducing the conditions and relationships of a family home and also including the use of new technologies;
(2) interventions for a temporary stay in a "extra-familial" context in order to face emergency situations, in accordance with the consent of the person with disabilities;
(3) measures aimed at creating family-type and co-housing accommodation solutions, which may include the payment of necessary costs and charges even supporting forms of mutual help among persons with disabilities; and
(4) programmes aimed at increasing awareness and developing skills for the achievement of the highest possible level of autonomy for people with disabilities.

The Fund was set to be €90 million for 2016; €38.3 million for 2017 and €56.1 million for 2018 (but subsequently cut by €5 million). With regard to 2019, the amount has been restored to €56.1 million.[20]

As specified by Act n. 112/2016, it is up to the Regions to define the criteria and modalities for distributing the funding and verifying its implementation.

B Establishment of Trusts and other Instruments of Allocation of Assets

Act 112/2016 also provides for tax breaks for the creation, in favour of people with disabilities, of instruments for allocation of assets.

The first instrument contemplated by Act 112/2016 is the trust. It is worth highlighting that the institute of trust has been recognised in Italy since 1989 with the adoption of Act 364/1989 ratifying the 1985 Hague Convention of the Law Applicable to Trusts and on Their Recognition. Yet, Italy has not yet adopted additional provisions aimed specifically at regulating this instrument in its national legal framework.

As the 1985 Hague Convention reads, the notion "trust" refers to the "legal relationships created – *inter vivos* or on death – by a person, the settlor, when assets have been placed under the control of a trustee for the benefit of a beneficiary or for a specified purpose" (article 2). The characteristics of the trust are:

(a) the assets constitute a separate fund and are not a part of the trustee's own estate;

20 As determined by the Italian Budget Act adopted in December 2018 (Act n. 145/2018).

(b) title to the trust assets stands in the name of the trustee or in the name of another person on behalf of the trustee; and
(c) the trustee has the power and the duty, in respect of which he is accountable, to manage, employ or dispose of the assets in accordance with the terms of the trust and the special duties imposed upon him by law (article 2).

With the creation of a trust, therefore, the settlor deprives himself/herself from the title to the transferred assets. At the same time, these assets are distinct from the personal assets of the trustee, who is merely required to administer the transferred assets in the interest of the beneficiary. Insofar as the assets put into a trust constitute a fund which is separated from the assets of the settlor and trustee, they are not affected by the changes to the personal or patrimonial circumstances of these individuals.

The "atypical" features of the trust make it a flexible instrument applicable to diverse situations,[21] including for the protection of dependent people, both in terms of economic and assistance support.[22] With the adoption of Act 112/2016, the national legislator has explicitly provided for the possibility to establish a trust in order to assist, take care of and protect people with disabilities, clearly recognising the application of this instrument in a field different from that of taxation.[23] Yet, as has been highlighted, the legislator has not provided any definitions nor addressed the effects of the application of trust in this ambit.[24] Therefore, it will be necessary to refer to national case law in order to deal with these issues.

The second instrument mentioned by Act 112/2016 is that of *vincoli di destinazione* (restrictions on use of assets), introduced to the Italian legal framework in 2005 via article 2645-ter. of the Civil Code. This rule allows for the setting of official deeds through which registered real estate assets or moveable assets may be designated – for up to 90 years or for the lifetime of the beneficiary of the deed – in order to fulfil interests worthy of protection concerning, among others, people with disabilities. Unlike the trust, which concerns any asset (including real estate, moveable assets, shareholdings, credit instruments), the instrument of *vincoli di destinazione* concerns only real estate or moveable assets enrolled in official registers. Furthermore, the assets bound by *vincoli di destinazione* cannot be subsequently increased.

The last instrument is the *fondi speciali composti di beni sottoposti a vincolo di destinazione e disciplinati con contratto di affidamento fiduciario* (special funds consisting of assets with a restriction on use and regulated with the contract of fiduciary entrustment),

21 M. Lupoi, *Trusts*, Milano, Giuffrè, 2001.
22 F. Vitulo, 'Il trust come strumento di tutela dei soggetti deboli', *in* E. Vivaldi (Ed.), *Disabilità e sussidiarietà. Il "dopo di noi", tra regole e buone prassi*, Bologna, Il Mulino, 2012.
23 G. Arconzo, 'La L. n. 122 del 2016: i diritti delle persone con disabilità grave prive del sostegno familiare', *Il Corriere Giuridico*, No. 4, 2017, pp. 515-523
24 Arconzo, ibid; T. Tassani, 'La fiscalità dei negozi di destinazione nella legge sul "dopo di noi", tra agevolazione e impatto sistematico', *Notariato*, No. 5, pp. 517-527.

which consists of agreements through which a person transfers to another person (the trustee) assets or rights in order to be managed for the benefit of the beneficiary, according to a specific programme that binds the parties, establishing their duration, obligations, conditions and procedures. Unlike *vincoli di destinazione*, in the case of the special funds the objects of the transaction are also movable assets not enrolled in official registers. According to Act 112/2016, the funds created in favour of non-profit organizations operating in the charity sector also fall within the *fondi speciali* for which this Act provides tax breaks.

Act 112/2016 identifies some conditions to be met in order to benefit from tax breaks in the creation of the above-mentioned instruments. In particular, these instruments must be established through an official deed and must be aimed at the social inclusion, care and assistance of people with serious disabilities, in favour of whom they have been set up. The Act also requires that: all the individuals involved and their respective tasks must be clearly identified; the specific needs of the people with disabilities must be set out; assistance activities for the care of people with disabilities and fulfilment of their needs must be indicated; and the legal obligations of the trustee, settlor and benefactor must be identified.

Furthermore, Act 112/2016 requires the identification of a protector carrying out the task of checking the fulfilment of obligations for the establishment of trusts or *vincoli di destinazione* or *fondi speciali*. While this constitutes an important provision, the legislator has not, however, defined the tasks of the protectors and has not illustrated how they should interact with other legal instruments aimed at supporting disabled people, such as the Support Administrator (*Amministratore di sostegno*) introduced by Act 6/2004.[25] Doctrine and case law will be called on to clarify these aspects.

With regard to tax breaks, Act 112/2016 (article 6) has established, among the other things, that since January 2017 the assets allocated in the aforementioned three instruments are exempt from succession and donation tax, and that mortgage and registry taxes apply with a fixed amount and not in a proportional way. In order to protect the families of people with serious disability, the legislator has clarified that these tax reliefs apply even in cases where the disabled person dies before his/her relatives who have established the trust or one of the other instruments mentioned in the Act. Yet, these facilitations dot not apply if the relatives who have established the trust or the other instruments have already died at the time in which the person with disability dies. The Act also introduces an exemption from stamp duty for the legal documents regarding the management of separate assets.

In addition, Act 112/2016 establishes that in the case of the transfer of real estate or real rights to the trusts or *fondi speciali*, the municipalities may establish reduced rates, deductibles or exemptions with respect to the municipal tax. Yet, given that this shall not

25 Arconzo, op cit, n. 23.

imply "new or major charges for public finance" (article 6), it is likely that the municipalities may have difficulties in applying these facilitations.[26] Act 112/2016 also introduces some facilitations in the case of free gifts or other free acts carried out by private individuals towards trust or special funds.

Finally, it is worth mentioning that Act 112/2016 (article 5) also provides for the possibility to deduct up to a maximum of €750 in relation to insurance premiums on the condition that these are life insurance policies for people with serious disabilities.

C *Information Campaigns*

Act 122/2016 also requires the development of information campaigns aimed at influencing public opinion at large around supporting the social inclusion of people with disabilities.

IV Living Independently and Inclusion in the Community through Individualised Projects and Deinstitutionalisation

While different legislative interventions have dealt with the right of people with disabilities to live independently and be included in the community since the 1990s, it is with Act 112/2016 that the national legislator addressed this right in an advanced way in line with what is set forth in the 2016 UNCRPD.

The main instrument introduced by Act 112/2016 to ensure the fulfilment of the right to independent living and inclusion in society is the above-mentioned Fund for the Assistance of Persons with Serious Disabilities Lacking Family Support.[27] There are in particular two related and central aspects of this instrument that need to be highlighted in this regard: first, the attention to the development of individualised projects for people with disabilities and second, the promotion of paths of deinstitutionalisation and community services.

As previously illustrated, Act 112/2016 states that its measures shall be integrated, with the involvement of the people concerned, in the individualised projects provided by Act 328/2000 concerning an integrated system of social services. The Ministerial Decree of 23 November 2016[28] – on the requirements to access the measures of the Fund of Act 112/2016 – provides more details in this regard. The Decree specifies that access to the interventions implemented through the Fund occurs after a multidimensional evaluation by a group of diverse experts in the field. This evaluation is aimed at defining an individu-

26 Ibid.

27 Ibid.

28 The text of the Decree is available at: http://www.lavoro.gov.it/documenti-e-norme/normative/Documents/2017/decreto-Dopo-di-Noi-registrato.pdf.

alised project for the person with disability, the goal of which is to identify the specific support and help that the person needs, including health and social services. This provision is particularly important as the creation of individualised projects, and therefore of individualised support services,[29] constitutes one of the main conditions for ensuring that people with disabilities can exercise their right to independent living and be included in society:

> Individualised support services must be considered a right rather than a form of medical, social or charity care. For many persons with disabilities, access to a range of individualised support services is a precondition for independent and community living. Persons with disabilities have the right to choose services and service providers according to their individual requirements and personal preferences, and individualised support should be flexible enough to adapt to the requirements of the "users" and not the other way around.[30]

In line with the principle "nothing about us, without us" advocated by the movement for the rights of people with disabilities,[31] and which also inspired the drafting of the 2006 UNCRPD,[32] both Act 112/2016 and the 2016 Ministerial Decree stress the active role that people with serious disabilities should have in defining the individualised projects concerning their lives, and therefore in imagining, outlining and building their future. In particular, the Ministerial Decree explicitly affirms that the personalised projects should be "defined guaranteeing the widest possible participation of the person with serious disability, taking into account his/her desires, expectations, preferences and also foreseeing his/her full involvement in the following monitoring and assessing phase".[33] Where persons with a disability are not able to fully express their will, they can be supported by their parents or by whoever protects their interests.

The Ministerial Decree also states that each individualised project contains a project budget (*budget di progetto*) defined as the whole of the economic, human and professional resources to be used in a "flexible, dynamic and integrated way" to implement the services provided in the individualised projects. The introduction of a personal budget, which is in accordance with Article 19 of the UNCRPD,[34] constitutes a fundamental means to empower people with disabilities to have increased levels of choice, guaranteeing them an

29 G. Arconzo, 'Il diritto alla vita indipendente delle persone con disabilità', *in* A. Morelli & L. Trucco (Eds.), *Diritti e autonomie territoriali*, Torino, Giappichelli, 2014, pp. 266-276

30 Committee on the Rights of Persons with Disabilities, op cit, n. 13, para. 27.

31 J.I. Charlton, *Nothing about us without us: disability oppression and empowerment*, Berkeley, University of California Press, 1998.

32 C. Colapietro, *Diritti dei Disabili e Costituzione*, Napoli, Edizione Scientifica, 2011, p. 48.

33 Ministerial Decree 23 November 2016, op cit, n. 28.

34 Committee on the Rights of Persons with Disabilities, op cit, n. 17.

equal right to choose necessary services, to make their own decisions and to participate in society. According to this model, the budget should be allocated to persons with disabilities on the basis of an assessment of individual needs and life circumstances, optimising the use of the resources in a non-fragmented way. As the president of the National Association of Families of Persons with Intellectual and/or Relational Disabilities has stressed,

> to speak about a project budget means that we do not think in terms of fees and beds but in terms of a life project: the project budget guarantees the economic resources to each person to be able to build 'the tailor-made suit', this is absolutely innovative because it is by no means on the other side.[35]

In conformity with an approach aimed at providing specific and individualised support to people with disabilities according to their needs, capabilities, requirements and preferences, Act 112/2016, as illustrated above, dedicates special attention to fostering paths of deinstitutionalisation and community services through the resources of the Funds for the Assistance of Persons with Serious Disabilities. As affirmed in Article 19 of the UNCRPD, the right to live independently and to participate in the community encompasses ensuring people with disabilities have the opportunity to choose and decide how, where and with whom to live. People with disabilities shall have the same rights as others in deciding their place of residence and living arrangements. They should not be obliged to live in an institution or residential facility.

It is worth mentioning that in Italy Act n. 180 of 1978 established the closure of psychiatric hospitals and the creation of alternative services, marking the passage from an approach in which people with disabilities were seen as a menace and tended to be isolated and segregated, to a vision aimed at their social integration. Nevertheless, to date the main pillar of policies on residential facilities for people with disabilities, especially in the case of people with serious disabilities, has been the institutionalisation of services without the implementation of effective paths aimed at overcoming segregation and isolation.[36] This trend has also been reported on with concern by the UN Committee on the Rights of Persons with Disabilities, which has recommended that Italy "redirect resources from institutionalisation to community-based services and increase budget support".[37]

In line with this, the above-mentioned Second National Biennial Programme on disability has also stressed the need to accelerate processes of deinstitutionalisation, by

35 S. De Carli, 'Firmato il decreto attuativo: il dopo di noi diventa concreto', *Vita*, 28 November 2016.

36 Initial report of Italy (CRPD/C/ITA/1), 2013. Available at: https://documents-dds-ny.un.org/doc/UNDOC/GEN/G15/044/22/PDF/G1504422.pdf?OpenElement. It should be emphasized that in 2014 Act n. 81 established the closure of the forensic psychiatric hospitals by March 2015 (*ospedali psichiatrici giudiziari*). Yet, the last forensic psychiatric hospitals were finally closed only in 2017.

37 Committee on the Rights of Persons with Disabilities, op cit, n. 17.

developing a range of residential, in-home and community support services adaptable to the individual needs of people with disabilities.

Against this background, Act 112/2016 constitutes an important step forward by clearly recognising deinstitutionalisation as a key issue for the wellbeing, autonomy and social inclusion of people with disabilities. The Act provides for the implementation of housing services, taking into account also the instruments offered by new technologies, and for the development of innovative residential solutions, such as co-housing. To counter conditions of isolation and segregation, these housing solutions, as the 2016 Ministerial Decree has significantly established, shall be located in residential areas, or more generally in non-isolated areas, in order to ensure the "affective and relation continuity" of the people hosted, creating an environment which meets and responds to their needs and preferences.[38]

V Act 122/2016: A Real Challenge for the "Familistic" Welfare State?

While Act 112/2016 can be considered innovative and a significant achievement in the path for the recognition of the rights of people with disabilities, especially with respect to the right to independent living and inclusion in the community, there are some problematic aspects that need to be stressed.

The first aspect open to criticism concerns the subjects of Act 112/2016. As illustrated above, the Act exclusively focuses on people with serious disabilities, "not caused by natural ageing or by diseases related to senility". It therefore excludes from its provisions all those persons with disabilities who, even if their conditions are not "serious", require continual assistance and support. This approach, which is in contradiction to the 2006 UNCRPD in which neither the type nor the degree of disability affecting a person have any relevance,[39] raises the question of the definition of the concept of disability, and in particular of serious disability.

As underscored in the Second National Biennial Programme on Disability, the Italian legal framework currently lacks adequate instruments to certify a situation of "disability" (serious or not). The concept of "serious disability" in fact corresponds, as in Act 112/2016, to the state of serious handicap defined in the afore-mentioned Act 104/1992 on assistance, social integration and the rights of persons with a disability. This definition, as highlighted above, mainly relies on a medical approach to disability, stressing the limitations of impairments and the consequent social disadvantage created by these. Thus, unlike the approach of the 2006 UNCRPD, this definition does not pay attention to the environment in which people with disabilities live, and to the interaction between people with disabilities and the social, cultural and practical barriers that impede their full and effective participa-

38 Ministerial Decree 23 November 2016, op cit, n. 28.

39 Bernardini, op cit, n. 10.

tion in society. From this perspective, the reference in Act 112/2016 to the definition of "serious handicap" contained in Act 104/1992 risks undermining the achievement of the aims of Act 112 itself, defined in accordance with the principle of the 2006 UNCRPD.

In addition to being in a situation of serious disability, the other requirement necessary to benefit from the provisions of Act 112/2016 is a lack of family support. In this regard, it is relevant to highlight that the Act seems to restrict the concept of family to that of parents, as it refers to: people with serious disabilities "lacking family support because they are missing both parents or their parents are not able to provide adequate support" (article 1). This approach, as Arconzo has stressed, seems to be in tension with recent case law of the Italian Constitutional Court that, in reference to the provisions of Act 104/1992, has extended the notion of family by granting de facto cohabitants the opportunity to have paid days of leave from work to assist people with disabilities.[40]

On the other hand, it needs to be highlighted that over recent years family networks in Italy have changed, becoming increasingly narrow and "long".[41] Indeed, while there has been an increase in the ageing of the population, there has also been a significant decrease in the number of family members and an increase in their geographical mobility. This has undermined family solidarity and, accordingly, those members (mainly women) who carry out care activities have found themselves even more alone in meeting the needs of dependent family members for care. In the absence of adequate welfare support, these changes in family structure, together with other factors such as the growth in female participation in the labour market, have fostered an increase in the outsourcing of (migrant) domestic/care work[42] while families have assumed the role of "care managers", managing the economic and bureaucratic matters related to the employment of care workers.[43] In this light, the choice of the legislator to limit the concept of family to the presence of parents can be viewed as an attempt to address the contemporary complexity and changes in family structure in a way that is in favour of people with disabilities: the adoption of this narrow conception of family makes it easier for them to meet the requirements to benefit from the provisions of Act 112/2016.

While Act 112/2016 is addressed to people with disabilities without family support, its measures – as specified in article 1– can also be applied in view of a lack of family support, through the progressive taking charge of the person concerned while their parents still remain present. This provision, which is also reaffirmed in the 2016 Ministerial Decree, recognises the need to sustain people with serious disabilities not only when they lack

40 Arconzo, op cit, n. 23. A. Cordiano, 'La dichiarazione di incostituzionalità della legge 104/1992 e l'estensione del beneficio del permesso al lavoratore convivente di fatto', *Forum di Quaderni Costituzionali Rassegna*, N. 4, 2016.

41 ISTAT, *Come cambiano le forme familiari*, Report, 2011.

42 Casalini, op cit, n. 2; Maioni & Zucca, op cit, n. 7.

43 M. Ambrosini, *Irregular migration and invisible welfare*, London, Palgrave Macmillan, 2013.

family help, but also in the phase of progressive separation from family support, ensuring them a continuity in the trajectory of their lives. Yet, by focusing on the so-called "after us" period and on the phase of transition towards this period, Act 112/2016 seems not to call into question a national welfare system which delegates to families the main role in providing care to their dependent members and/or in managing all the related economic and bureaucratic issues. In other words, the concern of the legislator is to address the moment in which families are no longer able to carry out their role as carers, or to carry this out adequately, and to make this transition more gradual and less painful for people with disabilities. The issue of how the state should directly and effectively take over the burden of care activities is, therefore, not addressed.

Closely related to this point is the fact that both Act 112/2016 and the 2016 Ministerial Decree do not make any reference to the tasks, responsibilities and rights of the care-givers, seeming in this way to overlook care work and the social, health and economic costs that it entails. In this regard, it is worth mentioning that currently the Italian Parliament is considering a bill concerning those who provide non-professional and free care for dependent people. Yet, as has been noted, this bill seems to consist merely of a formal acknowledgment of the role of care-givers, without recognising their rights and without challenging the central role of families in the Italian welfare system.[44]

With regard to the Fund for the Assistance of Persons with Serious Disabilities Lacking Family Support established by Act 112/2016, the fact that the resources of this Fund are mainly addressed to the development of individualised projects for people with disabilities and paths of deinstitutionalization undoubtedly constitutes progress for the realisation of the right of people with disabilities to live independently and be included in the community. Nevertheless, it is relevant to consider that there are no clear data on people with disabilities. The National Institute for Statistics (ISTAT) has indeed denounced the difficulties in identifying the number of people with serious disabilities as defined in Act 112/2016.[45] The lack of clear data makes it particularly difficult to establish investments and long-term plans, as well as to assess the congruence of resources allocated by Act 112/2016 and, accordingly, the real sustainability of the projects that the Act itself would like to assure.

Diverse associations have denounced the exiguity of the economic resources provided for the Fund.[46] Moreover, in 2018 the original amount of the Fund was reduced by cutting €5 million. Although the Budget Act for 2019 has established an increase of €5 million for each year of the three-year period 2019-2021, the resources are still inadequate and do not respond to the real need for care of people with disabilities in Italy. As the National Asso-

44 S. De Carli, 'Delude il testo unificato per il riconoscimento del caregiver famigliare', *Vita*, 28 September 2017; B. Casalini, 'Caregiver familiari, serve un vero riconoscimento', *Ingenere*, 5 May 2016.

45 ISTAT, *Nota sulla legge dopo di noi*, 2017, p. 5, available at: https://www.istat.it/it/archivio/200674.

46 See http://www.vita.it/it/article/2017/12/01/la-legge-sul-dopo-di-noi-e-operativa-solo-in-cinque-regioni/145290/.

ciation of Disabled and Civil Invalids has pointed out, the choice of the legislator to address the assistance and support of people with serious disabilities "through the use of variable, contingent and insufficient funds, and not through an institutionalised system of fundamental provisions, services and economic help to which it corresponds the full freedom of choice of people with serious disabilities or of the person who represents them" risks largely limiting the potentiality of the measures provided by the Act, putting into question the effective involvement of the state in addressing care issues.[47]

On the basis of these considerations, it is not surprising that, as a recent study has shown, the implementation of Act 112/2016 has thus far been slow and inadequate across the country, highlighting its limits in effectively promoting the development of a welfare system based on diverse and structural services for the care of dependent people. The Act, indeed, has been implemented in only a few Regions, such as Lombardy, that have already developed excellent systems of social-health inclusion for dependents through an integrated network of services widespread in the area.[48]

As for the provision of Act 112/2016 concerning tax breaks for the establishment of instruments such as trusts, *vincoli di destinazione* and *fondi speciali*, this measure addresses a relatively limited number of cases: it is applicable in those situations in which there are sufficient assets to be destined for guaranteeing adequate life conditions to a disabled person and therefore to be used for the creation of instruments such as trusts.[49] In this regard, it is worth noting that to date there has been little use of this provision.[50]

VI Concluding Remarks

Act 122/2016, providing measures on the assistance for people with serious disabilities lacking family support, constitutes significant progress for the rights of people with disabilities, especially for the fulfilment of the right to live independently and be included in the community as set out by the 2006 UN Convention on the Rights of Persons with Disabilities. This Act has provided for the establishment of a Fund, whose resources shall be used for the development of individualised projects for people with serious disability and, especially, for the promotion and paths of deinstitutionalisation in line with Article 19 of the 2016 UN Convention. The Act has also established tax breaks for the creation of instruments of allocation of assets such as trusts.

47 ANMIC, 'Riflessioni ANMIC sulla legge in materia di "dopo di noi"', 2016, available at: http://www.sanita24.ilsole24ore.com/pdf2010/Editrice/ILSOLE24ORE/QUOTIDIANO_SANITA/Online/_Oggetti_Correlati/Documenti/2016/09/08/DISABILI_DOPO_DI_NOI.pdf?uuid=AD0GwVGB.

48 Anffas, *Percorso di attuazione delle Legge 112/2016*, 2018, available at: http://www.anffas.net/it/chi-siamo/la-nostra-organizzazione/fondazione-dopo-di-noi/.

49 ANMIC, op cit, n. 47.

50 Anffas, op cit, n. 48.

These measures are certainly important for the realisation of the well-being, autonomy and social inclusion of people with serious disability lacking family support. Nevertheless, as this paper has sought to illustrate, they risk having a limited impact and, above all, not in effect challenging the model of the national "familistic" welfare system. The lack within the Italian legal framework of adequate instruments to certify a situation of "disability" (serious or not) in line with the 2016 UN Convention probably constitutes one of the main factors that affect the implementation of Act 112/2016 and that risk undermining the achievement of the aims of its provisions. On the other hand, there are some highly problematic aspects of the approach and measures of the Act itself. As pointed out in this paper, the legislator, importantly, has established that the measures of Act 112/2016 apply not only in the case of people with serious disabilities without family support but also in view of the lack of family support, through the progressive taking charge of the person concerned. Yet, by focusing on the so-called "after us" period (with "us" referring to the families) and on the phase of transition towards this period, Act 112/2016 seems not to call into question a national welfare system which considers families to be the main parties responsible for providing and managing care activities. In other words, the issue of how the state should directly and effectively take responsibility for the care of dependent people from birth, seems to have been overlooked.

This is also reflected in the measures provided by Act 112/2016. On the one hand, the choice of using variable and insufficient funds, rather than implementing a system of structural services and necessary economic help, seems not to ensure the real sustainability of projects for the independent living of people with serious disabilities. On the other, the provision regarding tax breaks for the creation of instruments such as trusts is likely to be of relevance to only a limited range of the population, to the detriment of people in disadvantaged economic conditions.

In order to effectively address the issue of the care and assistance of people with disabilities, in particular with respect to their right to live independently and be included in society, it is necessary to implement structural and concerted measures by developing a structured plan for people with disabilities, guaranteeing that each person is supported – from birth throughout the course of life – by various personalised and coordinated services, ensuring the right of self-determination and the respect for the freedom of choice of the person as well as the right of the members of his/her family to choose whether or not to provide for care, and how this should be done.

Taking Care of Rain Man:[*] Interaction between Parental Estate Planning and Disability Benefits

Veerle Vanderhulst[**]

I Introduction: Ageing Parents of Disabled Adult Children and their Concerns about the Future

"It is a cruel thing to say, but I hope my daughter dies before I do." These are the words of an ageing mother who lives together with her forty-year-old mentally handicapped daughter, in response to the question how she sees the future.[1] The quote is illustrative of the worries universally experienced by ageing parents of disabled adult children. Research shows that ageing parents of a disabled child worry about the future.[2] This is especially the case with regard to the time when the ageing parents will no longer be able to take care of their disabled child themselves or they die prior to their child, i.e. the so-called *l'après-parents* or *post-parent* age.

The fact that parents worry about *l'après-parents*, may not come as a surprise, as they often play a very important role in the care for their disabled grown-up child during their lifetime. Parents fulfil the role of actual caregiver, e.g. when they provide housing as they

---

* Movie lovers will recognize the central character of the 1988 Oscar winning movie of the same name: Raymond, a.k.a Rain Man, is an adult suffering from autism and a genius at maths. When his only remaining parent dies, he inherits from his father no less than $3 million under a trust favouring the institution where he resides. This parental estate planning angers his disinherited professionally successful brother, and in an attempt to get his hands on the $3 million he decides to kidnap his disabled brother, taking him on a road trip through the country. The adventures of the two brothers – although entertaining – are less relevant to this paper than the actual starting point of the story, which serves as the starting point of this paper, i.e. the attempt of a parent to care for his disabled adult child *after* both parents have died. See full storyline on: www.imdb.com.

** Doctoral student, Faculty of Law and Criminology, Free University of Brussels. This chapter won the International Society of Family Law's Early Career Researcher Prize at the 16th World Conference held in Amsterdam in 2017.

1 D. Serneels, *Bejaarde ouders met een thuiswonende mentaal gehandicapte zoon of dochter: omgaan met de toekomst*, Leuven, Universitaire Pers Leuven, 1994, p. 126.

2 See, for example, research on the situation of adults with disabilities living at home with their parents and the parents' views on the future: L. Bowey & A. McGlaughlin, 'Older Carers of Adults with a Learning Disability Confront the Future: Issues and Preferences in Planning', *British Journal of Social Work*, Vol. 37, 2007, pp. 39-54; H. Prosser, 'The Future Care Plans of Older Adults with Intellectual Disabilities Living at Home with Family Carers', *Journal of Applied Research in Intellectual Disabilities*, Vol. 10, 1997, pp. 15-32.

continue to live together as a family even after the child has reached majority. They act as supervisor or care monitor when they represent their adult child in the "care users' advisory board" of the care institution.[3] They finance care, especially when they pay for the expenses resulting from admission in a care institution. They act as administrator, such as when they are appointed guardian and make sure that the financial resources of their disabled offspring are used to pay medical bills. Along with the prospect of the parents' death, the big question is who will fill in the gap in care that arises from their passing away and who will take on the different care-related activities in succession to the parents.

Making plans for the future may bring peace of mind to the parents and may prevent crises resulting from the sudden loss of the parents' support following their death. Moulding these future plans into legally binding provisions and transforming the parents' estate into actual care arrangements that last beyond the parents' lifetime is the core business of such parental estate planning. It comprises the setup of a detailed plan that stipulates the different legal transactions to be carried out in a timely manner to provide care for the disabled adult child after the parents have passed away.

Given contemporary trends in society, proactive estate planning with the object of providing care for a disabled child is increasingly relevant. In recent years, it has become more likely that a disabled person will outlive his parents and enter into *l'après-parents*. Indeed, owing to medical and other evolutions, the life expectancy of disabled persons has increased,[4] in at least some instances (e.g. children with intellectual disabilities) in developed countries.[5] In addition, in the last decades family structures have changed:[6] nowadays, families are characterized by many vertical ties and relatively few horizontal ties.[7] This may affect the availability of family members (other than the parents) who are spontaneously willing to take care of their disabled relative after the parents have passed away. Also

3 In Belgium – at least in the Flemish Community, i.e. the Dutch-speaking part of the country – each residential care institution is obliged to install a "care users' advisory board" in order to receive subsidies by the government. Via this board, care users are actively involved in matters concerning the relationship between the care institution and the care users. See arts. 27 to 30, Decision of the Flemish Government 4 February 2001 concerning the general conditions for recognition by the authorities and the quality assurance of institutions and services providing care, treatment and support for persons with a disability, *Belgian Official Journal* 8 April 2011 (Belgium).

4 Serneels, op cit, n. 1, pp. 5-14, with reference to international scientific studies.

5 WHO, *World Report on Disability*, World Health Organization, 2011, pp. 60 and 142.

6 On changes in family structures, see e.g. F. Rothenbacher, 'Social Change in Europe and its Impact on Family Structures', *in* J. Eekelaar & T. Nhlapo (Eds.), *The Changing Family. Family Forms and Family Law*, Oxford, Hart Publishing, 1998, pp. 10-21.

7 P.A. Dykstra & E.A. Komter, 'Generational Interdependencies in Families: The MULTILINKS Research Programme', *Demographic Research*, Vol. 27, 2012, pp. 487-506; V.L. Bengston, 'Beyond the Nuclear Family: The Increasing Importance of Multigenerational Bonds', *Journal of Marriage and Family*, Vol. 63, 2001, pp. 1-16.

important is the shift from an institutional care model to a community-based care model.[8] Whereas an institutional care model locates care for disabled persons in an institutional and rather isolated environment exclusively relying on professional caregivers, a community care model encourages care to be provided by family members in a homely environment thus including disabled persons in society.[9]

This paper examines one particular aspect of parental estate planning in favour of a disabled adult child that deserves special attention, i.e. the uneasy relationship between parental estate planning and disability benefits provided by the state. It is not only the parents who are supportive of their disabled son or daughter: the state is too. In Belgium, as is the case in the majority of states worldwide,[10] people with disabilities may benefit from different types of disability benefits within the framework of collective social protection. The question arises whether the legal care arrangements of the parents influence the disabled child's entitlement to these disability benefits.

First, this paper takes a closer look at estate planning itself and the various legal tools available to shape such a plan (Section II). Subsequently, social protection by the state and its interaction with parental estate planning is considered (Section III). The paper ends with some concluding remarks and thoughts about future prospects (Section IV).

II Family (Property) Law and Care Arrangements for Disabled Adult Children

The following paragraphs explore what instruments and legal tools parents have at their disposal to shape estate planning in favour of their disabled adult child. A review of all the many permutations available in law is outside the scope of this paper; instead a generalised global overview is offered.

Planning opportunities in favour of children with disabilities may be subject to more limitations in comparison to planning opportunities in favour of children without disabilities, precisely because of the relative's disability. The law may impose procedural safeguards with respect to certain transactions involving the disabled child as beneficiary. In Belgium, for example, when the disabled child is subject to an adult guardianship measure, pure and simple acceptance of the parents' inheritance is allowed only if certain conditions are met.[11] These kinds of limitations are, however, unlikely to determine the actual content of the estate plan, but merely have minor practical implications for its actual realization.

8 See e.g. Communication from the Commission to the European Parliament, the Council, the European Economic and Social Committee and the Committee of the Regions. European Disability Strategy 2010-2020, *A Renewed Commitment to a Barrier-Free Europe*, 15 November 2010, COM(2010) 636 final.

9 WHO, op cit, n. 5, pp. 3 and 156.

10 ILO, *World Social Protection Report 2014/15*, International Labour Organization, 2014.

11 Art. 499/7,§2,5° Civil Code (Belgium).

However, the presence of the disability may have more far-reaching implications. In Russia, for example, adult children are entitled to a reserved portion of their parents' estate only if they are unable to work due to their disability.[12] Thus, the freedom of testation of the parent of an adult child depends on whether this child is handicapped or not.

Next, the question arises whether the law provides supplementary tools specifically tailored and exclusively available for estate planning in favour of adult disabled children, to the exclusion of abled-bodied children. In Belgian family (property) law, no such tools are to be found:[13] parents with children with disabilities have no extra auxiliaries or remedies at their disposal to shape their plan. However, in several other jurisdictions, the law does provide for specific instruments only to be employed for the benefit of disabled relatives. In France, for example, the "continuing powers of attorney for another person" (*mandat de protection pour autrui*) was introduced. This variant of continuing powers of attorney entails the designation by the parents – without any intervention of the court – of a person who will represent their disabled child after their death.[14] This allows parents to choose a person whom they trust to administer the child's fortune. Another example can be found in the USA, where parents of disabled children may establish a "special needs trust".[15] This is a discretionary spendthrift trust created for a beneficiary with a disability that supplements, but does not supplant, public benefits for which the beneficiary may be eligible.[16]

Finally, it is noted that several family (property) law rules, while not exclusively applying to disabled family members, may nevertheless be particularly relevant to them in this context. Indeed, in Belgium, exactly the hypothesis of a disabled child appears to be (part of) the underlying motive of some legal provisions, though their range of application is effectively much wider. This is, for example, the case for the rules on the reserved portion of children in the estate of their parent and the freedom of the legator to dispose of the remaining part, allowing the testator to favour one child (e.g. because of his disability)

---

12 Art. 1148 Civil Code (Russia); Commission on European Family Law, *National report on informal relationships: Russia. Report by M. Antokolskaia*, January 2015, p. 23, http://www.ceflonline.net/country-reports-by-subject; R. Frank, 'Family Solidarity in Support and Inheritance Law', *in* B. Verschraegen (Ed.), *Family Finances*, Vienna, Jan Sramek Verlag KG, 2009, p. 20 (footnote 92 mistakenly refers to art. 1128 instead of art. 1148).

13 Belgian marriage law includes some specific provisions dealing with the eventuality of one of the spouses becoming incapacitated. This paper does not examine these provisions, as they only apply in the context of marriage and are more likely to protect the household's interest than the individual's.

14 Art. 477 Civil Code (France). The Belgian law of persons includes what at first seems to be a similar provision: administrators – in the context of adult guardianship measures – can express their preference concerning the next-to-be-appointed administrator (art. 496/1 Civil Code (Belgium)). However, this expression of preference does not have the same status as the French *mandat pour autrui*, among other things because this preference merely serves as a guideline for the judge who will appoint the administrator in the context of a judicial protection measure.

15 42 US Code §1396p(d)(4)(A) *jo.* 42 US Code §1382c(a)(3) (USA).

16 R.P. Lacey & H.D. Nadler, 'Special Needs Trusts', *Family Law Quarterly*, Vol. 46, No. 2, 2012, pp. 247-67.

over another.[17] The underlying considerations mentioned in the preparatory proceedings of the Civil Code dating from 1804 come across as a pioneer example of parental estate planning in favour of a disabled child even before the term existed.[18]

To sum up, parents have various instruments or legal tools at their disposal to shape the plan for the future. In Belgium, there are no specific tools that exclusively apply to disabled children, so parents need to have recourse to classical instruments to set up the care arrangement, such as donations, bequests, life insurances, the establishment of a private foundation, etc.

III Disability Benefits by the State and Parental Care Arrangements for Disabled Adult Children

The following paragraphs consider to what extent such provision made by the parents is likely to influence the child's entitlement to disability benefits by the state. First, the right to social protection is briefly discussed (Section A). Subsequently, the complex relationship between state and family support is touched upon in a general way (Section B). Then, the interaction between the two levels of protection is discussed more in detail with respect to financial support (Section C) and support in kind (Section D).

A Right to Social Protection for Persons with Disabilities

Article 28 of the United Nations Convention on the Rights of Persons with Disabilities (CRPD) – one of the most widely ratified UN treaties[19] – refers for the first time in an international instrument to the right of disabled persons to social protection and links it to the right to an adequate standard of living.[20] States parties are obliged to "take steps to safeguard and promote the realization of this right".[21] Article 28, 2 enumerates five types of measures States Parties should undertake, including measures concerning services and

---

17 When the testator has two children for example, the legal portion of each of them equals one fourth of the estate. The testator may freely dispose of the remaining half of his estate.

18 See P.A. Fenet, *Recueil complet des travaux préparatoires du Code civil*, Tome III, Paris, Videcoq, 1836, p. 53.

19 G. Quinn, 'A short guide to the United Nations Convention on the Rights of Persons with Disabilities', *in* G. Quinn & L. Waddington (Eds.), *European Yearbook of Disability Law, Vol. 1*, Antwerp, Intersentia, 2009, p. 91.

20 Report of the Special Rapporteur on the rights of persons with disabilities (7 August 2015), UN Doc. A/70/297, p. 8; R. Sainsbury, A. Lawson & M. Priestley, *Social protection for disabled people in Europe: synthesis report. Report on behalf of the European network of academic experts in the field of disability (ANED)*, 23 January 2017, p. 4. At present, the convention has been ratified or acceded to by 176 states and by the European Union.

21 Art. 28, 2 UN CRPD.

devices for disability-related needs, income protection, disability-related expenses, housing costs and retirement benefits for people with disabilities. In this paper, the term "disability benefits" is used as an umbrella term referring to all kinds of measures that fall within the scope of the right to social protection.

In accordance with this common international framework, it is up to each state to include in its own manner and in its own domestic legal framework the right to social protection.[22] Thus, disability benefits may take various forms, depending on the objectives – i.e. the detailed enumeration of the different measures in article 28 CRPD – and on the specific societal context of the various states. In Belgium, people with disabilities may benefit from both specific regulations exclusively applying to the disabled (e.g. income replacement allowance, integration allowance, personal care budget, as explained below), and wider social security programmes. Furthermore, various measures are spread over a great number of statutes (e.g. in the field of social aid, housing, education, social work, tax regulations, etc.).[23]

Social protection programmes play a very important role in "alleviating and preventing poverty and vulnerability, promoting effective access to health care and other services, and foster inclusion and participation".[24] However, it is a common criticism – applicable to the Belgian scheme – that the level of benefits is too low.[25] Research shows that there is a high level of hidden poverty among people with disabilities. In general, though, the average income level is relatively high in Belgium, which can be characterized as a highly developed country.[26] About 23% of the population in working age (i.e. aged 16 to 64 year) are persons with disabilities.[27] About 5% of the Belgian population are recipients of disability benefits.[28] A survey carried out amongst 1,118 recipients of disability benefits showed 39% of the interviewees reported an income below the EU poverty line.[29] As far as access to services for disability-related needs is concerned, highly dependent persons face waiting lists for periods sometimes exceeding three years, due to the shortage of places in care institutions.

---

22 Report of the Special Rapporteur, op cit, n. 20, p. 14.

23 B. Van Buggenhout, 'Legislation concerning the Disabled: a Challenge for Developing Countries', *in* Instituut voor Sociaal Recht (Ed.), *Sociale Bescherming op nieuwe paden. Liber Memorialis Béatrice Van Buggenhout*, Leuven, Universitaire Pers Leuven, 2003, p. 568.

24 Report of the Special Rapporteur, op cit, n. 20, p. 5.

25 Sainsbury et al, op cit, n,. 20 p. 5.

26 World Bank Country profile of Belgium (http://data.worldbank.org/country/belgium). See also National Bank of Belgium Online Statistics (https://stat.nbb.be).

27 ANED, *European comparative data on Europe 2020 & people with disabilities. Final report prepared by Stefanos Grammenos from Centre for European Social and Economic Policy (CESEP ASBL) on behalf of the Academic Network of Europe and Disability Experts (ANED)*, December 2013, p. 21 (http://www.disability-europe.net/theme/statistical-indicators).

28 ANED, *Adequate standard of living and social protection (Article 28 of UN CRPD). Statistical Indicators. Final report prepared by Stefanos Grammenos from Centre for European Social and Economic Policy (CESEP ASBL) on behalf of ANED*, January 2016, p. 27.

29 ANED, *Country report on social protection and art. 28: Belgium. Report prepared by G. Van Hove, s.d.*, p. 5.

This situation lead in 2013 to a resolution of the European Committee of Ministers of the Council of Europe,[30] advising Belgium to bring the situation into conformity with the European Social Charter.

B The State vs. Mom and Dad?

Parents want the best for their child. From their point of view, it is understandable that they aim to create the best of both worlds by combining family protection (via their estate plan) and state protection (via disability benefits). Indeed, for most families the social protection offered by the state is of crucial importance, and the death of the parents will only increase this need. For example, as far as income protection is concerned, the level of protection provided by social allowances is nearly impossible to arrive at by family support only. Regarding disability-related services, it is questionable whether the supporting power of the family alone suffices to provide for day and night care for highly dependent people. In addition, the cash benefits provided by the state often enjoy an advantageous status as they may – as is the case in Belgium[31] – not be susceptible to seizure by creditors, an important advantage to adults suffering from prodigality or likely to (over-) indebtedness due to their disability. Furthermore, parents may hold the conviction that the social protection offered by the state – though vital – does not suffice and as a result try to "upgrade" the level of support by adding their own means as supplementary support on top of the social protection by the state.

However, the accumulation of family support and state support is not something to be taken for granted. Family protection and social protection relate to each other in a complex and multi-layered way. Ambivalence exists on which of the family or the state should be considered the primary care provider.[32] At the one end of the spectrum, the family is considered as the primary care provider. On that view, parental estate planning is likely to disqualify the disabled child for disability benefits, as on this view the available family resources should be exhausted first. At the other end of the spectrum, the state is considered the primary care provider. On that view, parental estate planning will have no effect on the eligibility for disability benefits by the state.

A question that relates to this controversy is whether care arrangements designed with the explicit aim of allocating the financial burden as much as possible on the state are reconcilable with the principles of public order and good morals. When the parents are very wealthy and in principle have sufficient resources, such planning could generate at

30 Resolution CM/Res ChS (2013) 16 of the Committee of Ministers (16 October 2013), International Federation for Human Rights (FIDH) v. Belgium.

31 Art. 1410, §2 Code of Civil Procedure (Belgium).

32 See the various contributions in M.T. Meulders-Klein & J. Ekelaar (Eds.), *Family, State and Individual Economic Security*, Brussels, Story-Scientia, 1988.

least some controversy in times of scarce state resources. The same question, however, has a different dimension when it comes to parents who have meagre resources and who want to use their limited resources as efficiently as possible to supplement the social protection. In Belgium, following German case law, legal doctrine assumes that such arrangements are entirely legitimate, regardless of the circumstances, though the question has not yet received much scholarly attention.[33]

C *Financial Support*

The support provided by means of parental estate planning may take various forms in order to improve or simply continue the care for the physical, mental and social well-being of the adult child. However, the plan may, for example, merely entail financial support, such as the donation of a considerable sum of money directly to the disabled person.

Logically, financial support by the parents is likely to affect the eligibility of the disabled person to disability benefits whenever the eligibility requirements relate to the financial situation of the disabled person. Usually, this is the case for cash benefits arising from non-contributory or distributive social protection programmes meant to ensure the maintenance of the disabled person, such as social assistance programmes that are fully financed by the state (as opposed to, for example, social insurance programmes).

In Belgium, the two main examples of means-tested allowances for people with disabilities are the income replacement allowance and the integration allowance. (By contrast, support with respect to services and devices for disability-related needs (e.g. access to specialized care in care institutions) is not means-tested.) The income replacement allowance applies to persons with disabilities who are unable to gain sufficient work income as a result of their disability, i.e. for people whose earnings capacity is reduced to a third or less of what a healthy person can earn in the general labor market.[34] The integration allowance is intended to compensate for the need for assistance from third parties and additional costs resulting from the impact of the disability on their independence in daily activities.[35] Indeed, research shows that the extra or additional costs may amount to 50% of an individual's income.[36] These income protection allowances are intended to ensure the livelihood of the disabled person. As a result, the allowances are not granted if the

---

33 See J. Bael, 'De planning van de nalatenschappen van de ouders van een gehandicapt kind anno 2004', *in* J. Bael, R. Deblauwe & C. De Wulf (Eds.), *Familiale vermogensplanning. XXXe Postuniversitaire cyclus Willy Delva. Familiale Vermogensplanning*, Kluwer, Mechelen, 2004, p. 469 with reference to German case law (Bundegerichtshof 21 March 1990 and Bundesgerichtshof 20 march 1993) and German doctrine.

34 Art. 2, § 1 Disability Allowances Act 27 February 1987, *Belgian Official Journal* 1 April 1987, *err.* 6 August 1987 (Belgium).

35 Art. 2, § 2, ibid.

36 Report of the Special Rapporteur, op cit, n. 20, p. 11.

person has access to other means to ensure this level of subsistence, even if his ability to gain income by work is lowered down to a third or he is confronted with additional costs for help with daily activities.

With respect to means-tested allowances, it is crucial to examine what exactly is considered as "means"'. In Belgium, the legislation on the income replacement allowance and the integration allowance uses the same concept of income that is used for income tax purposes. Without going into detail into all principles underlying Belgian income tax law,[37] one particular principle is of particular relevance, i.e. the legal distinction between capital and income. From an economic point of view, capital gains may increase a person's well-being and hence his ability to pay taxes, i.e. to contribute to the improvement of the well-being of less well-off people as taxes are being used for public services.[38] From a tax point of view, however, capital gains are not considered income. Hence, capital tax is not levied.[39] By introducing this concept of income in the regulation on social allowances, the legal distinction between capital and income is relevant to eligibility for social allowances as well as for the possible effects of parental estate planning on them.

Consequently, if financial support from the parents increases the capital of the disabled person, then eligibility to social allowances is unaffected. Beneficiary provisions that do *not* jeopardize the entitlement of the disabled child to social allowances comprise for example: first, a donation *inter vivos* or bequest of the parental home so the disabled child can continue to live in its familiar surroundings, as individuals do not need to pay taxes on income from real property that they use for housing purposes only;[40] second, the donation *inter vivos* or the bequest of a single sum of money outright, as this does not lead to an increase of taxable income but merely to an increase of capital.[41]

If the financial support from the parents leads to increase of income, then the measure risks reducing eligibility for the social allowances. Examples of measures that lead to a higher taxable income and thus may have a negative effect on the social allowances include: first, a donation *inter vivos* or a bequest of real property intended for rental purposes, thus providing the disabled person a monthly income by means of its taxable rental proceed-

37 For a brief overview of the general principles of tax law, see: P. Faes, *Belgian Income Tax Law: Principles and Practice*, Chichester, John Wiley & Sons Ltd, 1995, pp. 3-12; A. Spruyt, 'Taxation' *in* H. Bocken & W. De Bondt (Eds.), *Introduction to Belgian Law*, Brussel, Bruylant, 2001, pp. 348-356.

38 K. Holmes, *The Concept of Income. A Multi-Disciplinary Analysis*, Amsterdam, IBFD Publications BV, 2001, p. 572.

39 Ibid.

40 Art. 12, § 3 Income Tax Code (Belgium).

41 In Belgium, the interest that is yielded by the capital is taxable, yet these taxes are levied by means of *advance* tax payment and thus fall without the scope of the concept of income according to the regulation on social allowances.

ings;[42] and second, the interest included in the sum of money disbursed to the disabled child following a beneficiary provision in a life insurance.[43]

Following on from the concept of income, it is crucial to examine whether in addition to the disabled person's income, the income of other persons needs to be taken into account, such as the income of family members living together with the disabled person. When social protection programmes assume that the family to be the primary care-giver, it may not come as a surprise that the income of family members will be taken into account as well, assuming or imposing some solidarity on their behalf. If the death of the parents will have an effect on the actual living situation of the disabled person (e.g. when the disabled person after the death of his parents is supposed to move to a cohousing project living together with other disabled persons), the potential effect that this may have an effect on the allowances should be borne in mind.

In Belgium, both the income replacement allowance and the integration allowance vary according to the family situation of the disabled person. The disabled's family situation – living alone, living together with a relative, living together with a non-family member, or living in a care institution – determines the basic amount of the allowance and/or determines which income is taken into account when evaluating the available means of the disabled person. When a person, for example, lives together with a family member, the income of this relative is not taken into account, to encourage family members to take care of each other. However, the disabled person is only granted a limited income replacement allowance, barely sufficient to cover all expenses (i.e. €556/month). When the disabled person lives together with a non-family member, the income replacement allowance is higher, but then again, to determine whether the disabled person meets the income requirements, both his own income and the income of the other member of his household are taken into account at least to some extent.

D Support in Kind

Parental estate planning may result in support in kind as well. For example: the stipulation that part of the parents' estate after their death will be donated to a beneficiary who is charged with the burden to take care of the disabled adult on a daily basis, e.g. driving him to work every morning, or providing support in daily activities. From the point of view of the disabled child, such help will be regarded as benefit in kind.

---

42 Art. 7 Income Tax Code (Belgium). If the real property is rented to a person who does not use this real property for professional reasons, then the income is calculated on a lump-sum basis, the so-called "cadastral income" (kadastraal inkomen).

43 Art. 17, § 1, 4 Income Tax Code (Belgium).

Logically, the support in kind provided by the parents may have an effect on the disability benefits if the eligibility requirements of these benefits consider the extent to which the disabled person receives such support. The criteria that are likely to be influenced by support in kind are: requirements concerning the income of the disabled person and the evaluation of the disability.

From an economic point of view, benefits in kind may represent an increase of the recipient's net wealth.[44] As was pointed out earlier, this is particularly important for means-tested allowances, typical of non-contributory social protection programmes. Whether this support in kind is considered as leading to an increase of income according to the regulation on social allowances also depends on the legal concept of income used.

In Belgium, the concept of income used in the regulation regarding income replacement allowance and integration allowance coincides with the legal concept of taxable income. Benefits in kind do not fall within the legal concept of income,[45] and so support in kind does not lead to an increase of taxable income and will not jeopardize the entitlement of the disabled person to the social allowances mentioned.

The support in kind from the parents may have an influence on the evaluation of the disability itself. For example, support in kind may affect the disabled person's ability to gain income by work, thus possibly affecting eligibility to social allowances that are meant to protect income, consisting usually of benefits in cash. Support in kind may also affect how the disabled person is able to carry out daily activities, thus affecting the eligibility to social allowances that are meant to compensate for the extra costs covering support from others.

In Belgium, however, evaluation of the disability as a requirement for the income replacement allowance and the social integration allowance does not take into account possible help from others. The effect of the disability on capacity to earn money or to perform everyday activities is measured independently of any support. The evaluation of the disability of a person who lives with his brother who helps him every day to get dressed is carried out in exactly the same manner as the evaluation of a person who lives on his own and receives no help at all. The same goes for the evaluation of the disability with respect to gaining access to state-financed specialized support from care institutions.

Even though the disability is recognized regardless of available support, the presence of support in kind may nevertheless influence the actual grant of support by the state. The limited resources of the state may force them to build in some priority rules. In Belgium, there are no such prioritizing rules on the basis of available support in kind in relation to the income replacement allowance and the integration allowance. Conversely, such rules

44 Holmes, op cit, n. 38, p. 575.

45 Exception must be made in relation to benefits in kind granted by employers to employees. (Holmes, ibid, p. 575. Note that Holmes refers to the tax system in New Zealand, but the same applies to the tax system in Belgium.)

do exist – in the Dutch-speaking part of Belgium[46] – with regard to state-provided support in specialized institutions and services for disability-related needs. This kind of support is realized by means of a so-called personal budget: the "personalised annual sum which can be used by people with a disability to purchase care and support from within their own network, from volunteers, individual companions, professional carers and accredited care providers".[47] The designation of such a personal budget is considered to empower disabled persons and is a good example of demand-driven care. However, the state does not provide enough resources to grant such a personal budget to all people who require it. Consequently, the state has to decide which demands for care will be given priority. Interestingly, the rules to determine these priorities take into account the presence of support in kind in two different ways.

Firstly, the presence of support in kind may lead to a lower priority status. To determine priority status, the gap between the existing need for support and the support already available to meet those needs is measured. Support in kind by family or the informal network may bridge – or at least reduce – this gap as family members and the informal network are considered as fully-fledged levels of support. The care model that lies beneath the state policy assumes the existence and complementarity of different levels or circles of support, including self-care, family, informal network, general care and services accessible for all people and specialized care accessible only for persons with disabilities.[48]

Alternatively, from a long-term perspective, the provision of support in kind by family members may lead to a higher priority status. To determine priority status, the extent to which family members and/or members of the informal network have supplied care "beyond the usual" is taken into account. Care "beyond the usual" refers to the situation where family members living together with the disabled person have supplied care during a longer period of time and to an extent that could not reasonably be expected of them.[49] When they are unable to continue this kind of care, their efforts are 'rewarded' as the disabled person's need for care receives a higher priority status.

46 Belgium is a federal state, composed of communities and regions. The state-provided assistance and support in specialized homes, institutions and services for people with disabilities is not organized by the federal authorities, but by the communities.

47 Flemish Agency for People with a Disability, http://www.vaph.be/vlafo/view/nl/204726-The+Flemish+Agency+for+People+with+a+Disability+(VAPH).html.

48 It is based on the model of the American Association on Intellectual and Developmental Disabilities (formerly American Association on Mental Retardation). See AAMR, *Mental Retardation. Definition, Classification, and Systems of Supports. Workbook*, 2002.

49 Art. 2, Decision of the Flemish Government 4 March 2016 on the establishment of a regional priority committee, the allocation of priority groups, the determination of the social necessity, the guidance to support, the coordination and planning in the context of personal budgets for adults, *Belgian Official Journal* 20 April 2016. (Belgium).

IV Concluding Remarks and Future Prospects

In Belgium, family (property) law is characterized by a "general" or "inclusive" approach towards opportunities for care arrangements for the benefit of disabled children. Rather than including provisions that exclusively apply to disabled persons, the law provides tools that are applicable to all situations, including those that favour persons with disabilities. Inheritance law rules, for example, take into account the hypothesis that some family members need more protection than others, without providing rules that are exclusively applicable to disabled children. Over the past few years, consensus appears to be growing that the current opportunities and measures provided for in family (property) law do not adequately meet all the needs of parents who are making plans for their disabled children. Policy makers have announced that in the near future the law will be adjusted better to meet the parents' needs. In my view, three courses are open to policymakers.

First path: the introduction of new, tailor-made measures exclusively applying to disabled family members in order to suit their special needs. In that context, an important issue to be addressed is how and by whom it will be determined whether a person belongs to the category of "disabled persons", as the measure would exclusively apply to them. Several options are possible: the rules may align with the concept of disability used in matters relating to social allowances, or they may align with the concept of "legal incapacity" used in the law on adult guardianship measures.

Second path: leaving parents or families more freedom to handle the transfer of their estate after their death, regardless of the presence of disabled children. Some of the rules in inheritance law are considered to be barriers preventing parents from taking adequate measures of protection for (some of) their children. A recent law reform reduced the reserved portion of the children, thus enlarging the available portion and giving parents more freedom to transfer their estate after their death as they wish, including the possibility to leave a larger portion to the disabled child who needs more support.[50]

Thirdly: the introduction of tools that allow more efficiently the transformation of estate or assets into care. The central aim of parental estate planning is to guarantee continuity of care for the disabled adult child beyond the lifetime of the parents. Thus, such planning is first and foremost to be considered as *care* planning as it focuses on how all available resources can be used and transformed into care for the disabled adult child. Inspiration for such like tools may be found in inheritance rules that reward family members who performed care with an increased share of the estate,[51] as is the case for

50 Law 31 July 2017 on the modification of the Civil Code concerning the inheritances and the gifts and the modification of various other provisions in this respect, *Belgian Official Journal* 1 September 2017 (ed. 1), *err.* 7 September 2017, *err.* 21 February 2018 (Belgium).

51 Frank, op cit, n. 12, p. 17.

example in Germany.[52] The underlying mechanisms may serve as a source of inspiration for setting up a similar rule with regard to parents of disabled children encouraging siblings (or other relatives) to take care of their disabled sister or brother.

Estate planning in favour of a disabled adult child should take into account the disability benefits provided for by the state. Parents should at least proactively investigate the effect of the care arrangement on the eligibility for the state benefits to avoid unpleasant surprises. Due to the complex relationship between the two levels of protection, parental estate planning entails the risk of lowering the protection from the state, resulting in a status quo rather than a maximization of the support. Indeed, it is not easy to arrive at an arrangement that allows parental estate planning and disability benefits to join forces to maximize the support for the disabled adult child.

This paper showed how important the actual interpretation of the concept of income is, especially with respect to allowances that are means-tested. For that matter, in Belgium, remarkably the regulation on income replacement allowance and integration allowance ties up with the concept of income used for income tax purposes. Due to this connection, parental estate planning necessarily entails a fiscal point of view as well. Parental estate planning becomes a truly interdisciplinary undertaking and requires an interdisciplinary approach involving both family (property) law, social security law and taxation law.

Moreover, the entanglement between entitlement to social allowances and the legal concept of taxable income may reinforce the invitation "to taxpayers to apply strategies that convert otherwise taxable income into non-taxable capital gains", i.e. an invitation that arises from the traditional legal distinction between taxable and non-taxable income.[53] From an individual perspective, strategies aimed at increasing capital rather than income are likely to kill two birds with one stone: the disabled child-taxpayer pays no taxes and does not risk losing his entitlement to means-tested allowances. On a macro level, it is clear that the interplay between income tax law and social allowances is a research area still largely unexplored, including the consequences of the interplay on the macro level both for tax policy and social policy. In addition, it is to be questioned whether the best guarantee to continue care is an increase of capital, since the provision of a regular and steady income on a periodical and firm basis certainly has advantages too.

As far as the interaction between the two levels of support is concerned, the analysis of some disability benefits in Belgium showed that usually the interaction between family protection and state protection is of particular interest when they involve the same type of support. Indeed, financial support by the parents is likely to have a – negative – impact on cash benefits by the state that are meant as income protection, but does not seem to alter the child's entitlement to support in kind by the state in the form of access to spe-

52 Section 2057a Civil Code (Germany).

53 Holmes, op cit, n. 38, p. 574.

cialised care and services. Conversely, support in kind by the parents does not influence cash benefits by the state that are meant as income protection, but may have an impact on the entitlement to support in kind by the state in the form of access to specialised care and services. In Belgium – i.e. in the Dutch-speaking part of Belgium – this is the result of the care model that consists of different complementary circles of support, including family members and the informal network.

In conclusion, it may be observed that it is highly exceptional that parents dispose of a $3 million estate to take care of their "Rain Man". In reality, it is more likely that the resources of the parents alone do not suffice. This paper has made the case that parental care arrangements should take into account state protection as well, joining forces to maximize support on behalf of the disabled adult.

Printed by Libri Plureos GmbH in Hamburg,
Germany

9 789462 369276